MEN OF WAR

By the same author

Lord Byron's Jackal: A Life of Edward John Trelawny

The Kindness of Sisters:
Annabella Milbanke and the Destruction of the Byrons

Scott of the Antarctic:
A Life of Courage and Tragedy in the Extreme South

MEN OF WAR

*Courage Under Fire in
the Nineteenth-Century Navy*

DAVID CRANE

Harper
Press

Harper*Press*
An imprint of HarperCollins*Publishers*
77–85 Fulham Palace Road,
Hammersmith, London W6 8JB
www.harpercollins.co.uk

Visit our authors' blog: www.fifthestate.co.uk
Love this book? www.bookarmy.com

Published by HarperPress in 2009

Copyright © David Crane 2009

Maps © HarperCollins*Publishers*,
designed by HL Studios, Oxfordshire

1

The author asserts the moral right to
be identified as the author of this work

A catalogue record for this book
is available from the British Library

ISBN 978-0-00-725405-7

Set in Sabon and Photina MT display by
G&M Designs Limited, Raunds, Northamptonshire

Printed and bound in Great Britain by Clays Ltd, St Ives plc

For my Mother and Father

CONTENTS

ILLUSTRATIONS

HASTINGS

Frank Abney Hastings.

Willesley Hall, near Ashby-de-la-Zouch, family home of the Abney-Hastings. *(Lady Selina Newman)*

The stables, Willesley.

Bust of Hastings. *(British School of Archaeology, Athens)*

The *Hellas* and the *Karteria*.

The *Karteria*. *(Lady Selina Newman)*

Thomas Cochrane. *(National Portrait Gallery, London)*

The Battle of Navarino. *(National Maritime Museum, Greenwich, London)*

Commemorative medal presented to the Abney-Hastings family on the 150th anniversary of the Greek War of Independence. *(Lady Selina Newman)*

PEEL

The Gallant Peel, by John Lucas. *(National Maritime Museum, Greenwich, London, Greenwich Hospital Collection)*

The bombardment of Acre, 3 November 1840. *(National Maritime Museum, Greenwich, London)*

Clements Markham, aged fourteen.

Sevastopol, 17 October 1854. The first of three acts of heroism that earned Peel the VC. *(Illustrated London News/Mary Evans Picture Library)*

A Quiet Day in the Diamond Battery, by William Simpson, 15 December 1854.

The 'Swiss Cottage' at Sandy. *(Photograph by Nigel Morris)*

The *Shannon*. A rescue at sea on the voyage out to India. *(Rev. Jonathan Peel)*

Naval Brigade races. Lithograph based on a drawing by Captain Oliver Jones, RN.

The Relief of Lucknow, by Thomas Barker. *(National Portrait Gallery, London)*

Peel bringing his guns up in front of the Dilkusha. Lithograph based on a drawing by Captain Oliver Jones, RN.

Arabic prayer taken by Peel from the Zenana at Lucknow in November 1857. *(Rev. Jonathan Peel)*

Sir William Peel, VC, KCB, by William Theed, in St Swithun's church, Sandy.

GOODENOUGH

James Graham Goodenough.

The bombardment of Sveaborg, August 1855.

Fatshan Creek, 1 June 1857. *(Mary Evans Picture Library)*

The attack on Goodenough and his party. From a sketch by Lieutenant Harrison, RM, of HMS *Pearl*.

The funeral of Goodenough.

Letter of condolence from Queen Victoria to her goddaughter, Goodenough's widow.

Victoria Goodenough in 1897.

Posthumous portrait bust of Goodenough by Prince Victor of Hohenlohe-Langenberg, Count Gleichen. *(Conway Library, The Courtauld Institute of Art, London)*

LIST OF MAPS

INTRODUCTION

Hastings's Sword

My sword, I give to him that shall succeed me in my
pilgrimage, and my courage and skill, to him that can
get it.

John Bunyan, *The Pilgrim's Progress*

The boast of heraldry, the pomp of pow'r,
And all that beauty, all that wealth e'er gave,
Awaits alike th'inevitable hour,
The paths of glory lead but to the grave.

Thomas Gray,
'Elegy Written in a Country Churchyard'

I FIRST CAME ACROSS the idea for this book fifteen years ago in the
British School in Athens while working on a biography of Edward
Trelawny. I was going through the archive of the great philhellene
and historian of Greece, George Finlay, and in among his papers was
the draft will of an ex-English naval officer and hero of the Greek War
of Independence called Frank Abney Hastings.

It seemed that almost nothing was known of Hastings before he
arrived in Greece – aristocratic connections, Trafalgar at the age of
eleven, a row with his superiors that brought his career with the Royal
Navy to a premature end – but it was the will rather than the man
that grabbed my attention. Like almost every document that Hastings ever left it is heavily scored and corrected, but in among a few
minor bequests to a servant and friends was a single clause – the gift
of an inscribed sword with instructions that it was to be passed down
the generations from officer to officer in perpetuity – that seemed to
conjure not just a man but a whole world and tradition into vivid
and immediate life.

Memory has a way of improving, or at least 'tidying' things, and when I went back to the archive some years later the clause was both less elegant and more robust than I had recalled. In it Hastings nominates a man called Edward Scott, 1st Lieutenant of the *Cambrian*, 'the finest officer' he had ever served with, as his beneficiary, with the rider that

> he will cause to be inscribed on the blades of my swords and on the Barrels of my Fire arms the following words. Viz 'This /Gun/ Pistol or sword (as the case may be) was bequeathed by Frank Abney Hastings to his former Messmate Captain Edward Scott RN and I further request of the said Edward Scott that these arms and my Nautical Instruments and my watch, may never be sold but that he should bequeath them to that Naval Officer whose Skill and Valour he most admires.

There is something gloriously immodest and extravagant about this that is typical of Hastings – as if Achilles had bequeathed his shield and sword, and then, what the hell, thrown in his helmet and greaves for good measure – but for all that the idea is still a profoundly generous one. There was nothing unusual in one officer presenting a commemorative sword to another in this way, but what Hastings's bequest enshrines is not so much a memorial to himself as an idea of naval service that links generation to generation in an organic tradition of 'Skill' and 'Valour' in which he himself formed one small but brilliant link.

And in spite of the fact that Hastings is now virtually unknown in the country of his birth – and scarcely remembered in the country of his adoption – no nineteenth-century naval officer so boldly carried the torch. It used to be said by a rueful Spanish ambassador that every English captain an enemy faced was a Nelson, and if that is about as accurate as most generalisations about the Royal Navy, it is probably truer of Hastings than it was of any young officer of his generation who learned his trade during the last decade of the Napoleonic Wars.

'Who is the happy Warrior? Who is he, That every man in arms should wish to be?' asked Wordsworth, and almost a century before Herbert Read found his own savage answer in the trenches of Flanders, Hastings triumphantly filled the bill. It is possible that he had other interests than fighting and the art of war, but born as he was in the first year of the conflict with Revolutionary France he never knew or seemed to want anything else, fighting against Napoleon and the United States for as long as there were battles to be fought, before transferring his allegiances and genius to the nascent Greece in her struggle for independence from Ottoman oppression.

Hastings has only himself to blame that he is not better known, but as the architect and captain of the first successful steam warship and the great prophet of gunnery and total war, he was the unacknowledged godfather to everything that was bloodiest in the century ahead. 'Great Britain is especially called upon to acknowledge her obligations to Captain Hastings,' George Finlay wrote with premature optimism in 1845, at a time when the Royal Navy was tardily implementing the revolutionary lessons Hastings had given the world's navies almost twenty years before.

> By rendering naval warfare not only more destructive, but at the same time making it more dependent on a combination of good gunnery and mechanical knowledge with profound naval skill, he has increased the naval power of Great Britain, where all those qualities are cultivated in the highest degree. At the same time, the civilized world is indebted to him for rendering battles so terrible as to henceforth be less frequent, and for putting an end to naval warfare as a means of amusing kings, and gratifying the ambition of princely admirals, or vainglorious states.

It would have been fun to hear Hastings's response to these pieties – he could have started a sea battle in a dry-dock – but for all the brutal realism with which he approached the business of war, his friendship with Edward Scott suggests that he was not immune to the navy's more dashing and chivalrous traditions. 'SCOTT. (CAPTAIN, 1838)' Scott's entry in O'Byrne's 1848 *Dictionary of Naval Officers* begins, and nothing could speak more eloquently of the depths of the tradition he represented than that a career of such variety and distinction should now be so utterly and irrecoverably lost:

> EDWARD HINTON SCOTT was born about 1789. This officer entered the navy in May, 1798, as Fst. Cl. Vol. on board the ANSON ... With five of the [enemy] frigates ... she came, 12 Oct., singly into collision, and sustained a loss, with injury to her masts and yards, of 2 men killed and 13 wounded. On 18 of the same

month we find her, in company with the KANGAROO 18, endur-
ing a similar loss in a gallant action of an hour and a quarter which
terminated in the capture of *La Loire* of 46 guns and 664 men ...
While attached to the ANSON Mr Scott contributed, also, to the
capture of several fine privateers ... In the course of the same year
he commanded a rocket-vessel in Sir Sidney Smith's attack on the
Boulogne flotilla. On leaving the BLAZER he became Acting lieutenant of the SKYLARK 16; and while in that brig ... he had charge
of her boats in a running fight with a French cutter privateer of 8
guns and 48 men, whom, after having cut away her sweeps and
chased her for three hours, he drove under the guns of the
SKYLARK. On one occasion he landed at Flushing, spiked the 8
guns of a battery, and brought the guard off prisoners ... He was
frequently, in the SATURN, and her boats engaged with the
enemy's forts and armed vessels (several of which he captured).
During his servitude in the ORLANDO he took part in many boat-
affairs in the Adriatic and Chesapeake. He commanded her boats
too in several skirmishes with the Malay proas in the Straits of
Sunda and Malacca, and once succeeded in repelling an attack
made by them at night on a wrecked Indiaman, of which he had
been placed in charge. In the boats of the CAMBRIAN we find him
cutting out, in the Gulf of Athens, with much spirit and judgement,
a piratical schooner, carrying two long guns and 50 men, together
with three of her prizes ... He also assisted at the reduction of
Napoli di Romania and, at the head of a hundred seamen, landed
there at the request of the Provisional Government, had the good
fortune, when the troops entered the town, to save the lives of 2000
Turks, men, women, and children ... For these services ... was
presented with a sword by the Greek Provisional Government ...
For his conduct in jumping overboard from the ORLANDO and
saving the lives of four persons, Capt Scott (who is senior of 1838)
received the thanks of the Royal Humane Society.

In an ideal world it would be possible to trace Scott's inheritance
down the generations – in any decent fiction 'Evans of the *Broke*'
would be wielding Hastings's sword in the hand-to-hand fighting
with a rammed German destroyer in the Channel in 1917. (In any
fiction, on the other hand, it would now be rusting in shame on the
bed of the Persian Gulf.) But history is seldom so obliging. It seems
doubtful that the sword even got as far as Edward Scott, but the idea

of the bequest is too good to let go of; so what follows here, in the lives of Hastings and of two other figures who dazzled their generations – the brilliant William Peel, third son of the Prime Minister, and James Goodenough, the outstanding officer of his time – is a kind of *ideal* progress of the sword through the late Georgian and Victorian navy that answers to the spirit of Hastings's will with a faithfulness that no literal or historical descent could possibly hope to do.

There are various reasons for choosing these men in preference to more obvious candidates – Goodenough instead of his more famous contemporary Tryon, for instance – but the first and foremost is that they were, in that special sense of the word reserved to the armed forces, 'lucky'. In the century between the end of the Napoleonic Wars and the outbreak of the First World War the Royal Navy fought only one fleet-to-fleet action, but in an age in which many a gifted officer was doomed to fret on half-pay, Peel and Goodenough were fortunate enough to see action against the Russians and the Chinese, in ships of the line and in gunboats, at sea and in trenches, off the walls of Acre and on the walls of Canton, in the Baltic and the Crimea, in open boats against pirate junks and on open ground in front of Lucknow against sepoy mutineers.

These were the careers that every nineteenth-century naval or army officer wanted and *needed*, the opportunities for glory, distinction and advancement that were the life blood of both services. 'I stay in hopes that war may again break out in some part of our Indian territory,' one typical young ex-Harrovian, contemplating the horrors of peace, wrote from India to William Peel's future housemaster in 1829, 'or that the Russians, succeeding better than they deserve, will at last reach India, when a man who distinguishes himself may have a chance of being rewarded by an extra step in rank, or medal, or something of that kind, instead of, as it is now with us, receiving bare thanks from our worshipful masters the shop-keepers of Leadenhall Street.'

Whether or not it was entirely a matter of 'luck' that Peel and Hastings were in the right place at the right time when Russia and British India finally obliged is a nice question – there is at least half a case for arguing that the natural 'warrior' gets the wars he 'deserves' – but either way, they were born 'fighters' in the sense that Hastings understood the word. If this had simply been a matter of courage one could open any nineteenth-century navy list and stick in a pin to find his successors, but Peel and Goodenough were not just men who could and did fight – in Wilfred Owen's startling boast – like 'angels', but officers who in a period of institutional stagnation brought to the business of war all the intelligence, thought, empirical skills, leadership, ambition, aggression, imagination and 'thirst for glory' that had once characterised the Nelsonian service that shaped Hastings's ideals.

And if the absolute dominance of the Royal Navy during the nineteenth century – the French could never be relied on for a fight, and the Russians would rather sink their ships in the Black Sea than face battle – meant that they had to do their fighting in some odd places, they remained always loyal to that tradition. In many ways Peel's and Goodenough's careers might have been those of any Victorian army officer, but even when they fought as part of naval brigades hundreds of miles from their natural habitat, in the heat and dust of India or up the rivers of the Mosquito Coast, they remained as unmistakably the products of Hastings's navy as did the bluejackets under their command.

But while these three careers, spanning a period of seventy years that opens with Trafalgar and closes on the beach of a remote Pacific island, are a celebration of continuity and tradition, they equally reflect an age of rapid and radical change. When Hastings first saw action from the deck of a man-of war he would have approached the enemy at a slow walking pace; but by the time Goodenough took his place on the Admiralty Committee on Designs for Ships of War in the early 1870s, sail had given way to steam, wood to armour, and the *ad hoc* improvisations and confused hell of Trafalgar to dreams of choreographed fleet actions, centralised command, signalling hegemony and speeds of fourteen knots.

In a sense these technical developments left the subjects of this book relatively untouched: Peel did most of his fighting on land, and Goodenough died a very eighteenth-century death. But the navy has always been a microcosm of national life, and no one was immune to the wider social and intellectual changes shaping nineteenth-century Britain. Both Peel and Goodenough first went to sea in the last leisurely days of sail, but if they were Georgians by upbringing and age they were Victorians by instinct and high moral seriousness, and in crucial matters of temperament and faith as remote from Hastings as they were close to him in their gift for war.

And while there are certain men, as John Masters put it in his wonderful evocation of pre-Second World War soldiering with the

Indian Army, *Bugles and a Tiger*, who only come fully alive in battle, there are fewer who are prepared to admit it even to themselves. Over the middle years of the century both Goodenough and Peel would throw themselves into conflicts every bit as savage as anything Hastings knew, but even so they could no more have publicly signed up to his reductive vision of 'the art of war ... in other words, the method of killing men most expeditiously' than could the Christian country and governments that sent them into action.

Hastings had come of age in a war of national survival that left little room for moral reflection, and had fought for Greece in a savage war of liberation that left still less room for sentiment, but these were dispensations that the generations who fought for Turkey in the Crimea or in the Opium Wars against China never enjoyed. In every war there will always be men who fight for the sheer joy of stabbing and stabbing again the 'well-killed Boche', but for anyone else, anyone brought up within the framework of a Christian nation – and it is impossible to overstate the influence of religion on the national life of nineteenth-century Britain – the sheer thrill of battle and the Homeric lust for Glory and Fame that were the unashamed motives of Hastings's life had to be dissembled into more morally acceptable notions of 'Duty', Service', 'Patriotism' and 'Sacrifice'.

The fighting instincts were no less rampant – 'After all,' Thomas Hughes cheerfully asked in *Tom Brown's Schooldays*, 'what would life be without fighting, I should like to know?' – but no one who had had their first scrap at the back of Thomas Arnold's chapel at Rugby was ever left in any doubt of the need for a just moral cause. 'From the cradle to the grave,' Hughes went on, neatly subsuming the soul, the school playground and the killing grounds of the Alma and Inkerman into one moral universe, 'fighting, rightly understood, is the business, the real, highest, honestest business of every son of man. Every one who is worth his salt has his enemies, who must be beaten, be they evil thoughts and habits in himself, or spiritual wickedness in high places, or Russians, or Border-ruffians, or Bill, Tom, or Harry, who will not let him live his life in quiet till he has thrashed them.'

The pages of *Tom Brown's Schooldays* are as good a place as any to feel the moral change that had overtaken nineteenth-century Britain, and one of the fascinations of the three lives here is the ways in which natural warriors of successive generations justified to themselves Hastings's 'art of killing'. As a boy of seventeen William Peel would experience all the thoughtless excitement of action at the bombardment of Acre; but if that takes little understanding, what was it that enabled a man of his intelligence, piety, innate gentleness and background to fight with such brilliance in the Crimea in defence of an Ottoman Empire that was repugnant to every tenet he held?

Perhaps the first and most prosaic answer is that there was a burgeoning belief in the nineteenth century – and one to which Peel ardently subscribed – that God's Higher Purpose was to be worked out through British civilisation, British arms and British trade. Seldom can the long, disreputable history of the 'Just War' have been deflected to such improbable purposes. 'There cannot be a doubt that it is a just war we are engaged in,' wrote Captain Hedley Vicars, a natural warrior and Popery-hating zealot who in 1854 looked forward to Britain's triumph over the Russians in the Crimea as a portent of the imminent 'coming of the Son of Man'.

> There are some people, I know, who cannot imagine how any Christian could ever join the deadly strife of battle; but I can only say with such I do not agree, so I shall not flinch from doing my duty to my Queen and Country, the Lord being my helper ... I consider war to be ... as much a visitation from the Almighty as cholera or any other scourge; and as on the appearance of that dreadful malady, we do not sit quietly down and let it take its course, but very rightly (trusting in the blessing of God) use every precaution, and employ every means to drive it from amongst us, so in the case of this war with the Russian despot. He has made an aggression against a country (one of our oldest allies), which has given him no just cause of provocation, and has thus disturbed the peace of Europe and let loose upon us the horrors of war, and shall we Britons let him have his way, and tamely look on? God forbid! Rather will we, the Lord being our 'shield and buckler' crush the evil, and restore peace and quietness to the land.

There were other, and contradictory, strands at work too, and along-side this growing belief in Britain's Divine Mission was a lurking anxiety that the sinews of national life had been fatally softened by long years of peace. The triumphant success of the Great Exhibition in 1851 had demonstrated to the world the pre-eminence of British manufacturing, but what if there was a price to pay for prosperity and luxury in a decline of the 'Race' that only war could halt? 'Art?'

exclaims Stangrave in Charles Kingsley's *Two Years Ago* (1857), a
novel set against the background of a Devon village ravaged by
cholera and the mightier national struggle with the Russians taking
place on the shores of the Black Sea:

> What if the most necessary human art, next to the art of agricul-
> ture, be, after all, the art of war? It has been so in all ages. What
> if I have been befooled – what if all the Anglo-Saxon world has
> been befooled by forty years of peace? We have forgotten that the
> history of the world has been as yet written in blood; that the
> history of the human race is the story of its heroes and its martyrs
> – the slayers and the slain. Is it not becoming such once more in
> Europe now? And what divine exemption can we claim from the
> law? ... What if the wise man's attitude, and the wise nation's atti-
> tude is that of the Jews rebuilding their ruined walls – the tool in
> one hand, and the sword in the other; for the wild Arabs are close
> outside and the time is short, and the storm is only lulled a while
> in mercy, that wise men may prepare for the next thunderburst ...
> Armed industry, which tills the corn among the cannons' mouths
> ... knows that so long as cruelty and wrong exist on earth, man's
> destiny is to dare and suffer, and if it must be so, to die.

It was no coincidence that the two great, sacrificial periods of British
polar exploration – the search for Sir John Franklin in the early 1850s
and the first stirrings of interest in Antarctica at the end of the century
– coincided with two prolonged periods of peace, and war offered
opportunities for purging the nation's soul that not even the self-
induced miseries of 'man hauling' and starvation rations could match.
For Kingsley the conflict with Russia was nothing short of a waken-
ing 'to a new life – at least to the dream of a new life!', it was 'a discipline from heaven', an expiation for old 'sins', a purifying fire that
redeemed men and women alike from fripperies and ease. 'My health
is quite restored enough to enable me to walk up to a cannon's
mouth,' Major Campbell tells the beautiful Valentia St. Just before
sailing for the Crimea and a hero's death on 'Cathcarts's Hill', only
yards from where William Peel would win his Victoria Cross. 'There
are noble elements underneath the crust, which will come out all the
purer from the fire; and we shall have heroes and heroines rising up
among us as of old, sincere and earnest, ready to face their work, and
to do it, and to call all things by their right names.'

Along with this sense of national crisis went a growing obsession with masculinity and courage that seems from this distance a reflex of the same insecurity. 'To understand courage,' wrote Field Marshal Lord Wolseley – a companion-in-arms and admirer of Peel's – in a noxious article entitled 'Courage' that might have provided chapter and verse for everything that is most paranoid in the whole A.E.W. Mason canon,

> one must have thoroughly studied cowardice in all its phases and they are infinite. It is the most subtle of mental diseases, the existence of which may never be known to any but the man whose heart it gnaws at. When the day arrives on which all hearts shall be open, we shall, I am sure be astonished to find that many of those who have passed muster in our ranks as brave men will plead in extenuation of sins committed the astounding fact that they were cowards by nature.
>
> There are, of course, many degrees of courage, endless varieties in its manifestations, but my own experience leads me to believe that this virtue in men follows the same natural laws as obtain in the cases of horses and dogs. The better bred all three are the greater will be the innate pluck ...
>
> In our army – as indeed in nearly all good armies – there is a great gap between the social position of the officer and the private. Their education from early infancy has been as opposite as the poles ... For the officer to be suspected of any lack of nerve would be fatal to him. He would be shunned and boycotted as a leper, and he had better end his days at once by his own hand.

This, then, was the culture – a culture of national assertion and self-doubt – that shaped the mid-century experience of war, and twisting insidiously around Kingsley's visions of redemption and Wolseley's darker obsessions was that bizarre and very Victorian cult of Chivalry that found one of its most famous and handsome incarnations in Sir William Peel. The history of chivalry had already taken some very odd turns by the time of the Crimean War, but under Kingsley's and Thomas Hughes's influence 'the old chivalrous and Christian belief [in] the protection of the weak, the advancement of all righteous causes' was refined into a search for self-purification and 'self-conquest' that reached its highest pitch on the barren uplands above the city of Sevastopol.

'The annals of chivalry' had nothing to match the exploits of Peel and his young 'pages' in the Crimea, Lord Lyons, the Commander-in-Chief in the Black Sea, would tell an enraptured Guildhall audience at a banquet to celebrate the end of the Crimean War, and the greater the moral and physical degradation around him, the more brilliantly Peel's armour shone. Nobody who saw him under fire in the trenches of the Crimea would ever forget his air of quiet and inviolable self-mastery, and it would be the same again in India, where he could ride through a landscape of decomposing corpses and tree boughs heavy with hanged rebels as if it was some mythological world of chimeras and goblins conjured up by a Malory to try his knightly resolve.

If the face of heroism had changed between the Homeric code that Hastings embraced and the medieval code of a Peel, the life and death of the third of these naval officers provides perhaps the most vivid proof of how it would mutate again before the Victorian age was very much older. In the eyes of a man like Thomas Hughes there might have seemed no conflict between 'chivalry' and Christianity, but to a sterner moralist of Thomas Arnold's stamp the whole cult of chivalry – with its essential egotism, its elitism, its self-reliance, its glamorised brutality, its culture of 'honour' rather than 'duty' – was not some knightly expression of the gospels but the enemy and antithesis of those true Christian virtues that a Protestant England would eventually find in James Graham Goodenough.

The cultural divide between Peel and James Goodenough was not the same in either degree or kind as that between either man and Hastings, but it was in its way just as profound. It is always tempting to think of change in terms of generations or decades, but history rarely evolves so neatly, and although only six years separated the two men in age, the Britain that mourned Peel's death in India in 1858 was not the same country that would thrill to Goodenough's less than twenty years later.

When Peel died the country commemorated the life of a peerless knight; when Goodenough was killed it celebrated the death of a national martyr. In those two responses lies a world of difference. It was not that 'Holy Joe' Goodenough had been any less of a natural fighter than either Hastings or Peel, or had been engaged in 'better' wars, but that his 'heroic' death at the hands of a group of island 'savages' whom he refused to harm chimed not just with Britain's growing sense of its Sacred Mission but with the tastes, prejudices and religious instincts of an ascendant middle class ready to claim Goodenough as its own.

It was in some ways a curious claim to make on a man married to a goddaughter of the Queen, but in more important respects they had it right. By birth and education Goodenough might have sprung from an ethos of refined privilege, but in his faith, social conscience and his impregnable, teetotalling respectability he belonged squarely to that middle-class world – to a world that stretched from the products of Arnold's Rugby at one end to the chapel, mission and Low Church pamphleteer at the other – that was learning to look to its own kind for the embodiments of national greatness. 'The middle class of this country may well be proud of such men as these,' wrote *The Times* of Havelock, Nicholson and Neill, the heroes of the Indian Mutiny, 'born and bred in their ranks – proud of such representatives, such reflections of their own best and most sterling characteristics, – proud of men who were noble without birth, without the pride of connexions, without a breath of fashion, and without a single drop of Norman blood in their veins.'

But if in Goodenough the middle classes had, at last, the real thing, a Christian warrior who lived and died by what he preached, the concept of a 'naval martyr' was not without its difficulties. The sole reason that the public at large had been happy to indulge the chiliastic nonsense of a man like Vicars was that he could also fight like a lion, and if Sir Henry Havelock, the hero of Lucknow, was allowed to treat the world to the spectacle of an exemplary Christian death it was because he had made damned sure to precede it with a campaign of unedifying Old Testament ferocity.

Goodenough, though, was different, and if he chased Glory as assiduously as Hastings and Peel had done, it was the Glory of the next world and not of this. Throughout his long and distinguished career he did all he could to reconcile the conflicting claims of his faith and his profession, but when, finally, in the pursuit of Britain's Sacred Mission among the natives of the Pacific islands he had to choose between 'love' and 'duty', and paid for it with his life, a new and disturbing kind of naval hero was born.

There were those in the service who were dismayed by his choice, but if the sword that had been left to Edward Scott had come a long way in forty years to stay so firmly sheathed on a beach on Santa Cruz, Hastings would at least have recognised the forces that had brought Goodenough to such an end. In the years since his own death the whole concept of heroism might have changed, but if – to use George Finlay's phrase – those 'elements of true greatness' that had combined in him to produce a martyr to Greek freedom coalesced in Goodenough to create a profoundly different kind of hero, then the elements themselves remained just the same.

Courage, sacrifice, selflessness, ardour, energy, vanity, pride – the self-referential vanity of the hero, the spiritual pride of the martyr – they are all there, but if there is one key to the lives that follow it probably lies in the 'thirst for glory' that Hastings confessed was the driving force of his life. There are any number of reasons why men fight, and then there are the reasons that they give, but whether it was an earthly or a heavenly reward, the 'lustre of a name' that Peel spoke of or the lustre of a martyr's crown, the battles of the sea that were the only sort Hastings knew or Bunyan's battles of the soul, the pursuit of 'Glory' – whatever the price – was, in all three men, what Alexander Pope would have called the 'Ruling Passion'.

And no nineteenth-century naval officer needed to be reminded of where the paths of glory almost inevitably lead. 'There is no death so glorious, so much to be desired, as on the battlefield,' wrote Captain Oliver Jones, who had helped support the wounded Peel at Lucknow, and if an ironic fate robbed each of Hastings, Peel and Goodenough of that particular happiness, they were, like Tennyson's Sir Perceval, at least allowed to glimpse the Grail. In their last moments as fighting men each saw the glory that they had lived for, and none of them would have had it any different. For the Homeric warrior, the 'parfait gentil knyght' and the soldier of Christ alike, death – 'the experience of all experiences', as Charles Kingsley put it – was not the negation of hopes and ambitions, but what Goodenough, writing to a wife who would rejoice in his Christian triumph, called 'the happy crown of life'.

Hastings

The Happy Warrior

I

IN THE LATE AFTERNOON of 18 June 1819, a Royal Navy brig of war seven weeks out of England came into a busy Port Royal harbour on the island of Jamaica under a flamboyant press of sail. It was a manoeuvre her young commander had seen and admired in other captains, and as the *Kangaroo* came alongside the moored flagship, *Iphigenia*, he gave the order to shorten all sail and simultaneously let go her anchor.

It would have been a flashy manoeuvre in a vessel that handled better than the *Kangaroo*, and as she began to drift towards the *Iphigenia*, her commander found himself powerless to stop her. The First Lieutenant in the flagship had been engaged on the blind side of the quarterdeck as the *Kangaroo* came in, and the first he knew of the danger was when the shouting brought him across to the starboard rail to see the *Kangaroo* 'broadside on' and 'apparently drifting' under her own momentum athwart the *Iphigenia*'s cable. 'I instantly ordered the Boatswain to send out the Forecastle men to run in the flying Jib boom,' he recalled. 'Captain Parker gave orders for veering the cable which I went to see executed as the Kangaroo would certainly have been on board of us had it not been done.'

The incident and the danger were over in a moment, but the *Iphigenia* was neither the ship, nor *Iphigenia*'s captain the man to have affronted in this way. 'You have overlayed our anchor,' shouted the future Admiral Sir Hyde Parker – son of Admiral Sir Hyde Parker, grandson of Vice-Admiral Sir Hyde Parker Bt. 'You ought to be ashamed of yourself, you damned Lubber, who are you?'

It would be another thirty-six hours before Hyde Parker got a reply to his question, but the answer when it came was 'Lieutenant and Commander' Frank Abney Hastings, a fair-haired, jaw-jutting twenty-five-year-old veteran of the Napoleonic and American wars with the nose of a Wellington and rather more of his character than was good for a junior officer. He had taken over HM Survey Vessel *Kangaroo* in a murky Deptford Basin just five months earlier, and had brought to his first modest command all the enthusiasm and energy of a man who had lived for that responsibility since he had first gone to sea as an eleven-year-old on the eve of Trafalgar. 'I was a young officer,' he later pleaded in extenuation of his recklessness,

> and anxious to excel ... God forbid that I should for one instant attempt to justify in myself a conduct that I should not approve in another. I had quite recently observed with admiration the smart way in which some men of war in which I have been brought up have shortened all sail at the moment of anchoring and I was ambitious to imitate them. I feel now how injudicious it was to attempt such an evolution in a vessel like the Kangaroo.

Contrition did not come naturally to Frank Hastings, but more unfortunately it had not come early either, and long before this confession reached the Admiralty he had done all within his powers to ruin his career. On the evening of the *Kangaroo*'s arrival in Port Royal he had delivered the despatches he was carrying to the Commander-in-Chief as if nothing untoward had happened, and then like Achilles to his tent, had returned to the pregnant solitude of his captain's cabin to brood over the public nature of Parker's insult. 'When duty permitted me for a moment to reflect on the language used by Captain Parker,' he later wrote to the Lords Commissioners,

> my first impression was to apply for a Court martial ... there were officers of the army on board who could not be ignorant from its Publicity of the insult offered me & ... would have construed forbearance into cowardice ... in fact the short time I had to deliberate left me no choice but that of disgracing the Rank to which your Lordships had been pleased to appoint me or of adopting the proceeding which has unfortunately led to this explanation.

The following morning – a Sunday – he went on half-pay and, dressed in a plain blue greatcoat, had himself rowed across the harbour to Admiral Home Popham's flagship. There, on the *Iphigenia*'s quarterdeck, 'between three and four bells', he approached the officer of the watch, a Lieutenant Wood. 'Captain Hastings asked me if Captain Parker was on board,' Wood later testified: 'he at the same time gave me a note for Captain Parker saying it was from Captain Hastings. I went to the opposite side of the deck where Captain Parker was and delivered it to him, informing him it was from Captain Hastings. Captain Parker then opened the note and appeared to read it.'

'Port Royal Monday 20th June,' the hurriedly scribbled note read. 'You appear about to sail – time is precious tomorrow morning I must have that satisfaction your conduct on the 18th has rendered so indispensable. I am not provided with a friend so that I am myself the bearer of this. Frank Hastings late commander of the Kangaroo.'

It was the first in a chain of letters that would eventually stretch from Port Royal to the Admiralty and the Prince Regent. 'Sir,' Parker wrote the same day to Popham, enclosing Hastings's challenge, careful to embrace his admiral, his admiral's flagship and His Majesty's whole navy in the insult to his personal dignity:

> The day before yesterday in the evening a Brig of War, the Kangaroo, commanded by Lieutenant Frank Hastings came into Port Royal, in so unofficerlike manner as far as related to the respect which is due to all Flag Ships, and in so lubberly as far as relates to his professional duties as a seaman ... that I could not refrain from reprimanding the Officer, whoever he might be, in severe terms ...
>
> To my great astonishment however, this morning a person calling himself Capt Frank Hastings came aboard His Majesty's Ship Iphigenia and delivered the enclosed challenge ...
>
> I now most respectfully Sir, leave it to you to judge whether the discipline of the Service has not been insulted by such a proceeding ... I am satisfied that my Lords Commissioners of the Admiralty will upon this occasion approve of my conduct in bringing this Officer before a Court instead of accepting a challenge publicly delivered before the officers; contrary to the respect which is due to the Military discipline of His Majesty's Service.

As Popham's own chequered record would suggest, he was in fact a seaman of a very different cast – had Hastings issued his challenge in the first rush of blood, he later told him, he 'could almost have forgiven it the provocation was such' – but in a service that forbade duelling he had little room for manoeuvre. On the same day he instructed Commodore Sir George Collier to convene the senior captains in port aboard HMS *Sybille*, and when in another fit of hauteur and legalistic quibbling Hastings refused to attend a court that could have no jurisdiction over an officer on half-pay, the slow, deliberate processes of Admiralty justice ground into motion without him.

> 'Was the Commander in Chief's Flag flying on board the *Iphigenia* at the time the Kangaroo anchored?' Parker was asked on board the *Sybille*.
>
> 'Yes.'
>
> 'Did you consider the manner in which the Kangaroo came to an anchor Seaman-like or not?' they asked Mr Rent, the *Iphigenia*'s master.
>
> 'No – I could not avoid exclaiming – That's a lubberly trick and that I thought the Flag Captain would give it him.'

One by one – Flag Captain, Master of the *Tartar*, Master Mate of the *Kangaroo*, Master, First Lieutenant and Boatswain of the *Iphigenia* – they were all questioned, and when Lieutenant Hood reported that he had seen 'Captain Hastings shake his head in, as it struck me, a very disrespectful manner' at the retreating figure of Parker, the court's findings became a formality. '10th Aug,' John Wilson Croker – placeman supreme, model for the vile Rigby in Disraeli's *Coningsby*, and Tory Secretary to the Admiralty – scrawled crossways over the Port Royal court findings:

> This is an aggravated case of insubordination. The Board are indispensably called upon to remove Captain Frank Hastings from the list of commissioned officers in the Navy. Acqt. Sir H. Popham accordingly, & inform him also that their Lds. entirely approve the conduct of Capt Parker in refraining from noticing the challenge conveyed to him by Mr Hastings in any other manner than by transmitting it to the Rear Admiral for his information, and they desire it to be understood that even if it should be repeated at any future period, the acceptance of it on the part of Captain Parker would in their Lds' estimation be highly improper and would incur their severe displeasure.

It was the end of Frank Hastings's Royal Naval career.

II

If ever a man was doomed by birth it was Frank Abney Hastings. In the weeks and months after the *Kangaroo* incident, there was scarcely a day when one word of apology could not have saved his career, when a single gesture of moderation or even cautious self-interest could not have redeemed his reputation; but he was quite simply incapable of making it. 'Your Lordship may find officers that will submit to such language,' he wrote instead to Lord Melville, the First Lord of the Admiralty,

> but I don't envy them their dear purchased rank & God forbid the British Navy should have no better supporters of its character than such contemptible creatures. A great stress has been layed upon the circumstance of the challenge being delivered to Capt Parker on the Quarter deck, but ... why the contents of a sealed challenge should be known to bystanders any more than the contents of a dinner invitation I confess myself at a loss to divine.

If this was hardly the language of conciliation or compromise, the truth was that there was nothing in Hastings's temperament or background that would have counselled a place for either. For six hundred years the Hastings family had amassed titles and lands with a daring promiscuity, alternately the favourites and the victims of successive English monarchs to whom they were too closely related for comfort, safety or humility. 'Though the noble Earl was sprung from ancestors the most noble that this Kingdom could boast,' the *Gentleman's Magazine* wrote in 1789 on the death of Frank's grandfather, the 10th Earl of Huntingdon,

> Plantagenet, Hastings, Beauchamp, Neville, Stafford, Devereux, Pole, Stanley, it might be said also that they were most unfortunate. The Duke of Gloucester was strangled at Calais. The Duke of Clarence was put to death privately [fine word, 'private'] in the Tower. The Countess of Salisbury, his daughter, was publicly beheaded, as was also her son ... Henry Stafford, Duke of Buckingham, was beheaded by Richard III. Robert Devereux, the famous Earl of Essex, died on a scaffold in the reign of Queen Elizabeth. The untimely deaths of the gallant Nevilles are sufficiently

known. The founder of the Huntingdon family, William Lord Hastings, lost his head in the Tower ...

No family that includes Warwick the Kingmaker *and* Essex can put
such a record entirely down to ill-luck, and it sometimes seems as if
the Hastings went out of their way to import vices that were not
already indigenous to the tribe. From the sixteenth century onwards
there had been a distinct streak of religious extremism in the family,
and in the seventeenth fanaticism was wedded to real madness with
the marriage of the 5th Earl to Lucy Davies, a niece of the Lord
Castlehaven beheaded for sodomy and abetting the rape of his wife,
and the devoted daughter of that notorious prophetess, Bedlamite
and 'abominable stinking great Symnell face excrement' of Stuart
England, Lady Eleanor Davies.

To marry into one unstable family might be a misfortune, but to
marry into two smacks of something more culpable, and to the toxic
infusion of Castlehaven's Touchet blood in the seventeenth century
was added that of the Shirleys in the eighteenth. This latter alliance
came at a time when some of the old Hastings energy seemed at last
to be dissipating, but in the tyrannical and litigious Selina Shirley,
Countess of Huntingdon – cousin of the Earl Ferrers hanged for
murder, founder of the religious cult bearing her name and, by turns,
Wesleyan, mystic, ritualist and damnation-breathing Calvinist – the
Hastings could again boast a figure to hold her bigoted own with any
in the family's long and bloody history.

It is astonishing, in fact, how successfully the Hastings clan came
through an Augustan age of Lord Chesterfield, 'manners' and
rhyming couplets and emerged on the other side with all their traditions of violence and excess so wonderfully intact. In a letter to
Warren Hastings – no relative but a close friend – Frank's father once
cheerfully confessed to their 'naturally hot and spicy' blood, and
whether they were Calvinist or atheists, shooting themselves or shooting their steward, hanging rebels in America or being hanged at
Tyburn, the young Frank's immediate family bequeathed to him a
tradition of volatility that found its inevitable echo in his challenge
to Captain Hyde Parker.

Throughout his life Frank would be abnormally sensitive to the
claims of a family that, in its more modest moments, traced its ancestry back 'eleven hundred years before Christ', and for him there was
a twist that might well have added a morbid prickliness to the natu-

ral Hastings hauteur. From the first creation of the earldom in the sixteenth century the Huntingdon title had descended in more or less regulation mode to the middle of the eighteenth, but when the 9th Earl died of a fit of apoplexy in 1746, he was succeeded by a seventeen-year-old son whose well-publicised contempt for women of a marriageable class had soon eased him into the arms of the Parisian ballerina and 'first dancer of the universe', Louise – 'La Lanilla' – Madeleine Lany.

The result of that 'Philosophical and merely sentimental commerce', as his friend and moral guide Lord Chesterfield silkily put it, was a baby boy born on 11 March 1752. By the time this 'young Ascanius' arrived in the world 'La Lanilla' had already been abandoned, and while Huntingdon continued his philosophical and sentimental education on a diet of Spanish paintings and Italian women, the infant Charles was removed from France and sent over to Ireland to be brought up 'as brothers' with his cousin Francis Rawdon, the future 2nd Lord Moira in the Irish Peerage, Baron Rawdon in the English, 1st Marquis of Hastings and Governor General of India.

Of all the generations of Hastings who shaped Frank's future, Charles Hastings – his father – is infinitely the most engaging. There seems little now that can be known of his early childhood, but in 1770 he was bought a commission in the 12th of Foot, and over the next twenty years enjoyed as successful a career as was possible at that nadir of British army fortunes, distinguishing himself in America and at the siege of Gibraltar before finally rising by purchase and patronage to the rank of lieutenant general and the colonelcy of his old regiment.

With the powerful Hastings connections behind him, the friendship of the Prince of Wales, and a pedigree and personality that might have been designed for the louche world of Carlton House, the only things missing from Charles's life were the title that went into abeyance on the Earl's death in 1789 and the fortune and family seat that passed to his Moira cousin. He would have to wait another sixteen years for the minor compensation of a baronetcy, but in the year after his father's death he augmented his modest inheritance by marriage to a Parnell Abney, the sole daughter and heiress of Thomas Abney of Willesley Hall, a handsome but dilapidated estate with a landscaped park and ornamental lake just two miles south of the historical Hastings power base at Ashby-de-la-Zouch.

Charles was thirty-eight on his marriage, and still only forty-one in 1793 when war broke out with France, but to his deep frustration a Tory government could find no active use for him in the years ahead. The seven years between 1796 and 1803 were spent instead in command of the garrison on Jersey, and by the time his friends came into power, age, ill-health and a growing melancholy had reduced him to a kind of English version of Tolstoy's old Prince Bolkonski, brooding in his library over his maps and despatches as Bonaparte's armies redrew the boundaries of Europe.

It is hard to imagine what solace a world-weary free-thinker can have found in Parnell Hastings – 'a great bore' is the only surviving judgement on her – but the one thing they shared was a deep love of their two surviving children. It would seem that their eldest, Charles, was always closer to his mother than to his father, but if there were times when the old general thought a good dose of peppers in the boy's porridge would cure him of his 'milk-sop' tendencies, there were no such fears over his younger and favourite lad, Frank, born in 1794 and destined from an early age for a career in the navy.

With his father's royal and military connections – Lord Rawdon was Commander-in Chief for Scotland and Sir John Moore a close friend – it seems odd that Frank did not follow him into the army, and odder still when one remembers the grim reality of naval life in 1805. In May 1803 the brief and bogus Peace of Amiens had come to its predictable end, and for the two years since Britain's weary and overstretched navy had struggled from the Mediterranean narrows to the North Sea to contain the threat of the French and Spanish fleets while the country steeled itself for invasion.

It is only in retrospect that 1805 seems *the* year to go to sea, because with Napoleon abandoning his invasion plans, and the allied fleets holing up in Cádiz after their West Indies flirtation, the only certain prospect facing Frank as his father took him down to Plymouth was the 'long, tiresome and harassing blockade' work that had become the navy's stock in trade. 'I think it incumbent upon me to announce to you the disposal of my boy,' a grateful Charles Hastings wrote to Warren Hastings on 11 June 1805, a month after entering Frank as a Volunteer First Class under the command of one of Nelson's most bilious, courageous and uxorious captains, the solidly Whig Thomas Fremantle, 'whom you were so kind as to patronize by writing to Lord St Vincent. He is at present with the Channel fleet on board the Neptune of 98 guns commanded by my friend Captain

Fremantle. We have heard from him since, and he is so delighted with his profession that he declares nothing shall ever tempt him to quit it – I took him down to Plymouth myself.'

It would be hard to exaggerate how alien and hermetic a world it was that closed around the young Hastings when his father deposited him at Plymouth. As a small child growing up on Jersey he would have been familiar enough with garrison life, but nothing could have prepared him for the overpowering strangeness of a great sea-port during wartime, its utter self-sufficiency and concentration of purpose, its remoteness from the normal rhythms of national life, its distinctive mix of chaos and order, its forest of masts and myriad ships' boats, or the sheer, outlandish oddity of its inhabitants. 'The English keep the secrets of their navy close guarded,' the young Robert Southey, masquerading in print as the travelling Spanish nobleman Don Manuel Alvarez Espriella, wrote two years later of his attempt to penetrate the sealed-off worlds of Britain's historic ports. 'The streets in Plymouth are swarming with sailors. This extraordinary race of men hold the soldier in utter contempt, which with their characteristic force, they express by this scale of comparison, – Mess-mate before ship-mate, ship-mate before a stranger, a stranger before a dog, and a dog before a soldier.'

At the outbreak of the Napoleonic War the Royal Navy was quite simply the largest and most complex industrialised organisation in the world, and it was in the great south coast ports of Plymouth or Portsmouth that this took on its most overwhelming physical expression. 'A self-contained walled-town,' wrote Caroline Alexander in her magical evocation of the dockyards that serviced the world's greatest fleet – eighty-eight ships of the line in commission the year Frank joined, thirteen 'Fifties', 125 frigates, ninety-two sloops, eighteen bombs, forty gunbrigs, six gunboats, eighty-two cutters and schooners and forty-one armed ships,

> the great yard encompassed every activity required to send ships to sea ... There were offices and storehouses, and neat brick houses ... as well as the massive infrastructure required to produce a ship. In the Rope-house all cordage was spun, from light line to massive anchor cable, in lengths of more than a thousand feet, some so thick that eighty men were required to handle them ... Timber balks and spires of wood lay submerged in the Main Pond, seasoning until called to use. In the blacksmith's shop were wrought ninety

hundred-weight anchors in furnaces that put visitors in mind of
'the forge of Vulcan.' And on the slips, or docked along the waterfront, were the 180-foot hulls of men-of-war, the great battle-
wounded ships brought for recovery, or the skeletons of new craft,
their hulking, cavernous frames suggesting monstrous sea animals
from a vanished, fearsome age.

Along with all this industrial might came the people, the contractors
and tradesmen, the wives and prostitutes, the shopkeepers and clerks,
and the thousands of workers who kept the fleets at sea. 'I could not
think what world I was in,' another boy recalled his introduction to
this alien culture, 'whether among spirits or devils. All seemed
strange; different language and strange expressions of tongue, that I
thought myself always asleep or in a dream, and never properly
awake.'

If it was an alien world, though, with its own language and
languages – England, Ireland, Canada, America, the Baltic, Spain,
Portugal, Puerto Rico, Martinique, Sardinia, Venice, they were all
represented in *Neptune* – its own customs, and traditions, its own
time-keeping, arcane ways of business and overlapping hierarchies,
it was a world the young Hastings took to as if he had known no
other. 'Whilst on board with him (although only eleven years old last
month),' Sir Charles proudly told Warren Hastings, 'he offered to go
up the masthead without going through the Lubbers' hole which
however Capt Fremantle would not permit as I could not have borne
seeing him make the attempt – I have no doubt that he will do very
well if his education is not neglected but as there is a Schoolmaster
on board I entertain great hopes of him making a proficiency.'

There were thirty-four boys in all entered in *Neptune*'s muster
book – the youngest nine years old (there was a four-year-old girl in
Victory, born in HMS *Ardent* in the middle of the Battle of Copenhagen) – though only a handful rated 'Volunteer First Class' who
were destined to be officers. There was still such a wide divergence
of practice from ship to ship that it is impossible to generalise about
these boys' duties, but in a world of interest and patronage, the naturally symbiotic relationship of captain and volunteer was a well-
connected boy like Hastings's best guarantee of the training his father
had wanted for him. 'My Dear General,' – that 'most mischievous
political quack ... Mr Pitt' was still alive and the general as yet without his baronetcy – Captain Fremantle was soon writing to Frank's

father, conscientiously carrying out his side of the bargain: '... of your boy I can say nothing but what ought to make you and Mrs Hastings very happy, he is very mild and tractable, attentive to his books & *dashing* when with the youngsters of his own age. I declare I have had no occasion to hint even anything to him, as he is so perfectly well behaved.'

With all the 'dash' and patronage in the world, a man-of-war like *Neptune*, with her 116 marines and ship's company of 570 brawling, drunken, thieving seamen recruited or pressed from across the globe, was a tough school for any boy. 'Who can paint in words what I felt?' Edward Trelawny, whose path would later cross with Hastings's in Greece, histrionically recalled his first days as a thirteen-year-old midshipman in that summer of 1805. 'Imagine me torn from my native country, destined to cross the wide ocean, to a wild region, cut off from every tie, or possibility of communication, transported like a felon, as it were, for life ... I was torn away, not seeing my mother, or brothers, or sisters, or one familiar face; no voice to speak a word of comfort, or to inspire me with the smallest hope that anything human took an interest in me.'

Trelawny had his own sub-Byronic line in self-pity and self-dramatisation to peddle, but even in *Neptune* and under a captain like Fremantle, there were no soft edges to the gunroom. 'I thought my heart would break with grief,' William Badcock, a fellow 'mid' in *Neptune* when Hastings joined, recalled. 'The first night on board was not the most pleasant; the noises unusual to a novice – sleeping in a hammock for the first time – its tarry smell – the wet cables for a bed carpet ... Time however reconciles us to everything, and the gaiety and thoughtlessness of youth, added to the cocked hat, desk, spy-glass, etc of a nautical fit out, assisted wonderfully to dry my tears.'

And for all the brutal horseplay – 'sawing your bed-posts', 'reefing your bed-clothes', 'blowing the grampus' (sluicing a new boy with water) – and the ever-present threat of the 'sky parlour' or masthead for punishment, there was none of the institutional or private tyranny in *Neptune* so vividly recorded in Trelawny's *Adventures of a Younger Son*. A midshipman coming off watch might spend his first half-hour unravelling his tightly knotted blanket in the dark, but with cribbage and draughts to play, book work to be done and stories of Captain Cook to be wheedled out of the old quartermaster, Badcock did his 'fellows in Neptune the justice to say that a more kind-hearted set was not to be met with'.

Hastings did not have long in Plymouth to acclimatise himself to this new world. On 17 May, after a hasty refit, the *Neptune* was ready again for sea. 'I begin my journal with saying that I have passed as miserable a day and night as I could well expect,' Fremantle complained to his wife Betsey the same night, as his sluggish-handling new ship pitched and rolled in heavy seas and Plymouth, home and family slipped below the horizon:

> tho' I have no particular reason why that should be the case ... I dined with young Hastings only on a fowl and some salt pork, as triste as a gentleman needs to be ... my mind hangs constantly towards you and your children, and I am at times so low I cannot hold up my head ... my only hope is in a peace, which I trust in God may be brought about through the mediation of Russia. These French rascals will never come out and fight but will continue to annoy and wear out both our spirits and constitutions.

This two-month cruise with the Channel Squadron gave Hastings his first experience of blockade work, and after another brief refit at Plymouth he was soon again at sea. Fremantle had no more real belief in bringing the French out to battle than he had ever had, but by 3 August they were once more off Ushant and before the end of the month had joined Collingwood's growing squadron blockading the enemy fleets inside Cádiz. 'I am in hope Lord Nelson will come here as nobody is to my mind so equal to the command as he is,' Fremantle wrote to his wife on 31 August:

> it will require some management to supply so large a force with water and provisions, and as the combined fleets are safely lodged in Cadiz, here I conclude we shall remain until Domesday or until we are blown off the Coast, when the French men will again escape us. I can say little about my Ship, we go much as usual and if any opportunity offers of bringing the Enemy's Fleet to battle, I think she will show herself, but still I am not half satisfied at being in a large Ship that don't sail and must be continually late in action.

They might well have stayed there till doomsday, but while Fremantle fretted and flogged, a messenger was already on the road to Cádiz with orders for the French Admiral Villeneuve to take the fleet into the Mediterranean in support of the Emperor's new European ambitions. From the collapse of the Peace of Amiens Napoleon's naval strategy had been marked by an utter disregard for realities, but this time he had excelled himself, timing his orders to arrive on the very day before Fremantle and the whole blockading fleet at last got their wish for Nelson. 'On the 28th of September was joined by H.M. Ship Victory Admirl Lord Nelson,' wrote James Martin, an able seaman in *Neptune*, 'and the Ajax and the Thunderer it is Imposeble to Discribe the Heartfelt Satifaction of the whole fleet upon this Occasion and the Confidance of Success with which we ware Inspired.'

'I think if you were to see the Neptune you would find her very much altered since you were on bd,' Fremantle told Frank's father, sloth, dyspepsia and ill-temper all dispersed by a single dinner with Nelson and the promise of the second place in the line in any coming action. 'We are all now scraping the ship's sides to paint like the Victory [black, with buff-coloured stripes running between the portholes], the fellows make such a noise I can hardly hear myself. Pray make my respects to Mrs Hastings & beg her [to have] no wit of apprehension about her son who has made many friends here, & who is able to take his own part.'

Opinions were still divided as to whether or not the French would come out, but with five 'spy' frigates posted close in to the city, and Nelson's battle plan circulated among the captains, the fleet knew what was expected of them. In the brute simplicity of the tactics Hastings was to learn an invaluable lesson, but the great danger of breaking the line in the way Nelson intended was that it ceded the opening advantage to the enemy, exposing a sluggish handler like *Neptune* in the light October breezes to the full enemy broadsides for anything up to twenty minutes before she could get beneath a foe's vulnerable stern.

Nobody in *Neptune* was under any illusion as to what that would mean, but nothing could contain the excitement when the signal from the inshore squadron finally came. 'All hearts towards evening beat with joyful anxiety for the next day,' Badcock wrote on 20 October, as *Neptune* answered the signal for a general chase, 'which we hoped would crown an anxious blockade with a successful battle. When night closed in, the rockets and blue lights, with signal guns, informed us the inshore squadron still kept sight of our foes, and like good and watchful dogs, our ships continue to send forth occasionally a growly cannon to keep us on the alert, and to cheer us with the hope of a glorious day on the morrow.'

As partitions, furnishings and bulkheads were removed, decks cleared, livestock slaughtered – Fremantle had a goat on board that had provided him with milk – *Neptune* turned south-west to give her the weather gage in the coming action. From the signals of their 'watchdogs' they knew that the enemy were still moving in a southerly direction, and as dawn broke on 21 October, first one sail and then a whole 'forest of strange masts' appeared some eleven miles to leeward to show that the Combined Fleet was at last where Nelson wanted it.

The sun, William Badcock – midshipman of the forecastle and first in *Neptune* to see the enemy – remembered, 'looked hazy and watery, as if it smiled in tears on many brave hearts which fate had decreed should never see it set ... I ran aft and informed the officer of the watch. The captain was on deck in a moment, and ere it was well light, the signals were flying through the fleet to bear up and form the order of sailing in two columns.'

As the ship slipped into those atavistic rhythms that no one who witnessed them ever forgot, and hammocks were stowed, cutlasses and muskets distributed, powder horns and spare flintlocks issued, magazines and powder rooms unlocked, operating area prepared, and final letters written, full sail was set and *Neptune* strove to take her place in the line. In Nelson's original battle plan Fremantle had been ordered to follow *Temeraire*, *Superb* and *Victory* in the weather division, but with only the short October day ahead of them, and speed crucial if the enemy were not to escape, precedence went out of the window in favour of an *ad hoc* order that left the two columns to sort themselves out, as sailing capacities dictated, behind *Victory* and the *Royal Sovereign*.

It was now that the 'old *Neptune*, which never was a good sailer', as William Badcock put it, 'took it into her head to sail better that morning than I ever remembered', and at about 10 a.m. she came up alongside Nelson's *Victory*. Fremantle intended to 'pass her and break the enemy's line', Badcock recalled, 'but poor Lord Nelson hailed us from the stern-walk of the *Victory*, and said, "*Neptune*, take in your studding-sails and drop astern; I shall break the line myself."'

It was probably the eleven-year-old Hastings's sole glimpse of Nelson, but if he ever wondered what it was that gave him his unique hold over men, he did not have long to wait for an answer. As *Neptune* dropped astern of *Victory*, and the *Temeraire* slipped between them to take her place in the van, Nelson's last signal before the order to 'engage' was relayed through the fleet. 'At 11,' the *Neptune*'s log laconically noted, 'Answered the general signal, "England expects every man will do his duty"; Captain Fremantle inspected the different decks, and made known the above signal, which was received with cheers.'

He 'addressed us at our Different Quarters in words few', James Martin remembered, 'but Intimated that … all that was Dear to us Hung upon a Ballance and their Happyness depended upon us and their safty allso Happy the Man who Boldly Venture his Life in such a Cause if he shold Survive the Battle how Sweet will be the Recolection be [sic] and if he fall he fall Covred with Glory and Honnor and Morned By a Greatfull Country the Brave Live Gloryous and Lemented Die.'

In the heavy swell and light winds – and to the sounds of 'Rule Britannia' and 'Britons Strike Home' drifting across the water from ships' bands – *Neptune* closed on the enemy with agonising slowness. 'It was a beautiful sight,' Badcock wrote,

> when their line was completed; their broadsides turned towards us, showing their iron teeth, and now and then trying the range of a shot to ascertain the distance, that they might, the moment we came within point blank (about six hundred yards), open the fire upon our van ships … Some of them were painted like ourselves – with double yellow sides, some with a broad single red or yellow streak; others all black, and the noble *Santissima Trinidada* (158), with four distinct lines of red, with a white ribbon between … her head splendidly ornamented with a colossal group of figures, painted white, representing the Holy Trinity … This magnificent ship was destined to be our opponent.

It was not just a 'beautiful sight', but an exhilarating and terrifying one, and at the stately walking pace at which the fleets closed there was all the time in the world to take it in. At 11.30 *Neptune*'s log at last recorded the signal 'to locate the enemy's line, and engage to leeward', and as first *Victory* and then *Temeraire* broke through ahead, and *Neptune* prepared to receive her opening broadsides, Fremantle ordered everyone, except the officers, to lie down to reduce casualties.

Until this moment Hastings had been on the quarterdeck with Fremantle, an unusually small, frightened and superfluous spectator, neatly dressed in the new suit Betsey Fremantle had had made for him, but to his future chagrin the First Lieutenant now ordered him to a safer circle of hell below. 'A man should witness a battle in a three-decker from the middle deck,' a young marine lieutenant in *Victory* later wrote, struggling to evoke the blind, smoke-filled, deafening chaos of the battle that awaited Hastings as he made his way down to the lower decks of *Neptune*,

> for it beggars all description: it bewilders the senses of sight and hearing. There was the fire from above, the fire from below, besides the fire from the deck I was upon, the guns recoiling with violence, reports louder than thunder, the decks heaving and the sides straining. I fancied myself in the infernal regions, where every man appeared a devil. Lips might move, but orders and hearing were out of the question, everything was done by signs.

Even to those still on the quarterdeck, the smoke of battle and the tangle of fallen masts and rigging had already obscured *Victory*, but as *Neptune* closed on her target, the gap that Nelson had punched between Villeneuve's *Bucentaure* and *Redoubtable* widened to welcome her. For the final ten minutes of her approach *Neptune* was forced to take the combined fire of three enemy ships, until at 12.35 she at last broke through astern of *Bucentaure* and, in the perfect tactical position, delivered a broadside from thirty yards' range. 'At 12.35, we broke their line,' the log reads – a typical mix of understatement, spurious accuracy, guesswork and partial knowledge.

> At 12.47, we engaged a two-deck ship, with a flag at the mizzen. At 1.30, entirely dismasted her, she struck her colours; and bore down and attacked the Santa Trinidada, a Spanish four-decker of 140 guns … raked her as we passed under her stern; and at 1.50 opened our fire on her starboard quarter. At 2.40, shot away her main and mizzen masts; at 2.50, her foremast; at 3, she cried for quarter, and hailed us to say they had surrendered; she then stuck English colours to the stump of her main mast; gave her three cheers.

Neptune herself was in little better shape – 'standing and running rigging much cut; foretop-gallant and royal yard shot away … wounded in other places; fore yard nearly shot in two, and ship pulled in several places' – but as the smoke cleared they caught their first overview of the shambles around them. 'We had now Been Enverloped with Smoak Nearly three Howers,' wrote James Martin. 'Upon this Ships [*Santa Trinidada*] striking the Smoak Clearing a way then we had a vew of the Hostle fleet thay were scattred a Round us in all Directions Sum Dismasted and Sum were Compleat wrecks Sum had Left of Fireng and sum ware Engagen with Redoubled furey it was all most imposeble to Distinguish to what Nation thay Belonged.'

It was a momentary respite – 'but a few minets to take a Peep a Round us' – but in the midst of this chaos they could see *Victory* and *Temeraire* still 'warmly engaged' and, more critically, 'the six van ships of the enemy bearing down to attack' them. In his original memorandum Nelson had anticipated this second phase of the battle, and as separate ship-actions continued to the rear of them, *Neptune*, *Leviathan*, *Conqueror* and *Agamemnon* manoeuvred to form a rough line of defence. 'At 3.30, opened fire on them,' *Neptune*'s log continued, 'assisted by the *Leviathan* and *Conqueror*; observed one of them to have all her masts shot away by our united fire.'

With nearly all her own sails shot away, however, and not 'a brace or bowline left', *Neptune* was in no state to give chase when the remaining enemy abandoned their attack and escaped to southward. For another hour or so the fight continued around them in a mix of close actions and long-range duels, but for *Neptune* – and, at 4.30, just a quarter of an hour after she had ceased firing, Nelson himself – the battle was over. 'Three different powers to rule the main,' ran a popular song reflecting on the fate of the three 'Neptunes' that had fought at Trafalgar,

> Assumed old Neptune's name:
> One from Gallia, one from Spain,
> And one from England came.
>
> The British *Neptune* as of yore,
> Proved master of the day;
> The Spanish *Neptune* is no more,
> The French one ran away.

In the immediate aftermath of the battle, though, as carpenters and surgeons went to work with their knives and saws, corpses were flung overboard, and the news of Nelson's death spread through the fleet,

there was little temptation to triumphalism. During his last moments
Nelson had repeatedly enjoined Hardy to drop anchor at the end of
the day, and yet for some inexplicable reason Collingwood decided
against it, condemning his scattered and dismasted fleet itself to every
sailor's nightmare of a heavy swell, a freshening wind and a perilous
lee shore.

It would have been harder to say which stuck most vividly in men's
memories of Trafalgar, the battle itself or its terrible aftermath, as the
stricken members of the fleet fought for their lives and prizes against
a gale that was of a piece with everything that had gone before. In
spite of her damage the *Neptune* was actually in a better state than
most to ride it out, and after taking the *Royal Sovereign* in tow the
following day, she was deployed again on the twenty-third to counter
a bold enemy attempt to recapture what it could of its lost ships.

With the weather worsening again after a brief respite – the
barometer reading that night at the Royal Observatory just south of
Cádiz was the lowest ever recorded – and the shattered Combined
Fleet in no state to renew a general action, anxieties in *Neptune*
rapidly turned to their hard-won prize. From the moment they had
gone into action the towering *Santissima Trinidada* – the largest
battleship in the world – had been marked as *theirs*, and their first
sight of her after the battle, when a prize crew under William
Badcock went aboard to take possession, provided a bloody testament to the appalling destruction *Neptune*'s 'beautiful firing' had
inflicted. 'She had between 3 and 400 killed and wounded,' Badcock
told his father, 'her Beams where coverd with Blood, Brains, and
peices of Flesh, and the after part of her Decks with wounded, some
without Legs and some without an Arm, what calamities War brings
on.'

As conditions grew more desperate than ever, and self-interest gave
way to self-preservation, Collingwood gave the order to 'sink, burn
and destroy' all prizes, and Badcock's thwarted crew went to work
in the dark and mountainous seas. 'We had to tie the poor mangled
wretches around their waists, or where we could,' another of
Neptune's officers recalled, as lower gun ports were opened, holes
cut in the hull, and the last of the wounded winched off, 'and lower
them into a tumbling boat, some without arms, others no legs, and
lacerated all over in the most dreadful manner.'

There were 407 taken off in the *Neptune*'s boats alone – a last boat
went back for the ship's cat, spotted perched on the muzzle of a gun

as the *Trinidada* rolled helplessly in her death throes – and shortly after midnight the pride of the Spanish fleet and *Neptune*'s prize-money went to the bottom. 'I am afraid this brilliant Action will not put much money in my pocket,' wrote Fremantle – unusually benign for him, given that he had nothing more tangible to show for Trafalgar than the *Trinidada*'s pug dog (the cat had gone to *Ajax*),

> but I think much may arise out of it ultimately. This last Week has been a scene of Anxiety and fatigue beyond any I ever experienced … I am at present towing the *Victory* and the Admiral has just made the signal for me to go with her to Gibraltar … We have ten men killed and 37 Wounded, which is very trifling when compared to some of the other Ships, however we alone have certainly the whole credit of taking the *Santissima Trinidada*, who struck to *us alone*. Adml. Villeneuve was with me over two days, I found him a very pleasant and Gentlemanlike man, the poor man was very low! … This fatigue and employment has entirely driven away the bile and if poor Nelson had not been among the slain I should be most completely satisfied.

His letter is dated 'off Cadiz the 28th Oct. 1805'. He was right to be satisfied. By any other measure than a butcher's bill the *Neptune* had acquitted herself heroically. '7 November,' reads the ship's log ten days later, as they made passage for Gibraltar: 'Captain Fremantle read a letter of thanks from Vice Admiral Collingwood to all officers & men belonging to the Fleet for their conduct on the 21st Octo. Performed Divine Service & returned thanks to the Almighty God for the victory gained on the day.' Frank Hastings would have done well to have forgotten his father's atheism and joined in. At the age of just eleven he had survived the storm of the century and the greatest battle ever fought under sail. The next time – twenty-two years later at Navarino – there would be an action of similar proportions, his brilliance and daring would have gone a long way towards provoking it.

III

One of the great disappointments of Hastings's story is that there is neither a portrait of the unusually small, fair-haired lad who had fought at Trafalgar, nor any surviving account from him of his part in the battle. It is clear from the Fremantle correspondence that Frank wrote an indignant protest at being sent below, but it would seem likely that his disappointed father destroyed that along with all his other letters in the aftermath of the *Kangaroo* incident, reducing his boy at one embittered stroke to a silent and anonymous role in all the great dramas of his early life.

There is an unusually rich and varied archive to fill the gaps – captains' letters, testimonials, Admiralty minutes, ships' logs, tailors' bills – but nothing quite makes up for the absence of Frank's own voice. It is easy enough to follow the external outline of his career over the next six years, but the formative steps that operated on his genetic inheritance to transform him from the small frightened boy on the quarterdeck of *Neptune* into the commander of the *Kangaroo* remain frustratingly, elusively, out of reach.

By the time one hears his own voice, the movement and rhythms of a man-of-war, the mouldering damp and discomfort, the proximity of death and violence, the chronic sleeplessness and brutal intimacy that were the universal experience of any young officer were so much a part of his nature that they pass unnoticed. In the youthful letters of a Peel or Goodenough there is a vivid sense of what it was *like* to be a boy at sea, but when Hastings finally emerges from his midshipman's chrysalis it is as the finished product, as inured to the hardships and dangers of naval life as he is to the sense of wonder and curiosity that clearly once touched him.

There are times, in fact – so complete is the absence of 'colour', so absolute the sense of purpose and concentration in his adult letters – when it feels as though one is following a man through a sensory desert. Over the last ten years of the Napoleonic Wars he served and fought from the China Seas to the Gulf of Mexico, yet one would no more know from Hastings what it felt like to be shipwrecked in the icy black waters off Halifax than how shattering it was to drag a massive naval gun through the swamps and bayous of New Orleans.

The magical island fortresses of the Ligurian Sea, the baroque grandeur of Valetta, the feckless elegance of Nauplia's Palamidi fortress, the harsh and brilliant clarity of the Cyclades, the romance of the Dardanelles, the numinous charge that attaches itself to the landscape of Greece – these were the background to his fighting life, but one would need one's longitudes and latitudes to know it. It was not that Hastings was blind to either people or place – he was a naval officer trained to *see* and record – but where other men looked at modern Nafpaktos and saw historic Lepanto, Hastings looked at Lepanto and saw Nafpaktos; where other men saw the harbour from which the *Argo* sailed or the little ribbon of island on which Spartan soldiers first surrendered, Hastings saw only currents, breezes, lines of fire and anchorages.

It cannot have been always so – he was too intelligent, too widely cultured, too well-liked, too much a man of the Age of Byron for that – and no such child can have excited the intense affection and dread with which family and friends awaited the news from Trafalgar. The first despatches from Collingwood had reached Falmouth after a voyage of only eight days, but for the families in the great houses, cottages, vicarages and deaneries that serviced the navy the arrival of the schooner *Pickle* signalled just the start of the waiting. 'Thursday 7th Nov. I was much alarmed by Nelly's *ghastly* appearance immediately after breakfast,' Betsey Fremantle wrote in her journal, the day after Collingwood's despatches reached London,

> who came in to say Dudley had brought from Winslow the account that a most dreadful action had been fought off Cadiz, Nelson & several Captains killed, & twenty ships were taken. I really felt undescribable misery until the arrival of the Post, but was relieved from such a wretched state of anxious suspense by a letter from Lord Garlies, who congratulated me on Fremantle's safety & the conspicuous share he had in the Victory gained on the 21st off Cadiz … I fear the number of killed and wounded will be very great when the returns are sent. How thankful I am Fremantle has once more escaped unhurt. The accounts greatly shook my nerves.

For the Hastings family, immured in the middle of the English countryside with their maps and their fears, the wait was still longer. 'I should certainly not have delayed so long writing to you had I not so much leisure on my hands,' Frank's father at last wrote to Warren Hastings more than six weeks after the battle.

Great inclination to oblige, frequent opportunities of doing it and a thorough conviction of its propriety, all this made the matter so easy that I never failed every morning at breakfast to declare my intention, always however determining to put it off to the last moment of the post, in order to send you news, which not coming, I thought it hardly worthwhile to trouble you, and so it went on until the glorious victory of Trafalgar was announced when my anxiety for your little protégé my son Frank only eleven years old who was on board the Neptune so damped my spirits, & absorbed every other consideration, as to render me unfit for any other thing, and it was not till about ten days ago that our minds were set at ease by the returns of the Neptune at last arriving, and also seeing a letter from my little Hero which completely dissipated every anxiety.

The wait had put a strain on even his oldest and closest friendship – Lord Moira, thinking that Frank was with Cornwallis in the Channel had written flippantly to Charles Hastings – but when the news came everything was forgotten in the flood of relief and goodwill. 'Most truly do I congratulate you,' Moira wrote almost immediately again, '… on the safety of your Frank … When he comes to be prosing in his cane chair at Fourscore it will be a fine thing to have to boast of sharing the glory in the Battle of Trafalgar.'

'My Dear General,' wrote the Duke of Northumberland – another old soldier in the American Wars with a son in the navy,

I have longed for some time to congratulate you on the English Victory gained over the combined fleets of France & Spain, but could not do so till I saw an authenticated List of the killed and wounded. Last night relieved me from my difficulties, & brought me the Gazette Extraordinary, & I now therefore take the earliest opportunity of writing to say how happy I am that my friend your youngster has had his share in so glorious a Victory unhurt. I hope he likes the Sea as well as ever, and flatter myself, He will in time prove another Lord Collingwood. I should have said Nelson but that I would prefer his being a Great Living Naval Character, to a dead one.

There was more than a touch of Jane Austen's Mrs Musgrove about Parnell Hastings, and as the letters flowed in at Willesley anxiety gave way to a pride every bit as extravagant. 'Mrs Hastings is a great bore,' Fremantle wrote back to his wife, after she had complained of the Hastings dragging 'poor' Captain Arklom – previously in *Neptune* – to dinner to ply him with 'silly questions about their Boy'.

> I am afraid Hastings will shoot me, for the first Lieutenant think-
> ing such a small child could not be of use on Deck desired him to
> go below, which he did *without remorse*, but *is* now ashamed of it
> and have wrote to his father something on the Subject, you must
> call upon the Woman, and say what is really true that he is a very
> clever and well disposed boy, and very attentive to his Navigation,
> if you are half as fidgety about your Doddy who seems to occupy
> you so much, I will break every bone in your skin.

There is a foreshadowing here of the older Hastings – morbidly sensi-tive, proud, honourable, intense – and probably a glimpse, too, of the endless teasing and ragging that was part and parcel of a gun-room world that hovered between the chivalries of war and the brute realities of a floating prep school. 'Young Hastings get [sic] Volumes by every opportunity,' Fremantle wrote to his wife, as the *Neptune* resumed blockading duties off Cádiz. 'His mother put his letters to my address without an envelope, but the part opposite the seal concluded with your Affe. Mother it made no difference, as I did not read a Sylable [sic], indeed if I had I conclude it contained much what Mothers write to their Children at that age.'

Child or not, though – and Hastings was now just twelve – there was a career to be planned for him if he was to be a second Colling-wood, and on 2 June 1806 he was transferred by boat from the *Neptune* to the forty-two-gun *Sea Horse* under the command of Captain John Stewart. In his later years Hastings never forgot the seamanship and sheer endurance demanded by a winter blockade in *Neptune*, but the frigate and not the lumbering three-decker was the glamour ship of the navy, the vessel in which captains made their names and fortunes and young officers and midshipmen had their chance to punch above their rank and weight.

The move was the making of Hastings – the *Sea Horse* the perfect training in the kind of coastal warfare he would make his own – but before that there was convoy duty and a return to England for the

first time in eighteen months. 'My boy of Trafalgar is just arrived,'
Sir Charles wrote proudly to Warren Hastings from Willesley on 2
November, only five days after the *Sea Horse* anchored at
Portsmouth: 'he appears an unlicked cub – but is considerably
advanced in nautical knowledge for his age and time of service – he
is only thirteen [twelve in fact] last Febry has been but a year and a
half at sea, and is as capable of keeping a day's reckoning, putting the
ship about, in short navigating a ship on board, and that is according to the Capt's testimony.'

This was not all blind partiality – the only fault Captain Stewart
could find with his charge was that he would not *grow* – and Warren
Hastings was more than happy to respond in kind. 'I think you have
much happiness yet in store,' he wrote back. 'You will live to see one
of your sons a finished gentleman; and the other standing on the
summit of glory as a British seaman. Charles Imhoff [Warren Hastings's stepson] tells me he never saw a youth so much improved, in
knowledge, manners or manliness, as the latter in the short time in
which he has not seen him.'

Frank had just two months at Willesley – his first holiday at the
old Abney seat to which his parents had recently returned – and it was
probably as well that he could call on his blockading experience to
prepare him for the rigours of home life. He had been only two years
old when his father moved to Jersey, and the family's long absence
had left the house in a state of almost comic dilapidation, its roof leak-
ing, draughts howling, the beds a misery, and the dining table so small
– Sir Charles complained to Warren Hastings – that the family could
not dress for dinner until *after* dinner because they spent their meals
kicking each other under the table and filthying each other's clothes.

Almost nothing is left now of Willesley – the ornamental lake, the
contours of an eighteenth-century landscaped park – but a Vanbrugh-
esque stable gateway of Cyclopean proportions gives some idea of
what Sir Charles Hastings took on when the family returned to their
'ruined mansion'. A surviving estate book underlines how seriously
he took his duties, but if he did all he could to indulge his wife's and
his son Charles's passion for the place, he remained at heart the man
of affairs he had always been, stoically resigned to finding himself
dependent on the London mail or a sight of his boy, Frank, for proof
that there was a world beyond his Willesley exile.

He was determined, too, that Frank's future should not be forgotten while he was at home, taking on the best mathematics tutor that

he could find for him; but by the beginning of January 1807 the *Sea Horse* was being fitted for sea and the end of the holiday was in sight. 'I have been much more interested about the brilliant exploits of Sir J. Duckworth in the Archipelago, or rather against the Porte,' Sir Charles wrote rather prematurely to Warren Hastings on 17 April, after the *Sea Horse* had been diverted from the Far East to the Mediterranean to face a growing Turkish threat in the Aegean, 'and if it is true that he has forced the Dardanelles and destroyed the whole Turkish navy – Lady Hastings may sleep in peace for she has been much alarmed at the boy going up the Mediterranean and being taken by one of their corsairs and perhaps undergoing a certain operation that would fit him more for the Seraglio than the Navy.'

Frank was well out of the dismal failure of Duckworth's expedition, and if he had had to forgo Warren Hastings's Eastern patronage, the Hastings name worked just as well closer to home. 'I have much pleasure in acquainting you your Dear Frank is in the highest health and spirits,' General Sir John Smith, an old colleague of Frank's father on Sir Henry Clinton's staff during the American War of Independence, wrote from Gibraltar on 21 July: 'he dined with me about ten days since and Sailed again two days after to join Lord Collingwood ... I beg my Dr Sir Charles will rest assured that his old academical fellow poet – Jack Smith – will make a point of paying all possible attention to his son Frank Hastings and that he shall have a mother in Mrs Smith when necessary – anything you may wish to send him – direct to my care and he shall receive it safe.'

With the inevitable lag in news there would always be something for Lady Hastings to worry about, and Mrs Smith was already too late with her motherly attentions. 'We are just returned from a rather successful cruise,' John Stewart, another bold, intelligent and talented frigate captain, who had circumnavigated the globe with *Vancouver*, had written to Sir Charles a fortnight earlier,

and going to sail again in search of Lord Collingwood, who we conclude is gone up to attempt what I expect he will not succeed in, as the French influence will keep the Turks in a warlike temper ... We have been unlucky enough to lose a Lieutnt last cruise he was killed in a boat by a round shot which also took the arm of little Lord John Hay [aged fourteen] both of which things vexed me ... the former however could not have been prevented, but the little

boys were expressly forbid going, I found young Hay had been a
favourite of the poor Lieutnt [Young], & had been smuggled into
the boat.*

The incident was not enough to stop Hastings stowing away in the
ship's boat just five days later – 'I gave him a scold but could not be
very angry,' Stewart told Sir Charles – but a Mediterranean frigate
was no place to hide a boy. The injury to Hay had occurred in the
Hyères Roads while the *Sea Horse* was engaged with an enemy
bombard and merchantman, and over the next two years she was in
constant action, exchanging fire with shore batteries at Barcelona,
cutting out French vessels, capturing the castle of Pianosa off Elba or
destroying magazines and guns in a brilliant raid on Isola di Giannutri in the Ligurian Sea. 'All our frigate captains are great generals,'
an exhausted but grateful Collingwood, the commander-in-chief in

---

* 'As I may not have time to write in Malta,' Stewart began a second and fuller
letter to the Marquis of Tweeddale, Lord John's brother, that wonderfully
captures the ethos and conditions of frigate life in the Mediterranean for boys
like Hastings or Hay,

I do so now to tell you that Lord John is quite recovered after a very
dangerous operation which he underwent May 16th. He had unknown to
me (or indeed to any officer except the officer of the boat he went in) gone
in our larger cutter with the 3rd Lieut in charge of some vessels which we
were also chasing in the ship, upon seeing them run on shore we backed
& gave it up, unfortunately a round shot from a battery struck the
coxswain of the large boat & knocked him overboard with the loss of his
thigh, as the boat was going fast it was some little time before they could
pull around to pick him up, the next shot from the same gun struck the
Lieutnt in the very centre of the breast, went through a Marine's body &
carried off John's left arm close to the shoulder. I saw something was wrong
and sent the surgeon who found the Lieutnt & Marine quite dead poor
little John said you see Doctor I am wounded but poor Mr George is killed;
we got him on bd. & it was found necessary to take the arm out of the
socket which from the very shattered state of the parts was a very precarious operation; he underwent it with a fortitude which surprised us all &
never once called out except just saying as the Dr divided a large nerve 'O
kill me at once...' I suppose you will not think of taking him out of the
service on this account, at least I should think him quite as fit for it as ever,
he now again goes to school & in short is every way as capable as before
except wanting a left arm.

the Mediterranean, wrote: '… they have taken seven forts, garrisons, or castles, within the last two months, and scaling towers at midnight, and storming redoubts at mid-day, are becoming familiar occurrences. It is really astonishing, those youths think that nothing is beyond their enterprise, and they seldom fail of success.'

There could have been no better theatre for Hastings to learn the importance of this brand of warfare, and with the exception, perhaps, of Cochrane, few abler teachers than Stewart. In the scale of European events these victories might have seemed little more than pinpricks, but quite apart from the effects on national morale, the mayhem caused along the French and Spanish coasts by ships like the *Sea Horse* or *Imperieuse* demonstrated that under the right command naval power could exert a strategic influence on land warfare out of all proportion to numbers or firepower.

Hastings would never be averse to the kind of verve and élan that characterised these operations – the *Kangaroo* demonstrates that – but there were other lessons, too, of a dourer and more professional kind, that he was taking in. At the age of fourteen he had served under two captains of very different temperaments, and if there was one thing he had learned from both, it was that if there had to be war – 'the art of killing in the most speedy way possible', as Hastings bluntly put it – then it had to be fought with all the ruthlessness and efficiency that could be mustered.

Implicit in this credo was the conviction that the end justified the means – fireships, mortar ships, 'stink vessels', hot shot, anything – because wherever the Battle of Waterloo was to be won, Trafalgar had most certainly *not* been won on the playing fields of Eton. 'The objection of unfair is so ridiculous, and so childish,' Hastings would again write, haughtily showing just how well he had absorbed the lessons of the Mediterranean, 'that I should consider I was insulting the understanding of the public by mentioning it, had I not heard it reiterated so often, and by people whose opinions go for something in the world … I have heard pretenders to humanity talk of the cruelty of hot shot, shells, etc; it really appears to me the superlative of cant to talk of the art of war (or, in other words, the method of killing men most expeditiously) and humanity in the same breath.'

This might have been Cochrane talking, and with the political situation deteriorating – Portugal under threat, Turkey and Russia (a nigh impossible 'double') both hostile, Denmark implacable, Sicily in danger, America muttering, France threatening the Ionian Isles and

Britain without an ally to her name except the bizarre Gustavus of Sweden – Hastings would have found few dissenters in the Mediterranean Squadron. 'We have been out from Syracuse ten days looking after the Toulon fleet which is expected to be making for Corfu,' Captain Stewart – as ever spoiling for a fight – wrote to Sir Charles Hastings. 'Thornbrough is following them up & Ld Collingwood (with whom we are) sitting in their route, our force is five of the line, myself & a brig; theirs five of the line, four frigates & several corvettes besides transports in all 20 sail, we are full of hopes and ardour & night or day they are to be attacked the moment we can meet them.'

Stewart was disappointed of his 'Toulon Gentlemen', but by the time he wrote – 11 January 1808, dated '07 in error – the *Sea Horse* was in the eastern Mediterranean and facing a very different kind of challenge. Towards the end of the previous year Collingwood had negotiated an arrangement with the Porte to exclude Turkish warships from the Aegean, but as the Greek islanders took advantage of their masters' absence and Anglo-Ottoman relations hovered somewhere between war and peace, the *Sea Horse* found herself the solitary British presence in an exclusion zone that the Turks had no intention of honouring. 'You will expect me to say something about the Turks,' Stewart told Sir Charles, warming to a subject dear to every frigate captain's heart – prize-money –

with whom we have been Philandering for so long, in fact from the hour that Sebastiani [Napoleon's envoy to the Porte] knew of the Treaty of Tilsit, Sir A. Paget [Britain's Ambassador] might have departed, as it was (between friends) it ended in them at last sending him away & saying they would not receive any more flags of Truce from the ship he was in. We in my opinion did wrong in forbearing from making war on them during the negotiations ... had we done as we have since done, take burn & destroy, I seriously believe they *might* have made peace with us ... Now I understand they want to begin a negotiation, we are not now at war they say & it is no prize money to us Captains, but I would like to know what name can be given to our footing with that nation, we must coin a word. I alone destroyed or took twelve of their vessels, only four of which are in Malta, who is to account for the rest?

'Take burn & destroy' – it might have been the motto of the Mediterranean fleet – and whatever his fears over the legal status of his prizes,
they were never going to stop Stewart when the chance came. Through
the early months of 1808 the *Sea Horse* had been constantly engaged
in capturing or destroying cargo bound for Constantinople, and when
on 1 July, while riding at anchor off the island of Sira, wind came of
bigger game with the news that, in defiance of Collingwood's agreement, a substantial Turkish flotilla had come through the Dardanelles
to punish their rebellious Greek subject, Stewart did not hesitate.

The same day he began working the *Sea Horse* up from Sira against
a north-north-easterly, and at noon on the fifth he received confirmation of the Turkish movements from a Greek ship bound for Malta.
Taking advantage of a light south-easterly the *Sea Horse* immediately
made all sail, and at 5.45 p.m. saw between the islands of Skopelos
and Dromo two enemy men-of-war, the twenty-six-gun *Alis-Fezan*
and the larger and more powerful fifty-two-gun, 1,300-ton *Badere-
Zaffer*, Captain Scandril Kitchuc-Ali.

Stewart had, in fact, been expecting far longer odds for the forty-
two-gun *Sea Horse*, and faced with only two opposing vessels, closed
on the Turkish ships until at 9.30 he was near enough to hail the
Turkish commodore and demand his surrender. 'This Captain Scandril flatly refused,' William James, prize court judge, historian and
shamelessly partisan hammer of the American navy, wrote, 'and into
the hull of the Badere-Zaffer went a whole double-shotted broadside
of the Sea Horse. Nor was the Turkish frigate slow in returning the
fire. In this way, with the wind a light breeze about two points abaft
the starboard beam, the two frigates went off engaging; the Badere-
Zaffer gradually edging away to close her consort, who was about a
gun-shot distant.'

For the next half-hour the two ships manoeuvred for position, with
the heavier and better-manned *Badere-Zaffer* attempting to board,
and Stewart employing all his seamanship to fight the battle on his
terms. At 10 o'clock he had again got his ship on the larboard quarter of his enemy when the *Alis-Fezan* interposed herself, taking from
Sea Horse at a range of no more than a cable's length a devastating
starboard broadside that within ten minutes had driven her out of
the action.

As the *Alis-Fezan* limped burning into the Aegean night, her crew
decimated by the *Sea Horse*'s gunnery, her hull racked by explosions,
Stewart turned his attention back to the *Badere-Zaffer*. The Turkish

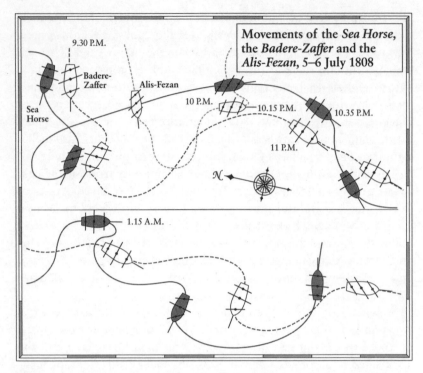

Movements of the *Sea Horse*,
the *Badere-Zaffer* and the
Alis-Fezan, 5–6 July 1808

9.30 P.M.

Badere-Zaffer

Alis-Fezan

Sea Horse

10 P.M.

10.15 P.M.

10.35 P.M.

11 P.M.

N

1.15 A.M.

captain was as determined as before to exploit his overwhelming advantage in manpower, but as the two ships ran before the wind exchanging broadsides and Captain Scandril again closed to board, Stewart swung the *Sea Horse* across the *Badere-Zaffer*'s bow – losing her gaff vangs and mizzen and starboard mizzen back-stays to the enemy bowsprit as he did so – and raked her crowded forecastle with grape from his stern-chase guns as she passed.

Outsailed and outgunned as they were, the *Badere-Zaffer*'s crew gave place to no one when it came to courage, and the two ships continued to exchange broadsides until the Turkish cannon at last fell silent. As the *Badere-Zaffer* settled helpless in the water, shortly after 1 o'clock in the morning, her mizzen, fore and main topmasts all gone, her hull so badly shot up she could barely float, Stewart brought the *Sea Horse* under her stern and hailed her to surrender. A desultory fire from her after-guns was the only answer, and with one last starboard broadside, Stewart, 'finding that his shattered opponent would neither answer nor fire, very prudently, and very humanely too, hauled off; and, after standing on a little further, brought to on the starboard tack to wait for daylight'.

It took one more broadside, and a mutiny of the *Badere-Zaffer*'s surviving officers – who hauled down her colours from the shattered stump of her mizzenmast while they held the half-mad Scandril in his chair – to end the engagement, but shortly after dawn it was over. 'Sent the 1st Lieut to take possession of her,' the *Sea Horse*'s log recorded, with a characteristically laconic indifference to the human drama: 'she proved to be the Badere Zaffer a large Turkish frigate, a complement of 540 men commanded by Scandali Kichuc Ali, Captain. Her consort's name was the Alex Fesan carrying 24 brass guns and two mortars. The enemy lost 170 killed and 200 wounded, ours 5 seamen killed [two next to Hastings when a gun blew up] & ten wounded and two dangerously.'

For all the good the *Badere-Zaffer* ever did the *Sea Horse*'s crew – the prize court refused to buy her for the navy – Scandril might as well have succeeded in a last-ditch attempt to scuttle her, but Stewart was determined to add her to the growing haul of bombards, brigs, schooners, wine, 'senna and austrich feathers' that he had already sent back to Malta. Over the next days her battered hull was made seaworthy enough to be towed, a skeleton crew was detained to man their prize on the voyage back to Valetta, and a Greek vessel bound for Constantinople 'co-opted' to repatriate their prisoners.

It was not long before the *Sea Horse* was following them, because with a demi-thaw in diplomatic relations between Britain and the Ottoman Empire, she was back again at Malta in September to receive on board another old friend of Sir Charles's, Britain's new ambassador to the Porte, Mr Robert Adair. Through the previous months the Turks had done all they could to stall negotiations, and even in a more conciliatory atmosphere it was the end of January 1809 before the ship's company was again manning the yards to salute 'His Excellency Mr Adair the Ambassador on his disembarking' at Constantinople. 'The walls of the Seraglio are like the walls of Newstead,' another young English aristocrat, Lord Byron, on his travels with his old Cambridge friend and future philhellene John Cam Hobhouse, recorded of his first impressions of the 'polis',

but the ride by the walls of the city on the land side is beautiful, imagine four miles of immense triple battlements covered with Ivy, surmounted with 218 towers, and on the other side of the road Turkish burying grounds (the loveliest spots on earth) full of enormous cypresses, I have seen the ruins of Athens, of Ephesus, and

Delphi, I have traversed great parts of Turkey and many other parts
of Europe and some of Asia, but I never beheld a work of Nature
or Art, which yielded an impression like the prospect on each side,
from the Seven Towers to the End of the Golden Horn.

To a young naval midshipman like Hastings, though, it was the
seaward defences of Constantinople that would have been of most
interest. The captains who formed part of Sir John Duckworth's
abortive expedition were adamant that the city had been there for
the taking if they had only been allowed, and over the next two
months of diplomatic inactivity and interminable salutes, Hastings
had all the opportunity he could want to assess those defensive frail-
ties that were still exercising his mind twenty years later.

These were all the more obvious, too, because the *Sea Horse* had
arrived at Constantinople at a juncture in the city's history that was
bloody even by its own violent and unstable standards. The contorted
negotiations with Britain had from the first been conducted against
a background of riots and rebellion, and a frenzy of beheadings,
strangulations, mutilations and traditional Ottoman family planning
– two hundred women of Mustafa IV's harem were drowned in the
Bosphorus – that had only paused for the murder of the Sultan and
the ascent to the throne of a man to whom terror was the supreme
instrument of policy.

With his jet-black beard, his great breadth of shoulder, an eye that
'awed' strangers and an 'air of indescribable majesty', as Hobhouse
put it, Mahmud II had the appearance to match his character. 'Those
who know him,' Adair's successor as ambassador to the Porte, Sir
Robert Liston, wrote of the man against whom Hastings would
expend his fortune and, ultimately, his life, 'say he had considerable
abilities, a vigorous and active mind, with such an idea of the elevation, perhaps of the sanctity of his station, and so strong a feeling of
personal superiority that he deems all opposition criminal, all resistance vain and ultimate disappointment on his part impossible.'

It would be intriguing to know what the young Hastings said of
him, and there is no doubt that he saw him at least once. 'Mann'd
the yards and saluted the Sultan with 21 guns upon his passing the
ship in his caique,' reads the *Sea Horse* log for 6 March, 'mann'd the
yards and saluted the Sultan on his return.' In its way, that glimpse
was as crucial as the single, fleeting vision of Nelson from the quarterdeck of *Neptune*. With great swathes of the city still smouldering

from the fires of the Sultan's mutinous Janissaries, and France and Russia both threatening Ottoman integrity, Hastings could be forgiven for underestimating the man, but he would have had no trouble in recognising a natural enemy. Corrupt, despotic, violent, vulnerable, Mahmud II was everything a young Whig aristocrat could ask for. And so, too, for a born incendiary like Hastings, was Constantinople. As the *Sea Horse* weighed for Malta, Robert Adair's mission accomplished, the memory of its burning suburbs, enfeebled defences and – still only a glint in the eye of even the most far-seeing naval moderniser in 1809 – its vulnerability to any ship capable of forcing the Dardanelles, left an impression that made those months among the most important of Hastings's life.

IV

For Frank and the *Sea Horse* the return to Malta in the spring of 1809 meant the welcome resumption of business as usual. After her long inactivity the ship finally quitted the Dardanelles at sunset on 29 March, and by 12 April was again in Valetta where Stewart mustered the ship's company to make 'known to them the Lords Commissioners of the Admiralty's approbation of their conduct in capturing the Turkish frigate'.

There was prize-money to be distributed – if not as much as they reckoned their deserts – but after three years in the *Sea Horse*, and *growing* at long last, as Stewart wrote to tell his father, it was time for the fifteen-year-old Hastings to move on. In July 1808 he had completed the requisite sea-time to be rated midshipman, and back in England Sir Charles was already mobilising old Jersey connections to secure his son's next ship. 'I shall be anxious to know when you have settled with Sir J. Saumarez about Frank,' Stewart wrote to Sir Charles from Sicily in December 1809, at the end of another success-ful summer and autumn cruise that included two brilliant assaults on the fortresses on Isola di Giannutri and Pianosa,

as unless something particular occurs I do not propose coming home next year unless it may be late in it & I would send Frank to you in April with a discharge into Sir J's ship which would secure his time: I have this last time at Malta given Frank a sum of money and made him buy his own clothes which by the by are now very expensive ... I have now wound up all his accounts to this day & find him still £16 in my debt but he shall not draw till he finally goes as he will necessarily want some more. I have been as moderate in his expenses as I could consistent with the high price of things and his going & living like a Gentleman. He behaves exceedingly well & I like him much.

If Admiralty records are to be believed, Frank was not discharged from the *Sea Horse* into *Victory* until 6 May 1810, but between the two ships there was Willesley, a 'delighted' mother and a determined father to see. He 'understood from Lady Hardy', Sir Charles was soon writing to Warren Hastings's son-in-law,

> that you and Lady Imhoff are both intimate with the Captain of
> Victory, on board of whom my son Frank is to go, will you have
> the goodness (previous to your quitting town) to leave him a letter
> of recommendation to your friend. He will find it very useful when
> on board as thro' the Captain's means he may be placed under the
> care of some Lieut. which is what I would wish as I cannot expect
> Sir James Saumarez will do any more than admit him on board.

After the excitements of the *Sea Horse*, and the light and the colour of Sicily, the Aegean and the Dardanelles, it was a return for Frank to the dull realities of home ports and blockade duties with the Baltic Fleet. In spite of the official entry date he did not join *Victory* until October 1810, and he was back at Willesley again by 15 December – 'the date of the Regency', as Sir Charles triumphantly dated Frank's arrival – putting his father to work to find him something more interesting than a winter's guard duty at Spithead. 'I have been in town for a few days in consequence of my youngest son,' Sir Charles wrote to Warren Hastings a month later, 'who required my exertions to place him on board a sloop of war to cruise the channel ... It was his own choice to employ the few months he has to finish his time in studying that most important though very dangerous navigation.'

This was a period of feverish political expectations for the extended Hastings clan, as Lord Moira came within a whisker of forming a government, but for Frank the next two years were probably the quietest of his whole career. It is difficult to trace his exact movements during this time through the usual Admiralty records, but by the autumn of 1812, after another summer at Willesley studying with a clergyman tutor, he was again exploiting family interest to smooth over the next step in his career. 'I am obliged to be in town the 1st week in Sept,' Sir Charles explained to Warren Hastings, 'on acct of my younger son, whose time of serving as a midshipman will be near expired and I must not be out of the way.'

The first great hurdle for any midshipman, ideally taken at the age of twenty after the requisite six years' sea-time, was the demanding examination to make lieutenant. In exceptional cases – or where powerful interest could be brought to bear – the age criterion might be fudged or falsified, but even a boy as well connected as Frank would seem to have had to do it the hard way, and to wait until just after his twentieth birthday in April 1814 for his promotion.*

Hastings was on the North America station at the time – the United States had declared war on Britain two years earlier – but it was only a matter of luck that he was alive to make lieutenant at all. Sometime late in 1813 he had taken a passage out to join the sloop *Atalante* under the command of Frederick Hickey, and early in November, as a nineteen-year-old acting lieutenant, found himself in heavy fog off Halifax when the distant sounds of a frigate's cannon were mistaken for the signal guns at the lighthouse on Sambro Island.

There was often clearer weather close in to shore at Halifax, and with lookouts posted on the bowsprit-end and jib boom, a leadsman in the chains taking constant soundings, and her signal guns firing every quarter-hour, the *Atalante* nudged under easy sail into the thickening fog. For forty-five minutes Hickey coaxed her towards the safety of harbour, and with the guns of Sambro Island – as he still fondly imagined them – silent, and the leadsman reporting nothing at twenty fathoms, had just begun to think his ship clear of danger when there was a sudden warning cry of 'Starboard the helm!' and the *Atalante* was in breakers. In a matter of minutes 'the rudder, the stern-post and part of the keel' had been ripped away by the rocks of the Eastern Shelf off Sambro Island, Hickey reported at his court martial, 'and perceiving immediately that there was no hope of saving the ship, my whole attention was turned to saving the lives of my valuable crew; to effect which, I directed, in the first place, the quarter boats to be lowered, and the jolly boat to be launched from the

---

* Admiralty records of his Lieutenant's Examinations have disappeared, and his own testimonials were lost in a shipwreck.

poop. I had also given directions for the guns to be thrown overboard; but the ship filled before any of them could be cut loose.'

There was just time to fire off a distress signal from the guns still
above the water, and to order his men to the exposed larboard side
of the ship, when with a crash of masts, the *Atalante* broke into three.
'In twelve minutes she was literally torn to pieces,' Jeremiah O'Sullivan, a passenger on board recalled, as the crew fought against the
crashing breakers to get to the ship's pinnace, tangled up helplessly
in the wreck of the *Atalante*'s booms, '... and to see so many poor
souls struggling for life, some naked, others on spars, casks, or
anything tenable was a scene painful beyond description.'

One of their boats had already gone down – not to mention Hastings's sea chest with all his possessions and papers – and with some
sixty of the crew struggling to get into the pinnace, it seemed only a
matter of moments before most of them went the same way. It was
rapidly obvious to Hickey that not all of them could possibly escape
in her, and ordering twenty or thirty of them out onto the booms, he
succeeded in freeing her from the wreckage and – 'in a most miraculous manner' – launching her to safety.

With the pinnace freed there was one last, desperate attempt to
lash the booms into a makeshift raft, but almost immediately they
began to drift into still heavier breakers. 'I signalled to the small boats
to come near us,' Hickey continued his evidence,

> and each to take in a few more men, distributing them with each
> other and the pinnace till I succeeded in getting every man and boy
> off the raft, when, with three cheers, the wreck was abandoned.
> After pulling near two hours without seeing the land, guided only
> by a small dial compass, which one of the quartermasters had in
> his pocket, we picked up a fisherman, who piloted the boat safe
> into Portuguese cove ... It now becomes a pleasing task to me to
> state in the fullest manner that the conduct of my officers and ship's
> company, under the most trying circumstances in which human
> beings could be placed, was orderly, obedient and respectful, to the
> last extremity.

The loss of the *Atalante* probably had as much to do with her seawor-
thiness as anything else, and if Hastings was lucky to get away with
his life and reputation – Hickey and his officers were honourably
acquitted of all blame at the court martial – it was an omen of things

to come. For the first seven years of his naval career he had known nothing but success, but over these next two he was to see the other side of his profession and learn the lessons of defeat in a war that exposed inadequacies in the Royal Navy that twenty years of almost seamless triumph had successfully masked.

There were any number of issues that lay behind the War of 1812 – the right to search and impressment, republican sympathies, Yankee designs on British Canada, mutual dislike – but at the heart of the struggle lay the system of economic warfare between Napoleonic France and Britain that threatened American merchant interests. In 1806 Napoleon had promulgated the first of his decrees designed to cripple British trade, and when Britain retaliated with her own Orders in Council that effectively closed Continental ports to neutral shipping there were inevitably a thousand potential flashpoints for war. 'With respect to America,' Stewart had written prophetically to Sir Charles Hastings in 1808,

> we may possibly by concessions put off the evil day but the arrogance, highhandedness & I may say ungentlemanlike conduct of that nation will sooner or later force us to quarrel with them; we have always put up with things from them we would not have suffered from any other nation in the world, many instances of which I saw in the last war, & our forbearance only increases the insolence of the mob, which seems to me the only real government in that country.

None of this can disguise what a 'bad' war the War of 1812 was, but to an ambitious young naval officer there is no such thing, and within weeks of the *Atalante* going down Hastings was lucky enough to join the newly commissioned *Anaconda* under the command of the twenty-eight-year-old George Westphal. There had been nothing wrong with Hickey – except that he seems to have been a permanently unlucky officer – but of all Frank's captains George Westphal, a protégé of the Duke of Kent and scion of an aristocratic German family of Hastingsesque antiquity, was by some margin the most remarkable.

As a young midshipman at Trafalgar he had lain next to the dying Nelson in the cockpit of *Victory*, and that was just the first and most romantic of his battle honours. In 1807 he had again been severely wounded and was captured after a long and bloody action, but making his escape in an open boat from a Guadeloupe prison ship, had worked his way back to England – courtesy of an American merchantman and an English privateer – in time to join in the reduction of Martinique and to take a prominent and heroic part in the attack on Flushing.

Fleet actions, espionage, ship-to-ship, siege work, land skirmishes, Westphal had fought in over a hundred engagements in all, and had continued in the same vein on American soil. 'On first landing,' a contemporary biography recorded one typical incident,

> Mr Westphal, having dismounted an American officer, set off on the captured horse in pursuit of the fugitives; forgetting, in the ardour of the moment, that it was not possible for his men to keep pace with him – a circumstance indeed that did not present itself to him until he found himself, unsupported, in the midst of a body of armed men. Firing his pistols right and left, however, and slashing his sword in all directions, he dashed through them and succeeded, although wounded by a shot through the hand, in effecting his escape, bearing away with him at the same time as his prisoner a Captain in the militia.

Hastings's new posting was doubly fortunate for him, because it was not as if the navy's performance against the Americans had been of a kind that would guarantee him a ship like the *Anaconda*, or a captain like George Westphal. For the previous decade the service had exercised a virtual mastery over its European enemies, but when in the first year of war English ships had taken on more heavily armed enemies with crews – as often as not British and Irish – of more or less equal skill, the result had been a series of defeats that became an equally fertile source of American myth-making and British soul-searching.

At the heart of the British performance – when all the socio-moral nonsense about Republican Virtue and New World Vigour is forgotten – were failures in long-range gunnery, and it was this that turned Hastings into the impassioned evangelist of gunnery reform he became. After twenty wearing years of warfare there were clearly other factors at work, but in a service in which 'any knowledge ... of gunnery [was] obtained gratuitously', as Hastings – precursor to all those prophets of gunnery change who would cry in the naval wilderness over the next hundred years – contemptuously put it, 'all the

Seaman's help in the world will avail little, if your artillery practice is inferior to the enemy'.

The war at sea had been largely turned around by the time Hastings joined the *Anaconda*, but though he got his fair share of prizes there was still one more brutal lesson before he could quit America. In the first twelve months after he had joined Westphal and the *Anaconda* he was principally engaged in the West Indies and the Gulf of Mexico, and as the conflict ground to its inevitable and pointless conclusion – the *status quo ante*, with no gains and no concessions on either side – he found himself at anchor with the main British fleet off the Louisiana coast in support of Britain's last punitive effort of the war.

If anything can epitomise the uselessness of the conflict, it is the Battle of New Orleans, fought at the beginning of January 1815, two weeks after the peace treaty had been signed at Ghent. For some months before this the opposition to war had been growing in Britain, but the abdication of Napoleon had given the government a belated opportunity to send out an army of Peninsular veterans under the command of Wellington's brother-in-law, Sir Edward Pakenham, to strengthen its position at the negotiating table.

In the middle of December 1814 the navy began to ferry the army to its advance base on the Île de Poix in Lake Borgne, but from the start the operation was bedevilled by delays – Pakenham had not even arrived – logistical shortages, command failures and overconfidence. After the pusillanimous American performance before Washington that last was at least understandable, yet as so often it was only the courage and endurance of the army's rank and file that redeemed a battle plan which condemned them to a sixty-mile slog across lake, bayou, bank, shoal, swamp and the mud of a half-cut canal in some of the filthiest weather Louisiana could throw at them.

It had never occurred to Andrew Jackson, in command of New Orleans's defence, that an attack could come from this quarter, but by December the British army and commander were at last united on a narrow strip of firm ground between the Mississippi on their left flank and a cypress swamp on their right, just seven miles downriver from New Orleans. 'In the endeavours to place the small vessels of war as near as possible to the point of landing,' Sir Alexander Cochrane, the Commander-in-Chief, wrote of the *Anaconda*'s role in the operation,

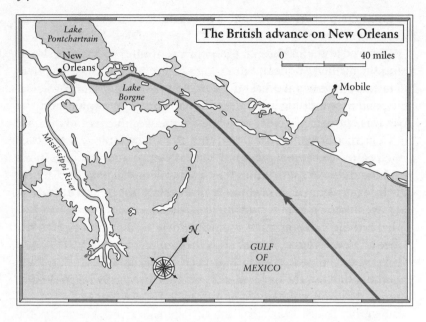

Captain Westphal was particularly conspicuous in his zeal and
success towards the effecting of this important object; he having,
by the utmost perseverance, skill, and exertion, hove the
ANACONDA over a bank nearly five miles in extent (upon which
there were only eight feet of water), into Lac Borgne, and there
occupied a station that enabled that sloop to render the most essential aid and protection to the open boats conveying troops and
supplies from the fleet; which were frequently rescued by her assistance from the imminent danger to which they were reduced by
the severity of the weather.

With Jackson's defenders now entrenched behind a strong defensive
wall stretching from river to swamp, however, and his right flank
supported by the naval guns of the *Carolina* and *Louisiana*, Pakenham delayed his final assault until more artillery could be brought up
from the fleet. Under the command of Sir Thomas Troubridge, a
naval brigade that included Hastings dragged and canoed their
cannon up from Lake Borgne, and on 27 December – using the hot
shot that would become so dear to Hastings's heart – set fire to the
Carolina and blew her out of the water in a matter of only minutes.
'His conduct as a *Gallant, able, attentive, Obedient,* and *Zealous*
young officer, claims my highest approbation,' Westphal wrote of

Hastings's part in the action. 'On several occasions his zeel [sic] &
activity attracted the notice of Sir Thomas Troubridge, who
commanded the Brigade of Seamen and of Lt Col Dixon commanding the artillery, both of whom caused me to express to Lieutenant
Hastings (on several occasions) their thanks for his persevering activity, and promptitude in the execution of the several tasks with which
he was entrusted.'

The spectacular destruction of the *Carolina* was the last real British
success of the campaign. A humiliating defeat in an artillery duel on
1 January gave a grim pointer to what was to come, but it was a
warning wasted on Pakenham. Reinforced by the arrival of two more
of Wellington's best regiments he ordered a frontal assault against
the entrenched American line for dawn on the eighth. It was an
assault that Hastings and the navy were well out of. The failure of a
diversionary attack across the river to go off on time, or an appalling
blunder that left the forlorn hope without fascines or scaling ladders,
might have deterred another commander, but Pakenham was made
of sterner stuff. With the morning light already streaking the
Louisiana sky he gave the command for the attack to begin.

The previous day Jackson had watched British preparations for
the battle, and as the rocket signal went up, and the fog cleared from
the British troops advancing in close order, the turkey shoot began.
At five hundred yards the first twelve-pounder exploded into life,
followed by the whole of the artillery and – at two hundred yards –
by Jackson's Tennessee riflemen. There was no missing and no escape.
The attackers were soldiers who had fought their way up Spain under
Wellington, but under the sustained fire of the whole American line
the right began to edge left and the British assault to falter. General
Gibbs got to within twenty yards of the defences before he fell with
four bullets in him. A few even made it as far as the ditch in front of
the earthworks before they died. As the troops fell back, they found
themselves caught between their own guns behind them and the
American in front in a chaotic shambles of their commanders'
making. And for once British troops were not going to bale their
generals out. 'For shame!' cried Pakenham, trying to rally them again,
'Remember you are British soldiers!' but it was no use. As he spurred
them on a bullet shattered his knee and brought down his horse.
Mounting another, he was immediately hit again in the groin and
spine and collapsed to the ground, his last, unavailing orders expiring on his lips with him.

This was the end of the assault, and at just 8 o'clock, and in spite of the eventual success of the diversionary attack, the effective end of the battle. At the cost of eight – or perhaps thirteen – casualties, the Americans had killed two thousand British troops in the most lopsided defeat ever inflicted on British arms. And with the coming of peace there would be no time for redemption. 'Hoisted the English and American ensign in conjunction,' reads the *Anaconda*'s log for 16 March 1815, '& fired a grand salute in commemoration of Peace with America.'

It was a bitter end to a criminally pointless war. And for Hastings it was not just the end of the war but, except for the odd skirmish with Malay pirates in the Far East, the last time he would see action as a Royal Navy officer. Family interest and family money would keep him from the fate of those thousands of lieutenants thrown on the scrapheap by Waterloo, but from now on he would have to go looking for his excitement. 'I feel that in addressing your Lordship I am taking upon myself an unwarrantable liberty,' he wrote to Lord Melville, the First Lord of the Admiralty, after sixteen months in the *Orlando* on the Eastern station and the best part of an uneventful year aboard the *Pelican* in the West Indies had brought him again to London with his begging bowl out:

> perhaps no excuse can easily justify it; I throw myself on your Lordship's well known clemency and trust that you will not attribute it to impertinence, but an anxiety to attain that eminence in any profession which is the object of every enterprizing officer ... this has emboldened me to solicit employment in the expedition which your Lordship may, perhaps, decline, to prosecute their discoveries to the Northward at a favourable season. If I am so happy as to enjoy a place in your lordship's good opinion, sufficiently favourable to induce you to grant my request, no exertion on my part shall be wanting to qualify myself for this arduous undertaking. Till the period of sailing my labours shall be directed to the acquisition of such knowledge as is likely to prove serviceable – you may perhaps find those more capable but none more devotedly willing to acquit themselves with credit.

It is a fascinating thought that Hastings might have ended up in the North-West Passage – the cradle and the grave of so many nineteenth-century naval reputations – but while there was no vacancy on that expedition Melville had not forgotten him. On the return of the *Pelican* in 1818 Hastings had gone up to Willesley, and while he borrowed his brother's gun and played the country gentleman – 'Frank is trying to be a sportsman,' his mother reported in a spidery hand made worse by gathering blindness, 'he has killed a hare & brace of Partridges' – Lord Melville's goodwill filtered down through the channels of Admiralty preferment: 'Lieut F. Hastings to be appointed to the Frigate destined to relieve the Forth,' a minute for 9 January 1819 reads, 'it being Ld Melville's intention to recommend the Lieut to the Bd on that station.'

A fortnight later, on 23 January, the appointment was ratified: 'Lieut Frank Hastings to be appointed to the command of the Kangaroo Surveying Vessel at Deptford.' Within another two weeks Hastings was in London, and on 8 February he began entering men into his new ship. At just twenty-four, he had his first command. Four months later it would come to its disastrous end in the harbour of Port Royal. How different the history of the nineteenth-century navy, possibly of Arctic exploration, might have been had John Barrow found room for him on his expedition to the North-West Passage is a matter of poignant speculation: how different Greek history would be is a matter of fact.

V

On 6 March 1821, a Russian general of Greek extraction crossed the River Pruth from Bessarabia into Moldavia, raised his standard emblazoned with a phoenix, and called on the Christian populations of the Ottoman Empire to throw off their Turkish oppressors.

At first glance, the banks of the Pruth might seem a perverse place to start a Greek revolution, but at the beginning of the nineteenth century the abject condition of Greece itself meant that any revival would have to come from without. In the early fifteenth century there had been one last, great flowering of Byzantine culture at Mystra in the southern Peloponnese, but over the four hundred years since Mystra's fall the geographical area of what is now modern Greece had sunk into a state of oppressed and degraded misery, its traditions of freedom withered to the bandit culture of the mountain regions and all memory of its political and artistic birthright buried under centuries of foreign tyranny.

It was inevitably from western Europe, where there had been a rebirth of scholarly interest in Greek art, that this memory was given back to Greece and to the scattered communities of the Greek diaspora. Throughout the eighteenth century these colonies had flourished at ports and cities throughout the mercantile world, and as this renewed sense of identity became a fixed part of the émigré consciousness, the fashionable Hellenism of the dilettante was transformed into a heady cocktail of political theory, revolutionary fervour and Byzantine nostalgia.

For the nineteenth-century Greek, it was supremely Constantinople – the '*polis*' – and not Athens that was the historical centre of the Greek world, and it was no coincidence that the movement for Greek freedom found its focus and leadership there. For the best part of four centuries the great Christian families of the Phanar* had arrogated to themselves all the tasks that Muslim indolence or fastidiousness would allow them, and it was the wretchedly inept son of one of these princely families, the one-armed Alexander Ypsilanti, who in the spring of 1821 crossed the Pruth to spark off a Greek revolt that only the Turks themselves cannot have seen coming.

Ypsilanti's campaign was a fiasco – by June it was over and he had shamefully fled to Austria – but as news of the uprising spread and the Greek flag was raised on Peloponnesian soil, fantasy had suddenly become fact. For centuries Greeks and Turks had been living within the empire side by side, and within weeks the Ottoman-Greek world was in flames, as community turned on community in a religious and racial war of a hatred and savagery that would have beggared the imagination of a Goya.

And as massacre followed massacre – Athens, Constantinople, Tripolis, Smyrna, Nicosia, Kos, Rhodes – it was inevitably the plight of the Greeks that excited the sympathy and indignation of the Christian West. In its earliest days European philhellenism was largely an academic pastime, but under the influence of Byron's verse it became a popular cause that within months had inspired the first volunteers – Swedes, Danes, Bavarians, Saxons, Prussians, Italians, Russians, French, British and Americans – to raise, beg and borrow the money to make their way east to save the cradle of Western culture and

---

* The district of Constantinople that gave its name to the great 'Phanariot' families who played such an important role in the Greek Revolution.

political freedoms. 'Fair Greece! Sad relic of departed worth!' wrote Byron,

> Immortal, though no more; though fallen, great!
> Who now shall lead thy scatter'd children forth,
> And long accustom'd bondage uncreate?
> Not such thy sons who whilome did await,
> The hopeless warriors of a willing doom,
> In bleak Thermopylae's sepulchral strait –
> Oh! Who that gallant spirit shall resume,
> Leap from Eurotas' banks, and call thee from the tomb?

'We are all Greeks now,' Shelley proudly proclaimed from the cosy safety of Italy, but if this sounded good, what was actually meant by it would have been hard to define. Among the first volunteers who sailed out to fight were refugees from monarchical despotism who would have thrilled to the language of Shelley's 'Hellas', yet side by side with them were academic dreamers and romantic fantasists, Byronic poseurs and aristocratic democrats, deluded Benthamites and disenchanted Bonapartists, charlatans and orthodox co-religionists, fortune-hunters, mercenaries and unemployed and unemployable military professionals, the flotsam and jetsam of a whole European generation who had known nothing but war. 'What a queer set,' the American doctor, Samuel Gridley Howe, one of the greatest of all philhellenes, wrote of these men – heirs at once in their mix of naïveté and depravity to the Children's Crusade and the *condottieri* of four-teenth-century Europe. 'What an assemblage of romantic, adventur-ous, restless, crack-brained young men from the four corners of the world. How much courage and talent is to be found among them, but how much more of pompous vanity, of weak intellect, of mean self-ishness, of utter depravity ... Little have Philhellenes done towards raising the reputation of Europeans here.'

The disappointment was not all one-way, because if these were seldom the kind of volunteers to inspire the Greeks with a keen sense of gratitude, the feeling of disillusionment on their arrival was invari-ably mutual. The one belief that sustained most philhellenes was the conviction that they were defending the heirs to ancient Greece, and when instead of Pericles and Epaminondas they found a nation of mountain bandit warriors as ready to behead, baptise or sodomise their Ottoman victims as the Turks were to enslave, circumcise and impale theirs, the revulsion was as intense and irrational as the enthusiasm it replaced.

In the whole history of the Greek War of Independence no more than a handful of foreigners ever bridged the cultural gap between the Greece of the imagination and the Greece of reality, and incomparably the greatest of these after Byron was Frank Abney Hastings. In many ways Hastings belonged to the mainstream of philhellene life, but even as a citizen with a grudge and a fighting man without a war there were crucial differences about him – differences of wealth, talent and temperament – that equipped him to survive a Homeric world of factionalism, greed, treachery and violence with a resilience that few other foreigners could match.

Glory, revenge and the joy of battle – the brazen tripod that holds up the Homeric world – these were the urges that drove Hastings, and the Greek War was as much made for him as he was for the Greeks. Like any good Whig aristocrat he was a firm believer in Greece's ancient liberties, yet if he fed off her classical past it was not off the Greece of Demosthenes or Aristogeiton – 'Harry Stodgiton' as one enthusiastic Scottish MP called him – but off an older and more elemental code. 'That Glory is in a great measure the object I propose to myself I cannot deny,' he would tell Lord Byron, '& I must acknowledge that independent of the satisfaction I should receive from establishing a European reputation ... 'twould be delicious revenge to prove to those who have deprived me of my rank in the British service that the object of their persecution is not altogether devoid of Naval merit.'

There seems no way of recovering the exact steps that led Hastings to Greece – he was in France, learning the language and 'qualifying' himself for the kind of foreign service Cochrane had made so glamorous in South America when war broke out – but the one certainty is that without the humiliation of the *Kangaroo* he would never have gone. 'My lord,' he had written pathetically to Lord Melville, 'only those who like me have thirsted for glory, who like me have lived in the anticipation of fame can tell how intolerable it is to find the tender bud nipped when about to bloom.'

It is arguable that Hastings never recovered from the humiliation of the Port Royal inquiry, and he certainly emerged from it a different man, less anxious to please, less open to people and in some ways less likeable than the small lad who made friends so easily in *Neptune*. It is possible of course that this was no more than the natural consequence of age, but between the 'gentlemanly' and 'exemplary' young officer all his captains spoke of so warmly in their testimonials and the often harsh, judgemental, self-sufficient loner who we at last get to know in Greece it is hard not to detect the shadow of the *Kangaroo*.

For all his sense of rejection, however, Hastings's dismissal from the service only confirmed and strengthened in him that blinkered obsession with his profession that had never left room in his life for much else. It is clear from the early diaries of Thomas Fremantle that the brothels of Naples were a staple part of a Mediterranean officer's world, and yet apart from a single woman's name scrawled in a pocket notebook – and she turns out to have been a boat moored in the Thames – there is not even a momentary hint among Hastings's surviving papers that he was any more interested in Mediterranean women than he was in his father's housemaids or those 'pretty daughters' of Halifax who 'made such sad havoc with the hearts of both the army and navy'.

Hastings was capable of strong and loyal male friendship – Edward Scott in the *Orlando*, to whom he would leave his sword, George Finlay later in Greece – but there seems no reason to read any more into this than into anything else. It is always possible that letters will turn up to reveal a lover or a brace of children somewhere in France or the Morea, but until they do nothing is going to crack the adamantine image of a man who sublimated all his energies and ambitions – sexual, social, emotional, professional – into the all-consuming business of warfare.

It was not that there was ever anything *cold* about Hastings – the Greek marble bust of '   ' gives very little away – on the contrary, he was a generous and highly-strung creature of endless moods, passions, angers, noble impulses and nervous energies. To the end of his life he would always crave recognition and fame, but as he sat in his metaphorical tent brooding or raging over real or imagined wrongs, his notion of achievement – like his idea of justice – went along with a profound sense of self that needed no grubby endorsement from the common run.

In this fierce and proud individualism, this refusal to sit at any bar but that of his own conscience, Hastings was supremely a child of his time – this is, after all, the age of Byron – and onto the natural hauteur of the eighteenth-century aristocrat was grafted the isolation of the romantic. 'It was not out of consideration for others, but respect for

himself, that he always bluntly told the truth,' the philosopher-novel-
ist William Godwin wrote of his fictional hero Borromeo – a portrait
of another Byronic philhellene, Edward Trelawny, that in important
respects is a far truer likeness of Hastings – '... Yet this man was
eminently a moral being. He had certain rules of right to which he
rigorously adhered, not for the sake of good to result to others, but,
as certain theologians inculcate in their systems, from the simple love
of justice, and without care for the consequences.'

It was, then, this Hastings – age twenty-seven, height five feet seven
inches, eyes blue, hair and whiskers fair, forehead bold, nose '*grand
et aquilain*', as his French passport describes him – who in March
1822 boarded a Swedish merchant vessel at Marseilles bound for the
eastern Mediterranean and Constantinople. From the earliest days
of the revolt Marseilles had been a popular staging post for philhellenes, and travelling with him in the *Trontheim* was another volunteer, a coarse-grained but insinuating anglophobe American zealot
blessed with just the right blend of physical toughness and moral
laxity to equip him for the intrigues, warfare and vermin ahead, called
George Jarvis.

From his father's will it is clear that Hastings had volunteered without his blessing, but with the security of his mother's marriage settlement – worth £5,000 – behind him and £300 in gold concealed round
his person, he was in a strong position to travel on his own terms. In
a typical piece of generosity he had paid for Jarvis's passage to Greece,
and on the evening of 3 April, after a journey of just over three weeks,
the two men were landed with all their baggage on the barren northern tip of Hydra off the north-east coast of the Peloponnese.

The Greece and the revolution into which Hastings and Jarvis
sailed in the spring of 1822 was in as precarious a state as it had been
at any time since Ypsilanti had raised his standard. In the first months
of the war the Ottoman government had been too busy with other
problems to give the rebels its full attention, but with Athens and the
historical fortresses of Nauplia, Patras, Rion, Modon and Coron –
the 'eyes of Venice' – still in Muslim hands, and two Ottoman armies
massing in the north-west and north-east to revenge the massacres of
1821, no newly arrived volunteer could be quite sure how or where
he would find the Greece he had come to save.

And if the Turks were at last taking their war seriously, the Greeks
were no nearer presenting a unified and coherent front than they had
been in the first confused days of revolution. At the beginning of 1822

an Assembly at Epidaurus had drawn up a modern constitution for the country, but while the laws might have been framed in the image of Greece's first president – the educated, frock-coated, bespectacled, Phanariot exile Alexander Mavrocordato – real power still lay with the island merchants, local primates, captains and klephtic chiefs whose loyalty to a central government or a united Greece was as notional as the constitution itself.

Hastings was not certain, until a group of islanders materialised out of the rocky landscape, whether Hydra was a part of the revolution, and even the offer of a boat and a guide to the town was not sufficient to still his suspicions. He had served long enough in these waters as a midshipman to be almost as wary of Greeks as of Turks, and when it transpired that there was room in the boat only for Jarvis and their baggage, he prepared himself for the worst. 'I was amongst three,' he wrote in his journal, 'each had a knife – it is true

I was armed "jusqu'au dent" but before I could have cocked a pistol, the man next me might have stabbed me & there appeared every probability I should pass the night in this bay – I therefore resolved to abandon my effects to their fate & go over land to the Town.'

This was easier said than done, but weighed down by his guns, sabre and gold, he hauled himself up the two hundred feet of almost sheer cliff and, 'fatigued to death', finally stumbled across a shepherd's cot 'and made signs for water'. For the first time since his landing he came across the other side of the Greek character, and strengthened by bread and cheese and the 'real disinterested hospitality' of the shepherd, made the last hour's 'painful march' across country with life and money still mercifully intact.

When the sun rose the next morning, Hastings found himself in one of the handsomest and most prosperous towns in the whole of the Levant. The merchant families of the island had done well out of the economic blockades of the Napoleonic War, and the neat white houses and great Genoese and Venetian residences of Hydra's 'primates' – great names of the revolution like Tombazis and Conduriottis – rose up from its secretive harbour in a natural amphitheatre that provided a gleaming contrast with the scenes of desolation only miles away on the coast of the Morea.

From the first months of the revolution the island had been one of the three centres of Greek naval power, but if Hastings imagined that his professional credentials or his knowledge would secure him a welcome, he was in for a rapid disillusionment. In the months he had spent in France he had been studying the latest developments in gunnery and ship design, and he arrived full of ideas and innovations, desperate to try out his new sights and paddle boats on an island community equally determined to resist the advice and habits of an English Messiah whose sole experience of command had ended in his dismissal for gross insubordination.

Perhaps only a young English aristocrat could have arrived with the confidence and assumptions that Hastings brought, but at the root of his dilemma was that same cultural gap that every philhellene faced. From the age of eleven he had known nothing but the disciplines and practices of the Royal Navy, and on Hydra he found a world in which war was a matter of profit and not honour, in which captains went to sea when and if they pleased, crews hired or withheld their services at their whim, and any notion of a 'fleet' – or cooperation between the islands – was more a voluntary and self-interested association of equals than a patriotic duty.

But even if this 'bigoted' Hydriot community was a world unto itself – impervious to anything Hastings had to offer, complacently sure of its own superiority, and independent of any central authority – it was still all there was, and at first light on 20 April Hastings and Jarvis sailed over to the desolate Corinth isthmus to present their credentials to Greece's new president. On their first arrival they were received with a distinctly cautious civility by Mavrocordato, but it was only after further audiences with the Ministers of Marine and War had produced nothing that Hastings learned why. 'Monsieur le Prince,' he immediately wrote in protest – and one can hear a certain irony in the use of that title from a descendant of Edward III addressing the heir to a long line of Turkish 'hired helps' in the Danubian provinces –

I have determined to take the liberty of addressing your Highness in writing, as I found you occupied when I had the honour of presenting myself at your residence yesterday. I shall speak with freedom, convinced that your Highness will reply in the same manner.

I will not amuse you with recounting the sacrifices I have made to come to serve Greece. I came without being invited, and have no right to complain if my services are not accepted. In that case, I shall only regret that I cannot add my name to those of the liberators of Greece; I shall not cease to wish for the triumph of liberty and civilization over tyranny and barbarism. But I believe that I may say to your Highness without failing in respect, that I have a right to have my services either accepted or refused, for (as you may easily suppose) I can spend my money quite as agreeably elsewhere.

It seems that I am a suspected person because I am an Englishman. Among people without education I expected to meet with some prejudice against Englishmen, in consequence of the conduct of the British government, but I confess that I was not prepared to find such prejudice among men of rank and education. I was far from supposing that the Greek government would believe that every individual in the country adopted the same political opinions. I am the younger son of Sir Charles Hastings, Baronet, general in the army, and in possession of a landed estate of nearly £10,000

a year. The Marquis of Hastings, Governor-General of India, was
brought up by my grandfather along with my father, and they have
been as brothers. If I were in search of a place I might surely find
one more lucrative under the British government in India, and less
dangerous as well as more respectable than that of a spy among the
Greeks. I venture to say, your Highness, that if the English government wishes to employ a spy here, it would not address a person
of my condition, while there are so many strangers in the country
who would sell the whole of Greece for a bottle of brandy ...

What I demand of your Highness is only to serve, without
having the power to injure, your country. What injury can I inflict
on Greece, being alone in a ship of war? I must share the fate of
the ship, and if it sink I shall be drowned with the rest on board.

Hastings was never to know that Jarvis was behind his cool reception – he had warned Mavrocordato against the help of Perfidious
Albion – but the letter had its effect, and on 30 April he at last got
permission to sail with the fleet in Tombazis' corvette, the *Themistocles*. He recorded his belated introduction to the *laissez-faire* time-
keeping of the Greek navy with characteristic irritation: 'In the
morning we commenced getting under way & hauling out of the
harbour. In fifteen years of service I never beheld such a scene. Those
of the crew who chose to come on board did so – the rest remained
on shore & came off as it suited their convenience.'

If Hastings's exasperation was understandable, it was hopelessly
academic, because by the time the Hydriot fleet finally sailed, they
were not just hours but weeks too late to prevent the single greatest
tragedy of the whole revolution. The initial object of the fleet was
the Greek maritime power base of Psara, but beyond that, just four
miles from the Asian mainland, lay another island with a profoundly
different tradition and population, whose name over the next months
was to become a byword across Europe and America for barbarism
and horror.

In the first stages of the uprising, Chios – the peaceable, mastic-
growing Shangri La of the Aegean where Occidental fantasy and Eastern reality came as close to being one as they ever have – had done
all it could to keep out of a war it could not possibly hope to survive.
In the years before the revolt the Turks had left the government of the
island more or less completely to its inhabitants, but Ottoman indulgence always came with a bow-string attached, and when in March

1822 the island was reluctantly sucked into the conflict, the Porte responded as only it could. 'Mercy was out of the question,' wrote Thomas Gordon, the friend of Hastings and great philhellene historian of the war, 'the victors butchering indiscriminately all who came in their way; shrieks rent the air, and the streets were strewed with the dead bodies of old men, women and children; even the inmates of the hospital, the madhouse, and the deaf and dumb institution, were inhumanely slaughtered.'

The Turks had landed on 11 April, and less than a month after a slaughter that had left 25,000 dead and slave markets from Constantinople to the Barbary coast glutted with Greek women and boys, all that was left of the old idyll was a wilderness of smouldering villages and unburied corpses. 'We landed contrary to my opinion,' Hastings wrote from the *Themistocles* on 8 May, his impotent anger, as it so often would, recoiling onto the Greek fleet and his fellow volunteers,

> for we had no intelligence & ... had reason to suppose the Turks were here in numbers ... We landed & I wished to establish some order – place a sentinel on the eminence ... keep the people together etc but I had to learn what Greeks were. Each man directed his course to the right or left as best pleased him. After rambling about without any object for two hours we reassembled near our boat & when about to embark, four refugees – men – appeared on the eminence above us creeping cautiously towards a wall & some muskets were seen. This was justly calculated to create suspicion. Our men called to us to get into the boat – we did so – all except Jarvis who always pretended to know better than his superiors & those who had seen service ... No doubt when Jarvis [the two men had already almost come to a duel] has seen some service he will learn that the duty for an officer is to provide for the protection of his own men as well as the destruction of the enemy. However the confusion I saw reign during this alarm disgusted me with Greek boating – every one commanded – everyone halloed & prepared his musquet & no one took the oars – nobody attempted to get the boat afloat, so the boat was ground fore & aft.

The men on the clifftop turned out to be Greek, but with Hastings and his party finding only three other survivors – two women and a child hiding among the decomposing corpses – revenge was only a matter of time. 'While I was on board the Admiral,' he wrote four days later, at sea again in the narrow channel between Chios and mainland Asia,

> I beheld a sight which never will be effaced from my memory – A Turkish prisoner was brought on board to be interrogated & after he had answered the questions to him, the crew came and surrounded him, insulting language was first used, the boys were made to pull him by the beard & beat him, he was then dragged several times round the deck by the beard & at length thrown living into the sea. During this horrid ceremony the crew appeared to take the greatest delight in the spectacle, laughing & rejoicing & when he was in the water the man in the boat astern struck him with the boat hook. This sight shocked me so much that I could not help letting them see I disapproved of it: but I was told it was impossible to prevent it & that letting the sailors see my disapproval would be apt to expose me to their revenge.
>
> Mr Anemet a gentleman serving on board the Minerva was on board the Admiral & gave me shocking details of the massacre of the men of a boat they took that morning; after sinking the boat with grape shot they picked up some of the wounded who floated, with two Greek women who were prisoners in the boat & escaped unwounded. The wounded were senseless, but the Greeks did not consider that to kill them at that moment was cruel enough; they therefore revived them & afterwards one of the women with her own hands cut the throats of two of them; the others after torturing greatly, they hung & even heaped their revenge on the bodies. The Turks I was told defended themselves with great courage. The one I saw massacred, uttered no complaint, made no supplication nor acted meanly in any way, true he trembled greatly, but it must be remembered he was surrounded, had already been half drowned & hauled round the deck by the beard; as it was it is not surprising that his nerves should have a little failed him.

'What marvellous patriotism is to be found in Greece!!!' Hastings was soon scrawling – the words heavily underlined – on the twenty-fifth, after a rumour reached the ship that the Ottoman fleet were planning an assault on the most remote and exposed of the three Greek naval centres at Psara.

> The report ... greatly alarmed the men on board our ship, who appeared resolved gallantly to run away & leave their countrymen to have their throats cut in case the attack should take place – quells animaux! ... I was sorry to find also that the Franks [i.e. the Western philhellenes] on board the other ships were conducting themselves in a manner not at all likely to gain the esteem of the Greeks, eating, drinking & smoking seemed to be their principal occupations.

All that Hastings asked was the chance to fight, but as the summer dragged on with only a single Greek success to show for it, that seemed as remote as ever. A half-hearted night attack on the Turkish ships under a bright May moon came to nothing, and after a stretch of blockading work off the Turkish-held Nauplia – where Hastings met 'the famed Baboulina', revolutionary Greece's bloodthirsty cross between a Parisian *tricôteuse* and a vision-free Jeanne d'Arc – he made a final, Cochrane-esque bid to bully Miaulis, the Greek commander, into action. 'I saw the Admiral this evening,' he wrote on 6 July, back at Hydra again, where he found himself stranded among the scheming philhellene 'scum of the earth' that had made it their home while he had been away with the fleet,

> and presented him with a plan for endeavouring to take a frigate – the idea was to direct a fireship & three other vessels upon a frigate during the night & when near the enemy to set fire to certain combustibles which should throw out a great flame; the enemy would naturally conclude they were all fire-ships ... However, the admiral returned it to me ... without even looking at it or permitting me to explain it to him and I observed a kind of insolent contempt in his manner, which no doubt arose from their late success [an action with a fireship against a Turkish vessel] – for the national character is insolence in success & cowardice in distress. This interview with the admiral disgusted me more than ever with the service – They place you in a position in which it is impossible to render any service, and then they boast (amongst themselves) of their own superiority and the uselessness of the Franks (as they call us).

There was in fact to be one last chance for Hastings, and it came almost before the vitriol in his journal had had time to dry. A couple of days after his rejection by Miaulis the *Themistocles* again put to sea, and on 15 July was giving chase to a small flotilla of enemy *sakol-evas* south of Tenedos, when a rogue wind took her close in under a cliff heavily manned by Turks. 'These troops opened a sharp but ill-directed fire of musketry on the deck of the Themistocles,' George Finlay later wrote – there is, typically, no mention in Hastings's journal of his own role in the action –

> and on this occasion a total want of order, and the disrespect habitually shown to the officers, had very nearly caused the loss of the vessel. The whole crew sought shelter from the Turkish fire under the bulwarks, and no one could be induced to obey the orders which every one issued ... Hastings was the only person on deck who remained silently watching the ship slowly drifting towards the rocks. He was fortunately the first to perceive the change in the direction of a light breeze which sprang up, and by immediately springing forward on the bowsprit, he succeeded in getting the ship's head round. Her sails soon filled, and she moved out of her awkward position. As upwards of two hundred and fifty Turks were assembled on the rocks above, and fresh men were arriving every moment ... her destruction seemed inevitable, had she remained an hour within gun-shot of the cliff ... Though they had refused to avail themselves of his skill, and neglected his advice, they now showed no jealousy in acknowledging his gallant exploit. Though he treated all with great reserve and coldness, as a means of insuring respect, there was not a man on board that was not ready to do him any service. Indeed the candid and hearty way in which they acknowledged the courage of Hastings, and blamed their own conduct in allowing a stranger to expose his life in so dangerous a manner to save them, afforded unquestionable proof that so much real generosity was inseparable from courage, and that, with proper discipline and good officers, the sailors of the Greek fleet would have had few superiors.

It was something, but not what Hastings had come east to achieve. But then, the Greece that was taking shape while he fretted away the summer on the *Themistocles* was hardly the country that even the most pragmatic philhellene had hoped for. Little might have happened at sea, but on land it had been a different story. On 16 July a philhellene army under the command of General Normann, a German veteran of the Napoleonic Wars who had fought at Austerlitz on the side of the Austrians, and on the retreat from Moscow with Napoleon, was destroyed at Petta, and with it went the last vestiges of authority remaining to the central government and the Westernised Mavrocordato. From now on the revolution and the new Greece would belong to the victors of Tripolis and a dozen other massacres – to the captains who had reneged on every guarantee of safe conduct they had ever given; who had roasted Jews at the fall of Tripolis, and transposed the severed heads of dogs and women; to the men who could spin out the death of a suspected informant at Nauplia for six days, breaking his fingers, burning out his nails and boiling him alive before smearing his face with honey and burying him up to his neck. It was enough, as one embittered English philhellene put it, to make a volunteer pray for battle, in the hope of seeing the Greeks on his own side killed.

VI

There is no year in the history of the Greek War of Independence so difficult to comprehend as that of 1822. In the first months of the rebellion the Ottoman armies had been too busy with the rebel Albanian Ali Pasha in Ioannina to give the Greeks their full attention, but from the day in early February that Ali's head was delivered to the Porte and two armies were despatched southwards from their base in Larissa – one down the western side towards Missolonghi, and a second down the east towards Corinth, Nauplia and the Morean heartland of the insurgency – Greece and the Greek revolt looked almost certainly doomed.

The stuttering failure of the western army would not directly involve Hastings, but the collapse of the eastern expedition under the command of Dramali Pasha was another matter. Early in July 1822 Dramali's army of 23,000 men and 60,000 horses had swept unchecked across the isthmus and on to Argos, but within weeks it had virtually ceased to exist as a fighting force, reduced by starvation, disease, incompetence and unripened fruit to an enfeebled rabble facing the dangers of a humiliating retreat through the passes, crags and narrow gorges of the Dervenakia to the south of Corinth.

The retreat of Dramali's army was to give the Greeks under Colocotrones – the ruthless scion of a long line of Turk-hating bandit chiefs

– their greatest victory of the war, and one that would have been still greater without the lure of the Ottoman baggage trains. With more discipline not a single Turkish soldier could have made it back to Corinth alive; even as it was the bones of Dramali's troops would litter the mountainsides and gullies for years to come, left to whiten where they had fallen, hacked down in flight or – a *tableau mort* that titillated the imagination of Edward Trelawny – perched astride the skeletons of their animals, fingers still clenched around the rotting leather of their reins.

The one great prize along the eastern coast still in Ottoman hands at the end of July was the citadel of Nauplia, and that too was only courtesy of their Greek enemy. If the Greek captains had honoured some of their earlier promises the town would have given in long before, but with nothing to hope for from surrender but death or worse, its emaciated garrison – too weak even to man the upper ramparts – had held on even after all hope of rescue was gone, a pitiable testament to the cruelty, ineptitude and greed of their besiegers.

And to their cowardice, Hastings reckoned, because in spite of its towering position, grace and size – partly because of its size – Nauplia's Palamidi citadel could never have been held by its Turkish garrison against any sustained assault. Hastings had first inspected the fortress from the deck of the *Themistocles* at the beginning of July, and in the last days before Dramali's retreat had quitted Hydra with a '*soi disant*' philhellene frigate captain and incendiary, Count Jourdain, to see if there was any more fighting to be had with the land army than there was with the fleet.

He and Jourdain had sailed to Mili, or 'the Mills of Lerna', on the western side of the gulf, and on 27 July were sent across to the tiny island fortress of Bourdzi to reconnoitre the position. 'We found an irregular old Venetian fortress,' Hastings noted of the island – the traditional home of the Nauplia executioner in peacetime and a suicidal death-trap to anyone trying to hold it in war –

mounting 13 guns of different calibres & in various conditions – it is entirely commanded by the citadel which could destroy it on any occasion – more particularly as all its heavy guns bear on the entrance of the harbour ... The shore on the Northern side of this fort is not distant more than two thirds gun shot, so that the enemy could throw up batteries there which could open a cross fire on this miserable place & destroy it in one day as the walls [are] in a state of decay & the carriages of the guns scarcely able to bear three discharges.

For the next week this dilapidated and useless fortress, floating only a few hundred yards offshore under the guns of the Palamidi fortress, was home for Hastings and a motley crew of Greek and philhellene companions. There seemed no earthly reason why he or anyone else should be asked to hold the position, but there was a streak of masochistic pride about Hastings that served him well under duress, and the more ludicrous the task and the heavier the fire the more determined he was to sit it out 'while any danger existed'.

The first incoming shots had been so wayward, in fact, that he assumed they were signal guns, but a 'smart & not badly directed fire' soon disabused him of that idea. 'Our guns opened in return,' he recorded, 'but want of order obliged us shortly to desist – The men were not stationed at the different batteries so that each went where they pleased & it pleased the greater number to hide them-selves.'

With their batteries ill-sited, the gradients sloping in the direction of the recoil, their mortars rusted through, Jourdain's 'inflamable balls' useless, and the carriage wheels broken, this was perhaps no surprise, and one more smart artillery exchange was enough to send the fifty Greeks who had reinforced the fort scuttling for the other side of the gulf. 'One of the Primates, Bulgari, observed that we were at liberty to quit or remain as we thought proper,' Hastings recorded that night in his journal, alone now except for four other foreign volunteers equally determined to brave it out, '& begged us to consider that we remained by our own choice – We remained though convinced we could do nothing unless we were furnished with means of heating shot red for burning the houses.'

At a severely rationed rate of seven shots an hour, they had shells enough for seven days, but the Turks were under no such restraint and a heavy bombardment over the next two days rendered the fort virtu-ally *hors de combat*. By 4 August Hastings was concerned enough to send a message across the bay that they risked being cut off, and two days later, to the distant sounds from the Dervenakia of the slaugh-ter of Dramali's army, he finally decided that they had done enough. 'The reiterated insults I had received made it painful to a degree to remain,' he wrote from the Mills after their escape in a Greek vessel,

& I should have left the place long ago, had the fire not been so
continually kept up on the place. At 4 therefore I quitted the fort
with the other gentlemen & proceeded alongside the Schooner but
here they would not allow us to approach, however being highly
outraged I seized a favourable opportunity & jumping from the
boat seized the chain plates of the Schooner & mounted on deck
– there I preferred my complaint to the Members of the Govt on
board, they replied as usual with a shrug of the shoulders saying
'what can you expect from people without education!!'

As Greece slid inexorably into chaos, with Colocotrones in the
Morea and Odysseus Androutses, the most formidable and devious
of the klephts, in mainland Roumeli, rampantly out of control, the
next twelve months were as bleakly pointless as any in Hastings's
life. After five fruitless days at the Mills he had decided that he could
be better employed on Hydra, but within the week he was again
back on land, crossing and recrossing the Morea in a restless search
for a leader who might impose some structure on the enveloping
turmoil. 'I was glad to find that Colocotroni' – the 'hero' of Tripolis and the Dervenakia – 'was disposed to make a beginning towards
introducing a little regularity,' he wrote on 5 October, in Tripolis in
time to witness the town *en fête* for the grotesque anniversary cele-
brations of the horrors of 1821, '& I find that having been Major
of the Greek corps in the English service [in the Ionian Isles], he is
able to appreciate the advantages resulting from regular discipline
… After mass we visited him, he appeared extremely acute & intelligent & perhaps (not withstanding the character which the Govt
give him) is better able to govern than they are – the abuse heaped
upon him by the Hydriots evidently arises from jealousy of his influence & success.'

For a good English Whig Hastings was perhaps becoming more
tolerant of despotism and 'strong government' than was good for
him, but then again a journey through the parched and devastated
Morea in the autumn of 1822 was not going to provide a lesson in
the virtues of constitutional government. After leaving Tripolis and
Colocotrones he made his way south-west to Navarino and Messina,
filling his journal as he went with anything and everything from the
number of trees in Arcadia (28,000) to the sight of a Kalamata beggar
– amputated feet in hands as he crawled through the marketplace –
or the latest example of Greek perfidy. 'The Turks had obtained terms

of capitulation,' he recorded of the surrender of Navarino's Turkish garrison,

> by which it was stipulated that the lives of the garrison should be spared, that they should be permitted to carry away ⅓ of their property & be transferred to Asia on board Neutral Vessels – But no sooner had the Greeks taken possession of the Fortress than they massacred the greatest number of the inhabitants & transported the rest to a rock in the harbour where they were starved to death ... It is confidently asserted that the bishop issued his malediction on those Greeks who failed to massacre the Turks.

The remarkable thing about all this is not how like every other embittered philhellene Hastings sounds in his journal, but how unlike them he acted. For most of his fellow travellers the shock of disillusionment was rapidly terminal, but it only took the slightest sniff of action or the sight of a fortress still in Turkish hands to bring Hastings back to the colours, as enthusiastic as ever.

If he had foreseen the role Navarino would play in the revolution, he might have paid it even more attention than he did, but it was above all Nauplia's Palamidi that exercised his mind. On his return from his travels he had gone back to his old base on Hydra, and on 9 November he was joined there by another shadowy foreign volunteer called d'André, who had sought him out with a proposition that between them they should equip and lead a party of a hundred Greeks to storm the Palamidi.

For all his doubts about d'André, it was a proposition that left Hastings feeling not 'a little ébloui' – *dazzled* – and that same day he purchased fifty muskets at forty-eight piastres each and embarked with his new colleague for the Gulf of Argos. At the Mills d'André wrote to a dubious species of military 'pimp' in the business of troop procurement, and by the next day Hastings had his company to command – or at least forty-five of the fifty soldiers he had been promised, which was all that a 'certain Mr Testat' could produce at such notice. 'I armed them,' he recorded, with an optimism that he could still, bafflingly, bring to his military dealings with the Greeks, 'causing to be read to them at the same time some articles by which they were informed of the conditions upon which I delivered them the arms.'

Although the government at Tripolis was prepared to grant Hastings a commission that cost them nothing, they were not

ready to feed his men, and while d'André headed with their
company for the Dervenakia, Hastings returned to Hydra for
more funds. 'I visited the Minister of War,' he wrote indignantly
on 30 November, 'who did not receive me too well considering
the expense I had been at – he seems to consider the arming of 50
men as something not worth the trouble of undertaking & urged
me to form a corps of 300 – I replied I would undertake it if he
would furnish me with the money – as to the money he said I could
easily raise that sum.'

In one respect, at least, the Minister was right, because for all the
good Greece or Hastings would get out of his investment he might
have saved himself the bother. The next day he set off to the north to
rejoin his troops, who were guarding the passes near Corinth, and
found Testat in a state of permanent drunkenness, his second-in-
command little better, and his unfed soldiers – 'one & all' – in such
a state of mutinous discontent that only Hastings's arrival came
between d'André and their bayonets.

The real problem, as ever with Greek irregulars, was not fear of
the Turks but the lure of plunder, and with rumours of the fall of
Nauplia reaching them with every messenger Hastings had no hope
of keeping them at their post. He managed to buy himself some time
by dismissing d'André, but when news at last reached them that the
Palamidi had surrendered without a shot being fired, there was nothing he could do but join in the general migration south and look for
a chance to regain his muskets. 'I made the soldiers pile their arms,'
he wrote on 20 December, grateful that he did not have 'to resort to
firing measures' against his own men, '& then applied to Colocotroni
who sent an officer who brought the arms & placed them in the room
where Colocotroni held his council … The measure was quite unexpected by the soldiers & surprised them so completely that they did
not even murmur.'

The absurd and the horrific were never far apart from each other
in this conflict, however, and Hastings was determined to get out of
Nauplia before the town fell to an expectant and mutinous army.
Through the last weeks of the siege the garrison had been too weak
even to climb up to the fortress, and as the Greek soldiers massed at
the gates, determined to beat their own captains to the plunder, the
Muslim sick and dying could only await their fate, eking out their
final hours in the hopeless search among the unburied corpses of their
dead children for a last, filthy scrap of food.

There is no doubt either – in spite of all the promises of safe-passage – that there would have been a repetition of Tripolis, Navarino, Athens and Monemvassia had not a British frigate, HMS *Cambrian* under the command of Captain Gawen Hamilton, sailed the next day into the Gulf of Nauplia. In these early years of the war there was a strong anti-English feeling in the Greek government, but even the most rabid anglophobe knew that in Hamilton they had a friend they could trust and an arbiter they could not ignore.

It is difficult, in fact, to believe that anyone else in the Aegean would have had the moral authority to impose his will in the way that Hamilton did at the surrender of Nauplia. 'He held a conference with Kolokotrones and the Moreot chieftains,' Finlay wrote,

> whose Russian prejudices induced them to view the interference of an English officer with great jealousy. He was obliged to tell them in strong language, that if, on this occasion they failed to take effectual measures for the honourable execution of the capitulation, they would render the Greek name despicable in civilized Europe, and perhaps ruin the cause of Greece. The chiefs respected Hamilton's character; the wild soldiers admired his martial bearing and the frankness with which he spoke the whole truth. He took advantage of the feeling he had created in his favour to act with energy. He insisted on the Greek government immediately chartering vessels to embark the Turks, and to facilitate their departure he took five hundred on board the *Cambrian*.

The news of the *Cambrian* reached Tripolis on 30 December, and that night Hastings recorded it in his journal: 'We were informed that the Greeks had entered Nauplia, & an English frigate of war was in the roads ... The Greeks of Tripolitza were in great choler agst the frigate for having insisted upon the immediate embarkation of the Turks & having declared that he would accompany them to their destination.'

It must have been a strange moment for Hastings, a poignant mix of pride, regret and alienation that the 'choler' of his new countrymen can only have heightened. There was a twist, too, awaiting him when on 1 January 1823 he made the long, bitter march through more than a foot of thawing snow to Nauplia and found there his old first lieutenant from the *Orlando*, Edward Scott. His journal does no more than note their 'great surprise' at the meeting, but the next day

he went on board the *Cambrian*, the first time he can have been in
an English man-of-war since his return from Port Royal more than
four years earlier. 'I went on board and saw Scott,' he noted. 'Much
difference of opinion existed among the Greeks on the conduct of the
English Capt but I feel convinced that he saved the lives of the Turks
by his prompt measures & that he did a great service to Greece.'

It had been an unsettling way to see out an old year that had
brought nothing and see in a new that promised less. There would
come a time when Captain Hamilton would willingly have given a
thousand pounds to be in Hastings's shoes, but as the *Cambrian*, with
its five hundred emaciated Turks, weighed for Smyrna, Hastings
could only reflect on how utterly alone he was. He had no Greek
friends, and a chance meeting with a party of Germans – some new
arrivals, some survivors of the original Philhellene Battalion desperate to escape a country they had grown to hate – was enough to
remind him how little he belonged to any philhellene world either. He
had, though, thrown in his lot with his adopted country, and he was
no quitter. 'I now resolved to go to Hydra,' he wrote the day after the
Cambrian sailed, and two days later, on 7 January, nine months after
his first arrival, he was back among the scenes of his first disappointment.

VII

The uncertainty that surrounded Hastings's life at the beginning of
1823 was no more than a reflection of the state of Greece itself as
it drifted towards the first of its civil wars. His courage in the
Themistocles the previous summer had belatedly won him a
Hydriot reputation of sorts, but as the stories emerged from the
Morea of Colocotrones's growing power and the endless rivalries
– government against captain, captain against captain, captain
against primate – an island exile seemed an indulgence that Hastings could not afford if he was ever going to get the chance to fight
again.

He had been invited by Emmanuel Tombazi, one of the leading
Hydriot captains, to join him on an expedition to Crete, but even
that was dependent on decisions taken elsewhere, and in the middle
of February Hastings returned to the Morea to be closer to the centre
of power. Before he could sail an accident with a pistol almost cost

him his head – and did cost him six teeth broken and two knocked out – but on the fourteenth he landed again at Nauplia, setting up house in a half-ruined shelter in the old town while he waited for government and island deputies to arrive for the second National Assembly.

With Colocotrones and his followers quitting Nauplia for Tripolis as soon as the deputies arrived, it was a miracle the Assembly met at all, but by mid-April the warring factions had at last buried their differences sufficiently to converge on Aspros on the east coast of the Morea. On the twenty-fifth of the month Hastings set off after them to fight his corner, and for the next week pitched his tent like some demented Viola in front of the house of the Cretan island's deputies, 'halloo-ing' his cause and credentials until he finally got the appointment he was after as 'Chef de l'état major de Artillerie' (sic) on the forthcoming expedition to Crete.

Hastings might have known from the spurious grandeur of his title that he was in for another disappointment, but before the end of May he had sailed along with 1,500 troops and two Germans he had taken into his service at Hydra. On 3 June the expedition disembarked near the citadel of Kisamos on Crete, and within days he was back into the familiar and desultory rhythms of Greek campaign life, with weeks of frustration and inactivity punctuated by sporadic fits of violence and treachery.

The Turkish garrison of Kisamos – ravaged by plague – succumbed without either a fight or the usual reprisals, but from then on it was the old story of confusion, inter-island dissensions, bad faith, broken paroles, massacres, 'atrocious treason' and 'cowardice'. 'It is plain that they will not fight in a position in which there is a possibility of their being killed,' Hastings was soon complaining, after his Greek soldiers had refused to sight his batteries in range of Turkish guns, 'and I cannot persuade them that amongst all the modern inventions there is no secret of fighting without danger.'

The longer he fought with the Greeks, in fact, the more clearly he saw the virtues of the Turks – 'a courageous and honourable people' – though one partial exception he would always allow was in favour of the Cretan soldier. 'A German arrived from Kiramos,' he noted in his journal:

he says that the quality most esteemed in a soldier here is to run
fast. When the gallant Ballasteros* was abandoned by his soldiers
& fell into the hands of the Turks who put him to death in the most
cruel manner the Greeks remarked that it was no loss as he was
worth nothing as a soldier [as] he could not run fast – I must
however acknowledge that I [had] a very different feeling at
Cadeno [on Crete]. As there was no cannon I took the musquet of
my servant & advanced into the valley to a short pistol shot from
the pyrgos – the Greeks then used all their endeavours to persuade
me to retire saying it was not my business to get killed & that I did
not understand their manner of making war & it would hurt them
very much to lose me citing with much regret the fate of Balleste –
this I must acknowledge gave me a favourable opinion of the
Cretans – fortunately for me Tombazi recalled me from this position & thus I was (perhaps) saved from Balleste's fate.

Hastings could have had no idea of it at the time but it was the last
occasion on which he would fight alongside Greek soldiers on land.
In the early days of the campaign fever had been rampant in the army,
and by 10 August he had joined a mounting sick list, 'suffering very
much' and the next day was still worse. 'During the night I was stung
by something in my handkerchief,' he wrote, 'and on the light being
brought I found a scorpion in my handkerchief. The pain tho' very
great lasts only 5 or 6 hours.'
   It would be another five weeks before Hastings was strong enough
to move, and by that time he would have been grateful for any excuse
to quit Crete with life and honour intact. In the early part of September a letter from Edward Scott had warned him of an Egyptian army
heading for the Morea, but even before that – before the expedition
had even sailed, in fact – a chance meeting with the indefatigable Irish
philhellene and serial activist Edward Blaquiere, travelling in Greece
on behalf of the newly formed London Greek Committee, had raised
possibilities that made the prospect of a foot soldier's death in a useless
war a criminal abrogation of all Hastings's headiest ambitions.
   One of the most puzzling and ill-explained aspects of European
philhellenism in the first days of the revolution had been the compar-

---

* The French Napoleonic veteran and philhellene Baleste, the first of the foreign
volunteers. He was killed in Crete, and his head sent to Constantinople.

ative indifference of Britain to affairs in Greece. In the historio-
graphy of the war there have been any number of reasons advanced
for this coolness, but whether the answer was domestic politics,
Castlereagh or simply some post-Napoleonic species of 'compassion
fatigue', the truth remains that for all the pamphlets, speeches and
moral indignation, no more than a dozen British philhellenes had
actually gone out to fight for Greece by the end of 1822.

There had never been any shortage of sympathisers, though, and
at the beginning of March 1823 an inaugural meeting of the new
London Greek Committee was held at the Crown and Anchor in
London's Strand. The moving spirits behind its formation were the
usual suspects associated with the liberal causes of the day, and their
manifesto lacked nothing of the woolly sentiment that characterised
the earliest 'friends of humanity, civilization, and religion'. It was
time to redress Britain's record, it announced, and 'time ... to make
a public appeal ... in the name of Greece. It is in behalf of a country
associated with every sacred and sublime recollection: – it is for a
people formerly free and enlightened, but long retained by foreign
despots in the chains of ignorance and barbarism!'

If this could just as easily have come from Boston or Berne as
London, there were forces at work within the Committee that poten-
tially distinguished it from its European or American equivalents. At
the core of the small active membership was a group of skilled and
practised politicians, and as Britain's foreign policy under
Castlereagh's successor, George Canning, began to thaw towards
Greek aspirations, the Committee found itself and its cause in an
unlikely – if undisclosed – harmony with British national interests.

Without the tacit connivance of the authorities the London
Committee could have done little, but in the short term of even
greater importance to Greece was the potential access to the London
money markets at a time when a drop in interest on government
bonds was making foreign loans an attractive proposition. In its early
days the Committee's attempts to raise funds from voluntary dona-
tions had been modest at best, but by 1823 a heady mix of idle money,
speculative greed and philhellenic high-mindedness had conjured up
dreams of a Greek gold bonanza on a scale to dwarf anything that
had gone before.

With the future colonial governor John Bowring, the radical MP
Joseph Hume and the politician-money man Edward Ellice all deeply
involved, there was no shortage of financial acumen available to the

Committee, but what was required was a 'name', and for that only one would do. From the first founding of the Committee its most famous member had been the exiled Byron, and in a spectacular propaganda coup Blaquiere had broken off his journey to Greece at Pisa in order to persuade him to take on the leadership of the cause his verse had done so much to popularise.

It did not matter that there was not a single original idea in that verse; it did not matter that the exiled poet would as soon have gone to Spain or South America; it did not matter that he was a faddish and overweight thirty-six; or that it would take him another five months to get even as far as Cephalonia: it was the Byron name that the Committee had been after, and Hastings's reaction showed how well they had gauged its effect. It would be hard to imagine anyone better equipped by birth or temperament to resist its lure, but from the day Hastings met Blaquiere the thought of Byron haunted his imagination, easing the frustrations and miseries of the Cretan campaign with visions of a role in the war and a strategy for winning it that suddenly seemed something more than dreams.

A 'violent and dangerous' relapse on his return to Hydra from Crete left it looking unlikely that Hastings would live long enough to see out the week, never mind to see Byron, but he had already prepared his brief. 'Lord Byron's companions Hamilton Brown & Mr Trelawny arrived & called on me,' he noted in his journal on 11 October, after a meeting with the two 'secretaries' Byron had sent on ahead of him to report back from the 'Seat of War'. 'I gave Mr Brown my letter for Ld Byron containing my views on Greece & he engaged to forward it safely.'

Hastings's letter had had a long and hard birth – draft after draft, heavily scored and annotated, survive among his papers – but the result is the most impressive and clear-sighted strategic document to emerge from the revolution. Behind it lies not just eighteen months' experience of Greece, but fifteen years' service in a navy whose strong empirical problem-solving tradition equipped him to move from the large picture to the detail with a persuasive authority.

'Firstly,' he wrote to Byron – having duly larded his arguments with the appropriate compliments to the 'First Genius of the Age', 'I lay down as an axiom that Greece cannot obtain any decisive advantage over the Turks without a decided maritime superiority; for it is necessary to prevent them from relieving their fortresses and supplying their armies by sea.'

The only weapon against Turkish fortresses that the Greeks had, Hastings argued, was famine, and without it they would have achieved nothing. In those outposts where the Turks could resupply their garrisons – Patras, Modon, Coron, Negropont – the Greeks had been powerless, and in a terrain that made movement and supply difficult, an army without artillery, engineers or the finance to sustain itself in the field for any length of time was never going to be the answer.

If this seems self-evident now, it did not then – any number of British or European officers thought the war could be won on land – but Hastings had not finished there. 'The localities of the countries are also such,' he went on presciently, 'and the difficulties of moving troops so great, that, without the aid of a fleet, all the efforts of an invading army would prove fruitless. But on the contrary, were an invading army followed by a fleet, I fear that all the efforts of the Greeks to oppose it would be ineffectual. The question stands thus, Has the Greek fleet hitherto prevented the Turks from supplying their fortresses, and is it likely to succeed in preventing them?'

The answer to both questions was 'no', and Hastings was one of the few to see that the comparative calm of 1823 had more to do with other pressures on the Ottoman Empire and the disastrous fire in her main arsenal at Tophana in March that year than with any real security. 'Is it likely that the Greek marine will improve, or that the Turkish will retrograde?' he asked, remembering, perhaps, that austere, relentless and unforgiving figure he had glimpsed from the deck of the *Sea Horse* thirteen years earlier.

> The contrary is to be feared. We have seen the Greek fleet diminish in numbers every year since the commencement of the war, while that of the Turks has undeniably improved, from the experience they have gained in each campaign ... Is the Greek fleet likely to become more formidable? On the contrary, the sails, riggings and hulls are all going out of repair; and in two years time thirty sail could hardly be sent to sea without an expense which the Greeks could not probably incur.

With the Ottoman fleet again at sea, and Ibrahim Pasha's Egyptians subduing Crete before turning their attention to the Morea, there was an unarguable force to Hastings's argument. But he also had an answer. 'We now come to the question, How can the Greeks obtain a decisive superiority over the Turks at sea?' he continued.

I reply, By a steam-vessel armed as I shall describe ... It would be necessary to build or purchase the vessel in England, and send her out to complete. She should be from 150 to 200 tons burden, of a construction sufficiently strong to bear two long 32-pounders, one forward and one aft, and two 68-pounder guns of seven inches bore, one on each side. The weight of shot appears to me of the greatest importance, for I think I can prove that half a dozen shot or shells of these calibres, and employed as I propose, would more than suffice to destroy the largest ship. In this case it is not the number of projectiles, but their nature and proper application that is required.

Although it would be another two years, and endless disappointments, refinements and changes, before Hastings got his steamship, here in essence is the vessel that made his name. Over the past generation there had been various experiments on both sides of the Atlantic with the military application of steam, but if Hastings could not claim absolute priority – Frederick Marryat, Cochrane protégé and future novelist, commanding the sixty-horsepower *Diana* in the First Burma War of 1824–26 has that – such a vast gulf in terms of scale, ambition and power separates the vessel Hastings was proposing from Marryat's that the age of steam in naval warfare only properly begins with him.

At a juncture in naval architecture at which the frigate was poised to reach its final, elegant apogee, in fact, there is something brutally modernist in Hastings's utter disregard for the aesthetics of sail and line. The potential advantages of steam power – independence, predictability – were all the more vital among the capricious breezes of the Aegean, and what it gave Hastings above all was a delivery system that would enable him to bring to bear against an enemy the full weight of his gunnery as quickly and effectively as possible. 'We now come to the plan of attack,' he continued to Byron, conjuring up some steaming whirling dervish of a vessel:

In executing this, I should go directly for the vessel most detached from the enemy's fleet, and when at the distance of one mile, open with red-hot shot from the 32-pounder forward. The gun laid at point blank, with a reduced charge, would carry on board *en rico-chetant*. I would then wheel round and give the enemy one of the 68-pounders with shell laid at the line of metal, which would also ricochet on board him. Then the stern 32-pounder with hot shot, and again 68-pounder of the other side with a shell. By this time the bow-gun would be again loaded, and a succession of fire might be kept up as brisk as from a vessel having four guns on a side. Here the importance of steam is evident.

There would be, of course, a danger of the engine being hit, he conceded,

but when we consider the small object a low steamer would present coming head on, and the manner in which the Turks have hitherto used their guns at sea, this risk really appears very trifling. The surprise caused by seeing a vessel move in a calm, offering only a breadth of about eighteen feet, and opening fire with heavy guns at a considerable distance, may also be taken in to account. I am persuaded, from what I have seen, that in many cases the Turks would run their ships ashore and abandon them, perhaps without having the presence of mind to set fire to them.

For obvious reasons the use of red-hot shot at sea had always alarmed the men who sailed wooden vessels, but Hastings had seen too clearly for himself the effects it could have on ships not to believe there were technical solutions to the dangers. 'Of the destructive effect of hot shot on an enemy's ship,' he told Byron,

it is scarcely necessary for me to speak. The destruction of the Spanish fleet before Gibraltar is well known. But if I may be permitted to relate an example which came under my proper observation, it will perhaps tend to corroborate others. At New Orleans the Americans had a ship and schooner in the Mississippi that flanked our lines. In the commencement we had no cannon. However, after a couple of days, two field-pieces of 4 or 6lb and a howitzer were erected in battery. In ten minutes the schooner was on fire, and her comrade, seeing the effect of the hot shot, cut her cable and escaped under favour of a light wind. If such was the result of light shot imperfectly heated – for we had no forge – what would be the effect of such a volume as a 32-pounder? A single shot would set a ship in flames.

The risks, too – introducing the red-hot shot before laying the guns, the problems associated with firing shells, the dangers of a shell rolling in a horizontal bore, the transport of shells around the ship – were all more apparent than real, but it seems unlikely that anyone with a boredom threshold as low as Byron's was still reading. The central message, though, had sunk in. Finlay once remarked that there was not one but two Byrons at Missolonghi: the 'feminine' (as he curiously and revealingly put it) Byron who performed in company – vain, frivolous, mercurial; and the 'masculine' Byron, all intellect and good sense, who came out in one-to-one conversation. It was this second Byron – whatever lies to the contrary were later told – whose attention Hastings had caught. It makes it all the more of a shame that the two men never met, but Hastings's letter would bear its posthumous fruit. As Byron moved from Cephalonia to Missolonghi and his own sacrificial death, harried and importuned on all sides, Hastings was about to discover the terrible irony of Byron's Greek adventure: alive, there was little the First Genius of the Age could do; dead, nothing he could not. All that Hastings had to do was wait. And in the meantime, another and closer death had already brought his vision a step nearer.

VIII

It seems impossible to know now what contact he had had with Willesley in the eighteen months since he had sailed for Greece but Hastings's departure had badly hurt his ageing father. For many years the old general had been living out his days with a more or less stoical patience, a spectator at a play that had long lost his interest, saddened by years of war, ill-health, the death of friends, the failing sight of his wife and disappointment in his sons. 'Were it not for the sake of my children I know not whether I should have taken that trouble' – of visiting Cheltenham for the waters – he had written as early as 1808, 'after all – for what? To prolong the dream a few years longer – and which dream after all has not been a pleasant one – no, I think I should prefer confining myself to my convenient room, surrounded by my family, books and maps, and strive to spin out this dream at least contentedly if not comfortably – so much for sermonising.'

It would be hard, he conceded in 1813, 'to quit the Theatre before the play is over and the curtain drops', but with the defeat of

Napoleon and the *Kangaroo* incident there was less and less to hold him. There is the occasional trace of him in the local newspaper – a bullock presented to the town for 'a patriotic feast' to celebrate Wellington's Peninsula victories, the festivities to welcome the Marquis of Hastings back from India – but from the odd letter that survives, the only consolations of his old age seem to have been laudanum and the presence at Willesley of a little girl, a natural daughter of Sir John Moore adopted by the Hastings family after Corunna. 'The young orphan who was a very bright, interesting and charming girl,' Baron Louis le Jeune, a French prisoner of war at Ashby and – in the easygoing ways of a provincial town far from the sea – a dinner guest at Willesley, recalled, 'was quite the life of the circle which her host and hostess gathered about them. The courtesy and kindness with which I was received did much to cheer my spirits, prisoner though I was.'

It is a poignant and elusive image – how she came, who her mother was, where she went, all seem mysteries – but whatever compensation the young Eliza Moore brought for the disgrace of Sir Charles's 'Trafalgar Hero' it was tragically not enough. 'My dear dear Mother,' Frank's older brother, Charles, wrote from Geneva on 9 October 1823, eighteen months after Frank's departure for Greece:

> This instant a courier has arrived with Mr McDonall's letter, & the most melancholy intelligence it contains the sudden manner of its communication to me has thrown me into the greatest grief & sorrow – I am fearful to agitate your feelings my dear Mother by giving vent to my own, & I hardly know what I write or how to express myself ... Keep yourself up my dearest Mother I beg of you ... It is to me a great consolation that no one can have a moment's doubt that my poor Father's mind was quite gone ...

The new Sir Charles might well have been right – 'Oct 2', the wonderfully named Derbyshire Coroner Charnel Bateman wrote in his accounts, 'Willesley to view the body of Sir Charles Hastings Bart, who shot himself, being at the time in a state of temporary derangement, 21 miles £1.15s 9d.' – but there was certainly nothing insane about the man who had made his will only months before. 'I desire my body may be opened after my death,' he declared, with the same robust, pagan instincts that made him so contemptuous that Bonaparte should have surrendered rather than fallen on his sword,

and buried without a coffin upon the Grove Hill on a spot marked
by me, wrapped up in either woollen, oil cloth or any such perish-
able materials as will keep my body together until deposited in my
grave by six of my most deserving poorest labourers to whom one
pound will be given ... and several acorns to be planted over my
grave that one good tree may be chosen [the rusting iron railings
still surround a tree near where Willesley Hall once stood] and
preserved and that I may have the satisfaction of knowing that after
my death my body may not be quite useless but serve to rear a good
English Oak.

The same mixture of singularity, clarity and generosity runs through
the rest of the will, and if Sir Charles Hastings died insane, then he
had probably lived that way too. There is a curious – and very *Hastings* – codicil disinheriting his elder son in favour of Frank should
Charles ever employ their old steward again, but the clause that most
affected his estranged favourite – and transformed his bargaining
power with his Greek masters – came right at the beginning.

As my youngest son Frank Hastings has been provided for by a
clause in the Marriage Settlement I shall entrust him to the care
of his Mother and Brother who will act towards him as he behaves
and I grant him my blessing and entire forgiveness ... I leave to my
eldest son Charles Hastings five thousand pounds to enable him
to pay his brother that sum due to him by the Marriage Settlement.

'I have written three letters to my brother,' Charles told his mother
in that same letter from Geneva, 'in which I urge in the kindest and
strongest manner I can his immediate return to England – & have
desired him to draw on me for any sums of money he may want. The
3 letters go by different channels, & I think safe one's [sic].'
    There is no mention of his father's death in Frank's journal –
although there is a copy of the will among his papers – but if it did
reach him before the end of the year his brother's plea went ignored.
It seems likely in fact that Charles's letters did not catch up with him
until well into the next year, because by the end of October 1823 he
had left Hydra for Athens, sailing north via Corinth with another
disenchanted product of the Royal Navy, Byron's secretary, imitator,
traducer and future biographer, Edward John Trelawny.

It says something about the diversity of philhellene life that two men as diametrically opposed in character and ambition as Trelawny and Hastings could find themselves on the same side, let alone in the same boat. They had entered the navy as boys in the same year, but whereas Hastings had served in the *Neptune* at Trafalgar, Trelawny – to his bitter regret – had missed out on the battle, beginning a downward spiral of resentments and failures that was made bearable only by a fantasy existence of sub-Byronic adventures that he half came to believe in himself.

There was no shortage of fabulists among philhellene volunteers, but what set Trelawny apart was his genius for co-opting others into his fantasy world. At the end of the Napoleonic Wars he had found himself in the same position as thousands of other unemployed lieutenants, but not even a humiliating marriage and divorce could keep him down, and in 1822, armed with little more than his dramatic good looks and a genius for story-telling, he succeeded in 'bamming' and talking his way into Byron's Pisan circle in time to preside at the cremation of Shelley's drowned corpse on the beach near Livorno.

It had seemed axiomatic to the Byron circle that Trelawny should fill the role – hadn't he, after all, burned the body of his Eastern child-bride after she had been attacked by a shark? – but while Byron remained fond enough of Trelawny to take him to Greece, the creature had soon outgrown his creator. He had crossed the Morea initially in order to report back on the political and military situation, but with every mile put between himself and Byron the old ties and loyalties had weakened, and long before Hydra Trelawny had resolved to throw in his lot with a man who was the antithesis of all that the dilatory Byron represented. 'I am to be a kind of aide de camp to [Odyssesus Androutses],' he proudly wrote to Mary Shelley in a characteristic blend of fact and fantasy. 'The General gives me as many men as I choose to command, and I am to be always with him … I am habited exactly like Ulysses, in red and gold vest, with sheep-skin capote, gun, pistols, sabre, & a few dollars or doubloons; my early habits will be resumed, and nothing new, but dirt and privations, with mountain sleeping, are a good exchange for the parched desert, dry locusts and camels' milk.'

Trelawny would not have known camel's milk if he had taken a bath in it – the Wahhabi–Ottoman desert wars, though, were prominent among his fictional battle honours – but his whole life is such a triumph of imagination over reality that it would be pedantic to hold that against him. From the first time he had read a Byron poem he had modelled himself on the Byronic hero, and here at last was the chance for life to catch up with art, for reality finally to deliver among the crags and bandit lairs of Parnassus the excitements and notoriety that ten years of the navy or Bristol boarding houses had so signally failed to provide.

Trelawny's hopes were to be realised, too – life was briefly, tardily but dramatically about to give him everything down to the statutory Byronic child-bride he craved – and even in embryo he was a riskily outlandish companion with whom to travel. He and Hastings had arrived at the Corinth isthmus on the eve of the formal capitulation of the citadel, and in the heightened tensions that always followed a surrender the mere appearance of anyone as theatrically exotic as 'Greek' or 'Turk' Trelawny was enough to get the pair of them almost shot as spies.

It cannot have escaped Hastings, however, as they picked their way through the whitening bones of Dramali's men and horses – 10,000 of them, he reckoned – and crossed for Athens, that for all his absurd posturing Trelawny was probably closer to the philhellene 'type' than he was himself. For the best part of two years Hastings had railed against Greek ingratitude, but with only one or two exceptions he remained as much a loner in volunteer company – coldly remote with his own countrymen, contemptuously suspicious of '*soi disant*' French 'experts', and perfectly ready, in the face of Jarvis's American vulgarity, to enforce a proper respect at the end of a duelling pistol if necessary.

There was as ever, though, a resilience about Hastings that kept him going, and with the imminent promise of 'English gold' he was no sooner in Athens than he was again writing to exhort Byron to prevent the money falling into a bottomless Greek sink. In the months since his first letter nothing had occurred to make him change his mind, but he had seen enough of the country's politics to know that with every snout in the trough – as he elegantly put it – it was going to be hard enough to persuade the Greeks to finance a single steamship, let alone a fleet, if they had control of their own gold.

£20,000, that was all he needed – all Greece needed if she was 'yet to be saved' – and for once Hastings seemed lucky in his timing. 'Trelawny gave a dinner to Goura' – just about the basest of all the Greek leaders – he noted on 13 December, exultant after hearing that Byron and Colonel Napier, the Resident on Cephalonia and a soldier with a distinguished past and a sinful future, had at last 'approved' his plan: '... in the middle Mr Finlay arrived ... Mr Finlay is quite a young man – he has studied in Germany & pleases me much ... Mr Brown informs me by letter that he is likely to return to England & I may get a steamer – I hope to God he may succeed and in that case it is not impossible I may be named to the command of her if so my destruction ... of the Turkish fleet must ensue in the summer.'

The young George Finlay had made an even stronger impression on Byron – he thought the ghost of Shelley had walked in when he first met him – and over the next four years he was to become Hastings's closest friend and ally in Greece. The following day the two men went to 'visit the antiquities' together, but it is a fairly safe bet that if Hastings had his way the conversation was all tactics, hot shot and the 'one or two Steam vessels' with which he had promised Byron he could destroy 'even Constantinople'.

It was a tragedy that it would take Byron's death in April 1824, and the subsequent wash of sympathy it caused, to realise Hastings's vision, but even with the arrival of the first £40,000 of the loan he was still made to wait. 'During the summer of 1824,' Finlay wrote,

Hastings endeavoured to impress the necessity of rendering the national cause not entirely dependent on the disorderly and tumultuous merchant marine, which it was compelled to hire at an exorbitant price. It is needless to record all the difficulties and opposition he met with from a Government consisting in part of ship owners, eager to obtain a share of the loan as hire for their ships. The loan, however, appeared inexhaustible; and in the autumn of 1824, Hastings returned to England, with a promise that the Greek government would lose no time in instructing their deputies in London to procure a steam-vessel to be armed under his inspection, and of which he was promised the command.

It had taken more than two years for Hastings to get the promise of his steamship. It was just as well that he did not know, as he disembarked in England at the end of 1824, that it would be another two before he would have the chance to fight in her.

IX

If Hastings knew the Greek government too well to imagine that his problems were over, even his cynicism can have done little to prepare him for the vexations ahead. He had sailed back to England in the company of Edward Blaquiere, and within days had exchanged the open corruption of Greece for the more impenetrable mire of Blaquiere's philhellene friends, the brazen robbery and violence of sectarian fighting for a financial world in which it is now almost impossible to define where greed shaded into outright criminality and incompetence into deliberate malpractice.

The sordid history of the English loan concerns Hastings only in so far as it affected the construction of the new Greek fleet, and all that needs stressing here is that of the £2,800,000 raised from British investors only a tiny fraction was ever converted into the arms or munitions that might have helped win the war. Hastings had himself promised £5,000 to the construction of a steam vessel, but even with that carrot dangling in front of them it was not until March 1825 that the Greek deputies finally authorised the construction of a ship on the Thames at Deptford and of an engine for her to be built by a man who would come to figure large in Hastings's pantheon of criminal incompetents, the Smithfield engineer Alexander Galloway.

The commission came just in the nick of time – a month earlier, and Hastings had been resolving 'neither to be a dupe or dupeur', a month later and he would probably have been back in the Royal Navy – but he knew himself too well to pretend he was done with Greece. 'I came to town at the instigation of my relations & Naval friends to endeavour to get re-established in the British Navy,' he wrote soon after getting the invitation to command the steamship.

> My brother had seen Lord Melville over the subject & there seems little difficulty attending it ...
>
> There is nothing I am aware of that would give me such sincere satisfaction as to aid the delivery of Greece & there never was perhaps an opportunity that offered itself of gaining such lasting renown at so little hazard – I mean there never was an exploit to which such credit was attached so easy of execution as the destruction of the Turkish fleet: & could I feel satisfied that the proper measures would be pursued for attaining that end I would not hesi-

tate an instant to resign my commission was I even Admiral in the British Navy for the purpose of carrying those plans into execution. [If they accept his plan] I shall be that instant ready to renounce the British service & lay down at your disposal the sum of money I had proposed to the Greek Government.

And for any non-establishment naval man, let alone philhellene, there was one further inducement to fight for Greece when her government appointed Thomas Cochrane, the 10th Earl of Dundonald, to command her new fleet. If it had done nothing else the appointment would have signalled the final shift from a military to a naval strategy that Hastings had long been advocating, but it was above all the name of Cochrane – the most brilliant and controversial of the young sea captains to make their reputations during the French wars – that would most vividly have caught the imagination of a born warrior and innovator like Hastings.

On an infinitely grander and more flamboyant scale, Cochrane's background, character, politics, cussedness, originality and naval career bear striking parallels to Hastings's own. The tall, red-headed, angular-featured son of an impoverished and eccentric Scottish earl, Cochrane had fought from the outbreak of the French wars, winning himself a reputation for brilliance and insubordination in just about equal measure until a stock market scandal gave his political and professional enemies the excuse they needed to have him drummed out of the service, ceremonially stripped of his knighthood in a midnight ritual of degradation, and thrown into prison.

There seems every possibility that Cochrane was in some way involved in the swindle that brought him down; but, supremely litigious and stubborn by nature, he fought to establish his innocence with the same dogged ferocity that characterised his seamanship. He would have to wait for another generation and a different England to regain his domestic honours, but by the time his and Hastings's paths crossed he had already made a second and even more glittering reputation in South America's liberation wars, in command of the nascent Chilean fleet against the Spaniards and then of the Brazilian ships in that country's struggle for independence from Portugal.

The only drawback to Cochrane, in fact, was that for all the grandiose titles that came his way – Vice-Admiral of Chile, Commander-in-Chief of the Naval Forces of the Republic, First Admiral of the Brazils and Marquess of Maranham – he had never

commanded anything that remotely resembled a fleet. The novels of
Frederick Marryat are evidence enough of his ability to inspire the
men under his immediate command, but Cochrane's virtues – audacity, ingenuity, courage, unorthodoxy, seamanship, individual flair
(and no one ever had them in greater measure) – were supremely
those of the frigate captain rather than admiral, the lone 'sea wolf'
rather than the politician needed to navigate the notorious shallows
of Greek naval life.

Given his impeccable radicalism, however, and his extraordinary
record in South America – with just a couple of ships and a limitless
supply of bluff he had achieved near-miracles – he was an inevitable
choice, and if he did not come cheap no one in the summer of 1825
with any imagination could have regarded the £57,000 Greece paid
him as anything but well spent. It might give some indication of the
scale of this investment if it is remembered that the Greek national
revenues for the same year were only £90,000, yet for that £57,000
they were getting the one man who, if past exploits were anything
to go by, could deliver on even the wildest and most ambitious of
the strategic promises Hastings had made in his letters to Lord
Byron.

The detailed and complete destruction of the whole Turkish fleet,
the liberation of Greece, the burning of Constantinople itself –
Cochrane instinctively saw the same possibilities that Hastings did
and, more importantly, the same methods to achieve them. 'I have not
been able to convince myself that, under existing circumstances, there
is any means by which Greece can be saved as by a steady perseverance in equipping the steam vessels,' Cochrane wrote to the Greek
deputies, warning them that he would not budge until he had six
steamships armed with Hastings's sixty-eight-pound long guns under
his command,

> which are so admirably calculated to cut off the enemy's commu-
> nications with Alexandria and Constantinople and for towing fire
> vessels and explosion vessels [Cochrane specialities] by night into
> ports and places where the hostile squadrons anchor on the shores
> of Greece.
>
> I wish I could give you, without writing a Volume, a clear view
> of the numerous reasons, derived from 35 years experience, which
> induce me to prefer a force which can move in the obscurity of the
> night, through narrow channels, in shoal water, and with silence

and celerity, over a naval armament of the usual kind, though of far superior force.

[The steam vessel] will prove the most formidable means that has ever been employed in Naval warfare. It is my opinion that 24 vessels moved by steam ... could commence at St Petersburg and finish at Constantinople the destruction of every ship of war in the several ports.

The agreement of the deputies to five new steamships seemed to clear the way to Cochrane's appointment and the fulfilment of Hastings's ambition, but nothing to do with the Greek Committee or the Greek deputies was ever as simple as that. It had taken almost three years' advocacy for Hastings to secure himself even a single vessel, and now suddenly he found himself facing the bitter prospect of seeing his own pet project losing out to the more grandiloquent demands of Cochrane's steam 'fleet'. 'I fancy you have lately received a letter from the Greek Deputies complaining of the delays of Mr Galloway in putting up the machinery on board of the vessel built by Mr Brent,' he was soon writing to John Cam Hobhouse, Byron's old friend and a leading member of the Greek Committee, '& I consider the conduct of Mr Galloway so totally devoid of candour that I also feel myself obliged to appeal to you on the subject.'

For Hastings and Greece time and not money was the issue, and the gist of his complaint was that Galloway was stalling on his vessel so that he could economise by fitting all six engines at the same time. 'The Greeks have long looked forward to a steam vessel as the arm that would assure them success,' he went on, in a disingenuous projection of his own hopes, '& have been daily led to expect the arrival of one; what then is likely to be the impression on their minds when they behold the Egyptian fleet with a steam vessel without having one to oppose it? The Greeks (like all barbarous people) are easily depressed; are easily elated and the sight of a steam vessel under this flag would inspire them with unlimited confidence, the sight of the enemy one will inspire them with a corresponding terror.'

With a son loitering in the 'flesh-pots' of Alexandria, as Hobhouse put it, Galloway's philhellene loyalties came under regular suspicion, but Hastings's more pressing concern was with an older and more familiar 'enemy' than the Egyptians. 'If six vessels are equipping & getting in a warlike manner at the same time,' he warned Hobhouse, 'such an act of impudence will again call forth some strong measure on the part of our Government – rely upon it the Government knows everything about this affair which it desires to know, & if it chooses to stop it, will do so in spite of us – if the existing laws do not suffice others would be enacted, & if driven to extremities they would direct their naval commanders to arrest us even out there.'

With a Foreign Enlistment Act forbidding British nationals from serving under foreign flags, and the government's continuing ambivalence towards the Greek insurgents, this was no idle fear. Since the suicide of Castlereagh in August 1822 there had certainly been a perceptible softening of official attitudes, yet at a time when Britain was seeking a negotiated settlement to the Greek problem, the prospect of British foundries producing weapons and British dockyards building ships to destroy the fleet and capital of an allied country was awkward enough without the inevitable publicity surrounding everything in which Cochrane was involved.

It would, in fact, have taken a brave government – probably braver than Lord Liverpool's at any rate – to have moved against Cochrane as it had done ten years earlier, but for once in his life he too was taking no chances. At the beginning of November he was warned by the opposition Whig politician Henry Brougham that he risked arrest if he remained in England, and on 9 November 1825 – the same day that Hastings was writing to alert Hobhouse to the danger – he slipped across the Channel with his wife and son to continue his preparations beyond the reach of a Tory establishment he had been hounding and exasperating for more than twenty-five years.

With Cochrane now constantly on the move, and coded letters, government spies, hand-delivered communications the order of the day, the delays endemic to everything to do with Greek affairs could only be exacerbated. 'My Lord, I had the honour of meeting your brother this day,' Hastings wrote to Cochrane at the end of November,

> who informed me that an opportunity would offer of writing to your lordship, so that I profit by it to inform you that the first vessel called the Perseverance is nearly ready inasmuch as it concerns Mr Brent. Mr Galloway is sadly behind – he now promises to be ready in one month, & his month may be considered as two. I have used every method & every argument to hasten him – the fact is the fate of Greece is in his hands & he will have a great responsibility on his shoulders if that cause is lost by his want of punctuality ... If

your Lordship would use your influence with Mr Galloway to
hasten the Perseverance you would render very important service
to the cause & to me if Greece is yet to be saved – but I fear 'tis too
late.

The guns were now ready, he told Cochrane – Hastings favoured
shipping them out to Greece via America – but even at his gloomiest
his estimates for the ship's completion were hopelessly optimistic. By
the middle of December Galloway's idea of a month had grown to
six weeks, and as February 1826 turned into March and April, the
engineer gradually metamorphosed from a self-deluding optimist into
the 'incorrigible ... impudent liar' and criminal incompetent of Hastings's increasingly furious complaints.

With the delays and setbacks to the engines, and the endless work
supervising the design and building of the ship's boats, or liaising
between the Greek Committee and their absentee admiral, it would
have taken a more patient man than Hastings to control his temper.
Galloway, he thought, should be hanged. Orlando, one of the Greek
deputies, was an 'insupportable blockhead' more interested – like all
the rest of them – in 'some affaire de putain' than in Greece. 'Before
I close this letter,' he wrote to Cochrane at the beginning of February – just about as close as he allowed himself to a warning shot
across the Admiral's bows – 'I must remark that Mr Hesketh
has conducted himself in a meddling interfering manner very ill-suited
to his station, & as I feel satisfied that such comportment is contrary
to your sanction I take the liberty of requesting you will instruct
him to limit himself in future to delivering your orders & reserve his
own opinions for those who value his opinions more highly than I
do.'

It is probably not just hindsight that detects a note of irony in a
reference to the 'great man' in his letters, but neither of them could
afford to fall out. Among the leading figures of the Greek Committee were several of Cochrane's old political allies, but when it came
to naval matters, he needed the 'indefatigable Hastings' just as badly
as Hastings needed Cochrane to stop a vacillating Greek government
from whoring after some crack-brained solution or Bavarian fanta-
sist to solve their military problems.

Hastings was also the one foreigner who had been able to give
Byron, Cochrane or the Committee a clear-eyed sense of the kind of
men they were dealing with in Greece. The two naval leaders of

whom he spoke most warmly were Canaris and Miaulis – 'a very distinguished worthy old man' – but for every Greek of ability or courage, there were half a dozen drunkards, pirates, cowards and rogues: 'a merchant of distinction but nothing more ... does not so much want talent as ferocity ... wants courage ... entirely ignorant ... consumes three bottles of Rum a day ... said to be a very great coward ... no consequence ... exceedingly intriguing ... undistin-guished except by a colossal stature & a ferocious countenance ... a great rogue ... detested but I know not why ...' 'The fact is that the Greek does not in general possess either courage, or generosity & scarcely patriotism,' he concluded, finding what comfort he could in so dire a catalogue of venality, greed and vice:

> his every action is subjected to the narrow views of self-interest alone. Fortunately providence has so ordained it, that moral evils arrived at a certain extent carry with them their own remedy & despotism debases the master even more than the slave; was it not so, despotism once established would be eternal; instead therefore of attributing the success of the Greeks to their Heroism, let us give it its real character, that of the degradation of the Turks.

And in spite of the Greeks, the delays and disappointments at the engine trials – only two of the ships under construction would ever make it out to Greek waters – the last week of May finally saw the completion of Hastings's *Perseverance*. Cochrane had originally planned on a grand entrance at the head of a united fleet, but with news of the war worsening with every post and the *Perseverance*'s sixty-eight- and thirty-two-pound guns already on their way to Greece, one ship – *any* ship, almost – was better than the finest fleet the Greek Loan could buy if it was going to languish at Deptford awaiting Mr Galloway's attentions.

And even if the *Perseverance*'s power – 'forty two horses' – was 'feeble', the engine still defective, and the charismatic Cochrane nowhere to be seen, it was *not* just any ship that made its 'unmolest-ed' way at 'about six miles an hour' downriver from her mooring. There might have been nothing new about the sight of such a vessel in the Thames by 1826, but one only has to translate her in the imag-ination – four hundred tons, 125 feet in length, twenty-five in breadth, paddles churning, tall, thin funnel, set well to the aft, belching smoke – from Deptford to the Gulf of Corinth and the waters beneath Delphi to see Hastings's vision, in all its barque-rigged, primitive and *shocking* ugliness, spring into vivid and brutal life.

The mounting of the guns, the alignment of the trunnions, the internal arrangement of the ship, the methods for safely handling and firing hot shot and shell in pitching seas, everything about her, as Finlay put it, was the brainchild not just of Hastings's strategic vision but of 'his extraordinary perseverance and energy'. 'The Karteria,' Finlay wrote,

> which was the name of the Perseverance in the Greek navy, was armed on the principle which Hastings had laid down as necessary to place the Greeks with small vessels on some degree of equality with the line-of-battle ships and large frigates of the Turks: namely, that of using projectiles more destructive than that of the enemy. These projectiles were hot shot and shells, instead of the cold round-shot of the Turks ... The Karteria was armed with sixty-eight pounders. Of these she mounted eight; four were carronades of the government pattern, and four were guns of a new form, cast after a model prepared by Hastings himself. These guns were seven feet four inches long in the bore, and weighed fifty-eight hundredweight.

It was not for nothing, either, that her English name was '*Perseverance*', and long before they reached Gibraltar and the Mediterranean Hastings would need all the reserves of it he could muster. The last time he took a ship downriver from Deptford had been the *Kangaroo* in 1819, and in spite of fine weather and fair winds the omens for his second command were not promising. The ship sailed well, and he had no complaints with his crew, but 'There never was a vessel sent to sea with an Engine in so discreditable a condition,' he complained after it had failed them a fourth time.

> From my experience of it I am satisfied we shall have to stop every two or three days to repair it & on our arrival at our destination I fear it will require a month to put into a fit state to go to sea with. The most lamentable incapacity has been shown by Mr Galloway in the conception of a variety of combinations ... [some remediable but others not] so colossal that I fear we shall not be able to make the alterations we desire particularly in the paddle wheels, which threaten to come to pieces every other day.

Another fortnight only made things worse – 'Galloway deserves to
be hung, & I would hang him if I had him here' – and Galloway's men
added further to Hastings's problems. 'Our voyage (thanks to Mr
Galloway & his) bets fair to be as tedious as that of Ulysses,' he
reported to Hobhouse on 10 July.

> The Engine, always defective, stopped altogether about a fortnight
> ago ... The total failure of the Engine has been the work of one of
> the Engineers [it was common practice for the engine builder to
> supply two engineers to maintain the machinery] who altered some
> of the screws of the Larboard side on purpose to ruin the Engine
> – I never liked taking Galloway's men after I found them dissatis-
> fied & had almost engaged a man from Taylor & Martin's which
> Galloway contrived to prevent. I shall discharge this man here &
> use my best endeavours.

The death of one of his officers, a Mr Critchley – masquerading under
the name of Thompson to protect his naval half-pay – added to the
gloom, and it was more than another two months before the *Karteria* (as she had now become) finally limped into Nauplia. 'All is
confusion here,' an aggrieved Hastings wrote again to Hobhouse on
5 October, 'with Athens ... blockaded ... The Egyptian fleet ...
expected ... with reinforcements ... The Greek Government (as I foresaw) [determined] to make a pleasure boat of me for their amusement,' and Cochrane nowhere to be seen. 'The absence of Ld C
astonishes and mortifies everybody,' Hastings continued, warming
to what would become his favourite theme over the next two years:

> for my part I do not know how he can exculpate himself, consid-
> ering the sum he has locked up & the period he agreed. I expect to
> get out of this without a sixpence of publick money. The Govern-
> ment has none, & if it had would not give any to me – I have bound
> myself responsible for three months wages for the Crew, to induce
> them to embark – (they saw that the Greeks would never pay them).
> As long as I have any money I will keep the crew together but my
> own funds will not go far in this, now is it fair that I should ruin
> myself while Ld Cochrane hanging back as he does is to receive
> such a sum. I should hope that you would see the propriety &
> necessity of finding funds for this vessel for at least three months
> more – then I must take by force part of the revenue of the islands

if not given freely, – & what with that, & occasional prizes I hope
to keep things afloat for a year or two if the war lasts ... Whatever
turns up rely upon it I will do my utmost to advance the interests
of Greece & should fortune not favour us I will be the last to quit
the wreck.

Hastings and the Greeks were not being entirely fair to their absentee admiral – it was not his fault that Galloway went on promising
more than he could deliver – but for all their own corruption and
greed the Greek government had every right to feel aggrieved. At the
end of 1825 they had a theoretical eight warships under construction, but a year later, and £155,000 spent in America alone, they had
just one American frigate to show for their money, one unreliable
steamer – the next two had proved completely useless, and two more
never left the Thames – and a £57,000 admiral who had got no nearer
an enemy ship than watching Mohammed Ali's new Egyptian men-
of-war rising on the stocks of the Marseilles dockyards.

There was one small glimmer of hope, when the Marseilles and
Paris Philhellene Societies suspended rivalries with London for long
enough to buy Cochrane a French brig, the *Sauveur*, but for the next
five months Hastings was on his own. 'To the Commander of the
First American or English vessel that arrives in Greece to join
the Greeks,' he addressed a letter at the end of October, too late in
the year to do anything more than prepare the *Karteria* for the coming
campaigning season:

An apprenticeship in Greece tolerably long has taught me the risks
to which anybody newly arrived & possessed of some place &
power is exposed. They know me, & they also know that I know
them, yet they have not ceased & never will cease intriguing to
get this vessel out of my hands, & into their own, which would
be tantamount to ruining her. Knowing this, I take the liberty of
leaving this letter to be delivered to the first officer in the command
of a vessel; to caution him not to receive on board his vessel any
Greek captain – they will endeavour under various pretences to
introduce themselves on board & when once they have got a footing, they will gradually encroach until they feel themselves strong
enough to turn out the original commander ... If you want seamen
– take none from Idra – Spetsia, Kranidid, Poros – the Ispariotes
may be trusted in very small numbers – take a few men from one,

a few from another island & thus you will be best enabled to establish some kind of discipline. Take a good number of marines – choose them from the Peasantry, & foreign Greeks, and you may make something of them ... You must see Sir that in this my advice ... I can have no interest any further than inasmuch as I wish well to the Greek cause & therefore do not wish to see a force that can render great service to the Greek cause rendered ineffective by falling into the hands of people totally incapable & unwilling to adopt a single right measure. In Greece there cannot be any artillery operations except such as are carried out by foreigners in their service.

It was not, perhaps, the triumphal return Hastings must have dreamed of, nor a document to inspire a sense of warm collaboration. But then charm or conciliation were never part of his prescription for success. Nor, in the fighting to come, would there be room for either if Greece was to be saved.

X

It would be impossible to exaggerate the dangers Greece faced over the winter of 1826–27. After a long and heroic resistance Missolonghi had at last fallen in April 1826, and with Athens under siege and Ibrahim Pasha's Egyptians well on their way to making good his promise to carry off 'the ashes of the Peloponnese', the rapidly shrinking enclave that was 'Greece' seemed to be facing extinction. 'The Morea has been devastated by the troops of Ibrahim in almost every direction,' one impassioned American philhellene wrote of the country:

All Messenia, part of Arcadia, Ellis and Achaia, presented a scene of utter devastation; it would seem as if the siroc had blown over it for years, destroying every vestige of vegetable, and had been followed by pestilence in its train, which swept away every living thing that had once inhabited it. Those delightful plains, which poets in all ages have sung ... were now barren wastes, where the roofless and blackened walls of the houses, the scathed and leafless trunks of the olive trees, and here and there the whitening bones of human beings, remained to tell that fire had passed over and blasted them.

This was the situation of at least one-half of the Peloponnesus; of its inhabitants many had been slaughtered, others carried off into slavery in Egypt, and the rest, where are they? Oh God! It is an awful question to answer, but it is a question which must one day be answered to Thee by this generation, who left thousands and tens of thousands of their fellow beings to be hunted like wild beasts; to dwell in the caverns of the rocks; to wander about, year after year, seeking for the roots of the earth, giving to their ragged and emaciated children sorrel and snails for food, unable to get enough of even this, and pining and dying – ay! Absolutely perishing from want, while the rest of the earth was full of fatness.

Here was a vision – with all its biblical and classical echoes – to stir the conscience even of governments, but whether it would do so in time was another question. From the very beginning of the war Greece's only real hope had rested with the Great Powers, but it was not until the summer of 1825 that a first cautious approach to London from the Tsar led in the following spring to negotiations at St Petersburg and a jointly signed protocol calling for mediation and an autonomous Greece under Turkish suzerainty.

Even the prospect of the 'barbarization' of the Peloponnese – Egypt's own Islamic take on seventeenth-century England's Irish solution – was never going to win over absolutist Austria or Prussia, but by the end of the summer France had joined the negotiations. Over the next twelve months the three powers would edge their way towards the document that would finally become the Treaty of London, but until that was signed and the original protocol had grown some real 'teeth', the problem facing them was always going to be in enforcing an agreement that was inimical to the ambitions of both warring parties.

The Greeks were in no position to argue with a protocol that offered more than they could ever win for themselves, but as Roumeli, the Morea and finally the town of Athens fell into Ottoman hands there seemed less and less reason for the Porte to tolerate any interference in its own internal affairs. A revolt of the Janissaries had given them problems of their own, but with only the beleaguered Acropolis in Athens standing between them, the isthmus and the last pocket of Greek resistance in the western Peloponnese, it was a fair gamble that they could finish off the war before the three signatories could muster the resolve or the unity to intervene.

As the Greeks and the Turks both knew, though, intervention was only a matter of time, and so by the end of 1826 the key to the whole war and the geographical scope of any future Greece had become the fortress at Athens. From the late summer of 1826 the insurgents had poured all their resources into her relief, though two abortive attempts in August and October, and a third in December under the command of that heroic relict of Napoleonic glories, Colonel Fabvier, had only succeeded in burdening a starving garrison with Fabvier himself and another five hundred Greek and French volunteers.

The failure of one philhellene never seemed to discourage the next for very long, however, and in the following February one of the most distinguished of all British volunteers agreed against his better judgement to try where the French had failed. Thomas Gordon had been among the first foreigners to join the Greek cause in the early months of the war, but, sickened by the horrors of Tripolis, had almost immediately quitted the country, driven out by that familiar combination of plague and moral disgust that had seen off so many romantic philhellenes in the opening days of the conflict.

But at that point the generalisations fail, because with his Eton and Oxford background, his experience with the British and Russian armies, his intelligence, linguistic abilities, independence and – above all – immense wealth, Gordon was made of very different stuff. In the years since he left Greece he had continued to play an influential role in European philhellenism, and even in absentia he remained one of the very few disinterested foreigners with the skills and the knowledge of both sides to make a genuine contribution to the war.

A sense of duty? The lure of Athens? A touch of philhellene vanity? It is unlikely that even Gordon knew what finally brought him back to Greece, but it certainly was not experience or judgement. During the five years since the fall of Tripolis he had successfully resisted every Greek blandishment, but for once his resolve failed him, and pressed again to give his services, he allowed the pleas of a desperate government to overcome every military and political instinct he had.

Gordon knew a direct assault on the enemy position made no strategic sense – he favoured attacks on the Turks' long and vulnerable supply lines – but he agreed all the same to a twin-pronged February landing at Piraeus and Eleusis, to the south and west of Athens. The experience of Fabvier in the open before Athens should have demonstrated once and for all the folly of any such strategy, but this was a war in which judgement was always at the mercy of fantasy, strategy in hock to politics, vanity, ambition, and the endless rivalries that set Greek against Greek, Greek against philhellene and philhellenes against each other.

If nothing else, the attack offered Hastings the chance at last to satisfy the enormous expectations that had surrounded the *Karteria* since her arrival in Greece three months before. 'All the world, men, women, children, old young, black and white, are coming on board to see the steamboat,' Samuel Gridley Howe, the *Karteria*'s new American doctor and one of the nineteenth century's greatest reforming philanthropists, had recorded in his November journal.

We have two Englishmen [officers], one German, one Frenchman, and one Greek; the Greek is the eldest son of Tombazi. Captain Hastings is a man who deserves the deepest gratitude and respect from the Greek nation. It is only through his exertion, his activity, and generosity, that this ship was ever got out. She was built under his own eye in London, and carries as much weight of metal as a thirty-six gun frigate; her engine, however, is not of the best. Captain Hastings, having on board about forty English and forty Greek sailors, is all ready to join the Greek fleet and engage the enemy. He sees the eyes of the whole people turned upon him – they are tired of waiting for Lord Cochrane and the rest of the vessels. Captain Hastings finds himself obliged to attempt something alone, and I doubt not, from his character, he will succeed or perish with the vessel. 'Tell Captain Hastings,' said Commodore Hamilton to me, 'that I honour and envy him for what others pity him: his situation is perilous, nay almost desperate, yet so glorious is the attempt that were I without wife or children, I would give £1,000 to be in it.' ... How my spirit springs with joy at being on our way to meet the haughty Turk. And though our fate is uncertain, it cannot be an inglorious one. To be engaged in something active and important, in so glorious a cause, in such consecrated regions, makes my heart beat with a wild enthusiasm, which to my sober senses seems boyish and romantic.

Over the next two months an endless stream of mechanical problems with engine, paddles, boilers, leaks, coal, guns and shells – the shells would not explode and all but one of the cannon were damaged by the shock of the charge needed to throw a sixty-eight-pound ball – dampened Howe's enthusiasm, but on 22 January 1827 the crew at

last learned that the *Karteria* was to see action. 'Even at this moment
the Greeks are struggling to repel the attacks of the Turkish hordes
which surround the sacred city,' an excited Howe wrote as six days
later the *Karteria* slipped unnoticed through the narrow western
straits between Salamis and Megara – the first man-of-war since
ancient times to effect the passage,

> but doubtless the sight of our vessel comforted them, and let them
> know that assistance was at hand. About 11 A.M. our engine got
> completely out of order, and there being not a breath of wind to
> break the glassy smoothness of the sea, we lay motionless; but in
> what a spot, and with what objects around us! I could not regret
> the delay which afforded me such a scene. Behind lay Aegina,
> with its slope to the sea, richly cultivated and interspersed with
> olives, while farther back rose its hills, crowned by the temple of
> Jupiter Pluvious, whose still standing columns were plainly to be
> seen. To the right lay Attica, stretching south and terminating by
> Sunium; high up was Athens, its Acropolis and Parthenon rising
> above the mist which floated over the town; Salamis was before
> us; to the left the Isthmus of Corinth, above which rose the
> ragged, almost perpendicular Acro Corinth, crowned by its
> fortress.

The potential fly in the philhellene ointment was as ever the *modern*
Greek soldier, and Gordon's battle plan was peculiarly designed to
bring out all his defects. He had already shown more than once what
a different proposition he was among the mountains of the Morea,
but as if no one had learned anything in the course of five years of
war, the attack on Athens again required him to face the enemy
infantry and cavalry out in the open.

At the beginning of February a force under the fat and bejewelled
Cephalonian Bonapartist Colonel Bourbaki was landed at Eleusis,
and two days later, on the afternoon of the fifth, Gordon's troops
began to embark in the small flotilla of boats that were to ship them
across to the mainland. Colours were blessed, saints invoked, and on
board the *Karteria*, Gordon, his second-in-command, the Bavarian
Colonel Heideck and the Greek leaders met Hastings to finalise
arrangements. 'The moon shone bright and clear,' Howe noted, and
after all 'the infernal delays of the Greeks', everything at last

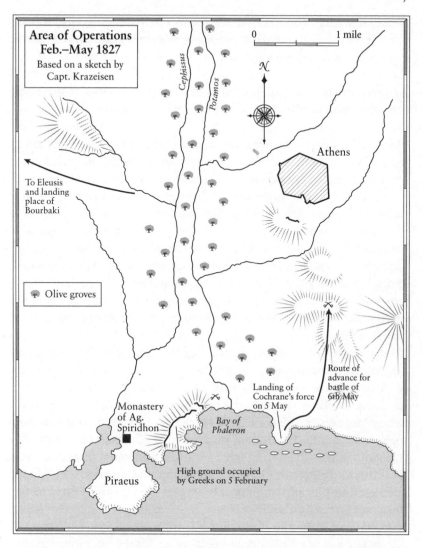

Area of Operations
Feb.–May 1827

Based on a sketch by
Capt. Krazeisen

0   1 mile

Cephissus

Potamos

Athens

To Eleusis
and landing
place of
Bourbaki

Olive groves

Monastery
of Ag.
Spiridhon

Landing of
Cochrane's force
on 5 May

Route of
advance for
battle of
6th May

Bay of
Phaleron

High ground occupied
by Greeks on 5 February

Piraeus

promised to favour our enterprise ... About ten the vessels were
all despatched in advance, and at eleven we got under way with
steam, and moving on rapidly soon overtook the little fleet, which
had but a light breeze. Off the Piraeus, having passed all the vessels,
we took a turn backward, sailed around then, and again took the
lead. The scene was exceedingly fine, – the night still and clear, a
slight breeze filling the sails of our little fleet, which lay about us
in every direction; the camp fires of the Greeks under Vashos and
Bourbakis upon the sides of the mountains; while from time to time

the launching of bombs from the enemy's batteries into the Acropolis marked the horizon with a long streak of fire, and showed that
the siege was still hotly pressed.

By three in the morning the moon had gone, and in a night black
enough to mask her approach, the *Karteria* anchored at Phaleron and
the first of Gordon's 2,300 men were rowed silently ashore. The
object of this first wave was the heights immediately above the landing place, but a sudden outbreak of musket fire and 'wild shouting'
from the ridge – almost certainly a Greek *feu de joie* to celebrate that
they still had their heads on their shoulders – was enough to panic a
dubious Gordon into thinking they had been thwarted. '"The Turks
are there! Our men will be cut to pieces! Back to the boats and take
them off,"' an indignant Howe wrote. 'These were the words of
Colonel Gordon, leader of the expedition, who seemed to be agitated
and surprised. Others [were] more cool, particularly Captain Hastings and Colonel Heideck, who besought him calmly to consider
whether he should not, instead of re-embarking, proceed to send more
men to their assistance.'

The bolder counsel prevailed, and by the end of the night the
heights of Munychia had been consolidated, with a traditional line
of earth and stone *tambouris* stretching out over a distance of eleven
or twelve hundred yards. In the early hours of the next morning the
first of Gordon's artillery pieces were dragged up from the beach, and
to a 'tremendous feu-de-joie of artillery and musketry' from the
Acropolis and an answering salvo from Gordon's guns on the heights,
the *Karteria* steamed around the headland and through the narrow
harbour entrance of the Piraeus to engage the Turkish centre in the
monastery of St Spiridon.

In half an hour the *Karteria* had dropped anchor, and from a
distance of about four hundred yards, firing for the first time with the
massive weight of her sixty-eight-pound guns, had soon reduced
whole sections of the monastery to little more than rubble. 'Two thousand men [had] stood regarding us with idle applause,' Howe wrote,
beside himself at the memory of the fancifully styled '300' assault
force staying firmly behind their *tambouris* when their time came,

but came down not. Such complete cowards are they that they will
never attack an enemy who is sheltered in such a way as to make
an attack in the least dangerous ... No, not they! They expected our

ship to march upon the land, enter the monastery, and drive out the enemy. Cowards I always knew them to be, and have often seen them show themselves, but never in a more shameful manner than to-day. In fact, my prediction will be accomplished: the country is too open for Greeks to fight in. At ten, we hoisted anchor and came just outside of the Piraeus, in order to prevent being caught by the enemy's bringing down cannon and placing it upon the entrance of the port, which is not more than fifty yards across.

Howe was no more tolerant of Gordon's generalship than he was of the Greeks, and the next day only reinforced his doubts. As soon as it was light the *Karteria* again steamed into the cauldron of the harbour, and boldly anchoring within musket range of the shore, resumed her solitary and futile small-arms and artillery duel with the heavily reinforced Turkish defenders. 'The Turks would only poke out their heads, fire their musquets, and retire,' Howe complained, vividly capturing the intense physical intimacy of Greek warfare, 'but one of them held out his head long enough for me to take aim at it and level him with a rifle-ball; he fell sprawling upon his face, and I hardly know whether pleasure or pain predominated in my mind as I witnessed his fall.'

After another two hours of shelling a signal came from Gordon to retire, and as Hastings ordered 'up anchor' the battle developed into a desperate race for the harbour mouth, with cannonballs 'whizzing about and striking the ship in all directions' and a force of cavalry dashing along the western shore of the port to cut off their retreat. 'Soon we were moving,' Howe recorded;

> the enemy saw it, and galloping rapidly down to the narrow part of the port, awaited us. Among them were many *Delhis*, with their tremendous long caps, I should think at least two feet and a half high. I plied my rifle as fast as possible, and luckily was not called to for one single wounded man, they being sheltered by the high sides of the vessel ... Our retreat was necessary, because we could not possibly do any good by remaining, but I could not help feeling shame as we moved off from a pursuing enemy hooting at us, and this in plain sight of the Greeks in the Acropolis and upon the hills.

A small dent in philhellene pride was neither here nor there – jeers
and insults were as ritual a part of Turko-Greek warfare as breaches
of faith or severed heads – but elsewhere in the battle it was a different story. 'The Turks from the monastery cried out to our men that
the troops under Vashos and Bourbakis had been completely routed,'
Howe continued.

> This I fear may be true. Vashos is an experienced Greek soldier and
> knows the *paliikaris* completely, and probably did not suffer much
> ... But Bourbakis is fresh from France, full of French notions, and
> though born a Greek, knows them not. He talked confidently of
> what he would do; nothing less than taking Kiutahi alive would
> satisfy him – and such nonsense. He is brave, and probably
> ventured upon the plain; the cavalry came upon him, his men ran
> away, and he was killed or taken prisoner; this we fear, but know
> nothing certain.

The reports were true – Vashos's 'poltroons' had fled, Bourbakis was
captured and beheaded for his pains, more than four hundred of his
regulars slaughtered – and with one army defeated the Turks were
now free to unleash the full weight of their cavalry and infantry
against the Greek-held heights of Phaleron. After the mauling the
Karteria had received in the first exchanges Hastings might have done
well to stay out of it, but these were precisely the kind of operations
for which his vessel was designed, and as his men watched successive
waves of Turkish attacks climb and break against the Greek defences,
he again ordered her to drop anchor within 'short musquet-shot' of
the Ottoman rear and open up with grape.

With the *Karteria*'s arrival the whole focus of the battle suddenly
shifted from the heights to the shore. From her deck Howe watched
a dozen men dragging a gun down to the water's edge, and within
moments a shell had 'burst amid twenty of us. I expected at least four
or five would have been killed, but my attention was drawn by the
shrieks and cries of a drummer boy. I saw him fall, terror and despair
in his countenance; seizing him in my arms, I carried him below ...'

The whole of the Turkish artillery was now turned on the *Karteria*, and as 'the balls ... began to whiz about the ship, to strike her
sides, cut her cordage etc', their position became increasingly desperate. The ship's guns had rapidly dealt with three of the enemy's
cannon, but two howitzers cleverly sited behind the walls of the

monastery soon had their range. 'I am told it was a rich scene to behold the mixture of dismay and gloom alternately reddening and whitening the cheeks of some of the Greek sailors,' wrote the English philhellene Thomas Whitcombe, impotently 'curling and twisting [his] mustaches' and 'biting [his] lips with vexation' up on the heights,

> as the worrying batteries' pitiless storm pelted in every direction round their vessel; – the jolly reefers wishing themselves all the while in the territories of Prester John, or any other outlandish quarter of the globe, rather than where they had found themselves. The hair-breadth escapes on board the Karteria were ... almost past belief, – flogging the doctrine of chances with unsparing thong ... Our maledictions, loud and deep, were denounced on the heads of those Europeans [servicing the Turkish guns] – Christians they presumed to call themselves! – who could thus unshrinkingly stain their name and birth-place with the indelible disgrace of pocketing the Seraskier's blood-steeped wages, in requital of tendering their arms and knowledge in aiding the suppression of the hallowed warfare of liberty and the blessed cross.

Up on the heights the battle was more or less won, and with the crew wilting and his boats shot to bits, Hastings's only thought was to extricate the *Karteria* while he still had the chance. 'To our dismay,' though, wrote Howe, back on deck after tending to the drummer boy – only very slightly wounded, as it turned out,

> on the word being given to start the engine it was found not to move. There was repetition of the order; it was shouted, but in vain; the engine would not start. Many a cheek blanched and many a lip quivered, for we were in a narrow port, exposed on every side to musquetry, and could see the enemy bringing down more cannon; to make it more dreadful, the anchor had been cut away, and it was whispered to me by the lieutenant that the ship's head was aground, – and she only a pistol-shot from the shore. The enemy apparently perceived this, and shouting and waving their sabres, they began to rush down, expecting to have us in a few minutes. I must say that a feeling of bitterness and almost agony came over me for a moment at the sight of these barbarians, who I expected would soon be mercilessly hacking us to pieces.

The one man on board who seemed unmoved by the danger was Hastings, and with 'much coolness and skill' he brought his frightened crew to order. For a few endless moments the *Karteria*'s fate hung in the balance, and then – very slowly – the engine began to move, the wheels turned back, the ship's head swung free and – 'Thanks to Mr Aeolus,' as the watching Whitcombe put it – the sails filled, and *Karteria* fought her way out through the narrow mouth of the port and into open water.

It had been touch and go, but the escape of the *Karteria* added the final touch to a day that had seen the Greeks put up their finest display in fixed battle of the whole war. It is arguable that only an Ottoman general could have ordered the attack on so formidable a position in the first place, but the casualty figures for the action – some three hundred Turkish dead to only fifteen Greek – had as much to do with the courage and defensive skill with which the Greeks fought behind their *tambouris* as it did with Ottoman obduracy and contempt.

In a sense, however, that was the problem – the Greeks had their bridgehead and the Turks had Athens – and faced with an inevitable stalemate and endless political dissensions, Gordon did what he should have done before the landings and resigned. He had at least kept his army intact, but that was all. The Acropolis, with Colonel Fabvier imprisoned inside it, was no nearer being saved; the Greek captains, euphoric at their 'victory', were no nearer to trusting Western tactics; and the *Karteria* no nearer to proving the decisive element in the war that Hastings had promised. It had not been a good campaign for philhellenism.

XI

If the winter of 1826–27 probably saw philhellene stock plummet to its lowest mark, there was one man whose absence through it all had only added to his reputation. Over the last months there had admittedly been a growing bitterness over Greece's missing admiral, but when on 17 March, 'after wandering about the Mediterranean in a fine English yacht, purchased for him out of the proceeds of the loan', as Finlay acidly and unfairly put it, Thomas Cochrane and the *Sauveur* at last arrived at Poros, all was forgiven in a surge of hope that the long-awaited Messiah had come.

With stalemate at Phaleron, Athens on the brink of collapse, civil war in Nauplia, open conflict brewing between the islands and rival 'governments' multiplying by the week, there could never have been a time when Greece was more sorely in need of a Messiah. 'This unhappy country is now divided by absurd and criminal dissensions,' Sir Richard Church, another aspiring saviour who had been waiting in the wings of Greek history for even longer than Cochrane, wrote to him. 'I hope, however, that your lordship's arrival will have a happy effect, and that they will do everything in their power to be worthy of such a leader.'

It was a challenge Cochrane rose to meet with his own inimitable brand of theatre and energy, immediately threatening Constantinople with a blockade, quoting Demosthenes at the Greeks, and refusing to stir until the rival governments of Colocotrones and Mavrocordato agreed to unite. There was never any likelihood that a truce between them would hold for very long, but under Cochrane's threats a temporary compromise was at least patched up and a new president elected whose most obvious virtue was his distance from everything that had happened before – the Ionian-born, Swiss-exiled, former Foreign Minister to the Tsar, Count John Capodistria.

A carefully preserved assassin's bullet hole, pockmarking the wall of St Spiridon in Nauplia, is a reminder of how well Capodistria would succeed in uniting Greece, but in the short term Cochrane had what he wanted. Within weeks of his arrival a new National Assembly had confirmed him grand admiral, and while they were doling out titles – real power, as Finlay bitterly noted, was not in their gift – appointed Sir Richard Church to the position he had coveted from the first days of the revolution, 'Generalissimo' of Greece's land forces.

After the long and testy business of the steam vessels, Hastings knew all too well what he was getting in Cochrane, but the new general would have been another matter. An Irishman by birth, Sir Richard Church had risen to the rank of lieutenant colonel in the British Army, leading with considerable success a Greek regiment raised to fight the French in the Ionian Isles, and forging with his men – including, crucially, Colocotrones – a mutual and quasi-paternalistic bond of affection and trust that was unique among philhellene sympathisers.

There can be no doubting the reality of Church's love for Greece, nor his courage – he had proved that in campaigns from Egypt to Santa Maura – but even among the ragbag of personalities and motives that made up the philhellene ranks he was a curiosity. After the end of the Napoleonic Wars he had joined the Neapolitan army with the rank of major general, and if that seems an odd thing for a philhellene to do there was clearly never any contradiction in his own mind – as William St Clair nicely observed – between championing Bourbon oppression in one country and revolution in another, in hanging rebels in Apulia and dreaming of the day he could lead them to freedom in Greece. 'One great and sublime idea occupies me,' he had written on the outbreak of the Greek insurgency, 'and renders me insensible to everything else. Conceive the great glory of being instrumental towards the Emancipation of Greece.'

Ardent, sentimental, chivalrous, self-deluding and 'philhellenic' in the purest of senses – these were hardly qualities likely to endear Church to the usual mix of Bonapartists, radicals, liberals, classicists, exiled revolutionaries and *Turcophages* already fighting for Greece, but they met an answering chord among the Greeks themselves. 'My soul has never been absent from you,' Colocotrones had written imploringly to his old commander. 'How has your soul been able to remain from us? Come! Come! And take up arms for Greece, or assist her with your talents, your virtues, and your abilities that you may claim her eternal gratitude!'

It was a fair enough question – 'How has your soul been able to remain from us?' – and one that is still not easy to answer. From the first time he heard that the Greek standard had been raised in the Morea Church had dreamed of little else, but for all his disinterested passion there was a streak of egotism about him, or if nothing so ugly, a kind of weak-minded vanity that had kept him out of the war until he could enter it with the éclat and prestige that the title 'Generalissimo' at last seemed to guarantee. 'Church was of a small, well-made, active frame, and of healthy constitution,' Finlay wrote of him.

His manner was agreeable and easy, with the polish of great social experience, and the goodness of his disposition was admitted by his enemies, but the strength of his mind was not the quality of which his friends boasted. In Greece he committed the common error of assuming a high position without the means of performing its duties: and it may be questioned whether he possessed the talents necessary for performing the duties well, had it been in his power to perform them at all.

Hastings had as little regard for society virtues as he did for titles – other families' titles at least – but for the time being his new admiral's plans kept the two men apart. 'You are hereby required and directed to proceed in the steam vessel under your command to the gulph [sic] of Volo and channel of Negropont,' Cochrane, on board the *Hellas* at Poros, instructed Hastings on 10 April 1827,

> where you will use your utmost endeavour to capture the provision vessels of the enemy destined for the supply for the army in the blocade [sic] of Athens. Previously to your departure you will inform yourself from the captain of the schooner lately arrived from that quarter, of the places and ports where certain provision vessels are said now to be collecting. You will remain on this scene for the space of fourteen days ... at the expiration of which you will return to this anchorage for further orders, leaving however the other vessels to continue the blockade.

This was the kind of operation for which the *Karteria* was designed, and the strategy that Gordon and Hastings had been advocating all along. The events of the previous winter had richly demonstrated the folly of any direct attack on Athens, but the Turks' long and vulnerable supply line across a ravaged countryside was a tempting target. 'This circumstance exposed their lines of communication, both by land and sea, to be attacked by the Greeks in many different points,' Finlay – once again with Hastings – wrote. 'Volo was one of the principal depots at which the supplies transmitted from Thessalonica and Constantinople were secured; and from this station they were forwarded by the channel of Euboea to the fortress of Negropont, and thence to Oropos. From Oropos the supplies were transported on horses and mules to the camp of the Pasha at Patissia, near Athens.'

Hastings's task was to disrupt the supply lines between Volos and Oropos – 'to use every exertion to capture their transports and destroy their magazines' – and after taking on more fuel at Scopulo, he steamed with the small flotilla under his command into the matchless natural amphitheatre that is the Gulf of Volos.

The Turkish-held fort of Volos lay in the fold of a well-defended bay at the northern extremity of the gulf. It was from this harbour that Jason had sailed the *Argo* into the Black Sea in search of the Golden Fleece, but if Finlay was dilettante and classicist enough to

savour the grim oddity of the *Karteria*'s eruption into a sunbathed
world of myth and legend, it was a refinement lost on Hastings. 'I
found eight vessels at anchor in the Port,' he dryly informed Cochrane
– equally oblivious to the placid beauty of a perfect early summer's
day or the wooded slopes that had once been the haunts of the
centaur Chiron:

> immediately I directed the Themistocles & Ares to anchor off the
> battery at the Point & cannonade it whilst I entered the harbour
> with boats & schooners. [the *Panagia* and *Aspasia*]. At 4h. 3om.
> they anchored with much gallantry [under] musket shot from the
> battery & soon silenced it. At the same moment I entered the
> harbour with the boats & schooners & we shortly took possession
> of seven Barges: they were all on shore & most without sails bent.
> However by 9h. PM we succeeded in getting out five prizes, three
> loaded with provisions & ammunition.

It was a language that Cochrane could understand – one professional
speaking to another – but its laconic understatement gives precious
little idea of the carnage the *Karteria* had wrought. The enemy transports had been crowded with soldiers to prevent their capture, but
nothing and no one could have stood up to the ferocious combination of shell and grape – three hundred two-ounce balls from each of
her guns – that Hastings poured into the ships and the shore defences.
The five vessels farthest from the land were soon captured and, after
a dour and bloody resistance, the two closest in followed suit. 'The
English boatswain of the Karteria,' Finlay – a newcomer to violence
of this intensity – recalled,

> who was first to mount the side of one, was wounded; but he
> succeeded in gaining the deck, and hauling down the Turkish flag.
> A Turk however, who had no idea of surrendering to an infidel,
> rushed at him, and fired a pistol at his head. The ball, fortunately,
> only grazed his forehead. The Turk then leaped overboard, and
> endeavoured to swim on shore; but one of the English sailors,
> considering his conduct so unfair as to merit death, jumped into the
> sea after him, and, having overtaken him, deliberately cut his throat
> with a clasp-knife, as he had no other weapon, and then returned
> on board. The Greek Revolution too often gave occasions for
> displaying,

The instincts of the first-born Cain,
Which ever lurks somewhere in human hearts.

The attack had taken just four and a half hours and was executed without a single death in the *Karteria*. 'The spectacle offered by the bay as it grew dark was peculiarly grand,' Finlay continued.

> On the sombre outline of the hills around the gulf, innumerable fires were seen; and a continued discharge of musketry was heard proclaiming the arrival of each little band of troops which reached the camp at Volo. The lurid light thrown out by the flames from the burning magazines, and the reflection of the blazing transports, which were quickly consumed to the water's edge, enabled the steamer, in departing, to destroy the carriages of two guns with which the Turks were endeavouring to salute the departing squadron.

The vessel Hastings had really been after was a Turkish man-of-war that intelligence suggested was at Volos, and as his triumphant squadron slipped away into the darkness, they were intercepted by a Greek fishing boat with the news that the ship had been moved to the safety of Tricheri, at the southern rim of the gulf.

As dawn broke the next day Hastings despatched his Volos prizes to Cochrane at Poros, and accompanied by the *Themistocles* – the vessel in which he had first made his name in Greece – the *Ares* and *Panagia*, stood into the bay to reconnoitre the position. And by the light of day he could see just how formidable it was. Covered by four captured Greek schooners, and mounting fourteen long twenty-four-pounders and two mortars, the brig of war had been anchored in a narrow bight, and attached by a gangplank to the rocks. On either side of her, cliffs rose steeply to give cover to a corps of Albanian troops. A shore battery close under her bows, and five more batteries positioned on the heights above, completed her defences.

With the four schooners lying safely beached, there could be no question of cutting out any of the enemy vessels, and Hastings decided instead to destroy them from a distance. Standing off some three quarters of a mile from the enemy shore, he ordered the *Karteria* into a wide and leisurely circle, firing off each of his long guns in turn as they were successively brought to bear on the Turkish brig. Then, like a snake backing off its prey while it waits for the venom to work, the

Karteria steamed out of range of the Turkish defences and watched. 'In about a half an hour, a quantity of smoke was observed to issue from the large Turkish vessel,' Finlay recalled, 'which the enemy appeared at first to disregard; but, in short time, they seemed to discover that their ship was on fire, for they were soon hurrying down and rushing on board in great numbers.'

The smoke was the sign Hastings had been waiting for. The steamship's carronades were loaded with shells, the long guns with grape, and *Karteria* closed in for the kill. Within minutes flames could be seen leaping up through the brig's deck, and as the rigging caught fire she was soon a ball of flame, her loaded guns going off at point-blank into the shore batteries until one last explosion in her magazine sent what remained of her burning hull and all her guns to the bottom of the bay. 'You will observe that in my letter respecting the affair of Trichery,' Hastings wrote with a certain justifiable smugness to Cochrane a few days later,

> [I] mention[ed] simply having burnt the Brig of War without saying how. That letter being a despatch for publication I thought it as well not to proclaim to the enemy the use we made of hot shot – 'twas by those I burnt the Brig & could quite as easily burn by the same means the largest ship ever built; might I suggest the advantage that would result from using the same projectile from almost every ship? Each vessel might as well as me have a furnace in her hold for the feeding of two of her guns – the effect would be tremendous.

It had been another brilliant action – the whole affair had taken less than an hour and cost only two lives among Hastings's men, one of them an Englishman, James Hall, cut in half by a round shot with the smile still on his face – but with the *Karteria*'s jib boom, main topmast, gaff and larboard cat-head all shot away there was no choice but to abandon station. 'Passing by Kunsi,' Hastings informed Cochrane on 26 April, confronted on the voyage back to Poros with the seamier side of Greek warfare,

> I observed several vessels at anchor there and a great number of large kyckes [sic] etc hauled up on the beach – I stood in & overhauled them & found as I suspected that a most scandalous and extensive commerce in grain is carrying on in that place with the

Turks chiefly in Greek vessels. A brig under Russian colours was chiefly discharged, an Opsarian schooner was nearly full – I set about loading the grain from the magazines but was unable to take off more than one third of what was in them, & have good reason for supposing the other magazines equally stored are to be found in the town ... The want of men, of time etc has prevented me putting a finishing hand to this infamous traffic but I have no doubt your Lordship will see the propriety of sending a Vessel of War without delay to destroy these depots. Tis idle to talk of blockading the Gulf of Negropont whilst such an extensive commerce is carrying on at other points of the island.

In letter after letter to Cochrane Hastings would ram home the same point, insisting that the only way to save Athens was by crippling the Turkish supply lines, but he might as well have saved his breath. 'The eyes of Europe are turned towards Greece,' Cochrane told the world on 14 April, desperate to announce his arrival with the dramatic capture of the prize that had eluded every other philhellene, 'and on the success or failure of the measures now to be adopted depends the support of your glorious cause, or its abandonment in despair.'

With a thousand Spanish dollars promised to the first man to raise the flag over the Acropolis, and ten thousand more to be shared among his companions, there was no shortage of volunteers to abet him in this folly. On 25 April Cochrane, armed only with his telescope, went ashore in time to inspire a small Greek victory near Athens, but it was a last, brilliant hurrah before reality in the shape of another shameful massacre kicked in. 'It was,' he declared, as he watched helpless from the deck of his schooner, the *Unicorn*, while his Greeks turned on the St Spiridon garrison who had surrendered under a guarantee of safe conduct, 'the most horrid scene I ever beheld – a scene which freezes my blood, and which cannot be palliated by any barbarities which the Turks have committed on you.'

It was less than a week before Cochrane and his fellow 'saviour' – the 'Dug-out Doug' of the Greek War, Generalissimo Sir Richard Church – were served with their second brutal lesson by the men under their command. On 6 May a force of three thousand men was landed to the east of Phaleron for a night advance on Athens, but by morning they were still there, the proposed *coup-de-main* unattempted, and – like every army before them – sitting targets in the open for the combined cavalry and infantry counterattack. The outcome of this 'insane project', as Gordon called it, was bitterly familiar. 'Fifteen hundred Greeks fell in this disastrous battle and six guns were lost,' wrote Finlay, who watched the engagement from the heights of Munychia. 'It was the most complete defeat sustained by the Greeks during the course of the war; it dispersed their last army, and destroyed all confidence in the military skill of their commander-in-chief, for even the shameful rout of Petta sunk into insignificance when compared to this terrible and irreparable disaster.'

Cochrane did what he could to cover the retreat to the boats, but 240 Greek prisoners were left behind to be beheaded, and Athens was effectively doomed. Within days Church's army of liberation had melted away to nothing, and on 5 July, after a siege that had lasted a year, the Acropolis was finally surrendered, Fabvier's garrison of 1,500 men, women and children marching out under a guarantee of safe conduct that, almost uniquely in this war, was faithfully honoured.

The surrender of the Acropolis spelled the end for Greek hopes of saving themselves, but for Hastings and *Karteria* it meant only a redirection of their efforts. In the run-up to the final battle for Athens Cochrane and Hastings had both looked eastwards and even to Constantinople, but with the loss of Greece's last mainland possession the strategic focus inevitably switched to the west and the south in the bid to carry the battle to the enemy that was untouchable anywhere else.

'Focus' is, perhaps, too charitable a word, because for the next weeks Hastings and his ship found themselves at the whim of an admiral desperately in search of the triumph that had eluded him at Phaleron. Throughout his career Cochrane had relied on reputation and the unexpected to achieve his goals, but with only two reliable ships, and scarcely two reliable crews, at his bidding he was increasingly reduced to a series of gadfly gestures that did nothing for his name and still less to placate his increasingly exasperated second-in-command.

There was no shortage of other anxieties for Hastings – fuel, men, money, masts, provisions, wages, fire-bars, paddles, prizes – but it was Cochrane's behaviour that most taxed his patience. It was probably the fault of neither man that a relationship of such endless promise should end in frustration, but Cochrane's very strengths as a subordinate – his unpredictability, his originality, his supreme individualism – were weaknesses in a commander who left the men under him to sink or swim in almost complete ignorance of his movements or intentions. 'He is an ingenious, restless, daring spirit,' Samuel Gridley Howe wrote in his journal, probably reflecting the views of his captain:

> He is fertile in schemes, acutely observant of men and things, a perfect sailor, a cool and hearty fighter; but he is *only* a fighter, a fine partisan leader, without the capacious and far-seeing mind which takes in a wide horizon and can make everything subservient to a great end. He could plan the details of a campaign, he would abound in happy thoughts, in daring, ingenious and brilliant schemes, and effect many a fine *coup de main*, but he could never plan or manage that campaign *en grand*.

It was, above all, the bewildering lack of cohesion or orders that most frustrated Hastings. 'I am anxious to receive from your Lordship an order respecting the distribution of prize-money,' he typically wrote, perhaps the mildest in a stream of pained requests that became icier by the letter.

> ... I am sorry to be obliged to remind your Lordship again ... It is disagreeable for me to torment your Lordship ... I had the honor of sending you a report of my proceedings since I left you & hoped to have found you here on my return to Poros that I might receive your further orders ... your Lordship may perhaps think it worthwhile to send a vessel here with orders for my further guidance ... In hopes of seeing your Lordship here I have waited two days ... If your Lordship remains long absent I shall be puzzled how to act ... I am delighted to find you have an expedition in progress ...

The expedition in question was just the last and most improbable of Cochrane's schemes for redeeming his name, and the folly that most nearly brought Hastings to resignation. On her way back from another wild-goose chase the *Karteria* had been severely damaged in a storm off Cape Malia, but by the second week in June was ready for sea again, and Hastings 'anxious to know how, when and where I can have the honor of rejoining your Lordship'.

Cochrane had in fact gathered a substantial force off the south-east point of the Morea, on his way to Alexandria to burn the Egyptian fleet, but Hastings was not to know that. Two days after his letter came a reply giving neither rendezvous nor target, and while the *Sauveur* and *Hellas*, with their squadron of fourteen brigs and eight fireships, sailed for the Egyptian coast, Hastings and the *Karteria* were left to wander the Mediterranean in a fruitless search for friend or enemy.

As it turned out the *Karteria* was well out of an Alexandrian fiasco that, if it was not entirely Cochrane's fault, showed how little he had learned from his Athens experience. In the old days he had planned and executed such attacks as a matter of course, but even if the Cochrane of 1827 had been the same man as the Cochrane of 1807, the men under him were not the British sailors and marines who had terrorised the French and Spanish coasts, but Greeks as little ready to risk their lives on a fire-ship as they were to take St Spiridon's at the point of the bayonet.

Perhaps Cochrane's greatest failure, in fact, was his inability to command the same loyalty from his men that Hastings inspired. It seems on the face of it odd that Hastings should have enjoyed a popularity he did so little to court, but 'leadership' comes in many different forms, and his combination of disinterested generosity and deliberate cold hauteur worked on a crew of mixed nationalities in a way that the Cochrane charisma never did.

It is impossible not to sympathise with Cochrane – 'See, my friend, see what it is to be a Greek admiral!' he remarked to the Swiss philhellene Dr Gosse as he showed him the loaded pistol he carried under his coat to protect himself from his own crew – but Hastings had been tried too far. 'I received a laconic order from his Lordship to join the squadron without delay,' he wrote bitterly to Finlay on 29 June, still at sea somewhere between Santori and Stampalia after another engine failure had left him at the mercy of the Egyptian fleet Cochrane had stung into action,

> this without any place being mentioned even in the date of the letter ... I find Lord C got off Alexandria and & sent in two fire ships who burnt a brig – the fleet then came out & chased him to the coast of Asia – All this is too ridiculous for contempt even if these freaks were not occasionally too serious – & I fear he will somehow contrive – (notwithstanding the fixed prudence of the Greeks) to make a second Athens business somewhere before he finishes – When I thus see Genius 'cut such fantastical tricks before high heaven' I bless my stars that I am but a simple matter of fact man without

pretensions to any more than common sense. I am now completely disgusted & shall quit a craft I feel it impossible to command with any credit to myself and advantage to the Greeks.

Hastings might have been unfair to Cochrane, but given the strain and expense he was under simply keeping the *Karteria* afloat, his bitterness is not surprising. 'It is with deep regret I see the extreme discontent existing on board the Sauveur Brig,' he had warned Cochrane two months earlier – just one of any number of letters carrying the same tale,

> which seems to me to be greatly augmented if not entirely owing to the Greeks being paid in advance & the English being in arrears of wages. In this country my Lord I must repeat that nothing can be done without regular payments. By paying out of my own funds when others could not be obtained I have established the confidence of the Greeks & English in this vessel as far as money is concerned, but I cannot continue to pay out of my own pocket. If funds are not forthcoming for the wages of this vessel I must beg leave to resign.

Hastings was not exaggerating his financial sacrifices – crew's wages, new masts, a hundred tons of firewood, a ransom to keep the head on a philhellene captured at Phaleron, all came out of his ever decreasing inheritance – but whatever the threats he was too honourable to resign. Over the next year his letters to Finlay would be filled with talk of Greek perfidy and resignation, but between a stubborn belief in the *Karteria* and a deeply unsentimental commitment to the Greek cause, he was – and the Greeks knew it, Cochrane knew it – there for the duration.

There was encouragement too, because on 6 July 1827 the Treaty of London, enshrining the intentions of the Great Powers towards the nascent Greece, was finally signed, opening up possibilities that even a month before could not have been dreamed of. The treaty proposed the establishment of a virtually independent Greece under Ottoman suzerainty, and called for an immediate armistice between Greek and Turkish forces that the three signatory powers – Russia, France and Britain – were prepared to impose by force if necessary.

And as sure as mobilisation would mean war almost a century later, no one could seriously doubt that the presence of the Powers' fleets in Greek waters would lead to armed intervention. The Russians certainly needed no encouragement to fight the Turks, Nelson's captains to fight anyone, and the French to protect their interests, and safe in this knowledge Cochrane, Church and Hastings moved to secure as much territory for any future Greece as they were able. At the end of August an expedition against Missolonghi under Cochrane's command was quickly aborted, but the following month, on 18 September, Cochrane unleashed Hastings and the *Karteria* with the kind of orders he had been waiting for. 'You have been good enough to volunteer to proceed into the Gulf of Lepanto,' Cochrane wrote from off Missolonghi, 'into which, under existing circumstances, I should not have ordered the Perseverance (Karteria.) I therefore leave all the proceedings to your judgement, intimating only that the transporting of General Church's troops to the north of the gulf, and the destruction or capture of the enemy's vessels, will be services of high importance to the cause of Greece.'

For Hastings the frustrations were at last over.

XII

Even the most 'cursory glance' at a map, as that passionate philhellene turned Turcophile, David Urquhart, wrote, will demonstrate the strategic importance of the Gulf of Corinth to any Greek war, and never was that more true than in 1827. During the first six years of revolution the one safe route between Continental Greece and the Morea had been by sea, but with 'the combined Mussulman fleets now anchored at Navarino, Patras, and Missolonghi' and their ships everywhere, the key to 'all communications' had become the Gulf of Corinth and the two castles commanding its western approach.

It was for this reason that Cochrane, desperate to foment and extend the war into western Greece before the Great Powers could enforce an armistice, despatched Hastings into the gulf to link up with the depleted rump of Church's army on its southern shore. On the basis of his own experience Hastings had as little faith in Church as in the feasibility of an enlarged Greece, but a Turkish squadron was too tempting a target to ignore, and on the evening of 21 September he made his first attempt at forcing a passage through the narrow 'Dardanelles of Lepanto' and into the enemy-dominated waters of the gulf.

By this time a squadron under the command of Sir Edward Codrington had successfully bottled up the Turkish and Egyptian fleets in the great, virtually land-locked harbour of Navarino, but that in no way lessened the dangers facing Hastings. The Dardanelles here are no more than a mile across, and on either shore stood a heavily armed fortress, the Castle of Morea, or Rion, on the Peloponnesian side, and Antirrion on the northern, mainland coast. 'I have the honor to transmit you a report of my proceedings from the day I left you,' Hastings reported to Cochrane:

> Capt Thomas of the Sauveur joined me the 21st & proposed with much gallantry to go into the Gulf in the day time – the wind being usually out at night. I consented with some difficulty in consequence of the little dependence I can place on my engine which might render it unprofitable for me to follow him immediately. The Sauveur with gun boat Bavarois in tow and accompanied by two schooners (you had left to keep the blockade at Missolonghi but who contrary to my knowledge thus disobeyed your orders) passed into the Gulf in most gallant style in despite of the enemy's very formidable batteries and one Brig of War & two schooners & several vessels at Lepanto. I attempted to steam in that night but the engine failed me within two miles of the Castles.

It seems woefully typical that the *Karteria* could not immediately follow Thomas, because if anyone deserved to share in one of the great symbolic moments of the war it was Hastings. 'A shout of welcome rose from the expectant host,' Urquhart wrote of the moment Church's army at Corinth first saw the *Sauveur*'s 'broad ensign display[ing] the silver cross on its azure field and the merry peals of the whole artillery of the citadel proclaimed, after two thousand years of subjection, the inauguration of the emblem of Greece on the waters of Lepanto ... The effect of the appearance of this vessel in the gulf was miraculous; the talisman of Turkish supremacy was broken, and the passage to western Greece opened. The palicari now flooded round General Church, urging him to lead them forward.'

Hastings was after the Turkish fleet, though, not the applause of Greece, and on the evening of the twenty-third, in defiance of a recently signed ceasefire brokered by the Powers, ran the gauntlet of the two castles with no more damage to the *Karteria* than a few cut riggings. The moment he was safely in the gulf he despatched a vessel

to Church to announce his arrival, adding a characteristic codicil that
left the 'Generalissimo' in no doubt as to either Hastings's priorities
or his autonomy. 'I shall proceed immediately to Salona,' – the
harbour under Mount Parnassus where the Turkish fleet was
anchored – he told Church,

> to ascertain how things stand there & afterwards proceed to
> Loutraki for water & to repair the boilers and communicate with
> you about our future operations. Lord C has given me Carte
> Blanche to remain in the Gulph: & as long as I can be of service &
> I can procure provisions & fuel, I will remain – fuel I shall soon be
> in want of – if you can procure me a good supply of good pitch pine
> timber it will remove the difficulty – Lord C caused some to be
> felled, I believe, near Megara – you can ascertain if that can be had
> & transported over the isthmus to me.

The habitually lordly tone Hastings took with Church would cause its
problems over the next six months, but for the moment his only
concern was Salona and the enemy squadron. Captain Thomas had
already tried ('impudently'? 'imprudently'? – it is hard to decipher Hastings's writing) to attack with the *Sauveur*, but contrary winds had
driven him back to Loutraki and on the twenty-sixth Hastings took
the gunboat *Philhellenic* and the ailing *Karteria* deep into the bay before
the Turks could reinforce its defences. 'We no sooner approached,'
however, he wrote to Cochrane on the twenty-seventh, 'than the wind
came so strong out that we could not keep the ship's head to the wind
& found it necessary to retire. The Turks have at Salona a very fine
Algereen Brig of 14 guns, a Brig of 16 guns bearing an Admiral's flag,
3 small schooners, 2 armed transport Brigs & two large boats with
guns & they have a battery on shore: there are three Austrians.'

The *Karteria*'s log reveals a rather hotter action than this suggests,
but their only casualty was an engineer slightly wounded, and
despatching a fast sailing vessel with orders for Thomas to join him,
Hastings set to work to prepare for another attempt. There were
further setbacks the next day when the captain of the *Bavarois*
resigned in disgust at his crew, but by the early hours of the twenty-
ninth all was again ready, with a new commander and crew in place
in the *Bavarois*, the *Karteria*'s engines and boiler repaired and the
first shells put in her fires for heating. 'During the night,' Urquhart
recalled of these last, tense hours of waiting,

the sounds of preparations on board the steamer floated on the still breast of the Gulf; and the watches of the two vessels, from time to time, enlivened their labours with answering cheers. The morrow was to be an eventful day for Greece: on its issue depended the mastery of the gulf, and all the advantage contingent on its possession; but above all was it to decide the highland chiefs, now wavering between Turks and Greece. But still more important and unforeseen results were in store.

It was a morning of cloudless blue skies and glassy stillness that no one in the ship or watching from the Greek camp on the shore of the Morea would ever forget. 'It was a curious sight,' Urquhart remembered – narcissistically determined to play actor and audience of his own unfolding drama,

> to see the black cloud from the funnel of a steamer driven by the breeze from Achaia towards the Delphic heights and Parnassus. It was strange to hear the patter of paddle-wheels sounding far and wide on the Corinthian wave … It was only then that we felt all the danger of the enterprise, or the consequence of a failure. With what anxiety did we watch the white sails and the black smoke, as they disappeared behind the low point! Of what suspense was that half hour that elapsed between that moment and the first distant peal of cannon that boomed along the water, and the mist of grey smoke that slowly rolled up from a hollow of the bay along the side of Parnassus.

It was 11 o'clock before Hastings's small flotilla finally disappeared from the view of the watching Greeks and the men on board gained their first sight of the task ahead. The sailors in *Karteria* and *Sauveur* had, of course, attempted the same attack less than a week before, but even in those few days the whole complexion of the bay had changed, with the enemy fleet – broadsides ready and 'dressed as for a gala scene in broad and bloody flags and long streaming pennants' – now made fast to the shore in front of a network of newly dug and heavily manned gun emplacements lining the beach. 'The shore also displayed flags of defiance where fresh earth works had been cast up; a goodly show of green tents and the glittering of arms enlivened the hills around, forming altogether a sight less enticing than picturesque.'

For Hastings's sailing vessels, however, there could be no turning back, as the leading wind that had taken them into the bay precluded any thought of retreat. At 11.30 Hastings took the *Karteria* in to within a cable of the enemy squadron, and anchoring stern and head to give himself a stable gun platform, opened up with a savage starboard broadside before the Turks could get off more than a single discharge.

Within fifteen minutes, as the log laconically notes, 'the Brig bearing the Admiral's flag' was seen to be on fire, and a schooner and transport brig soon followed, the transport sinking by the head with her stern aflame. As Hastings watched the first effects of his opening broadside, the *Sauveur* and the other smaller gunboats joined the action, anchoring just outside the steam vessel to add the weight of their own cannon to the *Karteria*'s overwhelming firepower.

By this time the crew of the large Algerine schooner had abandoned their stricken vessel, but with the musketry fire from the surrounding hills thwarting all attempts to board her, Hastings ordered the *Sauveur* in to counter it while he weighed anchor and moved in to secure his prize. Within minutes the worst of the Turkish fire had been silenced, but with only a fathom of water around the schooner and the tide falling, Hastings was forced to abandon his attempt to haul her off and to make do with burning her where she lay.

During this action the rest of the flotilla had not been idle, seizing the three Austrians as prizes, but with water low in the *Karteria*'s boiler and all the surviving shore batteries concentrating their fire on her, it was time to make their escape. At 5 o'clock Hastings cut the cable attaching them to the schooner and weighed for the open sea, leaving among the carnage of burning and half-sunk wrecks just one small schooner and boat to remind the Turks of the nine ships that had been so defiantly decked out only five hours before.

It had been the vindication of everything Hastings had ever preached, the triumph of steam over sail, of power and technology over mere numbers, of the future over the past. In an age before romance and science had parted company – Turner would have loved the *Karteria*'s black smoke rising against a Parnassan background – Hastings belonged to both, but in terms of naval warfare Salona unquestionably marked a watershed, offering a vision of battle that in its modernity and promise was closer to the kind of action planned for by Jacky Fisher than to the final great battle under sail to which it was the immediate prelude. 'The battle of Salona afforded the most satisfactory proofs of the efficiency of armament of steam-boats, with heavy guns, which Captain Hastings had so long and warmly advocated,' wrote Finlay eighteen years later. 'The terrific and rapid manner in which a force so greatly superior to his own was utterly annihilated by the hot shot and shells of the *Karteria*, silenced the opponents of Captain Hastings's plan throughout all Europe. From that day it became evident to all who studied the progress of naval warfare, that every nation in Europe must adopt his principles of marine artillery, and arm some vessels in their fleets on the model he had given them.'

It had been quite simply – as Hastings told Finlay – 'the finest day of [his] existence', and if Salona did not directly lead to what followed, Hastings's presence in the gulf most certainly did. It had never seemed to Ibrahim Pasha that the ceasefire was being policed with genuine neutrality, and on 1 October – the day after the battle – he ordered a squadron out of Navarino to take revenge on the Greeks for Cochrane's and Hastings's operations.

The squadron got no further north than Zante before it was intercepted by Codrington. By that time, though, the damage was done, leaving an outraged Ibrahim no readier to believe in British impartiality than Codrington was in Ottoman good faith. Another attempted breakout by Ibrahim's ships, and more of the usual Egyptian depredations in the Morea, pushed the two sides still farther apart, and faced with the prospect of a winter blockade, Codrington decided to force the issue. On 20 October the flagship *Asia* led the combined British, French and Russian squadrons though the narrow southern channel into Navarino Bay and, in a gesture virtually guaranteed to precipitate an action, dropped anchor deep within the enfolding crescent of the Egyptian and Turkish fleets.

The bay Codrington had entered is about three miles long and two miles wide, hemmed in on the western side by the island of Sphacteria, and accessible to ships only by that single south-western channel. Within it there was no room for manoeuvre and no possible escape for the hundred and more vessels that now faced each other. In sailing in as he did, Codrington had known exactly what he was doing, and if he had been relying on Ottoman indiscipline to provide the spark he was not disappointed. A boat was despatched from HMS *Dartmouth* to warn off an Egyptian fireship. A shot rang out, an allied officer was killed. A second rescue boat was fired on, an exchange of musketry rapidly escalated, and within minutes, in the coolly understated phrase of the *Asia*'s log book, 'the action became general'.

If Salona was the future, Navarino was the last savage hurrah of the past. Begun by accident, fought between friendly powers, slugged out at point-blank range, and devoid of movement or tactics, it was the strangest sea battle ever fought. Over the previous decade European officers had begun to make the Egyptian navy a genuinely formidable force, but when it came to weight of gunnery and sheer discipline it was no contest. By the time the last burning wreck had sunk beneath the waters of the bay, fifty-five of Ibrahim's ships had been destroyed, the rest maimed and more than six thousand men killed at a cost of just 176 allied casualties.

The political and moral ramifications of Navarino would rumble on in the courts of Europe for months to come, but no one in Greece cared a fig. If Codrington and his fellow admiral had exceeded even the covert intentions of their governments, Greek independence had been secured. Stripped of a navy, and cut off from their supply lines, Ibrahim and his Egyptian army were left helpless prisoners in a Morea that they had turned into a diseased and famine-racked desert. And no one had done more to precipitate victory than Hastings. 'I was once sitting' – reading the Philippics – '(near the ruins of a Temple) whereon it is said that the banished orator was wont to meditate on the perils of his country,' wrote Cochrane, stretching out the strict truth no more than any good philhellene romantic would do, when he recalled the advice of Demosthenes

> not to await developments, and then endeavour to counteract the enterprise of the enemy, but promptly to adapt a course [to] frustrate his measures. I was resolved to put this war counsel in succession, therefore having passed by Navarino, out of sight from its heights, and arrived at the Gulf of Lepanto, the steam vessel 'Enterprise' [Cochrane never got used to either its Greek or English name], the Sauveur Brig, and three Gun boats were sent in – under the command of the brave and zealous Captain Hastings – to destroy several small Turkish vessels of war and some Turkish ports ...
>
> Intelligence of this attack was quickly conveyed to Navarino ... and the decisive Battle of Navarino followed soon after. Thus, at the inspiration of two thousand years, the counsel of the most celebrated of persecuted Patriots (so arrogantly rejected when given)

may be said to have achieved the emancipation of his country from a yoke more cruel and degrading than the dreaded sway of the Macedonian monarch.

If this was not strictly accurate, it should have been. And if its combination of theatre, self-assertion, romance and economy of truth is pure Cochrane, Hastings for once would not have objected.

XIII

It would be another four years before the first King of modern Greece landed at Nauplia, but the only question after Navarino was not the existence but the extent of a free Greece. A month before the battle Cochrane had pointed theatrically to the north and declared it Greece's next goal, and with the freedom of the seas now suddenly theirs, nothing seemed to prevent a concerted attempt to bring the regions of western Greece and Roumeli within the boundaries of the future country.

Nothing, that is, except the usual failures of communications, leadership, cooperation, proper government, regional loyalties and money; but in the euphoria after Navarino, Hastings's was a lone voice of caution. 'If you have no hopes of provisions from Egina – Corinth etc,' he had warned Sir Richard Church just before the battle, 'permit me (as one tolerably experienced in Greek affairs) to advise you not to undertake anything – People will tell you plenty of provisions may be obtained in Roumilea [sic] – do not credit them – some deceive themselves, others wish to deceive you. On arriving there you will find nothing plentiful but stones.'

In a letter to Cochrane the same day, Hastings repeated his concerns, and even news of the victory could not shift them. 'Gen Church writes me that he positively intends passing into Roumeli & wants my aid,' he told him:

> ... he continues to apply to me for provisions and will soon probably for money. What am I to do about him? Although wishing to aid Gen Church & the service in all I can, I must acknowledge I have no confidence in his intended movements more particularly as he has no provisions and wants me to seize by force what I find in boats. – All I could get by this discreditable way of rais-

ing provisions would not certainly feed 100 men for three days
& therefore would not aid Gen Church & would be a gratuitous
vexation on these miserable peasantry. If Gen Church had money
& provisions much is to be done in Roumelia but without these
nothing can be achieved anywhere.

In the days after Salona there had been all the old, nagging problems
of ammunition, fuel, supplies and prize-money to strain Hastings's
nerves, but it did not take long for his irritation to coalesce around
the hapless figure of his commander-in-chief. 'I am ready to do all
or anything for the good of the service,' he wrote again to Cochrane,
just after the first news of Navarino had reached him, 'but I fear
Gen Church has no means. I had him on board for two days making
reconnaissances round the Gulph, & from what I can gather the
money said to be at Corfu is a Chimera – I suspect he has not a
shilling anywhere & cannot stir – he talks it is true of expeditions,
& I have always assured him of my readiness to aid but we cannot
be consuming month after month in the hopes of his receiving
supplies.'

There was nothing Hastings could do to shift the focus and direction of the war, however, and in the middle of November he prepared
to leave the gulf to carry Church's army from Cape Papas across to
the coast of Acarnania. 'I have the honor to announce to you that
after much delay and disappointment usual in Greece I am about to
proceed to Lepanto tomorrow,' he wrote again to Cochrane on the
seventeenth:

> I then go outside to pass Genl Church over to Roumelia and after-
> wards blockade Missolonghi, Patras & Lepanto ...
>
> I must also beg your Lordship to consider us in money matters
> – I am now seven thousand pounds out of pocket by Greek affairs
> and I am daily now expending my own money for the public serv-
> ice – our prizes are serving for transports for the army & I must
> either shortly abandon this important position or be paid.
>
> It is most likely that if all the important points I have mentioned
> could be blockaded the Turks would soon be reduced ... Without
> money you must be aware I cannot maintain this vessel & all to be
> expected from Genl Church you must be aware are plenty of prom-
> ises. The General is already overwhelmed with expectants & if he
> had millions would not be able to command a farthing – I will do

all I can but I must repeat it is not quite fair I should end a beggar after all the labour, vexation & disappointment I have experienced for so many years.

The one constant in all this, though, was Hastings's sense of duty, and the next day the *Karteria*, with her little flotilla of three prizes and a *mistiko*, sailed for Lepanto to finish off the job begun at Salona. There seems little doubt that Hastings could have repeated the dose if he had had the conditions, but finding the offshore wind too strong to press home his attack, he opted instead for a daylight passage through the narrows while he had conditions in his favour.

Hastings was always as loath as Cochrane to risk the lives of his men unnecessarily, but with the wind giving him little option, there was nothing for it but 'an act of rashness of which he would not willingly have been guilty'. With anything like good artillerymen in opposition the passage between the castles would have been suicide, and 'even with the gunners of Ibrahim Pasha's army' manning the batteries, a combined total of eighty-seven cannon of a calibre sufficient to straddle the whole strait made any attempt perilous. 'The little squadron of Captain Hastings approached the castles about noon on a beautiful day,' an exhilarated Finlay described it,

> the *Karteria*, leading with a favourable wind, and spreading an immense amount of canvas from her four low masts, glided along with the aid of her steam at an amazing rate. Her three prizes, followed with every sail set ... The moment the *Karteria* came within gun-shot of the Turkish castles, they opened their fire; and for some time the balls fell thick around her – those of both castles passing over her hull, and falling beyond their mark ... Fortunately very few shot struck the hull of the *Karteria*, yet the damage she received was not inconsiderable. The funnel was shot through, a patent windlass broken to pieces, and the fragments of the iron wheels scattered about the decks like a shower of grape. Several paddles were wrenched off the starboard paddle-wheel, and one shot passed through the side near the water's edge. Two of the best sailors on board were killed by a twenty-four pound shot, while working a gun on the quarter-deck. The hand of a boy was carried away by another, and yet all this loss was sustained ere the *Karteria* had reached the centre of the passage.

It was not so much the danger of the attempt, however, as the vivid colour and the timeless *intimacy* of it all, that dazzled Urquhart. 'There was a moment of beauty on the shore,' he later wrote – still hopelessly, romantically in thrall to a vision of Homeric warfare that even the belching funnel and hell-like furnaces of the *Karteria* could not dispel,

> with its rich and thronging costumes, glittering arms, and canopies of smoke. The proud excitement, the taunting gesture, the insult-ing scoff that characterises a warfare where system, undeviating discipline, and unfathomable counsels, had not rendered men machines – gave to that struggle all the play of the passions, and, to individual character, the development which rendered the wars of antiquity so poetic, and has caused the age, whose wars are described with greatest truth, to be called heroic.

Heroic or not, Urquhart would have been no less relieved than anyone else when in mid-passage the castle batteries suddenly lost their range and the *Karteria* slipped out of gunshot without any further casualties. The loss of two men was a blow that Hastings felt keenly, but the battering the *Karteria* had taken from the forts made him only more determined to reassert his ascendancy. 'He was sure,' Finlay recorded, 'that the Turks at Patras would soon receive an exaggerated account of the damage he had sustained, from their spies at Zante; and as this would embolden those who furnished their camp with provisions, he was extremely anxious to destroy any vessels that might be anchored at Patras, in order to convince the enemy that the *Karteria* was to be dreaded, even after receiving the greatest injury.'

The *Karteria* had attracted so much of the castles' fire that the rest of the flotilla passed through unscathed, and Hastings's luck contin-ued when he found anchored at Patras a heavily laden Austrian brig. The obvious option was to cut the vessel out where she lay exposed, but as preparations to take her began, a boat carrying the Austrian consul was seen approaching the *Karteria*. 'As Austrian consul,' Hast-ings hailed him,

> 'you must be aware that the Greek government have been blockad-ing Patras for some time, and that there is now a gun-boat cruis-ing off the port.'

Austrian Consul – 'My Government acknowledges no such authority as a Greek government, and, consequently, does not admit the validity of its acts.'

Hastings – 'My orders, however, are to enforce those acts ...'

Austrian Consul – 'I believe I am speaking to an Englishman; and neither Austria nor Turkey being at war with England, you are bound to respect the Austrian flag.'

Hastings – 'You are speaking, sir, to an officer in the Greek service, commanding the squadron blockading Patras; and if the Austrian brig does not place itself under my protection in five minutes, I shall fire into the Turkish camp, and it will be destroyed.'

For anyone wondering at the secret of Hastings's command over his Greek sailors, this exchange should explain it. Taking out his watch as the consul returned to the shore, he waited the five minutes he had promised him, and then seeing the brig's crew feverishly trying to haul the ship under the protection of the shore batteries, opened fire with a shell that ripped out her side and sent her to the bottom.

It almost went without saying – though that never stopped Hastings saying things – that having risked his neck on a daylight passage between the castles to rendezvous with Church's army, the general was not there when he arrived. Over the next days Hastings fired off letter after letter urging season and shortages in an attempt to inject some urgency, but it was still more than another fortnight before he was finally able to report that Church's force of twelve hundred men, half a dozen field pieces and sixty-odd horses had been safely landed at the beautiful natural harbour of Dragomestre on the Acarnanian coast.

By that time his mind was already on headier targets than the plodding Church, busy consolidating his base camp, was ever going to attempt on his own initiative. 'The [Egyptian] troops have all marched from Patra to Navarino, and nothing remains but some Albanians & the inhabitants,' Hastings urged Cochrane.

Lepanto is thinly peopled – all have little provisions as well as Missolonghi. From what I know of Lepanto or the Castles I am confident that if your Lordship was to attack it with the squadron you command and General Church was to make even a demonstration of attack by land it must fall within forty-eight hours – Lepanto lies on the face of a hill open to the sea, – every

shot & shell & rocket must tell somewhere & they would read-
ily capitulate – we must not take the Monastery of Piraeus as
our example – at Lepanto the Turks have their families – this
particular always operates upon them – but whether it did or
not – the place would be taken & I am not one to overrate the
capabilities of the Greeks.– I fear however that Gen Church has
other projects, and such as according to my opinion are very
unlikely to succeed.

Hastings certainly had no intention of hanging around Dragomestre
– 'lending [him]self to measures ... worse than useless' – but for the
time being he was forced to make do with the little island fort of Vasiladhi at the entrance of the Missolonghi lagoon that Cochrane had
tried to capture the previous September. 'I regret of all things not
having the flat bottomed boat,' he complained to him a week later
on 27 December, frustrated by both the shallowness of the lagoon
that allowed the *Karteria* no closer than a mile to the castle and the
bizarre atmospheric and water conditions that made a mockery of
their gunnery.

> With her we could have had the fort before this. General Church
> was to have attacked Anatolica [higher up the lagoon] & might
> have taken it in the first instance with little or no resistance; but he
> delayed too late & then came without an ounce of provisions &
> returned the day after to Dragomestre – this man is such an insuf-
> ferable Quack that I cannot act any longer with him; he affects to
> command the Navy as well as the Army ... though I have given
> him one or two rather rough lessons.

Church had rougher lessons ahead, but for the moment Hastings's
attentions were concentrated on Vasiladhi and the failure of their
gunnery. The problem had been that when they tried to ricochet the
shells the muddiness of the water caused irregular deviations, while
the higher trajectory fell prey to unpredictable air currents that
seemed to flow against the prevailing breeze at sea level. If they had
had the time – or more accurately, the provisions – to prolong the
blockade this would not have mattered, but with food among the
attackers running desperately low Hastings needed to blow rather
than starve the fort into submission. At last, on 29 December, after
a period of stormy weather, a day of clear blue skies and perfect calm

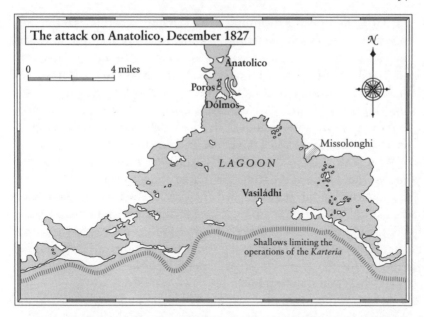

The attack on Anatolico, December 1827

0   4 miles

N

Anatolico
Poros
Dólmos
Missolonghi
LAGOON
Vasiládhi

Shallows limiting the
operations of the *Karteria*

gave him the conditions he was waiting for. The first shell fired from
the *Karteria* confirmed his optimism, and the fourth – aimed by Hastings himself and fired at a distance of about 1¾ miles – exploded in
the powder magazine, killing twelve of the fifty-one defenders and so
stupefying the rest that the castle was stormed and taken without
even a show of resistance.*

Given the range they had fired at, and the size of the little fort,
hunkered low in the reedy shallows of the lagoon, the capture of

---

* There was a touchingly comic codicil to this, when Hastings sent the
commander of the fort in a canoe to Missolonghi, to bring back flat-bottomed
boats to take away their Turkish prisoners in safety. The commander had seen
enough of the war to assume that this was a gentlemanly code for drowning,
and it was only very slowly that the dignified stoicism with which he accepted
his death sentence changed to a grave gratitude at the discovery that Hastings
meant what he said. 'The flat-bottomed boats arrived next day,' Finlay recalled,
'and took away the prisoners. They brought a sheep and a sabre as a present to
Captain Hastings from the Turkish commandant, accompanied by a letter
expressing his regret that the commander-in-chief in Missolonghi would not
allow him to come himself to visit his benefactor.' This incident compares interestingly with the practice of General Church, who was reduced to offering a
bounty on Turkish heads to get his men to fight.

Vasiladhi had been a stunning achievement – 'better practice has rarely been displayed', Hastings proudly told Cochrane – but it was typical that it should end in bitterness. 'I am full of misery,' he wrote hopelessly to Finlay on 7 January 1828, five days after handing over the captured fortress and its fourteen guns (four brass) and its fishing 'rights' to Church. 'I have not a dollar. I owe my people three months pay, and five-dollars a-head for the taking of Vasiladhi. I have no provisions, and I have lost an anchor and chain.'

With Vasiladhi in Greek hands, Hastings's next target was the Turkish-held base at Anatolico, situated some four miles farther up the shallow lagoon that guarded the coast. The town of Anatolico then stood on an island – now joined to the mainland by causeways – in the middle of a long finger of sea, and the only approach for an assault by boats was by way of a single narrow and difficult channel exposed for the greater part of its length to the combined guns of town, islets and flanking hills.

At the northern end of the channel, which ran only yards from the shore in places, the lagoon deepened again to give the Turks the added option of gunboats, but on either side the shallow water and deep mud made it a fraught and cramped approach. 'According to the wish of Gen Church,' Hastings wrote to Cochrane on 7 January – his last despatch before Cochrane suddenly, and without warning, quit Greece for England,

> I agreed to send all the boats at my disposal to attempt to capture an island named Poros commanding the entrance into the Lake of Anatolico where the Turks had a post & we heard he was filling up the passage & about to place guns on another island which would render him entirely master of the entrance. I soon discovered that what Gen Church calls the cooperation of the Navy is in reality the Navy executing the service & the Army looking on at its leisure waiting to take possession if success attended the arms of the former.

With only the haziest of intelligence to go on, no support, and half the promised boats, the night attack promised from the start to be the fiasco that Hastings had come to expect of all his dealings with Church's army. At half past three in the morning of the fourth he led his men in five boats up to the barrier that the Turks had thrown across the channel, and, jumping into the shallow water under a hail of musket and cannon fire, succeeded somehow in clearing away enough of a passage to press on with the assault.

The plan – if it could be called that – demanded at this point the mortar support of one of the brigs, but that was no more to be seen than Church's two rocket boats or the soldiers who had begun the attack with Hastings's men. 'We were now within pistol shot of Poros,' he continued – furious, as much as anything, that he had ever allowed himself to be persuaded into the attack, 'when I found to my surprise a fort on it which I had been assured there was not or I would not have attempted to attack, knowing that in our warfare these holds are not to be thus taken – seeing no reasonable hope of succeeding I ordered a retreat & having repassed by the way we entered I found Genl Church's detachment laying flat in the bottom of their boats out of gun shot.'

'I enclose you a copy of a despatch to Lord Cochrane,' Hastings wrote to Finlay on the seventh, anxious that there should be some other record of his conduct before Anatolico than the despatches that disappeared into the dead-letter office of the Greek admiralty, 'detailing a foolish affair I was pushed into against my own judgement by the Prince of Charlatans; we are now however on terms that we are not likely to meet again. In this affair of Poros I received a musket ball in the left shoulder, it tore my jacket but did me no further injury.'

It would have been well for Hastings if he had never seen Church again, but it would still take one more stand-off to convince him that there was nothing that could be done in western Greece. After the Anatolico failure he sailed the *Karteria* round to the army's base camp at Dragomestre, only to discover there that with Church's connivance his captains were lining their pockets by a trade with the very area around Patras he was trying to blockade. 'I hope this is the last time I shall be obliged to refer to this disagreeable topic,' he concluded another angry letter to Church on 14 February,

for I shall very quickly now quit this station. The length of time I have been upon it without receiving any order from my commander-in-chief, his temporary absence from Greece, the silence of the government, and the discretionary orders with which I was left by Lord Cochrane, all sanction my taking a step rendered necessary alone by your disapprobation of the manner in which I have conducted the naval affairs since I have been on this station.

If he had kept to his threat the history of the Royal Navy might yet have had a very different shape – there can be little doubt after Navarino that he would have been restored to the service – but in one way at least Hastings's Greek masters knew him better than he knew himself. It would have been hard enough for him in any circumstances to have 'quit the Theatre' – as his father put it – before the play was over, and for anyone as morbidly sensitive as Hastings the inexplicable defection of Cochrane made it well nigh impossible. 'A little being like me in the presence of King John is sure to have no will of his own,' he was soon writing slightly sheepishly to Finlay, after a summons by President Capodistria and the offer of some vague role in the formation of a new Greek navy left him as hopelessly entangled as ever. 'I foresaw this, & therefore wished to avoid a personal interview – he extracted a half-promise to render myself useful in any way for a few days [and offered] a sort of Admiralty Commission of which Toombasi and me are members. I see this is done as a kind of douceur to flatter my vanity – I am vain, certainly very vain, on some points, but not caught thus.'

He had, in fact, been 'caught' on the day, back in 1822, when he had first come ashore on Hydra, but Finlay, for one, was taking no chances. 'Your enemies are totally silenced,' he wrote to Hastings, adding his own dollop of flattery,

> & people begin to reckon Church not only a humbug but a little worse – he never goes near danger they say & spends all the money he can get, honestly or not, on uniforms & his table … Your vessel without flattery is the only one that can do anything … everybody demands you being at the head of the auxiliary squadron as they say you alone never meddle with affairs on shore ie you never have interrupted the Govt stealing – mind this is no compliment. They also say & it is a compliment & a very deserved one, that under you the Greeks behave well.

With the war in western Greece still spluttering on, it is hard to imagine that Hastings needed much coercing, and by the middle of May he had forgotten every resolution he had made to give Church and his army a wide berth. The Generalissimo had decided the previous month to make another attempt on Missolonghi, but before that could be taken it was essential that Anatolico and the route to the north that it commanded should be in Greek hands.

In terms of intelligence and knowledge of terrain, the Greeks were at least better prepared than they had been in January, and with the arrival of the *Karteria* at Vasiladhi, artillery batteries were erected and plans for the attack finalised. Hastings had brought with him a variety of different-calibre rockets, and a couple of hours before sunset on the fifteenth, under the covering fire of shot and rocket, advanced 'in a beautiful line' at the head of a little flotilla of boats. 'As night approached the scene became more and more interesting,' Church wrote,

> darkness fell altogether and then heaven itself seemed to be on fire as the tremendous firey [sic] tails of the rockets shooting upwards through the air descend[ed] again like lightning on the Town; the flash of the cannon from the land and from the lake and every now and then a tremendous crash produced by the falling of a house or roof ... the effect however of the rockets totally disappointed the expectations of all parties – at every considerable discharge of the large ones our men cheered both on shore and in the boats, and for a moment all was silence in Anatolico, but when the rockets fell without producing any remarkable effect the Turks in the Town cheered again and poured a fire of musquetry into our batteries.

The failure of their rockets was a matter of 'grief almost shame' to poor Church, and the next day Hastings returned to the *Karteria* to bring up two of the ship's sixty-eight-pounders to finish off the job properly. It was four or five days before the guns and ammunition could be ferried across the lagoon, but by 3 p.m. on the afternoon of the twenty-fifth the batteries were in place and all was ready for the two-hour barrage that would clear the way for a second attack. 'The 25th of May was fixed for the assault,' Finlay bitterly recorded,

> and Captain Hastings, who felt the necessity of enforcing order, and setting an example in so important a crisis, determined to direct the attack of the naval forces in person. Unfortunately, a division of the land forces, which were totally destitute of all discipline, and not even officered in a regular manner, had been embarked in the boats of some Greek privateers, for the purpose of assisting in the attack. The real object of these troops was to try to get first into the place in order to pillage. Before the artillery had produced any

effect, and before Captain Hastings had made all the necessary disposition for the assault, these irregular troops advanced to the attack.

With two of the gunboats following suit, Hastings now had no alternative 'between carrying the place' and witnessing the annihilation of a large part of the force under his command. 'As the scene of the action of the flotilla was close to the redoubt,' wrote Church, desperate to place as heroic a gloss on the whole fiasco as it would take, '... the gallant Commodore [promotion-creep to the fore] had only to step into his boat and with a couple of strokes of the oar to be in the midst of his boats ... In a moment passing with inconceivable velocity in a swift rowing boat bearing his Pennant, Hastings appeared at the head of the line of the flotilla and a thousand cheers saluted him as soon as his presence was observed.'

For the great technocrat, a rowing boat was a primitive way to attack; for the great naval moderniser, the muddy shallows of Anatolico a curious sort of battleground; but for the Homeric warrior that Hastings was, no place could have been fitter. In front of him, the whole of their fire now concentrated on his boat, was the enemy; to his side, the watching Greeks, cheering on their hero; and on the hillsides flanking the brightly lit lagoon, the brilliantly coloured Turkish cavalry, wheeling and spinning and counter-cheering in a scene of timeless and posturing theatre. As his boat advanced to the assault, the Cephalonians on the right who had precipitated the attack fell back under the first volley of musketry, leaving Hastings where he had wanted to be since he had first listened to Trafalgar raging around him from the lower deck of *Neptune*. Glory, he had told Byron, was what he wanted, and glory in one last apotheosis was what he would win. A rocket boat blew up, the captain of one of his gunboats was killed, and as, with 'invincible determination' and 'noble example' he pushed on to recover the situation, a musketball struck him in the left arm and 'the heroic Hastings fell!'

His fall was the signal for a general retreat, and the wounded Hastings was rowed back to the headquarters redoubt of his 'deeply afflicted friend and companion in arms' General Church. '"Make haste away Hastings for God's sake," said [and wrote] the General, as a barge blew up alongside Hastings's gig, it is nothing said Hastings alluding to his wound and I hope to be back in the Camp in ten days – please God that you may was the reply – the boat pulled off and Hastings was taken down to Vassiladhi and placed in bed on board of his own vessel at anchor.'

By a piece of ill-luck the *Karteria* was without a doctor – ironic that one of the two greatest philhellenes should die because he had too many doctors, and the other because he had none – and Hastings's crew were soon less sanguine. The musketball had struck him on the left arm 'a little above the wrist', and although he was well enough to send off a last characteristic despatch demanding the return of his sixty-eight-pounders, a succession of short but violent spasms was an alarming pointer to what lay ahead.

As fears among his crew deepened, and the talk turned to amputation, it was decided that the *Karteria* would make for Zante in search of a doctor. They had, though, left it too late. 'A sudden and unlooked for event plunged us into the deepest affliction,' a friend of Finlay's, Byron's old and trusted banker on Cephalonia, Charles Hancock, wrote to him on 2 June,

without a shadow of doubt to hang our hopes on – I dare say you have already heard that poor Hastings received a wound in his wrist some ten days ago in an affair before Anatolico wch was not considered serious – it appears however that about a week after it happened, spasmodic symptoms attacked the whole system – & he was brought over here for further surgical advice and assistance – he arrived here y'day afternoon – and was got into the Lazaretto with as little loss of time as possible but it was already too late – he was too much exhausted for amputation; the convulsive attacks were repeated & he died at ½ past 8 in the evening – Robinson & I are just returned from rendering him the last service in consigning him to the steamer's cutter – I need not tell you who knew him so intimately that Greece has lost one of the best and most efficient friends her cause ever had – We have taken no decision as to the place of interment of his remains – further than to approve of the body being taken on board the steam vessel to Egina. The officers seem to think & wish that the Greek Government may send his body back to England – We are of the opinion that the country he has been defending should be his grave ... We have provided a quantity of spirits & everything necessary to preserve the corps.

Hancock was to have his wish. 'The moment his death was known in Greece,' Finlay mordantly noted, 'the great value of his services was universally felt.' The President – 'King John' – decreed a public funeral and placed the 'sacred duty' of arranging it in the hands of Mavrocordato, Nicholas Kalergy, an old friend of Hastings's, and Finlay himself. The burial – long delayed, needless to say – took place on the island of Poros a year later. Tricoupi, the historian of the Greek revolution and future Greek minister in London, delivered the funeral oration, finishing, in the name of the whole Greek nation, with the following words:

O LORD! IN THY HEAVENLY KINGDOM REMEMBER FRANK ABNEY HASTINGS, WHO DIED IN DEFENCE OF HIS SUFFERING FELLOW CREATURES.

It was not the only service held in his memory. When men on Egina who had sailed under Hastings heard of his death, they paid the island's clergy to celebrate the funeral service 'with all the pomp and ceremony possible in those troubled times'. 'Never,' Finlay wrote, 'was braver man more sincerely mourned by a veteran band of strangers, who, in a foreign land, grieved more deeply for his untimely loss.'

Nor was it only strangers who mourned this difficult and honourable figure. 'On the 8th,' wrote Church, who had more reason than most to rue the 'hastiness of temper and manner' which had gone hand in hand with 'the noblest qualities of the head and heart',

the General had the melancholy duty of informing the President of the death of the gallant Hastings ... The death of Hastings was a great loss to Greece ... He was a man of the coolest intrepidity, great scientific and practical knowledge of his profession, ever ready for enterprise and of great perseverance – he was highly respected and esteemed by the Greeks and his military career in their service was marked by numerous services to his adopted country and by the acquisition of great glory to himself.

Without Hastings, Church continued, the *Karteria* was nothing. On board still were those tremendous guns which invented by Hastings had when directed by him, thundered fire and death upon the Turks in every direction – but he was no more – and the head which had directed, and the heart which stimulated the achievements performed by the Perseverance, having ceased to direct and to animate, her subsequent services with the army in Western Greece were as insignificant as they had previously been important and brilliant.

It was easy for Church to be generous – a dead hero, especially one of Hastings's stamp, has always been more comfortable to deal with than a live one – but the sense of loss was genuine. The historian of philhellenism, Douglas Dakin, once suggested that only a gap of language protected Hastings from the effects of his own gaucherie in Greece, but that is at the most only a very small part of the story. 'Nothing has been done about the interment of the remains of this devoted and gallant Philhellene,' Samuel Gridley Howe, a man equally deserving of Greek gratitude, wrote of him,

but his memory is deeply engraved in the minds of the Greeks; he will have a high rank in their history, and perhaps no foreigner deserves a higher. From his cold and ungainly manner, his want of address and of the common hypocrisy of society, he repelled acquaintance, he made few personal friends, and gave excellent opportunities to his enemies of injuring him, but his long, tried and entire devotion to the cause of Greece, his sacrifice of time, comfort and money, his perfect sincerity, his courage, his enterprise, his knowledge of his profession, and more than all, his daring and successful battles and his honourable death, have forced upon the minds of all Greeks [the conviction] that he was among their greatest and best friends. His name is never mentioned without an eulogium, and a regret that his merits had so long been concealed from them by his modesty.

The Greeks were right. In the year and more after Hastings's death there was a certain unseemly argument between the English executors of his original will and the acting executors of his Greek property, but they were only fighting over scraps. On 10 February 1829 an auction was held of 'the effects of poor Captain Hastings'. 'I bought Gibbon's "Roman Empire",' noted Howe (who had once picked up Byron's helmet in the same way to adorn his hatstand at home for another eighty years) 'at one hundred piastres; a Scott series in fifty-two volumes, 215 piastres; Shakespeare, two volumes, and Lempriere.' The rest of his books, charts, maps and instruments were also sold, and his clothes, plate and wine, as Hastings had wanted, went to his old servant, Alexander Ross. That, though, was about it. Greece had already had everything of value that he owned. He had spent his fortune and given his life in the service of a cause that he never confused with the failings of the Greeks themselves. He saw things clearly, he expressed them forcefully, and if that could some-times make him sound harsh it never made him act ungenerously.

No one served Greece more selflessly. No other foreigner could match his record of achievement. 'As nobody can have a better opin-ion of your military qualities, or take a greater interest in your success than myself,' Thomas Gordon wrote to him when the news of Hast-ings's great victory at Salona reached the north of Scotland, 'I saw with the greatest pleasure, that you had been instrumental in destroy-ing a Turkish squadron in the Gulph of Lepanto. Fortune seems to have reserved for you most of the trophies of the Greek war.'

Volo, Lepanto, Vasiladhi – Gordon was not exaggerating, but it had little to do with 'Fortune'. Hastings had the vision to see that the future of naval warfare belonged to steam and an overwhelming weight of fire, but that vision was rooted in a professionalism that left nothing to chance. It was not an accident that the *Karteria* – sunk by the Greeks themselves – was a cipher without him. 'Dear Finlay,' he had written only weeks before his death, with the good-humoured contempt of the professional for the amateur,

I sail tomorrow with the ship in high order – I wish you could see her, she is so smart now, & the thousand little improvements we made answer so well. Enough however about the Karteria. Now about yourself. Do let me recommend you not to go soldiering or sailoring: take a civil employment. I do not mean that you want military talents – on the contrary – you would have made either a good sailor or soldier had you served an apprenticeship – but with-out this, it is loss of time. When you reflect I am sure you must be convinced that talent has less to do with success in the military profession than being conversant with all the details of the trade. I do not hesitate to say that you would plan a battle better than Lord Nelson & on shore probably better than many generals – But you would be beaten nevertheless – because if you commanded all

the details would have been so overlooked that your better disposition would not compensate for defect of detail – It is by a scrupulous attention to detail that the British navy has often won battles
which certainly they never owed to the plan of attack chosen by the
admiral.

It says it all. Visionary and professional, Homeric warrior and utilitarian planner, leader and thinker, dreamer and pedant, Hastings was
the perfect product of the service that rejected him and perhaps the
greatest innovator the nineteenth-century Royal Navy produced. 'The
first steam-vessel armed with long sixty-eight pounders … the first
vessel from which eight-inch shells and hot-shot were used as ordinary projectiles' – they were large claims that George Finlay, writing
in 1845, made for Hastings, but ones that scarcely did more than
touch the surface of a restless and enquiring intelligence that left no
aspect of naval warfare or naval organisation unexamined.

As his friend in Greece, Finlay probably knew Hastings better than
anyone, but it can only have been as his executor that he realised how
wide-ranging that intelligence had been. Hastings only published one
slim pamphlet on gunnery in the last year of his life, but among the
papers Finlay collected up was a legacy that no one could have
guessed at and no one would enjoy. Peacetime recruitment, the aboli-
tion of the press gang, terms of service, pensions, prize-money distribution, entrance examinations, curricula reforms, residential staff
colleges, professional retraining – there were jottings, memoranda
and full-scale essays on all of them, anticipating reforms and changes
that would take another hundred years and the demonic energies of
Jacky Fisher to implement.

It is galling to think how differently the Royal Navy's history might
have evolved had there been no *Kangaroo*. If the Royal Navy's loss
was Greece's gain, however, Hastings belongs equally to both. His
body lies on Poros, resting place of that great hero of Cochrane's,
Demosthenes; his heart, though, is immured in the wall of the Anglican church in Athens. And if he would not be pleased that the light
in there filters through a window dedicated to that great philhellene
and 'insufferable Quack' Sir Richard Church, even that seems somehow as it should be.

HASTINGS

Frank Abney Hastings: 'Height, 1.70,' as his French passport describes him on his passage out to Greece, 'Hair and whiskers fair, Forehead large, Face full, Eyes blue-grey, Complexion high, Chin round, Nose *grand aquilain*'.

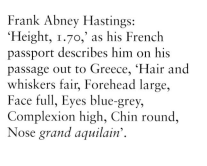

Willesley Hall, near Ashby-de-la-Zouch. 'An old crazy mansion', and family home of the Abney-Hastings.

The stables, Willesley – almost all that now survives of the 'castles in the air' improvements begun by Sir Charles Hastings to keep his wife and elder son happy.

The Greek hero:
the one volunteer 'in whose
character and deeds were the
elements of true greatness'.

The pride of the Greek navy. The American-built frigate *Hellas*, and the steam vessel *Karteria*.

The *Karteria*, Hastings's brainchild. 'The vessel from hell', as the Turks called her, and the ship that gave Hastings the 'the happiest day' of his life.

Thomas Cochrane: hero of the French wars, champion of South American liberation, High Admiral of Greece and the bane of Hastings's life.

The Battle of Navarino,
20 October 1827. The battle that
won Greece her independence, and
the strangest sea action ever fought

Timeo Danaos. A commemorative
medal presented to the
Abney-Hastings family on the
150th anniversary of the Greek
War of Independence. The unlikely
promise of an annual holiday in
Greece to be enjoyed in perpetuity
by the family lasted only as long
as the brutal dictatorship of
Colonel Papadopoulos.

PEEL

The Gallant Peel.
A posthumous portrait
commissioned by subscription
from John Lucas, and showing
Peel, complete with sword
and buttonhole, in action
before Lucknow. The original,
by order of the Lords
Commissioners of the
Admiralty, was hung in the
Painted Hall at Greenwich.
Prints were given to the
members of 'Peel's Brigade'.

The bombardment of Acre, 3 November 1840. This print, published to raise money for 'the relief of the widows, children and relations' of bluejackets and Marines killed in the campaign, was based on an original painting given by the artist, a shipmate in HMS *Charlotte*, to the seventeen-year-old William Peel.

Clements Markham, aged fourteen. Friend of Peel and Goodenough, he was 'the most beautiful as well as the most engaging boy' in HMS *Collingwood*.

Sevastopol, 17 October 1854. The first of three separate acts of heroism that earned Peel one of the earliest VCs.

'All will be serene.' *A Quiet Day in the Diamond Battery*, by William Simpson, 15 December 1854. Peel is standing next to a Lancaster 68-pounder. The 'Koh-i- Noor', Peel told his sister, was popularly known as the 'Dress Circle' and was 'quite the Haut Ton'.

'A bower anchor'. The 'Swiss Cottage' at Sandy that Peel had built for himself. 'You used that fatal word – bijou – own that it is not a bijou but a place that however pretty, would bear living in for months together.'

The *Shannon*. A rescue at sea on the voyage out to India. In command of the boat is Lieutenant Vaughan, while standing is the captain of the foretop, W. Hall, the first black winner of the VC.

Naval Brigade races. Lithograph based on a drawing by Captain Oliver Jones, RN.

Peel

A Verray Parfit Gentil Knyght

I very well agree with you in the hopes of him. It is a
gallant child; one that indeed physics the subject, makes
old hearts fresh. They that went on crutches ere he was
born desire yet their life to see him a man.

Shakespeare, *The Winter's Tale*

Whom the Gods love, die young.

Byron, *Don Juan*

I

IT IS HARD TO KNOW WHETHER to envy or to pity the third and
favourite son of Sir Robert Peel. From the day William Peel was born
at the family's London home in 1824 he moved in a world of wealth
and privilege, the gifted and beautiful child of a beautiful and devoted
mother, the darling boy of a father who did not, on the whole, go in
for 'darlings', the grandson on one side of a distinguished general
and on the other of a Staffordshire manufacturer with the energy to
create a fortune and the dynastic ambition to set his family on the
course that would take them from the industrial Midlands to Down-
ing Street and a position of power and respect unrivalled in nineteenth-century Britain.

There might well be men in every generation with the gifts of
William Peel, but to be born with the right talents at the right time
and in the right place is an altogether rarer blessing. If William had
belonged to an earlier or later generation of the Peels' evolutionary
cycle his fate and character might have been very different, but he
was born while the family fortunes were at their apogee, at that brief,
transitory moment in its history when everything was in place to

nurture success and nothing of the drive and purpose that had first
earned it had yet been forgotten.

In the classic paradigm of English social life, it has always taken
three generations to make a 'gentleman', but with the Peels the
process was slightly longer. The founder of the family fortunes in the
middle of the eighteenth century was a Lancashire cotton manufacturer known as 'Parsley' Peel, and even when his son – the first Sir
Robert, a Pittite MP rewarded for his loyalty with a baronetcy – sent
his oldest child, the future Prime Minister, to Harrow and Christ
Church there were still vowels to be smoothed and table manners to
be polished before a Peel could finally emerge from their manufacturing chrysalis as the 'beau ideal' of Victorian manhood.

The Peels themselves would always see something of his father's
look in the young William – 'the same glance of the eye, the same
lurking smile playing about the corners of the mouth' – but family
portraits tell a rather different tale. There is a wonderful Lawrence
of the first Sir Robert that captures all the shrewd acumen of the great
industrialist, but place it, or even the Linnel portrait of the young
Prime Minister Peel, alongside any likeness of William and the difference is plain – not just a difference of appearance, a refining of
features, a tempering of all coarseness, but a sort of thoroughbred
nervousness, an air of spirituality almost, that signals both the rise
of the family and the gulf that separates the age of Byron and Frank
Hastings from that of Thomas Arnold and William Peel.

With the brains of his father, the looks of his mother, the inherited
courage and energy of his ancestry, and a magnetism all his own,
William Peel has claims in fact to be seen as the fine point of a particularly English process of social evolution. In his *Memoir* of the great
Sir Robert, the French historian and statesman Guizot hazarded the
guess that 'God seldom accords to a man so many favours,' and that
might have been said with even more truth of the Prime Minister's
favourite son. To those who knew him, and perpetuated his memory,
the future Sir William Peel VC KCB seemed to have been given everything. Where his father was grudgingly admired or respected, William
was loved by everyone who met him. Where Sir Robert's massive,
slow-grinding, utilitarian intelligence took him reluctantly to unpalatable truths, William's quicksilver mind seized on opportunities.
Where Sir Robert's slow rise to the top was marred by bitter dispute,
William's brief career was effortless in its inevitability. When he wrote
his juvenile letters home, it went without saying that the Duke of

Wellington was given them to read. When he passed his exams with unparalleled speed and brilliance, nobody was surprised that speeches of congratulation were made in Parliament. When he spoke French, Frenchmen assumed he had been brought up in France. When he learned Arabic, he spoke it as well as he did English in six months. And when, at the age of thirteen, he entered the navy, its admirals merely awaited the time when he was to take up his predestined place at its summit.

If this seems too good to be the whole story, that is because it probably is; but what certainly remains true is that he arrived at a moment in history when the country at large was ready to embrace a Peel. The first Sir Robert had taken the family as far socially and politically as any eighteenth-century industrialist might well do, but by the birth of his grandson in the 1820s, the next crucial peak had already been conquered, with a Peel – the second Sir Robert – securely entrenched in the high office that a formidable career at Oxford and a typical and grimly formative political apprenticeship in Ireland had always promised.

And while all the great battles and achievements of Robert Peel's career – a police force, tariff reform, Catholic Emancipation, the Irish Church, the Corn Laws – still lay in the future, he was clearly the coming man. The long afterglow of Waterloo would always give the Duke of Wellington a unique position in public life, but with the transition from war to peace, and the gradual fading of a generation of politicians – Castlereagh, Liverpool, Canning, Eldon – whose careers and ideas had been shaped by the French Revolution and the Napoleonic Wars, there would be nobody on either side of the house for the next twenty-five years who could remotely rival Peel's abilities or authority.

It was not just in politics that the '20s proved a crucial decade for the Peel dynasty, because at the age of thirty-two Robert married a twenty-five-year-old heiress and beauty he had first met in Ireland called Julia Floyd. Julia was the orphaned daughter of a cavalry general whose career had stretched from the Seven Years War to the Siege of Seringapatam, and if the spirit she would show during the rural unrest of 1842 is any guide, was not just the source of her son's good looks but the conduit for that extraordinary physical bravery that marked his whole naval career.

It would be impossible to find a more devoted couple than Robert and Julia Peel, or fonder parents, and their thirty years of married life present almost a caricature of proto-Victorian domesticity. They had been married in Julia's stepmother's Seymour Street drawing room in June 1820, and a daughter – another Julia – was born the following year, followed in regulation succession by Robert, Frederick and – on 2 November 1824 – William, the last of the children to be born in Peel's old bachelor house before the family moved to the Whitehall home Sir Robert Smirke had built for them on the banks of the Thames.

There were two more sons, John and Arthur, and another daughter, Eliza, and from the glimpses of family life in correspondence, their early years were enveloped in a protective cocoon of love and attention. As the children got older they would inevitably be exposed to the fall-out of their father's politics, but in a succession of rented country houses and then in the great, ugly architectural mishmash that the ubiquitous Smirke built to replace the old manor at Drayton, Julia – the least political of political wives – did everything she could to provide a family retreat from the uproar over Catholic Emancipation, Maynooth or the Corn Laws.

But even at Drayton, where the portraits of Sir Robert's contemporaries stared down in admonitory gloom from the great gallery, there could have been no escaping the burden of *obligation* that came with being a Peel. 'I there saw Sir Robert Peel in the bosom of his family,' Guizot wrote some years later, capturing with a nicely Gallic touch the faintly claustrophobic Tory idyll in which the young William Peel was formed,

> and in the midst of the population of his estates: Lady Peel still beautiful, personably and modestly devoted to her husband; a charming daughter ... three sons ... Altogether, a beautiful domestic existence, grand and simple, and broadly active: in the interior of the house an affectionate gravity, less animated, less expansive, less easy than our manners desire or permit; political recollections perpetuated in a gallery of portraits, most of them of contemporaries ... Out of doors, between the landlord and the surrounding population, a great distance, strongly marked in manners, but filled up by frequent relations. Full of equity and benevolence on the part of the superior, without any appearance of envy or servility on the part of the inferiors. I there beheld one of the happiest examples of the legitimate hierarchy of position and persons, without any aristocratic recollection or pretentions, and amid a general and natural feeling of right and respect.

It says a lot for the moral and intellectual authority of Sir Robert Peel that his son William never consciously kicked against the political and social assumptions that underlay this idyll. The chequered careers of William's brothers, particularly the oldest, Robert, underline just how oppressive it might have felt, but from his earliest, precocious years the principal things that drove him – and the standards by which he judged himself – were the approval of his father and the recognition and acclaim of that public and masculine world that washed through Drayton.

It would arguably take the death of Sir Robert, in fact, to free him from the invisible strands of family expectations, but there was something about even the infant William that bedded down uneasily with his predestined role in life. 'I had a comfortless journey,' his father wrote home in 1828, in a letter that gives the first, unlikely glimpse of the future hero of Sevastopol and Lucknow, 'and really, at the first stage, had half a mind to return to you and those dear little ones that I left acting Thurtell and Weare. God bless little Julia, asking me who there was besides Hunt and Probert,* in order that she might find an appropriate character for little Willy. Poor little fellow, he is but a bad representative of a murderer.'

In many ways, in fact, the highly strung, physically delicate, fastidious and over-sensitive William would remain the most unlikely of killers. Throughout his life he suffered from bouts of depressive ill-health, and in some respects his whole career seems a triumph of willpower over temperament, a victory – if it should be seen as such – for the Peelite virtues of energy, ambition, power, duty and masculine virility over an innate softness of nature that would always make

---

* The 'Radlett Murder' of William Weare in 1823 was one of nineteenth-century England's most sensational crimes. Thurtell was hanged in 1824. Probert was hanged for stealing a horse the following year, and Hunt transported to Australia, where he became a police constable. The future Lord Melbourne was foreman of the jury, and Robert Peel Home Secretary at the time. 'They cut his throat from ear to ear,' ran one ballad,

His head they battered in.
His name was William Weare,
He lived in Lyons Inn.

The story was retold in several plays.

him more receptive to a pressed flower or a sister's ball dress than was customary in the Victorian hero.

He was a wonderfully spirited lad, and yet if there seems never to have been a time when he did not want to enter the navy, it is perhaps just as pertinent that there was never a time when his father did not want him to go into it. Sir Robert had himself grown up against the background of the struggle against Revolutionary and Napoleonic France, and he had enough of those Johnsonian instincts about the military life to push his spirited young son into fulfilling some of those dormant urgings that always left him in such awe of the Great Duke. 'I have always had a strong presentiment from my Boy's earliest infancy,' he wrote to the Earl of Haddington, on William's promotion to lieutenant, '(for his heart was fixed on the Navy when he was a child of 3 years old) that he was destined (if his life should be spared) to very great eminence in the Profession. He will most assuredly attain it.'

William was not the first child to be saddled with his father's martial ambitions – by the end of Victoria's reign it would become the stuff of A.E.W. Mason's novels – but in an age in which the boundaries between the 'masculine' and 'feminine' spheres of home and public life were ever more strictly policed, the pressures on a boy who might find 'the Duke' reading his letters must have been all the greater. 'My dearest Papa and Mamma,' he would write wistfully at the age of just seventeen, three thousand miles from 'dear old Drayton' and bound for the First Opium War, 'this is Christmas evening, and I indeed wish you a very merry and happy one. Though I cannot join the dear family circle which I hope is pressing at this moment round the cheering fire, yet I find it my greatest pleasure and real happiness to take up my letter and hold a distant correspondence with you, and think how happy you must be and what you are doing now.'

It is as impossible to quantify the cost of this kind of dislocation for William as it is for Victorian society at large, yet even at seventeen Eden and the prelapsarian world of his dearest Mamma and the dear family circle were only distant memories. By the time William was ten his father had already become Prime Minister for the first time, and if the real world was held at bay for a while by the Revd F.J. Faithful's private school at Hatfield, the respite was brief. By the age of twelve family theatricals, Mrs Faithful, 'thick trousers ... snowballing ... dreadful battles and armies' at Hatfield belonged to the past, and a very different and brutally masculine future was closing in. And if the second Sir Robert had been looking for a perfect induction into the casual savagery of life ahead for his favourite son, he could not have done better. He sent him to Harrow.

II

If there has ever been a good time to go to Harrow it certainly was not the 1830s. Sir Robert had been at the school at the beginning of the century in the golden age of Byron and Palmerston, but by the time William joined his brothers there a new headmaster was beginning his long and – if John Addington Symonds's fond memories of '"Bitches", onanism, mutual masturbation … and obscene orgies' are to be believed – losing battle for the souls and bodily temples of the uncontrollable sexual delinquents and future empire-builders in his charge.

Even as loyal and robust a Harrovian as Robert Peel would eventually be obliged by scandals, expulsions, falling rolls and suspicions of ritualism to remove his sons, but on 12 April 1837 William was taken down by his mother and placed in the unctuous care of the Revd William Whitmarsh Phelps at Harrow Park. The son of a modest West Country schoolmaster, Phelps had won a closed scholarship to Corpus in the summer of Waterloo, and after finding Christ Crucified at Oxford, had embarked on that classical Evangelical accommodation with the things of this world that would eventually lead him to Harrow, ownership of 'The Park' and an archdeaconry. 'Who is the tutor that would express indifference to a position of trust at one of our distinguished schools, as Harrow,' asked his Victorian apologist, the Slope-like Revd Charles Hole, 'while watching the early years of many bearing historic names, who might themselves be guiding the national destinies, and working in influential spheres of English welfare … Mr Phelps was not indifferent to any of it.'

It would have been hard in any circumstances for the son of a Prime Minister to have been unaware of his position, but the deference of the Revd Phelps cannot have helped. In many ways William would remain remarkably immune to the prejudices and assumptions of his class, but there was always an element of self-consciousness and entitlement about him – an awareness of the Peel name – that probably had as much to do with the clerical meekness of the Revd

Phelps as with the enlightened self-interest of naval captains anxious
to turn Sir Robert's son into a kind of glorified Admiralty pet.

It is difficult to gauge what other influence Phelps had on him –
on his English or Classics, none it would seem, on his intense and
distinctive spirituality probably just as little – but if another Peel was
precisely the sort of pupil he was after, he was not to have him for
long. 'I have only therefore to express my sincere thanks to you for
the care you have taken of my boys committed to your charge,' Sir
Robert was writing soothingly to him within the year, 'and my sincere
regret at the necessity of withdrawing them from your superinten-
dence.'

Sir Robert's regret did not stop him sending his younger boys to
Eton, or loosen the public purse strings when Phelps came looking
for preferment, but it is unlikely that he could have kept William at
any school for long. During the year William had spent at The Park
his father was already busy taking soundings among Admiralty
friends, and on 7 April 1838 – just four days after finally leaving
Harrow – William reported himself on board the *Royal Adelaide* to
sit his examination for 'Volunteer of the First Class'. 'Name, Mr
William Peel, Age 13', his certificate reads:

> Whether affected by impediments of speech, defective vision,
> Rupture or any other Physical insufficiency – No.
>   Can he write English from dictation and does he understand the
> four First Rules of Arithmetic Reduction and the Rule of Three –
> Yes.

The examination might have been a lot easier – Clements Markham,
a future shipmate, was made to write out the first part of the Lord's
Prayer and punched in the stomach for his medical – but if the young
Peel's grammar is any guide, standards were not tough. 'In reference
to your letter of the 4th Inst,' Admiral Beauclerk completed formal-
ities the following day – the interlocking machinery of naval admin-
istration and political 'interest' working smoothly – 'I transmit the
report Of Examination, and Qualification, of Mr William Peel,
Volunteer of the First Class appointed to the "Princess Charlotte" in
the Mediterranean; and acquaint you that he yesterday joined the
"Talbot" for a passage to her as directed.'

The 104-gun *Princess Charlotte* – Captain Arthur Fanshawe – was
the flagship of the seventy-year-old Sir Robert Stopford, Commander-

in-Chief in the Mediterranean, and an ageing veteran of the Basque Roads and the bombardment of Copenhagen. It is clear from a later letter that Peel was unhappier about leaving home than he ever allowed his father to know, yet even in the 'long lee of Trafalgar' the timeless rituals of a peacetime navy – drilling, mending, watering, sightseeing, shopping, cricket, partridge-shooting, regattas, diplomatic courtesies, climbing Vesuvius and waiting (as it would spend so much of the century doing) in eternal hope of a breakdown in the fragile relations between Britain and France – left a thirteen-year-old boy precious little time to mope. 'As I have not seen any more places since I last wrote to you I must tell you how my time passes,' Peel wrote home from Tunis – a letter that until he gets on to Herodotus and Euripides might have been written by almost any volunteer to any mother at any time and from any place during the long Victorian summer of British naval supremacy.

> We have got to keep watches up to 10 at night, so that we all get the middle watch but we have to get up at 4 o'clock every morning (of course I am talking of the volunteers) which although I did not much like at first comes now quite natural and I like it. There is a Chaplain on board as I told you before. At 7 bells am or at half past 7, we have to go on quarter deck, where the Chaplain reads some prayers every morning, then at 8 o'clock we have our breakfast and at half past 8 the drum beats to Quarters, which is this, to every gun there are 6 men and those men have got to stand at their guns in clean deck gowns and frock with their muskets cutlasses and Tomahawks, and Boarding Pikes, all properly cleaned and polished. There are so many officers appointed to each deck, I am on the Quarter Deck. This lasts about half an hour and at 10 we go into the schoolroom and we learn alternately Mathematics, Navigation, French and Italian. We are in the schoolroom till 12 o'clock and then we have our dinner which lasts an hour and then we have the afternoon to ourselves. But I asked the Chaplain Mr Kitson if he had any objection to my learning Latin and Greek, and he said no, and he should be very happy etc. As I have no books he lends me his and I go into the School Room after dinner and there I do a page of Herodotus and so many lines of the Epistles of Horace one day and the next a page of Euripides ... They laughed at me a little at first but they soon stopped and now they say nothing to it.

There were always cutlass and broadsword exercises at four with anyone disposed to go on laughing, but even at thirteen Peel had the strength of mind to follow his own path. 'I am sure you will be glad to hear that I have nothing but satisfaction from all the accounts I hear of William (my third boy),' Sir Robert proudly wrote to his son's old tutor:

> He has made a very favourable impression upon all who come in contact with him, and is confirming the hope I always entertained, that if it should please God to prolong his days and give him his health he will raise himself to eminence and distinction in the profession he has chosen. As he went out to the Mediterranean, to the great surprise of his companions, he applied himself to Grecian history, and told them that they would not laugh at him when they were off Greece and in the Archipelago and found how different from theirs the interest he should take in visiting the remarkable places they were about to see. His letters home are full of intelligence and a spirit of enterprise and [observation].

As the *Princess Charlotte* traded Tunis for the Aegean there was a chance to put his reading to use – a distant view of the Acropolis through a telescope, the Plains of Troy from the quarterdeck ('I would have given anything to go on shore ... but unluckily we were not allowed to go on account of the detestable quarantine') – but by the end of November she was back at Malta again, and at the heart of Britain's Mediterranean presence. 'On Thursday last at daylight we hauled down the quarantine flag, and are now in Pratique' – cleared to go ashore – Peel wrote to his mother from Valetta Harbour, where under the golden ramparts and the baroque splendour of Malta's turbulent and exotic past he was treated to his first, gloriously parochial demonstration of just how unbendingly *English* that presence was.

> Yesterday, Friday, the Hastings 74 with the Royal Standard at the main arrived. The Queen Dowager, I believe was very much delighted at the different things which the ships did. We all mounted guards, and directly the Hastings let go her anchor every ship together fired a Royal Salute of 21 guns, and for some minutes you could not see anything ... The next day Saturday ... we were saluting continually and on Sunday after Divine Service the Queen

Dowager and all her suite came on board us to see the ship. She was over every part of it, and was particularly pleased with our Gun Room where the Midshipmen live. While she was there the Queen Dow. sent for me and she held out her hand to me, and asked me several questions but told me in particular that you and dearest Papa and all were quite well ... after she left us she went to some other ships and the next time I was on board the Hastings to see Lord Howe [Queen Adelaide's chamberlain] the Dowager Queen sent for me and made me stop in her cabin some time, asking me several questions and showing me the different things she had collected on her passage. Her cabin was small but very comfortable and beautifully fitted out.

It was an object lesson – if he needed one after the Revd Phelps – in just how far and fast the Peels had moved in the four decades since Pitt had given them their baronetcy. As late as 1841 the second Sir Robert could still be nervous at his daughter's presumption in attracting the affections of Lord Jersey's heir, but for the fourteen-year-old grandson of a cotton spinner, blessed with William's looks, grace and easy assumption of *belonging*, there were no such worries. 'I had a luncheon on board there with Lord Howe and some others,' he continued to his mother. 'I saw Ldy G Curzon whom I scarcely remembered. I spent a capital evening there having plenty to say and talk about on both sides.'

'This evening yesterday the Queen,' – wintering in Valetta for her health – 'at least Lord Howe sent me an invitation to a dancing party or tea party, as the note called it,' he wrote again a fortnight later,

and as I was just shoving off from the ship the letter bags arrived from the steamer which had at last arrived and there were two letters for me from Dearest papa and you. I just read them over, saw that you were all quite well, put the letters in my pocket and arrived just in time at the Palace where I spent a very pleasant evening and danced several Quadrilles making a few mistakes in the first one, as I was quite out of time not having danced for a long time. I enjoyed it altogether very much.

Besides the dancing and sightseeing – his aesthetic tastes were as fallible as his father's – he was also taking drawing lessons and looking for someone to whom he might sit for a miniature, but it only took a missed mail packet or the thought of 'dear old Drayton' to dampen his spirits. 'Today we had such a merry Christmas,' he wrote bravely on his first Christmas away from home.

> I hope you all enjoyed and passed a merry one at Old Drayton ... Each mess had garlands of flowers with candles round them and all sorts of curious things such as Victoria etc and on the tables were placed large lumps of plum pudding when the band played for the ship's company to dine all the lower deck first were [fed] and the candles round the garlands lighted and all the crew began attacking their dinners they seemed all so happy and comfortable, in the gun room we also had excellent fun and in the evening got up a snap dragon and other sorts of games. Christmas day the packet is due and if we had but received our letters also on that day it would have been twice as nice. Today Wednesday the packet arrived but I am so sorry there is no letter for me. I suppose there must be some mistake in the delivery but I have inquired but there are none for me. It is a very great pity but I saw in the paper dearest Papa's name.

There was also no escaping another constant of naval life. 'This morning two men were flogged,' he wrote to his mother – the son of an unflinching 'hanger' of a Home Secretary jostling for mastery over a naturally tender young boy,

> and I will describe it to you ... A 5 bells AM which is half past 6 the whole ships company are ordered on deck, and all the officers in dress, and the culprit stands on one side of the main mast under a guard, waiting for the Captain to come. When the Captain comes on deck, he orders the man to be flogged, and the man takes off his frock and the man is shackled upon a grating ... and his hands and feet are shackled and tied. Then the quarter Master takes one step forward with the cat o nine tails lifted up in the air, and then lets it strike the man's back. It is dreadful, to hear the man cry out and to see his back after each strike, the man this morning received three dozen. I only waited for one man to be flogged, and then was obliged to go down, as I did not like the sight very much.

It was an ugly lesson, but one that the young Peel steeled himself to absorb. It was the third flogging he had witnessed in as many weeks, he told his mother, but they had 'all deserved it' and this man 'fully'. And if harder souls than his recoiled from the routine brutality of the peacetime navy, he need only have looked across to where HMS *Asia* – Sir Edward Codrington's flagship at Navarino – was anchored alongside the *Princess Charlotte* to be reminded of the grimmer realities that lay behind it. It would have been a reminder, too, of why the young boy, fed on a diet of Captain Marryat's adventures, had joined the navy in the first place. He wanted to fight.

III

At the end of the first year of William Peel's time in the *Princess Charlotte* Britain seemed as close to war as she had been at any time since Navarino. Over the decade since the end of the Greek conflict the fragile settlement in the eastern Mediterranean had all but unravelled, and with a belligerent Palmerston at the Foreign Office determined to uphold Turkish integrity and France's Prime Minister Louis Thiers supporting Mohammed Ali's dynastic and expansionist ambitions in Egypt and Syria, relations between two of the three powers that had won Navarino were as bad as they had been in a generation.

Behind this was the perpetual problem of nineteenth-century diplomacy – the decline of Turkey, Tsarist ambitions, British interests in the East – and with the advent of Mohammed Ali the permutations on the 'Eastern Question' had become more complex than ever. In any rational world France and Britain would have worked in concert to keep Russia out of the Mediterranean, but with Thiers bent on his own sub-Napoleonic agenda in Egypt and Palmerston prepared to get into bed with the autocracies if that meant preserving Turkey, 1839 closed with the bizarre probability that if there was to be a war in the east – and that seemed inevitable given Mohammed Ali's seizure of Syria the previous June – Britain and France would again find themselves on opposite sides.

There is a frustrating gap in William's letters for this period, but when they resumed in the summer of 1840, the *Princess Charlotte* was in the eastern Mediterranean, where she had been for most of the last year, lending some badly needed muscle to Palmerston's diplomacy. 'Since my last letter we have been cruising about,' William

wrote on 1 August from off Mount Athos, where Stopford had kept
his flagship while a powerful squadron under Commodore Charles
Napier cruised off Beirut in support of an insurrection against
Mohammed Ali's occupying Egyptians.

> We have had four very pleasant days at sea, and every evening a
> magnificent view of Mount Athos which rises to a great height
> from the sea, whilst the land round is too low to be seen ... The
> next morning ... a party including myself went ashore for a trip to
> the Plains of Philippi. Only three of us could get horses, so of course
> we young ones had to walk [25 miles, there and back, and the
> temperature on board ship 97 in the evening shade]. I enjoyed it
> all very much, particularly the first 4 miles which lead over the
> mountainous lands around and where one has a very pretty view
> of the town ... into the magnificent plain of Philippi [scene of the
> defeat of Brutus and Cassius] ... About 3½ miles on we came to
> an immense square block of marble 16 feet high and 9 broad, with
> an inscription on it, but which cannot be distinguished after the
> first four lines. It has a wreath round the top, and the block stands
> on a pedestal. There was once I believe a statue of Brutus on the
> top but we saw only the square hole in which it was fastened. We
> then went on and came to some very pretty ruins, the remains of
> an open assembly house, and close to the left there is a very steep
> rocky hill with an old roman tower on top ... Here one must have
> had a splendid view of the whole action. Something struck me at
> the time when I was looking down upon the field of Battle, which
> I dare say will strike dear Julia when she reads this letter, and sees
> that I have been on the 'Plains of Philippi', and which I will leave
> for her to tell you.

Peel was growing up – only fifteen still, but no longer the small boy
with only the barest scraps of schooling behind him – and with
Palmerston's patience running out it was just as well. 'It appears now
there is going to be no humbug,' Peel wrote from off Mitylene a fortnight later, after a visit to the Thracian birthplace of Mohammed Ali
at Kavalla, 'and that we are now to be in earnest. By the despatches
the Wasp brought we sent off immediately the Ganges and Thunderer
to Beirut. The Asia and Wasp sailed the next day for, I believe, the
same place. An Austrian steamer touched here, and a Turkish man
of war steamer ... carrying down the final proposals from the four

powers to Mehmet Ali which he was to accept within twenty days: and if not we were to force him.'

No one for a moment imagined that Mohammed Ali would accept a compromise – the man who raised himself from peasant origins, slaughtered his Mamelukes, sent his son Ibrahim to bring back the 'ashes of the Peloponnese' and tyrannised Egypt into the nineteenth century had not got where he was by moderation – but Stopford was prepared to give diplomacy one last chance. 'You will see by this letter that we are now at Alexandria,' Peel wrote again, while the fleet waited impatiently for the amnesty and final negotiations to run their course.

> August 24th at 4 AM we made sail and by daylight (it was my morning watch) we observed the top of Pompey's Pillar and a forest of shipping. We anchored off Alexandria that morning and found lying here the Bellerophon, Cyclops and Hydra. This is all our force at present, but the Austrians have two frigates and a corvette here. Mehmet has 19 sail of the line and as to Alexandria the whole is bristling with guns, and beautiful forts. He has, I believe, 14,000 regulars in garrison but including his fleet etc has to find food for 40,000 men … We cannot of course as yet expect to go ashore, and I hope when we do, it will be in a different manner than usual … We look very warlike as all our cutlasses are sharpened, and the guns loaded … As to the men, their ideas are that they are going to fight, but who they do not exactly know. The French fleet is still at Smyrna, but I suppose will be here shortly.

The last French papers Peel had seen were from 8 August, but from the tone of those France was clearly as 'talkative of war' as ever, and as the *Princess Charlotte* sat out its quarantine and the deadline on the ultimatum approached, excitement on board mounted. 'It is quite certain that he will not accept' the allied terms, he continued his letter on the twenty-fifth, 'and of course he will look to France for some hope. You have no idea how all hands wish to have war with France. The Austrians in their frigates are quite mad about it.'

Peel was to be disappointed by the French – the same day a steamer arrived with the news that they had hung their client pasha out to dry – but Mohammed Ali was made of sterner stuff, and on 5 September repaid Peel's faith in his intransigence by formally rejecting the allied ultimatum. It was what the fleet had been waiting for, and the next day, with diplomacy over, the *Princess Charlotte*, in company with the *Bellerophon*, *Zebra* and *Phoebe*, quitted Alexandria to join Napier's squadron off the Syrian coast. 'You see we are now at Beirut and hostilities commenced the moment of our arrival,' Peel wrote home as he watched preparations for the disembarkation of Napier's force of six thousand Turks and the fleet's marines – 'about 1400 in number as fine a body of men as ever could be found ...

> The whole point was covered with troops, which in the after-noon, appeared in large numbers as if to show their force to us. Then the first hostilities commenced ... Of course there was great excitement for the expedition, but the marines were the lucky ones. I was in great hopes, that the Field Piece was going in which case I should have gone with it, as I, I am glad to say, belong to it ... It was a glorious spiriting sight to see our 168 marines with knapsacks, haversacks, two days grub, water, carriers, etc fully armed and ranged up on deck for embarkations as they are a glorious set of fellows, and if they can get close to the Egyptians they will charge them, even so numerous, and make them open their eyes.

The hatred of the Egyptian occupation, and Ibrahim's traditional ferocity, had already provoked a native uprising, and Stopford intended Napier's force to join up with the rebel Druse, Moun-taineers, Maronites and any deserters they could attract. On the morning of the tenth a diversionary feint was made at the northern point of the bay, and at 'about 11 o'clock', as the Egyptian troops on shore swarmed to meet it, 'the Powerful Com Napier bore up', made the signal for the vessels to close, and, under a ferocious covering fire from *Edinburgh* and *Benbow*, 'put before the wind and, with the steamers, ran down to the bottom of the bay' – marked with an 'X' on his map by Peel – and disembarked his men.

Beirut's only defences were some old and impotent Venetian forts 'patched up with a few guns mounted', and Stopford had no wish to inflict any more damage than necessary. The fire of the fleet had been directed against the Egyptian soldiers and not the town, and with his men safely disembarked Stopford sent ashore a flag of truce, summoning its governor to negotiate its surrender. 'His excuse was that he could not understand it,' Peel continued when no governor appeared. 'It was then sent again in some other language and an answer was returned. I do not know exactly what it was but Soliman asked [to be given until] tomorrow morning to consider it.'

Intelligence of a thousand Egyptian cavalry only hours from Beirut explained the governor's dilatoriness, and at 6 p.m. *Bellerophon*, *Edinburgh* and *Ganges* opened fire on the now deserted town. 'And a dreadful one it was,' Peel wrote. 'The Austrian Admiral's frigate joined in. It was soon sunset and dark enough to make it almost a night cannonade, it was a magnificent sight, the fort returned a few shots but the first broadside from the Ganges totally destroyed it, all firing ceased at about 8 at which time the greater part of the place was destroyed.'

With Mohammed Ali's fleet under a tight blockade in Alexandria, and allied frigates free to range up and down the coast as they liked, Stopford was ready to expand the range of operations. On the four-teenth the *Princess Charlotte* moved from off Beirut to the nearby Antoura Bay, and under the cover of her guns Napier began to fortify his encampment and consolidate his land forces. 'We had distributed several thousand stand of arms among the Mountaineers,' Peel wrote home on the nineteenth, puzzled – as well he might be – at the shift-ing loyalties and religious complexities of Levantine politics,

> but it appears that the Druses still remain faithful to Mehmet Ali as none of them hardly has come over to us. The Maronites are our friends. They come down by the hundred every day to receive arms and come aboard to see the ships with their priests. They are a remarkably fine set of men, quite enthusiastic in the Turkish cause and have a deadly and joint hatred against the Egyptians and Alba-nians, particularly the latter who have committed the greatest cruel-ties upon them. They are, you know Roman Catholics, with the exception of course of the Pope. The Druses on the contrary are Mohammedans and are said to have among them still some remnants of the ancient paganism ...

It was frustrating for Peel to be stuck on board the flagship, but with the fleet's resources already stretched to the limit, there was always hope. 'The seamen as usual, distinguished themselves in dragging the guns up the rock when the Artillery had pronounced it as almost impossible,' he told his parents. 'I expect to be ordered to go with our field piece which is ashore in battery every day, as the Lieutenant in command of it, applied for me and you may be sure that I have been to Captain Fanshawe begging him to let me go, which he would instantly if it were not that there are not officers enough to do the duty aboard.'

Peel's hopes were unfounded – within the month northern Syria was under Turkish control without his assistance – but even with Ibrahim defeated on land and Beirut, Djebail and Sidon recaptured, there was one great prize still to come. On 31 October the *Princess Charlotte* weighed for the south, and two days later, a little after sunset on 2 November – Peel's sixteenth birthday – dropped anchor alongside the *Powerful* 84, *Thunderer* 84, *Bellerophon* 80, *Revenge* 78, *Edinburgh* 74, *Castor* 36 and *Carysfort* 28, two miles off the old Crusader fortress town of Acre.

That same night Stopford was joined by the rest of his force, and the next morning the fleet beat to quarters and cleared for action, knocked down bulkheads and cabins, sent 'all useful things below' and took their first proper look at Acre. It 'stands on the northern side of the bay', Peel explained to his father, 'situated in a sandy plain with high land all around it. It is very strong, particularly on the land side as the walls there are of immense thickness and mounted with heavy cannon. The sea wall is not so strong [one] being I believe 18 feet and the other 30. There was a large camp of cavalry round the town placed there, I suppose to prevent any of the garrison escaping.'

The fortress of Acre had in fact changed little in appearance since the days of Saladin and Richard I, with its limestone sea walls, washed to the south and west by the Mediterranean, jutting out to sea in the shape of a sharply angled redan. In more recent times the name was associated in British minds with the heroics of Sir Sydney Smith, and for those officers like Peel who had missed out on all the fun of Djebail and Sidon, it offered a last chance, as he disingenuously told his father, for the fleet's *ships* to distinguish themselves.

On the morning of 3 November – in one of those symbolic moments in nineteenth-century naval history that Frank Hastings should have lived to see – Stopford transferred his flag to the steamer *Phoenix* in order to take more effective control of the battle. In his initial plan he had envisaged a simultaneous attack on the two sea walls of the fortress, with a division under Captain Collier in the thirty-six-gun *Castor* dealing with its southern defences while his heavier ships led by Commodore Charles – 'Black Charley', 'Mad Charley' – Napier in *Powerful* engaged the stronger western flank.

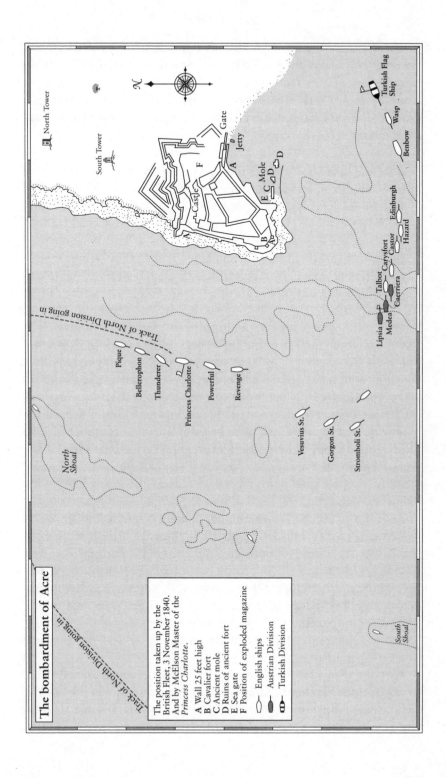

The bombardment of Acre

The position taken up by the
British Fleet, 3 November 1840.
And by McElson Master of the
Princess Charlotte.

A Wall 25 feet high
B Cavalier fort
C Ancient mole
D Ruins of ancient fort
E Sea gate
F Position of exploded magazine

⌒ English ships
⬗ Austrian Division
⬗ Turkish Division

North Tower

South Tower

Gate
Jetty
Castle
F
A
E C Mole
B
D
D

Turkish Flag
Ship
Wasp
Benbow

Edinburgh
Hazard
Castor
Carysfort
Talbot
Guerriera
Lipsia
Medea

Track of North Division going in

Pique
Bellerophon
Thunderer
Princess Charlotte
Powerful
Revenge

Vesuvius St.
Gorgon St.
Stromboli St.

North
Shoal

Track of North Division going in

South
Shoal

The vicious offshoot of a famous fighting family, the fifty-four-year-old Napier might have got his first nickname from his swart complexion, but the second he had earned on merit. 'About fourteen stone,' one not unsympathetic observer described the shambling, grubby, unkempt Hogarthian charms of the man entrusted with leading the action,

> stout and broad built; stoops from a wound in his neck, walks lame
> from another in his leg. Turns out one of his feet, and has a most
> slouching, slovenly gait; a large round face, with black, bushy
> eyebrows, a double chin, scraggy, grey, uncurled whiskers and thin
> hair; wears a superfluity of shirt collar and small neck-handker-
> chief, always bedaubed with snuff, which he takes in immense
> quantities; usually his trousers far too short, and wears the ugliest
> pair of old shoes he can find.

If it had just been his appearance his officers might have forgiven him – seen him, even, as a bruising throwback to less conformist times – but with his dirtiness and eccentricity went a vainglorious and contemptuous nature that could not let anyone share in the glory that was his exclusive due. From the day the *Princess Charlotte* arrived off Beirut Napier had resented the ageing and kindly Stopford's authority, and at every turn since had done his best to undermine it, disobeying orders, monopolising every glamorous operation and – worst of all in the eyes of a service that placed a high value on loyalty – conducting his own subversive and critical correspondence with Palmerston and the First Lord in London behind his Admiral's back.

As Stopford's second-in-command, though, Napier could hardly be denied the 'post of honour', and at 1 o'clock, as a fresh sea breeze sprang up, the *Powerful* bore up from the south, with the *Princess Charlotte* close astern. In Stopford's battle plan the *Powerful*'s station was off the southern fort of the western wall, but instead of dropping anchor to allow the squadron to pass outside him Napier continued northward in parallel with the seaward defences, before doubling back and taking up his own self-appointed station well to the north of his proper anchorage.

With the whole line cramped up behind Napier and a critical space left in front of him, it might not have been an auspicious start to the age of steam and command mobility, but one of the few blessings of being on the lower deck of a man-of-war in a fleet action was utter ignorance of a wider world. 'At about 1pm when the ship's company had dined on raw pork and we the officers on what we could pick up,' Peel wrote, oblivious to the confusion around him,

the Powerful 84 Commodore Napier which was the leading ship, bore up. The Princess Charlotte had the 2nd post of honour and followed quite close after the Powerful. I believe the Edinburgh [in fact, Thunderer] followed us, but as to the rest, I know nothing at all. It was at about 2.20pm that the Powerful and the batteries opened fire upon each other, the former, of course, as being end on only with a bow gun, but foremost guns then began to bear and fired as quickly as possible. Meanwhile the shots from the batteries kept whizzing by us and striking the water within a few yards off, but by the greatest good luck did not strike us. I belong to the After Lower deck Quarters where of course the largest guns are, and the finest men. We had just fired our guns when turning round I saw some men by the hatchway and going up to them saw they were lowering a dead man into the cockpit. He had been struck by a grape shot on the poop, and killed on the spot. We anchored about ½ past two and having our broadsides to the batteries opened fire within 800 yards and kept it up with the greatest spirit.

If the shallows had allowed it, Stopford would have had his ships at five hundred yards, but even at a distance of eight hundred they had gained an advantage of which they were only later aware. It had never occurred to the defenders that the attackers would be able to come in even that close, and their guns had been laid for a longer range, with the result – as a grateful Peel wrote – that they

luckily fired a great deal too high and all their shots went between the masts. The batteries kept up theirs with spirit, but in half an hour, it had considerably decreased and soon after was completely silenced with the exception of three guns which we could not silence till six. You can have no idea of the way in which we worked our guns, it was nothing but one continual roar with at intervals concentrated broadsides fired together ... We kept up firing till 5.30 when as it was dark, we only fired separate guns at those three that were the only ones remaining. On account of the immense smoke it was impossible to see the objects to fire at, and orders to cease firing to allow it to clear away were frequently given. At one of these times I was looking out of the port with a seaman trying to catch a glimpse at our position and where to fire at, when a sudden gust of wind blew us both in, and thinking it must have been the windage of a shot both of us turned round to see if the other was not struck. But finding us both alive we laughed heartily and supposed it had gone through the deck above. That same sensation struck everyone and it was found ... [that a] magazine ashore in the town had blew up and destroyed between 12 and 15 hundred men.

By seven in the evening every gun ashore had been silenced, and with nothing to be seen until morning, the *Princess Charlotte* hauled off and made sail for her old berth to wait for light. 'Most of the other ships did the same,' Peel continued,

and the next morning we saw several ships with a topmast or yard struck and repairing damage. Our own were very few, as I told you the enemy fired a great deal too high, and never corrected the mistake for there were shot continually whizzing between our masts. Our jolly boat was smashed by a large shot going through it. The dingy [sic], a small boat, also had a shot through her, three or four struck the poop, and the mizzen stay, and several back-stays, braces etc were shot away.

With only one death – Ed. Gordon (AB) – the *Princess Charlotte* had come out of an action in which she had fired 4,408 round shot lightly, but it was a bloodier story ashore. Stopford had intended to resume the bombardment the next day, but on the morning of the fourth a deserter from the town came aboard a Turkish man-of-war at the extreme east of the southern division with the news that Acre was defenceless and the battle over. Three hundred Turks were immediately landed to secure a base, and the following morning reinforcements poured ashore to occupy the town. Acre, they found, as they hoisted the Ottoman standard over the citadel, was still burning. 'I have not been ashore yet,' Peel wrote on the next day,

but those who have say the ground is covered with dead and dying men and animals ... The tremendous explosion must have weakened the garrison a great deal but it is impossible that any battery on shore can stand against the tremendous fire that comes from line of battle ships. The walls are shattered to pieces, the guns are dismounted and of course the houses of the inhabitants are pierced with shot ... We have made about 3000 prisoners and the remainder of the garrison who escaped with the governor are pretty sure to be captured by the Mountaineers. I am afraid that now Acre is taken, there is no other place along the whole coast where our ships can distinguish themselves, except Alexandria which is by nature almost inaccessible to ships of war.

Peel was right – his fighting was over – but a visit ashore two days after the bombardment had done something to cool a sixteen-year-old's blood lust. 'I am exceedingly glad we have left Acre,' he wrote home on 10 November from an anchorage 'in a bay called St George's where ... they say that St George killed the dragon':

We have all seen enough of dead men, for the beach for a long distance was covered with dead men, women, children, camels, donkeys ... It is wonderful to see the effect of the fire of the different ships. The walls are shattered to pieces and the embrasures particularly are completely knocked away ... Several of the guns have been completely cut in two, capsized or have their carriages knocked away ... But the worst part was that alongside the guns lay the bodies of the gunners ... After we had finished walking round the sea wall ... we then came to the place where the immense explosion was during the action, and where between 12 and 25 hundred men were so suddenly seen out of this world. The place looked exactly like the crater of a volcano. All round every thing had been levelled to the ground, and even the walls of the fortifications a long way off were split in all directions. There lay a mass of dead men and all sorts of animals at the bottom and the Turkish soldiers instead of removing them kept digging up the Egyptians for the sole purpose of taking the few piastres in their pockets.

There was a second disillusioning postscript to Acre, when the smouldering ill-feeling between Stopford and his second-in-command threatened to turn into a court martial and public scandal, but with Votes of Thanks, decorations and promotions in the offing, no one wanted to tarnish a victory that had demonstrated to the world the 'irresistible' power of the British Navy. 'L'éffet moral,' the Austrian Minister at Constantinople wrote to his government, 'que produira

cet événement est incalculable. St Jean d'Acre est regardée comme la
clef de la Syrie, dont les habitants se souviennent qu'il fallu à Ibrahim
Pasha une armée de 40,000 hommes, et dix mois de temps pour la
prendre, non sans essuyer des pertes considerables.'

And the Royal Navy had taken it in a day. Nobody in the fleet
forgot the cost – a large-scale painting of Acre, done by a shipmate
and given to Peel, was to be lithographed in England with the prof-
its to go to 'the relief of the widows, children and relations of the
Blue Jackets and Marines killed in the whole Syrian War' – but as
wars go, it had been pretty near perfect. The major European conflict
that Thiers confidently predicted had been avoided. The great problem of nineteenth-century diplomacy had been successfully put on
hold for another fourteen years. France – never an idle consideration
in naval circles – had been humiliated and Mohammed Ali successfully reined in. It had been achieved, too, with a speed and economy
of means that made it a model of its kind. Within a week Stopford
could report that there was nothing more for his ships to do, and by
the middle of January 1841 the Turkish fleet had been restored to
Ottoman control. On 13 July Mohammed Ali was recognised as
hereditary Pasha of Egypt under the suzerainty of the Sultan, the
Bosphorus and the Dardanelles were closed to warships, and Turkey
formally placed under the protection of the guaranteeing powers.
Palmerston's triumph was complete. 'Every country that has towns
within cannon shot of deep water,' he ominously announced, 'will
remember the operations of the British Fleet on the coast of Syria in
1840.' And if those were words that would come back to haunt the
navy fifteen years later in front of Sevastopol, there were few people
who would have taken exception to them in 1841.

IV

On 19 July 1841, a newly appointed midshipman dashed off a quick
note from on board his ship at Portsmouth for John Wilson Croker,
Peelite confidant and formidable Secretary to the Admiralty. 'My
Dear Mr Croker,' it read,

> I received your kind note this morning and was very glad to see
> you are so well. I shall have the greatest pleasure in accepting your
> invitation to dinner tomorrow Tuesday, but I am not certain about

being able to sleep out of the ship. I will not tell you any news about myself, and the ship, but will reserve it for your dinner table. I am quite well, and am glad to say have been so ever since I left England. So goodbye for the present, my dear Mr Croker, as I am

Yours sincerely William Peel.

There were not many people of three times Peel's age who would have felt confident in addressing Croker with such easy familiarity, but if at the age of sixteen he was as aware as Croker himself that he was not 'many people', it would be nice to think he also knew how lucky he had been. For forty years in the second half of the century the great Sir George Tryon would spend his life training and planning for a war that never came, but by the age of sixteen Peel had seen and survived his first major action, made his mark with his superiors and come home to an England in which his father – after six creative years in opposition, reconstructing a Conservative Party shattered by the Great Reform Act – was about to resume office as Prime Minister.

An enthusiastic Croker would soon be reporting to Drayton that William spoke 'with an intelligence and aplomb ... more like 26 than 16', but Peel's father needed no prompting. 'I can hardly justify on any reasonable grounds my early presentiments that my boy (if it pleased God to spare and protect him) will be a distinguished man,' he wrote to his old colleague and future Chancellor, Henry Goulburn,

but I must say that everything I have heard from him, or of him, since he entered his profession, has justified and confirmed it.

The kind interest you take about him encourages me to send you the two last letters which we have received from him. I showed them to two distinguished captains in the navy, who were very much struck by such a detail of naval operation from a boy, and by the combination of professional spirit and intelligence.

He could not resist sending them to the Great Duke either. 'I am very much obliged to you for having sent me the letters from your son William, which are very interesting,' Wellington wrote back from Walmer Castle with rather more judicious praise:

Encourage him by all means to write down his observations upon
the operations of which he is the witness, or in which he is an actor;
and above all to revise them after writing them, and correct any
error into which he may have fallen, leaving on the face of the paper
the error and its correction. This habit will accustom him to an
accurate observation and report of facts; which are most important,
destined as he most likely is to direct and carry on great operations.

The absurd pleasure this gave Sir Robert amused the vinegary old
Duke – it made Peel 'quite gay and *déboutonné*', he told a friend –
but Peel would have been as pleased to see his son if he had been
coming back from Harrow rather than Acre. He had only checked
himself from going to Portsmouth for fear of crossing with William
on the way, and sent instead fussy instructions on the best connections for Drayton – Portsmouth to London, and then Tamworth by
'the Birm. and Derby ... in six hours ... but the porter at Whitehall
will give you full directions'. 'I am in great hopes we shall be paid
off on Friday,' William wrote back, overladen with swag after three
years away from home and every bit as much the railway bore as his
father.

Julia has made out in her letter [complete with a piece of her
wedding cake] that it would be the quickest way to pass through
Bedford stopping at Middleton a night ... The poor porter in
London will not know what to do with the many boxes that I have
sent to him ... Did dearest Mamma get the orange trees, three in
number ... They were very carefully packed up and were in a high
state of preservation particularly the mandarin, notwithstanding
the rough treatment they necessarily met with in our bath on the
passage home.

William had missed his sister's wedding to Lord Villiers by only days,
but mere family news was soon competing with the more traditional
concerns of every midshipman. It was important to him that his time
of service should continue while he was at home, and he was keen to
be 'entered on the books of Some Flagship', he told his father, 'and
then have leave from that ship. I wish you would tell me what you
would prefer doing. There is no vacancy in the Queen at present or
in any ship here I believe.'

It seems very likely that his father overcame his scruples about interfering in his son's career, because after a short time in *Monarch* backdated to the day he left the *Princess Charlotte*, Peel was carried on the books of the royal yacht *William & Mary*, before joining the thirty-six-gun *Cambrian* bound for the China station and what he hoped would be a further chance to see action.

This was a reasonable enough hope, because for the past two years Britain had been shamefully mired in a war precipitated by a determined effort on the part of the Chinese to eradicate the import of opium. The trade in opium – carried out by the East India Company and independent merchants – had in fact been illegal since the eighteenth century, but a system of semi-official toleration, bribery and corruption had left it to flourish virtually unchecked, reducing anything up to ten million people to a state of hopeless addiction in order to fill merchant coffers and swell the revenues of the British government through its reciprocal duties on tea.

There was no great love of the trade in official circles, but when the first Chinese crackdown in 1839 resulted in the impounding of British goods, the arrest of British citizens and insults to the British flag, national indignation went into predictable overdrive. 'Our China merchants,' Thomas Macaulay declared, out-Palmerstoning Palmerston,

> belonged to a country unaccustomed to defeat, to submission or to shame; to a country which had exacted such reparation for the wrongs of her children as had made the ears of all who heard it to tingle; to a country which had made the Bey of Algeria humble himself in the dust before her insulted consul; to a country which had avenged the victims of the Black Hole on the field of Plassey ... They knew that, surrounded as they were by enemies, and separated by great oceans and continents from all help, not a hair of their heads would be harmed with impunity.

If it was neither a just war nor an equal one – a medieval army and a navy of war junks and fireships was no match for modern warships and an army of four thousand men – it was never likely to be a short one, with Palmerston on one side and the Chinese Emperor on the other. In its earliest, desultory days the campaign had been little more than 'a series of skirmishes', but at the beginning of 1841 Palmerston raised the ante by sending out a new commander, Sir Henry

Pottinger, with a punitive brief to open up four more trading ports, take Chusan island, secure the annexation of Hong Kong, extort a massive indemnity and demand the legalisation of the opium trade – a measure that, in Palmerston's words, would be in 'the interest of the Chinese government itself'.

It was at this stage in 'one of the most lawless, unnecessary and unfair struggles in the records of history' that the *Cambrian* weighed for the East. 'I have just been reading over the many kind letters I received from you whilst in the Mediterranean,' Peel wrote to his father and mother, untroubled, it seems, by anything more disturbing than leaving England again after only three months, 'and I find them always a never failing and most pleasing pleasure. How glad I am I brought them with me; and although they are only a selection, they take up a great part of my desk. They are quite a book of reference ... of all the happy events that are continually passing at home.'

He had a long voyage of five months ahead of him, but the newly built *Cambrian* – the frigate made famous by Captain Hamilton in the Greek War had foundered – was a wonderfully good sailor, and ship life was transformed by the presence of Lord Ellenborough, on his way out to India to succeed Auckland as Governor-General. 'Lord Ellenborough enjoys the most excellent health,' Peel reported on the waywardly talented, vain and grandiloquent son of Cochrane's old Stock Exchange nemesis:

> his kindness to me is excessive. I shall be quite lonely when he leaves us, and really, although anxious to arrive at Calcutta, I look to it also occasionally with great regret, as being the bounds to the happy hours I spend in his company. Every hour and even every minute not required for professional duties I pass in his own private cabins where he has an excellent library and where I have every convenience for reading as a small table and chairs are fitted round one of the port holes, and the gun removed forward. It is about the coolest place in the ship, which in the Tropics is the first consider-ation.

There was also the more traditional and forcible cooling, when Neptune and his court, 'rigged out in sheepskins and painted in all sorts of colours', came aboard at the equator to 'visit his children' crossing the line for the first time. Lord Ellenborough was allowed to buy his way out of the initiation with 'a tribute' for the old seaman playing Neptune,

> but we poor unfortunate fellows were shoved below under charge of several constables and were called up one by one to pass the dreadful ordeal. What they did to the men who had not passed before, was this. The man was blindfolded and led up by two constables, trembling from head to foot. The moment he reached the top of the ladder he became quite confounded by buckets of water thrown on him before he could recover from this shock a force pump was playing on his face, he was then seated on a three legged stool on the brink of the precipice where the water was confined in a large sail. The Barber then went up to him with a brush full of tar, dabbed it over his face, asked the poor fellow a question and as he answered the question, shoved it into his mouth. He then took a rough piece of iron with which he tore off the tar from his face and while the sufferer was endeavouring though in vain to extricate himself the three legged stool was tipped from under him, away he went head over heals [sic] into the large sheet of water, where three of the strongest men dressed up as bears were ready to pounce upon him and keep him under water.

The officers were treated rather less roughly, but it was another step in Peel's naval life, another boundary crossed, and he embraced it with the same enthusiasm he brought to every new experience. 'Although this station' – China – 'has the great disadvantage of being so very far removed from home,' he wrote with a mildly priggish earnestness that he never entirely lost, 'I think, when I return, I shall look back upon the short period I shall have spent in these countries with the greatest satisfaction. The seeing the principal places in India, Singapore and particularly China must give me great practical knowledge and experience.'

There could still be 'dear old Drayton' moments, prompted by the thought of taking the Sacrament at Christmas, or the sight of Orion in an unfamiliar sky as, cocoa in hand, Peel walked the forecastle on his night watches, but by 27 December he was happily writing home that they were 'safe and snug in St Simon's Bay'. 'The mist then cleared up,' he reported of his first excited impression of the Cape from the deck of the *Cambrian*, 'and gave us a beautiful view of Table Mountain, and the surrounding scenery. I could not before appreciate, as it deserved, the daring, skill and courage of those who first discovered this land and I can now indeed imagine their joy. The Cape itself is a mass of sharp and steep rocks, not very high, but it leaves its picture in my mind so strong that though in itself not very remarkable, I shall never forget it.'

The *Cambrian* was at Simon's Bay for eleven days, and as everywhere, the Peel name was guaranteed to 'ensure me wherever I go, kindness and attention'. On the second day he had ridden the twenty-three miles up to Cape Town to pay his respects to the Governor, and after signing the visitors' book at a pretty Dutch winery on his return was pursued back to the ship with the present of 'two casks of the best Constantia' – one for the Queen, and one for Sir Robert. 'I at first endeavoured quietly and very civilly to refuse his present,' he explained apologetically to his father, 'but finding him firm and very anxious I agreed to write a letter that should accompany it, and thanked him very much for the kindness and the great respect in which he held your name.'*

Mr S.V. Van Benen had other interests beyond his wine, and after showing Peel and his shipmates around the cellars, had taken them into 'a little room in which were perfectly exact full scale models, taken from life, of all the different tribes of savages that border on the frontier. They are wonderfully executed,' William wrote, opening up a curious window on the world of a young Harrovian Victorian empire-builder of more than average piety,

> look like life itself and give one an exact idea of what these savages are. They were so interesting, I could have stopped all day looking at them. The Bushman is the most curious. He is a *very small* man, face and particularly eyes flat, but with enormous sized muscles on his hips, so as to be quite a deformity … Of all these savages there was only one, that seemed naturally intellectual and capable of being civilised. The others must rank with the brute creation, or at most, be looked upon as the connecting link between man and the brute creation.

---

* It could cut both ways of course, and William would have to undergo a rigorous quizzing across the breakfast table from the Bishop of Calcutta over his father's position on religious matters: 'he had at length forgiven Sir Robert for his conduct on the Catholic question, but that it was long before he could forgive him…"What does your father mean to do with us"' he asked William.

On 6 January 1842 the *Cambrian* weighed again for Calcutta, and with 'Neptune and Aeolus' doing her no favours, and Ellenborough anxious to assume his self-designated role as India's new Akbar, even Peel could not wait to get there. 'Although I shall not look back upon this long voyage with any great degree of pleasure,' he wrote home a month later, with the Indian coast and Madras still twelve days away, 'yet I shall always feel the benefit of it, as, from there being nothing to distract the mind, and lead it to different pursuits, it has been a period of un-remitted reading of really valuable books.'

The *Cambrian* had originally planned on sailing straight on for Calcutta, but the news waiting at Madras of the slaughter of the retreating British column in the passes of Afghanistan put paid to that. 'I need not tell you how delighted I am to hear of the birth of the Prince of Wales,' Peel rushed off a short note on 21 February, before writing at length the next day a letter that reads more like a transcript of his Government House dinner than Peel himself.

> The Indian news is bad 500 men (but I suppose the truth is 3500) of the army ... including many officers of distinction, have been cut off by treachery and murdered. But of course, you will know all the details ... But what has most surprised me is the vile news-paper press. It is astonishing, that in such an immense country and population as this, when it is known that our chief stability rests in the good opinion and respect of the natives, and where we are but a handful, and have scarcely any real strength of our own, that persons should be allowed to publish what they please, and which must necessarily, as slander will always find more readers, and they are only intent on making money, turn with abuse and the most vulgar remarks upon the principal officers of the Government. All this abuse and everything that tends to lower the character of a public servant is ... translated into the native language by them and dispersed over the whole country by the swarms of Moonshees or description of agents who in all eastern countries, but particularly in this I believe, abound ... I hope you and Dearest mamma are quite well. Give my very best love to all, and tell Lord and Lady Jersey [Julia's new parents-in-law], from an eye witness at this very moment and same table, her son is looking quite well.

This is Peel's last extant letter from India, and after disembarking
Ellenborough and his suite at Calcutta, the *Cambrian* weighed for
Ichusan harbour, 'situated nearly in the middle of the Chinese coast'.
'I will not talk to you now about the Chinese war and politics,' Peel
rather grandly told his mother – letters that 'counted' were now
invariably to his father:

> You will be very curious to know the peculiarities of the China
> Coast ... It is very mountainous, or rather hilly and except in the
> valleys, apparently rocky or covered with a thin soil. The ingenu-
> ity and perseverance of the Chinese laugh at these natural difficul-
> ties, so that no country that I have ever seen, not even excepting
> the fine southern counties of our own land, shows such universal
> subjection to the hand of man as this.

It was just as well that Peel was so enamoured of the coastline,
because it was as much of China as he was going to see. The invaders
were so bitterly hated by the local population that no one could go
ashore except in a strongly armed party, and with a sliding bounty
scale calculated by rank for the kidnap or murder of any foreigner,
there was little encouragement for even a lowly midshipman to risk
himself.

It was not just the constraints of harbour life that irked Peel,
though, because after Syria and Acre his luck had run out. 'I am
most heartily sorry to say,' he told his mother without any obvious
irony,

> that instead of our being part of the attacking force for Nankin
> and Pekin we sail tomorrow for a place to the southward called
> Amoy where we shall be left in banishment ... neglected and passed
> over, while other ships are hurrying on in a blaze of conquest and
> distinction ... If I had an offer, I should endeavour to join some
> ship that will stop up here to the northward, but as report says we
> sail for our destination tomorrow, I must be dragged along with our
> unfortunate ship to our hopeless exile.

If this seemed grossly unfair to Peel – the *Cambrian* had been the first
of the fresh ships from England to arrive, and should have been
rewarded 'with the decided preference in any duty' – there was no
escape, and as Pottinger's troops fought, raped, burnt and pillaged

their way towards victory, a sulky Peel was forced to fester in the broiling heat of Amoy harbour.

And if it was not the heat it was the monsoon; if it was not the tedium of ship life it was restrictions on shore movements; if it was not the fatuity of taking and abandoning towns like Amoy it was Pottinger's strategic blindness; if it was not the dismal misery of Peel's exile it was the woeful inadequacies of Hong Kong as a future base for British operations. Every so often an incident or observation might still spark him into something like his old buoyancy, but for the first time in his letters one sees the volatility of temper, the extravagance of disappointment and – above all – the impatience with *time* itself, that seems something more than a mere adolescent moodiness.

'I wish I was anywhere else but here,' he was complaining to his father within days of arriving at Amoy, and with the fall of Chiankiang in July and the virtual collapse of Chinese opposition, his gloomiest fears proved justified. 'I hope all the articles in the Treaty as signed by Sir Henry Pottinger have met, not only your approval, but your approbation,' he wrote to his father without enthusiasm, when the first news of the secession of Hong Kong, $21 million compensation, open trading ports and equal diplomatic rights reached the marooned *Cambrian*.

> The Ransom money must be a most sensible relief to you, and its introduction into England gradually, and not in mass, will check the people from foolishly crying out for the reduction of the income tax [just reintroduced by Sir Robert the previous year] ... It is a great pity that Hong Kong is not better situated. I think we shall soon find it has many inconveniences, its harbour, at least that one at present occupied, could easily be made untenable by the Chinese in any future war, and no doubt will.

He was no happier about those heroic merchants of Thomas Macaulay for whom Britain had gone to war in the first place. 'Their profit and extortion are enormous,' he wrote of the masters of the opium clippers, who struck him as no better than 'the slavers on the coast of Africa'. 'I hope that our regular and honest trade will become so liberal and extensive as to drive this peculiar sect of traders entirely out of the market, though to prevent opium being imported, neither our own laws nor those of the Chinese would be of any avail. The opium smoker is like the confirmed drunkard, miserable and at last unable to live if he cannot indulge his favourite appetite.'

With the signing of the Treaty of Nanking, though, Peel's thoughts were free to return to a subject that had exercised him since his first months in the *Cambrian*. Even before the ship had reached the East he had been agitating over the route of his voyage home, and with letters taking five months to reach England – or the best part of a year for a reply if one came – he never missed an opportunity to repeat his request to be allowed to travel back overland from Calcutta. 'Remember what I have written in the proceeding letters about going home,' he wrote again in September, sketching out a sort of early Victorian 'gap year' for himself before settling back into the routines of naval life.

> I hope this time next year to commence my journey. In case these letters should have foundered, I will repeat what it is, to send me out my discharge or your private request for the Captain to give it to me, and then I would leave the ship in August to arrive at Madras or Calcutta in the beginning of September and starting from the latter place (for it would be easier to go up the Ganges by steam to Allamabad), get up as high as Delhi, and then go down to Bombay and on by steam via Alexandria to England.

The crucial factor in all this, however, was the sea time Peel needed to qualify as lieutenant, and as always his father had taken soundings among his naval connections before giving his answer. 'Dear Sir Robert Peel,' Robert Fitzroy, late of the *Beagle* and now a Member of Parliament, wrote back in response – the authentic voice of the old navy and the age of sail speaking:

> To the first – Shall he remain in China? I would reply in the negative. Every reason is *now* against him staying there.
>
> To the second – Shall he return here overland? I would answer *with less confidence* – I *think* he had better not.
>
> And to the third – Should he go from Amoy to the Cape Station – my reply would be – yes, and thence by the first *Man of War* to England.
>
> Letters sent now would probably reach the Cambrian in about five months. If Mr William Peel went immediately to Calcutta he would make his overland journey during the heat of summer – lose

two or three months sea *time* (for serviture of six years) unless specially arranged otherwise by the Admiralty, lose practice on board ship and see more than enough of steamers.

By returning to England in a Man of War he would be kept in constant practice as to navigation as well as seamanship and would be ready to pass his examination in England prior to going on again to South America, or some other station, in search of his Lieu-tenancy.

It was a disappointment for William, but with the violent summer heat giving way to the autumn monsoons, and virulent fever to ague, he would have happily settled for any route that would get him out of Amoy and the *Cambrian*. 'My good fortune has for the present left me,' he was still complaining in October, but at least he was to be spared another Amoy summer. The following April, nine tedious months after the end of a war that had passed him by, he received his orders for a passage back to England in the *Belleisle* troopship. It had been, he told his father, 'the dullest and most miserable [time] of my whole life'.

V

The England Peel returned to in September 1843 was on the eve of one of the great political crises of the century, but for a midshipman approaching his six years' sea time there were more pressing concerns. On his arrival back at home Peel had been placed for three weeks on the books of the *Camperdown*, and in November transferred for a gunnery course to the *Excellent*, the recently commissioned training ship at Portsmouth.

Moored out in the harbour, where it could fire out across the mudflats with complete impunity, and furnished – like the residual relic of a limb on a snake – with only a mizzen rigged for sail drills, the *Excellent* had been commissioned in 1830 to end those glaring inadequacies in naval gunnery that Frank Hastings had spent his life denouncing. Its aim was to provide the navy with officers and seamen

who would know the names of the different parts of a gun and carriage the dispart in terms of lineal magnitude and in degrees how taken, what constitutes point blank and what line of metal range, windage – the errors and the loss of force attending to it, the importance of preserving shot from rust, the theory of the most material effects of different charges of powder applied to practice with a single shot, also with a plurality of balls, showing how these affect accuracy, penetration and splinters, to judge the condition of gunpowder by inspection, to ascertain its quality by the ordinary tests and trials as well as by actual proof.

Peel was in his element in this sort of atmosphere, and passed out of *Excellent* with a speed and brilliance that gave Sir Robert the opportunity to bask in the congratulations of Parliament and the Service. 'The opinion I formed of your son from the conversation I had with him, prior to his joining this ship,' Thomas Hastings, captain of *Excellent*, wrote to him on 8 May 1844,

> & the strength of character ... has been fully supported.
>
> I was informed by the captains who examined him on seamanship that he passed with great credit.
>
> I can speak from my own knowledge as to his attainments in gunnery: the full numbers are 910, your son gained 908: the time allowed for going the full course is 14 months, your son accomplished it in 5 months & four days gaining a 1:1 certificate, which has not been affected by any other person in less than 8 months and 3 weeks.
>
> Today he finished his examination in navigation, obtaining 260 numbers, the full numbers being 270; for observations he has full numbers 60. For the additional questions set to test the candidates' knowledge of some of the principles on which the cases rest, which is optional for the candidates to work, & which in fact are not often worked, he has gained 40 numbers out of 56.
>
> Your son's conduct has been exemplary. I never met with any young man who entertained correcter principles or took better views of the discipline of the navy or who acted more steadily up to them. I cannot conclude without congratulating you on his success & expressing my conviction that should the future call for exertion from the Navy he will be found in the van of those distinguished in the service of his country.

It was all joy to Sir Robert's ears, but if he was like a cat on catnip as admirals, generals and statesmen queued to assure him of their 'strong conviction' of William's destiny, the best of it all must have been that his son's success had nothing to do with interest or institutional sycophancy. 'I have not the slightest hesitation in assuring you that had such a report as the one you have enclosed to me respecting your son,' Sir George Cockburn reassured Sir Robert, 'been received in the Admiralty in behalf of any other young officer, I should at once without reference to the rank or position of his father, have pressed upon Lord Haddington of the board of Admiralty the propriety of giving him immediate promotion to the rank of Lieutenant, as an encouragement to others to imitate such example.'

After all the attentions of Lord Ellenborough and Admiral Stopford, it must have been equally satisfying for William to know he could live without the safety net of family interest, but that did not mean it was not still there, or that he was not prepared to fall back on it when it suited his purpose.* 'My dearest father,' he wrote in August from on board the *Collingwood* at Spithead – a reluctant supernumerary on Sir George Seymour's flagship for a passage out to the *Cormorant* on the Pacific station –

the Collingwood is ready for sea at an hour's notice, but we are afraid our sailing may be put off to an indefinite period, keeping us the whole time in a state of uncertainty. I am very much pleased with everything I have seen on board the Collingwood. The officers are a remarkably good set, and the ship is in beautiful order. As I have not yet received a letter, I do not know whether there is a prospect of war with France or not. Of course if there is, I shall be very sorry to go to the Pacific, when I might easily be transferred to a ship in the Mediterranean or Channel ... I hope it will soon be settled when we are to sail, for nothing can be more irksome, at least to me as a supernumerary lieutenant, than to be holding on here, half on shore and half on board.

The war with France never materialised, and on 7 September, after a two-months delay punctuated by visits from the Duke of Wellington, Prince Albert and the future German Emperor, *Collingwood* finally

---

* The summer of 1844 was a 'Royal summer' in Britain, with the Emperor of Russia and the King of Saxony both visiting. It is indicative of Peel's standing that he was appointed to the *Black Eagle*, the steam tender to the royal yacht *William and Mary* in June 1844, to escort the Emperor across to Antwerp.

left Spithead for South America and her four-year cruise in the Pacific. This was the first – and as it turned out the last – voyage the *Collingwood* would ever make, and it was in its way a historical oddity, a last chance for its youngest volunteers and middies to experience the age of sail at its expansive best and a curious glimpse for its senior officers into the future of the Victorian Royal Navy.

It was not merely that the *Collingwood* was a kind of floating hatchery for its future leaders – half a dozen captains of major ships at the Spithead review of 1867 would be old 'Collingwoods' – but that something in the moral tone and earnestness of the wardroom and gunroom inexorably pointed towards a different age. There would still be enough drunkenness, brawling and flogging to show that the old order was not going to go down without a fight, but one only has to try to imagine the young Frank Hastings preparing himself for confirmation or poring over a 'treasured' prayer book in the gunroom to recognise the divide that separates his navy from that of young volunteers like James Goodenough or Clements Markham.

And in the decade of Disraeli's 'Young England' novels, of the Eglinton Tournament and dreams of chivalry, if ever a man was born to inspire these youths with his own blend of professional seriousness and high moral purpose it was William Peel. 'His looks and bearing were greatly in his favour,' one devoted acolyte would later write of him,

> for both in face and figure there was an appearance of what sporting men, in describing well-bred horses, call 'quality'. He was about medium height, with a head gracefully set on broad, well-turned shoulders, light in lower body, and with a dignified yet easy carriage; his dark brown wavy hair was generally carefully brushed back, showing an oval face, high square forehead, and deep blue-grey eyes, which flashed when he was talking eagerly, as he did when excited. His face when in repose had a somewhat austere look, with smooth and chiselled outline, a firm-set mouth which was the more noticeable because of his being clean-shaved.

With the looks and glamour of a 'silver-fork' dandy in fact, the unembarrassed ardour of a Daniel Deronda, the inherent priggishness of the age, and a debonair and worldly lightness that pulled him back from the brink of fanaticism, William Peel was all things to all youth. With the benefit of hindsight his life seems in many ways a battleground for these different and warring elements in his nature, but for the young 'mids' whose lives he moulded they seemed in perfect harmony, and Peel himself a heroic composite of Thomas Hughes's 'Old Brooke', Victorian Parfait Knight and something more emotionally, and perhaps sexually, highly charged.

There would be a long and spirited line of midshipmen who would think of Peel in these terms, and it was perhaps inevitable that the first of these to fall under his spell was the fourteen-year-old midshipman – and future President of the Royal Geographical Society, father of Antarctic exploration and fastidious gourmet of gunroom flesh – Clements Markham. The son of a Windsor canon and the grandson of one of the most unpleasant men ever to hold the see of York, Markham had been educated at Westminster, and even in a gunroom as full of promise as the *Collingwood*'s stood out for his volatile high spirits as much as he did for the delicate good looks that made him 'the most beautiful as well as the most engaging' boy in the ship.

It would be a relief to think that there has never been another child quite like Clements Markham, or one who has left so full a record of his myriad obsessions. From his earliest schooldays he had 'collected' the human race as another boy might beetles, and his notebooks and journals from the *Collingwood* are filled with the minutest details of the ship's company: their birthplaces and backgrounds, their physical defects, family connections, accents, mannerisms and peculiarities; the whole ship's company, too, from Captain Smart – 'Smart by name, Smart by nature' – to the lowliest boy or most heroic topgallant man. 'His noble thoughts and good advice sank into my heart gradually,' he wrote of Peel, 'as the golden fruit of much converse, for the most part light and merry. We often discussed Service questions, and he explained in detail numerous points in seamanship and gunnery which I had failed to grasp. At other times he dwelt upon the life-stories of naval worthies, discussing their relative merits and their battles. He also talked of friendships; how they were formed, and how they ought to be maintained.'

The two boys – because that, after all, is what Peel was still – would spend hours together, pacing 'up and down the forecastle ... during the long night watches' or out riding after the *Collingwood* reached Valparaiso. 'It was important,' Clements's cousin, that purveyor of Evangelical gloom and naval disasters Sir Albert Markham KCB, would later write of this intimacy,

for it was a friendship that did much to shape Markham's character, and one that exerted a beneficial influence on his after-life ...
Peel's view was that an officer in the Navy should devote all his
talents and energies to the Service; that his own interests, his aims
and studies, should be subservient to the navy. But he held that a
good naval officer, besides being a good sailor, must be well
informed, especially in history, geography and poetry. He recom-
mended Markham to read Milton's 'Paradise Lost', because, he
said, 'it is the grandest poem in our language, and it is the richest
storehouse of good English words and phrases'. He also advised
him to read all the most memorable voyages and travels, and
impressed upon him that a naval officer, who kept his eyes open,
possessed unequalled opportunities of becoming a sound geographer. He frequently dilated upon the rules of conduct which from
the first he had established for his own guidance in the Navy.

There was a long and honourable tradition in the navy of such friendships – a family might ask an older lieutenant to play 'sea-daddy' to
their son – but there seems little doubt that the younger boy's feelings at least were of a very different nature. A long and happy
marriage would never be quite enough to still the rumours that would
always surround Markham's sexuality, and for the rest of his life he
would scour the navy's gunrooms in search of another Peel, listing,
courting, encouraging, patronising, petting and sighing over generations of well-connected and good-looking middies who might fill the
void in his life left by the glorious young lieutenant he fell in love
with in the *Collingwood*.

'What tenderness and what devotion,' Disraeli wrote of such
schoolboy friendships in *Coningsby*, '... what ecstatic present and
romantic future ... what earthquakes of the heart, and whirlwinds of
the soul'; but if a number of things would fall conveniently into place
if Peel were homosexual – a certain sadness, inexplicable periods of
depression, a sense of frustration, an admiration for male beauty, a
coolness towards marriage – all that can be said is that there is not a
scrap of evidence for it. Throughout his career he liked to surround
himself with young middies of the Markham stamp, yet the one
certainty is that if he ever suspected any inclinations of his own, he
would have suppressed them as ruthlessly as he crushed his fears in
front of enemy guns or cauterised his own 'softness' in the burning
sands of the Nubian desert.

The son of a Home Secretary who had sent men to the gallows for the 'crime' could, of course, do no less, but to leave it at that would be to miss the point. In his later career Peel's closest relationship was with a young boy who had to flee the country for homosexuality, but his own behaviour and sense of self were always motivated by a chivalric code of self-discipline, prayer and service that enshrined bodily and mental purity among its highest ideals.

If this came at a cost, and lies behind the profound unhappiness that seems sometimes to have seized him – and there would be times when he seems to have actively courted death – it was a cost he was ultimately willing to pay. In his letters he would sometimes talk wistfully of a future wife and home, but the more likely truth is that naval service offered Peel not just a way of realising his father's expectations of him, but an escape from the complexities of his own nature into a world of institutionalised masculine loyalties. 'I am in perfect health,' he later wrote to his sister from the Crimea, 'hard and bronzed and *always* cheerful, not as too often in England, pale and thoughtful without thinking ... It is lucky I came away.'

The whole question is of interest solely for the light it throws on the complex bonds of service loyalties, and for the charismatic nature of Peel's leadership, but in 1844, as the *Collingwood* crossed the line and midshipmen danced with Sir George Seymour's daughters, bound for their new home in Valparaiso, his preoccupations were of a more prosaic and immediate kind. 'I am in the most excellent health,' he wrote home, tanned and fit again after the cold and damp of Portsmouth harbour, 'and like the Collingwood very much. Could you tell me in your next letter, if you think it possible that I may be promoted on the S.American station when I have served my time, and appointed to some vessel out there as her commander. It would of course be the best thing for me, as then I should lose no time.'

He need not have worried. If he had any fears that the wheels of preferment were not turning smoothly, he soon had proof that the Peel charm and name were still working their magic. After a voyage of just over three months the *Collingwood* anchored at Valparaiso in the middle of December, and following two pleasant enough months of cricket, opera, riding and the yarns of Cochrane's old officers, Peel took passage in the steam sloop *Cormorant* for a secret mission to report on the viability of preserving British interests along the disputed seaboard between California and the jointly held territory of Oregon. 'His distress may well be imagined,' Albert Markham later wrote of his cousin Clements – 'leaden hearted' and shedding 'bitter tears' at the separation,

> when he was informed by Peel himself, that the Admiral was about to send him to England as the bearer of important dispatches to the Admiralty, and that he would not, in all probability, return to the *Collingwood* ... [Markham] regarded this parting as the turning-point of his career. Peel was the one man to whom he invariably looked for support and advice, and he had a great influence for good over the young cadet ... He was a boy who really needed such a guide, and he felt without him it would be difficult to avoid going astray. He ceased all attempts to conquer his temper and his self-will ... His friend had been called away to fulfil a glorious destiny, and he felt hurt at not being able to share it with him.

That 'glorious destiny' still lay some way in the future, but as William ship-hopped his way north, the mere presence of a Peel in such sensitive waters was soon attracting nervous attention. 'When we find a brother of Aberdeen and the son of Peel in company we can [not] but wonder at it,' Thomas Larkin, the United States Consul General in Monterey, remarked after Peel had transferred to the *America* under the command of Captain John Gordon. 'I consider that Peel and Aberdeen hold more power over the whole world than the united strength of any three or four kingdoms or Empires.'

If foreign consuls had got the vapours every time a British ship carrying an officer of family and consequence came into port, the world would have been in a state of permanent panic, but Larkin's concerns were not entirely unfounded. Over the past sixty years Britain and America had already gone to war twice, and throughout the early 1840s a third conflict had seemed as likely as not, with territorial disputes west of the Rockies and along the eastern border of Canada and the United States providing both 'John Bull' and 'Jonathan' with all the provocation they could want.

It was lucky for both countries that Sir Robert Peel and Aberdeen were in office during this period, and in the teeth of the predictable Palmerston bluster, a compromise had been agreed over the eastern boundary that satisfied American sensitivities and did little harm to British interests. Sir Robert's instincts in foreign affairs were invariably peaceful where peace could be reconciled with 'national honour' in this way, but when in 1845 President James Polk came to power on the populist slogan of 'Fifty-four Forty or Fight' – a reference to a line of latitude in the west that would have given the United States a border well to the north of Vancouver Island – America's 'manifest destiny' and Britain's *amour propre* seemed again set on a course for collision.

As long as war remained a possibility, the interests of the Hudson Bay Company traders and settlers had to be protected, and on 28 August 1845 the *America* arrived off Cape Flattery at the southern entrance to the Strait of Juan de Fuca. 'The object of the vessel coming here,' the Chief Factor at Fort Victoria, the fur trader Roderick Finlayson, recalled, 'was to obtain full information & report to the English Government previous to the settlement of the boundary line. During my stay on board [the *America*] Capt. Parke of the Marines [and] Lieutenant Peel, a son of Sir Robert Peel, were sent across to the Columbia River to obtain information & report on the country in relation to its value to Great Britain.'

While Gordon stayed at Fort Victoria, famously complaining of the quality of the hunting and fishing – a country, he decided in which the salmon 'did not know enough to take the fly' was not worth 'five straws' – Peel and Parke embarked in the *America*'s launch on the first part of their mission. Gordon had given them orders to make their way down Puget Sound, with enough men to deter Indians but not enough to excite American resentment, and to continue for more than a hundred miles south to Fort Vancouver, to ascertain American military preparedness and 'the actual state of the Country on the Banks of the River Columbia, and the district called Oregon'. 'On the 8th September,' John McLoghlin, the Director of the HBC's Western department at Fort Vancouver, reported to London,

> Lieutenant Peel (son of the Rt. Honble. Sir Robert Peel) ... arrived here with a Letter from the Honble. Captn. Gordon of Her Majesty's Ship *America* ... by which I was most happy to learn that he was here to assure Her Majesty's subjects of 'firm protection in their rights' ... Lieutenant Peel and Captain Park accompanied by Mr Lowe (one of our officers I sent for the purpose) visited the Willamette, and ... appeared well pleased with the reception they received.

He might have been less sanguine about prospects if he had heard Gordon's opinions on the subject of Oregon, but McLoghlin did not need telling what the almost certain outcome would be. 'Unless active

measures are taken by the Government,' he warned in a letter carried
back by Peel, 'for the protection and encouragement of British influence, this Country will pass into other hands, as the overwhelming
number of Americans who are from year to year coming to the Country, will give an American tone and character to its institutions, which
it will be impossible afterwards to eradicate.'

Back in the *America* Peel wrote up his report for Gordon, detailing the military and geographical features of the territory, and sent a
second letter to Richard Pakenham, the British Minister in Washington responsible for negotiating an Oregon settlement. 'May I venture
to say,' Peel concluded this letter – a bold document from a twenty-
year-old lieutenant –

> as expressing also the opinion of my Captain, that if the 49th
> degree be the boundary determined on, it must not include the
> southern extremity of Vancouver Island. That point commands the
> navigation of the magnificent inlet and possesses a fine harbour.
> The Hudson Bay Co have seen its advantages and security, and …
> are preparing to change their principal seat of business from Fort
> Vancouver on the Columbia to this new settlement called Fort
> Victoria.
>
> The American settlements on the Willamette, running south, and
> those in the Sacramento running north will, I'm afraid, very soon
> unite – Their junction will render the possession of Port San Fran-
> cisco to the Americans inevitable, and that Harbour has so many
> advantages, is so safe from attack, and the land round its enor-
> mous girth is so rich and accessible, that when once in their posses-
> sion, it will I fear give the Americans a decided superiority in the
> Pacific. Having visited California and beyond I hope you will
> excuse me expressing these opinions, and believe that it is only
> from the advice of my friend Mr Barrons and from a feeling of
> duty, that I have ventured at all to send you this.

Peel and Parke were not the only British officers in the country –
they had met two army officers on a similar mission at Fort Vancouver – but Gordon was keen to get his own men's reports back to
London as quickly as possible. After leaving Vancouver Island he
sailed for Hawaii, and at Honolulu, Peel was transferred to an
American ship bound for Mazatlan, from where he travelled overland to Vera Cruz to take a mail packet for Havana and England,

reaching the Admiralty with his reports and despatches on 10 February 1846.

If Peel had come out of his assignment with great credit, he had returned to a crisis that dwarfed Oregon or even promotion. With unrest at home and famine in Ireland after a disastrously wet summer in 1845, his father had set himself to repeal that great Moloch of Tory protectionism, the Corn Laws, and William was back in time to witness the price of success. Just six days after he presented his reports at the Admiralty, a majority for repeal on a first reading of just ninety-seven – with 231 of Sir Robert's own Conservatives voting against him – spelled out what that price would inevitably be. 'The Manners, the Somersets, the Bentincks, the Lowthers and the Lennoxes' – like some latter-day Agincourt list, Disraeli watched the nobility and squirearchy of England filing into the lobby to vote Peel out of office, when, just two hours after the repeal of the Corn Laws, an Irish Life and Property Bill gave his enemies their chance of revenge,

> They trooped in: all the men of metal and large-acred squires, whose spirit he had so often quickened and whose counsel he had so often solicited in his fine Conservative speeches in Whitehall Gardens ... Sir Robert did not reply or even turn his head. He looked very grave, and extruded his chin as was his habit when he was annoyed and cared not to speak. He began to comprehend his position, and that the emperor was without his army.

If it was the end of Peel, however, it was also his finest hour, and waiting just long enough to hear from America that the US Senate had ratified the Oregon Treaty, he announced his resignation to Parliament. It must have been a particular satisfaction for him to think that his son had played some small part in the Oregon negotiations, and before moving on to the question of his own vexed legacy, he dwelt on the role of his Foreign Minister and the vision of British power and responsibilities that he had striven to inculcate in his son. 'He has dared to avow,' he said of Aberdeen,

> that he thinks in a Christian country there is a moral obligation upon a Christian minister to exhaust every effort before incurring the risk of war ... In relinquishing power I shall leave a name ... execrated by every monopolist who from less honourable motives clamours for protection because it conduces to his own individual

benefit; but it may be that I shall leave a name sometimes remembered with expressions of good will in the abodes of those whose
lot it is to labour, and to earn their daily bread by the sweat of their
brow, when they shall recruit their exhausted strength with abun-
dant and untaxed food, the sweeter because it is no longer leavened
by a sense of injustice.

Peel was right, though just how right only his death would show. But
already outside Parliament the crowds were waiting to cheer him as
he made his way home to Whitehall. Brought down by a mounte-
bank of genius in Disraeli, and succeeded by an 'insect' who could
not begin to compare with him in abilities or authority in Lord John
Russell, his ascendancy in Parliament was ended at that precise
moment when his place in the affections of the country was secured.
Without ever courting popularity, he had won it; without ever fully
sympathising with the currents of the time, he had successfully navi-
gated them; without knowing where he was going he had arrived,
inevitably, at the only place that intellect, moral courage, determination and great practical abilities could take him; and without having
a single jot of the martyr in his nature he had soberly embraced political martyrdom as the cost of his convictions. Work, duty, achievement, power, fame, sacrifice – and, ultimately, greatness: these were
a towering inheritance to leave to any son; and to a son like William
– all quickness, impatience, contradictions, emulation and ardour to
succeed – a burden that would prove increasingly difficult to live
with.

VI

For an impatient and ambitious young naval officer the 1840s were
not a good decade. In the year before Peel's return an invasion panic
had created a promising flurry of naval activity, but the French had
already demonstrated once in 1841 that they were not to be relied on
for a war, and the ageing Wellington's fears of enemy steamers attacking English ports proved no more accurate than the hopes that Louis
Philippe would have backed Mohammed Ali in Syria.

After a brief time on the books of the *Devastation* at Woolwich,
and the *Constance* at Plymouth, and nine months on half-pay, Peel
would have leapt at the chance of employment at any rate, and it

finally came in the following spring with his appointment to the command of the twelve-gun sloop *Daring*. The *Daring* was already on the West Indies station at the time, and it was the middle of April 1847 before he joined his new ship at Sacrificius, a small island just off Vera Cruz in the Gulf of Mexico.

During the previous month the *Daring* had been closely monitoring the conflict between Mexico and the United States, but by the time Peel arrived the immediate excitement was over, and a slight but perceptible vein of dissatisfaction runs through his one surviving letter home from this time. 'I hope you received a hurried note I wrote from off Bermuda,' he wrote to his father in June from Halifax.

> It was a great happiness to me receiving a packet of letters. I was as anxious to send the note, short as it was, as I was only just recovering from an attack of fever, and was afraid of the Packet taking you home reports of it. I am now, thank God, quite recovered, as strong as before, and greatly enjoy the sharp bracing climate of this place ... I received your two letters enclosing others, the one about my first Lieut, the other relating to Mr Fox [an application to Sir Robert to use his political influence in favour of a Captain Stoddart's nephew]. That gentleman is no longer on board the Daring having left some time previous to my joining. I am sure it was very kind of you to write so civil a letter in return to Capt. Stoddart's for I did not think his a proper one. I mentioned slightly the subject to the officer here and warned him that his friends would do more harm than good by such premature requests. I was afraid in my former letter to speak of the officers. They are an average set of men, who treat me with the greatest respect, and with whom I am very strict on duty. I believe they like me: yet of the three lieutenants there is not one I should care to follow me in a second ship. The ship's company, I am sure, are very much attached to me. Every one allows that the Brig is improved and very efficient ... The Admiral here is too old a man for me to make much impression on him either for good or bad.*

---

* The Admiral was Sir Francis Austen, Jane Austen's brother, and Peel's pessimism was not entirely unfounded. On 17 December 1847 Austen sent on a letter from Peel to the Admiralty, reporting on the state of the American–Mexican conflict and on a meeting with Commodore Perry, adding that in his own opinion it was 'very barren of interest'.

William's 'low spirits' were certainly enough to worry his parents –
or his mother at least – and this first experience of the 'loneliness of
command' was in its way as chastening as the months spent rotting
in Amoy harbour. It is clear from Clements Markham's journals that
Peel had everything required to win himself acolytes, but the qualities demanded of him in *Daring* were not those of mentor to brilliantly gifted middies of his own social standing, but of a young
commander dealing with older lieutenants who had none of the abilities or connections he had always taken for granted.

It is perhaps only imagination that detects a lack of sympathy for
their plight – for the plight, that is, of nine out of every ten lieutenants
in the Victorian navy – yet if Peel had a fault it was a lack of patience
with mediocrity. Nobody could have been more generous than he
was when it came to nurturing young talent, but the combination of
age and dullness would almost infallibly bring out the one flaw in a
character that was otherwise made for command.

It would be a mistake to make too much of this, but there is an
interesting illustration of Peel's lack of empathy in a brace of letters
he wrote to Sir Francis Austen in the wake of an expedition in the
Daring's boats up the San Juan river in Central America in February
1848. In his first letter Peel had clearly forgotten to single out any of
his men in the way that was expected of a ship's captain in such
circumstances, and even when he wrote again two days later to
correct his omission, it was more than he could do to bring himself
to mention any of the officers by name.

He was happy to name the Sergeant of Marines, the Master's Assistant, the Boatswain's Mate, the Foretop Man, a seaman gunner, and
above all the Boatswain – 'as he saved his Captain's life in one of the
rapids' – but his lieutenants and midshipmen had to make do with
his general approbation. 'In my [earlier] letter of proceedings,' he
wrote on 30 March, 'I forbore to mention any officer in particular
as deserving of praise, as it might have been invidious where all
equally shone. The fact of ascending the River in 8 days, in heavy
boats so deeply laden, could perhaps speak more strongly than I could
for their exertions.'

This letter followed an incident that brought the *Daring* closer to
action than at any other time during Peel's command. Over the previous years Britain had exploited political and tribal divisions in Central
America to promote her own mercantile interests, and in January
1848 had taken advantage of a border dispute between Nicaragua

and Mosquitian territory to occupy San Juan del Norte in order to ensure that any future canal linking the Pacific and Atlantic Oceans by way of the San Juan river and the Lake of Granada would be firmly in British hands.

The occupation was followed by an expedition up the river the following month, carried out by the boats of the *Alert* and *Vixen*, and although Peel was too late to take part in the one brisk action fought, it was not for want of trying. 'Though Commander Peel was not fortunate enough to be in time to assist in the Capture of Sera-pague,' Sir Francis Austen reported in more emollient mood to the Admiralty, 'yet the zeal displayed by himself, his officers, and men, is deserving of every praise and I have pleasure in bringing it before their Lordships.'

This expedition was an isolated incident in an otherwise dull command, however, and by the time Austen was replaced by an ageing Admiral of a very different stamp in Thomas Cochrane, now the Earl of Dundonald and restored to the service after years in disgrace, Peel was ready to move on. 'My Dearest Father,' he wrote from Drayton in January 1849, just over three months after quitting the *Daring*,

> I received today a very kind note from Admiral Dundas telling me that tomorrow (the 10th) he should sign my commission as Post Captain.
>
> I had always been told that Admiral Dundas was very friendly to me, but it has quite surprised me that he should avail himself of so short an interval of power in my favour during the vacancy of the First Lord's appointment.
>
> I am very happy at having attained the last and greatest step in our service that either interest or merit can bestow. I shall go to London, on receiving my commission, to pay my respects at the Admiralty.

There is something almost comical in the understatement of this letter, but as he made his way down to London as the youngest captain in the navy, it must have been hard for Peel to know whether he had his whole life in front of him or behind him. The step from commander to post captain was one that officers spent their careers struggling towards and never making, yet there he was at just twenty-four, with nothing more to prove, and little more to hope for than an extended period on half-pay and the distant prospect of a ship.

If it is hard enough in life not to get what you want, it is, in its own padded way, perhaps harder still to get it and to find that it is not after all what you wanted. From the age of three Peel and his father had been aiming towards this moment, but from the time he made post there was hardly a year in his life when he did not think or talk of leaving the service.

The key word in that last sentence is very likely 'father', because whether it is coincidence or not, the stream of dissatisfaction with naval life that fills Peel's letters gathers momentum at that precise moment when the man who had driven his early ambitions was suddenly taken away. In the early hours of Saturday, 29 June 1850 Sir Robert had risen in the Commons for the last time to speak in the Don Pacifico debate,* and late the following afternoon, after a meeting to examine Paxton's plans for the Great Exhibition glasshouse, had set out for a ride past Buckingham Palace and up Constitution Hill towards St George's Hospital.

His horse was newly bought, and a stranger in the park who recognised it was about to warn him against its temperament, when he remembered Peel's chilly reputation and thought better of it. As Peel stopped to greet two acquaintances the horse suddenly began to plunge and rear, throwing him over its head before stumbling over him and crushing his back as it fell.

The pain was intense – Peel had fainted by the time a carriage got him back to Whitehall – and the internal injuries critical. The fall had broken his collarbone and ribs, and brought up a large and dangerous swelling under his shoulderblade. For three days Peel lay on a mattress in his dining room, delirious or semi-conscious by turns as the silent crowds gathered outside and the Queen – the same Queen who had so hated him for his stiff-necked refusal to be everything

---

* The occasion of Palmerston's greatest parliamentary triumph, when he defended his use of force against the Greek government to protect the interests of a British subject of dubious reputation, David Pacifico. Palmerston famously declared that any British subject, 'like a Roman citizen of old, could rely wherever he was on the watchful eye and strong arm of England to protect him against injustice and wrong, declaring proudly, "Civis Romanus Sum"'. Interestingly, Hastings's friend George Finlay was also involved in the events that led to Palmerston's intervention.

that Melbourne had been to her when she first came to the throne – prayed for his recovery for herself and the country he had done so much to save from the anarchy that had convulsed the rest of Europe.

Peel's wife, Julia, collapsed under the strain, and with the unsatisfactory Robert in Rome, it was left to William and his young sister Eliza to run the stricken household. Through the Sunday and Monday a constant stream of carriages, friends, political associates and anxious well-wishers had made their way to Whitehall, but on Tuesday, 2 July, after what seemed a brief recovery, Peel relapsed and the Bishop of Gibraltar was summoned to administer the Sacrament.

By this time he was in little pain, but all hope was gone, and one by one his family were admitted to receive his blessing and say their goodbyes. Sometime during the evening his wife was led away from the room that had become a death chamber, and at around 9 o'clock that night, under the gaze of Reynolds's great portrait of Dr Johnson and surrounded by his brothers, three of his sons, his son-in-law, his great friends Hardinge and Graham and his doctors, Sir Robert Peel lapsed into an unconsciousness from which he never came round.

'I cannot bear even to think of losing him, it would be the greatest loss for the whole country and irreparable for us,' Victoria had written while Peel was still struggling for life, and three days later Aberdeen echoed the same sentiment. 'A great light has disappeared from us,' he wrote to Princess Lieven: 'never did I know such universal grief exhibited by every description of person; high and low, rich and poor, from the Queen to the common labourer; all feel alike and with good reason, for his services were equally rendered to all.'

'The country mourns over him as over a father,' the Queen wrote on the day of Peel's funeral, and for those to whom he actually had been a father or husband the suddenness of the blow was well-nigh unbearable. Throughout his political life this soberest of men had made a habit of the unpredictable, and as in life so in death – he had gone out for a ride one early summer's evening from his own house in Whitehall before dining with the Jerseys, and come back unconscious in a carriage to die – to leave, without warning or preparation, the woman to whom he had been 'the idol' and the 'beloved love' and the children for whom his achievements and presence had been the one fixed point of reference, authority, judgement, encouragement and example.

'Think what a Blank is here – how gladly would I now lie by the side of his hallowed remains in that sacred vault,' a prostrate Julia

wrote two months after his death – and of all her children
William was probably the one best placed to recognise the emptiness
she felt. 'My dearest Mamma,' he wrote to her in December, after a
truce in the hysterical row with her eldest son that had added to her
griefs,

> I cried like a child when I received your packet of kind letters this
> morning. I never would have thought you would have had such
> hard trials to sustain, but I thanked God also with a full heart for
> I see you will have a happy future. I read your last letter first, with
> the 'all well' to comfort me, and what you say of my dear brother
> Robert greatly charmed me. I am sure you will forgive all the Past,
> and be the mother of children who will rally round you in the
> worship of the memory of our father.

If William felt with his mother in all her harrowing loss, he would
not be the first son of a famous father to feel an unconscious sense
of release at his death, and it is significant that the letter is dated from
Cairo and not from Drayton or Whitehall. Throughout his father's
life he had dedicated himself to the profession his father had wanted
for him, but within weeks of his death he had thrown its shackles
off, and embarked on a journey for the Middle East to prepare
himself for a life of heroic exploration and missionary evangelising
that seems as great a *volte face* in its way as his father's 'treason' over
Catholic Emancipation or the Corn Laws.*

There can be nothing more impertinent than questioning the reality or validity of another man's interior religious life, but it is hard
not to think that Peel's rebirth was precipitated by the loss of the one
stable authority that had guided his path so far. For the son of so dry
a Protestant he had always been of an excitable disposition, and in
the wake of his father's death his religion seems to have taken on a
new intensity, arming him – in a classic mid-nineteenth-century Evan-

---

* There is a lingering suspicion that one desert, in Peel's eyes, was very much as
good as another. In February 1850 he had offered his services to the Admiralty
in connection with the search for Sir John Franklin and his crew, missing somewhere in the Arctic regions for the past three years. It is interesting that both
Peel and Hastings should have volunteered for the 'Grail'-like quest for the
North-West Passage that absorbed so much of the energies and talents of nineteenth-century naval officers.

gelical way – with a vivid and personal conviction of his relationship to God and of God's special purposes for him.

And if the will of God and the will of Peel seem to have been conveniently close when it came to the question of Africa, that would have come as no surprise to a generation that increasingly believed that God's providence was destined to be worked out through England and Englishmen. 'Its mission is not yet accomplished,' he would shortly write of the town of Khartoum, in a passage that yokes Carlyle and Kipling, Gordon, Disraeli and Lord Ellenborough, in a heady vision of empire that would have had Sir Robert turning in his 'sacred vault'.

It is waiting patiently to be the road to civilise Africa. But it is not an eastern nation, and not the Mohammedan religion, that can do it; and I am one of those who hope and believe that Providence will destine it for England. An English Government and a handful of Englishmen could do it. I will not dwell on those dreams of ambition that would turn the commerce of the East through Alexandria, and load the Nile with riches of unknown countries, in exchange for the industry of millions. Cities would rise up at Assouan and at Khartoum, whose influence would be felt over the whole interior. I know, alas! The spirit of the age is against such thoughts; and there are even men who would wish to abandon our empire; but I speak the voice of thousands of Englishmen, who, like myself, have served their country abroad, and who do not love her least, who never will consent to relinquish an empire, that has been won by the sword, and who think the best way to preserve it is often by judicious extension. England is too small for the energies of our youth – confined at home, and we should sink in luxury and corruption. Say you? We advance to a mighty crash. So pass all things away; but it will not be in our generation; we shall not live to feel its shame – a fallen race must read the epitaph of an empire:–

> Alas! not dazzled by the noontide ray,
> Compute the morn and evening of the day.
> The whole amount of that enormous fame,
> A tale that blends their glory with their shame.

If the extraordinary thing in this is how far and how rapidly William has travelled from the restraint of Sir Robert's foreign policy, the fact is that it was only with his father's death that he was able to achieve any real independence of thought or action. Till the end of his life he would always remain his father's son, yet in many surprising ways – in his blossoming imperialism, his volatility, his restlessness, his love of excitement, gesture, colour, youthful masculinity and dandified show – he was (cynicism apart) temperamentally and politically closer to Sir Robert's nemesis, Benjamin Disraeli, than he was to the man who had breathed his last surrounded by the portraits of Joshua Reynolds.

Where his grandiose ambitions came from – Ellenborough is the obvious suspect – or how long and private a gestation they had had, is impossible to know, but the one thing that is certain is that the catalyst for action was his father's death. Sometime in the early summer of 1850 Peel had found a young Lebanese Christian called Joseph Churi to teach him Arabic in London, but it was not until September of that year – two months after Sir Robert's funeral – that he asked Churi to accompany him on a reconnaissance through Egypt and the Holy Land to equip himself for the greater tasks ahead.

The twenty-three-year-old Joseph Churi – 'a more virtuous and religious minded man I never knew', Peel wrote of him – was a curious addition to the list of acolytes and knightly squires attracted to Peel's magnetic personality. 'You must know, gentle reader, that I am a Maronite of Mount Lebanon' – a fifth-century sect in communion with Rome – Churi engagingly began his account of their journeys together, 'and at the age of fourteen I was sent to the College of Propaganda, in Rome, to be educated in virtue and doctrine for the ecclesiastical state.'

Churi had spent seven years at Rome, studying rhetoric, logic, metaphysics and divinity, while adding Hebrew, Latin and the European languages to his native Syriac and Arabic. He had left the College because of illness in 1849, and after travelling through France, arrived in England to find among his earliest pupils when he began teaching an imperious young naval officer on half-pay determined to explore the Holy Places and to take Churi with him. 'I had some difficulty consenting to this project,' he later confessed, 'as I was unwilling to break off the lessons I was giving to other pupils, but finally I promised to go with him ... I will not give you a detailed account of the virtues of Captain Peel, lest I should offend him; but

I must say that besides his talent and excellent memory, he is very charitable towards the poor, and he has not those prejudices so common to the young men of his station.'

They had finally escaped from England and family disputes on 20 October – and there is something about the suddenness of the whole venture that makes 'escape' seem the right word – and after a thirty-six-day journey to the second cataract 'never equalled in the annals of the Nile', returned by way of Mount Sinai, Jerusalem, Nazareth, Bethlehem and Syria. 'My companion is most faithful and truly devoted to me,' Peel reported back to his mother midway through their travels. 'I hope all will go on well, and that you may see as confidently as I do how it will please God to give you from all these trials a spirit and enjoyment of this life that nothing but the depth of adversity could have refined. I see it myself, I see it in the solitude of my travels and I never lay down to rest without praying for this mercy towards you.'

This sense of spiritual certainty and peace might have grown in the solitude of the desert, but it clearly did not long survive his return to England in February 1851. He had embarked on his first journey in the teeth of his mother's fears, and it was not without a bitter fight with his family – and himself – that he prepared to carry out his more ambitious schemes of exploration and Christian regeneration 'before the years' had crept up on him and 'shaken the nerves of youth'. 'And now at the painful time of leaving,' he wrote elliptically to his brother from Southampton on 20 August 1851,

> I feel also the satisfaction of being held to my purpose without wavering. Success almost always attends that alone. But being free, having no master or office to control me, nor fear of the heartless or selfish smile if I turn back in failure are I believe the reasons why I go so calmly. However long in absence or in silence, never doubt that I am pursuing my way in peace perhaps in triumph for when Providence warns me I shall turn back.

It had been a fight to carry his wishes, but Peel was not going to shirk the call of God, Fame and England's providential birthright. 'The best feelings prevailed among the passengers through the whole journey,' he wrote in his account of his own seesawing moods of elation and despair on the voyage out, no little accident ever disturbed us, and many friendships were formed. Years must revolve before a kind fortune can bring us again together. Some have gone to India, some to Afghanistan, others to China and Borneo, – all to uphold the character of England, to administer justice, to extend commerce, or to defend and expand our empire. I embarked with the object of travelling in Soudan, hoping, by the blessing of the Almighty, to help to break the fetters of the Negro, to release him from the selfish Mussulman, from the sordid European; to tell him there is a God that made us all, a Christ that came down and died for all. Resolution stifled all objections and carried me aboard. We sailed, and then, knowing it could no longer influence my course, I gave way to the deepest despair. All that affection, all that temptation could hold out, rose in their most alluring form; and so time wore on, from the first few days very heavily. Till Cape St. Vincent woke me to other feelings, reminded me of the enthusiasm of my boyhood. Now all homesick, love-sick yearning vanished, and again I trod the deck with a high hope; my heart was lifted with England's honour. Then came Trafalgar. Would that Nelson had known the meaning of that name! It would have fixed a smile on his dying lips.

There was another relapse at Cairo, however, that almost spelled the end of his expedition before it had begun. 'I arrived here in such a weak state of health that I at once decided it was folly for me to proceed,' he confessed to his brother Frederick on 7 September. 'It was between Malta and Alexandria that it gave way and the doctor could only account for it by debility. I may tell you that my glands were all swollen so as to render movement painful. I think it came from the little appetite I had … Of course it acted on my spirits to find my body such a weak instrument of my will and I took it as a warning from a kind providence to keep me from danger.'

He was determined to return immediately to England, he told Frederick, but the depression was as temporary as his illness, and another four days in Cairo saw him ready to resume his journey. Before they left England Peel had dreamed of journeying the length of Africa to the Cape, but their first, more conservative, object was Khartoum, and on 11 September, armed with a firman and guide, and sent on their way with the good wishes of the Egyptian viceroy, Peel and Churi embarked at Boulac, the port of Cairo, for their journey up the Nile.

Their accounts of their Nile journey, of the river itself and their white-turbaned crew hauling tirelessly against the current, of the villages and markets, the beauty of the men and the hideous ugliness of the women, the 'horrible beauty' of naked dancing girls, of crops and rock formations, water volumes and temperatures, could safely be interchanged with those of any number of nineteenth-century travellers, but every so often there is a glimpse of Peel that makes them kindle into strange life. 'There is a melancholy in the Desert, and a gloom in the breast, that you cannot dispel,' he wrote after they had abandoned the river at Korusko to follow the caravan route south that cuts across the Nubian desert and bypasses the great westwards loop in the Nile.

Though lying in the vaulted chamber of the skies, the thoughts are not heavenly; they turn, they cling to all that is earthly. Why are they not heavenly? What is there between you and eternity? Are you not here alone. No, though you have left life behind you, you are not alone, Death is your companion. It stares you in the face at every step. Take care or you will stumble over its victims. Leave the road, you perish; follow the track of the caravan, and rotting carcasses are its mile stones. Why is the voice of the caravan so hushed, and why do you urge your camel's speed? See! your spirit is wounded; you are musing on a secret in your own breast, and yet it is known to all. Look at that horrid object that lay in your path, his head turned back, and his mouth wide open; he wanted water. Death has mocked him and choked it with sand; he wanted air, the wind is laughing through his ribs; he struggled to reach his journey's end, his feet are striking in the air. It is not Death that scares you; it is the insult that you cannot avenge; the curse of mortality, the disgust of Nature; it is corruption stinking in the nostrils of heaven. Happy are we who have been taught the blessed hope that this corruption is the seed of incorruption, the pledge of immortality.

There is something of Gerard Manley Hopkins in that last sentence – that final 'hope' carries as much conviction in the face of mortality as it does in Hopkins's 'Terrible Sonnets' – but even in the Sudan there was more earthly support for a traveller with the name of Peel. 'In Egypt I never mentioned my intention of travelling beyond the Pacha's territory, and I never asked for any assistance from the

Government,' he wrote to Frederick from the growing town of Khartoum, which he and Churi had reached just after sunrise – they travelled at night – on 23 October,

> but Abbas Pacha of his own accord gave me a Firman and one of his own people to attend me, and the Firman says that every one high and low is to pay me every attention, and to provide me with all I want, and who ever does not do it will be punished immediately … And so, please God, I hope to travel, passing from one country to another with the greatest dignity. I mention all this to show how different my position is from that of other travellers who had to submit to disguises of dress and figure to make their way among the people, and who can be surprised at their suffering from sickness and hardships under such conditions.

They must have made a bizarre pair, Churi and Peel, as they lurched their way on their camels across the scorching desert, the one, tiny, delicate and innocent, endlessly singing his canticles or intoning his prayers and Latin exultations; the other, the Englishman to his fingertips. 'My costume was not one which in general opinion is the best fitted to conciliate prejudices,' Peel conceded.

> I never would wear the slightest disguise, or even any part of the handsome Mahommedan dress, but wore a high broad-brimmed beaver hat with a cover that hung over the shoulders, white flannel jacket and trowsers, with strong half-boots. A short sword with steel scabbard, and a little pistol, were my constant weapons of defence for serious enemies, and a heavy hide whip had a salutary warning for dogs and boys. Besides this I carried a white double-lined umbrella to protect me against the burning sun, which also served at night as a tent to my head, when sleeping on the ground, and I also used to fold three or four white handkerchiefs round the hat to protect the temples.

Neither the name of Peel nor all the handkerchiefs in the world, though, were protection enough against the flies, thirst, miasmas and murderous heat of the desert, and as fever struck first Churi and then Peel a traveller less sure of the Almighty would have feared the worst. They had been warned as early as Khartoum that only beheading awaited them in Darfur, but it was not until Churi finally collapsed on their south-western journey across Kordofan that sense at last got the better of a quixoticism that bordered on madness.

But even in defeat there was an inner steel to Peel's character – the other side of that gentleness that could lead him to sacrifice his own precious water to revive a dying bird – and their return journey gave stark proof of it. The two men had got as far south as Labeyed before fever and ague had struck, and the moment Peel was well enough to travel again, he brutally forced the helpless Churi – no more than skin and bone – back onto his camel to begin the long journey north towards safety. 'A little after sunrise I got up,' Churi recorded,

> and attempted to cross the room, my legs trembled under me, and I had to lean against the wall ... The captain, seeing me on foot, called to inquire if I would be ready to set off the day after to-morrow ... 'Very well,' I rejoined; 'but you must take the trouble to bury me in the Desert, if you cover my body with sand and put my cross and Rosary near my head it will suffice.' He was displeased at my saying this, and I also, vexed, said 'he must be rather out of his senses, seeing that I could hardly stand on my feet to ask if I could travel in two days.' He left me, and I burst into bitter lamentations. 'O, Lord!' I exclaimed, 'consoler in all afflictions, do not abandon me! ... Blessed Virgin, remember that thou are called comforter of the afflicted; see in what trouble, anguish and oppression I am! Send joy and peace to my troubled heart, and drive away all sadness.'

If Peel's ruthlessness seems a long way from the image of Christian chivalry with which Victorian England invested him, it is the same Peel who made his men stand upright in the face of enemy fire, and in both cases there was arguably method to his actions. 'After a little time, the Captain asked again how I was,' Churi continued.

> 'A little better,'
>   Can you get to the next Holla?
>   I said, 'Yes,' for I was vexed at the impudence to say the least, of his making such a proposal when I was prostrate under violent fever.
>   He added, 'I do not think you can do it.'
>   'Yes, I can; for if I fall dead from a dromedary, God will have mercy on my soul.'

He was much displeased; but grumbling something left the hut.

I said to him. 'I don't think you have any right to be displeased with me. Why do you wish me to travel in such a state? Go yourself, if it pleases you. I will sleep here. I hope to do better tomorrow, and be able to follow you.'

After some minutes, he came back to me, 'Mr Churi, I think it will be best to go myself to the other holla and see if the camels are ready ...'

I thought for a little time on the conduct of the Captain, and felt deeply wounded by it.

The selfishness of youth, or the maturity of a natural leader? It is impossible to say with any certainty, but there seems little doubt that it was only Peel's harshness that kept his companion alive. Over the next week he would invariably ride on ahead in this way, and after eleven days in the desert – Churi 'burning with fever, tongue glued to my palate, head ... whirling round' and goaded on, one suspects, by an acute resentment of his master – the two men were rewarded with the sight of the White Nile that neither thought Churi would ever see again. 'He was so ill in Cordofan,' Peel wrote to his mother,

> I never thought he would have left it, and I at the same time for the space of three weeks was suffering severely from fever and ague, but, thank God, have never suffered from the slightest relapse. I had plenty of quinine and by a kind providence a most happy determination not to sink under it, but poor Churi was quite prostrate from its virulence. I got him back to the waters of the White Nile after a very painful march of twelve [sic] days in a desert, and then he began rapidly to recover.

With the Nile reached they were safe, and with Churi out of danger, Peel's impatience returned. Taking a boat as far as Barbar north of Khartoum on the river together, he travelled on by camel alone, instructing Churi – his hired assistant in these travels, it should be remembered – to follow on slowly with the baggage to Cairo, where there would be money waiting for the voyage back to England.

It was the end of their travels together, and if there seems a touch of the Napoleon about Peel's flight, abandoning baggage and loyal follower to the Egyptian desert, Churi was either wise enough or courtier enough to temper his criticism. 'Truly it was a great and noble enterprise that Captain Peel attempted,' he later wrote.

> There was every possibility of succeeding in our purpose if the condition the sine qua non of performing the journey did not fail; but this necessary condition was health. I am certain several have talked of Captain Peel's attempt, and perhaps judged ill. I know no one with so much decision, firmness and perseverance, to renounce the ease and pleasure, a civilised country, and the best and noblest society in the world which England affords, who was willing to sacrifice himself in attempting a difficult enterprise, honourable to himself and his nation, and useful to the whole world. Who would like to trust himself in a horrible desert? Who would voluntarily give up the delights and pleasures of his own native land to cross the Desert of Africa in summer, and bear a heat of 116, 118, 120, 125 degrees and that not for a few days only to lead a life that few can bear even for a day or two? Ought he who does such noble things, more for his country than his own honour, to be forgotten and put aside by those inferior in every respect to himself? No!

Perhaps. Born of the emotional turmoil of his father's death, measurable only in misery and suffering, and ending in disappointment, their journey had achieved nothing of note. They had witnessed with indignation the obscenity of the trade they had come to fight, the lines of men, bowed under their wooden halters, filing through Labayed, and been in no position to help so much as a single slave. They had added some wonderfully English prejudices to their repertoire and conceived a deep fear and hatred of Islam and its spreading influence in Africa. They had measured the volumes of the Blue and White Niles, taken temperatures, pressures, measured fossilised tree girths and charted mountain heights. Small returns for a vision that had promised the Cape, a slave-free Darfur and a population liberated from the tyranny of the Prophet and the Porte. They had, though, survived, and for that Peel could take the credit. If in some ways he had diminished, or at least hardened, as a man, he had grown as a leader. Churi might have bitterly resented him, but he kept going all the same, driven more by Peel's indomitable will than by any resources of his own. It was a lesson Peel never forgot. In mastering himself and his own 'weaknesses' he found he could master others.

It would be an invaluable asset in his career to come. And if the irony of it was that he would soon be exercising that talent in defence of a country and a religion he had come to hate, it was an irony that any Victorian naval officer would have happily swallowed. As Thomas Hughes put it: 'I'm as sorry as anyone to see folk fighting the wrong people and the wrong things, but I'd a deal sooner see them doing that, than that they should have no fight in them.'

VII

One of the great blessings of the system of naval half-pay and the Victorians' gift of self-censorship was that an aberration like Peel's journey down the Nile could be passed off as if nothing untoward had ever happened. It is clear from Joseph Churi's bizarre account that the journey came in for some adverse comment, but by the time the naval historian J.K. Laughton came to enshrine Peel's name in the *Dictionary of National Biography* all the emotional turmoil of these years has metamorphosed into a seamless transition from the *Daring* to his first appointment as Post Captain in the frigate *Diamond*.

It would in fact be another seventeen months before his appointment to the *Diamond*, and with a home of his own and a mother and an unmarried younger sister to think of, now that his brother was at Drayton, he was clearly flirting with the idea of giving up the service altogether. 'I have the honor to acknowledge the receipt of the communication your Lordship has caused to be addressed to me,' he wrote stiffly to Lord Hardwicke in September 1852, in response to the strange offer of a clerkship at the Post Office:

> I feel indebted to your lordship for your kindness in giving me an opportunity of entering the public service, but however much I am desirous of occupying my time I feel that from both my name and age I could not reconcile it to my feelings to accept of an office the emoluments of which are of so trifling a nature. It remains to thank your lordship very cordially for the consideration you have been good enough to show me and can only add how grateful I should feel if your lordship should still have the opportunity of promoting my interests.

He had put his finger on the problem, because while as a Peel he could hardly be expected to take a position below the family dignity, at twenty-eight he could not just sit back as an unemployed sixty-year-old admiral might, and wait indifferently for an appointment that might never come. With the death of his father he had bought himself an estate at Sandy in Bedfordshire, but if he ever seriously thought of dropping the 'bower anchor' and putting farming on a modern basis in the way he threatened, his appointment to the *Diamond* spared him the discovery that he had neither the temperament nor the modesty to bury himself in the 'bijou' Swiss cottage – as his sister disparagingly called it – that he was building in the depths of the Bedfordshire countryside.

The twenty-eight-gun frigate *Diamond* offered not just the prospect of his own ship, but, more crucially, of real fighting too, because the previous June Russian forces had moved into the Ottoman Empire's Danubian provinces and war had been declared between the two countries. The immediate 'cause' of the conflict lay in a dispute over the guardianship of the Holy Places and the Porte's Christian subjects, but behind these more or less specious pretexts lay those same historical issues of Ottoman decline, Russian expansion, French opportunism and British fears for her Indian empire that had given Peel his first taste of war off the Syrian coast twelve years earlier.

At the beginning of 1853 the Tsar had sounded out the British Ambassador to St Petersburg on a mutually beneficial termination for the 'sick man of Europe', but there was never the remotest chance of Britain allowing Russian control of Constantinople, with all the threat that entailed for her own interests in the eastern Mediterranean. In response to Russian aggression the Mediterranean fleets of France and Britain were despatched instead to the entrance to the Dardanelles, and in October 1853 – just as Peel was commissioning the *Diamond* at Sheerness for the Ionian Isles – ordered on the Sultan's invitation to pass through the Strait and anchor in front of Constantinople.

With war looming in the Black Sea, and naval operations bruited for the Baltic, the Ionian Islands might have been the last place Peel would have chosen, but that did not mean there were not important British interests to be protected there. During the struggle for independence thirty years earlier Byron and 'English Gold' had won Britain a temporary place in Greek hearts, but in any coming war over the Ottoman Empire, nationalism, religion and the old, heady dreams of Constantinople – the *Megali Idea*, the 'Great Idea' – were always going to put the newborn Greek nation on the side of Russia against Britain.

It is impossible to understand Greek nineteenth-century relations with its Russian co-religionists unless it is understood just how fierce a hold that 'great idea' had over the imagination of the country. In the years before independence idealists and theorists had looked to 'the City' as the centre of the Greek world, but in the decades since it had become a universal obsession, a cynical diversion for governments from the brigandage, economic failure, corruption and factionalism of domestic politics and a focus for all the aspirations and hopes that independence had so bitterly failed to satisfy. 'A Greek is not only a man who lives within this kingdom,' John Kollettis, Greece's Prime Minister in the 1840s, famously declared, 'but also one who lives in Janina, in Salonika, in Serres, in Adrianople, in Constantinople, in Smyrna, in Trebizond, in Crete, in Samos and in any land associated with Greek history or the Greek race ... There are two main centres of Hellenism: Athens, the capital of the Greek Kingdom ... and the "City", the dream and hope of all Greeks.'

This was a dangerously inflammatory doctrine at any time – it would prove fatal in the twentieth century – and at a moment of mounting tensions in the Black Sea it was one that was bound to put Greece on a collision course with Britain. Over the previous few years a string of incidents – most famously the 'Don Pacifico' – had already strained relations between them, and when Greece took advantage of Russian troops on the Pruth in Moldavia and a rebellion in Christian Montenegro to foment revolt across her borders, British patience with the country she had done so much to create snapped.

It was not a matter of right and wrong in any absolute sense – this was after all what Navarino had been fought for, what Hastings died for – but it left the authorities in the Ionian Islands in an impossible position. The Greeks certainly had an undeniable interest – there were more Greeks outside its 1832 borders than there were within – but as a guarantor of those borders and a champion of Ottoman territorial integrity Britain could not just stand back and wait while the traditional ragbag of klephts, freed convicts, deserters, looters, pirates, patriots, cattle thieves and regular army officers on half-pay poured into Epirus and Thessaly to bring them the blessings of '*enosis*' or union.

It is hard to imagine that there had been a messier time in twenty-five years for a man of Peel's ambition to be asked to hold the peace between two peoples he more or less equally despised. 'Albania is an unhappy country,' he wrote to his sister Eliza from Corfu soon after assuming his duties as senior naval officer in the Ionian Isles in February 1854, 'divided between two hostile races and religions, and it is a doubt which race is the most cruel and degraded. I rather believe the Greeks. No Greek can ever speak the truth, and I have never met one with an open honest face. Still the Turks, *our Allies*, are a hateful cruel race, the greatest curse and the greatest scourge to humanity that the world has ever seen.'

Behind this hatred of the Turks – part moral disgust at the slave trade, part religious zealotry – lay the experiences of his Nile journeys, and Peel had been left in little doubt as to how unpalatable a task lay ahead. 'The Lord High Commissioner desires me to state to you,' he was told on 6 February, just a day after the *Diamond*'s arrival, as news from the British Consul of growing unrest around the Gulf of Arta reached Corfu,

> his Excellency considers that this is a first attempt against the political rights of a Sovereign, whose authority Her Majesty is sustaining in the Black Sea with her whole Naval Power. He has very little doubt that this attempt has originated in foreign intrigues and is intended to cloak the designs of Russia under the semblance of a Religious & National struggle. He can conceive of nothing more embarrassing to the avowed policy of Her Majesty's Government which is to maintain the integrity of Turkey, than the success of this attempt ... His Excellency feels himself warranted, under these circumstances, in requesting you to detach at once, a portion of the force under your command to Prevesa, where there are both English and Ionian interests to protect ... and takes upon himself the responsibility with Her Majesty's Government, of requesting you to authorise the officer, whom you may select for the service, to do so: giving due notice to the Insurgent leaders, who up to this time are recognised by no known power.

It was one thing for His Excellency to authorise the use of force, it was quite another to persuade any Royal Naval officer – whatever the provocation – to turn his guns on Christian insurgents, and Peel saw it as no business of his to interfere in the internal security of the Ottoman Empire. He had no intention of ignoring the Lord High Commissioner's request for assistance, but despatching the *Shearwater* down to Prevesa he registered his own dissenting opinion with Admiral Dundas at Malta. 'A difference of opinion, if I may humbly say so,' he wrote without the slightest trace of humility – a son of Sir Robert Peel speaking, equal to equal, with his commander-in-chief over the head of some benighted local official, 'has arisen between myself and his Excellency, so, in the absence of any instructions, I hesitate to agree to His Excellency that I should, by force of arms, support the Turkish government against an insurrection of its own subjects. The occasion has not yet arisen, and may not arise, but I have told his Excellency when he represents to me that Prevesa is threatened with an attack, I will then give him my decision.'

Before he was a 'Peel', though, with his own matured opinions on foreign policy, he was a naval officer, and in the face of increased Greek aggression he was ready to act with ruthless decision. 'I am anxious to send at once to the Admiralty a full report of my proceedings in the Gulf of Arta,' he wrote from the *Diamond*, after sending the *Shearwater* to Prevesa to 'seize and detain' any Greek vessel found assisting the insurgents and his own pinnace and barge into the shallow waters of the Gulf in support, 'as they will doubtless be a subject of complaint by the Greek Government.'

> The connivance of the Greek Government with the Insurrection in Epirus is notorious ... and every assistance has been given in the supply of arms and ammunition. Indeed it is scarcely a true definition to call the present movement in Epirus an Insurrection; it is much more a Greek Invasion ...
>
> The Barge of the Diamond captured an Ionian vessel conveying seventeen soldiers of the 3rd Regiment of Irregulars, and the Pinnace in company with the Shearwater, captured two Greek vessels laden with Thirty three thousand Four hundred round of ammunition, two barrels of Gunpowder and four cases of Musket Balls, belonging ostensibly to the Greek Government.
>
> Lieutenant Ridge conveyed them to Prevesa, where in the presence of the Greek Consul, who had come to protest against my proceedings, I made the following disposal of them.
>
> The Boats and all personal property I restored to their respective owners.

The Soldiers I handed over to the Greek Consul without their arms or accoutrements, having ordered Lieut. Horton to see them delivered to the governor at Vonizza.

The ammunition I took on board for Corfu, where it is my intention to land it, until the leisure of Her Majesty's Government is known.

By the time this reached the Admiralty, the exasperated governments of Britain and France had sent troops into the Piraeus to give the Greeks something more than Peel to complain of, but that still left him with one unfinished piece of business on the Ionian station. In this last despatch from the *Diamond* Peel had reported intelligence of three Greek-owned, ex-Russian men-of-war at Trieste, and without waiting for instructions he had sailed north to intercept them, determined either to capture the ships if they had already put to sea or to demand of the Austrian authorities that they should be forced to leave the safety of a neutral port.

The last thing the British government wanted was a piece of Palmerstonian bullying that might alienate Austria, but naval officers had always operated in the creative space that long distances and slow communications gave them. By the time an alarmed Admiralty could send back a counter-order it was already too late, and Peel had shadowed his prey from Trieste to Gravosa, where he had bottled them up in the harbour and again gone ashore to demand that the authorities in Ragusa – modern Dubrovnik – should surrender them up to him.

It cannot have been every day that il Cavaliero Erco, the Maritime Inspector of Dalmatia, was required to negotiate with the son of a British Prime Minister, but with the aid of the Russian Consul to Montenegro and the slow workings of Austrian bureaucracy, he was able to spin the battle out for more than a week before finally giving in. Peel had initially tried to persuade the Greek commander that it would be more honourable to them both if he surrendered in open sea, but in the end he had to settle for seeing their vessels impounded for the duration of the war. The garrison commander 'told us that he had orders to dismantle the ships', Peel reported back to the Admiralty with the urbane assurance of a man dealing in a *fait accompli*, 'when I at once replied that though it would have given me more satisfaction to have captured them at sea, the object of my Government was equally accomplished'.

While the hunt for the three vessels had given the *Diamond* some sport – and there were certainly worse places for an early-summer cruise than the Dalmatian coast – it did not take a sighting of the Duke of Cambridge on his passage out to the 'Seat of War' to remind Peel that he was not where he wanted to be. The Queen had eventually declared war on Russia on 28 March, and as the great eastbound armada continued over the months ahead, and the men-of-war and troopships beat up round Matapan for the Dardanelles with all the flotsam and jetsam of humanity – the camp followers and Jewish traders, the unemployed officers and habitués of Maltese hotels, the Hungarian and Polish refugees, the wives, sisters, sightseers and 'Travelling Gents': with anyone, in fact, who could beg or buy a passage for Constantinople following in their wake – Peel was left to quiet his soul in the Gulf of Corinth. 'I don't know why I should bother you with these odious politics,' he had written restlessly to his sister three days before war was declared:

> Poor Ld Aberdeen must be very sad. How astonished I felt at reading Sir J Graham's speech at the Reform Club dinner. Surely our great Ministers commit greater blunders and follies than their subordinates. But what I smile at most is the credulity of the English People in supposing that their war (if there is one) will last only six months. It is more likely to be a six years war.
>
> There may be great changes, but I feel hurt at being in neither the Baltic or the Black Sea … Sevastopol is very strong, but I have looked at the plan and read its description, and feel *confident* that our ships could destroy its dockyard, and capture or destroy its fleet.

It would not have been like Peel, though, to waste his enforced idleness. 'I have with me a teacher of languages,' he told his sister. 'Arabic I speak now with almost the same facility as I do English, and I can also speak a little Turkish. In two months time I shall doubtless be very proficient. He lives with me and as I never speak to him other than in Arabic and am always learning the Turkish, I find my time passes well enough.'

There were other distractions, too – including a ball at Government House for the Queen's birthday – and there was nothing quite like a ball to bring out the other side of Peel's character. 'These little details which you apologise for were to me quite charming,' he replied to a letter from Eliza.

It is the only way of bringing things vividly before one. I felt almost as if in the Lodge, and almost but not quite a dressmaker ... I admired your dress very much and thought it beautiful, piquant and uncommon short. I hope to learn all about the ball in your next ... some young ladies would be very glad if the Diamond gave one. My cabin in this warm weather looks very beautiful, all white and gold, plenty of space, plenty of flowers, and yours and Mamma's cushions on the sofa.

Within a month the young ladies of Corfu had got their way, and so, more importantly, had Peel. 'My dearest Elise,' he wrote jubilantly on 23 June:

We are off to the Black Sea, and all the young ladies are in a flurry, for I give a grand ball before we leave. How I wish you were here to see it. The quarter deck will be quite clean and will form a tent of the flags of all nations, and give a space 80 feet long and 40 feet broad. The supper will be on the main deck and my cabin is for the ladies. Each one on coming on board will receive a bouquet ... and as soon as it is over, it will be Hurrah for the Black Sea and Corfu will soon be out of sight.

If the ball was a success – 'soft eyes looked love to eyes which spoke again', he assured Eliza – their departure was not without its drama. 'I can write you only a hurried line,' he wrote eleven days later, at last in Constantinople, springboard for the Black Sea and Crimea and seething wartime estaminet of allied life,

but as the postage is only three pence it does not matter. We arrived here yesterday from Corfu, in nine days, having left that place the day after the *Ball*, where 'the lamps shone on fair women and brave men etc, etc' ...

It was a grand ball, very successful and next day we got under weigh and as it was dead calm I had a steamer to tow her being very anxious to make a quick passage. She managed very clumsily and sent us almost on the rocks, I called her to cast off, and most fortunately, at that instant a sudden breeze sprang up to which we made sail, turned the ship's head, and sailed away almost literally scraping the rock. All the garrison with its band of music were there looking down on us, and when they saw us all safe, they gave us

most deafening cheers. We manned the rigging and returned cheer
for cheer. Really it must have been a beautiful sight. Archie [their
cousin] was there in a boat, and ought to describe it to you.

Peel's exile from the 'Seat of War' was over. And if he had been made
to wait, he had not yet missed out on anything worth Archie's telling.

VIII

If Constantinople, meeting point of East and West, the great '*polis*'
of Greek dreams – an Eastern Liverpool with a bit of Virginia Water
thrown in, as one Grenadier officer memorably put it – made an
impression on Peel he had little time to record it for his sister. The
Diamond had dropped anchor off the Golden Horn on 3 July 1854
after an uneventful passage through the Dardanelles, and by the fifth
was being towed up the Bosphorus by the steamer *Tribune* to join
the swelling mass of men and supplies converging on the allied camps
at Varna on the west coast of the Black Sea. 'You may be always
happy about the Diamond,' he finished off his news home: 'she is as
strong as a donkey, and almost as ugly, her guns are too small, she
could have carried heavier metal, but there is a general opinion, and
at Corfu, a certain prediction, that we shall not be in the Black Sea
for nothing.'

In terms of acknowledged war aims, the withdrawal of Russian
troops from the Danubian provinces had already removed the justification for an allied presence, but from the outset the British had
seen the destruction of the great Russian naval base at Sevastopol as
crucial to her future security. It is a moot point whether they would
have pressed on if they had known what miseries lay ahead, but
neither governments nor countries – and certainly not one as high on
'*gloire*' as the Emperor Napoleon's France – had any intention of
aborting a campaign that had already cost so much before the Russian bear had been taught his lesson.

Within days of Peel's arrival the allied commanders – Lord Raglan
and Marshal St Arnaud – had finalised a Crimean invasion plan, and
by the end of the summer an army of over sixty thousand had been
gathered at Varna to implement the allied war aims. 'Went yesterday
to Varna in a French steamer,' Peel wrote on 8 July, struck as every
visitor was by the difference between the 'wretched idleness' and the

lines of 'sick and dying' in the British camp and the elegancies of French life:

> called on Lord Raglan, who was very kind, and gave me a horse to see the Camps. Saw Zouaves, Chasseurs de Vincennes, Chasseurs d'Africque, Bashi Bozouks and other varieties, French, English and Turkish. The French camp was very good, they make charming bowers and are quite at home ... The bowers are for day time and the tents for night. They are placed in rows, the ground nicely swept, and the arms piled in front ... In the evening I dined with Marshall J Arnaud, and his staff, a very pleasant party, quite en famille, and no ceremony. I never spoke such good French, and was positively asked if I had not been brought up in France. He does not look strong, stoops a good deal from ill-health, and not from age.

It was not only the condition of Britain's army – generals who would have been better off at Bath, the absence of anything resembling a proper staff, the miseries of the common soldier, failures of cooperation, logistics, the commissariat – that appalled Peel. 'Our fleet here is playing a most inglorious part,' he was complaining again five days later, as unsympathetic as every young officer to the plight of the ageing Admiral Dundas working under the severe constraints of a difficult alliance, 'and there is considerable discontent about it ... I could never have believed such apathy. Here are actually four and twenty line of battle ships, French and English. In the winter the excuse for remaining at anchor was the bad weather, and now in the middle of summer, they are still at anchor. Sevastopol even is not blockaded, much less do they dream of attacking it.'

There is nothing unusual in Peel's frustrations – one could replicate them a hundred times in the correspondence of other officers – yet there is something about them that strikes a more personal and driven note. 'You must know,' he wrote to Eliza on 7 August, haunted as he always was by the mocking vision of his own mortality that he had confronted in the Nubian desert and the fear that he would never have the chance to show the powers he knew he possessed,

> that the command of a small frigate here places me in a very unfair position, the Admiral says he is afraid to send me out to sea for fear of being snapped up by the enemy's steamers, at which perhaps

you can imagine the sort of smile with which I receive it; and then when he does go to sea, because his ships are all line of battle ships or steamers, he sends me back to Baljick as not being worth the trouble of being towed. There has been such a scene between us, and we are on bad terms. I told him I served for honour and was in an unfair position, and that as soon as Sevastopol was taken, I should request to be superseded. Our inactivity to me is quite marvellous. We must be living on our capital, on the stock of reputation left to us as an inheritance by Nelson and others. The Admiral takes it quite easy, but how the Government or the people of England can stand it remains to be seen. I only hope they will not condemn all, at least I claim exception for myself.

There was worse to come, because if Peel was never afraid of death in battle – the only death he feared, his cousin recalled, was from disease – disease at Varna had become the allied armies' and navies' constant companion. 'Horrors occurred here every day that were shocking to think of,' wrote William Russell, the great *Times* correspondent, as cholera began to take its toll on an army already weakened by the chaos and overcrowding of the voyage out from England.

Walking on the beach one might see some straw sticking up through the sand, and on scraping it away with his stick, be horrified at bringing to light the face of a corpse which had been deposited here with a wisp of straw around it, prey to the dogs and vultures. Dead bodies rose up from the bottom of the harbour and bobbed grimly around in the water or floated in from sea and drifted past the sickened gazers on board the ships – all buoyant, bolt upright, and hideous in the sun.

'As you are sure to hear it by the newspapers,' Peel wrote in the middle of August, at sea off the coast at Varna in the hope of escaping contagion,

I may as well plainly tell you that the Cholera has broken out in both army and navy with excessive virulence. The French [army] have suffered dreadfully, their losses indeed are fabulous … The French fleet also suffered terribly. I do not know the total number, but in one night some of their line of battle ships lost twenty, thirty and forty men. They then put to sea, which is a certain remedy.

The English fleet also sailed as soon as the Cholera was striking down its victims; we are in company cruising on and off, to let the wind ventilate the ships ...

Is this not all very sad. The English entered upon this war with such boasting and after spending millions of money to equip their armies and fleets, these armies and fleets are discomfited.

'I must now give you some account of this Cholera,' he wrote in more detail to his brother Frederick ten days later from Baljick, as confidence in the panacea of the open sea guttered away and numbers like 'twenty' or 'thirty' seemed to belong to some golden age of health and optimism: 'We are now ... exactly a fortnight from its first appearance in the British Fleet, and up to today, the Britannia has lost one hundred and thirty two men, and has about 20 cases that will probably terminate fatally. The Albion has lost about sixty, the Trafalgar between thirty and forty ... the Montebello ... upwards of 200, the Ville de Paris 160 odd ... [and] for every dead man, you must reckon at least two that will be quite unfit for a long time to come, so you may imagine what our loss is.'

Peel's figures tell a horrifying story – and they are nothing like final – but what they do not capture is the lurching, unpredictable trajectory of the attacks that would skip one ship and leave the next unable to muster even a skeleton crew. 'One man would scream out in pain on the lower-deck at night,' a midshipman in HMS *Queen* wrote, recalling the terrifying speed with which the cholera, like some biblical plague, moving in 'a black cloud' across the waters of the Black Sea, laid waste the fleet,

> and his cries were generally followed by those of others. Thus the flagship lost 109 in a few days ... During the second week of August, Admiral Bruat, when leaving our ship after five o'clock tea, said he was thankful he had not a case. Next morning he sent to tell our Captain he had 140 cases, of which 40 were dead. His ship lost nearly 100 men in twenty-four hours ... and for many days after we returned to Baljik Bay, I was employed at sunrise and sunset, in carrying the dead of other ships out to sea for burial.

There was nothing biblical about it in Peel's view, however, nothing God-given in the condition of the allied armies and fleets; in his faith in hard facts he was still very much his father's son. The first two cases of cholera had actually occurred on his ship, but they had taken every precaution to ventilate and purify her, dousing the decks in 'Chloride of Zinc etc, etc', and had got away without a death. 'The Diamond has completely escaped, we were very healthy,' he could write at the end of August, 'as a proof we have but ten men on the sicklist out of 242, and those are many of them from trifling wounds and accidents. I earnestly trust that a strict enquiry will be held into all the circumstances of this dreadful visitation, for there are already some striking facts which would seem to afford a clue to its mystery no officers have died, or have even been attacked.'

It is clear that it was not just the *Diamond* that he had been ventilating. 'It has always been the habit and the *fashion* in this fleet to say that there was nothing to do, and it has been completely acted on,' he complained, before going on to sketch out a war strategy far more ambitious than anything the allies were yet envisaging.

> I need scarcely assure you how utterly opposite all this is to my own feelings and convictions. There is now talk of our going to Sevastopol, the sooner the better, but though some persons are very busy preparing for it, I shall never believe it till we actually sail.
>
> My own opinion is that our proper course now would be to have a large flotilla in the sea of Azoff, where *as yet we have never been*, to land at the Perkop, throw up strong entrenchments across the narrow isthmus, and then, raising the Musselman population, conquer the whole of the Crimea, it would certainly succeed. If we land, as is believed, close to Sevastopol, who knows what numbers the Russians may not be able to send by land along *excellent* roads from Odessa ... and from across the sea of Azoff, to force us to raise the siege. At least it is a question ... I am disliked by Com. In Chief, and I expect by many of the captains, so my position here is not pleasant, and I only tell them I wish they would do something.

If Peel may have ruffled some elderly feathers with his outspoken opinions, he was already making his reputation among the Young Turks of the fleet. 'After cruising for some days' off Sevastopol, where they had been assessing the defences, Evelyn Wood, a boyishly fresh-faced, unswervingly brave eighteen-year-old midshipman in HMS *Queen* recalled, 'Captain Mitchell as Commodore signalling HMS *Diamond* to take letters into Varna for the English mail, William Peel, her Captain, came on board for orders. All our officers were anxious to see him, for he already had a Service reputation as one of the best, though the youngest Post Captain ... I was evidently much struck with Captain Peel's appearance and manners, for I recorded in boyish language, "Captain Peel, very intelligent, sharp as a needle; I never saw a more perfect gentleman."'

It was a compliment Peel might well have returned, because if the future – and furiously mustachioed – Field Marshal Sir Evelyn Wood VC GCB GCMG was a warrior-gentleman rather than a gentleman-warrior, he was a boy made in his own image. On the outbreak of war Wood had found himself in the 116-gun HMS *Queen* under the command of his uncle, and while Peel and the *Diamond* were delivering mail and kicking their heels at Baljick Bay, had been fortunate enough to see what little action there had been.

The *Queen* had been part of the squadron that had reconnoitred Sevastopol and Balaclava, and she had also been at the bombardment of Odessa, where alone among a grimy flotilla of steamers pressing home the attack, the frigate *Arethusa* became the last major ship to fight an action under sail. 'Most of us have read thrilling descriptions of ships in action under *all plain sail*,' Wood proudly recalled forty years later, 'but few now alive can have seen, nor will anyone ever again behold, such a beautiful scene as that which riveted our attention, drawing all eyes away from the more destructive, but prosaic, duel between our steamers and the Mole forts.'

The *Arethusa* was the swansong of a navy that had all but disappeared, and as the weeks passed and Peel's gloomiest predictions for the invasion proved true, the 'capital' built up by Nelson and his captains seemed to be rapidly disappearing with it. There is little doubt that 'old Mrs Dundas' had been hamstrung by the demands of a difficult alliance, but at sixty-eight – and there only because he had been the man in place when war was declared – he lacked either the energy or the instinctive fighting talent to make the most of the navy's subordinate role, or the linguistic and diplomatic skills to punch his weight with the French.

It was as well for Peel that Dundas had only months left in his command, because his successor, Sir Edmund Lyons, was of a very different stamp. At sixty-three he was scarcely any younger than Dundas, but with something of the look and vanity of a Nelson went a fair share of his talent, and in a career that had begun in the last century at the age of eight he had shown precisely the kind of boldness, flair and willingness to exceed orders calculated to secure the loyalty of his youngest and most outspoken Post Captain.

'Lord Raglan and Sir E. Lyons are extremely kind to me,' Peel had reported home early in July, but, with the guns of the *Diamond* too light for her to play a part in any future bombardment of Sevastopol, there was little even Lyons could do for him. 'I must say that not only is this war most expensive,' he complained to his brother towards the end of August, as the campaigning season and the chances of glory inexorably contracted in front of him, 'but is also most inglorious. Do not suppose that except in the excitement of battle, war has any attraction.'

The position was dire enough for Peel to tell Eliza to start looking around for a wife for him – 'some one … that you think will do', as he unenthusiastically phrased it – but by the first week in September the armies were at last ready to move. 'No pen could describe its effect upon the eye,' Russell wrote, as the unparalleled armada of steam and sail began its task of transporting 30,000 French, 27,000 British and seven thousand Turkish troops across 250 miles of hostile waters.

> Ere an hour had elapsed it had extended itself over half the circumference of the horizon. Possibly no expedition so complex and terrible in its means of destruction, with such enormous power in engines of war and such capabilities of locomotion, was ever yet sent forth by any worldly power. The fleet, in five irregular and straggling lines, flanked by men-of-war and war steamers, advanced slowly, filling the atmosphere with innumerable columns of smoke, which gradually flattened out into streaks and joined the clouds, adding to the sombre appearance of this well-named 'Black' Sea.

It might have been 'interesting', as Wood nicely phrased it, if the Russian men-of-war had come out of Sevastopol to offer battle against the congested and slow-moving allied fleets, but the navy's reputation had not all gone yet, and on 11 September the signal was made for the transports to steer for Eupatoria. 'The impression as we drew near,' wrote Russell, as dawn broke the following morning, and a thin dark line just visible on the port side finally resolved itself into the coast of the Crimea, 'was that the coast presented a remarkable resemblance to the dunes of La Belle France. The country was flat, but numerous herds of cattle were to be seen in the plains and the salt marshes and the farm-houses became more frequent as we proceeded.'

The place chosen for the landing was a long shingle strip shelving back to a low sandstone cliff that formed a kind of causeway separating the sea from a stagnant salt-water lake behind. To the south of it was a sandy beach, and beyond that the low coastline stretched away as far as could be seen, until it faded into the hills surrounding Sevastopol some thirty-five miles distant. 'The country inland,' Russell continued, struck by the contrast between the allied armada and the autumnal, almost Keatsian rhythms of the scene ashore,

> was covered with cattle, with grain in stack, with farm-houses. The stubble fields were covered with wild lavender, southernwood, and other fragrant shrubs, which the troops collected for fuel, and which filled the air with an aromatic perfume. As we cruised down towards Eupatoria, we could see the people driving their carts and busy in their ordinary occupations.
>
> Now and then some Cossacks were visible, scouring along the roads to the interior. The post carriage from Sevastopol to Odessa was rolling leisurely along, and conveying, probably, news of the great armament with which the coast was menaced.

The planning for the invasion had been left to Lyons and his immensely able flag captain, William Mends, and at 9 o'clock on the morning of the fourteenth a single black ball was run up to the fore of the *Agamemnon* and a gun fired to reinforce the signal. Within minutes the inshore water was thick with gigs, launches, cutters, flats and horse floats, and under the passive gaze of a small party of Cossacks, watching from the ridge of the low cliff above the beach, the British disembarkation began. 'I can only write you a line,' Peel scribbled to Eliza on 16 September, forty-eight gruelling hours into the operation,

> hoping that you are all well, and to tell you that I am in excellent health. We have landed the Anglofrankishturkish army, and tomorrow they march for Sevastopol. The enemy have not as yet shown themselves, which in itself is indicative of weakness. Our only serious enemy is time, and a gale of wind that throws a heavy surf on the open coast, and for a time cuts off our communications ...

I have *many* friends here in the British army. Edward Peel is very
well as is Arthur Hardinge. Lord Raglan is the same as ever, and
right worthy to command a British Army.

I hope, please God, in five weeks time we shall have taken
Sevastopol. It may be sooner ... Every thing goes on wonderfully.

It might have been taken as an omen of things to come that the first
allied troops ashore had actually been French, and a closer look at
the army might have tempered Peel's optimism. The days at sea had
done something for its health, but the overcrowded expedition ships
had inevitably brought the cholera and dysentery with them, killing
or disabling almost five hundred men on the voyage and leaving the
rank and file put ashore too weak even to carry their knapsacks.

If the expedition had sailed at the height of the summer it might
at least have enjoyed a measure of surprise, but almost two months
of delay had given the Russians the respite they needed. Between the
allies and Sevastopol a series of rivers ran at right angles across their
line of march, and with all the freedom in the world to pick his time
and place the Russian commander, Prince Menschikoff, had deployed
his army of some 33,000 infantry, supported by more than three thousand cavalry and an artillery force of eighty-four cannon, along an
immensely formidable defensive position on the heights above the
River Alma seventeen miles to the allies' south.

On the right flank as the allies marched towards it, protected by
the sea and the guns of the fleets, were the French and Turks, on the
more exposed left the British, and for almost the last time in the war
they almost looked like the army that had embarked amidst such
enthusiasm from England five months earlier. Over the next year this
same force would disintegrate into the sartorial anarchy so poignantly
caught in the lens of Roger Fenton, the most famous photographer
of the conflict, but just as the *Arethusa* was the swansong of the old
navy then the Alma was to be the army's, the glorious 'scarlet, white,
blue, green, and gold', bear-skinned, feather-bonneted and parade-
drilled death knell of the Napoleonic age in 'full fig'.

And without any proper reconnaissance, without any adequate
idea of Russian numbers, without any serious allied cooperation, with
virtually no direction from start to finish, and no idea even of the
state of the river to be crossed, victory was going to demand the sort
of miracle that Raglan had always associated with the 'Great Duke'.
'On night of the 19th,' wrote the young Etonian signals officer George

Tryon, watching from the maintop of the *Vengeance*, anchored close to Peel's *Diamond* off the mouth of the Alma,

the army in full fig advanced (the fleets accompanying) and slept that night three miles from the Russians, stationed on the heights on the south bank of the River Alma, with seventy or eighty guns in position. We all anchored close to the shore in full view of everything. The next day at about eleven the army was seen to advance; the French and Turks, close to the shore, climbed up a very steep road, which the Russians were unable to prevent, as our guns would have been able to knock them over. The French rushed up most gallantly; the artillery had a tremendous drag to get up at all; twice we saw the French shelter under the brow of the hill, making a short retreat from the murderous fire, while their forces were increasing; when collected they rushed on, carrying everything before them.

Now, for our part of the field. Our men advanced, first coming to a village in flames, filled with sharpshooters, who were driven out by the Rifles, and were assailed by a storm of shot, shell, and grape. Now they came to a brook about 300 yards from the main Russian battery: it had very steep banks, and part of the men were up to their armpits; but nothing stopped them. They shoved each other up the opposite bank, and rushed on right in the face of a battery of twenty-four guns. Took it, guns and all, killing or driving out of the redoubt all the Russians, when some one hailed, 'You are firing on the French.' A bugler heard it, sounded cease firing, which was repeated down the line and obeyed. The 23rd leapt out of the battery; the Russians rallied, returned, retook their guns, and carried them off. In a few minutes the mistake was found out, but too late to save the lives of hundreds of brave men, who huddled together, afforded a fearful opportunity to the Russians to pour in a murderous fire. It was now the colonel and Radcliffe (a brother of the one who was in this ship, and eldest son of the Radcliffe papa met) fell; but our own men rushed up again as soon as the mistake was found out, captured two guns, and routed the Russians, who, like a flock of goats, now fled towards Sevastopol.

It is unclear how much of this the fleet could have seen from the maintops – Tryon had the benefit of a brother in the thick of the fighting – but it was only as the wounded were brought down to the allied ships the next day that the magnitude of the British victory became obvious. The far left of the army and the cavalry had played virtually no part in the battle, but under the withering fire of the Russian guns the centre and right had forded the Alma and fought their way up its slopes, taken the Russian batteries, retired, and then – in best Hyde Park drill order – recaptured them all over again in one of the supreme triumphs of courage over inept leadership that even British arms can boast.

If the victory had been followed up, and Raglan's cavalry let out of its infamous 'bandbox', then Peel's predictions for Sevastopol might have proved conservative, but with the defenceless city open to the north the allied commanders balked at their chance of ending the campaign there and then. For the next two days their armies sat instead on the heights of Alma and buried their dead, and when on the third day – to the 'infernal too-too-tooing' of French bugles and trumpets, as Raglan testily put it – the armies began a long and precarious flanking march of the city preparatory to a winter siege, the opportunity was gone.

If the cost of the victory at the Alma was measured in casualties – more than two thousand British dead or wounded alone – it would have been high enough, but the real price lay in this failure to follow it up. In a war in which the incompetence of the rival generals cancelled itself out, Raglan's men had done themselves no favours in bailing him out of trouble. They had, certainly, established a moral ascendancy over their Russian enemy that would carry them through even harder battles, but their own command was another matter. Ahead lay a winter campaign for which they, their generals, their commissariat and their medical support were desperately unprepared. As the allied armies and fleets prepared to part company, though – the *Diamond*, along with the *Agamemnon*, *Sans Pareil*, *Niger* and *Triton* to follow the coast south to their rendezvous with Raglan at Balaclava, the army to turn inland into the unknown hinterland of Sevastopol – there was at least one man for whom the campaign had been redeemed. In creating the conditions for a land war that would destroy his army Raglan had paradoxically found a role for the navy's guns. And if nobody, after the Alma, could ever again think that forty years in an office and an arm lost at Waterloo were adequate qualifications for the joint command of 60,000 men, Peel, for one, would always be too grateful for the opportunity to complain.

IX

The fortress city of Sevastopol – Russell's 'stately mistress of the Euxine' – stood beside a great natural harbour, almost a mile wide and five miles in length, on the south-western extreme of the Crimean peninsula. On either shore of this inlet were a series of stone-built forts, and on the southern side, clustered around a second harbour, called the Man of War, that ran south at a right angle from the main inlet, rose the city itself, a gleaming vista of white stone, of barracks and naval buildings, dry-docks, fortifications, churches and villas that climbed, like a sort of 'oriental Bath', towards the bare and undulating upland plateau that ringed it to the south and east.

There would have been few thoughts of Bath for anyone seeing Sevastopol for the first time from the sea, however, and especially not for a man who had cut his teeth at the bombardment of Acre. Even after six months of war the defences on the landward side were more or less negligible, but the sea defences Peel first viewed on 25 September were another matter, with a formidable complex of earthwork batteries and massive forts (with names – Constantine, 'Wasp', Telegraph, Alexander, Quarantine – that would all become grimly familiar to the allied fleets) commanding the entrance to the main harbour and its shallow sea approaches.

There had never been anything to fear, however, from the Russian navy – Menschikoff's decision to scuttle the front line of his fleet across the entrance of the harbour after the Alma had finally robbed the allies of any lingering hope of battle – and four days after their first leisurely look at Sevastopol, Peel and the *Diamond* were towed through a narrow gap in the cliffs to the south of the city to keep their rendezvous with Raglan's army. 'I never was more astonished in my life,' Russell wrote of his first sight of the tiny harbour of Balaclava, seen from the cliffs above before the squalor and miseries of the British occupation had changed its character for ever,

and looking down saw under my feet a little pond, closely compressed by the sides of high rocky mountains; on it floated some six or seven English ships, for which exit seemed hopeless. The bay is like a highland tarn, some half mile in length from the sea, and varies from 250 yards to 120 in breadth. The shores are so steep and precipitous that they shut out as it were the expanse of the harbour, and make it appear much smaller than it really is. Towards the sea the cliffs close up and completely overlap the narrow channel which leads to the haven, so that it is quite invisible. On the south-east of the poor village, which struggles for existence between the base of the rocky hills and the margin of the sea, are the extensive ruins of a Genoese fort, built some 2000 feet above the level of the sea ... its curtains, bastions, towers, and walls, all destroyed and crumbling in decay.

Russell might complain that the French were the first ashore at Calamita Bay, the first into action at the Alma – the first in everything – but Balaclava would prove the exception that the British soldier and sailor would come to rue. The army under Raglan had reached the harbour a day ahead of their allies, and at the urgings of the navy, who wanted its anchorage for their ships, had claimed rights of possession, ceding the left that they had held since Calamita – and with it the flank protection of the sea and the shorter and easier route up to the uplands – to their savvier French allies.

The sole anxiety among the fleet at this time, however, had been that the army would take the city before they could have a crack themselves, but on 1 October a signal from Balaclava instructing all 'Line-of-battle ships [to] send 140 men and proportion of officers for services with land-forces' put an end to fears that Raglan would do anything so precipitate. 'I write these lines in the greatest haste,' Peel wrote to his brother Frederick from the *Diamond* a week later,

> and shall feel very thankful if it pleases God to preserve my life through the next few days.
>
> I am with a thousand seamen to work batteries against Sevastopol, and though there is another Captain senior to me who commands the whole, I have seen enough in the last few days to know that it practically falls on me ...
>
> Our seamen are splendid fellows; we have great difficulties, and we manage to get over them.

Peel was perhaps being unfair about Stephen Lushington, the senior captain in command of this Naval Brigade, but he certainly had no complaints about the young midshipman, Edward St John Daniel, who he took ashore as the first of his aides-de-camp. The son of a Bristol merchant, Daniel had grown up among the Georgian grandeur of Clifton's Windsor Terrace, and after entering the navy at the age of thirteen had seen action with the frigate *Winchester* in the Second Burma War before joining Peel in the *Diamond*.

Over the months ahead – and whatever the dangers – the 'heroic boy' on the white pony could always be found at Peel's side, but in these first days it was a rather different sort of heroics Peel demanded. 'Probably no 1,200 men ever worked harder,' Evelyn Wood of the *Queen*, another of the young mids drafted into the brigade, recalled.

> We were told that the army could not assist with transport, but that it was most important to open fire on Sevastopol at once, and for the next six days our life was spent in dragging guns and ammunition up the Balaclava col or hill; on the 4th the brigade was divided, one half working from the harbour to the col, and the other from thence to the Light Division camp. The 68-pounder guns were dragged up on travelling-carriages lent us by the artillery, but they could not lend us enough for the other pieces, and nearly all the guns were dragged up the hill, and later down into the battery on their ships trucks [wheels] ...
>
> We breakfasted daily at 5, began work at 5.30, and, except for one hour at mid-day, worked till 6 P.M., doing the work of horses, the distance by the track from Balaclava to what was about to become the right attack being just 8 miles.

Even to this task the navy brought its own distinctive style, and the spectacle of Peel's tars – fifty to a gun, with a fiddler, fifer or tenor perched astride the barrel – hauling their massive weights onto the upland plain became one the 'sights' of the early Balaclava season. 'The tars are such jovial fellows,' Henry Jeffreys Bushby, a London barrister and the campest of camp followers and 'TGs' – 'Travelling Gents' – to come out to the Crimea, wrote home. 'They do everything to music and make work itself a kind of dance. There are four or five hundred at this moment hauling up a rope, with their feet tramping to the time of Rory O'More. In camp, where no fiddle was to be heard, they used to time their steps in hauling up the guns, by making one of their numbers sing.'

It was sometimes said of Sevastopol that the easiest way to take it would be to 'put up a grog-shop on the other side' and leave the tars to 'find their way through', but Peel at least was under no such illusion. 'We MUST take Sevastopol,' he told his brother on 8 October:

the enemy have made it very strong, and it will no doubt be a very severe affair. I shall look to you to put all things straight for me; and you must not on any account let our mother know that the next few days will decide everything.

PS Our guns, at least the 30 32Ps are up, with a good quantity of ammunition, though not nearly as much as we could wish. We have to drag almost everything ourselves, and it is six miles distant, I am this morning leaving the ship for good.

For the next eight months Peel's new home would be the bare and exposed upland plateau to the south and east of Sevastopol, over which sprawled the besieging armies of Britain and France. The area covered by the fifty-odd thousand men formed a roughly triangular tableland, dissected by a series of steep ravines and bordered along its eastern edge by a precipitous cliff that ran for eight miles south and south-west from the head of Sevastopol harbour to the sea-cliffs close to Balaclava. 'Nothing can be imagined more dreary and barren than the country in which the camp is pitched,' Henry Bushby wrote of this 'tawny Sahara':

The colouring of the scenery is simple enough – mainly plain drab ... the grass is scanty and withered. There are no trees, only here and there patches of short scrub oak. Even the withered grass and the scrub must be looked for. As a rule one sees nothing but bare brown earth, strewn with rough stones that set their faces against galloping Aides-de-Camp; or bristling with bunches of burnt-up, star-headed, thistles of which the best that can be said, is, that they now and again shade a misguided anemone.

With the French left flank resting on the sea and their right covered by their allies, and the British army defending an area that stretched from the Great Ravine to the Inkerman Heights in the north, there was no doubt who had been given what Raglan quaintly called the 'working oar'. By the end of the siege the roles of the two allies would be humiliatingly reversed, but in these opening months the French had the best of everything, with their overstretched and ill-equipped allies left to cope with a dangerously exposed right flank and a base at Balaclava that was vulnerable to a Russian army that might be just about anywhere.

It is fatuous to talk of a 'siege' when the route to the north and the Crimean interior was never sealed, but with the siege guns in place, the allied attacks formed a semi-circle at between a thousand and eighteen hundred yards' distance from the Russian land defences. In the first flush of enthusiasm Sir George Cathcart had famously dismissed these as no more than 'a park wall', but in the weeks since the allied landings Colonel Todtleben, the engineering genius in charge of Sevastopol's defence, had transformed them, creating a continuous line of reinforced earthworks that linked a series of forts running from the Little Redan in the north to – in anti-clockwise order – the Malakoff, Redan, Barrack, Strand, Flagstaff, Central and Quarantine batteries on the western flank of the city.

Of all these, the key positions, and the ones Peel was most closely involved with, were the Malakoff and the Redan, and on 8 October his men began to haul their ammunition and construct their

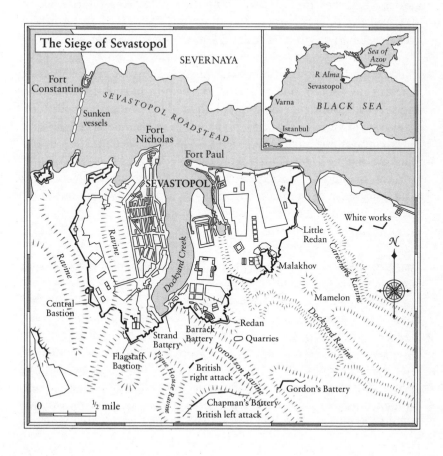

batteries on the forward slope of the Woronzoff Heights opposite them. 'We turned out daily at 4.30 am,' Wood remembered of the brutal work, made harsher still by the broken rocky landscape and thin crumbling soil that meant even the earth to fill their gabions – the cylindrical wicker baskets that reinforced the parapets – had to be hauled up into position on the heights, 'and with half an hour for breakfast and an hour's rest for dinner, all worked till 7.30 p.m., except the night parties, which rested from 2pm to 8pm, when they worked till daylight.'

It was not as if all the shovel and pick work was even done in any safety, because while the British and French guns remained silent, a barrage of shot and shell would greet the work parties' arrival and continue 'day and night' above the half-finished trenches. 'A few men [would be] placed on the look out, their heads a few inches above the work,' Captain Radcliffe of the 20th Regiment recalled, 'to give notice when they fired, by watching the smoke from their Guns by day and the flash by night & calling out "Shot" when all in the trenches lie down till it has pass'd and then resume their work.'

This did not stop a steady leak of casualties from both the 'Right' and 'Left Attacks' – the two British positions divided by the Woron-zoff Ravine – but in spite of deaths, exhaustion and continued illness, morale and confidence remained almost dangerously high. It must have been obvious to anyone who had approached the siege lines that there was nothing amateurish about Sevastopol's defences, yet it was hard for anyone in the British camp to remember the Russian collapse at the Alma and not anticipate the same again. 'I could not but feel a high degree of excitement,' wrote Fanny Duberly, that bloodthirsty bride of Bellona's least bellicose bridegroom, Henry Duberly, 'and I think it was not unnatural. We were standing on the brow of a hill, backed by our magnificent troops, and fronting the enemy; the doomed city beneath our feet, and the pale moon above; it was indeed a moment worth a hundred years of everyday existence.'

The confidence was so high, indeed, that the prospect of a flooded market had depressed the value of loot. 'On the 16th October' – the day before the proposed opening of the allied bombardment and infantry assault – Wood wrote, 'bets were freely offered in our camp that the city would fall in twenty-four hours. Some of the older and more prudent officers gave the Russians forty-eight hours, but no one thought they could withstand our fire longer. My older messmates would not allow me to buy a good Paris-made gold watch which a soldier had taken at the Alma and offered to sell for £1, saying, "In forty-eight hours gold watches will be much cheaper!"'

At six-thirty the next morning, just two and a half weeks after Peel and his Naval Brigade had disembarked, the seventy-two British and fifty-three French guns at last opened fire. 'The roaring and whistling of the shot, as they flew through the air on their course of destruction, surpassed anything ever heard before,' wrote Somerset Calthorpe, watching – or trying to watch – with Raglan through the thick pall of smoke that enveloped the two lines. 'About half an hour after we commenced "pounding" a breeze sprang up and cleared the smoke away for a short time; we had then an opportunity of seeing what we had done. The first thing we observed was the Malakoff tower quite silent, and the top of it all knocked to pieces ... Here and there also a gun had been silenced, but for the most part, no great advantage had been gained by either party.'

Inside the batteries, deafened by the roar of the guns and the shrieks of the wounded, blinded by the smoke and dust, or the atomised body of what only a moment earlier had been a seaman, it was as near to hell as anyone could imagine. 'Of all the dreadful places in the world,' a lieutenant in the 46th Regiment wrote, 'a battery under a ... heavy fire is the most dreadful. There is none of the excitement of personal combat; you become blackened with smoke, whilst every shot that strikes the parapet covers you with dust, and the heat and noise are almost unendurable. Then the nature of the wounds is so dreadful; you see men cut to pieces with a round shot, or blown up with a shell, so that there is no trace of there having been human beings left.'

Among all this 'tumult and confusion ... blood, groans and death', William Peel – still clean-shaven and dapper amidst an army that had almost forgotten what it was to shave or change its clothes – strolled about the twenty-one-gun battery in the Right Attack as if he was still in Corfu harbour. 'I can see him now,' the future Field Marshal Lord Wolseley, a devotee of the Carlyle School of Manliness if ever there was one, wrote many years later,

with his telescope under his arm in quarter-deck fashion, halting from time to time to watch the effect of his battery upon the enemy's works, or to direct the attention of his men in charge of guns to some particular spot or object in the Redan or Malakoff ... It was his particular practice to walk about behind his battery on the natural plateau of the ground, where he had little or no protection from the enemy's fire. This he did from no swagger, but to set an example to his own men of cool contempt for danger. He was thus always in view; his men could always see him, and as they were down in the trench before him, and so, in comparative safety, all felt that his eye was upon them, and that if he in that exposed position made so light of his great danger, they could not presume to wince under the shelter which the battery afforded them. He was not only always cool but most particularly courteous, and there was this well-known peculiarity about his grace of manner, that the hotter the fire and the greater the danger, the more suave, or as his men used to say, 'b—y polite,' he became.

Peel's men needed all the encouragement they could get, because by shortly after nine in the morning the *Diamond*'s contingent were desperately in need of reinforcement and powder. 'When we got about 5000 yards from the 21-gun battery,' recalled Wood, who, back at the brigade camp, had answered Peel's request for ammunition before anyone more senior could stop him,

> several round-shot and shell fired from the Redan, distant 2,000 yards, passed over our heads, making, I suspect, some of us less eager for the fray, than we were when in camp. Presently a shell burst immediately over the leading cart, and a fragment carried away one of the wheel spokes. The man in the shafts, and everyone at the drag-ropes, ran before my slower perception was acted on, and I was thus enabled to make a good start by peremptorily calling them to a sense of our duty. They returned with a higher opinion of their officer than he merited, as I saw clearly, before the idea of running occurred to me, that the danger was over.

Scrambling up the northern cliff of the ravine, Wood secured the powder in the caves used for a magazine, but he had no sooner made his way up through the covered entry and into the battery than, stooping to avoid a shot, he felt his foot slip on something soft under him. 'It was the stomach of a dead sailor,' he wrote, 'with nothing but trousers on his body, and stepping hastily forward I landed on another dead man – the Captain of the main-top! The shock to my feelings made me carry my head fairly erect for the next eight months.'

It was not just the shock to his feelings that made Wood stand and walk upright during his months in the batteries, because with Peel exposing himself to every shot, no officer of his would have dreamed of doing less. 'We were very proud of ourselves when we first opened fire,' Wood recalled, remembering the spirit that ran through Peel's 'Diamonds' as, hour by hour, they ground out their duel for supremacy with the guns of the Malakoff and Redan, 'and had adorned our battery with a board on which was printed "The Koh-I-noor Battery". This and a Union Jack hoisted behind the centre gun were soon knocked over – the name was knocked over but the flag-staff was replaced again and again. Captain Peel, whose idea it was, fixed it up twice the first day, but eventually nothing remained of the pole, and we fastened it to a spare rammer, stuck into a pyramid of gun-trucks.'

If there seems a touch of theatre about all this – the Koh-i-Noor was not known as the 'dress circle' for nothing – there was nothing contrived about Peel's reaction when a forty-two-pound shell from an eight-inch gun, fuse burning, smashed through the parapet and rolled into the middle of a group of sailors. The 'Diamonds' had already taken enough casualties to know precisely what carnage such a shell could do in a battery, but almost before the men could throw themselves to the ground Peel had it in his arms and, cradling it on his chest, had climbed onto the banquette and heaved it out of the battery a split second before it exploded.

It was no isolated incident – Wood would later look up to find that the man beside him, beating out flames next to a powder maga-zine while the shells poured in, was Peel – and at no time was this personal example so badly needed as on this first morning. After two and a half hours an explosion in a magazine announced the imminent collapse of the French bombardment, and with the British Left Attack running short of powder and faltering, any surviving hope for the planned infantry assault depended on the twenty-one-gun battery in the Right Attack.

The failure of the French guns had in fact already effectively doomed that – allied sensibilities precluded an all-British assault – and as the firing gradually died away all that was left to Peel's men was the bitter satisfaction of destroying the Malakoff's round stone tower and softening the Redan for an assault that would never come. 'Every regimental officer believed we could carry the Malakoff and Redan that evening,' Wood wrote forty years later, the disappointment as sharp as ever at the memory of a lost opportunity that would come back to haunt the allies, 'and this was not unreasonable, for they had all the confidence accruing from their recent success at the Alma ... but in combined operations concession is essential.'

It was an opportunity that was as transitory as it was real, because the next morning, after a night's heroic work rebuilding batteries and replacing guns, the Redan was as strong as it had ever been. It was a pattern that the British would see endlessly repeated, and the dawn of a realisation that what had once seemed Sevastopol's weakness was its protean strength. Like a boxer harmlessly absorbing punches on the arms – 'a Rumble in the Jungle' on the heights above Sevastopol – Todtleben's earthwork system could take all the punishment a labouring attack could throw, and simply wait for it to punch itself out. And punch itself out it soon did. 'The siege – or more properly, the bootless discharge of much cannon at mud banks – rubs on,' one Coldstream officer complained, but within forty-eight hours even that was scarcely true. On the afternoon of the seventeenth Canrobert, who had succeeded St Arnaud, had promised Raglan that his guns would be ready to resume the next day, but no one was surprised when they did not, and with each passing day Raglan had to watch his ammunition supplies dwindle and the return on the massive allied bombardment gutter away almost to nothing. By the twentieth the attack was over, and the greatest barrage in siege history had failed. The 'park wall' had held. And with the equally disastrous failure of an attack by the allied fleets on Sevastopol's massive sea defences, a long winter beckoned.

X

If there was one man who had come out of the disappointment of the opening bombardment smelling of Camelot it was Peel. 'To the best of my recollection,' Wood proudly recalled, 'the 21-gun battery was the only one that fired unceasingly till the 20th October inclusive. This was certainly due to our master spirit, Peel, not only by his providing the ammunition, but by the vigour he instilled into all his subordinates.'

There might be a temptation to take the testimony of Wood, writing with all the rheumy-eyed fondness of age for a boyhood hero, with a pinch of salt, but it is plain that among the ruins of allied hopes a Victorian myth was already taking shape. 'Every day, dearest Elise,' Peel wrote home with an artless pride to his sister, 'I have to go down into the trenches and stand for hours under an awful fire. My battery is the "Koh-i-noor" and I believe that it will live in history, and could you hear how I am spoken of myself by both soldiers and sailors, you would feel proud of your brother.'

It was not long before Eliza was able to hear, or at least read, of his exploits for herself. 'The blue-jackets were delighted with Captain Peel,' Russell wrote in *The Times*, after a mild censure for his reckless courage, 'who animated the men by the exhibition of the best qualities of an officer ... When the Union Jack in the sailors' battery was shot away, he seized the broken staff, and leaping up on the earthworks, waved the old bit of bunting again and again amid a storm of shot, which fortunately left him untouched.'

Russell was not the only man alarmed at his courage – Peel had to reassure his sister that he was not trying to get himself killed, whatever anyone thought – but there was already something other than dazzling heroics that had begun to cling about the Peel name. There would be many officers over the months to come who gained an equal reputation for their Christian valour, but in the language and imagery of the time, it was supremely Peel who emerged as the shining knight of Arthurian legend, the incarnation of a chivalric ideal of honour, service and manly nobility that was only heightened by the presence at his side of his devoted young midshipmen-squires.

There was nothing 'in the annals of chivalry that surpasses the conduct of Aides de Camp Messres Daniels [sic] and Wood', Sir Edward Lyons would tell a Mansion House audience, and Henry Bushby, for one, was another enthusiastic believer. 'What a softening, inexpressible grace is lent to a man-of-war by the middies,' he wrote from Balaclava, in a passage that might well have alarmed Victorian mamas more than it did.

The army has nothing corresponding to these pretty little fellows, who, with their rosy cheeks, resemble their mamas much more than the heroes they are one day to be. To meet them, too, in the midst of their work; and with the knowledge, that it was but the other day, that the poor boys were ducking their curly heads and laughing, amidst shot and shell, with about the same sense of adventure, as if it had been a game of snow-balls! Never dream of degeneracy

in a land where mothers thus devote their offspring. Talk of Sparta
– of Rome! England alone rocks her children on the wave, and War
is the 'wolf' which suckles them.

There was an intensity, a ferocity almost, about the devotion of these
'gallant youths' to Peel that now inevitably poses questions, but for
an age that had successfully de-sexed the Theban Band it simply
added to the myth. 'There is a special bond of comradeship between
those who have stood together in critical moments of war,' Sir John
Robinson, editor of the *Daily News*, wrote in a lushly Whitmanesque
passage quoted with approval by Evelyn Wood. 'Nothing can quite
approach it – they have been revealed to each other in a supreme test
of moral and physical value. They have been close to God, and have
seen each other as He and posterity will appraise them.'

   If the tortuous history of Victorian chivalry, with all its aberrant
twists, would brutally underline how many other and different
currents mingled with the ideals of Kingsley, Thomas Hughes or
Henry Bushby, myth and reality seemed for the moment to have
become one. 'Though all our officers were brave,' Wood remembered,
in a passage that invokes all those virtues – the disciplining and
subjection of the body, the protection of the weak – that Hughes saw
as central to that 'old chivalrous and Christian belief' at the heart of
Arthurian/Victorian legend,

   It was Captain Peel who inspired his followers with a part of his
   own nature. He exemplified the American poet's hero –

           'The bravest are the tenderest,
           The loving are the daring.'

This man, who never quailed, felt acutely every shot and shell
which passed near him. But the only outward effect was to make
him throw up his head and square his shoulders, yet his nervous
system was so highly strung that even a flesh wound became
dangerous in his case. In 1851, when crossing the Nubian Desert
... Peel dismounted from his camel to give water to a small dying
bird! To this tender-hearted man it appeared our bluejackets should
be encouraged to stand up to their guns like men.

For a sterner moralist like Thomas Arnold no two codes could have been farther apart than Chivalry and Christianity – the one all self-reliance, the other all submission – but as in so many things, Peel was a child of his times in his reconciliation of contradictions. 'I trust in God, and firmly believe he will bring me out safe,' he told his sister on 23 October, with the same mixture of faith and flash that had carried him through his Nile travels. 'You must not be alarmed all will end well or to use the expression of "Koh-i-Noor" Battery which I can assure you is quite the "Haut Ton" and is called by every one the "Dress Circle" "all will be serene" how I smile when I hear my noble blue jackets answer me that way, when no harm has been done.'

All might have been serene within the Koh-i-Noor, but with the failure of the bombardment and the indefinite postponement of plans to storm the city, there was no disguising the trouble the allies were in. There had been no expectation of a winter campaign when they had first landed in September, but even before the bitter Crimean cold had set in to weaken the suffering armies further, the cholera that had accompanied them from Varna continued its appalling ravages on an army now reduced to an active strength of no more than 16,500.

Things were to get a lot worse before they got any better, but with seven hundred men invalided to Balaclava in a fortnight, a constant bleed of another twenty or thirty casualties a day from enemy fire, ammunition, spare wheels and carriages for the guns all running low, and a Russian army threatening their rear, there was for the first time since the Alma a real military threat as well. There was a general feeling in the allies' camps that Balaclava itself could be defended against an assault, but the temptation to the Russians of a prize that would effectively spell the end of the allied campaign meant that an attack there was a matter of when and not if.

They had to wait only days, but if Peel was no more than a spectator at the Battle of Balaclava – with Raglan and the general staff he watched the heroics of Scarlett's 'heavies', Campbell's 'thin red line' of Highlanders and the unfolding tragedy of the Light Brigade from the Sapouna Ridge – he did not need the sound of Sevastopol's bells to tell him what a disaster it had been. 'What an anxious night,' Fanny Duberly could still write three days later, on 28 October, as with the Causeway Heights and Woronzoff Road now in Russian hands, she waited for a renewed attack, 'guns firing incessantly from the batteries around Balaclava! And occasional volleys of musketry,

seemed to say that the enemy were having another *try* for it. I lay
awake, a little anxious and doubtful. The harbour was astir – steamers getting up their steam, anchors being weighed, and all made ready
for departure. If they should be able to shell the harbour!'

Mrs Duberly was not alone in her fears – and the proximity of
ships carrying powder did little for her sleep – but the real weakness
of the British position had never been Balaclava, but at the opposite
end of the British lines, on the Inkerman Heights. Two days after the
battle Peel had optimistically written that their 'reverses' there might
at last 'be productive of good', but all the 'good' in the world was not
enough to change the simple fact that Raglan did not have the men
or the resources to prosecute a siege *and* defend his hopelessly
exposed right flank.

The failure of a strong Russian raid there on the twenty-sixth
certainly did nothing to inject a sense of urgency, but with his engineers constantly crying out for more 'working parties' and more
'covering parties', and Sir de Lacy Evans, the commander of the
exposed 2nd Division, complaining that he had 'only six hundred
men ... completely worn out with fatigue' to hold the forward positions, it was hard to see where Raglan was going to find his reserves.
'The failure to intrench at Inkerman,' Wood later wrote, was not so
much a matter of 'procrastination' or 'indolence', but 'was caused by
our having engaged in an enterprise entirely beyond our powers,
which the reflex action of public opinion from England would not
allow us to abandon, even if our leaders had been willing to do so ...
So Lord Raglan could only trust in Providence, in his own stoical,
courageous nature, and the, as yet, unconquerable fighting qualities
of our soldiers.'

If there was scarcely a man in the allied armies who could not see
this for himself, it was not going to take a Todtleben in the Russian
camp to identify the British weakness. The attack on the twenty-sixth
had admittedly been repulsed with minimum casualties by Evans's
men, but it had given the Russian commanders valuable intelligence
of the terrain and British dispositions that the arrival of reinforcements from Odessa at the beginning of November put them in a
strong position to exploit.

With the allies also planning a second bombardment it was a race
against time, and the first inkling Peel's men had that they had been
beaten to the punch came when out of the dark and rawness of early
morning on 5 November came the distant sound of an army march-

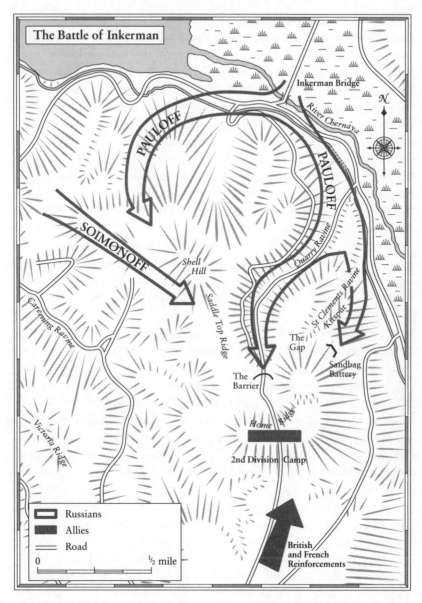

The Battle of Inkerman

Inkerman Bridge

River Chernaya

N

PAULOFF

PAULOFF

SOIMONOFF

Shell Hill

Quarry Ravine

St Clements Ravine

Careening Ravine

Saddle Top Ridge

Kitspur

The Gap

Sandbag Battery

The Barrier

Victoria Ridge

Home Ridge

2nd Division Camp

Russians
Allies
Road
0   ½ mile

British and French Reinforcements

ing. 'My relief breakfasted at 2.30 A.M.,' Wood remembered, 'and marched off to battery at 3.AM. It had been raining heavily during the night, and was still drizzling at dawn. There was a fog, which, though dense in the valleys, lifted occasionally on the hills. We could hear plainly the bells ringing in the city at 4 A.M., and some said they could hear the rumble of artillery wheels.'

The sounds came from the direction of the Inkerman slopes, some two miles beyond the position of Peel's battery on the British Right Attack. The contours of the land here gave the battlefield the shape of a rifle stock, with a massive tapering upland spur, defined on its eastern flank by the precipitous cliffs of the Tchernaya River and on its western side by the Careening Gorge, terminating abruptly at the northern – or butt – end above the great harbour of Sevastopol.

At its widest, at this northern extreme, the plateau is about two miles across, and at its narrowest, where the Nikirakoff Gully cuts in on the western side and the Quarry Ravine on the east, little more than a quarter. To the north of this narrow strip the ground slopes up to a central feature known as Shell Hill, and to the south broadens out and climbs again towards the Inkerman Crest, a negligible ridge some 1,200 yards from Shell Hill and thirty feet higher, that runs for four hundred yards in an easterly direction before turning sharply north along Fore Ridge towards the precipitous edge of the Tchernaya valley and the abandoned British gun emplacement of Sandbag Battery.

The two key features of this undulating upland were the scrubby, stunted oak with which it is covered, and the great ravines and tributary gullies that offered the only practical paths up onto the plateau. In the raid on 26 October the Russians had exploited the cover of the Careening Gorge to gain surprise, and the plan for the fifth was in essence the same, with a Russian army of 19,000 infantry and thirty guns issuing from Sevastopol under General Soimonoff, while a second army of 16,000 infantry and ninety-six guns under Pauloff was to cross the marshy ground at the head of the harbour and gain the uplands by means of the Volvia Ravine and the post road from the interior that winds up through the Quarry Ravine and emerges onto the plateau to the south-east of the Kitspur and Sandbag Battery.

Across the post road here, seven hundred yards from Sandbag Battery, the British had thrown up a low earth wall known as the Barrier – more a notional title than a real impediment – but their defensive strategy was essentially that which had just about served at Balaclava and on 26 October. The camp of the 2nd Division was pitched on the southern slope of the Inkerman or 'Home' Ridge only some half a mile behind this, but with a force of just 3,500 men under his command de Lacy Evans's only hope was to withdraw his pickets from the forward positions and defend the Home Ridge until reinforcements could be brought up to stem an attack.

This tactic had worked perfectly when faced with six and not forty thousand, but its inherent weakness – a weakness exacerbated by the diversionary threat of the Russian army that had fought at Balaclava to their rear – was always going to be the reaction time before any reserves could come to its aid. It had been mid-morning at Balaclava before the supporting infantry so much as reached the battlefield, but in the event the strategy was never to be tested at Inkerman, with a riding accident days before the battle meaning that the actual fighting was handled by a man to whom de Lacy Evans's sophisticated 'Fabianism' was utter anathema, his second-in-command, Major General J.L. Pennefather.

The Battle of Inkerman, fought in the fog and decided by a thousand different, chaotic and bloody hand-to-hand engagements, has been called 'the soldier's battle', but if anyone embodied its spirit, it was the hard-fighting and hard-cursing John Lysaght Pennefather. The son of a Tipperary clergyman, Pennefather was born in 1800, and like so many officers of his generation condemned to peace, had reached the rank of lieutenant colonel and the age of forty before he had seen his first and only action, with Napier at the pacification of Sind.

He might have had little experience, but the central tenet of Pennefather's creed – if 'you see a head, hit it' – had served him well enough when faced with odds of ten to one in the bloody fighting at Meanee in Napier's Sind campaign of 1843 for him to look no further now at Inkerman. If Evans had still been in control his forward pickets would undoubtedly have fallen back onto the Home Ridge, but from the moment the grey Russian columns spilled out of the fog and onto the crest of Shell Hill, Pennefather's one instinct was to reinforce his forward positions and counterattack whenever and wherever he could.

With complete surprise on his side, Soimonoff had rapidly established his guns on the crest of Shell Hill, and to the accompaniment of a one-sided artillery duel, sent his infantry into the thick mist and towards the narrow Saddle that would see so much of the fighting over the next hours. In the first stages of the engagement the fog and gloom had been all in his favour too, but as the battle rapidly degenerated into an inchoate series of bloody encounters, they came to the British aid, masking the hopeless paucity of their numbers, and magnifying – like some huge, vengeful Brocken spectre projected onto the swirling mist and drizzle of the raw November morning – the thin and broken lines of defenders into imaginary columns massing implacably behind the advancing first ranks.

If there was a shape to the battle, it was only one that was discernible later, and no one man's Inkerman was like another's, except in the bloody intensity of the fighting. 'Tactics there were none,' wrote Captain Wilson, as small groups – 'every man his own general' – cut off from their units in the mist, or broken up by the heavy brush, fought how and with whom they could. 'Amid a dense fog raged wholesale murder; the mortal strife was hand to hand, foot to foot, muzzle to muzzle, butt-end to butt-end ... now backward, now forward, now sideward.'

There might have been no discernible pattern to those who fired, hacked, bayoneted, punched and clawed at anything in their reach, but as the eerie November light strengthened it become clear that the first phase of the battle had gone the British way. The original Russian plan had predicated their two armies acting in concert, but while Soimonoff might well have been right to press home the attack across a ground too cramped for even *one* army to manoeuvre, the net result was that he had committed fifteen thousand men against the British left and centre with nothing to show for it.

With the failure of this first assault – and the death of Soimonoff – the focus of the battle shifted from the British left to the British right flank. As Soimonoff's demoralised army fell back to the north, the first eight battalions of Pauloff's army emerged from the Quarry Ravine on the eastern side of the plateau, pouring forward to take the virtually undefended battery perched on its own isolated ledge at the extreme forward right of the British position, known as the 'Sandbag'.

Situated some seven hundred yards to the right of the Barrier, and just forty steeply sloping yards above the precipitous cliffs of the Tchernaya valley, the battery had only marginal tactical value, but over the next hours attack and counterattack saw the bodies of both sides pile ever deeper around its ten-foot parapet as it repeatedly changed hands. 'They came on like ants,' wrote Private Hyde – one of the five hundred men of the 41st who had charged with Brigadier Adams to recapture it when first lost.

No sooner was one knocked backwards than another clambered over the dead bodies to take his place, all of them yelling and shouting. We in the battery were not quiet, you may be sure, and what with cheering and shouting, the thud of blows, the clash of bayonets and swords, the ping of the bullets, the whistling of the shells, the foggy atmosphere, and the smell of the powder and blood, the scene inside the battery where we were was beyond the power of man to imagine or describe.

With ninety enemy guns on Shell Hill, however, and nineteen thousand fresh troops, now under the command of Dannerberg, still to be committed to the battle, there could be no hope of holding it for long. It is virtually impossible now to establish – or believe – any strict chronology for Inkerman, but if Adams took the battery some time before seven-thirty, it was back in Russian hands by the time – well before eight – that the first swaying line of Grenadiers, their busbies visible above the scrubby undergrowth, appeared on the skyline to drive an enemy force of seven thousand out of the Sandbag for a second time.

In the long run there could be only one end to such bloodletting, and as the battery changed hands another four times, the British position became ever more untenable. In the dense fog the Russians pouring up the St Clements and Quarry Ravines were able to get within thirty yards of it before they were seen, and while they seemed to press on in inexhaustible numbers, every attack and counterattack took its toll on a thinning band of defenders reduced to standing on the piles of bodies for a makeshift banquette.

With a criminal counterattack down into the Tchernaya valley led by Sir George Cathcart – a bullet through the heart saved him for St Paul's rather than a court martial – wasting the last chance of plugging the 'Gap' between Sandbag and the Barrier, the position of the Duke of Cambridge's dwindling force became even more desperate. The sight of Cathcart's assault had proved too tempting for even Guards' discipline, and as his men threw themselves suicidally over the rim of Kitspur and into an enveloping Russian trap, the Duke found himself stranded with a ragbag of 150 men grouped around the Grenadiers' colours, and two enemy battalions swinging left out of the Quarry Ravine to cut him off from left and rear.

It was at this critical moment in the battle that a naval officer, wearing a tall, glazed pipe hat, armed with a field-glass and accompanied – like some medieval knight – by a young boy mounted on a white pony, casually sauntered up to the adjutant of the Grenadiers. 'The new arrival proved to be Captain Peel of the *Diamond*,' recalled Captain Higginson.

On my expressing astonishment at seeing him amongst us at such a moment, he simply remarked 'Oh there was nothing going on at my little battery on the hill behind; and as I heard you fellows had plenty to do, I thought I would come and look at you.' I replied with some gravity of manner that we were in a tight place await-ing a supply of ammunition and long expected support. While this conversation was going on, I felt a bullet pass behind through my bearskin cap, causing me for the moment to stoop forward. I exclaimed, 'This is rather hard lines! here are our own fellows mistaking us for the enemy, and firing upon us, instead of coming to our relief.' He turned his field glass in the direction I pointed, and said in a subdued voice, 'No, by heaven! It is the enemy getting around our rear.'

With only 150 men still with the colours, and scarcely a round of ammunition, every hand was welcome, and while the beleaguered Duke rode the gauntlet of Russian fire back to the Home Ridge, the tiny rump of his force prepared to fight its way back to safety. Split-ting involuntarily in the heavy smoke and fog into two groups, the smaller under the improvised command of a young surgeon charged their way up the slopes of the Fore Ridge, while Peel and the main party – colours aloft and ringed with a corona of bayonets – doggedly began their seven-hundred-yard fighting retreat along the plateau's edge. 'Happily the ground on our right was so precipitous as to deter the enemy from outflanking us on that side,' Higginson continued,

> as from time to time some Russian soldiers, more adventurous than their fellows, sprang forward towards our compact group, two or three of our Grenadiers would dash out with the bayonet and compel a steady retreat. Nevertheless our position was critical. By the time, however, we had traversed half the distance to the breast-work of the Second Division, the pressure on our rear and left was relaxed ... I shall never forget the cheer with which the returning colours were welcomed by all ranks, HRH being almost moved to tears, for, as they all said, 'We had given you up for lost.'

It was not quite the end of the battle – the British right had ceased to exist – but the belated arrival of the French and of two long-range eighteen-pounder siege guns gradually swung the balance the allies' way. To the very end it was there to be won if the Russians had only had the flair or imagination to seize their chance, but to say that is simply to repeat on a larger canvas the great puzzle posed by the rescue of the Grenadier colours – how was it that they were *not* lost? How was it that stubbornly brave Russian soldiers, led by officers every bit as willing to die as their British counterparts, could time and again fall back in the face of an enemy it outnumbered by thirteen to one?

The superiority of the new Minié rifle over the Russians' smoothbore muskets, the psychological mastery won at the Alma, the lumpen passivity of a conscript army, the arrival of the French, the British infantryman's 'unconcealed contempt for all foreigners and their ways', as Field Marshal Wolseley cheerfully put it – they all undoubtedly played their part in the victory of Inkerman, and if a proud Naval Brigade were largely ready to put it all down to Peel, that only illumined another more general truth. During the retreat from the Sandbag Battery and the last desperate defence of Home Ridge Peel had personally led seven separate attacks, and across the whole battlefield, from the first exchanges in the fog and dark of pre-dawn to the final repulse of Pauloff's Russians, it was the same story.

If every man was his own general, every general – every officer – was, equally, his own man. Of the ten British generals and their five replacements who fought at Inkerman, every one was either killed, wounded, or had his horse shot from under him. The Battle of Inkerman was no more a 'soldier's battle' than Waterloo, Albuera or any other static battle, that wonderfully brave and irascible fossil of older and more brutal days, Sir George Brown, complained:

> The description has been applied to the battle of Inkerman, I am aware, from a desire to flatter the *men* at the expense of their officers, but I suspect that Soldiers of the Army are by no means either sensible of, or grateful for the compliment thus intended to be paid them. Our men are as fine, generous, brave & manly fellows as are anywhere to be found in the world, but they always want to be led by their officers, & on no former occasion did the officers of the British Army ever exhibit a more brilliant example of gallantry, manhood & devotion to duty as was shown by them at Inkerman!!

And they had the men to lead. It was bitterly said on the Russian side that at Inkerman the French saved the British just as the Prussians had done at Waterloo, but if there is a certain reductive truth in that, it was pre-eminently a British victory. By the end of the battle men were falling asleep from exhaustion while still under attack, but for the best part of four critical hours the 2nd Division and its vastly outmanned and outgunned reinforcements had sustained the fight alone. 'If it is considered that the soldiers who met these furious columns of the Czar were the remnants of three British divisions,' Russell eloquently wrote,

> that they were hungry and wet, and half-famished; that they were men belonging to a force which was generally 'out of bed' four nights out of seven; which had been enfeebled by sickness, by severe toil, sometimes for twenty-four hours at a time without relief of any kind; that among them were men who had within a short time previously lain out for forty-eight hours in the trenches at a stretch – it will be readily admitted that never was a more extraordinary contest maintained by our army since it acquired a reputation in the world's history.

'*Vivent les Anglais, les plus meilleurs soldats du monde,*' the Zouaves had shouted as, vivandière to the front and rifles held high, they bounded like kangaroos across the slopes of Inkerman to drive the Russians off the heights; and they were not exaggerating. 'All honour & glory to you my dear old friend and gallant old comrade George Brown!', Sir George Napier – like most of the Napier clan no stranger to heroics – wrote when the details of the battle reached England. 'Never was a more brilliant Victory gained, nor a bloodier Battle better fought than that of Inkerman.'

If there is no battle like Inkerman, though, and no more astonishing victory in British military history, it had come at a terrible price. In the long run the courage and endurance shown here reaped its rewards for the British soldier, but as the artillery fire died out and the last of the Russian guns and men were withdrawn from Shell Hill, the battlefield told its own story. '*Quel abattoir!*' the French General Bosquet remarked as he stood among the piles of corpses where Peel had fought with the colours at Sandbag Battery. Around its parapets alone more than 1,200 Russian bodies lay, and at the Barrier and at the head of the Careening Gorge and along Home Ridge it was the same tale. *Abattoir* was the right word. Surgeons at the Peninsula had seldom had to deal with a bayonet wound, but at Inkerman they saw enough to last a lifetime. Men lay on the ground where they had been run through time and again, or knelt, still upright, British and Russian locked together in a ghastly tableau, each impaled on the other's bayonet. 'The thought of it made me shudder and turn sick,' Fanny Duberly wrote:

> ... the field of Alma was child's play to this. Compressed into a space not exceeding a square half-mile, lay about 5,000 Russians, some say 6,000; above 2,000 of our own men, exclusive of French ... lines upon lines of Artillery horses, heaps upon heaps of slain, lying in every attitude, and congregated in masses – some on their sides, others with hands stiffening on the triggers of their muskets; some rolled up as if they had died in mortal pain, others smiling placidly, as though still dreaming of home: while round the batteries, man and horse piled in heaps, wounds and blood – a ghastly and horrible sight!

It was not just the number of casualties that was so critical, but the quality of the soldiers lost. It is hard to imagine that Britain ever had a finer fighting army than that which sailed from Varna, and no raw recruits – boys many of them, with no more than weeks of service behind them – could provide any real substitute for the disciplined, battle-hardened army that to all intents and purposes ceased to exist at Inkerman.

With it went any lingering hopes of equality with their allies. As the Russians retired in good order, taking their guns with them, Raglan wanted to fight on, but Canrobert – Robert Can't, as he was popularly known by the British – refused, and his veto spelled out an irrevocable shift in the balance of power between the two allies. In all the major battles of the campaign Raglan's men had played the leading role, but for an army already decimated by sickness and casualties, Inkerman was the final blow, reducing it to a junior partner that 'in case of a row', as Henry Clifford put it, would have trouble putting 10,000 bayonets into the field.

And among those 10,000 there could be no elation that evening, no triumphalism – there were too many dead for that – nothing except exhaustion and a profound relief. There was no arguing with the fact that the Russians had got 'a hell of a towelling', as Pennefather put it, but in strategic terms it had not been so much a victory – not even a pyrrhic victory – as an evasion of defeat that left the enemy as strongly placed as ever to await those old historical allies of

Russia's, Generals January and February. But first there was a Crimean November to survive.

<h1 style="text-align:center">XI</h1>

The allies did not have to wait long to find out what the Crimea had in store for them. On the day after the battle the young Evelyn Wood had paid a seaman to scavenge him a pair of good Russian boots, and as the weather turned, and the warm October days that had followed Balaclava gave way to the incessant rains and bitterly cold nights of November, he and many others in the Naval Brigade had good reason to be grateful to the Inkerman dead.

Peel's sailors had been ashore for just on five weeks by this time, and, landed with only what they could carry, were as ill-equipped as the soldiers to face the rigours ahead. The conditions for the officers – navy or army – were harsh enough by any normal measure, but for men who might have been living in the same lice-ridden clothes since February it was infinitely worse, with 'rough, stony ground' for beds at night and 'continuous trench work by day' reducing 'their garments to tatters' before the Crimean winter had even properly begun.

The heavy rains started on 10 November, turning the clinging soil on the track up from Balaclava into a quagmire, but nothing prepared anyone for the glimpse into 'the End of all things' that was to come. On the tenth Wood had been forced to take to his bed with dysentery, and as he lay listening to the heavy gusts that buffeted his tent in the early hours of the fourteenth, had just about time to congratulate himself on escaping his battery duties for another day when the worst gale in Crimean memory hit Peel's camp with full force.

By five Wood's tent had joined the stream of flying debris that filled the air, and as crazed horses ran amok and drums careered wildly across the sky, the same story was repeated across the whole allied encampment. No one would have been able to say how many thousands of tents there were across the uplands the night before, but by the time the wind veered to the west and began at last to slacken, no more than a dozen were still standing, leaving the sick, the wounded and dying to the bitter sleet and snow, and the Naval Brigade to despair of the fate of their shipmates at sea.

If the havoc there was still more horrific – 'masts, spars, dead bodies, rum casks, dead cattle, hay, vegetables, & every item of wreck' filling the harbour and twenty-one ships wrecked off Balaclava alone – the long-term cost in terms of the army's suffering was to be incalculable. Among the vessels that foundered off Balaclava was one of the largest transports, the *Prince*, and as the battered troops came to terms with the devastation of their camps, the supplies, medicines, winter clothing and ammunition that could have meant the difference between life and death were lying at the bottom of the Black Sea.

'That storm was the beginning of misery so intense as to defy adequate description,' Wood remembered, and as scurvy was added to dysentery, cholera, frostbite, exposure, hunger and the daily miseries of hauling up rations and ammunition from Balaclava through mud that could suck a man's boots off, Peel's indignation fixed on the plight of 'England's little army'. 'I shall write you a foolish rankling letter,' he grumbled to his sister at the beginning of December, writing from the Brigade's new camp at the head of a ravine which ran between headquarters and the encampment of the 3rd Division,

> so please destroy it as soon as you have read it. The siege is at a standstill, and ... it is with great difficulty we can get the bare rations of food from Balaclava. All such other necessities as clothing, etc it is quite impossible to find transport for. The poor fellows, therefore, are very wretched, but one thing that will never fail them, and that is their courage. I have always laid great store on this courage of our men; would that I could equally praise our military science. Our chief engineer Sir J Burgoyne, a most excellent person, is I believe 77 years of age. How can Sir J. Graham reconcile it with his conscience in keeping Adm. Dundas in command of the fleet, or even in keeping certain captains in command of Line of Battle Ships, I do not wish to accuse our Gentlemen, but this I may fairly say that however passable they may be for ordinary occasions, they are not equal to our present difficulties.

'Our prospects are not encouraging,' he complained again to Eliza as winter gripped, and the incessant rain turned to snow, and men woke, if they woke at all, with their clothes as stiff as boards,

> for each day adds to my conviction that there is a lack of energy. I would not now direct that energy to taking Sebastopol, but to save the lives of the soldiers from the inclemency of the weather ... I am

shocked at the foreign enlistment Bill;* the Russians are strong through our own stupidity and what we want is not foreigners but kind hearted officers who will look after the health of their men and insist on their being well fed and looked after ... No men in the world, though they *were* made of wrought iron could stand the misery our troops were exposed to.

Peel was as good as his word, and if his Naval Brigade could not be insulated against suffering, the relative casualty figures over that winter show what could be done with the kind of care and officers he demanded. While the army was losing men at a rate that exceeded the Great Plague of 1665, Peel's brigade lost only 7 per cent in fatalities, a figure that was less than half that of the cavalry, a third that of the infantry, and only one tenth of the staggering 73 per cent mortality rate from disease alone suffered by eight of the hardest-worked battalions manning the trenches.

It did not make for glamorous soldiering, it was not the kind of warfare Peel craved, but the campaign could only be won by attention to the kind of detail that had so far been ignored. Peel was perhaps lucky that during the worst of the winter months the brigade was not as severely worked as some, but luck had nothing to do with the regime he enforced in the naval camp, with close attention to sanitation and clean water, the separation of latrines, the creation of a drying room, drainage for the tents, the supply of hot soup for every sailor returning from the batteries or – crucially – the compulsory quinine, cocoa and lime parades that left the men no opportunity to trade rations for an extra few minutes' sleep and a bout of scurvy.

It would not have been Peel, of course, without some more flamboyant demonstration of his qualities, and even at the slackest time of the siege there were dangers to bring them out. 'One day, in fairly quiet times, I was walking in [the twenty-one-gun battery] with him,' Field Marshal Wolseley, then a captain with the Engineers, wrote,

when we both heard the peculiar 'pich-ata-wich-ata' noise in the air which bespoke the approach of a large mortar-shell. We

---

* A Bill designed to recreate the British foreign legions of the Napoleonic age, recruiting mercenaries into the army from Italy, Germany and Switzerland to meet a chronic shortage of troops. The Foreign Enlistment Act received Royal Assent in December 1854, in the face of widespread opposition.

stopped to watch it, and to our horror saw it fall immediately in
front of us, upon the entrance to one of our largest powder
magazines, and not five paces off; the shell burst as it did so ...
The sandbag and apparently the passage timbers had been set
on fire, and in an instant a volume of smoke, laden with dust
from the explosion, issued from the interior. It was an appalling
moment and it must have seemed the end of this world to any
of us who still retained the power to reason at all. We were not
actually dead, but horror had for the second of time, as it were
killed our thinking faculties. We were face to face with death,
immediate death. I have often rubbed shoulders with that mocking monster, but I may without boasting say that upon no other
occasion which I can remember has he ever 'cow'd my better
part of man.' But Peel was 'all there' for in much less time than
it takes to tell this story, I saw him dive into the smoking magazine. This action on his part made men of us all in an instant, and
it was not long before every spark of fire there had been was
well trampled out.

And if there were no imminent dangers – no opportunities to excel –
then Peel's fertile brain was well up to creating them for himself. 'Our
army is in a critical position, and can never take Sebastopol except
at a fearful loss,' he had complained after Menschikoff had sunk his
ships across the harbour entrance – as indignant as any officer would
be who believed that an enemy's first duty was to provide the Royal
Navy with a chance of glory.

Now a Nelson in command of our fleet would come rally to their
rescue. I will never believe that the Russians can have made a
barrier across a harbour mouth nearly half a mile long so that our
ships can not enter. I may speak this, for what are sermons or
favours to those who are in the presence of death, and I would be
ready any day to take command of ... a line of battle ship, and rush
full open at their sunken ships and sunken chains in the full confidence that she would force her way through and snap their chains
like pack thread. Let four other ships only follow and they would
pour such an awful fire into the rear of all the Russian works that
our troops might storm with ease.

'His suggestion was to lash on either side of his own ship a laden collier,' Evelyn Wood elaborated, 'and then, sending every one else below, to himself steer the ship at full speed against the obstacle. It was calculated that the weight of the combined vessels would break the boom, and once inside, Peel intended to engage the forts, being supported by the whole of the fleet, which he proposed should follow him.'

If this – and another scheme to board the two Russian men-of-war in the harbour and take them with cutlass – was arguably more Cochrane than Nelson, that only reflects the curious mix of disinterest and exhibitionism that drove Peel's ambitions. In his letters to his sister he would constantly tell her that only 'Honour or Duty' kept him at his guns, but he was rather more open with his brother. 'My dear Frederic,' he wrote, touchingly revealing that very Tolstoyan – very Peel-like – blend of motives that lay behind his startling courage,

> I am very anxious you should enquire privately at the admiralty whether they ever received a despatch through Admiral Dundas *from* Captain Lushington, who commands the Naval Brigade, respecting my having thrown a live shell out of the battery. Capt. Lushington told me himself that he obtained all the particulars from an officer who was an eye witness, and sent them to the Admiralty.
>
> I have so little confidence in Adm. Dundas that I must believe he has withheld that despatch, and sent only a partial extract or some worthless statement of his own. If I am doing him an injustice in supposing him guilty of such measures, it is his own fault that he has not inspired those under him with sufficient confidence in his character.
>
> It can fall to the lot of very few, and to still fewer of high rank to do that of which I feel honestly proud, and as in this most arduous and protracted siege I may any moment be its victim, I naturally place a higher value on what would shed a lustre on my name.

'It is dreadful in our service,' he told Eliza in similar vein, 'to be always serving under men whose capacity you can measure as with a foot rule,' and every week of inaction offered some fresh irritation. 'Everything here is done too late,' he complained, angry at the allied lethargy and angrier still at not getting the credit that he believed his due.

It is well known that I was the first and long since I urged, in proposing the Railway from Balaclava, but begged that they should only write for a certain light description of rail and engaged that it should all be ready by the middle of January. The answer was that the proposal was not entertained. The other day we saw that Government intended sending out the material. If the idea did not originate in England, but came from here, the credit should be mine.

The only surprise of this winter, in fact, was that, frustrated on both sides as he was – convinced equally of the uselessness of the siege and of the personal vendetta that Admiral Dundas was waging against him – Peel's spirits remained as buoyant as they did. His health, too, was stronger than it had ever been, and his person as immaculately groomed as always, his sole concession to Crimean squalor being the addition of an unpleasantly dapper little moustache. He had found a washerwoman who could – to the amazement of the Russians at a ceasefire to bury the dead – starch his collars to his satisfaction, and had found himself a horse. 'This is new year's eve, just a twelve month since we parted at Portsmouth at the George,' he wrote wistfully to his sister.

To me it has been one of almost incessant work, except a few bright weeks among the Ionian Islands where all nature was in sunshine and flowers. There is no news here; so I shall tell you only of my having bought a most beautiful Arab horse, such a love, white, of faultless symmetry and enormous strength. We immediately made a wooden house for him, better than my own, and if he is not killed with kindness you shall see him and me together in England ... I intend if the weather sets in very severe, to make him wear trousers. He comes from Alesso, was the standard bearer horse of the Basho Bozorks under Oman Pacha, where he lost an eye, not a blemish but a honourable scar, and as his owner had returned to Asia, but could not obtain a passage for his horse, he came to me, and sold it as it stood, saddle bridle and all for what he asked £20.

And with moustache, starched collars and horse, he had also found himself a rather different admirer from the routine young midshipmen and Russian soldiers. He had – among the dangers of the Koh-i-Noor and the squalors of Balaclava – attracted the alarming attentions of a woman.

XII

With so many friends and acquaintances out in the Crimea – half of London society convened on the Upland – it had never been all work for Peel or the army, and a curious sidelight on his life out there is thrown by a source that never found a mention in his letters home. In the winter of 1854 his cousin Archie – the 'TG', as he was known in the family – had come out to stay in the *Diamond*, and on 26 December a rather rarer sort of tourist arrived at Balaclava, an attractive, spoilt, spirited girl of twenty-four with 'golden hair, great lustrous eyes ... high white forehead' and a 'small tight mouth clamped in an inflexible line' that might have told a warier soul than the young Archie Peel all he needed to know about her character and intentions.

The name of this visitation was Ellen Palmer, the daughter of an Anglo-Irish baronet, the sister of an 11th Hussars officer who had survived the Charge of the Light Brigade, and a distant relation according to family legend of the cuckolded husband of Charles II's Lady Castlemaine. Along with an aunt and her long-suffering father she had travelled across Europe to Constantinople in the summer of 1854, and after taking in the usual sights and studiously avoiding the less pleasant ones at Scutari, had procured a passage aboard Lord Raglan's yacht to launch herself, like some latter-day Louisa Musgrove, on her own hunt for a Crimean husband.

It seems a shame that the other campaign in front of Sevastopol was not fought with the single-mindedness that Ellen Palmer brought to the task, and by the time Raglan's yacht had dropped anchor at Balaclava, the *Caradoc*'s Samuel Derriman was already the first of her victims. The conquest of one rather junior lieutenant was never going to be sufficient for Ellen though, and her progress through the all-male world of the allied armies – she interestingly seems to have steered a wide berth of Mrs Duberly – was one long triumph, with lunch at Lord Raglan's and an escorted tour of the lines from Colonel Somerset being followed within the week by dinner with the most glamorous naval officer the Crimea had to offer, the twenty-nine-year-old William Peel. 'Wednesday 3rd,' her journal read: 'Rained all day so I was again disappointed of the excursion to Inkerman. Lord Lucan, Lord Bingham, Capt. Peel (of the Diamond) & his cousin dined here.'

There is no way of being certain what Peel made of her, but he was back on the *Caradoc* to play cards the following evening, at dinner again five days later, and within another fortnight had been persuaded into escorting her on a visit to the Koh-i-Noor. 'Monday 22nd,' Ellen wrote in her best Louisa Musgrove mode – for Jane Austen's Cob at Lyme read the twenty-one-gun battery under enemy fire:

> Captain Peel represented fully the danger we encountered, & everybody else held up their hands & eyes in amazement, however I was determined to go into the battery coute qui coute, & as Captain Peel had promised in an unguarded moment to show us his, the expedition was decided upon, & off we set ... The last part of our road lay through a road called 'the Valley of the Shadow of Death' from the immense number of people who have been killed there. The round shot & shell lay on the ground as thick as hailstones & one could hardly move without stepping upon them. We dismounted & went into the battery on foot & where the parapet was low we were obliged almost to crawl on all fours to avoid being picked off by the Russian riflemen who were posted about in all directions. One poor fellow was killed by them just before we came in. We walked through the whole of the battery regardless of the shot & our cannonballs flying about & shells bursting in all directions. I had been told of 'Whistling Dick' & now I heard the peculiar noise they make quite close to me. The firing grew heavier while we remained, so our homeward route was more hazardous than our approach to the battery had been ... We got home safe enough after all our risks, perfectly delighted that we had seen the trenches & been the first visitors to the celebrated 'Diamond Battery'. It is actual fact that nobody has ever ventured there unless called to it by duty.

It was perhaps as well for Peel that the Palmers were only there for the month, because not just Ellen but his cousin Archie had plans for him. To the end of his life Archie would always look back on William with something close to adulation, and while he fell hopelessly in love with Ellen Palmer himself, some bizarre 'beta cousin' instinct of deference meant that honour and self-knowledge obliged him to play second fiddle to William. 'He said he had confided his love to his cousin because his cousin had thought of me in the first instance,' Ellen wrote in her private diary after a desperate and lovestruck

Archie had followed her to Constantinople: 'he was helping him, until at last he was touché himself & then he owed it to him out of a feeling of honour. From all I can gather I fancy this caused a coolness between them. I think it could hardly have entered Archy's head to do this & risk his cousin's friendship unless he had really fallen in love with me.'

It is very possible that William had 'taken fright' after the battery visit – he would have done so if he had any sense – but judging from Ellen's diary, she had still not entirely despaired of him. During her last days at Balaclava both Peels were still at her side for clifftop walks and melancholy farewells, and if William's interest had cooled, he had obviously compromised himself enough to send after her a message that 'he hoped & didn't think he had been rude'.

It is perhaps only coincidence that dates a lifting of Peel's spirits to Ellen Palmer's departure – she wisely decided that a Peel in the hand was worth two in a battery, and grabbed his cousin Archie while she could – but things were at last looking up. 'Our army is improving,' he told his sister three days after Ellen sailed:

> the worst is past, even the severity of winter is gone ... The fire I was exposed to was the most wonderful storm of shot and shell I could ever imagine; it pleased God to spare me in it all, at Alma and at Inkerman and the Batteries. But though many people have thought that I wish to get shot, they are quite wrong and I could not go through such peril, unless Honour or Duty called me there. I expect to hear of an Armistice and the advent of Peace, or else to see us storm and take Sebastopol before three weeks are over.

He was being over-optimistic, but gradually things were getting better. There was more bitter cold still to come, the siege looked no more likely to succeed than ever, and the suffering of the troops continued. But with the fall of Aberdeen's government in England at the end of January 1855 and improvements in the organisation at Balaclava there were at least signs that Britain was beginning to take the plight of its army seriously.

For Peel, too, there was a brief respite from siege-work when he was transferred from the *Diamond* to *Leander* – one reason perhaps why he so warmly offered Ellen his old ship should she ever come back to the Crimea – but by 2 April he and two hundred of his new crew were back in the batteries. 'What a slap and a scolding I should get if I were in your reach,' he joked with Eliza twelve days later, after again failing to come up with the long letter he had been promising her.

> But you will understand now, dearest Elisa how I could not write, so fatigued as I have been by incessant exertions. The 'Leanders' have been as gallant as the 'Diamonds' and with the 'Queens' who formed the Right attack have fought most nobly. We have now gained the upper hand on our side, and the enemy's fire is wild and feeble. I will talk to you about all this, please God, on my return. The same kind mercy has protected me throughout. I was struck by a cannon ball full on the side of the leg just below the knee, which drove me back but never hurt me. The shot had struck outside the parapet and hopped over and its force was gone. It was very strange that it did not injure me. There, that is a little anecdote to interest you and I will reserve others.

After a night of incessant rain that flooded the batteries with a foot of water, this latest allied bombardment had begun on the ninth, with five hundred French and British guns taking the Russians by surprise. Two days later, early in the morning of the eleventh, Wood remembered:

> I was sent by Captain Peel from the 21-gun battery with a note for Captain Lushington, the Commander of the Naval brigade, and by him was ordered to take it on to Lord Raglan. Scribbled on a scrap of paper were these words: 'If the Allies intend to assault, a better opportunity than this will not offer. The fire of the Russian batteries of the Malakoff is completely crushed.' When galloping to Head-quarters my pony put his foot into a hole, and turning right over, rolled on me, covering my face, and clothes with mud. I thus appeared before Lord Raglan, who was in the farmyard at Head-quarters, casting troop horses, apparently belonging to his escort. He astonished his Staff by warmly shaking hands with the very dirty midshipman as he offered me breakfast. He then read the note, but merely remarked, 'Impossible, I fear.'

It was impossible for Raglan to move without the consent of his allies, and impossible for Canrobert to do anything without the blessing of the Emperor, but their inaction again condemned their armies to

another prolonged, ineffectual and costly artillery duel. 'It was important to observe the first impact of each shot,' Wood, in charge now
of three guns, recalled in a little vignette of battery life that conjures
up the grim physical reality so deliberately excised from Peel's letters
to his sister,

> which, with a steady platform for the telescope, I was able to
> effect, calling out '19 yards to the right.' Or '20 yards short' as
> it struck the parapet or ground. I was resting my left hand with
> the telescope on the 8-inch gun, and was steadying my right hand
> on the shoulder of Charles, 1st class boy, while I checked the prac-
> tice of the centre and right-hand gun, when a man handed round
> the grog for the gun's crew then out of action. The boy asked me
> to move my elbow while he drank his grog, so that he might not
> shake me, and on receiving the pannikin he stood up, and was in
> the act of drinking, when a shot from the Redan, coming
> obliquely across us, took off his head, the body falling on my feet.
> At this moment, Michael Hardy, having just fired his gun, was
> 'serving the vent.' This consists in stopping all current of air from
> the gun which, if allowed to pass up the vent, would cause any
> sparks remaining after the explosion to ignite the fresh cartridge.
> Hardy, like the rest of the gun's crew, had turned up his sleeves
> and trousers as high as could get them; his sailor's shirt was open
> low on the neck and chest. His face, neck, and clothes were
> covered with the contents of the boy's head; to lift the thumb
> from the vent might occasion the death of Nos. 3 and 4, the
> Loader, and Sponger, who were then *ramming home*; but he never
> flinched. Without moving his right thumb from the vent, with the
> left hand he wiped the boy's brains from his face and eyes as he
> looked round on us ... 'You — fools, what the hell are you look-
> ing at? Is the man dead, take his carcase away; isn't he dead, take
> him to the doctor.'

With the failure of the bombardment, life in the batteries and trenches
reverted to the familiar pattern of siege life. In the early weeks of the
campaign the allies had fought the kind of battles that would have
been familiar to their Napoleonic and eighteenth-century predeces-
sors, but as they inched forward towards the Russian defences, and
a spreading network of trenches, parallels and covered ways scarred
the Upland, the sorties, probes, night attacks, mining and countermin-

ing into which the war descended were closer to the fighting on the Western Front than anything known before.

But with the coming of summer – and colour to the dreary winter uplands – there were sports, band concerts, race meetings and the newly arrived Sardinian contingent to quicken the allies into fresh heart, and in the front lines the substitution of Canrobert by the more brute figure of Pelissier at last signalled a new urgency. On 6 June Peel made a final inspection of all the naval batteries in the Right Attack, and at three that afternoon, the first of five hundred guns stretching out across a front five miles broad opened up on the Malakoff.

As darkness fell there was a kind of Impressionist beauty to the scene, wonderfully caught by Tolstoy in his tales of Sevastopol life, but for those under the 'murderous' fire the 'havoc and ruin' defied belief. The guns in the Redan and the Malakoff had fallen silent even before sunset on the sixth, and by the afternoon of the following day the Mamelon and the 'White Works' to its left had ceased firing, their guns and gunners buried under the earth and rubble of their ruined parapets.

In the French and British lines, the single prayer was that this was 'the beginning of the end', but after the earlier bombardments everyone knew that the end could only come at the point of the bayonet. When the allied guns at last fell silent on the evening of the seventh, the men of the Naval Brigade watched the French filing into the advance trenches, and at just after 6 o'clock, as the signal rockets went up into blood-red sky, saw three columns – the 50th Regiment in the centre, the Zouaves on the left, Algerian troops on the right – burst out of their cover and up the slope into the shattered Mamelon on its summit.

The sight of a tricolore flying above the Mamelon raised British hopes, and even when it disappeared – to be raised and pulled down again – under the weight of a massive Russian counter-attack, a second wave of French troops, fifes and drums playing, could be seen advancing at 'a steady double' to the march 'Père Bougère' down the slopes of the Victorian Ridge. 'Just as the day closed in,' Wood wrote, the evening gloom thickened by smoke, 'we saw the French left and centre columns again advance from their trenches in our right front, while a heavy column of Algerian infantry moved on the Mamelon from the south-east, and in a few moments the sound of the fire, and the flash of muskets in the falling darkness, showed us that the Russians were once again retreating.'

The capture of the Mamelon had been the signal Raglan was waiting for, and as the ebb and flow of battle on the right continued, seven
hundred British troops advanced virtually unchecked against the
enemy rifle pits in the Quarries below the Redan. The Russian defensive strategy for Sevastopol had always been based on *recapturing*
rather than holding their forward trenches, so this was no surprise,
but as darkness fell a long and savage hand-to-hand battle for the
Quarries began. 'About ½ p 11,' General Codrington noted in stac-
cato form of the night's fighting,

> the Russians came out from the flank of the Redan in force, it was
> dark – no moon … and then there was hard fighting – hand to
> hand – firing at 30 yards – beat back and regaining the same
> ground, across the trenches … Bodies of our men and Russians
> lying thick. Again at ½ p. one or 2 in the morning, the same sort
> of desperate fighting: but we held our own, and the Russians, carry-
> ing off many dead in the night, left heaps, more than 300.

At daybreak the Quarries and other outworks were still in allied
hands, but the appalling casualties had given a grim foretaste of what
lay ahead. 'Every face was grave,' Wood remembered after he had
followed Peel into the ruins of the Mamelon that morning. 'Men
spoke in whispers even when transmitting orders. Inside the scene
was indescribable in its horrors. Dead men were lying heaped in every
attitude imaginable; some half-buried in craters formed by shells;
other bodies literally cut into two parts; and one I noticed had been
blown twenty yards by the explosion of a mortar shell. Some corpses
were lying crushed under overturned cannon, while others hung
limply over injured guns.'

With all the objectives of the 6–7 June bombardment now
achieved, nothing stood between the allies and the final assault on the
city. The day set for this was the anniversary of Waterloo on 18 June,
a date chosen in the hope that a victory would ease French memories
and provide a triumphant focus for what could still be an uneasy
alliance.

It was an appropriate gesture, too, because the heroism and *élan*
of the French – and in particular the Zouaves – in taking the
Mamelon had gone a long way to persuading even the most choleric
Peninsular veteran that this was now France's war. Since the Battle
of Inkerman, in fact, the French had been holding both the left and

right of the allied line, and with the contours of the land hampering any advance from the Left Attack, all that remained to the British in any future assault were the defences in front of the Right Attack.

That still left Peel's old sparring partner, the Redan, and as no-man's land contracted to no more than 450 yards, and the fort in all its formidable strength sprung into alarming focus from the British forward positions in the Quarries, no one was under any illusions as to what its capture would entail. Built on a ridge on the site of an old vineyard, just over three hundred feet above sea level, it formed part of a continuous curtain of defensive works that ran into the Middle Ravine and the Malakoff on its left flank and trended sharply west to link with the Barrack Battery on its right. The Redan itself was made up of two faces that met at an angle of sixty-five degrees, each seventy yards long and fifteen feet high, with a ditch immediately beneath them some eleven feet deep and fifteen to twenty feet across.

Fifty yards in front of the salient, an abatis of tangled branches – *ur* barbed wire – had been built on the natural glacis, and the whole approach was exposed not just to the guns of the Redan but to those of the flanking works to the north and west. The glacis itself sloped up to a ridge on the line of the capital, and this in effect meant that whichever flank a storming party chose, it would have to carry its ladders across four hundred yards of bare ground under the concentrated fire of either the Garden and Barrack batteries on one side, or the Gervaise and the Malakoff on the other.

The difficulties did not end there, because the design of the Redan – open at the rear to reinforcements and to the enfilading fire of the Barrack Battery – meant that even if captured it would be impossible to hold; but Wood, for one, never dreamed that either he or Peel would get that far. A week before the attack they had discussed which limb they would be happiest to lose – Peel had opted for a leg until it was pointed out that he would probably become very fat – but Wood and Daniel had already privately determined that as their 'Chief' was certain to die in the attack, they were going to die alongside him or live to carry his body back to their lines.

With Peel offering himself and the services of the Naval Brigade for ladder parties, this was no mere flight of morbidity, and in the naval camp odds were freely available about the death of his ADCs. 'Barring accidents, I bet I go as far as my chief,' Wood had responded to some mess-tent 'chaff' on the night before the assault: 'when another officer replied, "I'll lay £5 to £1 in sovereigns young Wood's killed to-morrow." Lieutenant Dalyell replied, "Done; bet's off if I am killed."'

It was nearly a matter of all bets off anyway, because Wood had been down with fever for a week, and Peel was as determined to keep his ADC out of the assault as Wood was to be in it. 'From some words I caught when entering his tent,' Wood wrote, after dragging himself out of bed on the seventeenth, and riding under shell fire to head-quarters before finally tracking his chief down to his tent,

> [I] gathered that he was arranging with one of the senior officers for the assault. He turned to me and said, 'Oh, Wood, you're not well today.' I replied, 'Not very well, sir, but not very ill!' to which he said, 'You had better go to bed, I shan't want you tomorrow morning.'
>
> 'I suppose, sir, by that we are going to assault?'
>
> 'Yes; and as you are not well enough to go up with us, you will please to stop in camp.'
>
> 'And are you going to take your other aide-de-camp?' I asked.
>
> 'Yes; I promised him a long time ago,' was the answer.
>
> I left the tent feeling very sulky, but Captain Peel called me back, and, to soothe my vexation, said, 'Well, you may go with us as far as the battery, but no further.' I immediately asked, 'Is the other aide-de-camp to go with you?' to which he replied in the affirmative.

This small exchange gives an intriguing glimpse into the rivalries that lay just beneath the smooth surface of mid-Victorian chivalry. It would be hard to conceive a more generous soul than Evelyn Wood, but in all his writings on the Crimea he could barely bring himself to mention the 'other aide-de-camp', either mis-spelling his name or silently air-brushing him out of the narrative altogether.

Wood was not the last of Peel's men to resent the favouritism shown to Daniel – though whether permission to storm the Redan counts as 'favouritism' is a moot point – but what lay behind Wood's reserve is less clear. The simplest explanation is one of good old-fashioned jealousy, and while that may well be true, it seems equally likely, given the disgrace that would envelop Daniel, that either some instinctive antipathy at the time, or a later fear of damning Peel by association, dictated Wood's silence.

It was certainly Daniel who would win the Victoria Cross and not Wood, Daniel on his white pony at Peel's side who would go down in Crimean legend, not Wood, and though that must have rankled at the time with the young boy, the mustachioed old general was too decent in his judgements to let it sour his history. For all his love of Peel, however, there had always been things about his hero that the simpler Wood never really understood, a 'feminine' side, as he put it – a tenderness for desert birds, an acute consciousness of danger, a dandyism, a physiological intolerance of pain (very feminine!) – that public revelations of Daniel's homosexuality must have forced him to look at in a different and disturbing light.

The story of Edward Daniel – stripped of his VC, driven out of the navy, shamed into exile and a pauper's grave in New Zealand – is one of the forgotten tragedies of Victorian England, but as Wood went to sleep on the night of 17 June it was with dreams of an Arthurian Idyll still intact. For a moment, too, any jealousies between Peel's two young squires were forgotten in the common cause, and as the camp began to rouse itself just after midnight, Daniel – in defiance of their chief's orders not to disturb him – came into Wood's tent to wake him from his heavy, laudanum-fuelled sleep.

There is something Shakespearean in Wood's account of his last battle alongside Peel – something that conjures up images of Brutus and the leaden-eyed Lucius on the eve of Philippi – but not even the Redan and duty could keep the boy awake. The moment Daniel left his tent he was asleep again, and it took the more robust offices of Michael Hardy, the Irish bluejacket who had wiped the brains of the boy off his face in the battery, before he could finally be dragged from his bed. The ladder party had already gone, Hardy told Wood, and to the response that he 'was too ill to go out', answered, '"Shure, you'll never forgive yourself if you miss this morning's fun"; and somewhat against my will, proceeded to dress me. Having accomplished this, he propped me up against the tent-pole while he got my pony, on which he put me, being obliged at first to hold me on to the saddle, for I was too weak to grip with my legs.'

It was a black night, and Wood and Hardy hurried after Peel's party as fast as the darkness would allow them, catching up with them outside the twenty-one-gun battery. Tethering his pony to a gun, Wood reported to Peel, who was telling off his sixty bluejackets into their ladder parties, six men to a ladder, and a petty officer to every pair. 'I asked my chief,' Wood wrote, 'if he had thought to bring down a Union Jack that we might have it up in the Redan before the Regimental Colours ... He regretted that it had been forgotten, but agreed it was then impossible to remedy the mistake.'

Peel was as determined as ever to keep Wood out of danger, and as he finished telling off the ladder parties he sent his ADC to the other end of the battery on the first of a whole string of spurious pretexts. In the darkness and confusion it was hard to find anyone, and by the time the exhausted Wood had made his way back again, Peel was already gone, moving forward with the ladder parties to a small hollow near the third parallel where their assault equipment had been stored.

The British attack was dependent on the French first capturing the Malakoff, but while Peel's men had a last tot of rum and watched for the signal flag to go up in the eight-gun battery, the allied assault had already begun to unravel. The initial plan had enshrined a final two-hour bombardment to silence any remaining guns, but at the last moment Pelissier – never a man to fight shy of a butcher's bill – had decided to dispense with it, sending his men across open ground against defences that had had all the time they needed to repair the previous day's damage.

With a botched signal flare compounding the error, Raglan and his officers could do no more than watch in helpless horror, complicit only in so far as Raglan's endless good nature had thrown no barrier in Pelissier's way, as wave after wave of French attacks broke on the Russian defences. 'I always guarded myself from being tied down to attack at the same time as the French,' he later wrote to Lord Panmure, explaining his decision to press on with his own attack when not a single French soldier had reached the Malakoff, '& I felt that I ought to have some hope of their success before I committed our troops; but when I saw how stoutly they were opposed I considered it my duty to assist them by attacking myself ... Of this I am quite certain that if the troops had remained in our trenches, the French would have attributed their non-success to our refusal to participate in the operation.'

It made no sense morally or militarily – the objectives could never be held with the Malakoff in Russian hands, the enemy were waiting and had brought up reinforcements, the artillery bombardment of the Redan had for some inexplicable reason stopped – but at five-thirty in the morning the signal went up and the attack designed to commemorate the success of Waterloo began. The planning for the assault had been put in the hands of Sir George Brown, and he had deployed his men in three columns, with troops of his own Light Divi-sion assisted by Peel's sailors attacking the northern flank of the Redan, while units of the 4th Division advanced on their left against its western junction, and a third column – never in the event used – waited in support.

The whole force – skirmishers, assault troops, 'wool-bag men', sappers, reserves, the lot – added up to barely 1,900, or less than a tenth of the 25,000 troops the French had committed to their abortive attack on the Malakoff, but even so it was more than Brown's woeful organisation could cope with. Many of the staff officers involved had no first-hand knowledge of the ground, and with no system in place to get the right men in the right parallels in the right order, no way of coping with the unsolicited 'volunteers' clogging up the advanced positions, no banquettes to help get the troops out in line, no clear orders at all for the third column and no artillery cover, there was chaos before the start signal had even gone up.

Among the naval contingent Wood had been the first to see the allied signal run up, and before it broke at the top called out to Peel 'Flag's up' and leaped after him onto the covering parapet and into a hale of grape and musket fire. 'It is difficult to picture its intensity,' Wood recalled. 'Various kinds of projectiles cut up the ground all round us, but yet not continuously in their fullest state. While there was no cessation of the shower of missiles, which pattered on the stony ground like tropical rain, yet every thirty seconds or so, gusts of increased violence came sweeping down the hillside, something after the fashion of a storm as simulated behind the scenes of a theatre.'

As the skirmishers to their front began to move forward in open order, Peel stood on the exposed parapet, brandishing his sword in the 'dim light' and calling on his sailors not to 'let the soldiers beat them'. 'Before we had advanced 100 yards,' Wood remembered, as Peel's bluejackets 'rose as one' behind him,

> several sailors had been killed, and I was struck by a bullet inside my thumb, and my sword was knocked five yards away from me. I thought my arm, which was paralysed by the jar, was off, and I instinctively dropped onto one knee, but looking down, I saw that it was merely a flesh wound, and jumped up hurriedly, fearing that any one seeing me might say I was skulking. On going to pick up my sword, I found it was bent up something in the shape of a corkscrew.

Without a sword or pistol – without any sort of weapon – Wood could only press on towards the shelter of the abatis, the sole officer from the naval party still effective. The senior lieutenant had been wounded almost as soon as the attack had begun, and within two hundred yards Peel had joined him, hit by a bullet which passed through his left arm and left him so faint that Daniel – his own uniform shredded by bullets and his pistol-case shot through – had to tie on a tourniquet under the withering hail of case-shot and rifle fire before he could support him back to the cover of the Quarries.

It was the end of the battle for Peel and Daniel, and for the rapidly shrinking rump of his bluejackets too, the end was only a matter of time. 'When I approached the abatis,' wrote Wood, 'there were only two ladders left carried by four and three men respectively. As I joined the leading ladder its carriers were reduced to three, and then the right-hand-rear-man falling, I took his place. The second ladder now fell to the ground, all the men being killed or wounded, and when we were about 30 yards from the abatis my fellow carriers were reduced to two.'

Scarcely had Wood picked up the ladder than the man next to him was killed, to be followed a moment later, as he turned to remonstrate with Wood for not holding up his end, by the last standing bluejacket of Peel's sixty men. 'I must admit a sense of relief came over me,' Wood remembered, luxuriating for one Tolstoyan moment in the strange, existential freedom of his position. 'I felt my responsibility was gone, as even the most enthusiastic Commander could scarcely expect me to carry the only remaining ladder, 18 feet in length, by myself. I was now lying within 30 yards of the abatis, under the slight shelter of which scattered soldiers were crouching; some were firing, and a great many shouting, while above us on the parapet stood Russians four and, in places, six deep, firing at us and calling sarcastically to us to come on.'

Wood did not have long to enjoy his moment of irresponsible relief, though. As he knelt over the body of a dying officer, hit in the stomach and screaming for his mother, a case-shot exploded through the abatis, hurling a shot of 5½ ounces – the weight of a cricket ball, in the sporty vernacular of the campaign – into his arm and knocking him insensible. 'How long I remained unconscious I cannot tell,' he wrote, but I was aroused by an Irish sergeant, shaking me by my wounded arm … and saying, 'Matey, if you are going in, you had better go at once, or you'll get begeneted [bayoneted].' My strongly-worded reply showed him that I was an officer, which he might well have been excused for failing to perceive, for I had little or nothing about me characteristic of the rank … The sergeant informed me that the 'retire' had sounded some minutes previously, and that all our people had gone back. He then, in spite of a shower of bullets fired at less than 100 yards distance, helped me up tenderly, taking great care this time not to hurt my wounded arm. Then, having put me on my feet, he, bending down his head, ran as fast as he could back towards our trenches.

It was more than Wood could do. The adrenalin and willpower that had carried him as far as the abatis was gone. Feeble from a week of fever and 'tinned milk and rice', faint from his wounds, he began the slow, unsteady walk back to safety through a storm of 'grape, case and bullets'. A shallow trench, thrown a hundred yards forward from the Quarries, gave him a momentary respite, but the shrieks of the wounded and dying that filled it seemed worse than the enemy fire. Crawling out again, he set his sights on

a place in the third parallel, where the parapet had been worn down, in order to avoid the exertion of going up even 4 feet, when a young soldier passed me on my left side, and, doubtless not notic- ing I was wounded, knocked my arm heavily, saying, 'Move on, sir, please.' As he passed over the parapet with his rifle at the trail, I caught it by the small of the butt to pull myself up. He turned round angrily, asking 'What are you doing?' and while his face was bent on mine, a round shot, passing my ear, struck him full between the shoulders, and I stepped over his body, so exhausted as to be strangely indifferent to my own life, saved by the soldier having jostled me out of my turn at the gap.

Wood was at last almost safe, but he had come to the end of his tether. Hauling himself over the parapet of the eight-gun battery, he collapsed and was carried in by two officers. He was given brandy, and a 'friendly doctor, whom I had known for some time, greeted me warmly with "Sit down, me dear boy, an' I'll have your arm off before ye know where ye are." I had some difficulty in evading his kind attentions, but eventually being put into a stretcher I was carried away by four Bluejackets ... We met the Commander of the Naval brigade, Captain Lushington, when I was being carried away, and to my great relief, he informed me that Captain Peel was alive.'

It was Peel's face that was the first he saw when he came round – his arm saved – from anaesthetic later that day. His chief had got no farther than halfway, and wanted to know how the rest had fared, but it was only the next day that the full scale of the disaster became clear. The left column, caught in a crossfire between the guns of the Redan and the Barrack Batteries, had if anything suffered even more severely, but of the sixty bluejackets under Peel's direct command in the right column, forty-eight were either killed or wounded, out of total casualties of one hundred officers and 1,444 other ranks. 'It was agonising to see the wounded men who were lying there under a broiling sun,' Russell wrote the next day, as officers and men crowded the front trenches waiting for the armistice that would enable them to perform 'friendship's last melancholy office',

> parched with excruciating thirst, racked with fever, and agonised with pain – to behold them waving their caps faintly, or making signals towards our lines, over which they could see the white flag flying. They lay where they fell, or had scrambled into the holes formed by shells; and there they had been for thirty hours. An officer told me that one soldier who was close to the abatis, when he saw a few men come out of an embrasure, raised himself on an elbow, and fearing he should be unnoticed and passed by, raised his cap on a stick and waved it till he fell back exhausted. Again he rose, and managed to tear off his shirt, which he agitated in the air till his strength failed him. His face could be seen through a glass; and my friend said he never could forget the expression of resignation and despair with which the poor fellow at last folded his shirt under his head to await the mercy of Heaven.

It had been for nothing, too. During a sullenly observed ceasefire that began at 4 o'clock the body of Michael Hardy was recovered from an embrasure of the Redan, the only man to make it across the abatis and the ditch. As soon as it was obvious that both right and left columns had been destroyed the centre was withheld, and Raglan ordered the bombardment of the Redan and the curtain walls that should have preceded and not followed the attack; but it was all too late. Over the seventeenth and eighteenth the Russians lost almost five and a half thousand men – a mirror-match for the combined allied figure – but the Malakoff and Redan were crucially still in their hands. The whole operation had been such a fiasco that it brought out a streak of gallows humour in the men, but among the officers and generals it worked, in Baring Pemberton's elegant phrase, 'like an emetic'. Captain Gerald Goodlake knew of at least fifty officers so disgusted with the handling of the attack that they had vowed to sell out, and for Brown and Pennefather (home), Escourt (cholera), and, above all Raglan (dead of a broken heart within ten days) the war was over.

For Peel and his two young ADCs it already was, and having fought in one of the greatest of all British victories at Inkerman, they went home with the bitter taste of humiliating defeat. Forty years later Wood was still worrying away at the errors and lessons of the allied failures, but none of the three men could have been sorry to have escaped a war that had bled the British army to death and exposed the inadequacies of a navy that had been living off the hard-won capital of the Nelson era for too long.

It was not as if, in Peel's own phrase, they were to be robbed of 'the fruits' either, because when Sevastopol finally fell almost three months later, the Redan, the great symbol of Russian defiance, remained uncaptured. A little under a month after the June assault the Russians had made one last failed offensive at the Battle of Tchernaya, that scarcely involved the British, and when on 8 September the French at last took the Malakoff, a British attack on the Redan that repeated all the errors of 18 June and added some more of its own was again repulsed with hideous losses. 'My head is throbbing, my ears are ringing with the booming of the cannon,' Henry Clifford wrote home that evening, 'with the whistling of the grape and the musket-ball, the wild shouts of the soldiers, the groans and yells of the wounded and dying, my eyes almost blinded with dust have before them the brave officers, waving their swords over their heads on the parapet of the Redan, *alone*, falling wounded ... And what almost breaks my heart, and nearly drove me mad, I see our English soldiers that I was so proud of, run away.'

Those soldiers, though, were not part of the old army that had died at Inkerman or perished from cold and cholera. They were instead raw recruits, brought up on the bad habits of trench warfare, and no substitute. But as humiliated officers counted the butcher's bill and pointed the finger of blame at their generals, and questioned the courage of the men, flames began to rise from different points across the city. 'Soon afterwards,' wrote an astonished Russell,

> wandering fires gleamed through the streets and outskirts of the town – point after point became alight – the flames shone out of the windows of the houses – rows of mansions caught and burned up, and before daybreak the town of Sevastopol – that fine and stately mistress of the Euxine, on which we had so often turned a longing eye – was on fire from the sea to the Dockyard Creek. Fort Alexander was blown up early in the night, with a stupendous crash that made the very earth reel ... In a moment afterwards the Redan was the scene of a very heavy explosion ... The Flagstaff and Garden Batteries blew up, one after another, at 4.45. At 5.30 there were two of the largest and grandest explosions on the left that ever shook the earth – most probably from Fort Alexander and the Grand magazine.

The Russians, as one English soldier put it, had 'done a Moscow', evacuating the city across the pontoon bridge over the Grand Harbour to the north, and torching it behind them. Victory, except for the looters, was as bitter as defeat. Everywhere was the evidence of the misery and horrors the siege had inflicted on the people of Sevastopol. In the suburbs beneath the Malakoff, the ruined houses were filled with the dead. 'The Russians had crept away into holes and corners in every house to die like poisoned rats,' continued Russell.

> Artillery horses, with their entrails torn open by shot, were stretched all over the space at the back of the Malakoff. Of all the pictures of the horrors of war which have ever been presented to the world, the hospital of Sevastopol offered the most heartrending and revolting. Entering one of [its] doors, I beheld such a sight as few men, thank God, have ever witnessed. In a long, low room, supported by square pillars arched at the top, and dimly lighted through shattered and unglazed window-frames, lay the wounded Russians. The wounded, did I say? No, but the dead – the rotten and festering corpses of the soldiers, who were left to die in their extreme agony, untended, uncared for ... some on the floor, some on ... pallets of straw, sopped and saturated with blood which oozed and trickled through the floor.

'If a few days before I had been told,' wrote Henry Clifford,

> 'On the morning of the 9th September, at five o'clock Sevastopol
> will be in the hands of the Allies and you will stand in the Redan
> held by the English,' I should have said, 'Oh that will be a proud
> and happy moment, that will repay us for all we have gone through,
> even the loss of so many lives, so much suffering and hardship will
> not have been thrown away in vain!' But no, I stood in the Redan
> more humble, more dejected and with a heavier heart than I have
> yet felt since I left home.

It was one fate, at least, that Peel was spared. By the time Sevastopol
fell he was at home. And if he would not live to see the lessons of the
Crimea produce the reforms he had predicted, he had returned to
England a man marked for the top. Lyons's despatch after the first
assault on the Redan had singled him out for his 'chivalrous gallantry
and cheerful readiness for every duty', and the honours flowed Peel's
way. 'I am commanded by His Royal Highness, The Prince Albert,
Grand Master of the Order,' the Lancaster Herald wrote on 20 July
1855, almost two months before Sevastopol had fallen, 'to transmit
to you the accompanying packet addressed to rear Admiral Sir
Edward Lyons, Bart GCB containing the Insignia of that Order for
the officers now serving in the Black Sea, named in the enclosed list
(16 in number) who have recently been appointed Companions (military division) of that Most Honourable Order.'

Among the new Companions of the Bath was William Peel, the
youngest recipient of the award. More honours were to come – a
Turkish award, the French Legion of Honour – and finally, in February 1857, the most prized decoration of all, the newly instituted
Victoria Cross. 'Sir Stephen Lushington recommends this officer,' the
official document read:

> 1st For having on the 18th October 1854, at the greatest possible
> risk, taken up a live shell, the fuze still burning, from among several
> powder cases, outside the magazine, and thrown it over the para-
> pet (the shell bursting as it left his hands) thereby saving the maga-
> zines and the lives of those immediately around it ...
>
> 2nd On 5 November 1854, at the Battle of Inkerman, for join-
> ing the officers of the Grenadier Guards, and assisting in defend-
> ing the colours of that Regiment, when hard pressed at the Sandbag

Battery. (Sir S. Lushington is authorised to make this statement by the Lieutenant General Commanding the Division, HRH the Duke of Cambridge, who is ready to bear testimony to the fact.)

3rd On 18 June 1855, for volunteering to lead the Ladder Party at the assault on the Redan, and carrying the first ladder until wounded.

Among the first recipients was also Edward Daniel, his name seemingly forever linked to that of Peel in the citation for his award: 'For devotion to his leader, Captain Peel, on 18th June, 1855, in tying a tourniquet on his arm on the glacis of the Redan, while exposed to a very heavy fire.' The young Wood, also put forward for the VC by Lushington, would have to wait. But he would not have to wait for long: for all three of them – all born warriors in their different ways – there was about to be a still bloodier war.

XIII

It is a terrible business … this living among inferior races. I have seldom from man or woman since I came to the East heard a sentence which was reconcilable with the hypothesis that Christianity had ever come into the world. Detestation, contempt, ferocity, vengeance, whether Chinamen or Indians be the object. There are some 3 or 4 hundred servants in this House [Lord Canning's]. When one passes by them salaaming one feels a little awkward, but the feeling soon wears off, and one moves among them with perfect indifference, treating them not as dogs, because in that case one would whistle to them and pat them, but as machines with which one can have no communion or sympathy … When the passions of fear and hatred are engrafted on this indifference, the result is frightful, an absolute callousness to the suffering of the objects of those passions which must be witnessed to be understood or believed.

Lord Elgin

Early in the morning of 10 May 1857 – a seemingly normal Sunday in the life of British India – a young Eurasian signaller at the telegraph station just outside the city walls of Delhi was about to close the office until the afternoon when he noticed a signal coming through from the military cantonment at Meerut, thirty miles to the north-east. The message was not an official one, but reported that there had been unrest the previous day over the introduction of the new cartridges to native troops, and that eighty-five sowars of the 3rd Light Cavalry had been imprisoned for their refusal to use them, and were – in the time-honoured traditions of the Moghul Emperors adopted by their British successors – to be blown from the guns in punishment.

The Indian Mutiny had begun, and while the mixture of hyperbole and fact contained in that signal was typical of what was to come, there was substance enough in it to make grim news for Delhi's British community. By the time the telegraph office reopened at 4 o'clock the line to Meerut had been cut, and when the next morning Charles Todd, the assistant in charge, set off to find and repair the break, he disappeared, never to be seen again, the first of Delhi's European victims of a rebellion that would provoke acts of an unspeakable cruelty and barbarism on both sides.

For all the readiness shown by either civil or military authorities, the Mutiny might have come out of nowhere, and on the morning that the news from Meerut reached Delhi, Captain William Peel VC CB was enjoying his last day at the Cape before weighing for China and the only war then registering on the British consciousness. It is hard to believe that he was any keener on the prospect of Amoy than he had been seventeen years before, but the Peel of 1857 was in many ways a different man from the frustrated *Cambrian* midshipman of 1840; different even from the man who sent his querulous letters back from the Crimea – more at peace with himself and more at peace with a world that had at last given him his due.

It is not that he was any less ambitious, less dismissive of his superiors, or that the demons that had driven him into the Nubian desert or the forlorn hope at the Redan were finally stilled, but he was no longer the son of Sir Robert Peel. He was now a figure in his own right. In his first months back from the Crimea he had battered away at the Admiralty with memos on French floating batteries and new naval technologies, but not even the typical failure of their lordships to rouse themselves to so much as an acknowledgement could dent Peel's fabled – and often fabulous – 'serenity'. 'I was pleased to see the Paper so fairly received,' he wrote to his brother Frederick, after bypassing the Admiralty to go straight to the War Office. 'The admiralty will never listen to it because they choose to assert that iron is unfit for war vessels; the trials on which this judgement was given, were not, I think, sufficiently matured. Wood is better than iron to meet solid shot, but for shells and other combustibles, iron is far superior.'

It had taken him six months to recover from his wound, but with his new estates to occupy him at Sandy, Buckinghamshire, and a mother and sister to care for, he was not short of occupation. The death of his father had left him and his brothers wealthy men by most standards, and he had clearly inherited all the old Peel talent for acquiring and improving land. 'In the middle of the month I spent a short but most enjoyable visit with Capt Peel at Sandy,' Evelyn Wood, who had transferred from the navy to the cavalry in search of another war, wrote.

> The morning after I arrived a deputation from Potton asked my host to link their village by tramway with the Great Northern Station at Sandy, a distance of about three miles. Having inquired the terms, he sat down and made his calculations, while they waited, and in less than an hour dismissed them with a favourable answer. He constructed the tramway, which was taken over by the Bedford & Cambridge Railway Company, when that was made five years later.
>
> Capt. Peel was as good at playing host as he was at fighting, and I left the place with an increased admiration of my late Chief's character. Three months later he came to see me at Dorchester, being anxious that I should study my new profession, and not content myself with sauntering through life in the Army.

The first engine built for Peel's line, launched by his mother – and still surviving as a museum piece at Didcot – would be named the *Shannon* in honour of the ship, but by that time Peel had already left Sandy to take command of the real thing. If he had been looking for some visible sign of his rising status in the navy he need have looked no further, because in the newly built, screw steam, six-thousand-horse-power, fifty-one-gun HMS *Shannon* their lordships had given him the perfect successor to the frigate that under Philip Broke had made the *Shannon* a household name during the American War of 1812.

There was nearly a watery grave for the new *Shannon* and her 510 officers, men and boys – including Edward Daniel – when she almost

foundered on the rocks below Bovis during her sea trials, but after
another scare off Ushant with the mainmast she was finally ready to
sail. As late as February 1857 Peel had still been hoping that she
would be sent to the Mediterranean, but in early March the orders
came through for the China station, and on the seventeenth – St
Patrick's Day – the *Shannon* weighed for the Cape en route to Singapore, where they were to take on board Lord Elgin, the newly
appointed Ambassador Extraordinary, for transport out to Hong
Kong to negotiate a peaceful solution to the latest breakdown in relations between Britain and China.

There were two fatalities from accidents on the voyage out, but
with the weather fine throughout, the performance of the *Shannon*
everything Peel could hope, and 'reading, chess, draughts (I am not
at all sure I have spelt that right) backgammon, boxing, dancing, etc.'
to keep a gifted and aristocratic gunroom happy, not even the first
'bad news of India' picked up from a passing steam packet was
enough to dampen spirits. 'The very day we arrived we received
invites to two balls,' Nowell Salmon – a young midshipman in the
Wood mould – wrote of their first cheery exposure to the imperial
round that centred on 'that jolly old fellow' Lord Elgin in Singapore.
'It was rather warm weather for dancing, as you may suppose, but I
managed to get on very well. I made friends with the two daughters
of the Colonel of the 14th, who had not long been out of England
where they were at school; they were very sprightly little girls and we
used to call them "Les petits Poulets". Their name I forgot to tell you,
is Pooley.'

If Salmon is to be believed, the only mild anxiety to cloud Singapore life was the daily loss of two – 'sometimes more, sometimes less'
– Chinamen to the jungle's tiger population, but above the level of
midshipmen's dances, picnics and riding parties things were crank-
ing slowly into grim and retributive life. On 23 June the *Shannon*
had finally weighed for China with Lord Elgin, but they had got no
farther than Hong Kong when an Indian steamer arrived from
Calcutta with more 'bad news with respect to the insurgent troops'.
'I rather think the contents of this letter will astonish you,' a delighted
Salmon wrote home from sea again on 8 August.

You know, of course, by this time all about the unfortunate state
of affairs in India. On the 16 July, we were in Hong Kong, having
just finished our preparations for the northern cruize when an order

came on board at 8 A.M. to prepare for sea immediately and embark 300 Marines that had just arrived in the *Sans Pareil*.

At 4 P.M. Lord Elgin came on board and we stood out of the harbour, not knowing till we were well outside that we were to go as hard as we could to Calcutta, where Lord E. is going to give Lord Canning the benefit of his advice …

But the most astonishing thing I have yet to tell you. Lord Elgin has given Captain Peel permission to offer the Governor-General the services of a Naval Brigade, which will consist of 300 bluejackets from this ship, and some from the Pearl who accompanies us.

The request had, in fact, come in the first place from the Indian authorities, but it is hard to believe Peel had not anticipated it. There would be a certain amount of chuntering back at the Admiralty over his decision to place the *Shannon* under civil command, but even in the age of the telegraph the latitude for initiative was still a healthy one, and Peel had no intention of allowing service punctilio or talk of proper distinctions between naval officers and 'Civil Authorities' to stand in the way of working under either Canning or the military powers.

After coaling at Singapore, and picking up a fair wind in the Straits of Malacca that stayed with them for the rest of their voyage, the *Shannon* reached the mouth of the Ganges Delta on 6 August 1857, and there waited in the deadening afternoon heat for a pilot to take her through the interminable twists and shallows of the Hooghly River. 'At length a smart little brig came under the Shannon's stern,' Edmund Verney, midshipman turned acting mate since passing his examination at Hong Kong, wrote of the oppressive prospect that Peel had last viewed as a young midshipman himself,

lowered a boat, and sent a pilot on board; and the frigate, furling sails, steamed through the dull and muddy waters of the Hooghly. The scenery at that part of the Delta formed by the mouth of the Ganges … is anything but inviting: from the masthead of a large ship, as far as the eye can reach, no rise of land is visible in any direction; at high water the sea is almost at a level with the tops of the innumerable mud islands, and which are uninhabited save by crocodiles and a few wild beasts; they are covered with a thick and almost impenetrable jungle, and there are seen the luxuriant vegetation of a tropical climate.

As they neared the city of Calcutta, perched on its ridge beside the Hooghly eighty miles from the ocean, first one, then a second, and finally a long string of English villas and pleasure gardens came into sight along the east bank, to provide English eyes in the *Shannon* with all the reason they could ever need to be there. From the deck of the ship the young Verney could make out the excited faces of English women and children peering out of the windows at them, and as they steamed slowly up past Bishop's College and the 'frowning batteries' of Fort William, cheer after cheer floated across the water to welcome them.

Even among the forest of merchant masts – 'French, Dutch, Yankee and all kinds' – crowding the waterfront opposite the Grand Parade the *Shannon* was a sight to cower or reassure, and as her nineteen-gun salute 'thundered through the sultry air' it was not just the imprisoned Despot of Oudh who heard 'a hint of England's might'. 'On Aug 7 telegraphs came all day of the progress of a great ship steaming up the river,' wrote a relieved Lady Canning, the 'beautiful and clever' wife of the Governor General, Charles Canning, son and heir – in brains, fun and capacity for work – of the great George Canning, George IV's Prime Minister, 'and the excitement grew when we knew it was the *Shannon*, and it reached its climax when we found it had brought Lord Elgin and 1,700 men. Next day he arrived in that beautiful Frigate – the largest ship, they say, that ever steamed up here. We were delighted to hear that William Peel was in command, and still more when Lord Elgin gave out his intention of leaving him to do us all the service he could with his heavy guns and crew.'

The relief in Calcutta was understandable, because if Canning had taken a haughty enough line with its panicking population in the early days of the outbreak, he had been able to do little since to quieten their fears. The rebellion had not and never would spread across the whole of India, but while the Madras army – the East India Company force was divided into three armies – remained loyal, and the Bombay relatively unaffected, it was a very different story with the powerful Bengal army, which could account for over half the total number of regiments in India.

The prompt actions of John Lawrence, Chief Commissioner of the Punjab, and Lieutenant Colonel John Nicholson, two of the most famous names of the Mutiny, had stifled unrest in the Punjab, but to its south-east all control had been lost. On the day after the outbreak at Meerut mutineers from the 3rd Light Cavalry had attacked and

taken Delhi, the symbolic and historic centre of Moghul power, and
by the end of June Cawnpore's population had been massacred and
the three-thousand-strong garrison and civilian inhabitants of
Lucknow besieged in the fortified Residency that was to provide an
outraged Britain with many of its most vivid and hagiographical
images of suffering, martyrdom and heroism.

No such sketch can give any idea of the violence and fear that
had convulsed India; of the isolated murders and atrocities or the
increasingly inhuman reprisals; of the bewilderment of officer after
officer who would have sworn to the loyalty of his native troops; of
the heat, thirst, exhaustion and disease that were the constants of
campaigning life – but it does at least isolate the theatre of war that
would exclusively concern Peel. From the start of the Mutiny
Canning had recognised that the key to Delhi and the Cawnpore–Lucknow axis was the control of the arterial Ganges water-
way, and the arrival of the *Shannon* with her immense weight of
artillery offered a possibility of recovering the lost ground of May
and June with a speed and firepower that his existing forces simply
could not match.

The debate over the causes of the so-called Mutiny is coeval with
the rebellion itself, but whatever the underlying reasons – religious
fears over the grease (rumoured to be pork or beef fat) for the new
cartridges, terms of service and pay, unpopular land reforms,
Company cupidity, Christian evangelism, nascent nationalism, the
arrival of the memsahib, the cultural remoteness of Company officers,
the dangerously unfavourable ratio of British (or Queen's) regiments
to native troops – the only aspects of the argument that now
concerned Canning and his generals were the chronic shortages of
European troops and artillery. 'I have further to acquaint you,' Lord
Elgin wrote to Peel on 10 August,

> that having learnt from the Governor General of India and Lieu-
> tenant Sir Patrick Grant that a body of Seamen and Marines, thor-
> oughly trained as Artillerymen, conveying guns of heavy calibre,
> and commanded by an officer of energy and experience, may render
> important Service at this juncture on the line of Communication
> between Calcutta and Delhi, and possibly at Delhi itself ...
>
> In removing [you] from the magnificent Ship under your
> command I make a considerable sacrifice: but I do so with the less
> reluctance because I am convinced that your conduct in the

discharge of the difficult and responsible duty about to devolve upon you, will be such as to justify the confidence in your distinction and ability which induce me to consent to it.

Naval forces had never been committed so far inland as Elgin was envisaging, but no one had more experience of the use of heavy naval guns in land operations than Peel, and he was quick to seize the opportunity. 'My dearest mother,' Salmon wrote home from Calcutta six days later:

As we anticipated, we are off up the country. We start at daylight tomorrow morning, for Allahabad, in a steamer, and a large flat boat. The Naval Brigade, commanded by Captain Peel, consists of 407 officers and men belonging to this ship. We take with us two field pieces and ten of our large eight-inch guns to form a breaching battery at Delhi, which is our ultimate destination, for we shall push on to Delhi as soon as we have a sufficient force to escort our immense train of guns, ammunition, etc. We take every grain of powder in the ship, and all the shot and shell for the eight-inch guns ...

It will take us twenty-one days to reach Allahabad, as we shall be obliged to anchor every night. Everything is topsy-turvy and the greatest excitement prevails. We take with us as little baggage as possible; each of us has a seaman's bag only, and a blanket, and we have no native servants, without whom *everybody* says we shall never get on. But it is on *that*, in great measure, that *we* rest our hopes of success, as we shall thus be dependent entirely on our own resources. No European regiment marches in this country without at least 2,000 native servants and camp followers.

I should not be in the least surprised to meet with some resistance before we have gone far from Calcutta, as the whole of Bengal is in the hands of the rebels, and I do not expect to see H.M.S. *Shannon* again for a year at least.

The *Shannon*'s officers still had a dinner of unimaginable dullness to endure at Canning's vast palace, visits from the Governor General to the ship, and a blessing from the eighty-four-year-old Bishop of Calcutta – incensed that his age prevented him from fighting with them – but on the twenty-first, after delays over transport, the brigade was finally ready to embark. 'Now that we are fairly off I must say something about the Hoogly,' Salmon reported home in a wonderfully period blend of open-eyed curiosity and inherited prejudice.

> On each side of the river in all the prettiest spots are ghauts, nicely
> built of stone, with generally a temple at the top of the steps. These
> ghauts, or more properly ghats, are built and endowed by the upper
> classes of the Hindoos, and it is considered a work of piety; some
> of them are very handsome. In the morning they are crowded with
> men and women bathing, and filling their chatties with water which
> they carry on the head; and as the attitudes of the women are gener
> ally graceful, it looks very pretty, but you must not take your glass
> to examine them more closely for the Indian women of the lower
> orders are, in nineteen cases out of twenty, most repulsive in their
> appearance, though among the unmarried women of the better
> classes you will occasionally see really beautiful features; but they
> marry at about 12 years old, and a year after that look old and ugly.

Everything about the Hooghly was new and 'delightful' to Peel's men
– the elephants with their 'gay howdahs', the monkeys swinging
about in the branches, the huge banyan trees as 'common as elms in
England', the myriad unknown birds, the distant sight of the
Himalayas lit by the morning sun – and even after they reached the
Ganges proper, and their steamer had to fight its slow way upstream
through the shifting sandbanks and floating corpses of hanged rebels,
standards and morale remained as high as ever. 'I have the honour to
inform your Excellency of my arrival here to day with a detachment
of the Royal Naval Brigade of 94 officers and men,' Peel wrote from
Allahabad on 3 October to Sir Michael Seymour, his old Admiral
from Collingwood days and now Commander-in-Chief on the China
station. 'The Bulk of the Brigade with all our siege train should arrive
here on the 6th inst: and the whole force will then be 390 officers
and men, but a reinforcement from the "*Shannon*" under Lieutenant
Vaughan, which must be close at hand, will make us 500 strong ...
The men are in excellent health, and manoeuvre with great precision,
and are in every way fit to take the field; their conduct is admirable,
and no departure whatever is allowed from the dress and discipline
of the service.'

The town of Allahabad had been captured and retaken in the first
weeks of the Mutiny, but the fort itself had never fallen, and had since
become the principal arsenal and base for British operations against

the rebel forces across the Ganges and to the north-west. 'The fort is a strange mixture of ancient and modern,' wrote Oliver Jones – a top-booted, frock-coated, spurred and scimitar-carrying half-pay naval captain, Crimea veteran and 'Travelling Gent' supreme, who had wangled a passage out to India 'for a *lark*', as he put it.

> It is situated at the apex of the Jumna and Ganges, and is in the form of a triangle, the two ancient sides facing respectively the Jumna and the Ganges, and the modern base fronting the land. The river sides are immense stone walls, of great height and thickness, with circular bastions at intervals, and machicolated crests, very picturesque, but utterly unfit against the battering cannon now used in sieges; the land face has all the modern improvements – low bastions and curtains, ditches, scarps and counterscarps, sloping glacis, and winding covert-ways.

The arrival of the Naval Brigade had freed four hundred men for action against the mutineers, but as one fourteen-year-old naval cadet, E.S. Watson, proudly wrote, Peel had not brought his men this far to carry out garrison duties, and he was soon again on the move. On 27 October a contingent of 170 men with a powerful siege train left with the *Shannon*'s gunnery officer, and on the following day a second party under Peel himself marched out to join a punitive British force now operating under the overall command of Sir Colin Campbell in the countryside around Futtehpore. 'I have just been turning out the guard to salute Captain Peel and his party as they passed out,' wrote Verney, bitterly disappointed to be left behind with the sick and the rump of the brigade: 'The Captain called out "Good bye, Mr Verney", which proceeding is contrary to all discipline.'

Peel's contingent of the Naval Brigade formed part of a column made up of a hundred-strong company of the 93rd Highlanders, sixty-eight men of the Royal Engineers, two nine-pounders of the Royal Artillery, and sixty men from various regiments under the command of Colonel Powell of the 53rd. The orders for the columns were to hunt down and bring to battle a large rebel force in the area, and on the afternoon of 1 November, after an exhausting march of seventy-two miles in three days, they found an enemy army of about four thousand dug in at Kudjwa behind some sandy hillocks.

The fighting had hardly begun when Colonel Powell was killed by a musketball, and Peel took over command of the battle. The

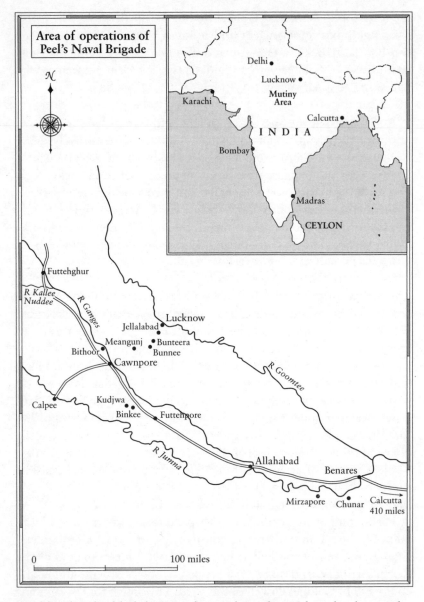

Area of operations of Peel's Naval Brigade

Highlanders had led the initial assault in skirmish order, but under a 'well served' artillery fire – invariably the rebels' strongest arm – the attack looked like faltering until Peel rallied as many fresh men as he could and succeeded in driving the mutineers out of their entrenchments. 'The enemy then retired in confusion, leaving us masters of their camp and with two of their guns and a tumbrel in our possession,' Peel wrote of a battle that in its formless – and oddly pointless – anonymity might stand surrogate for any number of similar engagements with an enemy that could simply dissolve back into the countryside from which it had emerged.

> The late hour of the evening (it was half past four when the enemy fired their last shot) and the excessive fatigue of the troops prevented any pursuit; we therefore spoiled their camp and, leaving it with cheers, formed on the road near the village and sent out parties to collect our dead and wounded.
>
> With the body of the Colonel on the limber of the gun he had so gallantly captured, we then returned and encamped near the village of Binkee. Our loss in the action was very severe, amounting to ninety five killed and wounded. The behaviour of the troops and the Naval brigade was admirable, and all vied with each other and showed equal courage in the field. The marching of the 53rd and the accurate fire of the Highlanders deserves especial commendation … I am much gratified with the conduct of all the Brigade, and there is no departure from the ordinary rules of the Service.

It had been no Inkerman, perhaps, but for most of Peel's men it was their first action, and with the praise of the Commander-in-Chief ringing in their ears, morale in the brigade was higher than it had ever been. The only naval fatalities had been one marine and a seaman, and as they marched into Futtehpore the next day with their fourteen wounded officers and men, Peel's bluejackets were 'received with great cheering'. 'Captain Peel arrived on the 10th with 100 men,' Salmon reported home ten days later, after the two advance contingents of the brigade were again united,

> having fought a very gallant action on their way up from Allahabad, in which our fellows behaved splendidly. Capt. Peel commanded after the death of Colonel Powell of the 53rd. Our men had been fraternizing with the 93rd Highlanders on their way up, and charged in line with them, every bluejacket picking out his own acquaintance to fight with. They had marched 24 miles in the heat of the day and were very tired, but that did not prevent them giving a good account of the niggers.

After giving his men a day's sorely needed rest, Peel left Futtehpore on 4 November for the fifty miles' march to Cawnpore, to join the large force massing under Sir Colin Campbell for the relief of Lucknow. 'At two in the morning the *reveillee* rang out,' wrote Captain Jones, recapturing the unforgettable rhythms and sounds of Indian campaign life with the Naval Brigade,

and immediately to my unaccustomed ears, began a noise most Babel like and extraordinary. Niggers chattering, horses neighing and stamping, camels grunting and gurgling, elephants blowing and trumpeting; some camels and elephants refusing to be loaded, and some straying about the camp, their drivers and mahouts running after them ...

The scene was very fine and grand, for the soldiers and camp-followers set fire to all the straw and litter; and all the various groups come out, some in strong light, when near the bright flame of the burning straw, others in the chiar-oscura of darkness visible, when farther from it; and the trumpets sounding, the soldiers, some assembling, some striking tents, and loading elephants with them, and bullocks, hackeries, and camels, with their bedding, officers riding about giving orders, the Artillery harnessing and preparing their guns, the baggage filing off the ground, and lastly – the order to advance – the measured tread of the infantry, the pattering of the horses' feet, the jangling of harnesses and accoutrements, and the rumbling of the gun-wheels, form altogether a scene most interesting and exciting ...

It was tiresome work, Nowell Salmon more prosaically told his mother, and with the Naval Brigade's massive train of guns and ammunition wagons, slow progress. 'Their big guns were drawn by thirteen pair of oxen, or by a couple of elephants,' Jones continued.

Along well-made roads, on good ground, where there are no nullahs to cross or obstacles to get over, the bullocks are much preferred; they go on steadily at a certain rate, about two and a half miles an hour, for from between twelve to sixteen miles per day for weeks together, without knocking up, and give very little trouble; but if the gun has to cross rivers, sands, nullahs, or broken ground, they are the stupidest beast in the world, pull different ways, or pull not at all, get their heads clear of their yokes, kick, butt, and give all manner of trouble, which with the cries, beating, kicking, and *tail-twisting*, inflicted upon them by their drivers, creates a Babel-like noise and confusion seldom to be enjoyed out of India. Meanwhile the gun sticks fast, and probably is sinking deeper and deeper into the sand or mud, or whatever it may be, till at length an elephant is brought up, who goes behind it and gives it a push or shove in the cleverest way; and when the strain is lightened, the bullocks are induced to renew their efforts; or, a couple of hundred men clap on the drag-ropes, and pull it out by main strength.

The post captain in Jones was equally taken with the strange metamorphosis of bluejacket into redcoat that Peel had wrought in only a few weeks. 'I was much pleased with the excellent order and discipline which was maintained, and the cleanliness and neatness which prevailed,' he wrote.

> The men in particular were as well dressed and as clean as they would have been on the *Shannon* herself, or any other man-of-war in good order.
>
> On parade they moved with the precision of a well-drilled corps, and they handled their arms as men who knew how to use them; and to see them 'march past' or advance in line, would have done a soldier's heart good.
>
> It appeared wonderful to me how sailors could be trained to be so steady, and the manner in which they worked their heavy guns was the admiration of every one, from the Commander-in-Chief downwards. In fact, the brigade was a credit to Captain Peel, his officers, and every man in it.
>
> The number of pets which the sailors had was marvellous – monkeys, parrots, guinea-pigs, dogs, cats, *mongoose* or *mongeese*, which you like, and lots of other creatures. Some of the monkeys were as tame and affectionate, and would follow their masters like dogs. Peel often said 'the *Shannon* would be a regular menagerie when they got back to her.'

Jones had marched up from Calcutta with the army, and had only caught up with Peel – out riding in the midst of 'his young folks' where there was anything 'historic' to see, or relaxed at the end of a day's march and telling stories 'rather in the Marryat style' – at the scene of the most notorious massacre of the Mutiny, at Cawnpore. 'The place was literally running ankle deep in blood,' wrote Major Bingham of the 64th, one of the first witnesses into the Bibighar, where 197 women and children had been held prisoner in stifling heat before being butchered, 'ladies' hair torn from their heads was lying about the floor, in scores, torn from their heads in their exertions to save their lives no doubt; poor little children's shoes lying here and there, gowns and frocks and bonnets belonging to these *poor, poor* creatures scattered everywhere. But to crown all horrors, after they had been killed, and even some alive, were all thrown down a *deep* well in the compound. I looked down and saw them lying in heaps.'

By the time Peel and Jones arrived the well had been filled in and the walls and floors scrubbed clean, but the impression the scene made was no less strong. 'On the wall behind the door was written with a pen or some sharp instrument,' Edmund Verney noted, 'Countrymen and women, remember 15 July, 1857. Your wives and families are here in misery, and at the disposal of savages who has ravaged both old and young, and then killed us. Oh! Oh! my child! Countrymen revenge it.'

It was a call that had been listened to only too well, and as the British force moved north-west towards Lucknow, its progress was marked by a brutalising regime of retribution, burning villages, murder, drumhead trials and executions that was to leave the moral balance sheet of the Mutiny pretty evenly poised. 'Let us propose a Bill for the flaying alive, impalement, or burning of the murderers of women and children,' the terrifying, complex, brutal, implacable, overpowering and tortured John Nicholson – feared, loved and quite literally idolised in about equal measure – had written after the massacres at Delhi. 'The idea of simply hanging the perpetrators of such atrocities is maddening ... We are told in the Bible that stripes shall be meted out according to faults ... If I had [the wretches] in my power today and knew that I were to die tomorrow, I would inflict the most excruciating tortures I could think of on them with a perfectly easy conscience.'

By the last months of 1857 the fatally wounded Nicholson had more or less had his way, with Delhi falling into British hands on 20 September after a bloody and ill-disciplined assault. With the capture of the city and Bahadur Shah – the eighty-two-year-old King of Delhi and Sovereign of the World – Canning had optimistically predicted the end of the insurrection, but great swathes of the country remained in rebel hands, and with Agra threatened and the beleaguered and sickening garrison at the Lucknow Residency under close siege, the end was still nowhere in sight.

The Residency at Lucknow, built on rising ground above the River Gumti and a sprawling, domed and minareted city of 600,000, comprised some thirty-seven acres within a perimeter of about a mile in circumference. Early in the Mutiny the garrison had recognised that only one position could be held and set to work on the compound, erecting gun emplacements and digging trenches, blocking windows and hoarding provisions, fortifying perimeter houses, throwing up palisades and earthworks, ransacking libraries for books to plug the holes – *Lardner's Encyclopaedia* could stop a musketball in just 130 pages – and pulling down any walls that could offer cover to an attacker.

A relief column under Havelock and Outram – the improbable-looking 'Bayard of the East' – had, in one sense, only compounded the problem by fighting their way into a Residency they could not evacuate, and as their men settled down to extend the defensive perimeter and countermine the besiegers' tunnels Lucknow's fifteen hundred European non-combatants steeled themselves for another agonising wait. 'Everyone is depressed,' one colonel's widow wrote – in its startling ingratitude the authentic voice of British India, 'and all feel that we are in fact *not relieved*. The fighting men we have are too few for our emergency, and too many for the provisions we have in the garrison.'

The shortage of supplies was not as parlous as had first seemed, and the garrison was still holding out when six weeks later the relieving army under Colin Campbell at last prepared to march. If Outram had had his way Campbell would have dealt with a rebel army to his rear and west before he worried about Lucknow, but the dictates of chivalry – or the lure of a peerage – won out over military logic, and on 9 November his patched and ragbag army of cavalry exquisites, Balaclava veterans and dispirited Delhi campaigners finally set out on the forty-five miles that separated them from the Lucknow Residency.

Even in an army decked out in a motley of old curtains, draperies and pyjamas, there can have been no sight stranger than that of Peel's bluejackets – '4ft high, 4 ft broad, long hair and dragging big guns!!' – drawn up for review on the banks of the Ganges. 'It was astonishing to see how well they performed,' Jones wrote of them,

with something of the amazement that Dr Johnson reserved for a
woman preaching.

> They looked more like a well-drilled corps than a body of Jacks,
> who, usually, cannot walk without rolling like a ship in the trough
> of the sea, nor stand without their legs apart at about the same
> angle as the shrouds of a seventy-four. It certainly reflected infinite
> credit upon Captain Peel and his officers, and upon the good-feel-
> ing of the men. The discipline was admirable; the men orderly,
> sober, clean, and respectful; and so great was the influence of ...
> Peel's high character and unflinching determination, that it was
> maintained with very little punishment.

Campbell was not everyone's favourite general – 'too cautious for
India, too selfish for any place' – but if he did have a peerage in his
sights the truth was that there was nobody on that parade whose mind
was not equally set on the Residency. On the following day Campbell
marched his troops as far as the Alambagh buildings to the south of
the city, and on the fourteenth, with an army now consisting of 4,700
men and forty-nine guns, began his final flanking advance on the Residency against a rebel force estimated at 30,000 strong.

The route Campbell's army took – a wide sweep to the east of the
city, bypassing the streets through which Outram and Havelock had
fought their way two months before at such a high cost – took them
through the lightly defended hunting box and deer park, known as
the Dilkusha, and La Martinière College, and by Lucknow's southern and eastern sides.

It had been done with minimal fuss, but the reconnaissance of the
canal and a diversionary barrage of rockets and shells had given Peel
the opportunity to display all his old *sangfroid*. 'We fell in and
advanced towards Banks' House, which stood as a prominent feature
beyond the canal,' the future Lord Wolseley wrote – as if, for all the
world, Peel was directing children over a zebra crossing. 'Captain
Peel's guns had come into action within a few hundred yards of it,
and as we came up and were about to pass to the front through them,
he held up his hand and said, with the cool affability which always
distinguished him, "One more broadside, if you please gentlemen."
The expression smelt of the sea, and amused us much. What a splendid fellow he was! We halted, he poured in his "broadside", and then
we doubled down to the canal.'

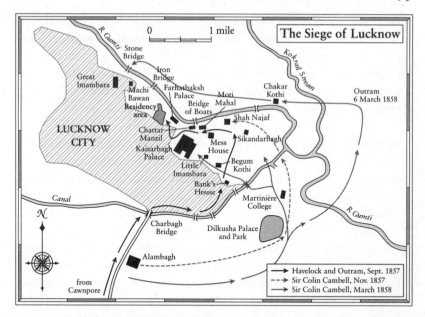

The real work, though, was still to come, and only began in earnest on the morning of the sixteenth. On crossing the canal near its junction with the Gumti, the attackers had followed the line of the river, before turning sharply left in the hope of bypassing the Sikandar Bagh, a strongly fortified garden enclosure, 130 yards square, surrounded by a massive, twenty-foot-high brick wall with pierced loopholes and circular corner bastions.

It was the end of Campbell's cakewalk into Lucknow, and as an 'incessant fire' poured in from houses and barracks on three sides and from the two thousand rebels in Sikandar Bagh beyond, the cavalry fell back on the congested body of infantry and artillery already crammed into the narrow lane behind. For a few chaotic minutes the whole advance was at a standstill, but as field guns were brought into operation and Peel's artillery rushed up, a company of the 53rd and the Highlanders of the 93rd clambered down through the rooftops to drive out the rebels at the point of the bayonet. 'This action of the highlanders was as serviceable as it was heroic,' wrote Roberts, 'for it silenced the fire most destructive to the attacking force; but for all that, our position was extremely critical, and Sir Colin, perceiving the danger, at once decided that no further move could be attempted, until we had gained possession of the Sikandarbagh.'

A spent bullet – having already gone through a gunner – hit and heavily bruised Campbell on the thigh as he directed operations, but by now the guns were battering away at the south-east corner of the Sikandar Bagh. 'In less than half an hour an opening three feet square and three feet from the ground had been made in the wall,' wrote Roberts, his blood still up forty years later.

It would have been better had it been larger, but time was precious; Sir Colin would not wait, and ordered the assault to begin. The infantry had been lying down, under such slight cover as was available, impatiently awaiting for this order. The moment it reached them, up they sprang with one accord, and with one voice uttered a shout which must have foreshadowed defeat to the defenders of the Sikandarbagh ... It was a magnificent sight, a sight never to be forgotten – that glorious struggle to be the first to enter the deadly breach, the prize to the winner of the race being certain death! Highlanders and Sikhs, Punjabi Mohomedans, Dogras [Rajputs] and Pathans, all vied with each other in the generous competition.

A Highlander was the first to die in the breach, followed by 'a man of the 4th Punjab Infantry', and as Sikhs, Scots, Bengalis, English, officers, men and boys – 'a pretty, innocent-looking fair head lad, not more than fourteen years of age' – rushed 'to pass that grim boundary between life and death', the overwhelming weight of attackers gradually began to tell. To the skirling of pipes, the crackle of flames, the screams of the dying and the ghastly chant of the psalms, the slaughter began. 'The scene that ensued required the pen of a Zola to depict,' wrote Roberts – carefully doctoring the horrors committed on the dead and dying by Campbell's enraged army.

The rebels, never dreaming that we should stop to attack such a formidable position ... were now completely caught in a trap, the only outlets being by the gateway and the breach, through which our troops continued to pour. There could therefore be no thought of escape, and they fought with the desperation of men without hope of mercy, and determined to sell their lives as dearly as they could. Inch by inch they were forced back to the pavilion, and into the space between it and the north wall, where they were all shot or bayoneted. There they lay in a heap as high as my head, a heaving, surging mass of dead and dying inextricably entangled. It was a sickening sight, one of those which even in the excitement of battle and the flush of victory make one feel strongly what a horrible side there is to war. The wretched wounded men could not get clear of their dead comrades, however great their struggles, and those near the top of this ghastly pile of writhing humanity vented their rage and disappointment on every British officer who approached by showering upon him abuse of the grossest description.

'The scene was terrible,' Lieutenant Fairweather wrote, 'but at the same time it gave a feeling of gratified revenge. You may think me a savage but I gloated over the sights of this charnel house. Who did not who saw the slaughter at Cawnpore.'

Peel's brigade had been spared the worst carnage of the Sikandar Bagh, but between Campbell's force and the Residency still stood the Shah Najaf, the 'handsome white-domed tomb' of the first King of Oudh. 'The day was rapidly drawing to a close,' Roberts recalled, after three bruising hours had brought them no nearer to taking the place.

A retreat was not to be thought of; indeed our remaining stationary for so long had been an encouragement to the enemy, and every one felt that the only chance for the little British army fighting against 30,000 desperate mutineers, with every advantage of position and intimate knowledge of the locality in their favour, was to continue to advance at all hazards; and this our gallant old chief decided to do. Placing himself at the head of the 93rd, he explained to the only too eager Highlanders the dangerous nature of the service, and called on them to follow him. There was no mistaking the response; cheer after cheer rent the air as they listened to the words of the Chief they knew so well, and believed in so thoroughly, assuring him of their readiness to follow whithersoever he should lead, do whatever he should direct.

With a twenty-foot, loopholed wall to climb, no scaling ladders and a murderous fire, no infantry attack could hope to succeed unsupported, and Peel acted as only Peel could. In the dust and smoke of the battle it was virtually impossible to see what was happening, but calling for volunteers to create a diversion, he ordered his heavy twenty-four-pounders forward into the vicious hail of shot, firing and advancing – firing and advancing – until they were in as much danger from the flying masonry of the Shah Najaf as from the bullets and grenades that rained down from above. 'Captain Peel led up his heavy guns with extraordinary gallantry within a few yards of the building to batter the massive stone walls,' Campbell wrote in his despatch. 'The withering fire of the Highlanders effectually covered the Naval Brigade from great loss, but it was an action almost unexampled in war. Captain Peel behaved very much as if he had been laying the Shannon alongside an enemy Frigate.'

In the end it was Peel's rockets and not his guns that turned the tide, terrifying the defenders with their wild careering path, but as the 93rd poured into the compound after the fleeing rebels, his spirit had become the brigade's. As one bluejacket cheered the 93rd forward, a round shot took his leg clean off above the knee, 'and although knocked head over heels by the force of the shot, he sat bolt upright on the grass, with the blood spouting from the stump of the limb like water from the hose of a fire-engine, and shouted, "Here goes a shilling a day, a shilling a day. Pitch into them boys, pitch into them! Remember Cawnpore! Go at them my hearties!" until he fell back ... dead.'

The Shah Najaf was in British hands. During the course of the night the wounded of the Naval Brigade were evacuated to the field hospital under the walls of the Sikandar Bagh, and the next morning, to the tune of 'The Campbells are Coming', the army resumed its advance. 'Today great cheering was heard all around which announced that communication had been opened with the Residency,' the *Shannon*'s chaplain wrote from the field hospital, 'Gens Havelock & Outram having met Sir Colin Campbell, & the women & children with the troops inside now considered out of danger. Cap Peel & the guns are well in front – the men behaving admirably.'

Freedom, though, had come at a high cost. 'His breast heaved with emotion, and his eyes filled with tears,' one witness wrote of the reunion of Havelock and his own regiment, the 53rd. '"Soldiers, I am happy to think you have got into this place with a smaller loss than I had." Hearing this I asked him what he supposed our loss amounted to. He answered that he had heard it estimated at 80, and was much surprised and grieved when I told him that we had lost about 43 officers and 453 men killed and wounded.'

Havelock did not have long to brood over the losses, or enjoy the news Campbell brought him of his knighthood. Six days later, after summoning his son to his bedside at the Dilkusha to see how a Christian could die, he succumbed to the dysentery he had contracted at Lucknow. Nor was he the only one. Among those who had held the Residency through the siege there was a certain bitterness at Campbell's decision to abandon it, but the death of Havelock only rubbed in what everyone should already have known. With a thousand sick and wounded and five hundred women and children to evacuate, a hopelessly outnumbered and depleted army, and an enemy force of 30,000 still in the field against them, he had no choice. On the morning of the nineteenth, under enemy sniper and artillery fire, the children and women – surly and ungrateful many of them – were spirited out of the relative safety of the Sikandar Bagh. The retreat from Lucknow had begun.

XIV

For three days the exodus continued. In the advance on Lucknow Peel's Naval Brigade alone had won four Victoria Crosses, and right through to the very end they remained in action, covering the retreat until midnight on the twenty-second, when in a preternatural silence that foreshadowed the withdrawal from Gallipoli, the last of the troops stole out from the Baillie Guard Gate of the Residency.

Leaving behind a force of four thousand under Outram at the Alambagh, Campbell's nine-mile-long train of soldiers, guns, baggage, wounded, sick, women and children started off on the slow, fraught march back to Cawnpore. The route took the column through enemy-infested country for some forty-five miles, and to compound Campbell's anxieties, Cawnpore itself, which he had left with only an understrength garrison under the command of Major General Windham, had come under assault from a rebel army estimated at up to 25,000 men and forty guns.

With a force of only eight guns and seventeen hundred infantry, many of them raw and ill-disciplined recruits, a better general than Windham would have struggled to hold Cawnpore for any length of time. The great fear for Campbell as he hurried towards Windham's rescue was that the bridge of boats across the Ganges would have gone, but as the van of his straggling column reached the river on the night of the twenty-ninth, he was relieved to see it still intact and in British hands.

The town, however, and the cantonment had fallen to the mutineers, and Windham's small force was pinned into the entrenchments
built four months earlier. Through the twenty-ninth and thirtieth
Campbell's column of troops and civilians streamed across the bridge
under the cover of Peel's heavy guns, and while plans were made to
evacuate the women and children to Allahabad and Calcutta – the
'ladies' had been downgraded to 'women' in Campbell's eyes by this
time – the army took up its defensive position near the entrenchments
to the south-east of the town. 'On the 29th Lascelles and I were looking over the parapet when we saw a round shot kick up the dust just
outside it, and over it came, *just* over us,' wrote E.S. Watson, one of
the garrison left behind at Cawnpore and the latest in a brilliant line
of young cadets to fall under Peel's spell.

> Lascelles slipped up and I bobbed to avoid it, and over we went
> both of us together! Such a jolly lark we had, and everyone laugh-
> ing at us. On the 30th Sir Colin Campbell from Lucknow, having
> heard the news of our being shut up, arrived with a large force to
> our rescue, with jolly old Captain Peel.
>
> As soon as ever *he* arrived he got two guns in position and began
> blazing away at them right and left, and I can assure you it did
> one's heart good to hear it. That afternoon the First Lieutenant
> came into the Fort to see us and gave us an order to join the
> Captain. We were so glad to see him, and he was delighted at our
> being in action. Lascelles and myself then joined him, and we
> moved out to this camp where the whole Army is except those left
> in the fort.

Over the next few days the artillery duels continued, with Lascelles
and Watson – 'fine little Mids, about fifteen years old', as Oliver
Jones described them, 'perfectly indifferent to the whizzing of
bullets or the plunging of cannon-balls' – sticking to Peel 'like his
shadow under whatever fire he went'. 'It is quite a sight to see the
Captain under fire, he is so cool,' Watson reported home. 'He was
leaning under a gun one morning looking through a telescope, when
a shell came and burst quite close to us, and he never even lifted his
head, but kept looking through the glass all the while. And when a
man behind us exclaimed that the bits were coming down like a
shower of rain, he said "nonsense, nonsense, it's only the dust and
dirt". I am getting quite used to the twang of bullets now and I

hardly care about them at all, but the round shot I have a great
dislike to.'

He might well have, too, as on 1 December he saw a single shot
take off the legs of three seamen. If he had any fear, though, he was
not going to show it, drawing much of his strength from the same
source as his chief. 'The firing goes on all through the night,' he wrote
on the third, 'and last night they tried to make an attack. Our lieutenant, who was commanding when we went out to attack them, was
wounded in three places, but, thank God, I have not yet got a touch.
I always say just a little prayer to myself before going under heavy
fire, and then I never lose my pluck. It is indeed a great cause of thank-
fulness that I have got through as far as this, and I hope that you will
thank God especially for it and pray that I may be preserved through
the rest.'

(He was.)

For Peel himself, he once told his cousin, a day was one long prayer
– his Bible was always open in his cabin – but if he never lost his faith
in God to bring him through a battle, he never forgot to do his own
bit to help. 'When the 24-pounders were put in Peel's hands, they
were not fitted with sights,' wrote Jones of the Hastingsesque professionalism that underpinned the Peel charisma,

> but he immediately had some made the best I have ever seen. A
> dispart was fixed on the muzzle of the gun, with a notch along it;
> the tangent sight was a long screw fixed into a hole bored through
> the cascable, pointed at the top, with a cross arm to turn it round,
> by which means the elevation was adjusted.
>
> Its advantages were, that there was the whole length of the gun
> between the sights, which made an error of pointing twice as easily
> corrected ... and the elevation could be, by the slightest turn of the
> screw, adjusted to the minutest part of a degree; and the result was,
> as Captain Peel observed, 'It should not be said of these guns that
> one can shoot with them as well as with a rifle, but rather one can
> shoot with a rifle as well as with them.'

With the revolutionary use Peel made of his heavy guns – handling
them with a Nelsonian swagger in front even of the advance skirmishers – he cannot have always needed his sights, but they were
typical of his whole detailed approach to warfare. 'Reduce our
squadrons on foreign stations and commission ten screw line-of-battle

ships, with a complement of 800 men each, for the purpose of furnishing a Naval Brigade of 5,000 men for service in India,' he began a long memo on the use of naval forces while still in the middle of the Cawnpore operations. 'Of these 3,000 should be for the Bengal Presidency and 2000 for Madras, the East Indian Navy giving its whole support to Bombay.'

The timing of the ships' arrival, the disembarkation of the men, the putative site of their headquarters, health, marching arrangements, ordnance, type of rocket, campaigning season – Peel considers it all before finishing with a characteristic flourish. 'The ammunition for these batteries should be at the rate of 600 rounds per gun or howitzer and 300 per rocket. I shall not, however, enter here into any details; they require separate consideration and it is on them that success depends, but of this I am certain, there is not a single difficulty or any accumulation of difficulties in the whole affair which could not be surmounted. W. Peel Captain RN. December, Cawnpore.'

The immediate difficulty to surmount was a rebel force – including the best of all mutineer troops, the Gwalior Contingent – that rested its centre on the town of Cawnpore and its left flank on the River Ganges. Through the early days of December the fighting continued around the clock, and on the morning of the sixth, after a diversionary feint against the enemy left and a massive bombardment of the town, Campbell attacked their right. 'My Dear Mama,' wrote Watson, in a breathlessly joyous account of the battle:

Now for it!!! December 6th.
    Early that morning we had just woke up in our tent when an order came to strike tents immediately. Up we all got, put our things in the hackery and everything ready. The men fell in and everything [was] done. The Captain called Lascelles and me up privately and said we were going to make the grand attack, and we were not to run and blow and go head over heels and get out of breath.
    Well, about nine o'clock we moved off with three 24-pounders, one 8-inch howitzer and two rockets, leaving two guns in camp and two at a battery. We halted when we had gone some way and waited for the troops.
    There were the 93rd Highlanders, 42nd ditto, 53rd and 23rd; they were the principal regiments. When everything was ready, we moved on, first with the guns away to the left. We soon got in sight of the enemy. There they all were, shoals upon shoals of them, most

of them half hidden among the jungles. We moved on, Captain Peel riding ahead to show the way for some time in sight of the enemy, without their firing a single shot, which I wondered at very much. We got our guns into position laid down and opened fire. There we were, quite by ourselves in a large plain with only the 53rd Regiment for our support, the whole Army drawn up about a quarter of a mile behind us in one long line.

We then opened fire, giving them the first shot, and they soon answered us. Captain Peel went galloping about all over the place, so I could but run after him like a groom! He told me to stick by the gun our First Lieutenant was commanding and to stay with him for the present. We blazed away for some time as hard as we could, they giving us shot for shot and bursting their shells beautifully.

But this did not last long. Our Marines and the 53rd charged and at the same time we gave them two rockets slap into the middle of them, and then with three good cheers we advanced our guns and they actually *ran*!!! Didn't we just yell and shout!

On we went up a road [the Calpee road] where they had two guns in position and they gave us a tremendous fire, and a good many stood their ground and gave us volley after volley of musketry. I expected to see some of our men drop every minute – the shot and shell came within an ace of us. I saw a Sikh knocked over close to us by a bit of shell but not one touched us. On we went, the brutes saw us still advancing and off they took their guns. On came our Infantry and we fairly set them running.

Captain Peel now dismounted and I went with him, and we came over a bridge on the road which went through a field crowded with sepoys. I can't tell you how jolly it was seeing the brutes run. I could hardly believe my eyes. I felt perfectly mad, and our men got on top of the guns, waving their hats and cheering and yelling like fun. It was most awfully exciting.

We pursued them to their camp, found it all deserted, tents, horses, ponies, baggage, bedding, swords, muskets, everything lying about, hackeries loaded with all manner of treasure, all left.

On we went still, right through the camp and after them across the fields and roads at a tremendous pace. I got fairly out of breath and the only way I could keep up when I was on a message from the Captain out of hearing, was to say to myself, 'Hoicks over, Hoicks over, Fox Ahead!' and I used to go along at double the pace.

We chased them for about ten miles along the road when we got
ordered to halt. We took seventeen guns, loads upon loads of
ammunition, all their luggage, treasure and everything – there's for
you! I could have got anything almost if I had chosen to pick it up.
Money was lying about the road, clothing of all kinds and almost
any imaginable thing you could think of. Panic was taken up by
those who were in the town and they all hooked up as fast as they
could go, so we got the place quite clean off them.

We returned quite late that night and bivouaced close to the
place where the enemy had their camp. The First Lieutenant,
Lascelles and I slept under a captured gun as comfortably as possible. Captain Peel was *so* delighted. He says the battle is the death
stroke to the rebellion.

Peel's optimism was premature, but the victory, followed up the next
day in another wild cavalry chase, was complete, and the Naval
Brigade's role in it as dashing as it had been at Lucknow. 'I must here
draw attention to the manner in which the heavy 24-pr. Guns were
impelled and managed by Captain Peel and his gallant sailors,' Campbell wrote in his despatch. 'Through the extraordinary energy and
good will with which the latter have worked, their guns have been
constantly in advance throughout our late operations, from the relief
of Lucknow till now, as if they were light field pieces, and the service rendered by them in clearing our front has been incalculable. On
this occasion there was the sight beheld of 24-pr. Guns advancing
with the line of skirmishers.'

'On this, as on every occasion in which danger was to be faced
and difficulty overcome,' a grateful Canning acknowledged, 'Captain
Peel, R.N., commanding the Naval Brigade, was foremost in intrepidity and resource. Lieutenant Vaughan and the other officers and
men of H.M.S. *Shannon* are worthy of their brave commander; and
it is a pleasure to the Governor-General in Council to declare its warm
admiration of their conduct.'

The credit belonged equally to officer and seaman, and with the
arrival on the twenty-second of the last contingent from Allahabad
– in 'floods of tears', half of them, at missing out on the fighting –
the whole Naval Brigade was at full strength for the first time in the
campaign. 'An Indian army on the line of march is a sight affording
much interest and amusement,' wrote Verney – a newcomer from
garrison duties to it all – as the brigade and army resumed their march

along the Grand Trunk Road to Futteghur, 'such a menagerie of man and beast, footman and cavalry, soldiers and sailors, camels and elephants, white men and black men, horses and oxen, Marine and Artillery, Sikhs and Highlanders.'

Verney was less amused by the preference that Peel continued to show Edward Daniel – seconding him for special duties whenever there was any call – but it is impossible to know whether fame in the Crimea had done its damage or this was mere jealousy. Even before the *Shannon* sailed Verney had hoped that Daniel would be kept in England, he had told his father, because otherwise 'the Captain would be sure to give him any little bit of duty that might end in promotion … Daniel greatly distinguished himself in the Crimea without doubt but I suspect is too well aware of it himself.'

It is little wonder if Peel did single out Daniel – the boy had saved his life at the Redan – and still less if Daniel had taken to the bottle, as Verney claimed, when those 'special duties' might include blowing away 'five or six sepoys from guns', and not even Peel was exempt from the degradations that accompanied the army's progress. 'There is a princi-pal street which runs the whole length of the town, which is divided by some six or seven gate-ways,' wrote Oliver Jones after he and Peel had watched the execution of '*Somebody* Khan', a rebel 'deeply implicated in the barbarities practiced upon our women and children'.

Close to the middle one grew a fine tree, and this, from its central position, was chosen for the place of execution, one of the branches of the tree being made use of for the gallows.

We found an immense crowd collected, both of natives and inhabitants, and of the idlers from the camp, beside a considerable military force to maintain order.

One would have thought, that, on so serious an occasion as that of an execution, especially of a person of rank, there would have been some decorum and decency of behaviour; but on the contrary most people seemed to think very lightly of it, and were cutting their jibes and cracking their jokes …

He was tied down on a charpoy – a sort of native bedstead – and carried under the fatal tree, upon which he cast an anxious look when he saw the noose suspended there from.

He was then stripped, flogged and hanged. He had on a hand-some shawl, which an officer took possession of on the spot – an action which requires no comment.

The man behaved with great firmness. While the rope was being adjusted, a soldier struck him on the face; upon which he turned round with great fierceness, and said – 'Had I had a sword in my hand, you dared not have struck that blow:' his last words before he was launched into eternity.

As Peel and I rode home to camp, we agreed that it would have been much better to have conducted the execution with more decorum; and that such a display of jesting and greediness, and the careless off-hand way with which it was done, were more likely to make the natives hate and despise us, than to inspire them with a salutary dread of our justice.

The more the Naval Brigade were exposed to the sahib and memsahib, in fact, the less sympathetic they became to the British India they had come to save, but if Peel could not see 'the wisdom or justice' of 'a policy ... far inferior to what might have been gained by other means than fire and sword', he could still forget himself in action. At the beginning of January 1858, news came through that the enemy had destroyed a suspension bridge over the Kali Nadi, and a column that included Lieutenant Vaughan and two naval guns was immediately sent forward under Brigadier Hope to repair it and secure the position.

When they arrived at the bridge they found that it had already been partially burned, and the first troops had no sooner made it across to the other side after a long night's work, than the sound of a bugle and the rumble of gun carriages gave unexpected warning of a rebel army of two thousand infantry, five hundred cavalry and nine guns. 'Is *Paal* with us to-day?' one officer heard a soldier of the 53rd – a predominantly Irish regiment at the time – ask another as the short-sighted Vaughan's guns went into action, '"No," said the other. "Who is it then?" "Why, sure it's the chap with glass in his eye – and he's *nearly as good as the other!*"'

He was right – Vaughan was 'a capital shot, and as cool when under a shower of bullets as if there was no such thing as gunpowder and lead' – but Peel had heard the sound of gunfire, and had no intention of missing out. 'There was a gun at the toll house at the entrance of the village which was doing mischief,' Jones wrote, 'and Peel took one of his 24-pounders (they are great iron siege guns of 50cwt.) up to the front line of skirmishers' and ordered his lieutenant to fire. 'Vaughan's first shot struck the roof of the house,' continued

Verney, 'his second the angle of the wall about half-way down, and the third dismounted the gun and destroyed the carriage. Captain Peel, who was standing by, said, "Thank you, Mr. Vaughan; perhaps you will now be so good as to blow up the tumbril." Lieutenant Vaughan fired a fourth shot which passed near it, and a fifth which blew it up and killed several of the enemy. "Thank you," said Captain Peel in his blandest and most courteous tones, "I will now go and report to Sir Colin."'

The duel turned into a charge, the charge into another wild cavalry rout that gave Roberts his VC, and a seven-hour battle that netted seven guns and three hundred rebel dead had been won at a cost to the Naval Brigade of just three wounded. 'We reached our camping-ground about 9.30 p.m.,' an exhausted and famished Verney wrote,

> and parked our battery in a ploughed field, but no baggage or provisions had arrived except the spirits, a cask of which is carried on an old limber and, under the charge of two quartermasters, is always foremost in the field on the march. We were each glad to drink our day's double allowance and even Captain Peel, who rarely drinks spirits, tossed off with gusto the abominable arrack that is served out in lieu of rum …
>
> At about midnight the elephants arrived with the tents which were immediately pitched in total darkness, but we had not a thing, not even a candle, till about four when the hackeries arrived with the baggage. Every tent was then illuminated and roaring fires blazed in rear of the camp, and at about five, as the first streaks of dawn hove in sight we sat down to a *late* dinner.

The battle was the last action before Futteghur, and the next day Campbell's force continued its advance through the grim evidence of their cavalry's work. 'The road from Kala Nuddee … and the fields on each side,' noted Verney, 'were strewn with dead bodies, some of old men, some of the young and some even of boys, covered with ghastly wounds, and one could trace the tracks through the fields of the flying sepoys pursued by the relentless Sikhs, and see the trampled ground where the short, final struggle had taken place. Some of the wells we passed were choked with corpses.'

By 4 o'clock that afternoon they had marched the last ten miles into the desolate town, only to find its churches pillaged, its neat bungalows ransacked, its gardens overgrown with weeds, the

Nawab's palace a smouldering ruin and the rebel force nowhere to be seen. In their haste to escape they had not even stopped to destroy the boat-bridge over the Ganges, and with their crossing secured and the fort – a large enclosure surrounded by high, thick mud walls under which flowed the river – occupied and strengthened, Campbell's army settled down to await a decision from Calcutta on their future strategy.

The 'crawlin' camel' himself was strongly in favour of operations to pacify Rohalkind first, postponing any move against Lucknow until the autumn, but Canning saw things differently. 'Every eye,' he wrote, 'is upon Oudh as it was upon Delhi: Oudh is not only the rallying-place of the sepoys, the place to which they all look, and by the doings in which their own hopes and prospects rise and fall; but it represents a dynasty; there is a king of Oudh "seeking his own". '

In the end it was Canning who prevailed, but it was another month before the army was ready to quit Futteghur. 'You will not fail to have observed the long inaction of our troops since the battle of 5th of December [the 6th in fact],' Peel complained to Sir Michael Seymour, 'as, with the exception of a slow march to Futtyghur and the capture of that place, little has apparently been done. I am afraid this inaction has been forced on us by political reasons, which required the combination of our forces with those of Jung Bahadoor [the Gurkhas] for the attack of Lucknow. But Jung Bahadoor has failed to keep time in his engagements, and the delay involves serious consequences.'

The delay was not all waste, and the captured eighteen-pounders from the battle of the Kala Nuddee – or more accurately, the twenty-four-pounder gun carriages on which they were mounted – gave Peel the chance to put a pet project into operation. He had brought his massive 55-cwt eight-inch guns as far as Allahabad without having the chance to use them, but he reckoned that, with some modification, the carriages and other roughed-out materials abandoned by the rebels could be employed to work them in the field with the same élan 'with which he had already astonished the army, and electrified and confounded the enemy' with his twenty-four-pounders. 'Our artillery consists of six 55cwt. 8-in guns, two 8-inch howitzers, eight 50 cwt. 24-pounders, two ship field-pieces, and a battery of eight rockets,' he excitedly told Seymour on 23 February, his vision stretching beyond the immediate campaign to the whole future of field artillery.

It is the most formidable field-artillery the world has seen, for it is a truth, and not a jest, that in battle we are with the skirmishers; and it is not from any foolish boasting, but from a proper estimate of ourselves and the enemy that I prefer the open ground, and avoid the confinement of a regularly constructed battery. The 68-pounders, or to speak technically, the 8-inch guns of the Shannon are as light in exercise as the 24-pounders … I trust that the results attending the employment of such guns as *field artillery*, will not be lost in England.

As long as the army idled at Futteghur, a desultory regime of village-burning, hangings (127 from one tree), peacock shoots, races (horses and water buffaloes) and the occasional skirmish left little scope for Peel's guns, and the nearest he came to danger was from a nest of snakes disturbed beneath an upturned boat. At the beginning of February the force was finally ready to march, and along with its massive artillery train – the Naval Brigade alone needed eight hundred bullocks to pull their guns and ammunition – Peel's men began retracing their steps past the whitened bones of rebel dead. 'I rode into Cawnpore this evening,' Verney noted on 10 February, and 'dined with Captain Peel who showed me a wonderful hen; every evening she comes into his tent and cackles until he places his portmanteau across one corner when she retires behind it for the night, and the next morning lays an egg'.

The plan of attack drawn up for Campbell's army – at 20,000 the largest and most varied British force ever put into the field in India – was different from those employed in either operation of the previous year. In the November relief Campbell had been able to benefit from the bloody experience of Havelock and Outram, and with a far larger force at his disposal he was now able to divide his army into two columns, the first under his own command to attack through La Martinière and across the canal, while the right wing under Outram crossed the Gumti in a wide sweep designed to bring it round to the more lightly defended north of the city.

Through the last days of February the massive army assembled, and by 2 March, after a last tortuously slow advance, hampered by mud, narrow lanes and recalcitrant animals, they were looking down from the Dilkusha to the rebel-held stronghold of Lucknow. 'There we saw,' wrote Jones, 'gilded by the rays of the setting sun, her golden domes, her slim minarets, her squares, her palaces, her earthen ramparts, raised by immense labour within the last three months, pierced by thousands of loopholes, bristling with many guns; and within the protected circle of which were, we knew, from fifty to one hundred thousand of those wretches who for months had vainly endeavoured to conquer the unconquerable garrison of the Residency.'

For Peel, with his experience of Sevastopol, it was another element of the defences that was most disturbing. 'We took this place on the 2nd with little loss,' he reported to Seymour on the seventh from the Dilkusha, 'a lofty solid Italian chateau in a beautifully elevated park, the grounds of which are to Lucknow what Hampstead is to London … I feel that Sir Colin Campbell has a difficult, anxious task. To my mind the cause of uneasiness is the sight of huge piles of gabions and fascines. The attack of Lucknow must never subside into a siege or into the hands of the professionals.'

Peel need not have worried. In the early hours of the ninth, long before daylight, the newly promoted Commander Vaughan supervised the brigade's six eight-inch guns, four rocket hackeries and two twenty-four-pounders as they were dragged into place for the attack on La Martinière. Shortly after daybreak the guns opened up, and though there were problems with both fuses and the rockets, 'the work went on well and merrily in the batteries'. 'Soon after the cannonading began,' reported the ubiquitous Captain Jones, who had attached himself to Peel as a supernumerary 'aide-de-camp',

Colonel Napier pointed out a wall that he wished breached, and Sir William Peel [he had just heard that he had been appointed KCB] ordered up two more of his guns, and selected an excellent position to place them in, some way to the left and front of the other battery; and when they were in position, and had opened fire, he went to a place about fifty yards more to the left, to watch the practice made by the guns.

In front of the Park walls were several rifle pits, and Peel, with his usual indifference to danger, thinking only of the effects of his shot against the breach he was making, and taking no notice of the bullets which were buzzing about our ears, was standing upon a little knoll, a fair target to the marksman. One could see the fellows lay their muskets along the top of the rifle-pit, then puff, a little white smoke; then bang, and whew-ew-iz, then sput against some stone as the bullet fell flattened close to our feet. At last one bullet, more true than the others, struck him, and he fell, saying, 'Oh, they've hit me!'

He had been hit high in the thigh, and as Jones bent down to bind the wound, Peel sent him for help. With some bluejackets to assist him, Lieutenant Young rushed across to carry Peel off the battlefield while Jones ran back to the Dilkusha to fetch a surgeon. 'Even now, as I am writing,' wrote Verney, as reports filtered back to the rear of the brigade, 'Watson arrives with the news that Captain Peel has been wounded. He went out with his usual nonchalance to find a suitable place for some guns ... when he was shot in the thigh by a musket ball. He was taken to the Dilkushah and the bullet extracted by the surgeon of the 93rd Highlanders. The wound is dangerous, it having been necessary to cut the ball out from the opposite side to which it entered.'

It was a bad wound, but with Peel initially 'cheerful' and the surgeon confident that he would be on his feet again in six weeks, the chaplain's main fear was that his 'excitable temperament will impede his progress to recovery very materially'. The next day Peel was moved from his tent to Campbell's bungalow, where it was hoped he would be more comfortable, but fever soon set in, leaving him too weak even to finish a despatch for Seymour. 'The halls of that Palace were crowded with sick sailors,' Verney wrote after visiting him on the seventeenth, the day the Naval Brigade fired its guns for the last time in the capture of Lucknow, 'most of whom were burnt all over from head to foot by the dreadful explosions that have taken place in the City. They were covered with cotton wadding, and by the side of each sat a native with a paper fan to keep off the flies. The sighs and groans of these poor fellows, reduced to mere pieces of burnt flesh, were those of men who literally felt life to be a burden, men without hope of recovery to whom death could but be a relief.'

Peel was at least recovered enough by now to ask Verney to procure him an enemy tulwar (a native sword) – a modest enough request given the orgy of looting that accompanied the assault – but it was another month before he was able to take up his despatch to Seymour. 'I attempted to write to you a few days after being wounded,' he wrote on 11 April, 'but a fever put me into such excitement that I was obliged to relinquish it ... On being wounded I placed myself in charge of the Field Hospital surgeons, and a medical board has ordered my return to England. Being unwilling, however, to give up the Shannon, and anxious to serve my time, I shall decide, or ask the medical men to decide again, on my arrival at Calcutta. The change of air and excitement of moving may restore me to health.'

The bloody fall of Lucknow did not spell the end of the Mutiny – Campbell's decision to allow the rebels to escape the net that Outram could have, should have and wanted to close tight saw to that – but it was the effective end of the Naval Brigade's involvement. In the days while Peel had been lying feverish at the Dilkusha his officers had fought their guns with all his old élan, and there is probably nothing that says so much for his leadership than that the brigade could function when he was not there just as it had under his direction. If Vaughan was almost as good as 'Paal', 'a better officer never existed' than Lieutenant Young, wrote Captain Jones, who had served with the brigade all the way to the Residency: 'the heavier the fire he was under, the cooler and steadier did he become, setting a good example to his men; indeed all the officers of the *Shannon* were men of the first stamp, and Sir William Peel often told me that though he had had nothing to do with choosing of any of them except his first lieutenant, that if he were offered the pick of the whole navy, there was not one there he would change for any of his officers'.

That said, there was never any mistaking that Peel was the figure who made the 'machinery' work, and his confidence in his men was reciprocated by an admiration and affection every bit as complete. In their last days in the city Verney had been sent into the Kaisar Bagh to loot one of the carriages of the King of Oudh for 'Captain Peel's conveyance to Cawnpore', and choosing the best he could find, had brought it back to camp for the brigade carpenters to 'customise'. They 'padded it', wrote Verney on 30 March, 'lined it with blue cotton, made a nest for his feet, and painted "H.M.S. Shannon" over the royal arms of Lucknow; when, however, he saw it to-day, he declined making use of it, saying that he would prefer to travel in a doolie like one of his bluejackets'.

It was a gesture typical of Peel, typical of his genuine simplicity, and of the slightly ostentatious turn it could sometimes take. When he had been praised to the skies in Campbell's despatch after the relief of Lucknow he had refused to read it out to the brigade on the grounds that it drew undue attention to himself, but had copies made for private reading. Complex to the end, he finally paid for his complexity, just as he had for his apparent indifference to danger and enemy fire. As late as 9 April he was writing back to Mr Waters, the

Irish master left in charge of the *Shannon* at Calcutta, confident that his strength was returning and 'hoping the youngsters are all well. My ten aide de camps,' he added, 'are much grown.'

It is Peel's last letter, preserved with a small envelope bizarrely stamped 'Cork District Lunatic Asylum'. That stamp is a tiny, salutary reminder of that vast, unknown hinterland of the past which remains the inevitable background to any life. The doolie Peel had been travelling in had been infected by smallpox, but why he had chosen a common doolie, or what was the exact chain of circumstances, unvarnished by sentiment, unadorned by hagiography, cannot be known. Where his family, determined to extract the last consolation from his end, got the story of him giving up his doolie to a sick missionary in one final gesture of Christian self-sacrifice, is similarly obscure. All that is certain is the grim fact that he got no farther than Cawnpore. He had come down from Lucknow with the army headquarters, and Roberts was with him. They reached the city on 17 April, and that night the two men dined together,

> when to all appearances he was perfectly well, but in going into his room the next morning I found he was in a high fever, and had some suspicious-looking spots about his face. I went off at once in search of a doctor, and soon returned with one of the surgeons of the 5th Fusiliers, who, to my horror, – for I had observed that Peel was nervous about himself – exclaimed with brutal frankness the moment he entered the room, 'You have got small-pox.' It was only too true. On being convinced that this was the case, I went to the chaplain, the Rev. Thomas Moore [a brave and old friend of the Naval Brigade] and told him of Peel's condition. Without an instant's hesitation, he decided the invalid must come to his house to be taken care of. That afternoon I had the poor fellow carried over, and there I left him in the kind care of Mrs. Moore, the *padre's* wife, who had, as a special case, been allowed to accompany her husband to Cawnpore. Peel died on the 27th. On the 4th May I embarked at Calcutta in the P. & O. steamer, *Nubia*, without alas! the friend whose pleasant company I had hoped to have enjoyed on the voyage.

For a man who wanted to die in battle, and feared only lingering disease, there could have been no more terrible fate, and no talk of Christian sacrifice could hide it. 'Alas,' wrote Oliver Jones when he heard the news – a warrior lamenting the death of a warrior in the same terms that Peel had apostrophised Nelson off Cape Trafalgar only seven years earlier –

far better for him would it have been to have expired with the sound of his cannon ringing in his ears. There is no death so glorious, so much to be desired, as on the battle-field ...

The service and his friends have sustained a great loss; his short but brilliant career has been marked by a devotion to his duty – a constantly doing what was right because it was right – always pressing forward in the path of honour, he served his country as well as she merits to be served. Brave but humane, daring but forethoughtful, he so perfected the means at his disposal, that when they were brought into the field they were irresistible ... In action cool, collected, and fearless, he led on his guns, and poured their well-directed fire upon the enemy, encouraging his men by his calm yet earnest manner, utterly regardless of danger, utterly unmoved by the iron storm often raging about him.

Highly educated and talented ... he was simple and unostentatious in his manner, friendly and conciliatory in his address, upright and honourable in his heart. His life, short as it unfortunately has been, has left behind it one of those beacon-lights of glory, one of those polar-stars of honour for future heroes to steer their course by; and his name is added to those of that glorious company so dear to every British heart – the naval heroes of England.

'We have been much distressed to learn of the death of our noble Captain,' Verney wrote in similar strain on the thirtieth, when only days later the news reached the Naval Brigade on their march to Calcutta. 'I cannot say what a sad loss we all feel this to be and how deeply his death is felt and regretted by every officer and man; the mainspring that worked the machinery is gone. We never felt ourselves to be *Shannon*'s naval Brigade or even the Admiralty Naval Brigade, but always Peel's Naval brigade. He it was who first originated the idea of sailors going one thousand four hundred miles from the sea, and afterwards carried it out in such an able and judicious manner.'

The eulogies continued, and not just from those who had fought with Peel. 'Sir William Peel's services in the field during the last seven months are well known in India and England,' the Secretary to the Government, speaking for Lord Canning, wrote, but it is not so well known how great the value of his presence and example has been, wherever this eventful period, his duty has led him.

The loss of his daring but thoughtful courage, joined with eminent abilities, is a very heavy one to his country; but it is the loss of that influence, which his earnest character, admirable temper, and gentle kindly bearing exercised over all within reach; an influence which was exerted unceasingly for the public good, and of which the Governor-General believes that it may with truth be said that there is not a rank or profession who, having been associated with Sir William Peel in these times of anxiety and danger, has not felt and acknowledged it.

And Calcutta itself joined in to pay its tributes. On 12 August his brigade – not the *Shannon*'s, that is, not the Admiralty's, but *Peel*'s brigade – paraded along a route lined by white-uniformed and red-turbaned and cummerbunded police and an 'immense crowd' to the bridge of boats that had been thrown out to the ship. 'The order was given to "Ground Arms",' Verney recalled, 'and the boatswains' pipes rang out "Hands Cheer Ship". In a moment our lower and topmast rigging were swarming with men and three such mighty English cheers rolled over that old Maidan as the Indian soil had never echoed to before and probably never will again.'

After the bullocks and camels, the elephants, dust and heat, Peel's bluejackets were back in their natural environment, but Calcutta had not forgotten what they had left behind. Four months earlier Verney had been immensely proud that the great guns of the *Shannon*, carved with the ship's name, had been left as a permanent memorial at Lucknow. And to those guns and the bones of 102 of his shipmates – officers, seamen, marines of the brigade who had died from wounds or disease – were now added the remains 'above all others', the Advocate-General, responding to the Gunner's toast at a farewell banquet for the Shannons, declared,

of your young, your noble, your heroic, your beloved Commander Sir W Peel. And let me express the deep sympathy which we, one and all, inhabitants of Calcutta, felt in the sentiments so touchingly and simply expressed, with the tenderness of true feeling, by my friend near me, the Gunner, for the loss of that much loved and lamented commander, a commander who at this time last year led

you forth ... a commander who has proved to Old England and the
world that her hearts of oak were as staunch when transplanted a
thousand miles from their ocean home as on the deck of their noble
vessel. We know that the memory of Sir William Peel will never be
forgotten by that gallant crew whom he taught, as Nelson did his
sailors and Wellington his soldiers, to go anywhere and do
anything. But I would also add that that crew should know that his
memory will never be forgotten in this city, which his presence
cheered and gladdened during his short stay and from which we
watched day by day with unflagging interest the tidings of his
achievements, more spirit stirring than those of romance and over
which the news of his untimely death spread a gloom and sorrow
I have never known surpassed. There was not a Christian, man,
woman or child, capable of understanding in Calcutta or in British
India, who did not feel – when the death of Peel was announced,
after all his successes and achievements, and while we fondly hoped
to welcome him here in triumph – as deep a pang as if some dear
personal friend had been lost.

This is not just the voice of officialdom – it is hardly as if India or the
Empire was short of heroes to mourn after the relief of Lucknow or
the recapture of Delhi – and the sharply personal note was almost
uniquely echoed in the Admiralty letter to Peel's brother, Sir Robert.
'In officially communicating to you the lamentable death of your
brother, Captain Sir William Peel,' the letter – a letter, too, that was
gone over and over again in draft – read,

My Lords Commissioners of the Admiralty command me to
observe that it is an occasion on which they consider that a departure from ordinary custom is dictated alike by feeling and duty.

My Lords therefore desire me to assure you that they consider
the premature decease of your distinguished Brother as a National
loss for which they feel profound regret. His heroic bravery,
displayed under unusual and most trying circumstances, and on
many hard fought fields, has excited the grateful admiration of his
country, while his generous and noble nature no less conciliated
the affection and devotion of his comrades.

At a moment when there was reason to hope that, recovered
from his wound, he would have returned to England to enjoy
temporary repose, and to receive a nation's gratitude, it has pleased

Divine Providence to remove him from the scene of his earthly glory.

My Lords further command me to request that you will communicate to his bereaved mother the assurance that they mourn in common with all Englishmen, the loss which our country has sustained by the loss of one of the brightest ornaments of the noble service with which their Lordships are associated; while they, individually, feel the sorrow in which Lady Peel has been so suddenly involved.

This is certainly not the language of the nineteenth-century Admiralty, but to ask what prompted this response across so wide a spectrum of public and private life is simply to come up against that peculiar, irrecoverable quality of *personality* that made Peel the leader he was. In a sense his talents as a *naval* officer must be taken on trust, but even if he had had the chance to command a ship or a fleet in action – or even to serve at sea in a battle after the age of sixteen – it is hard to believe that it would be as a strategist and organiser in the Tryon mould that he would now be remembered rather than as the leader of men he proved himself in the Crimea and India.

It is difficult to articulate this point without lapsing back into the Victorian cult of personality that inevitably softens the outline of the man, but Peel's genius was like that of Nelson as a trainer of officers. It is certainly true that his restless intelligence made him a moderniser and a technical innovator in the Hastings line, but what sets him apart from Hastings – what set him apart from any of his contemporaries – was his ability to inspire or awe men to his own vision of service and dedication.

It was once ruefully said by an opponent that when you faced any of Nelson's captains, you faced Nelson himself, and the same could have been said of the men who learned their trade under Peel. It is interesting that without Hastings the *Karteria* was nothing, and though he never had the calibre of officer that Peel commanded, he could never have left the same legacy of future leaders – Sir Nowell Salmon, Lord Walter Kerr, Field Marshal Sir Evelyn Wood – that Peel did.

There is nothing quite so hard to quantify as this kind of influence, but as the navy entered into its 'dark age' the memory of Peel was, as Jones put it, one of those 'beacon-lights of glory' that was never quite extinguished. 'When I came upstairs at 11.30, I found your charming letter to me,' Wood wrote in 1894 to Archie Peel, after the publication of Wood's history of the Crimean campaign. 'It is the more agreeable to me, that having lost most of my friends of 1854, I cannot expect the young folks to feel much interest in the "giants of those days." William Peel was my *beau ideal*. I have never known such another.'

Wood's scepticism about the 'young folk' was understandable, but in a navy in which Clements Markham scoured the gunrooms to send Peel's successors to the Antarctic, and Tryon's disciples would allow only one name to eclipse that of their own hero, unduly pessimistic. It is hard to imagine Peel settling down to the harbour duties for the Magdala campaign in the way Tryon did, but when Scott went south or 'Evans of the "Broke"' rammed and boarded a German destroyer in the Channel, they were conscious inheritors of a tradition of daring and aggression that traced itself back through Peel to men like Cochrane, Hastings and – another great captain of the *Shannon* during the post-Nelsonian era – Broke himself.

Peel was as conscious of this inheritance as he was of his legacy, as aware of what the *Shannon* meant historically as of any fresh lustre he might add to its name. And if he exerted such an influence on the men he commanded, it was because he had trained himself so assid-uously in the traditions to which he belonged. In the flood of eulo-gies and commemorative statues that followed his death his real personality was smoothed over, but the fascination of Peel is that his courage was not of the brutal, thoughtless kind of a Wolseley, nor his high-strung temperament – his femininity, as Wood labelled it – of the sort that was made for battle or the rigours of campaigning.

To say this is not to find another Victorian hero ripe for the Stra-chey treatment, but to recognise a far more interesting and fragile kind of greatness. From the moment Peel was conscious of who he was he must have been equally aware of the burden of expectation, and it was not a responsibility he bore as debonairly as observers believed. The eulogies that followed his death, the universal talk of his courage and daring, his fearlessness, calm and 'utter indifference' to danger, are testaments to how well he carried off the pose, but Evelyn Wood was not wrong when he wrote that Peel felt every bullet and shell fragment with a hypersensitivity almost incomprehensible to his own earthier nature.

And if nobody has ever written better or more generously about Peel one need look no farther than the life of his other ADC, Edward Daniel, to sense just how thin a crust separated a man of Peel's temperament from disaster in the bruisingly masculine world of the Victorian Empire.

Court-martialled for drunkenness within the year, driven from the service and the country for 'indecent liberties' with four subordinates within two, and stripped of his VC – the only officer ever to suffer the disgrace – and in a New Zealand pauper's grave within five, that life was the other side of the Imperial coin. Whether the drink that killed him was a symptom or the cause of Daniel's disintegration does not now matter, but what is telling is that he died, as he lived, in uniform. It might only have been that of the New Zealand Armed Constabulary Force, but that does not signify. Fighting was all he knew, and uniform – navy, Tanaki Military Settlers, constabulary – simultaneously camouflage and validation for those intense loyalties, needs and affections that had kept him at Peel's side under the withering fire of the Redan.

The same is probably true of William Peel, for whom war provided the context in which his complex, brilliant and impatient nature could find the closest it would ever know to peace. There were times in the Crimea when it seemed to watchers that he was trying to get himself killed, and if he denied this to his sister, it still suggests a truth of a kind: that for whatever combination of reasons – the need to prove himself, the need to subdue or discipline some part of his nature, the raw need for excitement, fame, honour, glory – death on the battlefield was for the patriot, Englishman, chivalric hero, imperialist, devout believer and troubled soul in William Peel the great adventure he was happy to embrace.

'All is serene' was the motto of the Diamond Battery, and if that serenity was the serenity of the swan rather than the marmoreal perfection enshrined in Peel's posthumous statue, it was a boast that he finally made true. It was inevitable that the Victorian age should turn him into the simple figure he never was, yet if only by accident they had got the 'right man', a man whose instincts of service, obligation, religion and honour drove him to make himself what his father, family, country and the age wanted him to be. And in India, in the middle of all the cultural and racial hysteria of the Mutiny, he became that ideal: not the William Peel buried like Daniel, the disgraced boy to whom he owed his life, in a lost grave thousands of miles from home; but, hand on sword-hilt, medals on chest, head proudly lifted, eyes staring confidently out, cannon and anchor strewn at his feet, the 'beau ideal' of William Theed's memorial statue in Sandy church: Sir William Peel, VC KCB.

Goodenough

The Sword of the Lord

I have thought of death sometimes with a weary expectant wonder, and now it is all so different. It seems more
like the happy crown of life.

James Graham Goodenough

I

ON THE GLORIOUS 12TH of August 1875, a Royal Navy steam
frigate under the command of Commodore James Goodenough CB
CMG dropped anchor off Carlyle Bay on the Pacific island of Santa
Cruz. Almost a year earlier another man-of-war had met with a
hostile reception in the same place, but as he watched the canoes
dancing out through the surf to greet them, Goodenough brushed
aside any forebodings he may have had to see what kindness rather
than force could do for the benighted islanders who had fallen foul
of the British navy.

It cannot have seemed an unreasonable wish – he had been cruising the islands of the Pacific in the *Pearl* for more than a year without harm – and there was just time while the two boats were lowered
to pen an optimistic few lines to his wife in Sydney. 'I am going ashore
to the spot where the Sandfly was lost last year,' he told her, 'to see
if I can't make friends with the unfortunates, who seem most friendly
and anxious to be civil, by coming out to us in canoes, and looking
as if they wished to please.'

Memories not just of the *Sandfly*, but of other outrages – the brutal
murder of the *Fanny*'s crew, the martyrdom of the missionary Bishop
Patteson in 1871, the attack on Albert Markham's *Rosario* – were
fresh enough to induce some caution, and as Goodenough saw the
size of his reception committee he signalled back to the ship for a

third boat to support them. He had originally ordered his boat crew
to aim for a spot some way to the right of their eventual landing place,
but as they approached the narrow strip of white coral sand, lapped
by the surf on one side and fringed with heavy, overhanging vegetation on the other, 'a native, waving a green bough' – the traditional
sign of friendship – 'motioned them to … a point on which the island's
canoes were rapidly and excitedly converging'. 'During the time I
have spent in the Pearl,' Alfred Corrie, a surgeon on the ship, recalled
of his first discouraging close-up of this welcoming party, 'I have had
the opportunity of visiting most of the islands in the South Pacific,
Fiji, New Hebrides, Savage Island, those belonging to the Banks and
Santa Cruz groups, and I must acknowledge that I have never, among
the hundreds of natives that I have met, seen any so savage or repul-
sive-looking as those I came across at Santa Cruz Island.'

Appearances apart, though, there still seemed nothing to raise
alarm, and if the natives looked nervous, that was only to be expected
when any white men they had previously come across were likely to
have been kidnappers supplying the illegal labour trade. 'As we drew
in to the shore canoes came about us, eager, vociferous, and friendly,
with a rather villainous look,' Goodenough wrote more temperately.
'They are big compared to some other islanders here, are not at all
dark, some being very light, and with very light hair … After touching the beach, I remained for some minutes in the boat, so as not to
alarm the people by too sudden moves or gestures, and gave away
some pieces of calico, bargaining at the same time a knife or two for
some pretty matting.'

Gradually the inhabitants became less nervous, beckoning Goodenough and his men to follow them to the nearby settlement, where
they took shelter against a sudden downpour under the roof of a half-
finished hut. Goodenough had taken the precaution of leaving the
third boat crew on the beach, but it was only after he had allowed
himself to be lured some way towards a second and larger settlement,
that it seems to have dawned on him just how exposed their position
had become. 'Oh! this isn't quite prudent,' he exclaimed, ordering
his men back to the beach.

As I got near the boats I said, 'Order everyone into the boats,' and
seeing every one near, turned to see if any were behind me. I saw
Harrison up a little passage between a stone wall and the side of a
hut, and just above the white coral sand beach, and went up to him

to see what he was about and to be with him. He was bargaining for some arrows with a tall man, who held his bow in his left hand, and was twiddling his arrows in a rather hectoring way, as I thought. Casting my eye to the left, I saw a man with a gleaming pair of black eyes fitting an arrow to a string, and in an instant, just as I was thinking it must be a sham menace, and stared him in the face, *thud* came the arrow into my left side. I felt astounded. I shouted 'To the boats!' pulled the arrow out, and threw it away (for which I am sorry), and leapt down the beach, hearing a flight of arrows pass. At my first sight of them all were getting in and shoving off, and I leapt into the whaler; then feeling she was not clear of the ground, jumped out, and helped to push her out into deep water, and while doing so another arrow hit my head a good sharp rap, leaving an inch and a half of its bone sticking in my hat.

Goodenough ordered his men to return fire, and as first one native dropped wounded from the dense foliage of a tree fringing the beach, and then a second was hit, the arrows gradually fell away. As the whaler's crew pulled for the ship, his secretary, William Perry, went to work on the wound in Goodenough's side, 'chewing and sucking' at it for poison until the ship's surgeon could properly cauterise and poultice it. 'The arrow seemed to have struck the rib,' Goodenough continued optimistically, 'and having been pulled out at once, no poison (supposing there to have been poison on them) could have become dissolved in the time.'

With six of his men wounded, however, an unwilling Goodenough decided '*à tête reposé*' that some mark at least of Her Majesty's displeasure had to be shown. There was a strong feeling in the ship that sterner retaliatory action was called for, but he was as reluctant to endanger the lives of 'the wretched islanders' as he was those of his own crew, and 'with wonderful Christian forbearance' contented himself with burning eight or nine huts in the village before weighing for Mota.

There was clearly a possibility that he and the other wounded were still in danger from tetanus, and Goodenough decided to head instead for the healthier climate of Sydney. 'The arrows did not look to have been poisoned, and if they were, were probably too short a time in the wounds to let the poison take effect,' he reassured his wife,

but ... should be guarded against ... To-day is Tuesday, just five
days; it seems but a day. In five days more we shall be able to say
that all danger of poisoning is over; but from the first moment I
have kept the possibility steadily before me, so as to be prepared;
it is very good to be brought to look upon a near death as more
than usually probable ... My only trouble is a pain in the small of
my back, which is a little against my sleeping. I am exceedingly
well ... I have asked Perry to put out a statement for the papers, so
that we may have no outrageously foolish stories. I can only imagine the motive to have been plunder, or a sort of running-a-muck.
I don't feel –

They were Goodenough's last written words. That same evening, in
the cool and fresh airs to the north of New Caledonia his condition
worsened, and after a restless night, it was clear that tetanus had set
in. 'He had desired some days before,' wrote his wife, 'to be told as
soon as any alarming symptoms should occur ... [and] received the
announcement in silence, and with perfect calmness, merely asking,
after a little while, how long it was likely to last; and as one or another
of his officers came in to see him he told them that he was going to
die, adding immediately that he had no fear, but perfect trust in God.'
    Through the rest of the day, while his officers took turns to sit with
him and read from the Psalms, and sleep was punctuated by spasms
of increasing frequency and intensity, Goodenough declined towards
his grave. By the next morning his breathing had become harder, and
after carrying him into the after cabin in search of fresher air, his officers were forced to take him back, exhausted, to his bed. 'He soon
... said to those who were with him,' his widow continued – Calvary
and orlop deck bedding down in a strange, inimitably Victorian
ménage, '"I gather from your manner that I am going to die soon; if
so, I should wish to see all the officers, to bid them good bye."

They all assembled, and he spoke to them at length, taking an affec-
tionate farewell of each, telling them how he had loved them all,
how he had seen in each something worthy to be loved; and saying
a kind and appropriate word of encouragement to each one, showing how well he knew their individual characters. He told them of
his happiness in his love of God, of his readiness to die: bidding
each one kiss him as a token that no hastiness on his part was
unforgiven by them. He then desired to take leave of the ship's

company, and insisted on doing so, though it was feared at first that it might hurt him. He said: – 'If I can only turn one soul to the love of God, if it were but the youngest boy in the ship, I must do it. Perhaps when they hear it from the lips of a dying man they will believe it.'

He was carried out in his chair, and, wrapped in blankets, laid on a bed on his quarterdeck, with the ship's company around him. He told his men that he was dying but that they were to smile and not look sad, and – his voice, weak at the start, gaining in strength all the time – that he was happy in his sense of God's love, that he exhorted them all to turn to God, and the older ones to guide the young. 'Will you do this for my sake?' he asked them, before finally begging their forgiveness for any mistakes he had made in his treatment of them, and assuring them that he had loved them all – 'even those among them that he had punished for that he had always seen some good even in the greatest offender. "As to those poor natives," he added, "don't think about them and what they have done. It is not worth while; they couldn't know right from wrong. Perhaps some twenty or thirty years hence, when some good Christian man has settled among them, something may be learnt about it."'

Shaking hands with each of his petty officers, and taking a last farewell of the weeping crew, he was carried 'through a lane of loving, pitying faces' to his cabin, where for another day he slid in and out of an opium-sedated sleep. Even in his moments of extreme pain the same smile of Christian acceptance remained on his face, and his greatest anxiety was that physical suffering might drag out of him language that he was loath anyone should hear on his lips. '"If bad words were heard from him,"' his officers were warned, '"those with him were to leave him, as it would not be his spirit speaking." Also that he had thought that, at the last, some dark picture of his life might rise up before him; instead of which God would only let him dwell on the words, "With whom is no variableness, neither shadow of turning." These words, he said, were a little window which God had opened to him in Heaven; and he said to the chaplain, "If in pain I cannot smile, let me see you smile, and do you repeat those words."'

At the last, even his anxieties that in his pain he would betray himself fell away. 'I have often used bad words in my life,' he said, 'but now though the pain is so great, I couldn't use bad words if I

wished; I'm not allowed to. Everything is so smoothed for me – the
pain only seems to come when I am able to bear it.'

Goodenough's trust and faith was rewarded. His end was as quiet
as the deepest piety could ask. The whole ship was silent save for the
sound of the engines, and at 4 o'clock they too were stopped. Sometime in the afternoon he confided his last 'earthly charge' to his
commander, and duty done, fell back onto his bed, slipping away so
peacefully that the 'exact moment' – a quarter-past five on the afternoon of Friday 20 August, 1875 – 'was only perceptible to him who
held his pulse'.

It was the perfect Christian end to a virtuous Christian life. The
Church Triumphant's gain, though, was the navy's loss, and whether
it was such an exemplary end for a commodore was another ques-
tion. It was a question that would reverberate uneasily through an
Imperial history whose milestones were the deaths of such men as
Vickers, Havelock and Goodenough. 'Under which king Bezonian?'
as Pistol might have asked: 'Speak, or die.' The Colt or the Gospel?
The Admiralty or the Mission? The Lord Jesus or the First Sea Lord?
It might have been as well for Victorian England if, ten years before
Gordon's death at Khartoum, it had found its answer. It would
certainly have been as well for the two seamen lying on either side of
him in his Sydney grave if Goodenough had not taken a lifetime to
find his.

II

James Goodenough was born on 3 December 1830 at Stoke Hill in
Surrey, the son of a Dean of Wells, the grandson of a Bishop of
Carlisle, and the great-grandson of the rector of Broughton Poggs in
Oxfordshire. For any boy with so remorselessly clerical a pedigree
there were only a limited number of professions open in the nine-
teenth century, and from the day of his christening, James Graham
Goodenough – like so many sons of England's rural rectories – was
earmarked by his father for the navy.

It is never clear whether at a later stage he had any say in this, but
with a background and a name such as his – Goodenough, with its
sturdily Bunyanesque ring to it, and James Graham after his godfather, First Lord of the Admiralty, Sir James Graham – it is unlikely
there was ever a time when he did not have the idea of two separate

The Relief of Lucknow, 17 November 1857, by Thomas Barker, based on sketches by Egron Lundgren, a Swedish artist working in India during the Mutiny. At the centre, shaking hands, are Outram, Havelock and Campbell. Peel is the fourth figure to the right of the grey at the centre.

1. Sir Henry Havelock 2. Sir James Outram 3. Sir Colin Campbell 4. Capt. Roberts 5. PEEL 6. Brig. Hon. Adrian Hope 7. Capt. Watson 8. Sir Robert Napier

Peel bringing his guns up in front of the Dilkusha. Lithograph based on a drawing by Captain Oliver Jones, RN.

Loot. Arabic prayer or invocation of Imam 'Ali ibn Abu Talib, the Fourth Caliph, whose followers belong to the Shi'a sect. 'You are Lord, O 'Ali, Peace be upon you,' reads the main text. The script is Persian and the date 1259 AH (or 1843 AD). On the back, in Peel's hand, is written: 'Taken by me from the Zenana at Lucknow. November 57, W. Peel RN. May it be more true to its present owner. W.P.' Peel had it sent back to his mother before his death.

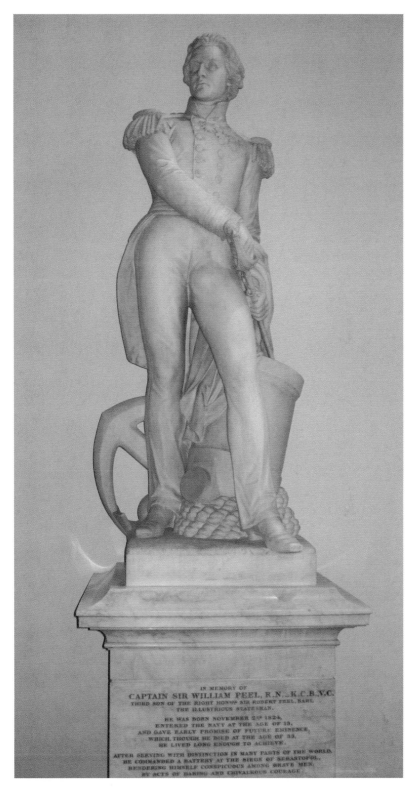

The Victorian hero. Sir William Peel, VC, KCB, by William Theed, in St Swithun's church, Sandy.

GOODENOUGH

James Graham Goodenough: 'a keen and deep set piercing eye, a prominent chin, which spoke the iron nerve he possessed, while the sinews of his mouth revealed from time to time the tenderness of his heart'.

The bombardment of Sveaborg, August 1855: '11.30 anchored out of range in 12f & observed tremendous explosion in Sveaborg as if a magazine had blown up.'

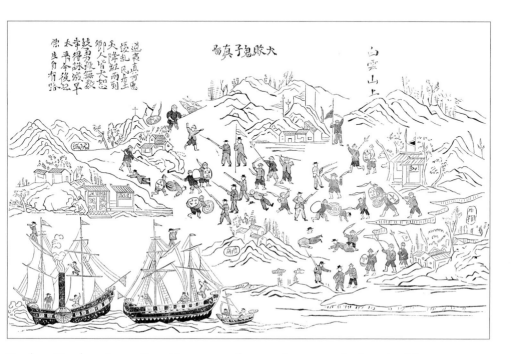

Fatshan Creek, 1 June 1857: 'As pretty a boat action as can be imagined.'

The making of a martyr. The attack on Captain Goodenough and his party. From a sketch taken on the spot by Lieutenant Harrison, RM, of HMS *Pearl*.

Last rites. The *Pearl*, with crossed yards in mourning; the landing of the bodies at Milson Point, Sydney; and the funeral procession.

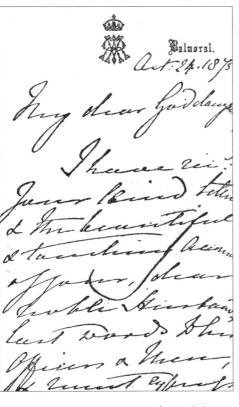
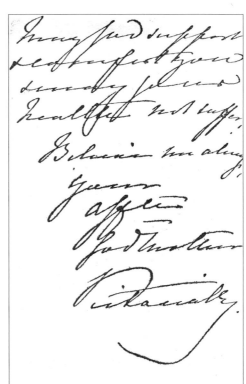

A nation mourns. Letter of condolence from Queen Victoria to her goddaughter, Goodenough's widow.

The widow: Victoria Goodenough in 1897.

Posthumous portrait bust of Goodenough, by Prince Victor of Hohenlohe-Langenberg, Count Gleichen: sculptor, admiral, and Goodenough's messmate in *Raleigh* during the *Arrow* War.

Masters firmly in his sight. 'From his earliest years he showed determination and strength of character,' his future wife wrote, yoking
from the very first the iconography of Christian self-denial to the
demands of his future career. 'Even his elder brothers and sisters were
accustomed to abide by his decision in undisputed matter, always
recognising his desire for justice; and they remembered that when
only about eight years old he for some time voluntarily contented
himself with dry bread at the school-room breakfast, in order to
harden himself, and make himself more fit to encounter any difficulties he might meet with in the profession which had been marked out
for him.'

One of the great problems for Anglican hagiographers was that
they had to make do with some fairly thin gruel – any self-respecting
Catholic saint would have been subjecting him or herself to infinitely
harsher rigours than dry bread – but there seems no doubting the
young Goodenough's moral character. 'He was, as a boy, what he
continued to be as a man,' Clements Markham, a lifelong friend,
recalled nearly forty years later: 'honourable, true, tender-hearted,
modest, brave, and a hater of all things evil. There was something in
his society which raised others unconsciously, yet he was not one of
those boys who were never to be found out of bounds or in the fighting green. On the contrary, while joining heartily in all that other
boys did, he kept all real evil from himself and his companions by a
sort of natural force. Every one liked him, and rejoiced at his successes
at school and on the water, which were extraordinary for so young
a boy.'

Goodenough's first years were spent in the shadow of Wells Cathedral, where in 1831 his father had been appointed Dean, but at the
age of nine and a half he followed in the family tradition and entered
Westminster School. During the 1770s his grandfather had been there
under Dr Markham, and with Goodenough's father, the Dean, a
former headmaster, he would have had as little say in the matter as
he did in his future career. 'On the morning of his entry he was
conducted, according to custom, "up school", and directed to sit
behind the examination-table,' Sir Albert Markham recalled of the
ritual induction of his cousin Clements – a process that would have
been all the more intimidating for a boy two years younger and less
supremely self-opinionated than the eleven-year-old Great Panjan-
drum-in-waiting of late Victorian England.

To a boy of his age the whole procedure was a very awe-inspiring
ordeal. The vast size of the room, with its lofty and open roof; the
masters and scholars around him, attired in their college caps and
gowns; the Latin prayers – all filled him with awe and wonder ...
Then his name was called in a loud and commanding voice by the
Head-master, who interrogated him as to his general knowledge.
The result of this examination was that he was placed in the 'Upper
School' in the 'under fourth form'.

In Goodenough's case he was placed in the third form – he rose eventually to the 'shell' – but his first days at Westminster would have
been the same. 'According to the rules and regulations of the school,'
Sir Albert continued with a baleful relish for all those inanities of
public school life – running everywhere, even to a flogging – that
provided so ideal a preparation for a career in the Markham navy,

> a boy in the same class as that to which the new boy is appointed
> was selected by the usher to act as his *Substance*, and to see him
> the new boy became a *Shadow*. It was the duty of the *Substance* to
> initiate the latter in all the ordinary details connected with his
> school-life, and to see that his *Shadow* was in possession of the
> necessary books and other indispensable properties required for
> his education. The *Substance* had also to explain the localities of
> the various places frequented by the boys outside the precincts of
> the school, such as the shops where bats and balls, sweets, cakes,
> and other articles dear to a schoolboy's heart, were sold. It was
> also his duty to point out the limits that constituted 'out of bounds',
> and other important details of a similar nature – such, for instance,
> as the hard-and-fast rule laid down by the boys themselves, that
> none but a sixth form boy was privileged to walk on the west side
> of Abingdon Street. In a few days the new boy was fully initiated
> into all the customs and routine of the school, and consequently
> ceased to exist as a *Shadow*, reverting again to a material body.

In the years to come instinct and intelligence would invariably put
Goodenough on the side of the progressives and modernisers, but a
public school education in the first half of the nineteenth century was
something he never regretted. He had gone up to Westminster with
the last of the Hanoverians only just in the grave, and it was still in
the old protectionist world before the repeal of the Corn Laws, that

at the age of thirteen, on 7 May 1844 – the same day and place that William Peel was sitting his Lieutenant's exams with such dazzling success – he went down to Portsmouth for the ritual entry farce into the old navy. 'The examinations in those days were not what they are now,' his widow wrote. 'He ... should have gone on board the "Victory" to be examined; but, as it was blowing hard, he was desired to sit down in the flag lieutenant's office, given a sum and a piece of dictation to do, and the examination was over.'

Goodenough might have been one of the Young Turks of the mid-Victorian navy, but he would always be grateful to have first gone to sea during the final undisputed heyday of sail. On passing his examination at Portsmouth he had been appointed to the newly commissioned HMS *Collingwood*, and after a long summer of delays – passed by the thirteen-year-old Goodenough in preparing for his confirmation – finally prepared to sail in the early afternoon of 7 September for the Pacific station and three years away from home and family.

The Goodenoughs had taken a house on the Isle of Wight for the summer, and their little yacht, the *Traveller*, with the Dean, his wife and their sons and daughter on board, had become a familiar sight to the men and boys of the *Collingwood* as they 'daily hovered around the great ship'. On the afternoon of the seventh they were again there to accompany her out to sea, and as she slipped her mooring at Spithead and moved down the Channel – 'canvas swelling out before the breeze', 'the blue flag of Sir George Seymour at the mizzen' and a small flotilla of boats, yachts and cheering families in her wake – 'the Dean followed her far out to sea, very loath to lose sight of the new floating home of the boy whom he loved so dearly'. 'How willingly would one dispense with these farewells,' Robert Falcon Scott would later write of this immemorial rite of passage, as the *Discovery* made her way towards the Needles Channel and the 'Old Country' 'gradually shaded from green to blue', until it had finally vanished in the distance, 'and how truly one feels that the greater burden of sadness is on those who are left behind! Before us lay new scenes, new interests, expanding horizons; but who at such times must not think sorely of the wives and mothers condemned to think of the past, and hope in silent patience for the future, through years of suspense and anxiety.'

Goodenough would never see his father again, and his mother too would die while he was at sea, but for the moment any apprehension or homesickness was forgotten in the novelty of it all. The *Collingwood* was never in fact as good a sailor as affection and distance would paint her, but it is questionable if any peacetime ship boasted a more varied complement of officers, from the new Admiral of the Pacific station, Sir Michael Seymour himself – a veteran of the Basque Roads, 'a tall, handsome man in spite of the disfiguring marks of a severe wound on one side of his mouth', not much rated outside the service but loved within it – down through Captain Smart and the young Lieutenant Peel, to a future general, a commander of irregular Turkish cavalry and any number of middies who would make their names in the Arctic Circle or the Crimea.

With Sir George Seymour taking out his family – wife, three daughters, a young son and five maids – there was waltzing, quadrilles and polkas on the quarterdeck in the evenings to ease the tedium of the long Atlantic crossing. The only anxiety of the whole voyage was in wild weather rounding the Horn, and with fishing from the bowsprit for bonito and dolphin (Goodenough could not eat salt-beef, so the fresh fish was a welcome relief), floggings, drownings – one of them a 'little 2nd class boy ... a very good little boy' who fell from the fore-rigging and was never seen again – 'crossing the line', at which the dresses of the ladies' maids really came into their own, and lowering one of the Admiral's geese over the side, Goodenough's first taste of gunroom life cannot have been much different from that of any other young volunteer in the last years of sail. 'In addition to carrying out his duties as a watch-keeping officer' – Goodenough had also volunteered for night watches – Albert Markham described the midshipman regime in the *Collingwood*,

> which necessitated him being on deck about eight hours out of every twenty-four, he had to attend school under the Naval Instructor from 9 to 11.30 a.m. every day except Saturdays and Sundays. At 11.30 every morning the midshipmen assemble on the poop with their sextants or quadrants (as the case might be) for the purpose of observing the meridian altitude of the sun. The afternoons were devoted to the carrying out of various drills, such as gunnery, cutlass, and rifle exercises, seamanship, including knotting and splicing, and so forth.

At the heart of his new world was the gunroom, and in physical terms at least, it again presents a familiar picture. 'Beer abounded in large jugs,' Walpole, another shipmate, wrote of the *Collingwood*'s gunroom, on an occasion when the two large deal tables had been cleared aside to make space for a fight. 'Admiring gazers on the fight sat round, drinking the same; in the ports men of milder mood were solacing themselves with pipes and cigars. One or two, fresh from quieter scenes, were persevering trying to read a book … the gifts of tender mothers, perhaps, or of fathers who hoped for clever sons, were piled in the corners, together with boat gear, sword-sticks, and heaps of other things past mentioning.'

There is no doubt where Goodenough would have fitted into this vignette, and the dedication at the front of Walpole's account of their voyage – 'To you its better parts are all their inspiration, a higher tone of feeling and of hope being raised in me' – is certainly addressed to him. 'As a midshipman young Goodenough fulfilled all the promise he had given as a boy at Westminster,' Clements Markham – the same intake into ship as well as school – wrote of him.

Always modest and unassuming, he naturally took the lead in everything; the best as a linguist, in navigation, in seamanship, in gunnery, and all exercises, and among the foremost in all expeditions. He took to sea with him Burney's collection of voyages in the South Sea, which he read carefully, and he thus acquired a love for such narratives and for the achievements of daring navigators and explorers, which continued to the day of his death. His messmates looked to him as their leader, almost as their guide; and none of them ceased to look back with regret to those four happy years.

If Goodenough plainly had the instincts and natural authority of a leader, he was lucky to begin his naval career in a ship where the moral tone so perfectly chimed with his own. It is not difficult to imagine a nineteenth-century gunroom in which his determined piety would have set him apart, but in Markham he had a friend and messmate of almost identical pedigree – a bishop and a dean apiece in their immediate family – in their Naval Instructor a teacher keen to encourage Goodenough's remarkable linguistic skills, in Smart a captain 'of the purest integrity and elevation of character', and in Sir George Seymour a *preux chevalier* of the old school' – or an 'old dotard', depending on your take – whose paternalistic interest in his young officers stretched to every aspect of their moral and physical well-being. 'On hoisting his flag on board the *Collingwood*,' Albert Markham wrote with approval, Seymour issued a memorandum denouncing smoking as 'a deleterious and filthy habit that destroyed the inner coating of the stomach and rendered the smoker unfit for social purposes'. With regard to the officers, the Admiral expressed a pious hope that they would not 'practice this dirty and disgusting vice. If any officer was unable to exist without smoking, he was to report himself to the Admiral, when a time and place would be allotted to him for the purpose of indulging in this pernicious habit.'

Like the beautiful ship full of beautiful and finely bred young boys that she was, the *Collingwood* took an equally dim view of ugliness – two ill-favoured cadets who joined her later (one who 'squinted frightfully', and the other who looked 'like a white nigger') were instantly packed off to other vessels – but here again Goodenough seems to have more than passed muster. For some reason there is no physical description of him among the obsessive jottings of Clements Markham, but Goodenough's widow would remember him as 'a man of middle height, of a spare and nervous frame', sharply defined features, 'a keen and piercing deep-set eye', and 'a prominent chin, which spoke of the iron nerve which he possessed, while the sinews of his mouth revealed from time to time the tenderness of his heart'.

If this is a description of the adult Goodenough and not the boy, the child universally and predictably known as 'Goodie' was not so much father to the man as his miniature likeness: 'On every emergency Goodenough's first thought was for others.' Markham recalled one typical incident, when the *Collingwood* was visiting Robinson Crusoe's island.

> Once he and another youngster [Markham himself, in fact] took a long excursion among the wild ravines of Juan Fernandez. Scrambling through masses of huge leaves, which concealed everything in front, Goodenough was a few paces ahead. Suddenly his companion heard a crashing sound, and as he crept forward Goodenough's warning voice urged him anxiously not to follow. At the moment he must have been in great agony. He had fallen down a sheer precipice, and had sprained his ankle, besides being severely cut, crushed and bruised.

Goodenough had landed on a narrow ledge, two hundred feet above the bottom of the ravine, and spent the night there, listening in the dark to the shrieks of owls and the distant calls of the rescue party that Markham had rushed back to the ship to fetch. It would have been hard enough for them to find the spot in daylight, but at night it was impossible, and it was only the next day, after Goodenough had managed to crawl along the ledge until it widened into a spur, that Sir George Seymour – who had joined the search with everyone else from the ship – blundered across him. 'It was twenty-four hours before he could be found and extricated,' a grateful Clements Markham later recalled. 'His companion never forgot that warning cry, which probably saved his life, and which added a feeling of reverence to his love for such a messmate. But such was Goodenough's character, in pain or in danger his first thought was for others.'

This is not all posthumous piety – 'honourable, true, tender-hearted, modest, brave, and a hater of all things evil' was the young Markham's verdict on him – and four years together in the same cramped gunroom was long enough for him to know what he was talking about. In many ways it seems odd that two boys of such different temper as Markham and Goodenough should have been so close, but in the wake of Peel's departure for Oregon, it was left to the younger Goodenough to exert his influence and force of character to save Markham from the worst consequences of an uncontrolled and uncontrollable temper. 'On one occasion', Albert Markham recalled – an incident that might have come straight out of *Tom Brown's Schooldays* – the two boys 'decided to have a good long ride' towards Santiago, and after thirty-five miles found themselves, hot and exhausted, at the mercies of 'a plump and charming' innkeeper determined to keep them for the night.

> Markham willingly assented, but Goodenough, here as always, stepped in as his guardian angel, and insisted they should return at once. He knew full well that his friend would only get into trouble again if he broke his leave. Sore and tired himself, he ordered the horses to be brought out, and compelled Markham to mount ... On reaching the wide plain ... a gaucho riding at full gallop made a dash at Markham, trying to unhorse him with his knee. Goodenough charged him, and he galloped away across the plain ... At length, weary and sleepy, they reached the first post-house, where Markham besought Mrs. Diggles [the black-eyed wife of a violent escaped convict] to get a bed ready for him, as he could proceed no farther. But here again Goodenough put his foot down, and said that whatever happened they must go on, for he was determined that so long as Markham was with him, he should do his utmost to prevent him from getting in another scrape. At length, more dead

than alive, they reached Valparaiso, and got on board the ship at about 10'30 p.m. This long ride together, and the firm attitude for his good taken by Goodenough, cemented, more solidly if possible, the friendship that already existed between the two boys. They became much more intimate, and frequently talked and exchanged ideas with each other ... It was a friendship that continued to the end of their lives, becoming more real and indissoluble as the years went by.

In spite of Peel's departure and Markham's turbulent temper – a temper he was as likely to indulge at seventy as at seventeen – the *Collingwood* remained an extremely happy ship. The Valparaiso station was generally regarded by naval officers as the worst on the globe, but within a month of arriving the *Collingwood* was at sea again, on its way to Callao, the seaport for Lima, for the beginning of a wandering commission that took them to Tahiti – in the middle of a crisis over the establishment of a French protectorate – and the Sandwich Islands before returning, in January 1846, to Valparaiso to commence a second grand sweep of the Pacific.

The Galapagos with Sir George Seymour, the ravines of Juan Fernandez, the coasts of Mexico and California, Hawaii, Tahiti, even the cathedral at Lima to rob the mummified Pizarro of a finger joint for a seal (fair game, presumably, to English Protestant piety) – by the time Goodenough finally returned to England in July 1848 after almost four years from home he was a midshipman of two years' seniority and had completed a voyage of 83,000 miles. For the last seven months of her commission the *Collingwood* had languished at Callao waiting for the *Asia* to relieve her, but if this was an inglorious end to so richly varied a voyage, Goodenough was not the only one who looked back on her with an affection that no other ship could inspire. 'The *Collingwood* never had another commission,' Clements Markham wrote of her, with an inimitable blend of waspish snobbery and sentimentality that perfectly conjures up the world and ship – part man-of-war, part private yacht – in which Goodenough first went to sea. 'It was as if the desecration could not be allowed of other men with lower tone and other ways in the same ship which once gloried in the presence of the Seymours and their friends. One such commission was to stand alone, and the beautiful hull was left for years to come as a sad monument to its glories.'

III

It is not clear when Goodenough would have learned of his father's death. The Dean had collapsed suddenly while walking in the fields near Wells in May 1845, and had been dead for more than three years by the time his son James made his way up from Portsmouth to his widowed mother and his sisters' new home at Loughton in Essex.

For any boy going to sea in the nineteenth century such sudden upheavals – emotional, financial, geographical – must have been the rule and not the exception, but there can be no questioning how great a loss his father was. From the age of seven James had been away at either school or sea, but if he had not even seen his father since he was thirteen, his own deeply Christian cast of mind and range of secular interests unmistakably bear the imprint of Edmund Goodenough's moral, intellectual and aesthetic influence. 'The Dean directed his children's education, and made them share in his pursuits,' Goodenough's widow would later write,

> whether of natural history, architecture, or music; and no doubt this assistance, the early associations of home, and the interest and beauty of Wells Cathedral and the surrounding scenery, cultivated in James the love of architecture and music, and that taste which could not be satisfied with anything short of the best and purest in art, and which formed a source of enjoyment to him through life. He often recalled in later years one of his earliest lessons in perseverance and hardihood. When about seven years old he used to ride with his father. His pony had been in the habit of bolting in at the stable gate, instead of coming round to the front door; and on one winter evening the Dean insisted on the little boy riding up and down the road, till long after dark, and till he had mastered his pony, and made him quietly pass the stable door.

This is all so instantly recognisable in its saccharin tone, its penchant for the improving moral fable (the same sort of story would be told of Captain Scott), that it is easy to forget how unusual in fact Goodenough's background was. During the nineteenth century the Church of England was still one of the great 'feeder' institutions for the Royal Navy, but it would be a mistake to look at Goodenough's pedigree – three generations of churchmen – and see nothing in it but that familiar and genial tradition of impoverished gentlemen-clergymen who, decade in and decade out, stocked the gunrooms of the Victorian men-of-war.

Edmund Goodenough might have ended his life a Dean of Wells, but he had been, successively, a Fellow of Christ Church, Oxford, a University Examiner in mathematics, headmaster of Westminster School and a council member of the Royal Society, and earnestness and high intelligence ran in the family. In the last quarter of the eighteenth century James's grandfather, Samuel, had been a notable figure in the intellectual world of the capital, a founder, treasurer and vice-president of the Linnaean Society and a vice-president of the Royal Society on merit long before the influence of his aristocratic old pupils at Westminster raised him to the bench as Bishop of Carlisle. ''Tis well enough that Goodenough/Before the Lords should preach,' ran one famous epigram, celebrating the implausible sight of a man of his learning casting his scholarly pearls before Parliament's lordly swine, 'But, sure enough, full bad enough/Are those he has to teach.'

It must be more than a coincidence, too, that Samuel Goodenough had been at the Royal Society during the long reign of Sir Joseph Banks, because in many ways his grandson James seems a throwback to the age of Banks, Bligh and Captain Cook. Throughout his life he would always have the *future* of the service clearly in his sights, but in a profession that was inexorably evolving into the navy of 'Pompo' Heneage and Lord Charles Beresford, Goodenough was the equal and heir to that breed of naval captains who, in their range of scientific and geographical interests, belonged to the intellectual elite of their day.

At the age of just seventeen, though, he had more mundane matters to concern him, and after only six weeks at home he was again at sea, bound in the steam frigate *Cyclops* for Sierra Leone and the West African coast under the command of that zealous flogger, Captain The Hon. G.F. Hastings. 'Of all the warlike operations which have been carried on under the British flag,' the Victorian historian C.D. Yonge wrote in 1863, with a Gilbertesque pride that was for once justified,

> there are none which rebound so greatly to our credit as a nation as those which have been undertaken for the suppression of the slave-trade. They have been engaged in from no motive of self-interest ... They were dictated by no real or fancied obligation to

enforce our laws ... They were not even prompted by any desire to preserve our own reputation from taint ... But they owed their origin and their persevering resolute continuance to a pure unselfish philanthropy; and they also owe the great (alas! that we cannot say the entire) success which has attended them to the conviction, which even the nations most addicted to the trade are unable to resist, that our motives are as blameless, as honourable, as our exertions have been untiring.

If there was a theatre of warfare that might have been designed for Goodenough, one that uniquely combined a sense of high purpose with the small-boat scale of action in which a young officer might excel, it was the West African station; but disinterested high-mindedness in the nineteenth century seldom precluded ambition. The *Cyclops* had sailed for Sierra Leone at the start of a three-year commission, but within just over a year he was back in England, 'his desire for advancement' leading him 'to compete at the Royal Naval College for the lieutenant's commission which was then annually given to the mate who after a year's study passed the best examination'.

It was an understandable move, because a young officer with a widowed mother and a large number of brothers and sisters, and neither the vast fortune nor the raft of interest on which the young Peel's career was floated, needed to seize every advantage going. 'It is a time of confusion,' Goodenough would write feelingly of the difficulties of combining ship and study duties on a station like Sierra Leone, 'during which the conflicting claims of duties on board and in boats, duties of detail which should be given to petty officers, lessons in the practice of gunnery, lessons in mathematics, frequent parades, musters and inspections, jostle and hurry in desultory and harassing succession.'

Goodenough returned to England in December 1850, and after the compulsory six months in *Excellent*, the gunnery school in which Peel had performed so brilliantly, preparing for his mate's certificate, entered the Naval College at Portsmouth, where in July 1851 he gained the 'only prize of scientific merit' that the navy at that time had to offer, in the shape of his lieutenant's commission. 'There are few, if any,' a rival officer, in competition for the same lieutenant's commission, recalled of Goodenough,

the delineation of whose character should be more inspiring to
young men who are seeking after the best and noblest things in this
life and that to come ... The time we spent together in 'Excellent'
and at the Royal Naval College, was one of close study and
constant companionship, but was very much without incident; we
taught in the Sunday schools together; we read and prayed together
every night, and what little time was snatched from study was
generally devoted to walks in the country, to which a little sketching and a little botanising added interest.

'It was my good fortune to have known him since the year 1850,'
another fellow student wrote. 'Then I saw what a man amongst men
he was, that his actions were all guided by the purest Christian principles ... a man who was ever manly, gentle, and kind, an officer as
smart, and a seaman as able as ever lived.'

His actions might well have been guided by the purest Christian
motives, and his aspiration 'to make God his *Summum Bonum*',
but that did not make Goodenough any more immune than Peel to
the frustrations of a peacetime navy. 'I think with you that it would
not be right to ask for a recall without a definite appointment,' he
wrote to his mother with that over-scrupulosity that was typical of
him:

> What I have wished you have divined and done, viz., to make my
> name known as an individual wishing for employment in the
> surveying branch, being in a manner adapted to it by the advan-
> tages often enjoyed in the college and elsewhere ... To you, dear
> mother, to whom I wish all my thoughts and doings to be known,
> I must say that I fear I have wished too much for this change, and
> that I have thought and talked a great deal too much of myself to
> the exclusion of others. So a truce to it.

It would have been interesting to know what Clements Markham
would have made of his ambition to enter the surveying branch, but
Goodenough was spared the pain of ever finding out. At the end of
his time at Portsmouth he had sailed for South America in the
Centaur, bearing the flag of Rear Admiral Henderson, but in February 1854, with war against Russia looking increasingly likely, she
was ordered back to England and her ship's company dispersed
around the fleet for active service in the Baltic.

In the national consciousness the war with Russia has always been 'the Crimean War', but for the navy at least it was a conflict that extended from the Black Sea and the Sea of Azov to the Baltic and the Pacific. The operations in the Pacific were admittedly only negligible, but with a strategy that envisaged an assault on Russia at her two most vulnerable points – Sevastopol on the Black Sea and its main fleet and fortresses in the north – there was never anything of the 'sideshow' about the Baltic operations Good-enough's godfather had planned. 'No fleet has ever quitted England with such marked honours,' Yonge wrote of the departure of the Baltic fleet from Spithead, more than a fortnight before the actual declaration of war.

> The day that it sailed, the 11th of March, the Queen, who was at Osborne, came herself alongside it in the Fairy yacht, and she received the Admiral and the different Captains on board; and it was amid royal salutes, almost overpowered in their roar by the cheers of the seamen as they manned the yards, and the music of the bands, playing that noble air which never falls lifeless on an English ear, and while the Queen herself, from her own quarter-deck, waved her heartfelt farewell to her loyal champions, that the gallant fleet weighed anchor, and sailed for the Downs.

With nineteen ships of the line – two thirds of which were screw steamers – eleven frigates, and a corresponding number of smaller vessels, the only thing that seemed to stand in the way of the most powerful fleet ever to sail was the man the Admiralty had placed in its command. At the age of sixty-eight Sir Charles Napier had lost none of his old boastfulness – he promised his audience at a Reform Club dinner that within a month he would be in Kronstadt or in heaven – but even on his own unpleasant and blustering terms he was only a shadow of the man he had once been, indecisive where he had once been hasty, and oddly fearful where he had once been so violently and overweeningly self-assertive.

'Most men of sixty are too old for dash and enterprise ... When a man's body begins to shake, the mind follows, and he is always the last to find it out,' Napier had once written, and over the summer of 1854 his words came back to haunt him. The fleet had left England with such high expectations that they were almost bound to be disap-pointed, and by August of the brief campaigning season, nothing except a blockade of the Baltic and the odd strategically unimportant operation had been even so much as attempted by Napier.

If this was galling for the country and for a government readying itself to throw its admiral to the dogs, it did at least assuage some of the disappointment Goodenough felt at being kept out of the action. On his return from South America he had desperately tried to get himself transferred to a ship bound for the Black Sea, but as the officers and crew of the *Centaur* were dispersed among the fleet, he found himself – 'with some surprise and disappointment' – languishing instead at Devonport in the eighty-four-gun guardship, *Calcutta*.

There were compensations – the launch of the Royal Yacht *Albert* with a 'very pleasant' gaggle of girls 'ready to flirt with anybody' (a detail ruthlessly excised from the printed journal) – and escape finally came in June when 150 officers and men of the *Calcutta* were lent to the *Royal William* to transport French troops from Calais for a proposed attack on the Russian island fortresses of Bomarsund. The next weeks were spent by Goodenough in the feverish preparations for the voyage, but by early July powder and three thousand shot had been taken on – not to mention 'wine and private stores ... *Nothing* was refused in the way of private stores' – and by the middle of the month they were anchored with the rest of the convoy off Calais. 'The church is simple plan & has an immense picture of "La Reprise de Calais par Henri II des Anglais, et la consequente Restoration de cette ville en Catholicisme",' Goodenough noted –

> very bad ... At noon the Emperor embarked in the 'reine Hortense' his screw yacht and went out to the 'Hannibal'. The people thronged both sides of the Quai and quantities of pretty people both French and English waved as he passed ... The tide was running very strong and his boat could not get up so the 'Corse' took him in tow till close to the ladder, wetting all hands well. The Empr. stood up and gave all orders himself and after getting out of the boat on the ladder saw all of his staff out before he went up himself. Poor old Marshal Le Vaillant was plunged to his hips in water and his red trousers came out brown. He only made a short visit.

Over the next days stores and ammunition were loaded, troops embarked, sentries posted in a losing battle to keep the French from smoking on the lower decks, and at 6 o'clock on the morning of the sixteenth, with a five-knot breeze behind them and the *Royal William* in the van, the convoy weighed for the Baltic. 'It was such lovely weather that the ports were always open,' Goodenough noted, 'the people well and the decks clean. We found that the soldiers had quantities of Lucifer matches and were obliged to keep a sharp looked out to prevent them smoking … One fine looking corporal of Chasseurs sang very well and led better. As he began to sing in the centre of his surrounding chorus, he threw his capote over one shoulder, his whole face lighted up with pleasure and animation.'

At daylight on Saturday, 22 July they entered the Great Belt and by that evening had safely negotiated the passage. 'We went to divisions and had service on the Quarter Deck,' Goodenough wrote the next day.

> The French soldiers crowded on the boats, hammock nettings and guns, while the officers sat on the track of the poop, and all behaved with the greatest respect and order throughout. It was an interesting sight. Like a great many others, they are by name Roman Catholics and in reality nothing. Many of them have said to me 'Si j'avais besoin d'une religion, je serai Protestant, mais je me prise toutes ces choses la.' Our lovely little Corsican Chasseur said, 'You pray for your Queen, your country and ministers and very justly and sensibly, but we pray for the Saints. Who are they, I should like to know? I never met one of them.'

The Baltic Sea divides halfway along its length into two unequal arms, with the smaller Gulf of Finland leading eastwards to the great fortress of Kronstadt and St Petersburg, and the fortresses of Bomarsund and the Aland Islands guarding the approaches to the Gulf of Bothnia and the north. It had long been clear that all talk of attacking Kronstadt itself had been no more than talk, but the fortress at Bomarsund – vulnerable to attack from its lightly defended land side – offered Napier's frustrated navy the chance to accomplish at least something before the summer was out.

The British army was too stretched by its commitments in the Black Sea to be able to spare any troops for the operation, and Goodenough was no happier at leaving the lead role to their allies than Peel would have been. 'The fort is in the form of a segment of a circle,' he noted, as the *Royal William* prepared to disembark her complement of the

nine-thousand-strong French force some fifteen hundred yards to the
south-west of the main fort:

> ... the centre and left are armed by 72 and 80 guns, in double tier
> of casements ... It appears to me, that as the bay contains no
> dangers, in the vicinity of the place, that six line of battle ships
> (screw) might have gone in with advantage, & have engaged the
> fort, broadside to its front, using cold shot guns only, and distant
> charges. If the enemy were obstinate enough to retreat to the
> towers, guns could then be landed, cavalier batteries erected with
> the materials of the fort, and they would soon be compelled to
> yield. An escalade would probably be successful with seamen
> trained to the use of ladders.

The distant sound of the bombardment he had been asking for was
as close as Goodenough would get to the assault on Bomarsund, and
by 16 August it had fallen to a combined naval and land attack at a
minimal loss of allied life. Among the seventeen French dead – the
intercession of the saints notwithstanding – was the 'merry Corsican
Chasseur' who had fuelled Goodenough's sturdily Protestant prejudices on the voyage out, leaving him to find what consolation he
could in the local flora on walks ashore – 'lily of the valley, prim-
roses, cowslips, wild strawberry, dewberry and wortleberry, hare-
bells, cistus & campanula' – and the looks and antics of the 750
Russian prisoners brought onto the *Royal William*. 'I came down
from Bomarsund with several women who wanted to see their brothers, fathers and so on,' he wrote on the seventeenth, sounding more
like a distressed travel rep dealing with a disgruntled Saga group than
a nineteenth-century naval lieutenant.

> Two or three were quite pretty ... The Russian officers [who] had
> been taken in the round tower wh was taken by our marines, and
> having their wives on board, objected strongly to taking them to
> France, and at last that they would not take their wives at all in a
> French ship, that they would not leave Termagent unless they were
> bound hand and foot and carried away
> The Adm yielded and their wives remained with them.

With outbreaks of cholera in the ship and a polyglot bag of prisoners – Finnish officers and sharpshooters, Cossacks, Russians, Poles,
Livonians, Jews, Circassians, Germans, Orthodox, Catholics, Luther-
ans, Mohammedans, convicts – and most of them demanding to be
segregated from the rest, it was a voyage home for the social anthropologist rather than the naval officer. 'Off Selsey Bill we were met
with orders to go to Plymouth,' Goodenough wrote, reflecting sadly
on the one passion – hatred of the French – that seemed to unite their
prisoners,

> and the Russians who had been afraid of going to France were
> delighted, thinking that it was now sure they would go to England.
> On the following evening ... we learnt that they were to go on
> Sunday ... to Brest. The Russians were much cut up. Old Col
> Tamerlan could not help saying before me 'C'est une chose infame'
> and some came up in tears. In the forenoon they begged to go on
> leave to do nothing but touch the English soil, but the Adm. who
> was on board would not allow it ... Col Klingstedt embraced
> Yatnall as he had Capt Wilmot and our old Gramalkin Schimonoff-
> ski could only press our hands and say with tears in his eyes,
> 'Inglsk! Very good!' ... Schukoff told me when I saw a geranium
> to think of 'Animtianiglacki' the Russian name for it wh means
> 'Annette's eyes' and think of him ... It was quite sad to see them
> leave so much against their will, and to have to tell them against
> hope, 'No doubt you will like France and then you will be as well
> off there as in England.'

It is interesting that neither evidence of the hatreds engendered by
war – and the longevity of passions that still fed off memories of 1812
as insidiously as 1914 France did off defeat in 1870 – nor the
complaints of Swedish farmers at the economic distress caused by
Britain's Baltic blockade seems to have caused any moral qualms in
the young Goodenough. It was very hard for anyone to see what
Christian Britain was doing propping up a corrupt and despotic
Turkey, but whatever scruples the twenty-four-year-old, single Goodenough had over the 'close season' of 1854–55, they were of a more
traditional and personal kind. 'My Dear Journal,' he addresses his
diary after a pause following an entry on the 'exceedingly pretty faces'
to be found among the 'lower classes – dressmakers &c' of Falmouth,

I wish that I had kept on writing you, even tho' I had nothing of stirring interest to pen. In those times of quiet, you would have served as a means of meditation and retrospect, at a time when I shut my eyes a good deal to the inconsistency of my dealings.

If all that I have done since I last wrote were known, how could I answer or indeed, how could I face, my dearest friends: I imagine that they now rather like me and I am fancying continually that I am looked up to by some. If it were so how I ought to hide my face, how to blush and weep for shame. I feel as though I were getting hardened and that some calamity is about to befall me.

Peel's answer to every crisis was activity, and for all their differences of temperament Goodenough was not so very different. The attack on Bomarsund had been virtually the last operation of 1854 in the Baltic theatre, but by the following February he had managed to wangle himself a transfer from the *Calcutta* into the sixty-gun screw steamship *Hastings* under the command of Captain Crawford Caffin. 'Well I shall never catch myself up in this journal of mine,' he wrote on 16 June 1855, after three busy months fitting out the ship for the Baltic and a similar blank in his diary:

> Here we are at Kiel, just the old feeling on arriving at a new place. A rush of bumboats and washerwomen in the morning, an enthusiastic feeling of admiration at the delicious morning air, and pretty coast, milk for breakfast and a general feeling that everybody must rush out of the ship as fast as he can ... Our mess is most pleasant so far as its members are [concerned]. I never met a pleasanter fellow than Jackson the chaplain, his manliness and simple earnestness are most attractive ... He preaches good practical short sermons, and last Sunday there was evening service in the cabins, which few men attended besides the boys and mids who were ordered.

With a change in command, and a new sense of purpose about, the *Hastings* was never going to be the summer cruise that the *Royal William* had been, and the removal of bulkheads – something Goodenough had 'long had an instinctive dread of' – was his first intimation of things ahead. As soon as the ice had broken up in the Gulf of Finland an advance squadron had carried out a reconnaissance of Kronstadt with complete impunity, but the more realistic target for

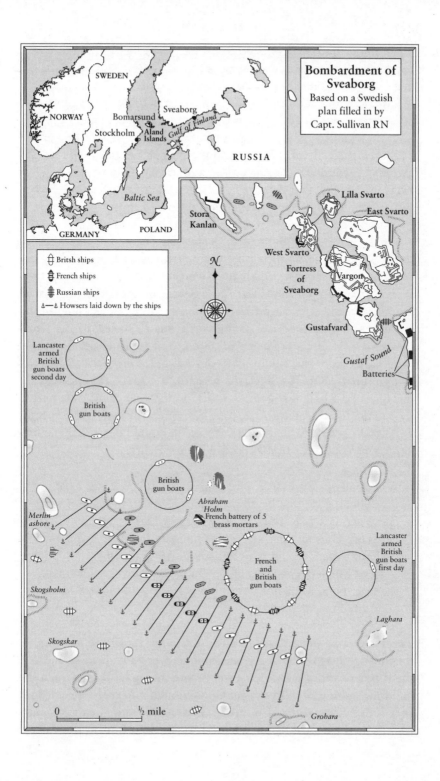

Bombardment of Sveaborg
Based on a Swedish plan filled in by Capt. Sullivan RN

SWEDEN

NORWAY

Bomarsund   Sveaborg

Stockholm   Åland
              Islands   Gulf of Finland

                             RUSSIA

Baltic Sea

GERMANY   POLAND

Lilla Svarto

East Svarto

Stora
Kanlan

West Svarto

Fortress
of
Sveaborg   Vargon

Gustafvard

⊕ Britsh ships
⊜ French ships
⊕ Russian ships
⚓—⚓ Howsers laid down by the ships

𝒩

Gustaf Sound

Batteries

Lancaster
armed
British
gun boats
second day

British
gun boats

British
gun boats

Abraham
Holm
French battery of 5
brass mortars

Merlin
ashore

French
and
British
gun boats

Lancaster
armed
British
gun boats
first day

Skogsholm

Laghara

Skogskar

0   ½ mile

Grohara

the summer had always been Sveaborg, the complex of stone and earthwork batteries guarding the entrance to Helsingfors harbour and dockyards on the northern side of the gulf.

The main defences of Sveaborg were constructed on a tight cluster of five heavily fortified islands, with the narrow channels between them blocked by sunken ships or barred by the broadside guns of anchored men-of-war. The previous summer Captain Sullivan had carefully reconnoitred the position, and it was in almost every detail his plan of attack that Admiral Sir Richard Dundas – Napier's successor in command of the Baltic fleet – prepared to put into action at the end of the first week of August.

On the seventh the Baltic fleet, which had been lying at Nargen on the southern side of the gulf, weighed for Sveaborg, and by the evening of the eighth, when they were joined at anchor by their French allies, preparations were complete. Dundas had brought with him a powerful squadron that included six ships of the line, but as in Sullivan's plan the bulk of the work was to be left to the fleet's mortar vessels, anchored in a shallow crescent at just under four thousand yards from the enemy batteries behind a protective screen of fast gunboats. 'On Tuesday', the seventh, 'I went to try and find the distance of a Russian frigate,' wrote Goodenough of his own part in the meticulous preparations for the bombardment – the mortar vessels had been attached to hawsers so they could be hauled in closer '*au besoin*' – and his first exposure to enemy fire:

> While pulling near I saw a white stake and thinking it was a beacon on a shoal, got some brushwood and tied it on to make it more conspicuous, while I took angles wh shewed the frigate to be 3000 yards off. On sounding we got five fathoms and then pulled away … The Russians thought this rather too strong and fired … 15 shot some of which pitched very close. On the island where I landed … the gigs found a quantity of well flavoured wild raspberries and good sized red currants.

The attack had been scheduled to begin at 2.30 on the morning of the ninth, but with the delays endemic to every allied engagement in the Russian war, it was after seven before the signal flag to open fire and four sighting shells brought Goodenough into real action for the first time. The principal point of assault was the cluster of main islands at the centre of the enemy fortification, but on the eastern

flank of Sveaborg were the batteries of Sandhamn, and it was towards
this heavily fortified and closely supported island that the *Hastings*
and her ship's boats steamed for the attack. '7.25am mortar vessels
etc opened fire,' reads the ship's log:

> 7.27 signal to weigh. 7.44 weighed & proceeded, beat to quar-
> ters. 8.5 opened fire at 2500 yds and edged in towards batteries
> fort guns as they would bear. 8.7 Amphion opened fire. 8.8 Ten
> gun fort on Sandhaven returned fire. 8.16 Four gun fort on Stock-
> holm opened fire. 8.30 Fort on extreme right opened as well as
> other forts to the west. Shot passing over but shell bursting short.
> 9 wore with head to the north and opened fire with starboard guns
> standing along the line of the coast. 10. gun boats 4 in no hove in
> sight between Stockholm & Ertholm & opened fire on us. Shot
> falling short about 50 yds. Turned after 10" gun upon them and
> drove them off. 10.25 main topmast backstay shot away. 10.50
> ceased firing per signal. 11.30 anchored out of range in 12f &
> observed tremendous explosion in Sveaborg as if a magazine had
> blown up.

Throughout the day the gunboats and mortar vessels had kept up an
unprecedented rate of fire, but as the darkness of the short summer's
night fell on Sveaborg, and the fires raging through the defences lit
up the sky, it was the turn of Goodenough to go in close under the
Russian batteries with the rocket boats. They had approached to a
little more than two thousand yards of the Russian frigates moored
in the channel between the island and shore, when – the story of the
rocket from Anatolico to Lucknow –

> a rocket burst … and the tube was rent to pieces. A piece of it struck
> Bowles across the back and a piece of shell of the rocket struck
> Hopkinson inflicting a severe wound on the shoulder blade … The
> men who had rather shirked their work before as the tube was
> unavoidably on the weather side of the boat … nearly threw them-
> selves overboard and it was some few seconds 'ere they recovered
> themselves enough to pick up the wounded men and haul them
> into the Cornwallis.

It was effectively the end of the battle for the *Hastings*, and if the rockets had been as 'wild' and ineffectual as usual, it scarcely mattered, because by nightfall on the tenth Sveaborg was one continuous sheet of flame. Dundas had decided against bombarding Helsingfors in order to minimise civilian casualties, but even so the toll in the forts and batteries was terrible, with the best part of a regiment of a thousand men at Gustafsvard, and an even higher number on the more heavily defended Vargon and Svarto, perishing at the cost of not a single allied dead.

If the naval attack on Sevastopol would have had Hastings turning in his grave, this destruction of Sveaborg on the Gulf of Finland, along with the attacks on Kinburn and Odessa in the Black Sea, had been the justification of everything he had preached on the conjunction of massive firepower and steam mobility. It also reinforced the pre-eminence of the Royal Navy as an instrument of foreign policy. There had been no fleet-to-fleet action of the kind that the public and the captains craved, but the destruction of Russian fortresses, the invisibility of Russian fleets, the unchallenged domination of Russian waters, the disruption of Russia's trade and the promiscuous liberties which British ships could take along an enemy coast had demonstrated the power of the Royal Navy as categorically as the more glamorous actions of the Napoleonic Wars had done.

Between the bombardment of Sveaborg and an assault on Kronstadt planned for 1856 fell the Treaty of Paris, and Goodenough's war was over. It was a war, too, that ended for him as bathetically as it had begun. On 13 August 1855 the *Hastings* weighed for the Nargen Roads, and five weeks later struck on one of those Baltic sandbanks that had given Sir Charles Napier such nameless fears. It took two days to float the sessel off, and it was only after jettisoning coal and hoisting off the ship's guns that the *Hastings* was able to limp back to The Nore with a badly damaged keel. For his part in the attack on Sveaborg, though, Goodenough had been gazetted, and he had already made the kind of impression he was to repeat throughout his career. 'He was always my friend and counsellor in every scheme for the good of the junior officers and crew,' the ship's chaplain recalled – no glimmer of contradiction in sight.

> He was genial, kind, and sympathetic, and would help me at all times to gain the end I had in view, without violating ship's rules and naval discipline. He supported me in introducing the celebra-

tion of the Lord's Supper, then almost an unknown thing on board a ship. By all of us he was much beloved, and though a strict officer, and very particular in matters of duty, he was known to be so conscientious and scrupulous about doing his own work thoroughly, that all admired and many emulated his high tone of doing everything as unto God and man.

Twenty years have passed since then, but I have the impression still very distinct that I never met in my naval career one whose religious feeling impressed me so deeply, or any one of whom I felt more sure that if life should be spared he would rise to greatness in his profession.

IV

With the benefit of twenty years of hindsight, and the noise and eulogies surrounding his hero's death on Santa Cruz, the *Hastings*'s chaplain might confidently have predicted greatness for the young Goodenough, but to the man himself in the spring of 1856 it cannot have been quite so obvious. During the summer he had spent in the Baltic his mother had died of TB in Spain, and the appointment to his first command in February 1856 – the two-gun, sixty-horsepower screw steam gunboat *Goshawk* – is unlikely to have given him any inflated sense of the prospects of a junior naval lieutenant without either family or wider 'interest' to support him.

A collision with the mercantile brig *Dove,* and a strong reprimand for 'want of care and mismanagement', can have done little to add to his confidence, but as he took the *Goshawk* into the Channel for the Great St George's Day Review to celebrate victory over Russia the future must at least have seemed rosy for the service itself. Among the younger captains like Peel there was still no shortage of muttering against the dead weight of age and incompetence at the Admiralty, but for the public at large the sight of six miles of warships crowding the Solent, and the first ever night illumination of the fleet, was all the proof it could possibly want that Victoria's navy was everything it had ever been.

With the Alland Islands demilitarised by the terms of the treaty, in fact, the fortifications of Sevastopol demolished, Russian warships excluded from the Black Sea and France an ally, the only real problem facing the navy lay in finding itself a worthy opponent. Throughout the period piracy and the slave trade could always provide a risky source of opportunity for a young officer, but in 1856 – a year after the effective end of the war with Russia, and a year before the Indian Mutiny gave it something else to think about – deteriorating relations with China seemed to offer an expectant nation the solitary hope of one of those major victories that, forty years on, the Poet Laureate Alfred Austin would sit in his English garden and dream of.

For one man in particular, the noisily flamboyant, heavy-drinking, newly appointed Commodore Henry Keppel, sixth son of the 4th Earl of Albemarle, grandson of the 20th Lord de Clifford, and second-in-command on the China station, the coming war might have been made in heaven. For the best part of 150 years the Keppels had played a leading role in British naval and military history, and Harry Keppel was to the manner born, inheriting from his ancestor, the 1st Earl – who had come over with 'Dutch William' – all the geniality and charm that went with the fighting genes that had taken the various Keppels to Oudenarde, Ramillies, Dettingen, Culloden or Quiberon Bay.

On 4 September 1856 Keppel had watched his broad pennant being hauled up by the Raleigh's boatswain's wife – 'good-looking woman, ought to bring luck' – but the arrival of James Goodenough from the Goshawk as his new First Lieutenant suggested that he had left little else to chance. Over the previous thirty-three years Keppel had made a formidable and noisy reputation as a fighting sailor, and if the Raleigh's officers and midshipmen were a set made in his own aristocratic image – Lord Charles Scott, Hon. Victor Montagu, Lord Gillford (the future 4th Earl of Clanwilliam), Victor Ferdinand Franz Eugen Gustaf Adolf Constantin Friedrich, Prince of Hohenlohe-Langenberg and son of a half-sister to Queen Victoria – there were enough serious professional men among them to make the son of a Dean and headmaster feel immediately at home.

As a veteran of innumerable boat actions against pirates, of the Baltic campaign and the Black Sea, where he had succeeded Stephen Lushington in command of the Naval Brigade, Keppel knew what he was talking about when he said that 'a finer crew never left a port', and for a while even his faith in the boatswain's good-looking wife looked well-placed. The Raleigh had weighed for the Far East on 19 November, and after a rapid passage via the Cape had just made land to the south of Macao, when shortly after noon on 14 April 1857 – just as Keppel was finishing signing returns for the day – he was stopped by a sudden, juddering thud as if the *Raleigh* 'had struck some floating timber'. 'We were heading up for Hong Kong and twenty five miles from it, when we felt a heavy shock,' wrote Goodenough, in his cabin working on his journal as she struck. 'I just said, "there, she is on shore this time at all events," took my cap and went on deck where I met a crowd of pale enquiring faces ... Smith, the gunner's mate was close to & said with a long face, "ah, she gave an awful blow just under our mess." All the men about were looking fearfully about & so I merely said aloud. "Ah! She'll stand many another blow like that" & turned aft to the binnacle.'

Goodenough was over-optimistic – they had hit a submerged rock, not wood – and going below again 'jumped into the gloryhole' to find the inner planking started over an area eight feet by four, and the water pouring in. It was soon clear that the damage was too extensive for even temporary repair, and while one watch was detailed off to man the pumps and the other to work the ship, Goodenough supervised the preparation of an improvised collision blanket to be thrown over the bow.

With the water gaining fast on the pumps, and the ship still twenty-five miles from Hong Kong, Keppel was worried this would stop her dead, and ordering the guns to be taken aft, the ensign to be hoisted Union flag downwards, and minute guns to be fired, conned the ship himself through a maze of shoals and tiny islands towards the relative safety of a sandbank. 'After a while, from the hammock netting where I stood,' recalled Keppel – never one to allow a matter of tedious fact to get in the way of a good story,

> a ship at anchor off Macao was seen. With a glass we made her out to be a frigate flying the French Admiral's flag. The first lieutenant was ordered to lower fore royal, hoist French flag and fire a salute ...
>
> The frigate was the *Virginie* carrying the flag of Rear-Admiral Guerin, who came himself to see how he could help us. His officer met him at the gangway and without delay explained what had happened. The gallant Guerin no longer thought of nationalities. He embraced and kissed me, exclaiming, 'C'est Magnifique! A British frigate saluting the French flag while sinking!'

Help had arrived just in time. 'In the three hours and a quarter between striking the rock and taking the ground she had made ten feet of water against all our endeavours,' Goodenough wrote rather more soberly. 'This had deepened her till she drew twenty-six feet of water, and as we were in only eighteen feet, she appeared pretty safe. Five minutes afterwards the Commodore sent for me to assist in speaking to the French Flag Lieutenant who had come on board, and told me to go to the French Admiral, ask for the Catinat steamer to take me to Hong-Kong and there tell the Admiral what had happened and ask for assistance.'

It took Goodenough the rest of the day to track down the Admiral, who seems to have been ashore rather than embracing Keppel, but by three the next morning he was at Hong Kong reporting to Sir Michael Seymour, and by four that afternoon was back again with assistance. 'I could not believe my senses,' he continued, when he saw what twenty-four hours on the sandbank had done to the *Raleigh*.

> She had sunk in the mud up to her main-deck guns, and I could see no one moving on board. I found the Commodore on board, his secretary, the chaplain, a guard of marines, and a boat's crew. They told me that on the night that I left she began to settle in the mud, and at seven o'clock the water came up on the lower deck. The men took their clothes and mess-traps on the main deck, and the officers' things were moved out of their cabins into the Commodore's. My old servant and my boy worked nobly, and saved nearly everything for me, except some books. At eleven the water was over the lower deck.

It was the end of the *Raleigh*, and while Keppel – generously supplied with eggs, bread, cooked fowl and 'some uncommon good claret' by the French – presided over the last rites from a raised platform above the bridge, everything that could be salvaged from the ship was taken on shore at Koko Island. During the next hours and days much of the work and responsibility again devolved on Goodenough as First Lieutenant, but by the sixteenth Seymour himself had arrived, and two days later, while Chinese divers continued retrieval operations in the stricken hulk, the first 338 of the *Raleigh*'s crew were transferred for transport to Hong Kong.

It would be impossible to tell from Keppel's own jaunty memoirs whether the fact that none of his men or none of his Madeira was lost was cause for the greater satisfaction, but it meant the breaking up of a ship's company that in the long passage out had found a strong common identity. During his early years Goodenough was lucky enough to serve under some outstanding commanders, but whether because of Keppel's infectious enthusiasm or the shared trauma of the ship's loss, there always remained as strong a bond between 'Raleighs' who found themselves together in other ships as there was between old 'Collingwoods' who had sailed on her one Pacific voyage.

The break-up of the *Raleigh*'s company was a particular disappointment to Goodenough, too, because during the voyage from England hostilities had again broken out with China. The immediate cause of a conflict known as the '*Arrow* War' was the impounding of a merchant vessel – the *Arrow* – carrying the British flag at Canton, but like so many bad wars its deeper historical origins lay in the unfinished business of a previous conflict and the unjust peace that the victor had forced on a helpless enemy.

The First Opium War was as shameful as any Britain has fought, and was concluded with a peace that did her as little credit. In 1839 Palmerston had taken Britain to war in the name of trade, and by the terms of the 1842 Treaty of Nanking China was compelled to open five ports – Canton, Amoy, Foochow, Ningpo and Shanghai – to foreigners, and concede Britain the rights to consular representation at each of them.

Even with the addition of a punitive indemnity and the secession of Hong Kong, there was never any more chance that these terms would satisfy British merchants than that the Chinese would comply with them, and with piracy rife, and real and imagined slights constant, the *Arrow* War was a conflict that could have broken out at any time in the fifteen years since the treaty was signed. It might have been better for Britain's international standing if she had found some more plausible pretext for war than the dubious status of a Chinese-owned *lorcha*, but for the acting consul on the spot, the young, intensely religious Imperial *devot* Harry Parkes, and Sir John Bowring, Benthamite reformer, ardent philhellene and radical turned Governor of Hong Kong, any excuse that meant they could tackle the wider question of Canton's 'open' status was good enough.

The Treaty of Nanking was open to varying interpretations, and the most contentious of these concerned the status of Canton, the one port in the years before the First Opium War open to foreign merchants. The British trading interest naturally wanted full and free access to the city itself, but in a characteristic masterpiece of stonewall diplomacy, the Chinese had pleaded the implacable and uncontrollable hostility of their people as an excuse for restricting foreign merchants to the narrow and uncomfortable strip of land, warehouses and extemporised dwelling places sandwiched between the walls and the river and known as the 'Factories'.

This festering grievance was bad enough in itself, but it became doubly so when all negotiations had to be conducted with one of the great hate-figures of Victorian imperialism, the formidable and repellent Imperial Commissioner for Foreign Affairs, Yeh Ming-Chen. Over the previous two years Yeh had executed more than 70,000 rebels in his province, but if an average working day might end with a hundred heads littering the execution grounds of Canton as proof of his domestic zeal, it was, as one American put it, in 'his insane and insufferable conduct towards foreigners ... that His Excellency Yeh [stood] alone and pre-eminent'.

The difficulties of dealing with such a man were further compounded by the fact that it had to be done at a distance, but with his vast girth, his hugely fat neck and face, his steeply receding forehead, protruding jaw, rotten teeth and eyes that inspired a 'feeling of repulsion' that familiarity could never deaden, 'invisibility' was perhaps not entirely a bad thing. 'No one can look upon that face without feeling that he is in the presence of an extraordinary man,' the *Times* correspondent, who would have all the leisure of a ship's voyage together to observe him, wrote. 'There is a ferocity about that restless roving eye which makes you shrink from it. It is the expression of a fierce and angry but not courageous animal – while the long nails of his dirty fingers are trembling upon the table, and his eyes are ranging into every part of the room in search of every face, his pose of dignity is too palpably simulated to inspire respect even if you could forget his deeds. But no one can look upon him with contempt.'

Yeh had in fact responded to British demands for satisfaction over the *Arrow* incident with every show of reasonableness, but with Parkes and Bowring determined to make open access to Canton an inseparable part of any settlement, hostilities became inevitable. In the early months of the standoff the British forces did not have the strength to hold the city even if they could take it, but on 23 October 1856, three weeks before the *Raleigh* and Goodenough weighed for the East, Sir Michael Seymour had led an expedition up the approaches to Canton, and captured or destroyed a number of forts and war junks before finally bombarding the city itself.

It could be no more than a gesture – Yeh was contemptuous enough of threats or blockades to offer a sliding-scale bounty on British heads – but there seemed little Palmerston's unenthusiastic government could do to halt the conflict without seriously prejudicing British influence in the East. The distance between Hong Kong and London meant that it had always been Parkes's and Bowring's war, but a practical sense of its wider responsibilities to Britain's representatives left a vulnerable government with little option other than to endorse demands it had never initiated and face the inevitable backlash at home. 'Never will England stand higher in the world's estimation,' a hostile Lord John Russell told the Commons, when in the wake of a narrow government victory in the Lords at the end of February 1857, the great Anti-Corn Law League campaigner and anti-interventionist Richard Cobden – that old ally of Bowring's in many a radical cause – introduced a resolution demanding an explanation of British aggression against China,

> than when it can be said that though troublesome and meddlesome officials prostitute her arms and induce a brave admiral to commence hostilities which ought never to have been begun, yet the House of Commons, representing her people, have indignantly declared that they will be no parties to such injustice; and that neither for commercial advantages nor for political advantages, nor for any other immediate advantages to their country, will they consent to stain that honour which, after all, has been and must be the sure foundation of her greatness.

A speech of towering moral grandeur from the half-mad Gladstone, and an unusually thoughtful contribution from Disraeli, were more than an ailing Palmerston could combat, but before anyone on the China station could learn of the government's defeat, a general election and British public opinion had come to the war party's rescue. 'An insolent barbarian wielding authority at Canton has violated the British flag,' 'old Pummice-stone' – back to his best fighting form again and sure as ever of 'John Bull' – had told the Tiverton voters, 'broken the engagements of treaties, offered rewards for the heads of British subjects in that part of China, and planned their destruction by murder, assassinations and poisons.'

The consequence of Palmerston's victory was not just to prolong the war against China, but effectively to extend its scope beyond anything either Bowring or Parkes had imagined. In their negotiations with Yeh the two men had never really looked any farther than Canton for satisfaction, but when in April 1857 the government despatched Lord Elgin as a special plenipotentiary it was with express instructions to base any future peace on the regularisation of British diplomatic and trading relations on terms of equality and guaranteed access to Peking.

If the despatch of Lord Elgin for the mouth of the Peiho River – traditional gateway for foreigners to China's capital – was unlikely to rob Keppel and Goodenough of their war, it was still a relief that Bowring's and Seymour's fixation on Canton and Yeh guaranteed that they would not have to wait for his arrival to see their first action. By the end of May all the stores that could be saved from the wreck of the *Raleigh* had been salvaged, and with a court martial exonerating her commodore and officers of any blame for her loss, 'the time had arrived', as Keppel grandly put it – as though the whole war had simply been awaiting his arrival to start in earnest – 'for the destruction of the Chinese fleet' in the Canton River.

It was more than sixty miles upriver to Canton, and with its innumerable shallows and mudbanks, its fortified islands and heavily armed shore batteries, its creeks, channels and difficult tides, the burden of any fighting in its waterways inevitably fell to the tenders, gunboats and ships' boats. During the previous autumn Sir Michael Seymour's small craft had distinguished themselves in innumerable actions against war junks, and with the force he had gathered by the end of May he at last had the numbers and the firepower for an attack on the formidable enemy fleet assembled in the Fatshan Creek.

There was a successful rehearsal against a powerful Chinese force on 25 May at the entrance to Escape Creek, and over the last days of May a fleet of eleven gunboats, fifty-odd ships' boats and two thousand men under Seymour assembled for the assault. 'All the Captains and Commanders were with their men,' wrote Yonge, as partisan as ever,

> and yet, large as the force was, to any one who did not know what English seamen could do, it might well have seemed too small for the work before it; for the enemy against whom it was advancing far exceeded it in numbers, and far more in apparent power and all

the appliances of war. Above six thousand carefully picked sailors and warriors manned eighty junks, the smallest of which was above double the size of those that had been destroyed in the preceding week; and their armament amounted to above eight hundred guns, many of them being 32-pounders of European manufacture.

The enemy had taken up an immensely strong defensive position, with their war junks, posted in two divisions and defended by fortresses on either bank of the creek, drawn up side by side to command the stream at a point where its channel is divided by a long, low island some three miles from the main river. There had been some hope on the British side that a night attack might at least give them the advantage of surprise, but for once in the war the Chinese had not been complacent about the barbarians, and as Sir George Seymour's *Coromandel* nosed into the creek in the early hours of 1 June a barrage of gunfire and signal rockets from the shore batteries told him that they were expected.

Immediately behind the *Coromandel* was the *Hong Kong*, a hired paddle steamer placed under the command of James Goodenough, and awaiting him an enemy and a kind of warfare that was utterly alien to anything in his experience. For those in the *Calcutta* boats it might all have been familiar enough by now, but in the clash of gongs and the beat of tom-toms, the hail of round shot, grape, canister and nails, the flying streamers and banners, the boarding nets and the smell of 'stink-pots', East met West with a colour and din that was worlds away from the Baltic or anything that Goodenough or most of the 'Raleighs' had ever seen before.

There was the river to contend with, too, because while Seymour had been wise to time his attack for dead low water, trapping the junks where they were and enabling any grounded boats of his own to refloat on the rising tide, this immediately brought its problems. 'All Sunday [Sir Michael preferred not to fight on the Sabbath] I was running up and down the river on various duties,' Goodenough, bearing the Commodore's pennant in *Hong Kong*, wrote,

and on Monday, at half-past four in the morning, weighed to go into action, to take some junks anchored in the Fatshan Creek ... The junks were protected by a fort and this was first stormed by Captain Elliot after a small resistance. We then advanced on the junks with four other gunboats, towing all the boats of the squadron, silenced a four gun battery on our way, and were just within range when we got onshore. Can you conceive anything more disappointing? The Commodore, who had his pendant in me, jumped into his boat, and away went all the boats to the attack. The other gunboats passed me, and I felt thoroughly sold.

If Goodenough felt cheated, Keppel was in his element, and as the first division of junks fell to the attackers he pressed on up the creek as fast as he could go. It was 'as pretty a boat action as can be imagined', he wrote with his usual disarming brag to his sister Mary.

> From the heights the Fatshan Creek affair must have been a beautiful sight. My broad pennant was hoisted on board the *Hong-Kong*. The shallow water caused her to ground; she would otherwise have been in front. Took with me Prince Victor of Hohenlohe, having previously been commanded by Her Majesty, through Sir Charles Phipps, to take care of him, and left Victor Montagu, my proper gig's mid, on board; but the lifting tide soon put him in the midst. We took the lead. The first division of the Chinese were attacked simultaneously by about 1900 men. I had not more than a quarter of that number to attack the second division, which was three miles higher up the river in a well-selected place, evidently the *elite* of their fleet. The junks numbered twenty in one compact row, mounting about fourteen guns each, removed to the side near us, those in the stern and bow being heavy 32-pounders ... Nearly the first poor fellow cut in two by a round shot was an amateur, Major Kearney, whom I had known many years. We cheered, and were trying to get to the front when a shot struck our boat, killing the bowman. Another was cut in two. A third shot took another's arm off.

Though one would not guess it from his account, this second Chinese squadron had come as a surprise to Keppel, but while his attack was faltering, Goodenough had succeeded in bringing up the *Hong Kong* past the other stranded gunboats in support. 'The boats had pulled on after the capture of the first body of junks,' Goodenough continued his account, after again extricating himself from the mud,

> ... and ignorant of the existence of these twenty, in front of whom three or four light leading boats suddenly found themselves at a turn of the river ... A round shot struck the Commodore's galley, and she began to fill. He stepped on the thwart to keep dry till another boat came up, and another shot passed under his feet and went through the bottom of the boat. Victor was with him, binding the stump of a fine young Isle of Wight man's arm. Another man had both his legs taken off, and two others were wounded as

she sank from under them. The Commodore called out to save his pendant, and stepped into Captain Tourneur's cutter, shaking his fist at the junks, promising to pay them out for this in the afternoon. Graham, close to me in the pinnace, had his jacket riddled by grape, and his legs blackened by the wind of a round shot. Two men's heads were taken off by his side, and the blood from their poor trunks literally covered him; three or four more were wounded in his boat, and the Commodore was persuaded to retire and reform.

While the small boats dropped to safety astern of the *Hong Kong*, Goodenough was left entirely exposed, forbidden to advance and a sitting target for an enemy who had got his range. Within moments one of his crew had lost a leg and his boat had been hulled a dozen times, and for the next half-hour he remained where he was, exchanging shot with the war junks while he prayed indifferently for the reappearance of Keppel or the first sign of a crack in the enemy's resolution. 'At this moment,' Keppel himself wrote, as he drew up again alongside the *Hong Kong* with his flotilla of small boats,

there arose from the boats, as if every man took it up at the same instant, one of those British cheers, so full of meaning, that I knew it was all up with John Chinaman. They might sink twenty boats, but there were thirty others who would go ahead all the faster. It was indeed an exciting sight. A move among the junks! They were breaking ground and moving off, the outer most first. This the Chinese performed in good order, without slacking fire. Then commenced an exciting chase for seven miles. As our shot told they ran mostly on the mud banks, and their crews forsook them ... Seventeen junks were overtaken and captured. Three only escaped. Before this last chase my poor Spurrier was shot down. I saw his bowels protruding, with my binoculars in the middle, as he lay at the bottom of the boat, holding my hand. He asked if there was any hope. I could only say, 'Where there is life there is hope,' but I had none!

Spurrier did – astonishingly – survive, but as Goodenough broke off the chase in the shallow waters of the creek and returned to the main stream of the river, there was no escaping the cost of victory. 'I had received many more wounded, nearly all very badly so, and so I was ordered to take them straight to Hong Kong at once, and passed a horrid night on the bridge,' he wrote. 'Put the sick on board the hospital ship at seven in the morning; coaled, watered, and started again at six in the evening, passed another night on the bridge, piloting the ship, and reported myself to the Admiral at nine o'clock the next morning. I never was so beat in all my life. All the way down I had the ringing of shot in my ears, and the groans of a poor fellow with half his skull fractured and carried away.'

It seems to have done nothing to dent his enthusiasm, and four weeks later he was gazetted for capturing a pirate junk – 'a very pretty boat of four guns ... like the plates of Venetian galleys' – while under the command of the ambitious and violent-tempered veteran of the North-West Passage, Sir Robert McClure. It was the first of two occasions within as many months that Goodenough would be singled out, and at the end of September he was given command of the gunboat *Bittern* before transferring in the middle of October as Second Lieutenant to Sir Michael Seymour's flagship, *Calcutta*.

The timing was opportune, because after a diversion to India in William Peel's *Shannon* on the outbreak of the Mutiny, Elgin was at last in China to give his reluctant authorisation for the capture of Canton. At the beginning of December the usual ultimatums were issued to Yeh, and when these were met with the usual prevarications British and French squadrons – France had been drawn into the war by the barbarous murder of a French missionary – occupied the nearby islands and prepared for a bombardment and landing.

If Yeh had been less complacent or indolent about blocking the river, or offering any obstruction to allied preparations whatsoever, the city should have been impregnable, and even as it was it represented a formidable challenge. The great advantage the allies enjoyed lay in the naval firepower they could bring to bear, yet with a garrison of 30,000 troops and a population of one and a half million secure within six heavily fortified miles of walls, Canton still ought to have been able to withstand an enemy of fewer than six thousand men. '28th. [twenty-seventh in fact] Fancy what I have been doing for the last two days,' Goodenough wrote home, after a bizarre limbo of a week ashore ahead of the bombardment and assault:

Bill-sticking! I have been with H. Parkes, the consul, sticking bills up in Chinese, within 150 yards of the walls, telling the people that we begin to fire to-morrow, and that the city will be ours. We call on the good citizens to assist us, when we shall be in possession, to maintain order and to keep up the police of their districts. The people pressed round to get the proclamation, and eagerly joking and talking to Parkes. At one place we stuck them up on a triumphal arch, created in honour of our having been kept so long out of the city ... We shall not be engaged for two days; we scale the wall which is twenty feet wide, and go along it till we reach a gate which we open for artillery, and then wait for orders. I do not expect fighting till we enter the city.

On 28 December the bombardment at last began, and as the guns from the boats and island batteries kept up a ceaseless fire against the walls and outlying fortifications, the allied force spread out unchallenged across the ground to the east of the city and settled down to wait for morning. 'We sailors thought that the most honourable position of the day was given by the Admiral to the Calcutta's guns,' recalled one old bluejacket as, sword in hand, eyes momentarily closed in prayer, 'Holy Joe' Goodenough – as those 'not afraid to speak evil of dignities' called him – took his place at the head of the sixty men and five guns under his command. 'We were placed in front of 4,000 marines, stretched out on a beautiful plain in three long lines, before two forts on hills outside the city, and when the bugles sounded the advance we scoured along the plain in front of all and scaled the wall with ladders, some getting through one of the gates – curious gates those eastern cities have – and dragging our guns after us.'

The Linn Fort – the first object for the Naval Brigade – was soon taken and, with scaling ladders up and – shades of the Crimea – the French first onto the walls, Canton was doomed. By 9 o'clock in the morning of the twenty-ninth the perimeter was securely in allied hands, and though the teeming city within was too big and dangerous to occupy, the fighting was effectively over, leaving a ring of allied guns and men staring down from the broad walls onto an eerily mute Canton.

It had gone more smoothly than Elgin, who had finally arrived in Hong Kong on 20 September, could ever have hoped, and the bloodiest fighting had taken place outside the city walls, when a fierce counterattack by Tartar troops briefly threatened to turn the allied right where Goodenough and the one gun he still had with him were positioned. 'I have often read with admiration the story of Gideon and his 300 chosen Israelites,' the same bluejacket, equally happy to see Tartar or Midianite fall before 'the sword of the Lord', wrote of this action.

> Comparing small things with greater, I have often thought this brush at Canton was of that ilk ... The Chinese came trotting up the hill, waving flags, &c, and we had expended every shot and shell with the exception of three rounds of canister, with one of which our gun was loaded. After the discharge, the rush at the foe was made, Lieutenant Goodenough, singling out a big Tartar Mandarin. While fighting with him his field-glass, which was slung round his neck, got in the way, and by sheer strength he broke the leather strap and flung it away. When the enemy were scared away we sought for and obtained it again. There was a tall tartar soldier who had a wound in his thigh. Lieutenant Goodenough, I remember well, poured the contents of his water-bottle in his mouth. That man's look was reward for all the self-denial; if a painter could have painted such a look it would have created a sensation.

Old Testament or New? – Gideon was rather closer to Yeh than to Goodenough in the way he treated captured enemies, but as the allies settled down to govern the city through the existing authorities and Yeh was packed off to Calcutta as a prisoner, humanity and common sense alike counselled moderation. Goodenough was always 'a good example to me', one officer wrote of his influence over these next days, a tense time when looting might at any moment destroy the fragile calm of Canton. 'During the excitement of operations before the enemy ... I have often seen him exercise his influence in checking licences occasioned by the inexperience of young hands, unaccustomed to victory, and commended afterwards by the older and superior bystanders.'

With the Hong Kong merchants, and even London, railing against Elgin's leniency, and negotiations with Peking faltering, it was only a matter of time before hostilities were resumed. Goodenough's services in front of Canton had won him immediate promotion to Commander – confirmed by the Admiralty and backdated to the fall of the city – and on 25 March 1858, after what seemed to the exasperated Elgin a criminal delay, Sir Michael Seymour's *Calcutta* with its new commander weighed for the Peiho River in the north to enforce Britain's treaty demands. 'Nothing to do but meditate on the

folly of this charming colleague my admiral,' Elgin wrote, as he sat
out the vicious squalls of the gulf and waited for the gunboats he had
been promised for over a month to arrive. 'He must be in his dotage.
It is stupidity beyond anything I have ever met with in my public
career ... I have a perfect driveller for an admiral, a general not much
better, a sot for a commodore, and an old woman for the second in
command up here ... I am like a person in a bad dream.'

For Goodenough it was more like waking from a bad dream. 'At
sea at last, in real truth,' he wrote, free of the channels and mudbanks
of the Canton River and of the interminable delays: 'for the first few
days it gave me an inexpressible feeling of relief to feel the ship
moving under me, to be able to look round without seeing that horrible Victorian peak over one's head. The north-east monsoon is not
yet over, so we are beating up, and in our zig-zag course have sighted
'Lurzon' various islands with grassy knolls and ravines, full of dark
scrubby trees, and to-day we are in sight of the north-end of
Formosa.'

For a man like Goodenough everything was of interest, yet there
was something about the Chinese landscape that seemed to fail his
very Victorian moral and poetic aesthetic. 'How I envy any one even
of your fellow-travellers in Italy,' he wrote to his family, travelling
through Europe as another old shipmate of his made his last, jolting
journey in a doolie down from Lucknow.

> The scenes and climate, and, above all, the associations must be
> delightful. This country is totally wanting in the last. There are no
> scenes one remembers with interest, no people who have spirited,
> free, or gentle natures to give one an *intérêt de Coeur*. The little one
> knows of the past history here excites no interest or reverence ...
> The country ... is pretty and varied, but never gets beyond the
> *petitesse* of the willow pattern. Does not this account to you for
> their cramped, dwarfed style of art? They have nothing that is really
> stupendous or magnificent to set against the work of their own
> hands – dykes and canals – which are stupendous as works of
> human labour, and in their intense self-love they prefer to portray
> the quaint, grotesque weavings of their own fancies to copying the
> beauties of nature, or rather of God's hand.

The canals and fields might have failed the Wordsworth test, but there was as little sign of willow pattern as there was of the hand of God waiting for them at the mouth of the Peiho River when the *Calcutta* finally dropped anchor off the Taku forts at the end of April. A long bar out to sea prevented the approach of anything bigger than a gunboat, but even the most cursory examination would have revealed what lay ahead, with a continuous and brutish line of earthworks, batteries and parapets stretching along both banks of the river for the best part of a mile.

And with a strong boom of spars, chains and hawsers thrown across the entrance to the river, stakes driven into the banks to impede any attempt at an allied landing, a newly arrived Tartar encampment in the rear, and the muzzles of 136 large guns covering the approaches, it was clear that there had been a method to Chinese diplomacy. 'The lessons taught by the campaign on the Chukiang [Canton] had, however, not been lost on the British Admiral,' Yonge wrote, smoothly skating over the dilatoriness of Seymour that had reduced Elgin to such a fury of impatience.

> He was confident in his own skill and the discipline and courage of his followers and allies as amply sufficient to counterbalance even greater odds than those to which he was now opposed. He even felt that there was some advantage in the length of time that had been afforded to the Chinese to complete their preparations for defence; since it would only make their discomfort more signal, and impress upon them a deeper sense of our invincibility than they would have felt, could they have made the excuse to themselves that they had been in any degree taken by surprise.

His confidence was infectious, and on the night of the nineteenth the storming parties held 'a jovial party ... to wish success to the under-taking'. The following morning Seymour and the French Commander-in-Chief hoisted their flags together on the *Slaney*, and at a few minutes after ten ordered their fleet into action. 'The boom,' recalled William Kennedy, a young and recklessly brave lieutenant in the *Calcutta* in command of one of the landing parties along with Goodenough,

> ... was sufficiently strong to keep out boats or junks, but not a steam vessel going at high speed. The *Cormorant*, Commander Saumarez, led the way in gallant style, snapping the chain like

thread. The forts opened fire on her as she passed the barrier; but
no shot was fired in reply till the Admiral made the signal to
'engage,' when each vessel hoisted a yellow flag at the mast-head,
and the action commenced.

   The *Cormorant* was followed by a French gunboat, then by one
of ours, then another Frenchman, and so on alternately. As each
vessel passed the narrows where the boom had been she received
a heavy fire, as the Chinamen had concentrated their guns on that
spot, and did not seem able to fire in any other direction ... It was
a lovely sight, the little gunboats making excellent practice, bursting their shells over the parapets and in the embrasures. The Chinamen stuck to their guns well, and returned the fire with spirit,
hulling each vessel repeatedly as she entered the river; but once
inside, they turned their attention to the next.

'For some time,' as Yonge wrote, 'nothing was seen but the smoke,
nothing was heard but the roar of such a cannonade as the Peiho had
never yet re-echoed in the two thousand years' since the Chinese had
invented gunpowder. For over an hour the forts gave as good as they
got, but as the earthworks literally began to crumble under 'the terrible hail which was poured upon them', their batteries at last fell silent.
'The boats were then ordered to land the storming-parties,' Kennedy
continued:

   we were put ashore in a paddy-field, where we sank up to our knees
   in mud, and having formed our men in as good order as we could,
   we rushed the forts. Fortunately for us, the Chinamen no sooner
   saw us coming than they bolted, the mandarins leading the way on
   horseback. The head mandarin was struck by a bullet and fell off
   his horse, and before we could come up to him to take him prisoner he drew his sword and cut his throat from ear to ear, and fell
   back dead in the mud. In a few minutes from the time of the landing the forts were in our possession, and the English and French
   flags were floating from the parapets.

With the fall of the Taku forts, the way was open to Tientsin, sixty
miles up the winding and uncharted Peiho River. 'The river was full
of large junks,' Goodenough reported home, after making the slow,
tense journey up to Tientsin in the *Coromandel,*

which had brought and discharged grain from the southern provinces. As the mandarins might at any moment set them on fire, and send them on top of us or sink them to block up the river, we turned them out ... On arriving at Tientsin we found a white flag flying; soon two deputations of merchants and tradesmen came off with petitions, setting forth that they had heard that the ship of our honourable nation being refused leave to enter the river, had come in by force. Now had we come to trade or to make war?

It was a good question, but until the arrival of Lord Elgin it was one to which no one was quite sure of the answer. In his decent, liberal way Elgin genuinely had the interests of the Chinese people at heart, but his less sensitive henchmen were never going to allow anything so woolly to impinge on negotiations conducted from such an overwhelming position of strength. 'On June 26,' Goodenough's shipmate, Lieutenant Kennedy, recorded of the final peace ceremony, conducted in the brilliantly decked out joss-house – temple – of the 'Supreme Felicity',

> Lord Elgin arranged to meet the Chinese commissioners to sign a Treaty of Peace ... Having donned our full uniform, we joined the procession, his Excellency Lord Elgin leading the way in a sedan chair followed by the Admiral, his staff and the rest of the officers. The ship's band and marines accompanied us, and everything was done to make the ceremony as imposing as possible. On arriving at a joss-house, Lord Elgin was received with a guard of honour and a burst of Chinese music. We were shown into a room illuminated with Chinese lanterns. Three tables were arranged side by side. Lord Elgin took his seat in the centre, the Admiral and the highest mandarin on the right, the second highest mandarin on the left. These two officers were said to be the highest in the empire, and wore the pink opaque button, denoting their rank.
>
> The ceremony occupied a very short time, after which tea and cakes were handed round, the band struck up 'God save the Queen!' and the treaty of peace with China was concluded.

It was a treaty that gave the West – including the Russians and Americans, who for all their *faux* high-mindedness stood to gain equally from every concession conceded to the British – everything that it demanded, but whether it was a 'peace' was another matter. The sticking point throughout the negotiations had been the foreign right of access to Peking, but while Elgin had stood firm on that to come away with an agreement that trebled the trading ports, guaranteed the rights of Christian missionaries, opened the city of Canton, extended the right of travel to the interior, legalised the opium trade and secured indemnities for the original 'outrage' suffered by the British merchant community, the year's gap scheduled between signature and actual ratification left every opportunity for the kind of misunderstandings, duplicities and imagined slights that had sparked the war in the first place.

Those problems, though, were no longer Seymour's or indeed Elgin's, he having left the ratification process to his brother. With hostilities seemingly over, temperatures on the Peiho regularly touching 110 degrees, the smallest exertion virtually impossible until evening, and fever and sunstroke rampant, Goodenough was not the only one who had had enough of China. They were not home yet, though. After one, more congenial diplomatic mission to Nagasaki in the *Calcutta*, the first line-of-battle ship to visit the city, the hazards of the Peiho were exchanged for those of Hong Kong – '*Mihi Hodie, Tibi Cras*' (Me Today, You Tomorrow) read the cheerfully prophetic inscription over the gateway to the Happy Valley cemetery – and the stifling inertia of colony life. '2 November', reads one note in the *Calcutta*'s captain's hand – and when it comes to boredom, a ship's log never lies:

> found Lt the Hon JB Vivian asleep under the poop when in charge of the watch … Reprimanded to be more careful in the future …
>
> 21 Jan In consequence of it having come to the Captain's knowledge that the Ship's Company are in the habit of selling, bartering and trafficking grog with the knowledge & consent of the petty officers … the Petty Officers' mess assembled on the quarter deck were warned that should any case of drunkenness occur for the future that both they & the Ship's Company should drink their grog at the tub.

As officer in charge of burials, the young Kennedy was soon a regular at the cemetery at Happy Valley, but on 19 March 1859, with fifty-nine men on the sick list, the *Calcutta* finally weighed for Singapore on the first leg of her voyage home. On 1 April, an apt date if Elgin is to be believed, Seymour addressed the ship's company for the last time before hauling down his flag. And four months later, on 30 July, after a visit to Napoleon's recently emptied grave on St Helena and one last death – a popular old sailor famous for teaching the parson's parrot to blaspheme and last seen 'scudding along on the crest of the waves' in a hulled coffin that refused to sink – the *Calcutta* anchored in Plymouth Sound. Goodenough might have taken less satisfaction in paying off the ship's crew if he had known that he would be posting stickers for a new one of his own and a return to China within five weeks.

V

On 25 June 1859 a force of sixteen warships, including thirteen gunboats, under the command of Sir James Hope, waited impatiently at anchor within the bar off the mouth of the Peiho River. Just over a year earlier Sir Michael Seymour's far smaller force had found little difficulty in capturing the Taku forts, and now Sir James – saddled with the task of escorting Frederick Bruce to Tientsin to ratify his brother's treaty – had been confident enough of a repeat performance in the event of Chinese resistance to ignore the evidence of reconstruction that he could see and take on trust his ability to deal with any firepower that he could not.

At 2 o'clock in the afternoon, with the guns of the forts completely silent, the first of his gunboats bore down unchecked on the reinforced boom that stretched across the river. In the gunboat *Banterer*, seeing action for the first and almost only time in his career, was a young midshipman, Jack Fisher. 'My dear Mams.,' he wrote the next day, irrepressible as ever after the worst single disaster in British naval history between the end of the Napoleonic War and the First World War:

By some wonderful means I have escaped unhurt, although my dear old Skipper has been very badly wounded in the foot, a large ball still being in it. I don't know whether I can give you a description of it, I feel in such a state of excitement ... There are very few wounded, I fancy, in comparison to those killed. In the *Plover*, the next gunboat to ours, 26 men were killed and wounded out of 36 men and officers, the Admiral being one of them. Rason, her Commander, was smashed to atoms. So was Mc Kenna, the Military Secretary, and all the Admiral's staff nearly ... but what could we do against such a fearful number of guns? And us poor little gunboats inclosed in such a small place, not much broader than the length of our ship ...

I never smelt such a horrid smell in my life as on board the Coromandel bringing the wounded out yesterday afternoon. Abaft the mainmast it was nothing but blood and men rolling about with arms and legs off, nearly all round-shot wounds. No one takes account of people dead inside here. We pitch them overboard as they are killed or dead. One soon gets used to it ... The old Admiral behaved splendidly after he had part of his thigh and leg shot away. He had a cot slung to a pole and was carried about in a boat from the *Plover* to the *Cormorant* to encourage the men, and then was hoisted up on the bridge till he was hit again, and then was laid down on the quarter-deck, where he remained till night ... Major Fisher of the Engineers told me the forts were splendidly built, we couldn't have built better ... I had to fling all my arms away coming back from the forts and was nearly smothered once, only one of our bluejackets was kind enough to haul me out. You sank up to your knees *at least* every step, and just fancy the slaughter going 500 yards in the face of that fire of about 30 pieces of artillery right in front of you and on each flank. It was dreadful, horrible work but, thank God, I came out all right ... They had horrid fire-balls firing at us when we landed. I saw one poor fellow with his eye and part of his face burnt right out ... It is a sad business, is it not, Mams?

With almost a hundred killed and over 350 wounded, it was a 'sad business' that inevitably played even sadder at home. There can be no doubt that an almost criminal complacency lay behind the disaster, but pride, loyalty and a sense of mortification that British arms had been humbled by an effete and opium-riddled enemy all meant that revenge for a perfidious act of Chinese 'treachery' became a sacred national duty. 'Our defeat had been attended by no disgrace,' wrote Yonge – content to forget the fact that Hope knew that the forts would be defended, or that an overconfident British command precipitated an action they were certain they would win.

No one could reproach the Admiral for conducting the attack in a way which had never failed against the Chinese before; and in the long and glorious records of the British navy more dauntless

THE SWORD OF THE LORD

courage and more unshaken resolution had never been displayed. There could be no disgrace in such a defeat, provided that those who did not sustain it did not sit down to lament it in tame despondency, but like men exerted themselves to retrieve it ...

The news of our defeat at the Peiho, except in the hearts of those whose friends had fallen in the conflict, did not so much awaken sorrow as for a misfortune which it would be hard to remedy, as indignation at the treachery of the Chinese ... No one blamed those who had suffered the defeat; for all felt that, had they been in their place, they themselves would have acted, or would have wished to have acted like them. But at the same time all likewise felt that the national glory had received a wound which could only be healed by a decisive triumph on the same spot.

'I hope you will have half expected what I am going to tell you,' Goodenough wrote apologetically to his sister on 18 September, just five weeks after he had finished paying off the *Calcutta*. 'When I heard of the terrible news from China, I could not do otherwise than offer my services to go out there again. I went to the Admiralty therefore, yesterday, and saw Sir Michael Seymour, who happened to be there, and he told me that I should in all probability be employed.'

There was a strong sense of duty at work, and the old desire for action, but Goodenough's feelings about another dose of China were clearly more ambiguous than he let on. 'Sept 22nd,' he noted in his diary, just four days later: 'Hungerford came to my attic with my appointment in the Times in his hand. I felt a sudden chill. It is hard to go, tho' it be entirely by my own request.'

The 'reward' for his patriotism was the command of the two-hundred-horsepower steam sloop *Renard*, fitting out at Sheerness, and after a snatched leave with the Markhams in London – long sermons and Arctic talk – and a massed family farewell he was again at sea. 'We are in free and exhilarating air,' he was soon writing, uncertainties forgotten and hopeful – *mutatis mutandis* – that tensions with Napoleon III's France in the aftermath of Solferino might provide him with something worthier than a Chinese war junk to fight.

The weather is so lovely that I am beginning to paint and polish ship and guns, and to exercise, and shall pop at a target the first fine day. I have been thinking of what I should do if we find we are

at war, and if I fall in with a French steam gun-vessel, and I have
decided on having my long guns on the bow, and short ones on
bow and beam, commence firing and close; load the last round
when at 600 yards with round shot and grape, and fire at 200
yards, then prepare to board, load short guns again with grape,
run alongside, fire, and board.

The French were no more obliging for Goodenough than they had
been for Peel, though, and if the log is any guide, the only threats to
his well-being seem to have been the dirt of a steam-powered vessel
and his wretched Steward. '21 October broken by accident in the
Captain's cabin 1 vegetable dish and cover,' it reads.

> 22 October broken by accident in the Captain's cabin 1 small saucer
> 23 October broken by accident in the Captain's cabin 1 wine glass
> 25 October broken by accident in the Captain's cabin 1 wine glass

It did not seem to matter whether they were at sea or anchor – wine
glasses, teacups, soup plates, breakfast cups, vegetable-dish covers,
saucers, large plates, small plates, glass tumblers, milk jugs all came
alike, and long before the Cape Goodenough was laying his own
dinner table to preserve what remained. 'Very grumpy with my Steward who really does not keep things clean,' he confessed to his journal. 'He on my sending dirty things off my table respectfully asks to
leave me after two months. "Yes if I can find anyone to take your
place." Oddly enough I had been thinking if it were possible to get
anyone at Ascension.'

Endearingly with him, however, complaints invariably mutate into
remorse by the time they have reached his journals, and they are as
full of improving maxims as a collection of old samplers. 'For every
ill beneath the Sun,' Goodenough cautioned himself,

> There is some remedy – or none
> Should there be one – resolve to find it
> If not – submit – and never mind it.

It was one thing to admonish himself, it was another to live up to his
precepts, and time and again a note of irritability that is ruthlessly
kept out of the journal edited by his widow breaks through. 'Never
so tired of anything in my life,' he wrote on 17 November, still a week

short of Ascension and, presumably, done with Thackeray's *The Virginians*, which had kept him up reading till four in the morning. 'I can't yet get reconciled to the perpetual motion & the entire want of exercise. The motion quite prevents study drawing & together with the heat leaves me in a lethargic state of disgust at everything. The dirt too of this detestable steamer, is not pleasant.'

One hears the unmistakable voice of the old, unreconstructed navy there, the authentic voice of an old 'Collingwood' who had learned his seamanship in the age of sail, and Goodenough was not averse to its disciplines either. '13 July,' records the ship's log – not an isolated incident in Goodenough's China service – 'read sentence of court martial on John Dallinger (PRM) to Ship's Co, sentenced to be hanged at 1.30 on board HM Gun Boat Leven.' 'Goodenough was a man not thoroughly appreciated by those who did not know him intimately,' one of his officers in the *Renard* recalled, in an interesting glimpse into his 'command style' before the imminence of death liberated him from the emotional straitjacket of his naval training.

His manner on duty could be as uncompromising as his actions, and it required a man to know him well to understand fully the stern truth with which he could reprove negligence or wilful default; but to those who had the privilege of serving with or under him, his manner, whilst never passing over a lapse of duty, was signally loving and attractive. There are many officers now serving who date their best feelings for the honour and well-being of the service from the time when they first came under Goodenough's fostering care. One only had to try to do one's duty to ensure his kindly smile, his readiness to condone any error in judgement, and his pleasant way to show the right thing to do.

As the *Renard* arrived on the China station, it became clear that duty rather than glory was all they were going to get in a war that was rapidly outgrowing its gunboat days. On the last day of the old year Goodenough received an Admiralty telegram instructing all ships of the *Renard* class to proceed to Penang for towing duties, and for the next six months that was to be his lot, a transport and logistical support role in the allied build-up as they assembled the sort of army that the end of the crisis in India had at last made possible for another assault on the Taku forts. 'It is all over,' wrote Goodenough on 22 August 1860, no more than a frustrated spectator as an Anglo-French army stormed the forts in a brutal assault from the land side that cost seventeen dead, 183 wounded and won seven Victoria Crosses – the most in any one action until Rorke's Drift nearly twenty years later,

> and except some half-a-dozen gunboats, no naval men have heard the whistle of a shot. I am just recovering from the labours of the day before yesterday. The road was in capital order, and I walked to the camp, and as near as possible to the point of attack [the inner fort on the left bank]. I intended to go right on, but a guard and a staff-officer had been left behind at the camp, with orders that no-one was to pass except on duty, and all the troops not engaged were confined to their own camps. I was sold, for I had just put a bottle of claret, a tongue, and half a cheese in my wallet to share with Berry of Bedingfeld. The next best thing to do was to sit in the gate, and hear what was going on from passers-by, staff officers, wounded men, or artillery officers going to the camp for ammunition.

It had been as vicious a battle as the defeat in the mouth of the river the previous year. 'Cold shot, hand-grenades, stinkpots, and vases of lime were showered on the crowd of besiegers,' a breathless Thomas Bowlby, the *Times* special correspondent brutally executed by the Chinese only months later, wrote of the hand-to-hand fighting for the inner fort on the northern bank.

> The ladders placed against the wall were pulled into the fort, or thrown over, and in vain did man after man attempt to swarm through the embrasures. If the defence was desperate, nothing could exceed the gallantry of the assailants. Between English and French there was nothing to choose. A Frenchman climbed to the top of the parapet, where for some time he stood alone. One rifle after another was handed up to him, which he fired against the enemy. But his courage was unavailing, and he fell back, speared through the eye. Another, pickaxe in hand, attempted to cut away the top of the wall. He was shot, and Lieutenant Burslem, of the 67th, caught hold of his pick and continued the work ...

Burslem was among those who won the Victoria Cross, and with the capture of the inner fort, the key to the whole defensive complex, Chinese resistance disintegrated. The outer fort and its garrison of two thousand men fell without a single shot fired, and by the next day, as the allied forces entered the deserted defences on the southern side of the river, the four Taku forts, and with them the command of the Peiho River and the road to Peking, were once again in allied hands.

The British and French demands were much as they had been before the signing of the Tientsin Treaty – with the addition of reparation and 'an ample and satisfactory apology' for the fiasco of the previous year – but even with the Taku forts captured negotiations with the Chinese went no smoother than they had ever done. By 30 August the *Renard* had joined Admiral Hope and Harry Parkes at Tientsin, and three weeks later, as Elgin's patience finally ran out, Goodenough was despatched upriver to reconnoitre its northerly reaches for an allied advance on the capital itself. 'I started early ... and rowed, or tracked, my boats as high as a place called Tungtsum by 10 P.M., forty miles,' he wrote on 22 September.

> I went on till twelve, and then slept rather uncomfortably in the stern of the boat till 5 A.M., when I was rewarded by a sight of the splendid range of hills at the back of Pekin ... I tracked on till eight, and was then obliged to return to time, having discovered beyond a doubt, that small boats and large river barges could convey the army so far. I was on board my ship in forty-eight hours from starting, having done ninety miles at least.

'The river transport is now in full force,' he wrote again two weeks later, as he retraced his reconnaissance journey with the supply barges diverted by the allies from their usual function in the salt trade,

> and we have about two hundred boats, manned by eight hundred natives, and kept in order by two hundred seamen and their officers ... At first the boats were sent in small divisions in charge of a lieutenant, but a fortnight ago a rumour came of bands of Tartars on the left bank, and it was thought necessary to form a grand flotilla of three divisions, with an escort of two hundred men. I went with a division of ninety boats in all, taking my gig, and sleeping in a covered boat which contained some cargo ... The alarm about Tartars proved false, and I had no hesitation in walking along the banks. After two days constantly journeying through corn, I was glad to see the hills which I had caught sight of at my highest

point on my first trip ... I came on a curious sort of flood-gates, apparently for irrigating a neighbouring district. It was faced through with capital granite, and had a well-finished marble monument on its mound to the north, standing on the back of a tortoise. The monument is in three pieces: the upper represents twining dragons, the next has an inscription, with a border of crabs and lizards in bas-relief, and the foot is a fine large tortoise. I have seen such things elsewhere, but never so good and perfect as this one ... I felt very much inclined to make a prize of him for Sydenham, but was deterred by the idea of 'barbarians' stripping the country, as well as by his serious weight.

It would have been as well if the rest of the allied force had shared Goodenough's sensibilities, but at least his transport duties spared him any share in probably the most shameful act of barbarism in European history since the sack of Byzantium. By the middle of September the outline of an agreement had been hammered out with the Chinese, but after further prevarications, the torture and murder of a number of British, French and Sikh prisoners – including Bowlby, the *Times* correspondent – led Elgin to order the firing of the Summer Palace at Yuan Ming Yuan by way of reprisal.

'*C'est détruire pour le plaisir de détruire,*' complained one French officer, and spread over eighty square miles of park, and comprising two hundred main buildings alone, pavilions, temples, lakes and gardens, audience halls and imperial suites 'into the adornment of which had been poured the wealth and ingenuity of successive Emperors', there was plenty to destroy and loot. '*Je prends la plume, mon bon père, mais sais-je que je vais te dire?*' wrote another overwhelmed officer. '*Je suis ébahi, ahuri, abasourdi de ce que je'ai vu. Les mille et une nuits sont pour moi une chose parfaitement véridique maintenent ... de soieries, de bijous, de porcelaines, bronzes, sculptures, de trésors enfin! Je ne crois pas qu'on ait vu chose pareille depuis le sac de Rome par les barbares.*'

What was not taken went up in flames. 'You can scarcely imagine the beauty and magnificence of the places we burnt,' Charles Gordon – the future Gordon of Khartoum – told his mother. 'It made one's heart sore to burn them; in fact, these places were so large, and we were so pressed for time, that we could not plunder them carefully. Quantities of gold ornaments were burnt, considered as brass. It was wretchedly demoralising work for an army. Everybody was wild for plunder.'

Perhaps the most surprising aspect of this piece of vandalism was that it came on the orders of Lord Elgin. For more than two years he had attracted the suspicions and opprobrium of ministers, merchants, consuls, admirals and generals for his liberalism and moderation, and it is a bitter irony that the one man who genuinely hated and feared the racial intolerance and arrogance of his countrymen in India or China should have ended his Peking mission by adding the Summer Palace to the dubious cultural battle honours already linked to the Elgin name.

'I hope for once we may do these people a service without alloy, and be able to leave them with a feeling that we have benefited them,' a rueful Goodenough wrote at the end of the campaign, but after what had happened it was a fatuous ambition. His duties with the transports and the provisioning of Tientsin had spared him the disgrace – and booty – of the Summer Palace, but as he moved first back to the Gulf of Pecheli, and then, as senior officer, to Shanghai, the conclusion of peace only brought with it a curious realignment of British interests and a fresh source of difficulties. 'The scoundrel rebels have come here again,' he wrote from Shanghai, as the allies, in a belated attempt to shore up the imperial power they had done so much to undermine, threw their support behind the Emperor against his semi-Protestant Taiping rebels, 'and are burning villages in the neighbourhood. They have excited our anger by enticing away a number of seamen of the fleet as well as of merchant ships, by offering them sixty dollars down on the nail, and sixty dollars a month pay. I suspect that the former is all that they will get.'*

'I have had an eight days' trip into the silk country, which has been exceedingly interesting and curious,' he wrote again, 'curious, as I have been issuing my commands at various places to the rebels, or Taepings, as though I was their chief.'

They had thought fit to interfere with people of ours and boats bearing an English flag, and had taken a quantity of silk which they were obliged to restore ... The Changmaws (long-haired ones)

---

* The Taiping Rebellion was the most serious uprising in nineteenth-century Chinese history. It is a matter of debate whether or not it was a genuinely popular movement, but it certainly suited the Western Powers to support a weakened imperial power rather than risk the consequences of a successful rebellion.

have nearly all the country, and though infinite rascals, will over-run it without a check. I was mistaken for a rebel myself, at a place where there were seventy boats of braves of the Imperialist side; they fled at the sight of my four-oared gig, drowning several people in their panic, but when they saw my boat was quite alone, and found out that I was a friend, wanted to make me responsible for the death of the drowned, blew up their matches, flourished swords, cut at me, and for two minutes I was thinking how many of them I should be able to dispose of if I lost my temper. Fortu-nately I kept it, and my revolver in my pocket, and only flourished my umbrella, and, thanks to an ebb current, drifted away from the place and the tumult while talking to a magistrate who came down to see me.

From Shanghai Goodenough went to Ningpo, to put the 'place in order against the rebels – though I am forbidden to take an active part, *i.e.*, to fire on them', he added regretfully – and violence was never far beneath the surface. 'I see strange sights,' he wrote in Octo-ber 1861 from Nankin.

Turning a corner on Saturday, I saw two men struggling, and became aware that one man had the pigtail of another strongly twisted around his left hand, while with his right he was chopping off his head with a big knife. He managed this in about a dozen blows, severed the remaining flesh, and chucked the head away, leaving the trunk in the middle of the street. A bystander went up to the head, lifted it by its tail, and looked it in the face, to see if he knew it, but apparently did not, dropped it, and went his way – and there it lay ... a small boy smilingly volunteered the infor-mation that the beheaded one, who was well dressed, was a thief, and had stolen 'quite a number of dollars'.

This was not what he had joined the navy for, and with the war over, China was no more a place for an ambitious young officer than it had been for Peel twenty years earlier. 'People are quite right in saying a return home damages one's prospects,' Goodenough wrote from the Gulf of Pecheli, conscious that he needed to be in the thick of whatever intellectual activity was stirring in the primordial sludge of naval life, and so it does if one's prospects are all included in the word promotion. But there are so many things besides promotion which affect one's welfare that that ought not to have too much weight. It would be better to defer one's advancement for two or three years than pass them in inaction. I feel very decidedly about the benefit of a return home, not for the health of my body, but of my mind ... Therefore I shall stand by my intention to come home overland, if the *Renard* is not ordered home by the mail of about March 10th. I shall never wait for bad health, for I am sure that if that fail it will be altogether, and then it will be too late.

There was the added incentive of seeing his two surviving brothers, and in November 1861 he prepared to leave the *Renard* for the mail boat to Ceylon and Egypt. 'Came back to the ship,' he noted in his journal on the twelfth, 'drank a glass of champagne with the officers, who wished me a very kind goodbye. People manned rigging and cheered.' While in Egypt Goodenough took the opportunity of inspecting progress on the construction of the Suez Canal, but by February 1862 he was back in England, and six months later, after the longest leave he had enjoyed since he had first gone to sea as a boy, found himself serving again under an old 'Collingwood' as commander in Admiral Smart's flagship, HMS *Revenge*, with the Channel Squadron. After a frustrating year in the Far East he was again where he ought to be.

VI

In the plethora of small wars that seems the dominant theme of nineteenth-century naval life it is easy to forget that the real business of the Royal Navy lay elsewhere. During the course of the century the navy would win more than forty VCs in various campaigns on land and at sea, but for all the gunboat diplomacy and small boat actions in the rivers of Burma or along the coast of Africa, and for all the lives lost in fighting piracy or the long, drawn-out and unglamorous battle against slavery, the *raison d'être* of the navy ultimately resided, as it had always done, in the strategic security of Britain and the implementation of her foreign policy.

The fact that there was no major fleet-to-fleet action involving the Royal Navy between the Battle of Navarino in 1827 and the outbreak of the First World War almost a century later is a testimony not to any temporary suspension of this truth but to its supremely successful fulfilment. In 1861 the threat of a German navy still lay well in the future, yet for any thinking officer burdened with the duty of maintaining this superiority in the face of the triple challenges of France, Russia and America, the crucial battles were those that could be lost to stagnation before they had ever been fought.

Among the most influential of these young officers, urgently concerned with the opportunities of steam power, with developments in gunnery and ship-building, with the handling of fleets in action, the recruiting and service conditions of a new navy, and the education of an officer cadre capable of embracing the challenges of technology, was Goodenough, and the *Revenge* was just the first of a series of appointments to reflect this rising status. In May 1862 he followed Smart out to the Mediterranean as his flag captain, and over the next decade his time in *Victoria* and then in *Minotaur* with the Channel Squadron under Sir Thomas Symonds, would put him at the very heart of those fleets and developments in signalling and 'Steam Tactics' that made the 1860s so seminal a decade in nineteenth-century naval history.

There had never been 'a happier ship' than *Victoria*, Albert Markham reckoned – and never a more fashionable fleet than the Mediterranean – but Goodenough's experience during these years was not confined to fleet manoeuvres and the occasional leavening of royal duties that was part and parcel of Victorian naval life. 'I have the honour to transmit to your Lordship a copy of a very able and interesting report which Captain Goodenough has been so good as to make to me of the result of his inquiries respecting the naval establishment of the United States,' Lord Lyons – Peel's old commander-in-chief in the Black Sea – wrote to Lord Russell in May 1864.

It shows that the Government of the United States is steadily making preparations to enable it to engage with advantage in foreign war, and that its means of carrying on a naval war are becoming every day more formidable.

I am afraid that there can be little doubt that these preparations are made mainly with a view to a war with England, and that in the present temper of the American people, advantage would be eagerly taken of any conjuncture of circumstances which would

enable a declaration of war against England to be made with toler-
able safety.

The report on which Lyons based this verdict had been sent to him
on 9 April 1864, at the end of a tour that at his own instigation Goodenough had made of the dockyards and arms manufacturers of the
United States. He had sailed from Liverpool to Boston the previous
December, and from there had travelled on to Washington, securing
official permission to visit the Union's navy yards and the college at
Newport, Rhode Island, before moving on to Pittsburgh for the gun
foundries and to the Federal army at Charleston, South Carolina.

The main thrust of the American naval effort in 1863, two and a
half years into the Civil War, was, predictably, aimed at the Confed-
eracy, but beyond the ships designed for blockade duty and the
narrow creeks of the east coast Goodenough descried a more sinis-
ter long-term threat. His report presented a detailed breakdown of
the present and predicted capacity and ordnance of the United States,
and from a mass of technical, professional and political data he
extrapolated a conclusion that foreshadowed the emergence of a
major naval rival across the Atlantic. 'They will not form a fleet properly so-called,' he wrote of the diverse range of vessels, all with their
specific purposes, widely varying sea capabilities, weight of gunnery
and speeds, that would constitute a United States navy, 'for their
object will never be to be in each other's company, but thrown out
as a chain across the great lines of commerce; they will be able to
destroy an enemy's merchant-ships, or, if the latter be convoyed, will
be able to hang about the convoy, cut off stragglers, and evade the
pursuit of more-heavily armed vessels accompanying it.'

It was not so much the description of vessels the United States
already had, or any superiority in construction or gun design that
alarmed the Admiralty, though, but the political intent latent in the
account Goodenough gave of the Secretary of the Navy's most recent
report to President Lincoln. 'Finally,' wrote Goodenough,

Mr Welles ... has informed the President in his report on 7 December 1863 that he contemplates building 'vessels of greater size than
any turreted vessel yet completed, to maintain our maritime position and for predominance upon the ocean.

'Not only must they carry guns of a heavier calibre than have
heretofore been used at sea, but in order to make long cruises, and

to cope successfully with any force, these vessels must have all possible strength, endurance, and speed. Being without distant Colonies where coal depots can be established on the shore of almost every sea, we must build ships with capacity sufficient to take on board fuel for a long cruise.'

It is curious to find Goodenough feeding anti-American paranoia in this way – and feeding it so effectively – because in a decade that saw the building of the coastal fortification known as 'Palmerston's Follies' he never belonged to the hysterical school of national defence. It seemed ludicrous to him that the country should indulge in the 'wild schemes' that had become the fashion, when what was needed was a steady and rational programme of expansion immune to either press agitation or political opportunism. 'I am always sorry for these party attacks,' he would later write from Australia – more prophetically than he would live to know:

> They divert the proper attention of conscientious friends of the Navy from the real needs of the service, and cause those disquieting spasmodic leaps in naval policy which are barren of real progress ...
>
> The definite and resolute plan fixed upon by the German government is very instructive to us in that respect. The German government have now three times laid down a *Flottengrundung*'s plan, each time preparing for its naval development over a period of eight to ten years, and have gone on 'ohne hast und ohne rast' till we are one day amazed at their success. This sort of programme is one which would confer the greatest benefit upon the future naval construction of the country.

His subsequent appointment as Naval Attaché to the Maritime Courts of Europe – St Petersburg, Odessa, Venice, Trieste, Vienna, Berlin, Wilhelmshaven, Paris – did nothing to change his mind, but it was never more, or bigger, ships or defensive forts that Goodenough saw as the pressing need of the age. During the dozen years between China and his posting to the Australian station he took an active part in the technological and tactical transformation of the service, but while he reported on the American navy and sat on the Admiralty Committee on Designs for Ships of War, he was never the zealot about *matériel* or Steam Tactics that he was about the one great passion of his professional life, education.

THE SWORD OF THE LORD

'It seems to me that education is the great question of the day,' he wrote in 1869, 'the question I should study most if I thought I could get into Parliament.' If he was thinking well beyond the navy when he wrote that, it was in the navy that he had elected to do what good he could do in life. 'I have been asked to offer to the members of this Institution and through this Institution to the Naval service,' he began a talk at the United Service Institution four years later, 'some remarks on preliminary naval education. They are the results of many years' observation, and of much thought on the training of naval officers, in the course of my service in the largest ships of Her Majesty's navy, during which time I have become convinced of the necessity of our providing a much more careful and methodical course of instruction for our officers than now exists, or has before existed.'

At the core of Goodenough's argument were two propositions: the first that the navy took its officers too young and too early; and the second that the education the modern naval officer received was woefully inadequate to meet the demands of an increasingly technical service. In the days of sail, Goodenough conceded, the experience of a lifetime might provide all the practical education required, but over the previous thirty years, while 'all other circumstances of life at sea' had changed, the one thing that had not was the 'preliminary training of our officers'. 'I have been told,' he went on – irony and argument nicely weighted to reassure that larger and dimmer audience that lay beyond the progressive elite in front of him,

> that it is not desirable to make the navy a scientific service. Science indeed! We are far from that – we are safe enough from any danger of that sort. I only wish for such an education and training as shall enable our officers to understand a few elements of the laws by which their ships float, and move, and are guided; such an education that will stop them from asking the impossible in a ship, while it prepares them to comprehend the simple phenomena and acts of nature ... Don't suppose that I speak of science. I speak of things which concern the safe navigation, or, at least, the economic navigation of ships. I speak of the bare elements, and not of any deep scientific acquirement. And if I go a hair's breadth away from practical professional topics, I may ask, What is the knowledge of military law? – what is the knowledge of the leading principles of the rules of evidence? – what of political geography? – what of our own mercantile marine? – what of maritime law – I leave these questions

to be thought over by those who have sat as members of a court
martial – by those who have found themselves the servant of a
consul at some unexpected political crisis, or who have been face to
face with mutinous merchant ships. It is then too late to look into
the elements which should have been acquired in youth ... Are we
who go down to the sea in ships, and occupy our business in great
waters, are we alone of all men only to see the works of the Lord
and His wonders of the deep, and not to comprehend them?

Goodenough was not the only voice, and by no means the angriest,
demanding a more systematic and relevant education for the young
officer, but in his demands for an older entry age the tone and concern
is unmistakably his. Throughout the century this was a question that
split the service down the middle, and if there were distinguished officers who reckoned there was nothing that could be done with a boy
after the age of thirteen, there were equally men, like the Etonian
George Tryon, whose careers suggest that the good Jesuit doctrine of
getting a child young and moulding him into conformity was the
mortal enemy of the initiative, originality and flexibility of mind that
the modern navy so badly needed.

There can be no hard and fast answer – the different roads by
which Hastings, Peel and Goodenough found their way to
Portsmouth surely show that – but Goodenough's concern was not
with the outstanding young officers of their generations, but with the
hundreds and thousands of midshipmen and lieutenants who would
fight in Britain's fleets and patrol her Empire and protect her trade
and find themselves in positions of responsibility for which their
education provided so little guidance. 'It has been said that early entry
into the Service is associated with all the traditions of the navy,' he
argued,

is in accordance with its historical recollections, and is in unison
with the general tone of professional feeling on the subject; that it
insures the obtaining a supply of young officers at a time when
their minds, being plastic and docile, and their habits and modes
of thought yet unformed, they can be more easily inured to the
peculiar habits of sea life, be more accustomed to its unavoidable
privations and occasional hardships, be trained up in attachment
to their profession, and be induced to adopt it heartily as their voca-
tion in life.

It did not seem to Goodenough that there was anything in a public school education inimical to this, nothing in the rigours of naval life that a boy of seventeen or eighteen fresh from Rugby or Westminster could not adjust to, but his real argument lay elsewhere. 'I regret the loss of individuality,' he went on, comparing the standardised product of a Dartmouth naval background with that of public school boy liberally educated to an age at which he might then usefully absorb the professional training required for the sea,

> which is inevitable when all young gentlemen are passed through the same course from the age of twelve. Captain Sherard Osborne, an officer of eminence, and of distinguished merit in our profession as a man of varied experience of the world, and an instance of most successful self-culture, and to whose opinion I therefore attach great value, advocates early education apart from special training, and deprecates the loss of individuality which ensues from long continued running in the same groove.

There was probably nothing in this that would have antagonised a naturally sympathetic audience, but at the heart of Goodenough's argument is a paradox of which neither he nor it were probably quite aware. During his time with the Mediterranean and Channel Fleets he must have searched as assiduously as anyone for the elusive Grail of choreographed fleet manoeuvres, yet in the very regularity and robotic control to which they aspired, in their promise of a mathematically predictable world in which 'every movement, every change of course, speed or formation, would be ordered and executed by flag signal', there was something not just at odds with his cult of liberal individualism but harshly alien to the sensibilities and 'Hopkinsian' sense of wonder that made Goodenough the man he was.

If nothing fancier, there was a breadth and depth to Goodenough's cultural interests that would not have made him immediately at home in an increasingly philistine service in which the 'three oner' – the naval version of the prep-school swat – was an increasingly risible figure. From the day he first opened his eyes he had been lucky enough to awake to a world of cultural and intellectual privilege, and the physical and aesthetic influences of childhood, the attraction of architecture and art, the sense of the numinous and the historical, the intellectual and scientific curiosity of the family milieu, had all combined to produce a character supremely at odds with the kind of officer the navy seemed bent on producing in their thousands.

It went deeper than this, though, because if Goodenough wanted a more 'scientific' training, he was no rationalist of the sort his fellow modernisers envisaged – of the kind that HMS *Vernon*, the torpedo training ship, would attempt to turn out – and had no desire to be. In all his lectures and papers on the subject he would go on hammering out the same old message, but it is hard not to feel that if he had been given everything he asked for – or if, say, he could have been transported ten years into the future to see a *Britannia*, the Royal Navy's training ship for its future officers, delivering every syllabus reform that his fellow Young Turks were campaigning for, his own profound discontent with naval education and the navy itself would have remained untouched. 'I have been in the classes of midshipmen in their recitation rooms,' he had written from America during his tour there.

> One class was at mechanics, and another was at moral philosophy, of which I have never read a word, nor do I ever wish to. It seems so odd to hear certain rules laid down drily, as guides for our action, without *any* reference to Christianity at all. A young fellow stood up, and was asked what guide he would take to determine his course of action under certain circumstances. 'My conscience.' 'Are you quite clear on that point, Mr. K.?' 'Yes, sir,' How incomplete – is it not? And how different from 'If any man lack wisdom let him ask of God, who giveth to all men liberally and upbraideth not.' I could not help saying so to my friend the commandant, who accompanied me.

Here at last, in that single word 'Christianity', deployed so naturally, so inevitably by Goodenough in the context of a naval academy, can be glimpsed the real gap that was opening up between the world he had entered at the age of thirteen and the man he had become in his mid- and late thirties. Throughout his career he had always stood out for his piety, but with age and maturity a faith that had once cheerfully squared a moment's prayer with the work of Gideon had deepened into a more radical, questioning and *demanding* thing. 'I say nothing about war,' he wrote from Vigo in 1870, on the news of the outbreak of the Franco-Prussian War. 'What can I say? It fills me with grief and confusion to see the best passions – not the worst, as writers say – supporting the continuance of war. Whichever side wins, it is grievous and horrible. Feelings are blunted, unfair dealing is suggested and believed in, a contact with each other, which ought to dispel prejudices, is likely to engender more hatred than at first. It is awful and horrible.'

There are perhaps few fighting men who would not sign up to a horror of war, and some who actually feel it, but 'Holy Joe' Goodenough had come a long way from the young commander who had been itching for a run-in with a French gunboat. In his talk to the United Service Institution he could still console an impatient generation of young officers with the promise that 'The Danes always land,' but whether as flag officer or attaché, it was international understanding and the prevention of war that became the driving force of his professional life. 'What a glory if we could lead the world in knowledge,' he wrote in 1871 from St Petersburg, which – when he could drag himself away from the Rembrandts, De Hoochs and Ruysdaels in the Hermitage – he was visiting in his capacity as Naval Attaché to the Maritime Courts of Europe, 'in justice, in brotherly kindness, and in *goodness*, – what an end to work and live for, or to die for, even to contribute in the least towards.'

These are not the kind of sentiments often heard in a British man-of-war, but whether he recognised it himself or not, the truth was that Goodenough was no longer the sort of man who would have been at ease in a warship. Intellectually, a gap had opened up between the navy and the man that he could perhaps bridge; morally, a contradiction had been exposed between his professional duties and his deepest convictions that would prove harder to resolve. It is not clear if anything had 'happened' – there seems to have been no 'conversion' of the classic evangelical kind – but a change had undoubtedly occurred. He had opened the decade – a decade of great outward, professional success – clutching a bottle of claret as he wandered off to watch the battle for the Taku forts, and ended it dedicating himself to a very different vision of British global power. And in the middle of it he had found a woman to share and confirm those convictions that would only surface publicly five years later on the quarterdeck of the *Pearl*.

VII

It would be uncharitable to think that Victoria Hamilton was born for widowhood, but even in an age which turned it into an art, few women can have embraced the role with so deadening a sense of its duties. In the year after Goodenough's death she published a *Memoir* that was everything piety could demand, but in squeezing the life out of him she did so successful a job on herself too that she comes off the page as leadenly and unloveably dead as the monument of blameless and sanitised goodness into which she turned her late husband.

It is lucky that we have his journals – unrecognisable, almost, in their tone, their range, their intemperance, their *liveliness*, from her carefully bowdlerised version of them – but there seems nothing to do the same service for her. It is possible of course that she always was the woman who wrote the *Memoir*, yet there is something so touching in his devotion to her, so unqualified in his gratitude for her love and support, that it is hard not to want to believe that – like some ardent and courageous Shavian zealot – there was once something else there that is now irretrievably lost. 'It is a happy thing,' he could write in absolute confidence on the voyage out to America in 1863, only a short time after they had become engaged,

> to begin a day with such vivid poetry, so rich and full of meaning, as that 5th Chapter of Isaiah, especially in the dreamy life of a passage, when one's thoughts are not violently disturbed. How immensely humbling and still how soothing they are ... I was reading yesterday of Johnson's intense dread of death, – as death, the end – and of his saying that every one feared death whose thoughts were not occupied by some stronger feeling which, displaced, did not conquer that one. I think that saying quite true, and that the fear of death can only be blotted out by looking beyond and upwards to the Hands which will help us over. You don't mind me talking of death; for you would have me be brave, and the only real bravery is that which can look quite calmly and in cold blood upon it.

It might not be easy to warm to Victoria Hamilton, but one cannot ignore her, and she clearly brought a clarity and certainty to Goodenough's life that had not always been there before. From his earliest days in the navy he had always been ready to profess his faith and teach his Bible classes, but under her influence – and as a daughter of a President of the RGS and of a former lady-in-waiting to the young Queen, she is a wonderful example of the strange channels down which Victorian philanthropy ran – those accommodations and compromises that he had muddled along with before marriage were swept away. 'He came to the conclusion,' she would later write of his stance on alcohol – and one can see the pursed lips of Victorian rectitude shaping the words – 'that he could not, consistently with his own idea of right and wrong, continue to advise people to do what he did not do himself. Having become much more firmly impressed with the advantages of total abstinence from intoxicating liquors – an opinion which gained strength with every year that he lived – he from that day, though he took no pledge, gave up the use of all wine, beer, or spirits; and except in case of illness, continued to do so all his life.'

It was inevitably a marriage conducted at a distance – a honeymoon in Switzerland, time together between sea appointments, a sight of his first son at Malta, a winter with their two young boys at Lisbon, another, crowded season in London – but she was there at his side when the end of his appointment as flag captain to the Channel Squadron gave them the chance to volunteer for the relief work that was being organised in Britain for French victims of the war with Prussia. In his younger days Goodenough had been no more averse to the idea of a war with France than any naval officer, but as a fluent French-speaker, cultural Francophile and humanitarian, the thought of French men, women and children suffering on the other side of the Channel while a 'Pharisaical' Britain, gorged on a sense of its own virtues and 'self-contentment', sneered at the French incapacity for sacrifice, was more than he could stomach.

If *The Times*, though, did not 'believe' in the French people, the *Daily News* had set up its own French Peasant Relief Fund, and on 8 November 1870 Goodenough and his wife set off for the Belgian town of Bouillon, ten miles from Sedan. 'In the dreariest period of the gloomiest of Novembers,' Bullock Hall, the director of the relief operation, recalled five years later,

> when autumnal rains were giving place to snow, and sleet, and frozen winter fogs, and we whose business it was to convey food and clothing over the slippery and almost impassable roads to the

destitute in the villages about Sedan, were almost in despair at the task we had undertaken, and were in sore need of encouragement, there came in answer to our appeal for volunteers, a man, the very sight of whom at once communicated new life to us. Here was a man, the very model of an Englishman, with unbounded energy, and combining extreme gentleness with an iron sense of duty; born to command, and with a genius for communicating the love of order and regularity, which characterised him; a man before whom one could only feel inclined to bow down; here was this man come to place himself meekly under orders, and to go plodding day after day through snow and slush.

Travelling on foot from village to village, liaising with Catholic *curés* and Protestant *pasteurs*, and armed against Prussian or French shells only with the Union Jack flying from his relief wagon, Goodenough threw himself tirelessly into the work. In many ways he remained as averse to 'mere charity' as any good Victorian, but if one can strip away the period rhetoric it is possible to glimpse during these weeks something of the man Bullock Hall spoke of after his death. 'His sermon was on 1 Tim ii.1,2,' Goodenough wrote memorably of a service in the Protestant church at Bouillon in the middle of November,

and he began by referring to his last sermon, in which he enjoined the practice of charity among the many poor, and desired his hearers not to be disheartened at being deceived and imposed on by people who sometimes came to them ... Then he went on to bid the congregation pray for all men – for kings, remembering that while St Paul wrote, Nero was emperor; for all people – for both peoples in the great war; for the extension of brotherly spirit and kindness, which would prevent the possibility of future wars, and breathe a spirit of humanity into the conduct of this war; for peace ... And shall we not pray for our own dear country – that this war may do us some good? ... And before peace is made, before we are quite triumphed over, may we not pray for a little success for our country? 'Oh, God! A little success, only a little, so that we may be not utterly humbled and despised in the eyes of surrounding nations.' It was this cry of nature that was so touching to listen to. All his sermon had been so wise, and so temperate – not clever, but excellent, and all eloquence restrained by practical earnestness; and this little cry from the heart was enough to bring tears to one's eyes.

If it brought a tear it was because it was a strangled cry between patriotism and universal Christian love that went to the heart of Goodenough's own predicament as a Christian and a fighting man. For a few weeks in France he could forget it in disinterested philanthropy and hard work, but as he returned to London to take up his place on the Admiralty Committee on Designs for Ships of War the contradictions of a professional life devoted to killing – as Hastings would unblinkingly have put it – and a marriage grounded on his deepest faith cannot have escaped him.

There was something else, too, because for all his genuine Christian humility and his desire to shape his life to God's purpose, the old Adam in Goodenough would not entirely die. It is never easy for a man of his abilities to mould himself to the demands and mental restrictions of service life, and neither committee work nor the appointment as attaché to the Maritime Courts of Europe could answer his restless and almost pro-consular sense of an officer's duties and powers. 'It is weakening the desire for knowledge and self-improvement in naval officers,' he said of the existing system of training in his address to the United Service Institution.

It is tending to narrow and circumscribe the idea of responsibility of a naval commander for all things coming within his ken, and to lower his conception of his own position from that of representative of his country in all parts of the world, and agent of her policy and a guardian of her commerce, to that of being a mere executive tool, whose only argument is force. The naval reputation of this country has not been achieved by men who held so mutilated a notion of their duty as to be mere executioners of their country's judgements. I believe that I may say that we have scarcely a man in our naval history, distinguished as a naval commander in action, who has not been distinguished in some other pursuit, professional or otherwise, practical or scientific; but if we continue to acquiesce in the meagre education which is at present permitted to naval officers, we must resign ourselves to the position of a Chinese military mandarin, and be at the beck and call of civilians and consuls, and to be hustled and forced into perpetual mistakes in war.

If this was heady, even dangerous stuff – and in an age of encroaching democracy, increasing standardisation and improving communications, curiously old-fashioned – that only reflects the ambiguities that ran deep through Goodenough's character and career. For the past ten years his professional interests had been shaped by the corporate dictates of fleet life, but he had gone to sea in a different navy and a different age, an age of sail in which a man like Michael Seymour could exercise across the Pacific frontiers of civilisation just those consular functions that Goodenough saw as the naval officer's natural remit.

And if there was anywhere on the planet to feel the draw of that 'Frontier World' – and it was still there in the 1870s – it was London. Over the next year Goodenough's commonplace book would be filled with details of business and committees, but in between the sketches for hydraulic designs and Admiralty discussions, the visits to galleries and theatres, the meetings of the Biblical Society and Temperance Society, the sermons, dinners and family engagements are the constant reminders of that wider world which had always beckoned men of his temperament. 'Clerk made clever speech about the slave and coolie trade ... Walked with Clem to the India Off ... In morning to St Peter's to hear Selwyn Bp of Lincoln on mission to Melanesia ... To Geog Soc & heard Rawlinson on Central Asia ... to Clem M to see Arctic dissolving views ... Geog Society's dinner & sat next to Collinson ... the Congo ... a manly speech ... to Geog Soiree *where were all the world ...*'

Goodenough was not exaggerating – this was the Imperial capital that Jan Morris conjured into such brilliant life, a city of visiting 'lions', travellers and global experts where one was as likely to sit down to dinner next to a missionary just back from the Sandwich Islands as to a man bound for the Congo – and in spring 1873 he at last found that 'round hole', as one fellow naval officer put, for which he was supremely well fitted. 'Captain Goodenough [had spent] the winter in London,' his widow recalled, laying, as only she could, the dead hand of sober duty on an appointment that fulfilled every demand and ambition Goodenough had,

> studying, attending lectures, working both at gunnery and other things connected with the naval service, till, in April 1873, he received from the First Lord of the Admiralty the offer of going to Australia as Commodore in command of H.M.S. 'Pearl'. This was

a command which for some years he had looked upon as one which would especially interest him, and he at once began to prepare himself for his new work, trying to learn as much as he could of those seas, then quite unknown to him, as he wished to arrive on his station possessed of all the knowledge of it which he could obtain.

For a sailor who looked to Cook rather than Nelson as his model, for the evangelising Christian, philanthropist, linguist and geographer, the attractions of the Pacific islands were obvious enough, but the added lure for the ambitious consul-in-waiting in Goodenough came with his instructions to report on the possible annexation of Fiji by the British Crown. Within days of hearing the news of his appointment from Tryon Goodenough had gone 'all over' the *Pearl*, and he was soon immersing himself in Pacific politics and history, collecting everything he could find in the way of accounts of old voyages, taking soundings at the various mission societies and briefing himself, above all, on the question of enforced labour that lay at the moral and economic heart of the challenge facing him.

There was even time to get Thomas Carlyle's views, and the Sage of Chelsea was as free with them as ever. 'I said I was going to Australia for 3 yrs & he said. What is your work there?' Goodenough noted on 5 May, after meeting Carlyle at a mutual friend's house.

I said to command the Naval Station & to suppress the kidnapping of Polynesians, and he said, 'Yes, ye'll have a good work to do, and ye'll see some of those new settlers who are turning the cannibals into civilized beings. I sd. Yes! In Fiji now there are 2000 to 3000 Europeans chiefly English who have colonized Fiji & our Colonial Office is afraid to acknowledge them.

He said. That Colonial Minister is a wonder to me. It is not possible to conceive a better work than that of taking people from where there is no room and no land for them, and to remove them to another where there is plenty, and yet our Govt seem to wish to estrange our colonies, to say 'don't come too near us, you may hurt us.'

'There was something self conscious, and ... painful in his manner & way of contemning mankind's follies,' Goodenough wrote that night. 'He must be accustomed to having people about him listening &

MEN OF WAR

hanging upon him.' From a naval captain that is rich, but if things
had been as easy as Carlyle suggested, Goodenough might just as well
have stayed at home. He had not long to wait, though, for a reminder
that it was not going to be so simple. 'Today as chronicled in The
Times,' he noted a week later, 'a deputation went to Ld Kimberley to
urge the annexation of the Fiji islands & presented memorials from
the Colonial Institute & the Aboriginal Protection Society.' The forces
of interest and self-interest were massing. There were last-minute
meetings with Lord Kimberley, the Colonial Secretary, and Gladstone
– 'most kind and charming in manner – exceedingly courteous',
Goodenough wrote of the Prime Minister – and on 11 June the *Pearl*
weighed for the Cape on her passage to New Zealand and Fiji. Goodenough's time had come.

VIII

Seventeen hundred miles to the north-east of Sydney, and sprawled
across an area some three hundred miles from east to west and 250
miles from north to south, lie the three hundred or so volcanic islands,
coral atolls and uninhabited outcrops that together make up the Fiji
Islands. The largest of these – Viti Levu and Vanua Levu – add up
between them to over six of the seven thousand square miles of the
islands' total area, but in a group that covers so vast an area of ocean,
straddling the 180° meridian between the 15th and 22nd parallels, it
is inevitably complexity and diversity – ethnological, geological, mete-
orological, racial – rather than homogeneity that characterises the
history of this frontier land of Polynesian and Melanesian cultures.

Complexity was never something to which early European traders
were over-sensitive, however, and from the first sustained contacts
with the 'Cannibal Isles' the seeds of their future problems were sown.
During the first half of the nineteenth century relations with Europeans had been limited to a primitive trade in sandalwood, *bêche-
de-mer* (sea-cucumbers) or tortoise shells for the notoriously choosy
Chinese market, but from the 1850s onwards – and particularly in
the 1860s, when Civil War in America caused a world cotton shortage – a different and more permanent influx of European settlers,
bent on carving out plantations for themselves from Fiji's fertile allu-
vial plains, arrived to destabilise an already 'Hobbesian' world of
inter-tribal and inter-island wars and rivalries.

The arrival of the European settlers, diseases and missionaries – always ready to take sides – and of Western firearms not only added a new potency to these conflicts, but also had the effect of concentrating power in fewer and fewer hands. In terms of real authority the forty or so chiefs who dominated the whole of Fiji in the 1860s could have been reduced to a dozen, and by the time Goodenough sailed all petty tribal rivalries had effectively been subsumed within one overreaching struggle between the two great figures of island politics: the highly competent Ma'afu, the dominant influence in the eastern islands, and the exotic reformed cannibal Cokobau (the 'C' is pronounced 'Th'), chief of Bau, a small island off the eastern coast of Vita Levu, and self-appointed 'Tui Vitu', or King of Fiji.

This concentration of native power had its obvious advantages for Europeans, and as early as the 1840s and '50s, visiting warships, or aspiring settlers in search of land, had found it convenient to recognise a 'kingship' that was a lot more circumscribed by geography and tradition than Cokobau's title would suggest. It was clearly in everyone's interest to have a single point of authority for negotiations, but the limited scope of Cokobau's effective power, the mountainous nature of an interior that placed an effective block on his authority and, above all, the complexities of tribal land ownership meant that settlers often found themselves purchasing land to which neither buyer nor seller had any rights.

As the European settler population grew during the 1860s – thirty or forty in 1860, something around two thousand in 1870 – and the disputes and violence over land ownership grew with it, so too did the need for plantation labour. The earliest planters had confidently predicted that the Fiji Islands themselves could supply all the labour that would ever be needed, but as it became clear that the native inhabitants were culturally antipathetic to plantation work, a system of imported island labour that shaded darkly into a new form of slavery became a feature of Fijian and Pacific life.

It was this trade in labour, morally questionable at its mildest, and vile at its worst, that most attracted British concern and made 'intervention-creep' in Fiji inevitable. In 1858 William Pritchard had been appointed the first British Consul to the islands, and although he had no magisterial powers, his mere presence there and the looming authority of the power he represented – visible in the occasional visit of a man-of-war – gave him a *de facto* role in regulating disputes between settler and settler, and settler and native chief, that imperceptibly nudged Britain towards a more influential role in island politics than she would have wanted.

As early as 1859, under Pritchard's zealous influence, Cokobau had been induced into an offer of cession that he was in no position to deliver, and Britain's rejection merely postponed an intervention that a decade of mass settlement made increasingly urgent. It needs to be remembered that there was a genuine hostility in British political circles at this time to colonial expansion of any kind, but successive governments could neither ignore the behaviour of British citizens to each other, nor – of far greater importance to the philanthropic and missionary lobbies that shaped the national conscience and drove forward policy in such fields – tolerate the ill-treatment by British traders or settlers of the native populations of the islands.

During the 1860s there were attempts by the settlers, and by a handful of influential European 'advisors' who attached themselves to individual chiefs, to regulate for themselves their relationship with the islanders. In the east the Lau Confederation went some way to formalising the authority of Ma'afu, while in the west, in 1867, a ludicrously elaborate and idealistic constitution was established under 'Cokobau I' and his successors that gave Fiji a constitutional monarchy and a system of native 'governors' that bore no resemblance to any actual or traditional reality.

In an island group where new war canoes were still launched across the bodies of prisoners used as rollers, the corner posts of a chief's house were supported by men buried alive, and cannibalism was flourishing in the mountain areas, it was not surprising that a constitution calling for a Secretary of State, a Minister for War, a Minister for Police, a Collector-General of Revenue, the control of land sales, labour contracts and self-taxation and the right to happiness should fail. Within four years a second and even more luminously Benthamite fantasy had similarly imploded, and by 1873 the tensions endemic to the islands had brought Fiji to the edge of anarchy.

There were all the old, historic, indigenous fault lines still, and those newer tensions between planter and merchant, planter and native, 'government' and missionary and 'government' and taxpayer, but the real split was between those who, either through disinterest or calculation, supported the natives and those who looked forward to their extirpation. During the years of constitutional experiment the 'government' had of course been carried out in the name of

Cokobau, but the real power during this time lay with the small cabal of Europeans who ran – and if their enemies are to be believed, exploited – his government in the face of a mounting tide of hostility from the disaffected majority of Fiji's foreign community.

Among this small group of advisors, the most interesting and important figure in the annexation story was a man called John Bates Thurston – the future Sir John Thurston KCMG – Cokobau's secretary and *de facto* ruler of Fiji. Thurston had been born in London in 1836, and after a period with the merchant service and a brief spell sheep farming in New South Wales, had set out on a 'botanising' expedition among the Western Pacific islands that ended in shipwreck and an eighteen-month exile on the then virtually unvisited island of Samoa before, in 1860, a Wesleyan missionary ship had rescued him and taken him to Fiji.

To any modern ear, sensitised by even a modicum of post-colonial guilt, Thurston's is the one voice among the Fijian planters that speaks a language that is even remotely sympathetic. During his eighteen months in Samoa he laid down the foundation of a profound knowledge of island life, and however inevitable the note of paternalism in his tone, or however much – as his enemies insisted – personal vanity and ambition played their part in his actions, his policies in Fiji were the only ones aimed at protecting the native Fijian against the domination of the white settler. 'While the Fijians have benefited by civilization the British subject has benefited by becoming the possessor of large tracts of land,' he explained for London's benefit in October 1873, intra-colonial snobbery and genuine concern nicely balanced: 'many such subjects of Her Majesty who a few years ago were ordinary seamen in colonial merchant vessels, are now the proprietors of whole islands, petty principalities, and have removed, or are now striving to remove the inhabitants. Thus in many cases the benefits derived from the settlement of civilised man has been bought at a high cost, and in many cases it is open to doubt whether the Fijian has received anything but a spurious article.'

It was his insistence on native rights, and his willingness to mobilise the native majority enshrined in the 1871 constitution to get them, that brought Thurston to the edge of civil war with the discontented rump of the white community. In the eyes of his enemies his idealism was no more than a cover for his own ambitions, but the more likely truth is that he had the zealot's adamantine belief that he and his cause were one. 'I have no doubt that he is perfectly honest in his views and desires for a native Government,' Goodenough would write of him after their first meeting, 'but he implies, and evidently thinks, that no one but Ministers have any political honesty at all, and he has told me in conversation that all the white men in Fiji are alike – missionaries, merchants, and all, in their resolve to suppress the self-government of the natives ... self-government of natives being, in his view, the direction of affairs by himself, Mr Woods, and Dr Clarkson [two other European members of the government], who, like many other bold, confident men, believe that they alone are honest, and have the secret of ruling.'

In Thurston's eyes, faced as he was with this determination of the white settlers not to be governed by 'an inferior race', the only alternatives were an independent Fiji with a constitution that guaranteed native control through native chiefs, or annexation by Britain. On 31 January 1873 he had persuaded Cokobau to renew his appeal to London for Fiji to be taken under British protection, but he was too wily a politician to leave it at that, and over the succeeding months had carefully prepared his fallback position, drafting and promulgating, without consultation, a new constitution that firmly tilted the balance of power in the direction of his native constituency.

It was into this cauldron of discontent, political posturing, Lilliputian constitutions and Klan vigilantism – part Gilbert and Sullivan operetta and part looming tragedy – that Goodenough, in advance of the new consul Edgar Layard, headed in the late autumn of 1873. The *Pearl* had made a leisurely passage as far as the Cape, and after a rapid voyage down to New Zealand to assume his new command, Goodenough had touched on Savage Island and Samoa before arriving on 16 November at Levuka, the thriving commercial centre on the eastern coast of the small island of Ovalau, off Viti Levu.

Only the presence of a British man-of-war, HMS *Blanche*, and the prompt actions of her Captain Simpson in upholding Thurston's authority, had contained the unrest provoked by the constitutional crisis of 1873, and Goodenough could not have found a challenge so perfectly fitted to his consular ambitions. In his last meeting in London Gladstone had spoken 'seriously of the great disadvantages' of annexation, but while Goodenough could have had no doubt about the strict limitation of his brief, thousands of miles of ocean and delayed communications between London and Fiji gave him a tempting and dangerous freedom of action.

The only real concern in London, in fact – luridly publicised after the murder of Bishop Patteson by islanders to whom every white man was a kidnapper and slaver – was the labour trade; but it was one thing in Goodenough's view to take a cavalier view of Fijian internal matters from the safety of the Colonial Office, and quite another when faced with the scale of unrest and potential violence on the spot. 'Captain Simpson was called upon to deal with circumstances which had probably never before presented themselves to an English Naval Officer,' Goodenough reported back to the Admiralty in his first letter from Fiji on 27 November, before – mentally, as it were – departing from his predecessor's stance and clearing the decks for action.

> There is ... now an unusual state of things here ... and the taxes ... have been exacted ... by the aid of British naval forces on this station, and could have been collected in no other way short of the employment of Fijian soldiery, armed and commanded by English-men, against the majority of white settlers, of whom five sixths are also Englishmen ...
>
> Such a condition of things cannot be allowed to continue. I could not allow a new arrangement [native voting rights and a built-in native majority to keep Thurston in power] to be promulgated without protest, when it is certain that its authority could only be maintained by means of a native armed force led by British subjects; nor could I continue to countenance the present irresponsible form of Government, under which a few British subjects demand taxes from other British subjects, and spend money so obtained under the protection of the British flag; without which protection, collision, and probably bloodshed, would be sure to ensue.
>
> In accordance with Mr. Thurston's wish, I received him on board the 'Pearl' on the 26th instant, and had a conversation with him, in which I pointed out that ... it was absurd for him to suppose ... that the foreign residents generally could be expected to submit to the despotic rule of two Europeans.

It had not been a comfortable meeting, because if Goodenough had not made up his mind in favour of annexation before he even left London, it did not take him long to do so. On the face of it one might have expected him to side with Thurston, but with the missionaries and the vast bulk of the white population equally hostile to the Secretary, Goodenough moved swiftly to block any new constitution and withdraw the *de facto* legitimacy of Cokobau's government. 'I thought it right to inform him pointedly that every British subject employed in [a Fijian] force, seniors as well as juniors, by whose orders any act leading to bloodshed might be committed, ought to be informed that he would be held responsible before the Supreme Court at Sydney,' Goodenough wrote.

> Mr. Thurston objected that it was very hard that a *de facto* Government, recognised as such by Her Majesty's Government, and carried on by Englishmen whose denationalisation had been virtually assented to ... should be threatened with the supreme court if they attempted to maintain the independence of their adopted country; and I informed him that it was not so, and that it was most proper that British subjects, who had taken upon themselves to employ large numbers of uneducated irresponsible natives, in opposition to a majority of their fellow-countrymen, should have a severe check placed upon their actions.

Goodenough was taking a lot on his shoulders – Thurston had a perfectly legitimate point, and he himself had sailed under specific instructions to recognise the *de facto* government – but he had no intention of allowing orders conceived in ignorance of the proper state of affairs to stand in the way of duty. 'Much correspondence has passed between Mr. Thurston, The Chief Secretary and myself, with which I need not trouble their Lordships,' he wrote loftily a fortnight later,

> consisting of queries from Mr. Thurston as to whether I still acknowledged the *de facto* Government of Fiji ... I have answered that I do not recognise the *de facto* Government.
>
> ... in his letters, he speaks of the white population as turbulent, treacherous, and threatening personal violence, and even assassination to the Ministers ... I have seen a great many of the British and other settlers, and the above is not the impression I have formed of them. The great majority of those whom I have seen only wish for the security of a strong Government to enable them to prosecute their industrial pursuits; and I have received all who have come to see me, comprising merchants, planters, and missionaries of both denominations.

There can be no question that Goodenough took his soundings
conscientiously, and if the conclusion he was inexorably moving
towards was at odds with traditional British policy, that again seemed
to him only an index of official ignorance of the true state of Fijian
affairs. 'I have had the opportunity of seeing a Mr Swanston' – 'a
native Minister and ... a fearless and straightforward man, with no
interest to advance' – he reported to the Admiralty, highlighting the
gap that existed between any theoretical notion of island 'government' and the chaos that existed, who had

> just returned from an expedition in the interior of Viti Levu, under-
> taken ostensibly to punish the murderers of some white settlers ...
> but really to subjugate the tribes who had never 'lotu-ed' (accepted
> Christianity and a teacher) or acknowledged Cocobau's rule. In the
> course of operations many towns have been burnt, and cannibal-
> ism has been returned to among the auxiliaries to the drilled Fijians
> employed on the Government side, in spite of all endeavours of
> white officers to suppress it.
>   The mountaineers who escaped with life were at first ordered
> to divide themselves among the peaceable villages nearer the
> coast, by Mr Swanston, who had the entire management and
> direction of the undertaking. But King Cocobau's Ministers, being
> pressed for money to pay the heavy expenses of Government,
> determined, in Mr. Swanston's absence, to endeavour to obtain
> money for the treasury by the conviction of these men as rebels
> and traitors, and then by hiring them out as convicts to the white
> settlers.

'I am informed on good authority,' Goodenough immediately wrote
to Thurston, again arrogating to himself an authority that went some
way beyond his brief,

> that some 800 prisoners of war – including men, women and chil-
> dren – are to be tried before the judges of Fiji, during this week,
> for the crime of rebellion, and that these people, if found guilty,
> will be sent into servitude for terms varying from three to four
> years ...
>   You have referred to the subjugation of these mountaineers as
> an evidence of protection given to British settlers by the Fijian
> Government, and I therefore must dispel ... any belief which the

> Fijian Government may have of these trials being viewed with satisfaction by Her Majesty's Government. Most of these men never owned the authority of the Chief of Bau [Cokobau], or the establishment of the Kingdom of Fiji ... They have been subdued by King Cokobau's Government, and made to acknowledge his authority, when fighting for their independence. It may be an object of military necessity to remove them from their mountain homes, whence they might have made raids upon peaceable villages, but they have not committed the crime of rebellion, and I protest against their being treated as rebels.

He was equally peremptory in his proclamation to the white planters. 'It has been represented to me, that various prisoners of war, taken in arms ... are now to be tried at the Island of Goro for the crime of rebellion,' he warned them, leaving no one in any doubt that it was Her Majesty's Navy and not Thurston's government that was in control. 'I hereby warn all British subjects that the hiring or engaging of these men is an act of slavery, under 6 & 7 Vict., cap. 98, and will be so regarded by me.'

During these first weeks Goodenough had necessarily acted alone, but at the end of December, Consul Layard, his co-commissioner on the annexation question, arrived to take up his duties, and on 1 January 1874 the two men formally announced to Cokobau the nature of their mission. In their future despatches to London the pair of them almost invariably write as 'we', but it is impossible not to hear in their reports the dominant voice of Goodenough and the retrospective justification for the freedom with which he had exceeded his instructions during his first month in the islands.

He and Layard had been sent to observe, take soundings and report, and not to initiate policy, but his reasoning again was that events had outstripped their instructions before they had even arrived. 'We have found the Government in these islands to be in a far less settled state than we had supposed it to be,' he informed Lord Kimberley on 13 February.

> We had been inclined to believe that we should find union, at all events among the Chiefs, in their desire for a general Government; and also that the majority of the planters would be found in favour of the present Ministers ... Moreover, we were severally enjoined, by our instructions, to recognise a Government as *de facto*, whose

Ministry and formation were, in some sort, known to her Majesty's Government.

The above anticipations have not been realized.

There were crucial moral issues at stake, of course – the treatment of the native inhabitants and the issue of plantation labour – but there were also urgent economic considerations that in Goodenough's eyes demanded annexation. During the first half of the 1860s a booming cotton industry had seemed to promise prosperity to the islands, but the collapse of the market at the end of the decade, and the difficulty of attracting fresh investment to so politically fraught a situation, had made it almost impossible for the swelling influx of settlers to start up new enterprises. 'We are aware that your Lordship will expect from us, in our general Report, a detailed statement of the finances of the Islands,' Goodenough and Layard wrote by way of explanation. 'We have not been able to obtain any statements from the Government, but we believe that the total indebtedness amounts to not less than 75,000 l., bearing interest at 10 per cent., which appears to have been spent, in addition to the revenue raised. The planters seem to be aware that this is about the amount, and seem to be willing to increase their present rate of taxation if the Islands be annexed to Great Britain.'

It is hard to know to what extent Goodenough and Layard found what they wanted to find, and ignored what did not fit in, but in the six weeks between Layard's arrival and this first report they had mustered all the support they could want from settler and native. In so far as it actually meant anything the two men continued to recognise the *de facto* authority of Thurston's government, but with every meeting Goodenough's own private convictions took on an increasingly *ad hominem* note. 'Got heap of letters from Thurston, confound him ... 4 or 5 letters from Thurston, hang him ... Is he capable of a lie – oh yes ... Thurston and Woods to dine, jovial & patting each other on the back & more distasteful to me than before even; Quite disgusting ... Cur & blackguard ... that liar is a good deal cleverer than I am, having the native chiefs at his back.'

He was scarcely more complimentary in private about 'Old Layard' and his 'absurd' manners and uniform – 'I see I shall have to tell Layard what to do in everything' – or his new master, Ward Hunt, at the Admiralty – 'fat vulgar fellow!' – but neither the enemy nor his own side was going to deflect him from his agenda. 'Commodore

Goodenough and Consul Layard are the two Chiefs sent out by Her Britannic Majesty the Queen of England to visit Fiji,' he explained to Cokobau, loading the dice heavily in favour of a policy antipathetic to the wishes of his own government:

> These two Chiefs desire to consult with the King and Chiefs of Fiji fully and clearly, that they may know what they (the Chiefs) desire, or prefer ...
>
> Should it be their true minds (the King and Chiefs of Fiji) to give Fiji to England, that it should become the Queen of England's to govern, there is but one object and desire sought – Fiji's peace and welfare in all time, – that the King and Chiefs, with all their people, and the inhabitants of the land, may live in peace and prosper. This, and only this, is the desire and object.
>
> It is no new thing for England to govern islands like Fiji. She owns and governs in several parts of the world, a great number of similar islands to Fiji, and it will be very easy for her to govern Fiji also, and to preserve its peace and promote the welfare and pros-perity of its people.

Cokobau was no more in a position to understand the nature of a British Protectorate than he was the constitutions promulgated in his name, but with all the evidence they needed of island unrest and polit-ical failure, Goodenough and Layard were ready to act. 'Affairs being in this state,' they concluded their report to London, serving on Lord Carnarvon, Lord Kimberley's successor in Disraeli's new government, what amounted to a virtual *fait accompli*,

> we have informed King Cocobau that he should consult the foreign Consuls prior to giving effect to any act of his Government; and we are prepared, although with great reluctance, to assume the temporary Protectorate of the islands should it be necessary, as any further acts of the Ministers would probably lead to confusion, and possibly to bloodshed. The necessary interference of the Senior Naval Officer here, during the past year, has already amounted at times to a virtual Protectorate.
>
> Your Lordship will gather, from the slight sketch we have here given of the state of affairs, that there seems no way at present out of the difficulties in which the community is plunged, and no Secu-rity for the future, but in Her Majesty's Government taking a much

stronger interest in the Government and welfare of British subjects here than has heretofore seemed expedient; and the formation of the Fiji group into a Crown Colony seems to us, even at this early period of our inquiry, the surest and best mode of doing so, if the resolution of the King and Chiefs would show, as we do not doubt it will, their desire for annexation.

'It [was] not in accordance with their instructions for them to issue such a document,' Lord Carnarvon irritably complained of Goodenough's and Layard's offer of a protectorate, but by the time the news of it reached London it was already too late. There was one last throw from Thurston, and a series of ludicrous demands – yachts, titles, pensions – from the chiefs that delayed negotiations, but by 21 March Goodenough had got his way, and Cokobau had signed an unconditional cession agreement that left all such ancillary measures 'to the justice and generosity of Britain'.

'Now I must work heart & soul to get the Govt to take the islands,' Goodenough noted in his journal that night, 'or all that will be worse than before, a good deal worse', but the only risk he actually ran was in overplaying his hand. Carnarvon was no different from any other minister in objecting to having policy forced on him by a junior, and if there was very little he could do to reverse the process Goodenough had begun, he could at least register his displeasure by refusing him the public fruits of victory. 'I share the usual fate of the naval officer,' Goodenough wrote huffily in his journal six months later, as he prepared to escort Sir Hercules Robinson, the Governor of New South Wales, out to Fiji to provide Carnarvon with a 'second opinion' before accepting cession, 'Viz, to be buoyé on the wheel of difficulty for a civilian to come and pick my brains afterwards.'

It might have been more graceful if Goodenough had left it at that, but what was at risk was not so much annexation as his *amour propre*, and he seems to have been incapable of leaving the matter alone. 'I think the Lord Carnarvon has behaved rudely to me – very rudely ... in treating me *de haut en bas*, as though I had nothing to do with the matter,' he wrote in his journal, and he was prepared to make his resentment official. 'That paper, – the version of the negotiations and correspondence printed for Parliament, –' he complained in a draft letter to Carnarvon preserved in the archive of the Melanesian Mission,

presents to Parliament a view of the proceedings of myself and Mr
Layard which does not give an accurate impression of our actions
in Fiji ... I do not presume to dictate the manner in which the Secretary of State should make an official communication, but I am
bound to express my regret that the execution of the service
entrusted to me and Mr Layard was thought by Lord Carnarvon
to have been of so little significance as not to require even the notice
which a disapproval of our acts involves.

He was talking nonsense – he had loaded his enquiries and report
shamelessly in favour of annexation – and if there was any doubt of
that the gratitude of the planters would soon dispel it. 'On Monday
morning a deputation of gentlemen waited on Commodore Goodenough,' the *Fiji Times* recorded the following year, on the occasion
of Goodenough's return to the islands,

> on board the Pearl, to present to him a very beautiful illuminated
> address as an emblem of the respect he was held in, and the serv-
> ices he has so generously rendered to the Europeans resident in Fiji
> by so nobly aiding them to achieve annexation with Great Britain
> ... 'We the undersigned, residents in Fiji [ran the address from the
> settlers], beg to express our appreciation of your services ... for the
> purposes of enquiring into the condition of this country. The happy
> result of which has been the annexation of these islands to Great
> Britain, brought about mainly by the firmness, diplomacy, and
> untiring zeal which you evinced while carrying out the duties of
> your commission ... Your uniform unvarying kindness and cour-
> tesy has won for you the esteem and respect of all.'

It was not an exaggerated tribute. The annexation of Fiji is often
portrayed as a watershed in colonial history, but while it was certainly
a move that heralded the arrival of Disraelian imperialism on the
political map, it had taken some very old-fashioned and autocratic
naval virtues to help bring it about. The irritation in London and the
venom of Fijian opponents were as much proof of that as the gratitude of the settlers. 'The high and mighty autocrat distinguished by
a broad pennant,' was how one newspaper cutting preserved by the
Commodore described him, and Carnarvon had not finished with
him yet either. 'Disgusting CMG has come uppermost in my
thoughts,' Goodenough wrote in his journal, at the end of a

prolonged and losing battle to reject a second exquisitely pitched rebuff that the government had dealt him for his part in annexation,

> but a thought with it to explain how I regard it. I am reminded of a young Chinese lady whom I once saw at a Taouist [sic] temple near the North Gate of Ningpo. She had bought a number of incense sticks to correspond with the number of gods wh. lined the sides of one chamber of the temple & had lit and stuck one up before the figure of each. There still remained one in her hand and she stood in the middle of the hall pressing the remaining stick to her lips, as an English lady does her knitting needle when counting or accounting for her stitches, and nodding her head gently at each grotesque looking god. At last she makes a shot and lighting her stick at random sticks it into the hollow stomach of the god wh. she fancies she may have missed ... taking the offer of CMG at its best Ld C is like the young lady in the carelessly perfunctory offer & I am as indifferent as the grotesque joss.

It would be nice to think he meant it, but it was probably as well that he did not live long enough to see his old enemy become Sir John Thurston KCMG. 'Read my letters to Thurston,' he wrote some months after it was all over, 'what a waste of time & trouble.' It was a sadly sour end to a venture that had engaged him as nothing else in his career, but he had done what he thought right, and that was enough. And besides, he had long outgrown any narrow 'mandarin' concept of 'duty' as a Kimberley or Carnarvon or any mere politician might conceive it. 'Some one spoke the other day of love and duty,' he had written to his fiancée almost ten years earlier, 'and which was the higher motive. I think that love is the stronger, higher motive, and that perfect love replaces duty. As it casts out fear; and if my love was always fervent enough, I should never feel it necessary to obey a call of duty.'

He was about to discover the consequences of that conviction. If he had known what those would be in advance, though, it would not have deflected him. '*Aut Caesar aut Nihil*' – Either Caesar or nothing – Byron had once remarked tellingly of himself, and there was a trace of the same pride in Goodenough. A CMG had never been his idea of a corruptible or an incorruptible crown.

IX

In the middle of April 1874, after a stay of five months among the Fijian islands, and almost a year out of England, HMS *Pearl* at last weighed for Sydney. There is an inevitable tendency with a story like Goodenough's to allow death to cast its backward shadow, but while the note of reverence in his widow's memoir thickens with every day that Santa Cruz creeps closer, bathing every chance encounter in significance, cherishing every fresh proof of his goodness, hoarding every encomium of friend and casual stranger, it is a temptation that needs resisting.

With the annexation of Fiji Goodenough had certainly completed his most important work, but he had no intention of breaking his staff, and at the age of forty-three he was a man at the height of his powers, a naval commodore to his fingertips, full of ambition, confident in his authority, happy in his appointment, strong in health, critical of all shoddiness and stern as a disciplinarian. 'If he had got overcome in jolly company,' he wrote after his steward had been found drunk only days after Goodenough had instituted a Temperance Offensive,

> it would have been my duty to punish him, but I shd have thought less of it. But this was a case of a man taking a part of the ship's stores of which he had charge & in private & alone sucking at it for pleasure & excitement of tickling his throat & going to bed stupid – I had no sympathy with a case of this kind at all ...
>
> Algernon preached most unluckily on the parable of the unjust steward wh was the Gospel for the day ... Fortunately the Stwd was not in church.

The widow's vision of the *Pearl* as a supremely happy ship, ploughing the oceans and exploring the wonders of the deep in God's name, is one that Goodenough's unexpurgated journals hardly bear out. It is impossible to tell at this distance whether he had simply been unlucky with his ship's officers, but few of them did not at some stage or another feel the rough edge of his tongue: 'I spoke to [Reade] & he said he had so many things to look after – I couldn't help saying that so had every officer since Noah,' he noted typically. 'He is a thoroughly bad officer, as bad as can be, & knows nothing of his work – How am I to get rid of him? ... Payton, Eyre and Carslake came to dine with me, the latter is a stupid ass – not a high form at all ... I inspected marines at dawn. *Dirty dogs!* ... reproved Carslake for sitting about and talking to a mid ... Reade is a useless ass ... that poor little wretch Fullerton as bad. Hay is the only Lt worth a straw ...'

Even the Hon. and Revd Algernon Stanley – the 'connection', as Goodenough's widow grandly put it, 'whom he had asked to accompany him to Australia' – and his endlessly 'incomprehensible' sermons did not escape. But nothing could dent Goodenough's enthusiasm for long. During periods of adverse squalls he would sing '*La Donna è mobile, come il* [sic] *vento*' to himself, and the old sense of wonder that had filled his letters to his wife from the Mediterranean was as strong as ever. 'So delightfully cool ... moon & Venus at 4.30am ... a bright meteor ... like a firefly in colour.'

And in the rich variety of the islands' cultures, their flora and fauna and geological formations, the beliefs and practices of the indigenous peoples, their dress, weapons, sexual practices, abortions, infanticide, cannibalism and, above all, languages – he seems to have spoken seven fluently – there was always something to engage the curiosity of a man like Goodenough. 'As the day broke,' he wrote on 24 April 1874, when some eight hundred miles to the west of Fiji they sighted the land of New Caledonia, complete with the French settlement and penal colony from which Victor Rochefort, the notorious aristocratic author, polemicist, anti-Bonapartist, communard and future anti-Dreyfusard had only just escaped,

we saw the small sandy islets covered with fir trees, and forming such a contrast to the cocoa-nuts of Fiji ... The whole place looks as if French money was being spent with both hands and I heard soon after that the home government spends about 4,000,000 francs a year on the transportation service. This for 8000 *transportes* or *condamnes*, and 300 *deportes*. Of the *transportes* there are 2000 on the island of Nou, of whom 1600 are sick, invalids, old, or incorrigibles; in short all the worst of them ...

The Governor says he has more than 10,000 people to feed ... Beef is now 7½ d, and mutton 3½ per pound. This is at all events cheaper than at Fiji by 2½d. The 10,000 persons to be fed are the confined portion of the 8000 *condamnes* and 3,500 *deportes*, also 1500 troops, infantry and artillery. Arranged to go to the Convict establishment at Nou to-morrow.

'Some splendid bunyan trees' in the hospital garden and an 'old professor of mathematics at Paris, who had taken part in the Commune' caught his eye; but the most 'interesting object' was undoubtedly an ex-naval lieutenant called Lullier. 'He was a general under the commune,' Goodenough noted,

> and was always a fellow of great energy. On being put on board the transport, he refused to put on a convict dress; no other was given him, and he remained in a cell, with a floor eighteen inches wide (against the side of the ship) for the whole passage, with a blanket for his entire covering. He has been in a cell for the whole of his stay here, five months; altogether eight or nine months of cell. The doctor said to him the other day, 'You had better come to hospital, your legs and feet are swollen, and your face too; you are a subject for treatment. You will have to put on the hospital dress;' which is a convict hospital dress. 'No,' he said, 'I won't, *J'aime mieux crever.*' They say he is at times mad.

After their brief stay on New Caledonia, the *Pearl* anchored at Sydney in May 1874, and while the ship underwent a two-month refit, Goodenough settled with his wife and two young sons, who had followed him to Australia, into the 'first and only established home' of their married life. 'I am first of all delighted with Trollope's great accuracy of impression and honesty in conveying it,' he noted after reading the novelist's recent account of his Australasian travels. 'Generally one feels very much as one did in most towns of the United States, that with an abundance of social good-nature there is a lack of culture, and a dearth of subjects of general interest, especially among the colonial born. I should fear that another twenty years will sensibly lower the highest grade of both the social and political tone, while perhaps the lowest may be raised.'

'All is failure here,' he wrote of Dalrymple, Tasmania, 'poverty and misery, added to the bad type they have sprung from – viz., the convicts', but it was only a part of the picture. 'I am bound to say that the great impression produced upon my mind after seeing a little of this colony, and these colonies,' he wrote, 'is a feeling of intense pride at what has been achieved by Englishmen, and of pleasure at the sight of so much physical well-being and independence of character – with less ostentation in our class, and far less independence of manner (in the bad sense) among the other, than I had expected.'

The one thing on which he disagreed with Trollope, in fact, was not convict labour or what they both saw as the inevitable eradication of the Aboriginal people, but Trollope's insistence on the necessary severance of the colonies from Britain. 'The flattering attentions with which you receive us, and almost overwhelm us,' Goodenough declared, when answering at a banquet the toast of 'The Navy', induce us to hope that we may really be links in a great chain of sympathy which binds the Mother country to Englishmen in either hemisphere; and if this be so, and if we succeed in fulfilling such an office, may I be allowed to carry the metaphor further, while I suggest that these great communities are in some sort anchors, by which the great vessel of the English state shall be moored and secured in future times of political and social strife.'

It was fitting that Goodenough should be speaking, because the banquet was held in honour of the annexation of Fiji, at which King Cokobau and Sir Hercules Robinson were the principal guests. 'I am very glad to have this opportunity of publicly acknowledging how much the success of my recent mission to Fiji is attributable to the skilful preparation of the ground by those who preceded me,' Robinson had told his audience, paying a handsome, if belated, compliment to a man London still seemed determined to slight.

> The labours of the late Commissioners – my friends Commodore Goodenough and Mr Layard – extending over five months, have not yet, I think, received the appreciation they deserve ... To them we are indebted for the very complete information as to Fiji we now possess ... Indeed, I can only say that I have often felt ashamed during the progress of my negotiations, of the extent to which I was profiting by the result of the labour of those who preceded me. You, many of you, I dare say, have seen what a good man the Commodore is across country [hunting was the only sport Goodenough pursued with any passion]. Well, I felt when I was in Fiji, as if I were riding after him over a stiff country, and that he having broken the top rails, I was triumphantly galloping through the gaps.

'In the course of my visits to the South Seas,' Goodenough told the dinner when it was his turn to speak, spelling out for them what he saw as the responsibilities of colonialism,

I have found that there is a prevailing conviction of British even-
handed justice, and I trust, that that being so, the recent acquisition we have made of new territory may be regarded as the fruit
of the confidence in that justice, which has prevailed in these
islands. It rests with the people of New South Wales especially,
who will have connection with these islands, either by family relations, or by commercial relations, to justify the confidence which
has hitherto been exhibited. I trust, that throughout the inter-
course of the people of the colony with the native races, will
justify that confidence. It is not sufficient for government to exercise its power to secure even-handed justice to both races which
are under its sway, but it is also necessary for those who go to Fiji
for a time, to have higher interests and desires than those of
making money, and to endeavour to secure the welfare of the
people living there.

It is interesting to hear Goodenough articulate his exalted faith in
colonialism and the obligations of colonialism so clearly, because it
is a reminder of just how firmly he belongs to his age. It would be
impossible to imagine a man more open to the island cultures of the
Pacific, but anchoring it is that same core paternalism, that same ultimate faith in the benevolence of British intervention and of the Christian mission, that had put him instinctively on the side of the settler
and the cessionist in Fiji. 'Now how great is the change!' he lectured
one group of islanders on Nive whose ancestors had driven off Cook.
'Instead of spears & axes I see everyone well clothed & well taught
& living in good houses. To whom do you owe this & how has it
come about? You owe it to the men who come from England to teach
you and live among you.'
     He would not always be consistent in this – he particularly liked
the Tongans, the 'snobs' of the Pacific, for their refusal to ape Western ways – and the longer he was among the islands the more clearly
he saw the dangers inherent in white domination. 'Suppose you offer
a man a canoe,' he reported Cokobau saying to him as he came on
board the *Pearl* on the day of the signing of the Deed of Cession, 'but
say, you shall have such a man for your steersman you shall use such
a rope and sail and so on. At last the man says, "Hang your rope.
Hang your canoe! Who asked for it!" He had come on bd in a black
coat against Thurston's wish saying, "This is the day of the white
man and I will put on a black coat."'

The sight of Cokobau in Western dress cannot have made easy viewing for a man who had done so much to bring annexation about, and there was not much comfort to come. 'Sir A [Sir Arthur Gordon, the first Governor of Fiji] shewed me a bit of correspondence between various people on Fiji,' Goodenough wrote some nine months later.

> His instructions are now injurious as to the native population – carping at Cocobau's salary, disposing of the land in the coolest way – such phrases occur as 'the natives must be taught as soon as possible.' The whole paper breathes a spirit of superiority of race & superlative condescension wh looks ill for the future.
>
> The tone of the whole paper is 'The natives are to live hereafter by our permission. If they die out so much the worse for them.' All this is very sad. I see everyone ready to cheat the natives of their lands. Some en gros and some en detail.

'It is evident that Fiji now palls greatly upon me & I am tired of the whole affair, having ... no responsibility in the matter,' he wrote after playing ferryman to the new governor, but official duties still had their more congenial side. 'Ladies and gentlemen,' he told his audience in a speech crowded with unrecognised ironies, when he was invited to unveil a statue to his hero James Cook:

> As you are doubtless aware, on this day, 146 years ago, the great navigator, whose statue has just been uncovered, was born in the small village of Marton, near Whitby, in Yorkshire. On the 21st of February, 1779,* Captain Cook met his death at the hands of the natives of a then obscure and just-discovered island of the South Seas. During the short fifty-one years between those two dates, a life was lived, and a character was developed, which has served, and will long serve, as an example for all Englishmen living in both hemispheres. The life was an example of diligence, of industry, and of devotion to duty; and the character which was thus developed was one which shows perseverance, constancy, courage and generosity ... If we could imagine Captain Cook ever returning to earth, with Mr Banks and Dr Solander to botanise once more on the shores of Botany Bay, with what delight would they look round

---

* Actually 4 February 1779.

on this vast assembly which I see before me; with what intense delight would they look upon the comfortable houses, numerous churches, and noble buildings which everywhere surround us! Captain Cook, as a man of great humanity, had an intense love for his fellow creatures, and with what feelings would he compare the mud and wattle cottage in which his father lived with the comfortable cottages which every industrious man can obtain for himself with fair labour ... You should consider your condition, and honour the name of the great captain who first brought ships to these shores!

Goodenough seems to have been incapable of public speaking without preaching, but if he was offering Cook as an example to his colonial audience, the great navigator also had a more personal relevance as a role model. During a few intense months in the Baltic and China Goodenough had probably seen as much action as most mid-century officers can have done, but at the dawn of an age in which the mere presence of the Mediterranean Fleet was enough to dispel the threat of war, it was more than ever not Nelson but Cook who seemed to offer a template of 'diligence', 'industry', 'courage' and 'devotion to duty' round which he could cut his own peacetime cloth. 'The islands had a special charm for the Commodore,' recalled the *Pearl*'s chaplain – on his day as 'incomprehensible' as Stanley in Goodenough's opinion. 'Imbued with the records of early discoveries, admiring Captain Cook as a true pattern of a discoverer, as brave yet prudent, high-minded, accurate, truthful, the Commodore seemed to think it a worthy aim to try and supplement the discoveries of his great predecessor.'

With the illicit labour trade as great a challenge as ever, there was enough to keep him busy as well, with the added spice of cannibalism always in the background to add a certain *frisson* to the *Pearl*'s work. 'The master of the Sybil told me that he had picked up a boy who had swam to him from the rocks of Nguna,' Goodenough noted from the New Hebrides group after he had been asked to take the same child, the only survivor of a cannibal attack on a group of escapees from a labour ship, back to his own island of Pentecost. 'By 10.15 we reached Mr. Milne's (the missionary) house, small but well built on a concrete foundation, in a nice garden fifty yards from the beach, quite pretty,' Goodenough continued.

He had heard of the landing and killing of these boys of Pentecost, and had no doubt that if killed it was for the sake of eating ... and said, that though the people near him would not eat men, those at the other end would do so directly. A lot of savage looking rascals had followed us from the boat to the house, and sat there listening. I asked Mr. Milne to let them know what we were talking about; and they declared that they never eat men, that what happened at the other end of Nguna they knew very little about. One carried on a conversation by signs with my Pentecost man ... ending by biting his own wrists, with upraised eyebrows, as a sign of interrogation; and on receiving an affirmative sign of upraised chin from the latter, putting on a look of well-assumed repugnance. The mouth and wrinkles of the nose would have made a splendid article for Darwin's 'Expression of the emotions in Man and Animals'.

Goodenough might not have believed the men, but they were too frightened to act as his guides, and so, returning to the ship, he steamed around to the north-west of the island, going ashore again with a party of eight men armed with revolvers and a back-up party in a second cutter. They made their way up a narrow path that climbed gently up from the beach, and eventually, after a steeper climb, came to a level platform used as a sacred dancing ground and, two hundred feet above it, among great boulders of volcanic tufa and a luxuriant riot of hibiscus, draecaenas, crotons and ferns, the village they were looking for.

From behind the trees, women – all of them ugly, 'some what we should call hideous' – peered out at them, while the men, their faces painted black and red, the septums of their large, wide noses pierced with bones or shells, their limbs decorated with tortoiseshell, plates and shells hanging from their necks and bamboo combs in their hair, stood their ground. 'I found the chief and shook hands,' Goodenough wrote,

and the interpreter began his story. The men looked rather fine, and bigger than Vate men; but great brutes and rascals I should say. My interpreter had evidently sold himself to these fellows, and was intending to make all square. He said what I had to say in a very few words ... and then replied for them. 'He say, canoe come, seven or eight men. Canoe break, men run away bush. He no kaikai

him. He say, long time before he no kaikai man. See he build house
for Mr. Milne. You see him.' All of which was undoubtedly lies; but
there was no help for it after some cross-questioning, but to say, in
a fatuous way, that man-eating was a very bad thing, and go away
to look at the surroundings. There were three old skulls, and fourteen lower human jaws, near the end of the hut … I never saw a
more curious and picturesque place, or one with so decided a
flavour of heathenism.

It was the white labour traders, however, and not the cannibals, who
angered Goodenough, the more so as there was often little enough
he could do. 'How do you recruit them?' he demanded of one English
captain of a French schooner, equipped with all the requisite paper-
work to pursue his trade with impunity.

'I pull along shore, I, or the mate, and a boy buy some yams or
what not, and then I offer them a knife or two knives, or a knife
and a tomahawk to come, and they give it to their friends, who
come down with them, and they come with me.' The Master of the
May Queen and of the Sybil had repeated exactly the same thing
to me, so that the voluntary recruiting is all rubbish, and engagement is all nonsense. These people neither understand why they
go, nor where, or what they are to do, or when return.

For the best part of April and May 1875 Goodenough cruised among
the New Hebrides, 'collecting information, aiding missionaries, trying
to do justice for traders and natives' – 'making his office a real power
felt for good', as his chaplain optimistically put it – and after a brief
return to Sydney to ferry Sir Arthur Gordon to Fiji he was again back
in the New Hebrides. The effects of the labour trade were once more
brought home when they landed on 22 July on Vate, where the children and women, the latter smeared with turmeric and ochre, and
'so filthy and hideous' to be 'quite shocking', frightened by the sight
of white men ran away on their approach.

There was a rather more friendly welcome for Goodenough a few
days later, but while the barter was good and the natives adamant that
they had turned their backs on killing, there was invariably some little
reminder to help concentrate the mind. 'I saw by the way a skull
which Perry brought,' Goodenough noted wryly, 'and at the chief's
house, a piece of human thigh-bone, shaped off to ape out the inside

of a cocoa-nut, and well polished. Coming off, Messer told me that, while sketching, a boy stole up to him and measured his nose with a straw, broke the straw off, and went gently and thoughtfully away.'

It would seem, however, as if Goodenough was as confident as Cook in his dealings with the islanders, though his confidence was of a different origin. 'At each place he would land first,' his chaplain recorded,

> for he would never allow others to run a risk he would not share himself; then by giving presents, of which he always had an abun-dance, and by a frank and friendly manner, would always estab-lish confidence ... He believed that open dealings would always be successful, and unconscious of a hostile motive himself ... He never believed there was a danger in landing within sight of the ship, in a confiding, unsuspicious manner, and so would go, with his boat's crew unarmed, alone or with officers whom from time to time he asked to accompany him.

Goodenough's confidence in the infinite power of goodwill was dangerously increased when, on 11 August, the inhabitants of Vanikoro, a notoriously hostile island, proved welcoming, but as the *Pearl* ran down to Payon – where the *Sandfly* had been 'insulted' by a skull impaled on a point – the sight of the same skull and deserted village stirred a vague melancholy that was very unlike him. 'The people of the village,' he noted in his journal,

> probably sixteen or twenty, including women and children had all vanished (as they did to-day) up the stream in a canoe. After look-ing about, and leaving a sulu* on a stick, we went on, seeing no hut, or canoe, or sign of inhabitant, till past the extreme where were two houses and a hut for dead men's skulls, abandoned, as I suppose six or eight months ago. The whole of Vanikoro at a greater rate than this cannot have more than six hundred people on it of any sort. Where are they? ... None of it looks fit for man at all ... In a very few years the last man will vanish. And then?
>
> Came away at about 4.15 P.M., and stood under sail in nice smooth water right over the reef, carrying three feet, and getting

---

* A length of cotton, as in a sarong – presumably used as a marker.

to the ship at about 5.15, tremendously burnt by the sun. Ran away
towards Santa Cruz under top sails, four and five knots.

It was the last journal entry before Santa Cruz. With its mundane
details of ship life, it is particularly fitting. 'Teach me to live that I may
dread/The grave as little as my bed,' Goodenough had inscribed at
the front of an earlier journal sixteen years before, and he had lived
up to his precepts. On the night of the eleventh, as the *Pearl* continued down to Santa Cruz, Goodenough was a sailor; twenty-four
hours later he was ready to take his place among the Christian
Martyrs of nineteenth-century Imperial hagiography.

X

On 23 August 1875, HMS *Pearl*, sails furled, yards scandalised,
ensign and broad-pendant flying at half mast, steamed into Sydney
harbour, with the first stages of a very Protestant beatification all but
complete. During his last lucid moments in the ship Goodenough had
ordered that a telegraph should be sent on ahead to forewarn his
wife, and within hours a Gazette Extraordinary was carrying the
news. 'His Excellency the Governor, with feelings of deep regret for
the public loss, announces to the Colony … the death of James G.
Goodenough, C.B. C.M.G., Captain and Commodore commanding
the Australian Station. The funeral procession will move from
Milson's Point, North Shore, at three o'clock P.M. to-morrow, August
24th, and his Excellency, with a desire to show every possible respect
to the memory of the deceased, directs that the public offices should
be closed, and invites the attendance of all officers of the government.'
    Goodenough had given instructions that he was to be buried at St
Leonard's cemetery on the north shore of the harbour, and from an
early hour the next day, while businesses and offices stood silent and
empty, steamers carried the thousands of mourners across to Milson's
Point, Goodenough's body was brought across the water in his own
gig, towed by a steam launch, and followed by his wife and sons and
the state barge of the governor. On reaching the point, his coffin was
placed on a gun carriage draped with the Union Jack. On it were put
his sword, epaulettes and medals, and then, followed by a second
gun carriage bearing the coffins of the two seamen killed with him,

and the 'dense concourse of people' – a crowd of thousands – Goodenough's body was drawn the two miles from the landing place to the
grave dug for him by marines from the *Pearl*.

There would be a burst of anger when the first news reached
England, an irritation in *The Times* that a man of such promise 'had
fallen a victim to his own imprudence', and a fury in professional
quarters that Goodenough's solicitude for 'races scarcely human' had
brought about the tragedy; but with his widow, fellow officers and
the crew of the *Pearl* all in Sydney, the 'agenda' was inevitably set
there. 'Mrs Goodenough is most grateful for Her Majesty's kindness,'
Captain Hastings telegrammed the Admiralty on her behalf, 'She is
resigned & supported by the knowledge of his triumphantly happy
death.' 'God of the world, Thy ways are strange!' an 'In Memoriam'
published the day after the funeral declared:

> ... Thou takest thus the man
> Whose noble life would seem the most to help in Thy great plan,
> Of good for all Thy erring children – one whose very face
> Spoke of strong Godward aim, with calm soul-winning grace –
> A chief who held as holy charge all those beneath his power.
> Who judged their souls – not mere machines – with the immortal
>   dower
> Of choice between right and wrong ...
>
> ... No, we cannot see Why,
> The Wherefore of Thy work Earth's shadows dim the mortal eye;
> We can but trust the all-wise Father, and e'en by that very death
> Of peace and love – when, Christ-like to the end, with ebbing
>   breath,
> He all forgave his foes – perchance some wakened hearts were
>   blest,
> Whom their loved Commodore shall watch with joy from his far
>   rest.

If the Sydney poet clearly went to Tennyson for his Doubt, he had just
as plainly gone to the *Pearl* for his interpretation, and what we
already have here is the party line on Goodenough's death. Over the
next weeks a whole range of accounts would emerge from the *Pearl*,
and what is striking about them – suspicious almost – is a uniformity
of tone and incident that is not just a long way from the synoptic

gospels that provided them with so much of their iconography, but also from the contradictions and inconsistencies that invariably surround the telling of any historical event.

Had the officers of the *Pearl* sat down to agree their stories, they could hardly have come up with a more homogenised narrative, or one that seemed so completely watertight. There might well be professional doubts in Britain about the wisdom of Goodenough's actions in landing unarmed on Santa Cruz, but until the following year, when the senior naval surgeon in the *Pearl*, Staff Surgeon Messer, puzzled by some unexplained aspects of the tragedy, turned his attention to the medical details of the case, there was nothing to ruffle the picture of an orderly and well-run British man-of-war, momentarily touched by sorrow and grace, that had become the accepted orthodoxy.

It is not what had been told – the quiet of the ship, the prayers around the bedside, the psalms, the final farewells, the tear-stained faces, the Petrine anger of his officers and the Christ-like forbearance of Goodenough – but what was *not* told that lingered in Messer's mind, and his attention focused immediately on the nature of the wounds. Over the previous months he had been exploring ideas about the psychosomatic effects of fear on a patient's health, and in the deaths of Goodenough and his two seamen in circumstances that conjured up all the atavistic dread of a primitive, heathen culture, he had been handed on a plate the *locus classicus* he was looking for.

The particular interest of Messer was in the weapons that were used in the attack, because if the clubs, spears and throwing stones of the natives might interest an anthropologist like Goodenough, the 'poisoned arrow' had achieved a very different status in the Western imagination. The effects of any poison seem to have had a special fascination for the Victorian mind, but among sailors in the Pacific a particular terror had fixed itself to the native poisons, and the mere sight of the arrows as they were brought on board the *Pearl* – heavy and long, each with a piece of painted hardwood fixed to the end of the shaft, and a splinter of human bone, maybe eight inches in length, and sharpened to a fine, brittle point, firmly spliced on to it – had been enough to spark off a fear every bit as potent as anything with which the weapons might have been tipped.

According to popular lore, the human bone, which invariably splintered in the wound, leaving some fragment behind, was generally smeared with 'the kidney fat or other part of a dead, decomposing human body', and in the nature of ship life this kind of legend lost nothing in the telling. Among the crew of the *Pearl* was a man who had been in the *Rosario* when an orderly had been killed by arrow two years earlier on Nukapu, and if there was one thing certain about the Santa Cruz incident, it is that those who were wounded in the attack would have been well and truly primed as to their likely fate.

This same seaman used to tell 'marvellous stories' of the attack on Nukapu, of the agonies of death from tetanus; and the effect, as Messer revealed, was not the calm of *Pearl* hagiography, but an irrational panic that seems to have gripped half the ship. In the Admiralty files on the *Pearl* is a commendation of Goodenough's secretary for heroically sucking the wound with an ulcerated mouth, but the reality seems to have been very different, with one officer, hardly even grazed by an arrow, so convinced of his danger that he rapidly developed his own strange and imaginary symptoms of tetanus, and 'becoming extremely excited and, affected by the belief that he must die ... adopted strange and eccentric methods to prevent his jaw being locked'. 'The most strange example of the mental shock,' though, Messer found,

> was in an officer who received a slight prick on the finger in some unknown way, and who gradually, under the existing excitement, began to believe that in handling some of the arrows brought on board he had wounded himself. His fear and nervousness became so intense, and were associated with such strange creeping and twitching sensations near the wound, that he firmly believed he was affected by tetanus and should shortly die; and to such an extent did his morbid sensations lead him that he was actually considered insane by more than one medical man, and was ultimately invalided from the effects of this nervous shock. In another instance a person who had sucked one of the wounds became so alarmed and nervous as to be unable to sleep, eat, or do anything but walk up and down in expectation of an early and painful death. Other slighter cases of nervous or hysterical tetanus appeared at this time, showing how powerful was the mental influence at work.

It seemed overwhelmingly likely to Messer that the effects of the arrows were psychosomatic rather than physical, and no experiment that he carried out for himself with 'poisoned arrows' could kill so much as a bird. The wounds received at Santa Cruz were all of a very slight nature, and while he could envisage blood poisoning setting in, there seemed nothing in the nature of the injuries to induce tetanus in the way they had done without the mind playing a powerful supporting role.

There was only one aspect of the problem that puzzled him, because while most of the cases – though not all – followed a course he might have predicted, the one glaring exception to this was Goodenough himself. It was a commonplace of missionary and medical opinion that the 'ignorant and savage races' could kill themselves with fear, but if there seemed one man in the whole Pacific with the intellect, culture, experience and scientific knowledge to shake off the dread and superstitions that clung to the words 'poisoned arrow', it was the man who most publicly, immediately and serenely embraced the absolute certainty of his death.

There was no real evidence that a 'poisoned' arrow was more likely to cause tetanus than any other scratch, or even that the poisoned arrow was poisonous at all, yet from the moment Goodenough was hit his mind dwelled on the imminence of his death to the exclusion of all else. In the first few hours after the attack he appeared to see how remote the threat was, but at some deeper level – transported either by visions of a heavenly crown or broken by the thought of his own carelessness in sacrificing his men's lives – mind and bacterium would seem to have been set to work in perfect harmony to produce a fatal result.

He must have known, too – he was a naval officer of the old school, after all, a stickler for discipline and impatient of fools – that however tightly the forces of decency would close ranks around his memory, the questions and the doubts would be there. 'A thrill of sorrow went through the Service,' the *Army and Navy Gazette* would begin its obituary notice – and Goodenough, slipping in and out of consciousness, his mind filled with his Bible, might well have seen the words taking accusatory shape on his bulkhead.

When it was announced on Tuesday morning that Captain Goodenough ... had been murdered by one of the miserable savages of an island well known to the kidnappers, who have, by their barbarous conduct, instilled into the minds of all the inhabitants of the unexplored islands of the Pacific a horror and a dread of the approach of white men ... If the boat's crew had been provided with revolvers, or if a few Marines, well armed, had landed, no blood would have been shed, and we would not now be regretting the loss of one of the most rising men in the Service, whom we could ill afford to lose ... success is likely to attend a conference with savages if those who conduct it be provided with the handy little invention of Colt or of Adams than if they be merely ornamented by dirks or swords.

There was enough truth in this to sicken any man – 'Oh this isn't quite prudent!' Goodenough had cried even before the first arrow had been fired – and he was not just any man. For a punctilious and exacting professional the idea of his own fatal 'imprudence' on the island would have been bitter enough, but for a man as obsessively self-questioning as Goodenough was, as fastidiously – even morbidly – conscious of the various and unworthy tangle of motives that lay behind even the noblest action, the prickling suggestion that his own pride and egotism had caused the tragedy would have been even harder to bear.

From his earliest days in the navy he had dedicated himself, in 'Dr Milner's homely phrase', to making God his '*Summum Bonum*', but he was clear-sighted enough to know that the 'paths of glory' lead to other vanities and chimeras than the worldly or Homeric fame so desperately sought by a Hastings or a Peel. During his final cruise among the islands he had absorbed himself in *Middlemarch* and its devastating exploration of evangelical hypocrisies, and it is hard to believe that in those last days, as he prayed that no bad words should issue from his lips in public, the thought never crossed his mind that his own lofty sense of rectitude and Christian virtue – like that empty 'Joss' or idol he had likened himself too – had replaced God as his '*Summum Bonum*'.

And which in the end drove him – hope of the martyr's crown or guilt, Christian courage or flight – it is impossible to say, but as panic seized on his officers, and the two seamen, hidden from him, succumbed to tetanus, Goodenough put the final touches to his earthly legacy and prepared himself for his spiritual home. 'Well,' he said, as his officers carried him back to his cabin after his last farewell to his ship's company – those 'blackguards', 'asses' and 'dirty dogs' who had enlivened his journal and would dig his grave – 'I suppose there is nothing more to be done now, but to lie down and die quietly!' He was right. For the Commodore and the martyr alike, it was the only path left. And if to some in the service the notion of a Royal Navy captain expiring in a mist of Christian *agape* while his

murderers went unavenged was more than could be borne, England
– the England alike of the Anglican establishment and the dissenting
chapels, the England of the missions, of the Empire, and of the Queen
herself – was ready to enshrine him in its growing Imperial Mar-
tyrology. 'He rests far away, with other gallant sailors, in the burial
ground in Sydney,' Dean Stanley – pupil and biographer of Thomas
Arnold, panegyrist of David Livingston and Anglican Keeper of the
Religio-Patriotic Flame at Westminster Abbey – declared in the
sermon he preached for All Saints that year.

> But he, though dead and far away yet speaks to us here. He tells
> us by his life what a happy and glorious thing is a good and Chris-
> tian service of our country and our fellow-creatures. He tells us by
> his death that it was the great love of God that sustained him in
> that happy life, and in that agonising but triumphant death.
> Englishmen! – young Englishmen ! – soldiers! – sailors! – yet not
> soldiers nor sailors, nor young men only – take courage from his
> example. When you are tempted to think goodness a dream, or the
> love of the Almighty a fable, when you are tempted to think lightly
> of sin, or to waste your time and health in frivolous idleness, or to
> despair of leading an upright, pure, and Christian life – remember
> Commodore Goodenough; and remember how in him self was
> absorbed in duty, and duty was transfigured into happiness, and
> death was swallowed up in victory.

It was a fitting day – All Saints – to preach on Goodenough. 'Duty',
some might have argued, lay buried on either side of him in his remote
Sydney cemetery, but that had long been left behind for higher things.
And if 'The Sword of the Lord' – last used on the Peiho River seventeen years before – rested, along with the medals of a long and distinguished career, on his coffin, it lay there firmly sheathed.

EPILOGUE

For Lycidas is dead, dead ere his prime,
Young Lycidas, and hath not left his peer:
Who would not sing for Lycidas?

John Milton, 'Lycidas'

They shall grow not old, as we that are left grow old.
Age shall not weary them, nor the years condemn.

Laurence Binyon, 'For the Fallen'

THERE IS A MEMORIAL INSCRIPTION on the grave of a small child
in an Oxfordshire country churchyard that provides a sobering warning to anyone tempted down the 'What if?' paths of history. The boy
can scarcely have been out of his infancy when he died, but that was
not going to deter his grieving parents, who charted in painstaking
detail the future their son would never have, tracing his laurels-strewn
ascent through school, university and his chosen profession – various
options considered – to a position of honour, eminence and the grateful esteem of a nation that would never know he had so much as been
born.

If nothing could be more destructive, more stubbornly wrong-
headed, the temptation to weep for the young Lycidas is hard to resist.
E.M. Forster once wrote that there is a natural desire for any novelist to give his characters a happiness that 'real' life denies them, and
the imaginative divide between biography and fiction is not so great
that the urge to redress the accidents of history and grant the dead
the 'justice' and fulfilment that chance or early death denied them is
any less strong.

The future for both Peel and Goodenough looked so certain too,
so bright, and even for Frank Hastings it is hard not to feel that in

1828 the end to the long years of anger, exile and frustration was in sight. It is almost certain that he would have been restored to his old rank in the navy had he lived, and with his reputation high among Codrington's officers in the Mediterranean, his Whig friends about to return to office, a new professionalism abroad in gunnery practice and the triumph of steam imminent, his time had surely come.

Before one resurrects a sixty-year-old Goodenough as First Sea Lord, though, or projects Peel into the command of the Mediterranean Squadron and Hastings to the Black Sea fleet in front of Sevastopol, it would be wise to recall the fate of Thomas Cochrane during the Greek War of Independence. In 1824 it would have been difficult to find a single man on either side who would not have confidently predicted success for him, but by the time he finally reached Greece in 1827 the years had taken their toll, hardening the follies of youth into the vices of age, and its virtues of daring, decision and flair into a blustering and hollow caricature of themselves.

Alongside the gloomier effects of age, the thickening arteries, the loss of flexibility, the advent of caution, also lurked the dangers of institutional thought and practice in a navy increasingly determined to clone its officers. In 1879, just four years after Goodenough's death, an American professor named James Solely was sent to Europe to study the different systems of naval training, and in a critical analysis of British practices concluded that 'it seems impossible that the injurious effects of the methods of training pursued with young officers during the first eight years of their professional life should not be felt by the vast majority throughout their whole career ... One is led to the conclusion that the high scientific and professional attainments of many English naval officers [he had the *Excellent* and its offshoot, *Vernon*, in mind] are not in consequence, but in spite, of their early education.'

This might have been Goodenough himself speaking, and as an indication of how little either man was listened to, the bleak self-analysis of another naval officer whose life and achievements were eclipsed by his death would be hard to beat. 'Do you understand a little our naval machine?' Captain Robert Falcon Scott would ask his fiancée on the eve of the First World War, almost thirty years after Goodenough addressed the Royal United Service Institution on the state of naval education in Britain: 'from midshipman to Admiral cast in a mould to make parts of a whole – so that having a fine thought or quality is condemned because it does not fit. And the machine grinds on with wonderful efficiency because it is unyielding and like nature itself atrophies the limbs for which it has no use however great their beauty ... Here I see this level, it is the dreamer, the enthusiast, the idealist – I was something of each once – and now it gives me the feeling of being old!'

Even if Hastings had escaped the hazards of age and narrow institutionalising – and here again it is worth remembering that the wonderfully brave Lord John Hay, the young boy who had his arm amputated on the *Sea Horse* without complaint, lived to become as dull and reactionary an admiral as the service could boast – he would still have been as much in the hands of chance as any nineteenth-century officer. At the time of his death Hastings was just thirty-four, and even if he had enjoyed a 'good' war against the Egyptians in Syria or the Chinese in the First Opium War he would still, at sixty, have been too young for high command in the Crimea, and too old to be let loose in the Sea of Azov to terrorise Russia's lines of communications as he had done those of the Turks more than twenty-five years before.

The imaginary 'future' of such a man, though, would not just have been a matter of luck but of character, and is there any reason to think that a forty-year-old Hastings would have been any more tolerant of incompetent superiors than the young 'lieutenant and commander' who ruined his career in the *Kangaroo*? It was hard enough for a junior captain like Peel to put up with the dead wood that clogged the avenues of promotion, but the idea of a man who had reinvented naval warfare while Peel was still playing 'murderers' in the nursery suffering gracefully under the gerontocracy of 'old mother Dundas' or Sir Charles Napier strains the imagination.

And that is the problem. A small 'tweak' here, Forster would have argued, a little 'adjustment' there – an element of caution in the approach to Anatolico, perhaps, a different doolie on the journey back to Calcutta, a Colt in Goodenough's hands as they approached the beach on Santa Cruz – that is all that is needed; but as Forster knew perfectly well, there is nothing minor in such 'tweaks'. It is certainly true that Hastings might well have survived his wound had Howe still been the doctor on board his ship, but if 'drama' is 'character in action', then his 'glorious' death at the head of his flotilla of boats was as inevitable and intrinsic to the man's whole life and personality as was the infected carriage to Peel's or the sacrificial débâcle on Santa Cruz to Goodenough's.

It was not a matter of mere chance that they all died so young –
Hastings thirty-four, Peel thirty-three, Goodenough forty-four – and
to want them to have lived longer is to want them to have been different men. There is no reason to think that any of them went out of his
way to anticipate the 'happy crown of life', but death in one form or
another had been the constant companion of their fighting lives, the
essential and familiar counterpoint to the boldness, ambition and
courage with which they had courted risk and danger on battlefields
from the Crimea to India and from Greece to the walls of Canton.

Whatever the temptation, then, it is probably wrong to think of
them as men who were robbed by early death of fulfilment, but rather
of lives that were ended while they were still at the peak of their
powers. If the three biographies demonstrate anything, it is that there
is no single key to leadership; but while Peel's charismatic charm was
as far removed from Goodenough's stern exterior as it was from Hastings's nigh-autistic incapacity for ordinary human relations, the one
common denominator they shared was youth, and that particular
brand of fearlessness that – like 'the God Hercules' leaving Mark
Antony on the eve of Actium – could eventually desert even a natu-
ral-born killer like 'Black Charlie' Napier.

Age brings with it no inevitable diminution of courage, of course –
junior officers had no monopoly on that in either the nineteenth-
century navy or army – but of that decisiveness, rapidity of thought
and capacity for surprise that, in Jacky Fisher's words, were the
offspring of 'Imagination' bred with 'Audacity'. The generals who died
at Inkerman fought every bit as furiously as any of their men, but if,
again, there is a single theme that presents itself most persistently
through this book – whether in western Greece with 'Generalissimo'
Church or the Alma with Lord Raglan, the Baltic under the command
of Napier or the advance on Lucknow with the 'Crawlin' Camel' – it
is that of youthful impatience with the dilatoriness and caution of age.

There is a revealing parallel here with the world of Polar exploration, which for the nineteenth-century navy was not just a testing
ground of manhood, but a substitute and a training for war. 'He
should be a naval officer,' Clements Markham – friend of Peel and
Goodenough and high priest of the cult of youth – wrote in the 1890s,
as he searched the Navy Lists for the young officers who would lead
the assault on the South Pole: 'he should be in the regular line and ...
not more than 35; but preferably some years younger than that. All
previous good work in the Polar region has been done by young offi-

cers ... Old officers, all past 40, have failed and have been unable to take the lead in expeditions they nominally command.'

Parry was just twenty-nine when he did his best work in the Arctic, Markham noted, McClintock twenty-nine, Osborn twenty-eight to thirty-two, Mecham twenty-two to twenty-six, Vesey twenty-one to twenty-five, Franklin thirty-three, and beyond that there was very little to be expected of any man. It is interesting to think that if Hastings and Peel had sailed for the North-West Passage when they applied they would have been twenty-five and twenty-six respectively, and if the 'Markham Scale' is any sort of guide both men were actually at the very limits of their 'productive' fighting lives at the time they died.

There is at least something in this, too, because while it is just possible to see Hastings grown old – cantankerous and opinionated in the Cochrane mould – or Goodenough dividing his time between the Admiralty and the Royal Geographical Society, an ageing Peel is almost unimaginable. In a memoir written by Goodenough's son there is a photograph of a sixty-odd-year-old Lord Walter Kerr surrounded by the officers on his flagship, and one only has to picture Peel in such a group, a thickening, slab-bearded relic of the *Shannon* brigade surviving into a different age, to realise how much of his influence and charisma as a leader was tied up with the cult of youth and glamour he embodied.

It was the *young* Peel, with his virtues of ardour, courage and daring, who Oliver Jones called a 'beacon light' to future generations, the *young* Peel who Wood and Daniel swore to die with, the *young* Peel who, like Binyon's eternally youthful dead, filled Markham's imagination, the image of the 'gallant' young Peel, quite literally, that his 'Shannons' retained to the ends of their lives. 'I can suppose, Sir,' one such old sailor, an ex-bluejacket turned schoolteacher called Edward O'Leary, wrote from East St Louis, Illinois, in 1904 to another grimly bearded fossil of 'the Mutiny', the once-brilliant Sir Nowell Salmon VC,

that in your active life full of national import, the incidents of over forty-five years ago may have become hazy as you reach back in memory to the past. I therefore beg your indulgence while I recall to your memory some events ... which, though not bringing me personally to your memory, will serve to prove that I was one of the crew of the frigate *Shannon*, and under the 'Gallant Peel' fought

at your side at Lucknow ... I have a nice family and home; Capt.
Peel's portrait, 'Leading the Naval Brigade into Action,' hangs in
the place of honour in my library, a steel engraving from a picture
by a London painter of note.

If exploration and war were both young men's 'games' to the Victorians, it is arguable that the tragedy of Goodenough's death was not
that he died young, but that he did not die young enough. It was a
bitter shame that his wide intelligence was lost to the service at a time
when it was so badly needed, but in its very different way age had
disqualified him for war as surely as it had Cochrane, robbing him
of those brutal warrior instincts so absolutely central to Hastings's
'art of killing'.

The Goodenough who had once fantasised of conflict with France
would not have made the hash he did of the landing on Santa Cruz,
but he was no longer that man. At forty-four, with his faith deepened, his humanity matured and his sympathies broadened, he hated
killing and war. There was again no slackening of courage, but it was
not now the fighting courage of the Christian Warrior wielding the
'Sword of the Lord' under the walls of Canton, but the quiescent
patience of the 'Christian Martyr'. 'It seems almost too sacred to
write about,' Algernon Stanley – occasional incomprehensible
preacher in the *Pearl* and future Roman Catholic bishop, *in partibus*,
of Emmaus – wrote of the events on Santa Cruz:

> We [Stanley and Goodenough's widow] have talked constantly of
> him and there is more exaltation in what she says than of any other
> feature. She likes to see officers who were with him, and of course
> the hardest task is not to envy them the happiness of being with him
> at the end. You know how I loved him and how worthy of love he
> was. I always knew he was a good man, but I did not know the
> depths his religion reached. I cannot imagine anything more touch-
> ing or more grand than the account of his last days.

This was all as it should be for a martyr, but as the Mission and the
Church enrolled Goodenough among their saints, and his young
widow, sleeping at night beneath his broad pendant, settled down to
a lifetime of mourning and black crêpe (it was twenty-six years before
she moderated her dress to grey for her son's wedding), it was perhaps
as well that the navy found itself in the hands of a man who never

confused Christian love and the business of war. 'There was a discussion at Lord Rosebery's dinner-table on the action of Admiral Togo in sinking the *Kouching*, a merchant vessel carrying goods of a doubtful nature in the Chinese–Japanese War,' Sir William Goodenough – Goodenough's son and Commodore of the Second Light Cruiser Squadron at Jutland – recalled approvingly. 'Lady Fisher upheld that if Togo had been a Christian he would never have done it. "You wouldn't have done it, Jack," she said across the table. "Indeed I would," said Lord Fisher; "but then, I'm not a Christian."'

Almost exactly a century after Hastings had first seen battle at Trafalgar, the wheel had come full circle. With a man in charge of the navy's future who worshipped his God as he might have done Moloch, the sword that lay sheathed on Goodenough's coffin was again bared. Necessity, the struggle for survival – the first genuinely national war since Napoleon – had again returned warfare to its most brutal and elemental shape. And the navy was – just in time – ready. When Scott went south to 'fight' against the 'mighty powers' of nature he did not take his New Testament with him but his *The Origin of Species*. When 'Evans of the *Broke*' forged through a sea of wounded and drowning German sailors in the Channel he called out from his bridge, 'Remember the *Lusitania*!' and ploughed them under. And when in the smoke, half-light and confusion of Jutland, Sir William Goodenough – in so many ways his father's son – momentarily wondered whether a three-funnelled ship in front of him was friend or foe, he fired anyway. 'I must say I was never so impressed in my life with hideous strength,' wrote 'Birdie' Bowers, the God-fearing Antarctic explorer, as, on the eve of the First World War, the tiny wood-built *Terra Nova* steamed through the lines of warships that the demonic Jacky Fisher had created in his own appalling image.

> The new monsters are ugliness itself but for sheer diabolical brutality in ship building some of the Dreadnought Cruisers take the cake. The look of them is enough to scare anything & when you pass close enough to look into the muzzles of their guns the effect is something to be remembered. Much as I love ships & particularly HM ships, there was something about the look of this squadron that was Satanic.

Hastings – the man who designed, commanded and fought the vessel that the Turks called 'the ship from hell' – would have been at home.

ACKNOWLEDGEMENTS

I WOULD LIKE TO THANK the following for permission to quote from material in their collections: the Trustees of the National Library of Scotland; the Huntington Library, San Marino, California; the Melanesian Mission; the British School of Archaeology, Athens. I am also grateful to the State Library of New South Wales for making material available from its James Goodenough archive, and to the staffs of the library of the School of African and Oriental Studies, London University, the National Archives of Scotland, the British Library, the National Archives at Kew, the University of Loughborough Library, the National Portrait Gallery, the Derbyshire County Record Office and the Ashby-de-la-Zouch Museum.

I am especially grateful to the Reverend Jonathan Peel for allowing me to use William Peel's family letters, and for his kindness throughout; Lady Selina Newman for giving me access to material still held by the Abney-Hastings family; the Earl of Dundonald for generously granting permission to quote from the Dundonald Papers; Amalia Kakissis and the staff at the British School at Athens, for all their assistance and hospitality while I was staying at the school; Peter Funnell at the National Portrait Gallery for his assistance with pictures; Robert Clerk for coming to my technological rescue on more than one occasion; Alan Petty for reading the book in manuscript and suggesting improvements; and Francis Hamilton, and Perran and Suno Wood, for their generous loans of Crimean War material. I would also like to thank the Reverend Janet Mackenzie of St Swithun's, Sandy; David Friswell, Kenneth Hillier, Martin Beckett, Celeste Goodridge, Neville Chiavaroli, Clare Asquith, Eric and Joyce Willcocks and Peter Darling, who have all helped with either research questions or illustrations. While every effort has been made to contact holders of copyright material, in a few cases this has not proved possible. I would welcome the opportunity to rectify any omissions in future editions of this book.

There has been very little written on any of the lives covered here, but I am still conscious of the debts incurred in writing this book. I hope the notes and bibliography will make the extent of these debts clear, but there are certain outstanding acknowledgements that need to be made. The work of William St Clair remains as indispensable as ever to anyone writing about the Greek War of Independence and philhellenism. David Brewer's cogent history of the Greek War has also been of great help. For Peel, Norman Gash's work is still essential reading, but I am particularly grateful to Douglas Hurd, both for his fine biography of Sir Robert Peel and for his kindness in pointing me in the direction of unpublished sources. There is a large and growing body of work on the issues raised by the life and death of James Goodenough, but I would particularly like to acknowledge the contribution of Jane Samson to this debate.

I would like to thank the Society of Authors, whose generous grant made possible much of the research for this book. Derek Johns has been as imperturbable as always and Robert Lacey, at HarperCollins, more patient than any editor should have to be. I would also like to thank Arabella Pike for her support in the early stages of this book. Lastly, as ever, I would like to thank Honor, who has worked on it with me at every phase.

NOTES

ABBREVIATIONS

Askwith: Askwith, Betty, *Crimean Courtship*, Salisbury, 1985

BL: British Library

BSA: British School of Archaeology at Athens (H: Papers of Frank Abney Hastings)

Bushby: Bushby, Henry Jeffreys, *A month in the camp before Sebastopol by a non-combatant*, London, 1855

Churi: Churi, J., *Sea Nile, the Desert and Nigritia*, London, 1853

Crane, *Scott*: Crane, David, *Scott of the Antarctic*, London, 2005

Duberly: *Mrs Duberly's War: Journals and Letters from the Crimea, 1854–1856*, ed. Christine Kelly, Oxford, 2007

Finlay, *Blackwood's*: Finlay, George, *Blackwood's Edinburgh Magazine*, Edinburgh, 1845

Finlay, *History*: Finlay, George, *History of the Greek Revolution*, London, 1971

Gash: Gash, N., *Sir Robert Peel: The Life of Sir Robert Peel after 1830*, London, 1972

Gough: Gough, B., 'Lieutenant William Peel, British Naval Intelligence and the Oregon Crisis', *The Northern Mariner* IV, No 4, 1994

Guizot: Guizot, M., *Memoirs of Sir Robert Peel*, London, 1857

HA: The Huntington Library, San Marino, California, Hastings Collection

Hastings: Hastings, Frank Abney, *Memoir on the use of shells, hot shot and carcass shells, from ship artillery*, London, 1828

Hero: Anon, *The Christian Hero of Santa Cruz*, London, undated

Hibbert: Hibbert, Christopher, *The Great Mutiny*, London, 1980

Hill: *The Illustrated History of the Royal Navy*, ed J.R. Hill, Oxford, 1995

Howe: Howe, S.G., *Letters & Journals of Samuel Gridley Howe during the Greek Revolution*, Boston, 1907–09

HP: Hastings Papers, Loughborough University Library, microfilm

Hurd, *Arrow*: Hurd, Douglas, *The Arrow War*, London, 1967

Hurd, *Peel*: Hurd, Douglas, *Robert Peel*, London, 2007
James: James, W.M., *The Naval History of Great Britain*, London, 2001
Jones: Jones, Captain Oliver, RN, *Recollections of a Winter Campaign in India*, London, 1859
Journal: Journals of James Graham Goodenough, Mitchell Library, Sydney (Microfilm MAV FM4/1766–8; MLMSS 889/1–11)
Kennedy: Kennedy, Vice-Admiral Sir William, *Hurrah for the Life of a Sailor*, Edinburgh, 1900
Keppel: Keppel, Sir Henry, *A Sailor's Life under Four Sovereigns*, 1899
Lovell: Lovell, William, *Personal Narrative of Events 1799–1815*, London, 1879
Markham: Markham, Sir Albert, *The Life of Sir Clements R. Markham, KCB, FRS*, London, 1917
Massie: Massie, Alastair, *The National Army Museum Book of the Crimean War*, London, 2005
Memoir: *Memoir of Commodore J.G. Goodenough, RN, CB, CMG*, edited by his widow, London, 1878
NA: National Archives
NAS Dundonald: National Archives of Scotland, Dundonald Papers
NRS: Salmon, Nowell, in Navy Records Society, ed. D. Bonner-Smith & E.W.R. Lumby, London, 1947
O'Byrne: O'Byrne, W.R.A., *A Naval Biographical Dictionary*, London, 1849
Peel, *Ride*: Peel, Capt, RN, *A Ride through the Nubian Desert*, London, 1852
Pemberton: Pemberton, W. Baring, *Battles of the Crimean War*, London, 1968
PL: Peel Letters (Private Collection)
RGS CRM: Royal Geographical Society, Markham Papers
Roberts: Roberts of Kandahar, Field Marshal, *Forty-one Years in India*, London, 1898
Rodger: Rodger, N.A.M., *The Wooden World*, London, 1988
Russell: *Russell's Despatches from the Crimea*, ed. N. Bentley, London, 1970
St Clair: St Clair, William, *That Greece Might Still be Free*, London, 1972
Spilsbury: Spilsbury, Julian, *The Thin Red Line*, London, 2006
Trafalgar: Clayton, Tim and Craig, Phil, *Trafalgar: The Men, the Battle, the Storm*, London, 2004
Urquhart: Urquhart, David, *The Spirit of the East*, London, 1835
Verney, *Devil*: Verney, Major-General G.L., *The Devil's Wind*, London, 1956

Verney, *Shannon*: Verney, Edmund, *The Shannon's Brigade in India*, London, 1852

W. Goodenough: Goodenough, Admiral Sir William, *A Rough Record*, London, 1941

Whitcombe: Whitcombe, Captain Thomas, *Campaign of the Falieri and Piraeus in the Year 1827*, ed. C.W.J. Eliot, New Jersey, 1992

Wolseley: Wolseley, Field Marshal Lord, 'Courage', *Fortnightly Review*, August 1888

Wood, *Crimea*: Wood, Field Marshal Sir Evelyn, *The Crimea in 1854 and 1894*, London, 1895

Wood, *Fortnightly*: Wood, Field Marshal Sir Evelyn, *Fortnightly Review* CCCXXXIV, London, 1894

Wood, *Midshipman*: Wood, Field Marshal Sir Evelyn, *From Midshipman to Field Marshal*, London, 1906

Wynne: *The Wynne Diaries*, ed. Anne Fremantle, London, 1940

Yonge: Yonge, C.D., *History of the British Navy*, London, 1863

INTRODUCTION

2 the finest officer ... BSA H.4 Book D

3 Great Britain is ... Finlay, *Blackwood's*, p.519

3 SCOTT. (CAPTAIN) ... O'Byrne, p.1040

5 I stay in hopes ... Hole, Rev Ch., *The Life of the Reverend and Venerable Will. Phelps MA*, London, Vol II, p.49

7 the art of war ... p.34

7 After all ... Hughes, Thomas, *Tom Brown's Schooldays*, London, undated, p.242

8 There cannot be a doubt ... *Memorials of Captain Hedley Vicars*, by the Author of *The Victory Won*, London, 1861, pp.122–204

8 'Art?' exclaims ... Kingsley, Charles, *Two Years Ago*, London, 1881, p.381

9 to a new life ... Ibid., pp.358–9

9 My health is quite ... Ibid., p.253

10 To understand courage ... Wolseley, pp.280–1

10 the old chivalrous ... Girouard, Mark, *The Return to Camelot*, New Haven, 1981, p.142

11 The annals of chivalry ... Wood, *Midshipman*, Vol I, p.114

12 The middle class ... *The Times*, quoted in Dawson, Graham, *Soldier Heroes*, London, 2005, p.107

13 There is no death ... Jones, p.174

HASTINGS

15 I instantly ordered ... NA ADM1/270

15 You have overlayed ... BSA H.11 (12)

16 I was a young officer ... Ibid., (16)

16 When duty permitted me ... Ibid., (12)

16 between three and four bells ... NA ADM1/270

17 Captain Hastings asked me ... Ibid.

17 Port Royal Monday ... Ibid.

17 Sir, The day before yesterday ... Ibid.

17 could almost have forgiven ... BSA H.11 (18)

18 Was the Commander in Chief's ... NA ADM1/270

18 This is an aggravated ... Ibid.

19 Your Lordship may find ... BSA H.11 (18)

19 Though the noble Earl ... *Gentleman's Magazine*, October 1789, p.959

20 abominable stinking great ... *Dictionary of National Biography*, 2004

20 naturally hot and spicy ... BL AddMss 29175/f6

20 eleven hundred years before ... BL AddMss 29190/f283

21 first dancer of the universe ... Crane, Arthur, *The Kirkland Papers*, Chatham, 1990, p.4

21 Philosophical and merely ... HA13730

21 as brothers ... HA9488

22 milk-sop ... BL AddMss 29175/f6

22 long, tiresome and harassing ... Lovell, p.15

22 I think it incumbent ... BL AddMss 29180/f235

23 The English keep ... Southey, Robert, *Mr Rowlandson's England*, ed. John Steel, Woodbridge, 1985, p.187

23 A self-contained ... Alexander, Caroline, *The Bounty*, London, 2003, p.181

24 I could not think ... Rodger, p.37

24 Whilst on board with him ... BL AddMss 29180/f235

24 My Dear General ... HP, Box 110/3325

25 Who can paint in words ... Trelawny, Edward, *Adventures of a Younger Son*, London, 1891, p.61

25 I thought my heart ... Lovell, p.3

25 fellows in Neptune ... Ibid., p.4

26 I begin my journal ... Wynne, Vol. III, p.166

26 I am in hope ... Ibid., p.198

27 On the 28th ... Trafalgar, p.81

27 I think if you were to see ... HA3325

27 All hearts towards evening ... Lovell, p.44

28 forest of strange masts ... Ibid.
28 looked hazy and watery ... Ibid.
28 old *Neptune*, which never was ... Ibid., p.45
29 At 11, Answered ... Ibid., p.47
29 addressed us at ... Trafalgar, p.148
29 It was a beautiful sight ... Lovell, pp.47–9
29 to locate the enemy's line ... Ibid., p.45
30 A man should witness ... Trafalgar, p.177
30 At 12.35 ... Lovell, pp.47–9
30 standing and running rigging ... Ibid.
31 We had now Been ... Trafalgar, pp.216–17
31 but a few minets ... Ibid., p.239
31 the six van ships ... Lovell, p.49
31 At 3.30, opened fire ... Ibid., pp.47–9
31 a brace or bowline ... Ibid., p.49
31 Three different powers ... Ibid., p.55
32 She had between 3 and 400 ... Trafalgar, p.319
32 We had to tie ... Ibid.
33 I am afraid this brilliant ... Wynne, Vol. III, p.221
33 7 November, Captain Fremantle ... NA ADM51/1545
35 Thursday 7th Nov ... Wynne, Vol. III, p.216
35 I should certainly ... BL AddMss 29181/f348
36 Most truly do I congratulate ... HA5138
36 My Dear General ... HA10150
37 Mrs Hastings is a great bore ... Wynne, Vol. III, p.260
37 Young Hastings get ... Ibid., p.274
38 My boy of Trafalgar ... BL AddMss 29181/f316
38 I think you have much ... HA6152
38 ruined mansion ... BL AddMss 29182/f254
39 I have been much ... Ibid., f144
39 I have much pleasure ... HA10971
39 We are just returned ... HA12708
40 I gave him a scold ... Ibid.
40 All our frigate captains ... Rodger, p.555
40 As I may not ... SNL, Tweeddale MS 14449f3
41 the art of killing ... Hastings, p.22
41 The objection of unfair ... Ibid.
42 We have been out ... HA12707
42 You will expect me to say ... Ibid.
43 This Captain Scandril ... James, Vol. V, p.59
44 finding that his shattered ... Ibid., p.60
45 Sent the 1st Lieut ... NA ADM51/1914
45 senna and austrich feathers ... Ibid.

45 His Excellency Mr Adair ... Ibid.

45 The walls of the Seraglio ... *Byron Letters & Journals*, ed. Leslie
    A. Marchand, London, 1973, Vol. I, p.251

46 Those who know him ... Mansel, Philip, *Constantinople*,
    London, 1991, pp.234–5

46 Mann'd the yards ... NA ADM51/1914

47 known to them ... Ibid.

47 I shall be anxious ... HA12710

48 understood from Lady Hardy ... BL AddMss 29185/f194

48 I have been in town ... BL AddMss 29186/f9

49 I am obliged to be in town ... BL AddMss 29187/f206

49 Starboard the helm! ... NA ADM1/5439/337

50 In twelve minutes ... O'Byrne, p.234

50 I signalled to the small boats ... NA ADM1/5439/337

51 With respect to America ... HA12707

52 On first landing ... O'Byrne, p.1274

52 all the Seaman's help ... Hastings, p.3

53 In the endeavours ... O'Byrne, p.1274

54 His conduct as a *Gallant* ... BSA H.4 (6)

55 For shame ... Lord, Walter, *The Dawn's Early Light*, New York,
    1972, p.334

56 Hoisted the English ... NA ADM51/2194

56 I feel that in addressing ... BSA H.11 (1)

57 Frank is trying ... HA5836

57 Lieut F. Hastings ... NA ADM3/192

57 Lieut Frank Hastings ... Ibid.

59 Fair Greece! ... Byron, Lord, *Childe Harold*, Cantos I and II,
    Poems, London, 1812

59 We are all ... Shelley. P.B., *Hellas*, in *Selected Poetry*, Oxford,
    1968, p.275

59 What a queer set ... Howe, p.333

60 That Glory is in a great ... BSA H.4 (31)

60 My lord only those ... BSA H.11 (23)

61 pretty daughters ... Lovell, p.93

61 It was not out of consideration ... Crane, D., *Lord Byron's
    Jackal*, London, 1998, p,299

63 I was amongst three ... BSA H.2 (Journal pp.1–2)

64 fatigued to death ... Ibid., p.2

65 Monsieur le Prince ... Finlay, *History*, Vol. II, pp.343–4

66 In the morning ... BSA H.2 (Journal p.7)

67 Mercy was out of the question ... Brewer, David, *The Flame of
    Freedom*, London, 2001, p.158

67 We landed contrary ... BSA H.2 (Journal, pp.8–9)

68 While I was on board ... Ibid., pp.10–11
68 What marvellous patriotism ... Ibid., p.19
69 I saw the Admiral ... Ibid., p.23
70 These troops opened ... Finlay, *Blackwood's*, p.502
72 We found an irregular ... BSA H.2 (Journal, p.31)
73 while any danger existed ... Ibid., p.32
73 Our guns opened ... Ibid., pp.33–4
73 One of the Primates ... Ibid., p.25
73 The reiterated insults ... Ibid., pp.37–8
74 I was glad to find ... Ibid., p.54
74 The Turks had obtained ... Ibid., p.61
75 a little ébloui ... Ibid., p.68
75 I armed them ... Ibid., p.75
76 I visited the Minister of War ... Ibid., p.76
76 one & all ... Ibid., p.77
76 I made the soldiers ... Ibid., p.81
77 He held a conference ... Finlay, *History*, Vol. I, p.300
77 We were informed ... BSA H.2 (Journal, p.82)
78 I went on board ... Ibid.
78 I now resolved ... Ibid., p.83
79 Chef de l'état ... Ibid., p.92
79 It is plain ... Ibid., p.198
79 A German arrived ... Ibid., pp.103–4
80 During the night ... Ibid., p.106
81 friends of humanity ... St. Clair, p.142
82 Lord Byron's companions ... BSA H.2 (Journal, p.108)
82 Firstly, I lay down ... Finlay, *History*, Vol. II, p.335
83 The localities ... Ibid., p.336
83 Is it likely ... Ibid.
83 We now come to the question ... Ibid.
84 We now come to the plan ... Ibid., p.338
85 but when we consider ... Ibid., p.339
85 Of the destructive effect ... Ibid., p.338
86 Were it not ... BL AddMss 29183/f284
86 to quit the Theatre ... BL AddMss 29188/f257
87 The young orphan ... Crane, Arthur, *The Kirkland Papers*, Chatham, 1990, p.63
87 My dear dear Mother ... HA4644
87 Willesley to view ... Derbyshire County Record Office, Coroners' Expenses 1820–3, Q/AF 818
87 I desire my body ... NA PROB11/1676
88 As my youngest son ... Ibid.
88 I have written three letters ... HA4644

89 I am to be a kind ... Crane, D., *Lord Byron's Jackal*, London,
      1998, p,101
90 Trelawny gave a dinner ... BSA H.2 (Journal, p.112)
91 visit the antiquities ... Ibid.
91 one or two ... BSA H.4 (32)
91 During the summer ... Finlay, *Blackwood's*, p.503
92 neither to be a dupe ... BSA H.4 (35)
92 I came to town ... BSA H.12 (4)
94 I have not been able ... NAS Dundonald, GD233 Box 43 Bundle
      14
95 I fancy you have ... BL AddMss 36461/f278
95 The Greeks have long ... Ibid.
95 If six vessels ... Ibid.
96 My Lord, I had ... NAS Dundonald, GD233 Box 43 Bundle 14
97 incorrigible ... Ibid.
97 insupportable blockhead ... BL AddMss 36462/f149
97 Before I close ... NAS Dundonald, GD233 Box 43 Bundle 14
98 a very distinguished ... BSA H.3 (3)
98 The fact is ... BSA H.3 (1)
98 forty two horses ... BL AddMss 36462/f187
99 The Karteria ... Finlay, *Blackwood's*, p.501
99 There never was ... BL AddMss 36462/f251
100 Galloway deserves to be hung ... Ibid., f305
100 Our voyage ... Ibid., f331
100 All is confusion here ... Ibid., f360
101 To the Commander ... NAS Dundonald, GD233 Box 43 Bundle 16
102 The Morea has been ... Howe, pp.193–4
105 All the world ... Ibid., pp.187–9
106 Even at this moment ... Ibid., p.203
106 The moon shone bright ... Ibid., p.206
108 The Turks are there ... Ibid., p.207
108 Two thousand men ... Ibid., p.208
109 The Turks would only ... Ibid., p.209
109 Soon we were moving ... Ibid., p.210
110 The Turks from the monastery ... Ibid., p.211
110 burst amid twenty ... Ibid., p.214
110 the balls began ... Ibid.
111 I am told ... Whitcombe, pp.99–100
111 To our dismay ... Howe, pp.215–16
112 Thanks to Mr Aeolus ... Whitcombe, p.99
112 after wandering about ... Finlay, *History*, Vol. II, p.137
113 This unhappy country ... Thomas, Donald, *Cochrane*, London,
      1978, p.301

114   One great and sublime ... St. Clair, p.320
114   My soul has never been absent ... Ibid., p.321
114   Church was of a small ... Finlay, *History*, Vol. I, p.418
115   You are hereby ... NAS Dundonald, GD233 Box 43 Bundle 18
115   This circumstance exposed ... Finlay, *Blackwood's*, p.506
116   I found eight vessels ... NAS Dundonald, GD233 Box 44 Bundle
      21a
116   The English boatswain ... Finlay, *Blackwood's*, p.506
117   The spectacle offered ... Ibid., p.507
118   In about a half ... Ibid., p.508
118   You will observe ... NAS Dundonald, GD233 Box 44 Bundle
      21a
118   Passing by Kunsi ... Ibid.
119   The eyes of Europe ... Thomas, Donald, *Cochrane*, London,
      1978, p.302
119   It was the most horrid ... Ibid., p.304
120   Fifteen hundred Greeks ... Finlay, *History*, Vol. I, p.431
121   He is an ingenious ... Howe, p.335
121   I am anxious ... NAS Dundonald, GD233 Box 44 Bundle 21a
121   anxious to know how ... Ibid.
122   See, my friend ... Thomas, Donald, *Cochrane*, London, 1978,
      p.308
122   I received a laconic ... BSA H.3(37)
123   It is with deep regret ... NAS Dundonald, GD233 Box 44 Bundle
      21a
124   You have been good enough ... Finlay, *Blackwood's*, pp.509–10
124   the combined mussulman ... Urquhart, Vol. I, pp.20–1
125   I have the honor ... NAS Dundonald, GD233 Box 44 Bundle
      21a
125   A shout of welcome ... Urquhart, Vol. I, p.26
126   I shall proceed immediately ... BL AddMss 36544/f163
126   We no sooner approached ... NAS Dundonald, GD233 Box 44
      Bundle 21a
126   During the night ... Urquhart, Vol. I, p.26
127   It was a curious sight ... Ibid., pp.29–30
127   dressed as for a gala ... Ibid., p.29
128   the Brig bearing ... BSA H.5 (*Karteria* Log)
129   The battle of Salona ... Finlay, *Blackwood's*, p.510
129   the finest day ... BSA H.3 (50)
130   I was once sitting ... NAS Dundonald, GD233 Box 44 Bundle 20
131   If you have no hopes ... BL AddMss 36544/f180
131   Gen Church writes ... NAS Dundonald, GD233 Box 44 Bundle
      21a

132 I am ready to do all ... Ibid.
132 I have the honor to announce ... Ibid.
133 an act of rashness ... Finlay, *Blackwood's*, p.513
133 The little squadron ... Ibid.
134 There was a moment ... Urquhart, Vol. I, p.35
134 He was sure ... Finlay, *Blackwood's*, p.513
134 As Austrian consul ... Ibid., p.514
135 The [Egyptian] troops ... NAS Dundonald, GD233 Box 44
       Bundle 21a
136 lending [him]self to ... Ibid.
136 I regret of all things ... Ibid.
137 The flat-bottomed ... Finlay, *Blackwood's*, p.519
138 better practice has rarely ... Ibid.
138 I am full of misery ... Finlay, *History*, Vol. II, p.25
138 According to the wish ... NAS Dundonald, GD233 Box 44
       Bundle 21a
139 We were now within pistol shot ... Ibid.
139 I enclose you a copy ... BSA H.3 (62)
139 I hope this is the last time ... Finlay, *History*, Vol. II, pp.344–5
140 A little being ... BSA H.3 (75)
140 Your enemies are totally ... BSA H.4 (16)
141 As night approached ... BL AddMss 36505, pp.247–9
141 The 25th of May ... Finlay, *Blackwood's*, p.516
142 As the scene of the action ... BL AddMss 36505, p.270
142 invincible determination ... Ibid., p.272
142 Make haste away ... Ibid.
143 A sudden and unlooked for ... BSA H.4 (53)
144 The moment his death ... Finlay, *Blackwood's*, p.517
144 OH LORD IN THY ... Ibid.
144 Never was braver man ... Ibid.
144 On the 8th ... BL AddMss 36505, p.309
144 hastiness of temper ... Lane-Poole, Stanley, *Sir Richard Church,
       CB, GCH, Commander in Chief of the Greeks in the War of
       Independence*, London, 1890, pp.66–7
145 Nothing has been done ... Howe, p.334
145 the effects of ... Ibid.
146 As nobody can have ... BSA Finlay Papers, E9 (11)
146 Dear Finlay ... Ibid., A16 (3–4)
147 The first steam-vessel ... Finlay, *Blackwood's*, p.519

PEEL

150 the same glance ... Peel, Sir Lawrence, *A Sketch of the Life and Character of Sir Robert Peel*, London, 1860, p.277

150 God seldom accords ... Guizot, M., *Memoirs of Sir Robert Peel*, London, 1857, p.3

152 I there saw ... Ibid., p.338

153 I had a comfortless journey ... *The Private Letters of Sir Robert Peel*, ed. George Peel, London, 1920, p.109

154 I have always ... BL AddMss 40608/f336

154 My dearest Papa ... PL, 25 December 1840

154 thick trousers ... PL, January 1839

155 'Bitches', onanism ... Crompton, Louis, *Byron and Greek Love*, Los Angeles, 1985, p.80

155 Who is the tutor ... Hole, Rev. Ch., *The Life of the Reverend and Venerable Will. Phelps MA*, London, Vol. II, p.92

156 Name, Mr William Peel ... NA ADM1/891/B225

156 In reference to ... Ibid.

157 As I have not seen ... PL, 11 August 1838

158 I am sure ... Hole, Rev. Ch., *The Life of the Reverend and Venerable Will. Phelps MA*, London, Vol. II, p.128

158 I would have given ... PL, 28 August 1838

159 I had a ... Ibid.

159 This evening yesterday ... PL, 14 December 1838

160 dear old Drayton ... PL, 1 December 1838

160 Today we had ... PL, 14 December 1838

160 This morning two men ... PL, 13 August 1838

161 Since my last letter ... BL AddMss 40608/ff2-3

162 It appears now ... Ibid.

163 You will see ... BL AddMss 40608/ff6-7

163 It is quite certain ... Ibid.

164 You see we are now ... PL, 11 September 1840

164 about 11 o'clock ... Ibid.

164 His excuse was ... Ibid.

165 And a dreadful one ... Ibid.

165 We had distributed ... PL, 19 September 1840

165 The seamen as usual ... Ibid.

166 stands on the ... PL, 5 November 1840

168 About fourteen stone ... Napier, General E., *The Life and Correspondence of Admiral Sir Charles Napier*, London, 1862, Vol. II, p.126

168 post of honour ... PL, 5 November 1840

169 At about 1pm ... Ibid.

170 Most of the other ships ... Ibid.
170 I have not been ... Ibid.
171 I am exceedingly glad ... PL, 10 November 1840
171 *L'éffet moral* ... Yonge, Vol. II, p.548
172 the relief of ... PL, 10 November 1840
172 Every country ... *The Illustrated History of the Royal Navy*, ed
          J.R. Hill, Oxford, 1995, p.171
172 My Dear Mr Croker ... BL AddMss 40485/f236
173 with an intelligence ... Gash, p.178
173 I can hardly justify ... *Sir Robert Peel from his Private Papers*,
          ed. Parker, Ch., London, 1899, Vol. II, p.452
173 I am very much obliged ... Ibid.
174 quite gay and *déboutonné* ... Gash, p.178
174 the Birm. and Derby ... PL, 20 July 1841
174 I am in great hopes ... BL AddMss 40608/f29
174 entered on the books ... Ibid.
175 Our China merchants ... Hernon, p.310
176 the interest of ... Ibid., p.321
176 one of the most ... Ibid., p.298
176 I have just been reading over ... PL, 7 February 1842
176 Lord Ellenborough enjoys ... Ibid.
176 rigged out in sheepskins ... PL, 23 December 1842
177 but we poor unfortunate ... Ibid.
177 Although this station ... Ibid.
177 safe and snug ... PL, 23–27 December 1841
178 ensure me wherever ... PL, 2 January 1842
178 two casks of ... Ibid.
178 a little room ... Ibid.
178 he had at length ... Peel, Sir L., *A Sketch of the Life and
          Character of Sir Robert Peel*, London, 1860, p.277
179 Although I shall not ... PL, 7 February 1842
179 I need not tell you ... PL, 21 February 1842
179 The Indian news ... PL, 21–22 February 1842
180 I will not talk to you ... PL, 29 May 1842
180 I am most heartily ... Ibid.
180 with the decided preference ... Ibid.
181 I wish I was ... PL, 13 June 1842
181 I hope all the articles ... PL, 11 September 1842
181 Their profit and extortion ... Ibid.
182 Remember what I ... Ibid.
182 Dear Sir Robert Peel ... PL, 1 December 1842
183 My good fortune ... PL, 3 October 1842
183 the dullest and most ... PL, 11 September 1842

183 who would know ... Hill, p.257
184 The opinion I formed ... BL AddMss 40608/ff330–2
185 I have not the slightest ... BL AddMss 40354/f139
185 My dearest father ... BL AddMss 40550/f168
186 His looks and bearing ... Wood, *Midshipman*, Vol. I, pp.25–6
187 His noble thoughts ... Markham, Sir Albert, *The life of Sir Clements R. Markham, KCB, FRS*, London, 1917, p.39
187 up and down ... Ibid.
187 It was important ... Ibid.
188 What tenderness ... Disraeli, Benjamin, *Coningsby, or the New Generation*, Oxford, 1982, p.38
189 I am in perfect health ... PL, 9 July 1854, 19 January 1855
189 I am in the most ... BL AddMss 40551/f233
189 His distress may well ... Markham, A., p.40
190 When we find ... Gough, B., 'Lieutenant William Peel, British Naval Intelligence and the Oregon Crisis', *The Northern Mariner* IV, No 4, 1994, p.4
191 The object of the vessel ... Gough, p.7
191 did not know ... Ibid.
191 the actual ... Ibid.
191 On the 8th ... Ibid.
191 Unless active ... Ibid.
192 May I venture ... NA FO5/457
193 The Manners, the Somersets ... Hurd, *Peel*, p.367
193 He has dared ... Ibid., p.370
195 I hope you received ... BL AddMss 40598/f364
195 very barren of interest ... NA ADM1/5887
196 as he saved ... Ibid.
196 In my letter ... Ibid.
197 Though Commander Peel ... Ibid.
197 My Dearest Father ... BL AddMss 40609/f332
199 I cannot bear ... Hurd, *Peel*, p.385
199 The country mourns ... Ibid.
199 the idol ... Ibid., p.387
199 Think what a Blank ... Ibid.
200 My dearest Mamma ... PL, 18 December 1850
201 Its mission ... Peel, *Ride*, p.64
202 You must know ... Churi, p.2
202 I had some ... Ibid.
203 My companion is ... PL, 18 December 1850
203 before the years ... PL, 16 August 1851
203 And now at ... PL, 20 August 1851
203 The best feelings ... Peel, *Ride*, p.3

204 I arrived here ... PL, 7 September 1851

205 There is a melancholy ... Peel, *Ride*, pp.31–2

205 In Egypt I never ... PL, 26 October 1851

206 My costume was not ... Peel, *Ride*, p.110

207 A little after ... Churi, pp.203–4

207 After a little ... Ibid., p.231

208 burning with fever ... Ibid.

208 He was so ill ... PL, 26 January 1852

209 Truly it was a great ... Churi, p.301

210 I'm as sorry ... Hughes, T., *Tom Brown's Schooldays*, London, 1857, p.242

210 I have the honor ... BL AddMss 35799/ff220–1

212 A Greek is not only ... Boatswain, T. and Nicolson, C., *A Traveller's History of Greece*, Gloucestershire, 1989, p.176

213 Albania is an ... PL, 24 March 1854

213 The Lord High ... NA ADM1/5631

214 A difference of ... Ibid.

214 I am anxious ... Ibid.

215 told us that ... Ibid.

216 I don't know why ... PL, 24 March 1854

216 I have with me ... PL, 23 June 1854

216 These little details ... PL, und. May 1854

217 My dearest Elise ... PL, 23 June 1854

217 I can write ... PL, 4 July 1854

218 You may be always ... Ibid.

218 Went yesterday ... PL, 9 July 1854

219 Our fleet here ... PL, 14 July 1854

219 You must know ... PL, 7 August 1854

220 Horrors occurred here ... Russell, p.55

220 As you are sure ... PL, 15 August 1854

221 I must now give you ... PL, 25 August 1854

221 One man would ... Wood, *Fortnightly*, p.476

222 The Diamond has ... PL, 25 August 1854

222 It has always been ... Ibid.

222 After cruising for some days ... Wood, *Fortnightly*, p.476

223 Most of us ... Ibid., p.472

224 Lord Raglan ... PL, 7 August 1854

224 I must say ... PL, 9 July/24 August 1854

224 some one ... PL, 9 July 1854

224 No pen could ... Russell, p.57

224 The impression as ... Ibid., p.59

225 The country inland ... Ibid.

225 I can only ... PL, 16 September 1854

226 scarlet, white ... *History of the British Army*, ed. Peter Young & J. P. Lawford, London, 1970, p.154

226 On night of the ... Fitzgerald, C.C. Penrose, *Life of Vice Admiral Sir George Tryon*, London, 1897, p.47

228 infernal-too-tooing ... Hibbert, Christopher, *The Destruction of Lord Raglan*, London, 1961, p.93

229 stately mistress ... Russell, p.256

229 oriental Bath ... Ibid., p.169

229 I never was ... Ibid., p.100

230 I write these lines ... PL, 8 October 1854

231 Probably no 1,200 men ... Wood, *Fortnightly*, pp.464–5

231 The tars are such ... Bushby, p.107

231 put up a grog-shop ... Ibid.

231 We MUST take ... PL, 8 October 1854

232 Nothing can be imagined ... Bushby, p.50

234 We turned out daily ... Wood, *Fortnightly*, p.488

234 A few men ... Massie, p.66

234 I could not but feel ... Duberly, p.82

234 On the 16th October ... Wood, *Fortnightly*, p.488

235 The roaring and whistling ... Spilsbury, p.129

235 Of all the dreadful ... Campbell, C.F., *Letters from Sevastopol 1854–5*, London, 1894, p.238

235 tumult and confusion ... Spilsbury, p.130

235 I can see him now ... Wolseley, p.286

236 When we got ... Wood, *Fortnightly*, p.490

236 It was the stomach ... Ibid.

237 We were very proud ... Wood, *Fortnightly*, p.492

237 Every regimental officer ... Ibid.

238 The siege ... Spilsbury, p.134

238 To the best ... Wood, *Fortnightly*, p.492

239 Every day ... PL, 23 October 1854

239 The blue-jackets ... Russell, p.113

239 in the annals of chivalry ... Wood, *Midshipman*, Vol. I, p.114

239 What a softening ... Bushby, p.110

240 gallant youths ... NA ADM1/5651/N548

240 There is a special bond ... Wood, *Midshipman*, Vol. I, p.46

240 Though all ... Wood, *Fortnightly*, p.495

240 old chivalrous and Christian ... Girouard, Mark, *The Return to Camelot*, New Haven, 1981, p.142

241 I trust in God ... PL, 23 October 1854

241 What an anxious night ... Duberly, p.97

242 only six hundred men ... Wood, *Fortnightly*, p.696

242 The failure ... Ibid.

243 My relief ... Ibid., p.694
245 you see a head ... Pemberton, p.134
246 Tactics there were none ... Spilsbury, p.219
246 Amid a dense fog ... Ibid., p.214
246 They came on ... Ibid., p.211
247 The new arrival ... Higginson, General Sir George, GCB, *Seventy One Years of a Guardsman's Life*, London, 1916, p.191
248 Happily the ground ... Ibid.
249 unconcealed contempt ... Wolseley, p.292
249 The battle of Inkerman ... National Library of Scotland, Correspondence of Sir G. Brown, MS1860p.37
250 If it is considered ... Russell, p.146
250 *Vivent les Anglais* ... Pemberton, p.167
250 Never was a more ... NLS, MSS 1850, p.52
251 The thought of it ... Duberly, p.100
251 in case of a row ... Spilsbury, p.246
251 hell of a towelling ... Pemberton, p.173
252 rough, stony ground ... Wood, *Fortnightly*, p.614
252 masts, spars ... Duberly, p.104
253 That storm was ... Wood, *Fortnightly*, p.845
253 I shall write you ... PL, 2 December 1854
253 Our prospects ... PL, 7 January 1855
254 One day ... Wolseley, Field Marshal Viscount, *The Story of a Soldier's Life*, London, 1903, p.129
255 Our army is ... PL, 2 December 1854
256 His suggestion ... Wood, *Crimea*, p.292
256 My dear Frederic ... PL, 8 December 1854
256 It is dreadful ... PL, 7 January 1855
257 This is new year's eve ... PL, 31 December 1854
258 golden hair ... Askwith, p.27
258 Wednesday 3rd ... Ibid., p.72
259 Monday 22nd ... Ibid., p.84
259 He said ... Ibid., p.121
260 he hoped ... Ibid., p.96
260 Our army is improving ... PL, 2 February 1855
260 What a slap ... PL, 14 April 1855
261 I was sent ... Wood, *Crimea*, p.252
262 It was important ... Wood, *Fortnightly*, p.872
263 havoc and ruin ... Ibid., p.116
263 the beginning of the end ... Ibid., p.114
263 Just as the day ... Ibid., p.118
264 About ½ p 11 ... Massie, p.194
264 Every face was grave ... Wood, *Fortnightly*, p.120

265 Barring accidents ... Wood, *Crimea*, p.294
266 From some words ... Ibid., p.293
267 Shure you'll never ... Wood, *Fortnightly*, p.289
267 I asked my chief ... Ibid.
268 I always guarded ... Massie, p.198
269 It is difficult ... Wood, *Fortnightly*, p.299
269 let the soldiers ... Ibid.
269 Before we had advanced ... Ibid., p.300
270 When I approached ... Ibid., p.301
270 I must admit ... Ibid.
270 How long ... Ibid., p.303
271 tinned milk ... Ibid.
271 a place in ... Ibid.
271 Sit down ... Ibid., p.304
272 It was agonising ... Russell, p.218
273 like an emetic ... Pemberton, p.217
273 My head is throbbing ... Spilsbury, p.314
274 Soon afterwards ... Russell, p.257
274 The Russians ... Ibid., p.259
275 If a few days ... Spilsbury, p.317
275 chivalrous gallantry ... NA ADM1/5651/N730
275 I am commanded ... NA ADM1/5669/PromN435
275 Sir Stephen Lushington ... NA WO98/3
276 For devotion ... Ibid.
276 It is a terrible business ... Hurd, *Arrow*, p.108
277 I was pleased ... PL, 20 February 1857
278 In the middle ... Wood, *Midshipman*, Vol. I, p.101
279 reading, chess ... NRS, p.260
279 The very day ... NRS, p.262
279 sometimes more ... Ibid.
279 bad news ... National Maritime Museum, Jod/93/1
279 I rather think ... NRS, p.263
280 At length ... Verney, *Shannon*, p.3
281 frowning batteries ... Ibid., p.3
281 a hint of England's might ... Ibid.
281 On Aug 7 ... Verney, *Devil*, p.46
282 I have further ... NA ADM1/5684
283 My dearest mother ... NRS, p.264
283 Now that we ... NRS, p.265
284 I have the honour ... NA ADM1/5684
285 The fort ... Jones, p.36
285 I have just been ... Verney, *Devil*, p.60
286 The enemy ... Ibid., p.65

287 received with great cheering ... National Maritime Museum Jod
         93/1
287 Captain Peel ... NRS, p.270
288 At two in the morning ... Jones, p.81
289 I was much pleased ... Ibid., p.59
289 his young folks ... Ibid., p.56
290 The place ... David, Saul, *The Indian Mutiny*, London, 2002,
         p.255
290 On the wall behind ... Verney, *Shannon*, p.44
290 Let us propose ... Hibbert, p.293
291 Everyone is depressed ... David, Saul, *The Indian Mutiny*,
         London, 2002, p.318
291 4ft high ... NRS, p.23
291 It was ... Jones, p.113
292 too cautious for India ... Hibbert, p.334
292 We fell in ... Wolseley, Field Marshal Viscount, *The Story of a
         Soldier's Life*, London, 1903, p.298
293 This action ... Roberts, p.179
294 In less than half ... Ibid., p.180
294 The scene ... Ibid., p.182
295 The scene was ... Hibbert, p.341
295 handsome white-domed ... Roberts, p.183
295 The day was ... Ibid., p.185
296 Captain Peel ... Verney, *Devil*, p.77
296 and although ... Hibbert, p.343
296 Today great cheering ... National Maritime Museum, Jod 93/1/2
296 Soldiers, I am happy ... Hibbert, p.345
298 On the 29th ... Verney, *Devil*, p.92
298 fine little Mids ... Jones, p.73
298 It is quite a sight ... Verney, *Devil*, p.93
299 The firing goes on ... Ibid.
299 When the 24-pounders ... Jones, p.62
299 Reduce our squadrons ... BL AddMss 49460/ff189–90
300 The ammunition ... Ibid.
300 My Dear Mama ... Verney, *Devil*, p.97
302 I must here ... NRS, p.22
302 On this ... Ibid.
302 floods of tears ... Verney, *Shannon*, p.38
302 An Indian army ... Ibid., p.55
303 the Captain ... Winton, John, *The Victoria Cross at Sea*,
         London, 1978, p.29
303 five or six ... Verney, *Shannon*, p.55
303 There is a ... Jones, p.87

304 the wisdom ... Yonge, Vol. II, p.786
304 Is *Paal* ... Jones, p.70
304 a capital shot ... Ibid., p.71
304 There was a gun ... Ibid.
304 Vaughan's first shot ... Verney, *Devil*, p.110
305 We reached ... Verney, *Shannon*, p.113
305 The road from ... Ibid.
306 Every eye ... Roberts, p.216
306 You will not fail ... Yonge, Vol. II, p.786
306 with which he ... Jones, p.95
306 Our artillery ... Yonge, Vol. II, pp.786–9
307 I rode into ... Verney, *Devil*, p.121
307 There we saw ... Jones, p.155
308 We took this place ... Yonge, Vol. II, p.788
308 the work went on ... Jones, p.172
308 Soon after ... Ibid.
309 Even now ... Verney, *Devil*, p.128
309 excitable temperament ... National Maritime Museum, Jod
    93/1–2
309 The halls of ... Verney, *Devil*, p.139
309 I attempted to ... Yonge, Vol. II, p.789
310 a better officer ... Jones, p.178
310 Captain Peel's conveyance ... Verney, *Shannon*, p.123
311 are much grown ... National Maritime Museum, 50 MS0115
311 when to all ... Roberts, p.230
311 Alas ... Jones, pp.174–90
312 We have been ... Verney, *Devil*, p.148
312 Sir William Peel's ... Ibid., p.149
313 The order was given ... Ibid., p.158
313 above all others ... National Maritime Museum WAT 5/press
    cutting
314 In officially ... NA ADM1/5698
315 When I came ... *Recollections of Lady Georgiana Peel*, compiled
    by her daughter, Ethel Peel, London, 1920, p.96

GOODENOUGH

319 I have thought ... Memoir, p.62
319 I am going ashore ... Ibid., p.207
320 a native, waving ... Ibid.
320 During the time ... *The Times*, 18 October 1875
320 They are big compared ... Memoir, p.207
320 Oh! this isn't quite prudent ... Ibid., p.209

321 The arrow seemed ... Ibid.
321 the wretched islanders ... Hero, p.25
321 The arrows did not look ... Memoir, p.210
322 He had desired ... Ibid., p.211
322 He soon said ... Ibid., p.212
323 As to those poor natives ... Ibid., p.213
323 through a lane of loving ... Hero, p.9
323 If bad words ... Memoir, p.214
323 I have often ... Ibid., p.215
324 exact moment ... Ibid.
325 From his earliest ... Ibid., p.2
325 He was, as a boy ... Ibid., p.3
325 On the morning ... Markham, p.12
326 According to the rules ... Ibid., p.13
327 The examinations in those days ... Memoir, p.4
327 daily hovered ... Markham, C.H., *A Brief Memoir of
        Commander J. G. Goodenough, CB, CMG*, Portsmouth,
        1877, p.7
327 canvas swelling out ... Markham, p.21
327 the Dean followed her ... Markham, C.H., *A Brief Memoir of
        Commander J. G. Goodenough, CB, CMG*, Portsmouth,
        1877, p.7
327 How willingly would one ... Scott, R.F., *The Voyage of the
        Discovery*, London, 1905, Vol. I, p.90
328 a tall handsome man ... Markham, p.17
328 a little 2nd class boy ... RGS CRM 2 p.6
328 In addition to carrying out ... Markham, p.27
328 Beer abounded in large jugs ... Walpole, Frederick, *Four Years in
        the Pacific*, London, 1849, p.2
329 As a midshipman ... Memoir, p.7
329 of the purest integrity ... Ibid., p.5
329 *preux chevalier* ... Markham, p.99
329 On hoisting his flag ... Ibid., p.24
330 squinted frightfully ... Ibid., p.84
330 a man of middle height ... Memoir, p.190
330 On every emergency ... Ibid., p.8
331 It was twenty-four hours ... Ibid.
331 honourable, true ... Ibid., p.3
331 On one occasion ... Markham, p.73
332 The *Collingwood* never ... Ibid., p.98
333 The Dean directed ... Memoir, p.2
334 'Tis well enough ... *Dictionary of National Biography*, 1921
        reprint

334 Of all the warlike operations ... Yonge, Vol. II, p.500
335 to compete at ... Memoir, p.9
335 It is a time of confusion ... Goodenough, J.G., 'Education in the
       Navy', *Fraser's Magazine*, 1871, p.609
335 the only prize ... Memoir, p.11
335 There are few ... Ibid., p.9
336 It was my good fortune ... Ibid., p.10
336 to make God ... Ibid., p.12
336 I think with you ... Ibid.
337 No fleet ever quitted ... Yonge, Vol. II, p.586
337 Most men of sixty ... *Edinburgh Review*, CXVIII, p.179
338 with some surprise ... Journal: ML FM4/1766/p.9
338 very pleasant ... Ibid., p.11
338 wine and private stores ... Ibid., p.16
338 The church is simple ... Ibid., p.23
339 It was such lovely weather ... Ibid., p.32
339 We went to divisions ... Ibid., p.38
339 The fort is in the form ... Ibid., p.53
340 lily of the valley ... Ibid., p.59
340 I came down ... Ibid., pp.59–72
341 Off Selsey Bill ... Ibid., p.98
341 My Dear Journal ... Ibid., pp.104–7
342 Well I shall never ... Ibid., p.119
344 On Tuesday ... Ibid., p.150
345 7.25am mortar vessels ... NA ADM53/4938
345 a rocket burst ... Journal: ML FM4/1766/p.154
346 He was always ... Memoir, p.13
347 want of care ... NA ADM196/36/541
348 good-looking woman ... Keppel, Vol. I, p.325
348 a finer crew ... Ibid.
349 had struck some ... Keppel, Vol. I, p.335
349 We were heading ... Journal: ML FM4/1766/p.241
349 jumped into the glory hole ... Ibid.
349 After a while ... Keppel, Vol. I, p.336
350 In the three hours ... Memoir, p.18
350 I could not believe ... Ibid.
350 some uncommon good ... Keppel, Vol. I, p.336
352 his insane and insufferable ... Hurd, *Arrow*, p.20
352 There is a ferocity ... Ibid., p.129
353 Never will England ... Ibid., p.62
353 An insolent barbarian ... Ibid., p.76
354 the time had arrived ... Keppel, Vol. III, p.1
354 All the Captains ... Yonge, p.728

356 All Sunday ... Memoir, p.21
357 as pretty a boat action ... Keppel, Vol. III, p.2
357 The boats had pulled on ... Memoir, pp.21–2
358 At this moment ... Keppel, Vol. III, p.4
359 I had received many more ... Memoir, p.22
359 a very pretty boat ... Ibid., p.25
359 Fancy what I have ... Ibid., p.28
360 We sailors thought ... Ibid., p.29
360 I have often read ... Ibid.
361 a good example to me ... Ibid., p.30
361 During the excitement ... Ibid.
361 Nothing to do ... Hurd, Arrow, p.141
362 At sea at last ... Memoir, p.30
362 How I envy ... Ibid., p.24
363 The lessons taught ... Yonge, p.744
363 a jovial party ... Kennedy, p.95
363 The boom ... Ibid., p.96
364 For some time ... Yonge, p.745
364 The boats were then ... Kennedy, p.97
364 The river was full ... Memoir, p.34
365 On June 26 ... Kennedy, p.102
366 2 November ... NA ADM56/6311
367 My dear Mams ... *Fear God and Dread Nought: The
    Correspondence of Admiral of the Fleet Lord Fisher of
    Kilverstone*, ed. Arthur J. Marder, London, 1952, p.27
368 Our defeat had been ... Yonge, p.766
369 I hope you will have ... Memoir, p.39
369 Hungerford came to my attic ... Journal: ML FM4/1766/p.308
369 We are in free ... Memoir, p.42
370 21 October broken ... NA ADM53/7644
370 Very grumpy with ... Journal: ML FM4/1766/p.352
370 For every ill ... Ibid., p.365
370 Never so tired ... Ibid., p.345
371 13 July ... NA ADM53/7644
371 Goodenough was a man ... Memoir, p.41
371 It is all over ... Ibid., p.45
372 Cold shot, hand-grenades ... Hernon, Ian, *Britain's Forgotten
    Wars*, Stroud, 2003, p.380
373 I started early ... Memoir, p.46
373 The river transport ... Ibid., p.48
374 *C'est détruire* ... Hurd, Arrow, p.226
374 *Je prends la plume* ... Ibid., p.228
374 You can scarcely ... Hernon, p.389

375 I hope for once ... Memoir, p.50
375 The scoundrel rebels ... Ibid., p.54
375 I have had an eight ... Ibid., p.56
376 place in order against ... Ibid.
376 I see strange sights ... Ibid., p.58
376 People are quite right ... Ibid., p.55
377 Came back to the ship ... School of Oriental and African Studies,
        Melanesian Mission, MelM2/21
378 a happier ship ... Markham, M.E. and F.A., *The Life of Sir
        Albert Hastings Markham*, Cambridge, 1927, p.36
378 I have the honour ... NA FO881/1254
379 They will not form a fleet ... Ibid.
379 Mr Welles ... Ibid.
380 I am always sorry ... Memoir, p.139
381 It seems to me ... Ibid., p.76
381 I have been asked ... Ibid., p.96
381 I have been told ... Ibid., p.102
382 It has been said ... Ibid., p.100
383 I regret the loss of ... Ibid., p.101
383 every moment ... Gordon, Andrew, *The Rules of the Game*,
        London, 1996, p.183
384 I have been in ... Memoir, p.64
384 I say nothing about war ... Ibid., p.80
385 What a glory ... Ibid., p.105
386 It is a happy thing ... Ibid., p.63
387 He came to the conclusion ... Ibid., p.78
387 Pharisaical Britain ... Ibid., p.80
387 In the dreariest ... Ibid., p.82
388 His sermon ... Ibid., p.83
389 It is weakening ... Ibid., p.99
390 Clerk made ... Journal: ML FM4/1766/pp.418–539
390 Captain Goodenough [had spent] ... Memoir, p.109
390 round hole ... Journal: ML FM4/1766/p.535
391 I said I was ... Ibid., pp.540–1
391 There was something ... Ibid., pp.542–3
392 Today as chronicled ... Ibid., p.549
392 most kind and charming ... Journal: ML FM4/1767/p.23
395 While the Fijians ... NA CO881/4
395 I have no doubt ... Ibid.
396 seriously of the great ... Journal: ML FM4/1767/p.27
397 Captain Simpson was ... NA CO881/4
398 I thought it right ... Ibid.
398 Much correspondence ... Ibid.

399 I have had the opportunity ... Ibid.
399 I am informed ... Ibid.
400 It has been represented ... Ibid.
400 We have found ... Ibid.
401 We are aware ... Ibid.
401 Got heap of letters ... Journal: ML FM4/1767/pp.341–617
401 absurd manners ... Ibid., p.433
401 fat vulgar fellow ... Ibid., p.636
401 Commodore Goodenough and ... NA CO881/4
402 Affairs being ... Ibid.
403 It [was] not in accordance ... Ibid.
403 to the justice and ... Legge, J.G., *Britain in Fiji*, New York, 1958, p.132
403 Now I must work ... Journal: ML FM4/1767/p.627
403 I share the usual ... Journal: ML FM4/1768/p.80
403 I think the Lord Carnavon ... Ibid., p.122
403 That paper ... School of Oriental and African Studies, Melanesian Mission, MelM2/22
404 On Monday morning ... Memoir, p.195
404 Disgusting CMG ... Journal: ML FM4/1768/p.427
405 Read my letters ... Ibid., p.122
405 Some one spoke ... Memoir, p.65
406 If he had got overcome ... Journal: ML FM4/1767/p.68
406 I spoke to ... Ibid., pp.57–152
407 So delightfully cool ... Ibid., p.50
407 As the day broke ... Memoir, p.134
408 He was a general ... Ibid., p.137
408 first and only ... Ibid., p.138
408 I am first of all ... Ibid., p.142
408 All is failure ... Ibid.
409 The flattering attentions ... Ibid., p.154
409 I am very glad ... Ibid., p.155
409 In the course of my visits ... Ibid., p.154
410 Now how great ... Journal: ML FM4/1767/p.218
410 Suppose you offer ... Journal: ML FM4/1768/p.149
411 Sir A shewed me ... Ibid., p.459
411 It is evident ... Ibid., p.474
411 Ladies and gentlemen ... Memoir, p.146
412 The islands had ... Ibid., p.187
412 The master of the Sybil ... Ibid., p.178
413 I found the chief ... Ibid., p.180
414 How do you recruit ... Ibid., p.182
414 collecting information ... Ibid., p.187

414 filthy and hideous ... Ibid., p.201
415 At each place ... Ibid., p.186
415 The people of the village ... Ibid., p.204
416 Teach me to live ... Journal: ML FM4/1766/p.307
417 dense concourse ... *Illustrated Sydney News*, 18 September 1875
417 had fallen a victim ... *The Times*, 28 August 1875
417 races scarcely human ... *The Times*, 26 August 1875
417 Mrs Goodenough is most ... Journal: ML FM4/1768/p.664
417 God of the world ... Memoir, p.217
419 The most strange example ... *The Times*, 29 January 1876
420 A thrill of sorrow ... *The Times*, 26 August 1875
421 Well, he said ... Memoir, p.213
422 He rests far away ... Ibid., p.221

EPILOGUE

424 it seems impossible ... W. Goodenough, p.56
424 Do you understand ... Crane, *Scott*, p.361
426 'Imagination' bred ... W. Goodenough, p.60
426 He should be ... Crane, *Scott*, p.81
427 I can suppose ... NRS, pp.283–5
428 It seems almost ... W. Goodenough, p.11
429 There was a ... Ibid., p.59
429 mighty powers ... Crane, *Scott*, p.143
429 I must say ... Ibid., p.408

SELECT BIBLIOGRAPHY

Manuscript Sources
The principal manuscript sources for the life of Frank Abney Hastings are contained in five major collections: the Hastings and Finlay Papers in the archive of the British School of Archaeology at Athens; the Hastings Collection in the Huntington Library, California; the British Library; the Dundonald Papers in the National Archives of Scotland; Admiralty records in the National Archives.

For William Peel the main manuscript sources are the family letters in the possession of the Reverend Jonathan Peel; the British Library; Admiralty and Foreign Office records in the National Archives; National Maritime Museum, Greenwich.

For James Goodenough the main manuscript sources are his journals held in the Mitchell Library, State Library of New South Wales; records of the Melanesian Mission, School of Oriental and African Studies, University of London; Admiralty and Colonial Office records in the National Archives.

Published Sources
Alexander, Caroline, *The Bounty*, London, 2003
Anon, *The Christian Hero of Santa Cruz*, London, undated
Askwith, Betty, *Crimean Courtship*, Salisbury, 1985
Bentley, N., ed., *Russell's Despatches from the Crimea*, London, 1970
Booth, Martin, *Opium: A History*, London, 1997
Brewer, David, *The Flame of Freedom*, London, 2001
Bushby, Henry Jeffreys, *A Month in the Camp before Sebastopol by a non-combatant*, London, 1855
Campbell, C.F., *Letters from Sevastopol 1854-5*, London, 1894
Churi, J., *Sea Nile, the Desert and Nigritia*, London, 1853
Clayton, Tim & Craig, Phil, *Trafalgar: The Men, the Battle, the Storm*, London, 2004
Crane, Arthur, *The Kirkland Papers*, Chatham, 1990

Crane, David, *Lord Byron's Jackal*, London, 1998

Crane, David, *Scott of the Antarctic*, London, 2005

Crompton, Louis, *Byron and Greek Love*, Los Angeles, 1985

David, Saul, *The Indian Mutiny*, London, 2002

Dawson, Graham, Soldier Heroes, London, 2005

Elliot, C.W.J., ed., *Campaign of the Falieri and Piraeus in the Year 1827*, Princeton, 1992

Ffrench Blake, R.L.V., *The Crimean War*, Barnsley, 1971

Finlay, George, *Blackwood's Edinburgh Magazine*, Edinburgh, 1845

Finlay, George, *History of the Greek Revolution*, London, 1971

Fitzgerald, C.C. Penrose, *Life of Vice Admiral Sir George Tryon*, London, 1897

Francis, Martin, 'The Domestication of the Male? Recent Research on Nineteenth and Twentieth Century British Masculinity', *Historical Journal*, 45, 3 (2002), Cambridge

Fremantle, Anne, ed., *The Wynne Diaries*, London, 1940

Gash, N., *Sir Robert Peel: The Life of Sir Robert Peel After 1830*, London, 1972

Girouard, Mark, *The Return to Camelot*, New Haven, 1981

Goodenough, J.G., 'Education in the Navy', *Fraser's Magazine*, 1871

Goodenough, Admiral Sir William, *A Rough Record*, London, 1941

Goodenough, *Memoir of Commodore J.G. Goodenough, RN, CB, CMG*, edited by his widow, London, 1878

Gordon, Andrew, *The Rules of the Game*, London, 1996

Gordon, T. *History of the Greek Revolution*, London, 1832

Gough, B., 'Lieutenant William Peel, British Naval Intelligence and the Oregon Crisis', *The Northern Mariner*, IV, No 4, 1994

Guizot, M., *Memoirs of Sir Robert Peel*, London, 1857

Haigh, J. Bryant, 'The Disgraced VC', *Bulletin of the Military Historical Society*, Vol.XXII, No. 86, November 1971

Hastings, Frank Abney, *Memoir on the use of shells, hot shot, and carcass shells, from ship artillery*, London 1828

Hernon, Ian, *Britain's Forgotten Wars*, Gloucestershire, 2003

Hibbert, Christopher, *The Destruction of Lord Raglan*, London, 1961

Hibbert, Christopher, *The Great Mutiny*, London, 1980

Higginson, General Sir George, *Seventy-One Years of a Guardsman's Life*, London, 1916

Hill, F.R., ed., *The Illustrated History of the Royal Navy*, Oxford, 1995

Hole, Rev. Ch., *The Life of the Reverend and Venerable Will. Phelps MA*, London, 1878

Howe, S.G., *Letters & Journals of Samuel Gridley Howe during the Greek Revolution*, Boston, 1907–09

Hughes, Thomas, *Tom Brown's Schooldays*, London, 1857

Hurd, Douglas, *The Arrow War*, London, 1967

Hurd, Douglas, *Robert Peel*, London, 2007

James, W.M., *The Naval History of Great Britain*, London, 2001

Jones, Captain Oliver, RN, *Recollections of a Winter Campaign in India*, London, 1859

Kelly, Christine, ed., *Mrs Duberly's War: Journals and Letters from the Crimea, 1854–1856*, Oxford, 2007

Kennedy, Vice-Admiral Sir William, *Hurrah for the Life of a Sailor*, Edinburgh, 1900

Keppel, Sir Henry, *A Sailor's Life Under Four Sovereigns*, London, 1899

Kingslake, A.W., *The Invasion of the Crimea*, Vols I–VIII, London, 1866–87

Kingsley, Charles, *Two Years Ago*, London, 1881

Lane-Poole, Stanley, *Sir Richard Church, CB, GCH, Commander in Chief of the Greeks in the War of Independence*, London, 1890

Legge, J.G., *Britain in Fiji*, New York, 1958

Lloyd, Christopher, *The British Seaman*, London, 1968

Lord, Walter, *The Dawn's Early Light*, New York, 1972

Lovell, William, *Personal Narrative of Events 1799–1815*, London, 1879

Mansel, Philip, *Constantinople*, London, 1991

Marchand, Leslie A., ed., *Byron Letters & Journals*, London 1973

Marder, Arthur J., ed., *Fear God and Dread Nought: The Correspondence of Admiral of the Fleet Lord Fisher of Kilverstone*, London, 1952

Markham, Sir Albert, *The Life of Sir Clements R. Markham, KCB, FRS*, London, 1917

Markham, C.H., *A Brief Memoir of Commander J. G. Goodenough, CB, CMG*, Portsmouth, 1877

Markham, M.E. and F.A., *The Life of Sir Albert Hastings Markham*, Cambridge, 1927

Massie, Alastair, *The National Army Museum Book of the Crimean War*, London, 2005

Napier, General E., *The Life and Correspondence of Admiral Sir Charles Napier*, London, 1862

O'Byrne, W.R.A., *A Naval Biographical Dictionary*, London, 1849

Parker, Ch., ed., *Sir Robert Peel from his Private Papers*, London, 1899

Peel, Captain, RN, *A Ride through the Nubian Desert*, London, 1852

Peel, George, ed., *The Private Letters of Sir Robert Peel*, London, 1920

Peel, Sir Lawrence, *A Sketch of the Life and Character of Sir Robert Peel*, London, 1860

Pemberton, W. Baring, *Battles of the Crimean War*, London, 1968

Percy, Algernon, *A Bearskin's Crimea*, Barnsley, 2005

Roberts of Kandahar, Field Marshal, *Forty-one Years in India*, London, 1898

Rodger, N.A.M, *The Wooden World*, London, 1988

Roper, Michael and Tosh, John, *Manful Assertions: Masculinities in Britain Since 1800*, London, 1991

St Clair, William, *That Greece Might Still be Free*, London, 1972

Samson, Jane, 'Hero, Fool or Martyr? The Many Deaths of Commodore Goodenough', *Journal for Maritime Research*, Greenwich, February 2008

Scott, R.F., *The Voyage of the Discovery*, London, 1905

Spilsbury, Julian, *The Thin Red Line*, London, 2006

Stanley, George F.G., *The War of 1812: Land Operations*, National Museum of Canada, 1983

Steel, John, ed., Southey, Robert, *Mr Rowlandson's England*, Woodbridge, 1985

Thomas, Donald, *Cochrane*, London, 1978

Trelawny, Edward, *Adventures of a Younger Son*, London, 1891

Urquhart, David, *The Spirit of the East*, London, 1835

Verney, Edmund, *The Shannon's Brigade in India*, London, 1852

Verney, Major-General G.L., *The Devil's Wind*, London, 1956

Walpole, Frederick, *Four Years in the Pacific*, London, 1849

Whitcombe, Captain Thomas, ed. C.W.J. Eliot, *Campaign of the Falieri and Piraeus in the Year 1827*, New Jersey, 1992

Winton, John, *The Victoria Cross at Sea*, London, 1978

Wolffe, John, *Great Deaths: Grieving, Religion and Nationhood in Victorian and Edwardian Britain*, Oxford, 2000

Wolseley, Field Marshal Lord, 'Courage', *Fortnightly Review*, August 1888

Wolseley, Field Marshal Viscount, *The Story of a Soldier's Life*, London, 1903

Wood, Field Marshal Sir Evelyn, *The Crimea in 1854 and 1894*, London, 1895

Wood, Field Marshal Sir Evelyn, *The Fortnightly Review*, CCCXXXIV, London, 1894

Wood, Field Marshal Sir Evelyn, *From Midshipman to Field Marshal*, London, 1906

Yonge, C.D., *History of the British Navy*, London, 1863

Young, Peter, and Lawford, J.P., eds, *History of the British Army*, London, 1970

INDEX